METROPOLITAN CHARTERS

Joseph F. Zimmerman, Editor

Graduate School of Public Affairs
State University of New York at Albany
Albany, New York

Printed in the United States of America
by the V-B Printing Company, Incorporated, Albany, New York

Foreword

The development early in the twentieth century of metropolitan areas and the absence of a unit of local government with adequate authority and resources to solve area-wide problems have been responsible for numerous proposals for the reform of the governmental system of the metropolis.

The early metropolitan reformers tended to view the basic metropolitan problem in terms of a multiplicity of local governments which resulted in conflicts of authority, duplication of services, financial inequities, a long ballot, inadequate service levels, lack of area-wide planning and programming, and other problems.

The fragmented government of the metropolis, in the view of the reformers, was dysfunctional and met service needs in an uneven manner and in many instances failed completely to meet service needs. A problem of metropolitan responsibility also was identified by reformers as citizens have no one government in a balkanized political system to hold responsible for metropolitan failures.

Advocates of metropolitan reform call for a comprehensive approach to the solution of area-wide problems and the devising of rational governmental structures adequate to deal with the problems of urban growth. The prescription for improved metropolitan health issued by reformers has varied from one area to another but involves the creation of a single government or a two-tier system of government for the metropolitan area.

A number of the early reformers recommended the use of annexation as the most effective means to create a metropolitan government. A root cause of the metropolitan problem, it has been suggested, was the failure of annexation to keep pace with urbanization. With a few exceptions, annexation today is not considered to be a feasible means of creating a metropolitan government.

Current interest in the one government approach to the solution of area-wide problems is represented by charters which provide for city-county consolidation—complete or partial. Complete consolidation provides for a new government formed by the amalgamation of the county and all other local governments. Under one form of partial consolidation, most county functions are merged with the local governments to form a consolidated government, but the county continues to exist for the performance of functions which are required by the state constitution. The second form of partial consolidation involves the merger of most but not all municipalities with the county.

City-county consolidation was facilitated in the nineteenth century by state laws which did not require a popular referendum on the question of consolidation and a majority affirmative vote in both the central city and the balance of the county to effectuate consolidation. Consolidation occurred in four areas: New Orleans (1813), Boston (1822), Philadelphia (1854), and New York City (1898).

Complete city-county consolidation has the advantages of simplifying the governmental structure, consolidating responsibility, eliminating duplication, and increasing popular control of the governmental system. If the metropolitan area falls entirely within the confines of a single county, complete city-county consolidation provides a single government with adequate powers to ensure the orderly development of the metropolitan area and the resolution of its problems. Yet only three proposals for city-county consolidation reached the ballot in the twentieth century prior to 1947 and all were defeated. Since 1947, partial city-county consolidation has been implemented in only two areas of the United States—Baton Rouge and Nashville.

The two-tier approach to the resolution of metropolitan problems is represented by the metropolitan county, metropolitan federation, and metropolitan special district—each involves the sharing of governmental power between an area-wide government and other local governments. Consequently, each plan is faced with the problem of determining the division of functions between the area-wide government and the other local governments. Although the three plans are basically similar, they differ in that the county plan does not involve the creation of an additional unit of government—the metropolitan government—and the special district plan usually assigns fewer responsibilities to the area-wide government than the other two plans.

The practical political obstacles to the reform of the government of the metropolis by consolidating existing local governments or creating a new unit of general local government with area-wide powers have led a number of observers to conclude the most feasible method to create a metropolitan government is the reform of the existing county government which generally has limited authority and an outmoded organizational structure. Most Standard

Metropolitan Statistical Areas fall within the confines of a single county and organized county government exists in all states except Alaska, Connecticut, and Rhode Island.

Metropolitan federation is patterned after the federal relationship which exists between the national government and the states in the United States, and is a compromise between total amalgamation of the units of local government and the existing fractionated system of local government. Existing local governments may be continued, partially consolidated, or replaced by new units of local government. Responsibility for area-wide functions is assigned to the newly created metropolitan government.

Metropolitan federation is found in the Toronto and Winnipeg areas in Canada and the greater London area in England, but has not been adopted in the United States although interest in federation is strong. Federation should not be confused with the New York City borough plan in effect from 1898 to January 1963. It had the superficial appearance of federation because each borough was responsible for a few functions: construction and maintenance of streets and sewers, enforcement of the building code, and maintenance of public buildings. The boroughs, however, lacked legislative powers.

The failure of most comprehensive metropolitan reorganization plans to win voter approval has stimulated the creation of metropolitan special districts. Creation of a special district is facilitated in many states by laws which do not require a popular referendum on the question of its creation. Most special districts are uni-functional and existing local governments continue to perform all their regular functions with the exception of the one assigned to the special district. The Metropolitan District Commission in the Boston area is one of the few multi-functional districts and it has been assigned responsibility for water supply, sewage disposal, and certain parks and recreational facilities.

The purpose of Metropolitan Charters is to make available for ready reference in one volume the charters as amended of the principal metropolitan governments in the United States, Canada, and England.

This volume is one in a series of publications focusing on metropolitan areas published by the Graduate School of Public Affairs. In 1962, the Graduate School's Local Government Studies Center incorporated the major functions of the Conference on Metropolitan Area Problems which had been organized in 1957 by the Government Affairs Foundation to focus attention on metropolitan problems.

Albany, New York   Joseph F. Zimmerman, Director
March, 1967   Local Government Studies Center

Contents

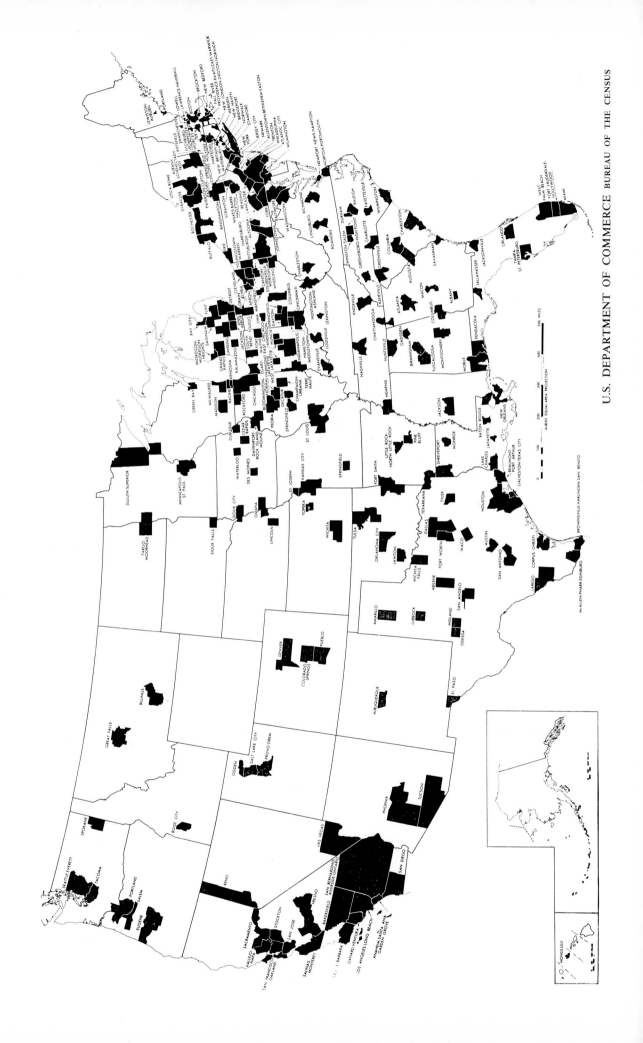

STANDARD METROPOLITAN STATISTICAL AREAS

AREAS DEFINED BY U.S. BUREAU OF THE BUDGET TO APRIL 8, 1966

U.S. DEPARTMENT OF COMMERCE BUREAU OF THE CENSUS

The Plan Of Government Of The City Of Baton Rouge And The Parish Of East Baton Rouge

In 1946, Louisiana voters, by a vote of 69,894 to 18,886, approved a constitutional amendment authorizing the drafting of a county home rule charter for the Baton Rouge area which would become effective upon approval by a majority of the voters in the area; separate majorities in the City of Baton Rouge and the remainder of the Parish were not required to effectuate the consolidation.

In an August 12, 1947 referendum, with one-third of the voters participating, a charter providing for the semi-consolidation of the City of Baton Rouge and the Parish of East Baton Rouge was approved by a vote of 7,012 to 6,705, effective January 1, 1949. The constitutionality of the new plan of government was upheld in 1949.[1]

The charter retains the city government, parish government, and two small municipal governments, but prohibits the incorporation of new municipalities or the territorial expansion of the two small municipalities. The City-Parish Council is composed of seven members of the City Council and two members from the outlying areas. The chief executive of the City and City-Parish is the Mayor-President. The area of the City of Baton Rouge was increased from approximately five to thirty square miles and its population was increased from approximately 35,000 to 105,000.

Two years subsequent to the adoption of the Plan of Government, an eleven-member study committee was created to review the Plan. Six of the seven amendments proposed by the committee were approved by the voters on July 29, 1952.

A second study committee in 1956 proposed seven amendments which were approved by the voters on November 6, 1956. Nine proposed amendments were submitted to the voters on November 3, 1964 and eight were approved. Four other proposed amendments were approved by the voters on November 8, 1966.

Chapter 1

GENERAL PROVISIONS

SECTION 1.01. UNITS OF LOCAL GOVERNMENT. There shall henceforth be within the limits of East Baton Rouge Parish, as the same are now established, a parish government and such other units of local government as are provided in this plan of government.

SECTION 1.02. THE PARISH. East Baton Rouge Parish shall continue to be a political subdivision of the state and through the governing body thereof shall have all the privileges, powers and duties, not inconsistent with the provisions of this plan of government, heretofore possessed by East Baton Rouge Parish or the governing body thereof, or which may hereafter be conferred or imposed on parishes or the governing bodies hereof by the constitution and laws of the state and, in addition, such other powers and duties as are specifically conferred or imposed on East Baton Rouge Parish by this plan of government.

SECTION 1.03. CITY OF BATON ROUGE. The City of Baton Rouge shall continue its existence as a political subdivision of the state and a body corporate under its charter as heretofore enacted except as the same is inconsistent with the provisions of this plan of government. The boundaries of the City of Baton Rouge are hereby extended to include, and shall henceforth always coincide with, the boundaries of the urban area as they are defined in this chapter and as they may be further extended in accordance therewith.

SECTION 1.04. SPECIAL DISTRICTS. The road, sewerage and drainage districts established within East Baton Rouge Parish prior to the first day of January 1949, whether within or without the City of Baton Rouge, shall continue to exist as on

that date constituted to effectuate the purpose for which each was created, to complete any works begun or authorized therein, to pay the debts of the district, and to levy such taxes and other charges as many have been or may be legally authorized in each such district. There shall also be within East Baton Rouge Parish such other districts as may be established by the governing body of the parish or city in accordance with the constitution and general laws of the state.

SECTION 1.05. INCORPORATED TOWNS AND VILLAGES. The incorporated town of Zachary and the village of Baker shall be parts of the rural area as defined in section 1.08 and shall continue in existence as municipalities subject, except as specifically provided in this plan of government, to the general laws of the state relating to incorporated towns and villages respectively, and may enlarge their boundaries as provided in such laws. No additional city, town or village shall be incorporated in East Baton Rouge Parish.

SECTION 1.06. INDEBTEDNESS OF THE CITY OF BATON ROUGE. All bonded indebtedness, including excess revenue bonds, of the City of Baton Rouge, outstanding on the first day of January 1949, shall be paid by taxes levied on taxable property within such city as constituted prior to such date, and the governing body of the City of Baton Rouge is hereby expressly authorized and required to levy annually on such taxable property taxes sufficient to meet principal and interest requirements on such indebtedness as such principal and interest become due.

SECTION 1.07. TRANSFER OF PROPERTY AND OBLIGATIONS. There are hereby transferred to the City of Baton Rouge, as of the first day of January 1949, the property and obligations of the Fire Protection District Number One of East Baton Rouge Parish, and the incinerators, dumps, other lands and equipment belonging to East Baton Rouge Parish used in the col-

---

[1] *State ex rel Kemp v. City of Baton Rouge*, 215 La. 315 (1949).

lection and disposal of garbage and other refuse. There are hereby transferred, as of the first day of January 1949, to East Baton Rouge Parish the use of all lands, buildings and equipment, belonging to the City of Baton Rouge, used in the construction, maintenance, repair and cleaning of the streets, boulevards, parkways, bridges, alleys and other public ways. There is also transfererd, as of the first day of January 1949, to the recreation and park commission for the Parish of East Baton Rouge all equipment belonging to the City of Baton Rouge and used exclusively for recreational purposes or the maintenance of parks, playgrounds and playfields.

SECTION 1.08. URBAN, INDUSTRIAL, AND RURAL AREAS. There shall be in East Baton Rouge Parish the following areas:

(a) Urban Area. There shall be in East Baton Rouge Parish an urban area in which, because of the congestion of population therein, there shall be supplied by the City of Baton Rouge, unless supplied by districts established in accordance with the constitution and general laws of the state, police protection, fire protection, garbage and refuse collection and disposal, street lighting, and the maintenance and operation of sewers and sewerage works. The urban area shall be bounded as follows: Beginning at a point three hundred feet north of the junction of the northern line of Goudchaux Street and the east line of the right-of-way of the Kansas City Southern-Louisiana and Arkansas Railway; thence easterly along a line parallel to and three hundred feet north of Goudchaux Street to a point three hundred feet east of the east line of Scenic Highway; thence southeasterly along a line parallel to and three hundred feet east of the east line of Scenic Highway to a point three hundred feet north of the north line of Airline Highway; thence easterly and southeasterly along a line parallel to and three hundred feet north and northeast of the north and northeast line of Airline Highway to the south R/W line of Ulysses Avenue; thence easterly along the south R/W line of Ulysses Avenue to a point 1148 feet west of the east R/W line of Airway Drive; thence northerly along a line parallel to and 1148 feet west of the east R/W line of Airway Drive extended to the north line of Section 64, T6S-RIE; thence easterly along said section line to the east R/W line of Airway Drive extended; thence southerly along the east R/W line of Airway Drive extended and Airway Drive to the north R/W line of Jones Creek; thence westerly along the north R/W line of Jones Creek to a line parallel to and 1000 feet northeast of the northeast R/W line of Airline Highway; thence northwesterly along said line parallel to Airline Highway to the northwest line of Lot 3, Square 3, Goodwood Homesites; thence southwesterly along said lot line to a line parallel to and 300 feet northeast of the northeast R/W line of Airline Highway; thence southeasterly along a line parallel to and 300 feet northeast of the northeast R/W line of Airline Highway to the north line of the Baton Rouge Water Works Company 29.43 Acre tract in Section 69, T7S-RIE; thence easterly along the north line of said Baton Rouge Water Works property to the west boundary of Oak Villa Subdivision; thence northerly, easterly and northerly along the west, north and west boundaries of Oak Villa Subdivision to the south boundary of Villa Del Rey Subdivision, first filing; thence northerly along the west boundary of said Villa Del Rey, first filing, to Jones Creek; thence continuing northerly along the extension of said west boundary of Villa Del Rey Subdivision, first filing, to the south right-of-way line of the Baton Rouge-Hammond and Eastern Branch of the Illinois Central Railroad; thence easterly along the south right-of-way line of said railroad to the east line of section 68, T-7-S, R-I-E extended northerly; thence southerly along the extension of said section line and the east line of section 68, T-7-S, R-I-E to the north boundary of Villa

Del Rey, fourth filing, being the south right-of-way line of Jones Creek; thence westerly and southerly along the south and east right-of-way line of said Jones Creek, being the north and west boundaries of Villa Del Rey, fourth filing to a line parallel with and 150 feet north of the north R/W line of Cuyhanga Parkway; thence easterly along said line parallel with Cuyhanga Parkway to the east R/W line of Sierra Vista Drive; thence southerly along the east R/W line of Sierra Vista Drive to the north R/W line of Cuyhanga Parkway; thence easterly along the north R/W line of Cuyhanga Parkway to the west R/W line of San Jauquin Drive; thence northerly along the west R/W line of San Jauquin Drive to a line parallel to and 116.14 feet north of the north R/W line of Cuyhanga Parkway; thence easterly along said line parallel to Cuyhanga Parkway a distance of 203.50 feet to the east boundary of Villa Del Rey Subdivision; Third Filing; thence southerly along the east boundary of said Villa Del Rey Subdivision, Third Filing to the north boundary of Greenoaks Memorial Cemetery; thence easterly along the north boundary of said Cemetery to the west boundary of Milnor Subdivision, First Filing; thence southerly along said west boundary of Milnor Subdivision and said west boundary extended to the north boundary of the Mary Bess Sharp Poirrier 27.87 acre tract; thence westerly along the north boundary of said Poirrier Tract and said boundary line extended to the common property line between the J. I. McCain Tract and the Parker and Manson Tract; thence southerly along said common property line to the north right-of-way line of Florida Boulevard; thence easterly along the north right-of-way line of Florida Boulevard to the intersection of the north right-of-way line of Florida Boulevard with the common property line, as extended, between J. D. Sharp and Mrs. J. D. Sharp, Sr., as shown on "Final plat of North Broadmoor, Second Filing," dated June 23, 1953, revised September 21, 1953, made by Mundinger, Dupree & Cooper, C. E., said map being recorded in the Office of the Clerk and Recorder for the Parish of East Baton Rouge; thence southerly along said common property line as extended to the north line of North Broadmoor, 2nd Filing; thence easterly along the north line of North Broadmoor, 2nd Filing and North Broadmoor, 3rd Filing to the west right-of-way line of Sharp Road; thence southerly along the west right-of-way line of Sharp Road to the south line of Broadmoor Terrace, 3rd Filing; thence westerly along the south line of Broadmoor Terrace, 3rd Filing to the east line of Broadmoor Oaks, thence southerly along the east line of Broadmoor Oaks to the north line of Broadmoor Terrace, 5th Filing; thence easterly along the north line of Broadmoor Terrace, 5th Filing, to the west right-of-way line of Sharp Road; thence southerly along the west right-of-way line of Sharp Road to the southeast corner of Broadmoor Estates, 2nd Filing; thence westerly along the south boundary of Broadmoor Estates, 2nd and 1st Filings to a point 150 feet west of the west R/W line of McMichael Drive; thence southerly, westerly and northerly along the east, south and west boundary of Broadmoor Estates, 1st Filing to the south R/W line of Browning Drive; thence westerly along the south R/W line of Browning Drive to the east boundary of Broadmoor Jr.-Senior High School site; thence southerly and westerly along the east and south boundaries of said Broadmoor Jr.-Senior High School site to the east boundary of Broadmoor Place, 3rd Filing; thence southerly along the east boundary of said Broadmoor Place, 3rd Filing to the centerline of Harelson Branch of North Branch of Ward Creek; thence westerly along the centerline of said Creek to the northeast corner of Hillcrest Acres Subdivision; thence westerly along the north boundary line of Hillcrest Acres Subdivision to a line parallel with and 30 feet west of the west boundary line of Broadmoor Place Subdivision, 1st Filing; thence northerly along said line parallel with Broadmoor Place, 1st Filing and along the west line of South Broadmoor, 2nd and 1st Filings and Broadmoor Elementary School Site to the south line of East Broadmoor, 8th Filing; thence westerly along the south line of East Broadmoor, 8th Filing to the west line of East Broadmoor, 8th Filing; thence northerly along the west line of East Broadmoor, 8th Filing to the south line of Broadmoor, 5th Filing; thence south-westerly along the south line of the drainage servitude which is the south line of Broadmoor, 5th Filing, and said line extended to the west right-of-way line of Airline Highway; thence northerly along the west right-of-way line of Airline Highway to its junction with the south right-of-way line of Florida Boulevard at the southwest quadrant of the Florida Boulevard-Airline Highway Traffic Interchange; thence westerly along the south right-of-way line of Florida Boulevard to a junction with the northerly extension of the east subdivision line of Parkland Terrace Subdivision; thence southerly along the east line of Parkland Terrace Subdivision extended and Parkland Terrace Subdivision to the southeast corner of said Parkland Terrace Subdivision; thence westerly along the south subdivision line of Parkland Terrace Subdivision and said line extended to a point 300 feet east of the east right-of-way line of East Airport Avenue; thence southerly along a line parallel to and three hundred feet east of the east line of East Airport Avenue and East Airport Avenue extended to a point on the north boundary line of Charmaine Subdivision; thence easterly along the northern boundary line of said Charmaine Subdivision to the northeast corner of said Charmaine Subdivision; thence southerly along the eastern boundary of said Charmaine Subdivision to a point on the north line of Lasalle Avenue; thence westerly along the north line of Lasalle Avenue to a point three hundred feet east of the east line of the eastern-most leg of Carter Avenue; thence southerly along a line parallel to and three hundred feet east of the east line of Carter Avenue and Carter Avenue extended to a point three hundred feet south of the south line of Old Hammond Highway; thence westerly along a line parallel to and 300 feet south of the right-of-way line of Old Hammond Highway to the east boundary of Palm Hills Subdivision; thence southerly, westerly and northerly along the eastern, southern and western boundary of Palm Hills Subdivision to a point 300 feet south of the south right-of-way line of Old Hammond Highway; thence westerly along a line parallel to and three hundred feet south of the Old Hammond Highway to the northeast line of Jefferson Highway; thence southeasterly along the northeast line of Jefferson Highway to its junction with a line parallel to and two hundred feet east of the east line of McCarroll Drive extended; thence southerly along a line parallel to and two hundred feet east of the east line of McCarroll Drive extended and McCarroll Drive to a point two hundred and forty feet south of the south line of Richards Drive; thence westerly along a line parallel to and two hundred and forty feet south of the south line of Richards Drive to a point three hundred and nine feet west of the west line of Murphy Drive; thence northerly along a line parallel to and three hundred and nine feet west of the west line of Murphy Drive to a point two hundred and five feet north of the north line of Boyce Drive; thence easterly along a line parallel to and two hundred and five feet north of the north line of Boyce Drive to the west line of McCarroll Drive; thence northerly along the west line of McCarroll Drive to its junction with a line parallel to and three hundred feet southwest of the southwest line of Jefferson Highway; thence northwesterly, westerly and northwesterly along a line parallel to and three hundred feet southwest, south and southwest of Jefferson Highway to a point three hundred feet south of the south line of College Drive; thence westerly along a line parallel to and

three hundred feet south of the south line of College Drive to the eastern boundary of Glenwood Subdivision; thence southerly along the eastern boundary of Glenwood Subdivision to the southeast corner of Glenwood Subdivision; thence westerly along the southern boundary of Glenwood Subdivision to the center of Wards Creek; thence northerly along the centerline of Wards Creek to a point three hundred feet southeast of the southeast line of College Drive; thence southwesterly, south erly and southwesterly along a line parallel to and three hundred feet southeast, east and southeast of College Drive to the southwest line of the right-of-way of the Kansas City Southern-Louisiana and Arkansas Railway; thence southeasterly along the southwest line of the right-of-way of the said railroad to a point three hundred feet southeast of the southeast line of Glasgow Avenue extended; thence along a line parallel to and three hundred feet southeast of the southeast line of Glasgow Avenue to the northeast boundary line of Glasgow Junior High School site; thence southeasterly, southwesterly and northwesterly along the northeast, southeast and southwest boundaries of Glasgow Junior High School site to the southeast right-of-way line of Brame Road; thence southwesterly along the southeast right-of-way line of Brame Road to the northeast boundary line of Hyacinth Terrace Subdivision; thence southeasterly and southwesterly along the northeast and southeast boundaries of Hyacinth Terrace to the northeast boundary line of Meadow Lea Subdivision; thence southeasterly, southwesterly, southeasterly and southwesterly along the northeast, southeast, northeast and southeast boundaries of Meadow Lea Subdivision to a point on the south bank of Bayou Duplantier; thence southeasterly along the south bank of said channel of Bayou Duplantier to a point three hundred feet southeast of the southeast line of Nelson Drive extended; thence southwesterly along a line parallel to and three hundred feet southeast of the southeast line of Nelson Drive extended, Nelson Drive and Nelson Drive extended to the northeast bank of Bayou Fountain; thence northwesterly along the northeast bank of Bayou Fountain to a point three hundred feet southeast of the southeast line of East Boyd Drive; thence southwesterly along a line parallel to and three hundred feet southeast of the southeast line of East Boyd Drive to the northeast line of the right-of-way of the Illinois Central Railroad; thence northwesterly along the northeast line of the right-of-way of said railroad to its junction with the south line of Gourrier Avenue; thence due west to the west boundary of East Baton Rouge Parish; thence north along the west boundary of East Baton Rouge Parish to a point due west of the zero mile post of the Illinois Central Railroad; thence following the southern and eastern boundaries of industrial area number one, as described in subsection (b) of this section, to the point of beginning.

(b) **Industrial Areas.** There shall be in East Baton Rouge Parish two industrial areas predominantly used for industrial purposes and in which areas there shall be privately furnished the following services usually provided by local governments: the construction, maintenance and cleaning of streets, street lighting, sewers and sewerage works, fire protection, police protection, and garbage and refuse collection and disposal. None of the above services shall be supplied by the parish or city within the industrial areas except police and fire protection in case of grave emergency, as provided by agreements between property owners within the areas and the City of Baton Rouge for mutual assistance in such circumstances. It shall henceforth be unlawful in the industrial areas to construct or alter any building for use in whole or in part for residential purposes. No portion of the industrial areas, so long as the above conditions are observed, shall be added to the urban area. If an industrial area or any portion thereof shall at any time cease to provide at the expense of the industry or industries located therein any of the services or facilities enumerated in this subsection, which are necessary in such area, and these facts are determined after public hearing by the parish council, such industrial area or portion thereof in which such service or facility is not provided at the expense of the industry or industries concerned shall cease to be an industrial area or part thereof and may, without petition by the property owners therein, be added to the urban area by the city council, subject to appeal to the district court as provided in the case of other additions to the urban area. The boundaries of the industrial areas shall be as follows:

(1) Beginning at a point on the west boundary of East Baton Rouge Parish due west to the zero mile post of the Illinois Central Railroad; thence due east to the east line of the right-of-way of the said railroad; thence northerly along the east line of said right-of-way to the junction of said east line of said right-of-way with the north line of Choctaw Drive extended; thence easterly along the north line of Choctaw Drive extended and Choctaw Drive to the west line of Daisy Avenue; thence north along the west line of Daisy Avenue to the north line of Chippewa Street; thence easterly along the north line of Chippewa Street to a point one hundred and seventy-six feet east of the east line of Daisy Avenue; thence northerly along a line parallel to and one hundred and six feet east of the east line of Daisy Avenue to the north line of Ontario Street; thence easterly along the north line of Ontario Street to the east line of Arbutus Street; thence southerly along the east line of Arbutus Street to the north line of Chippewa Street; thence easterly along the north line of Chippewa Street to the east line of Phlox Avenue; thence southerly along the east line of Phlox Avenue to the north line of Choctaw Drive; thence easterly along the north line of Choctaw Drive to the west line of Lockwood Avenue; thence northerly along the west line of Lockwood Avenue to the north line of Seneca Street; thence easterly along the north line of Seneca Street to a point one hundred and fifty feet west of the west line of Lockwood Avenue; thence northerly along a line parallel to and one hundred and fifty feet west of the west line of Lockwood Avenue to a point one hundred and fifty feet north of the north line of Ontario Street; thence easterly along a line parallel to and one hundred and fifty feet north of the north line of Ontario Street to the west line of Lockwood Avenue; thence northerly to the north line of Standard Heights subdivision; thence easterly along said north line of said subdivision to the west line of Scenic Highway; thence northerly along the west line of Scenic Highway to the center line of Monte Sano Bayou; thence in a general southwesterly direction along the center line of Monte Sano Bayou to the east line of the property of Copolymer Corporation; thence northerly along the east line of the property of Copolymer Corporation to the south line of Shada Avenue; thence westerly along the south line of Shada Avenue to the east line of the right-of-way of the Kansas City Southern-Louisiana and Arkansas Railway; thence northerly along the east line of the right-of-way of the said railway to a point on such right-of-way where the same would be crossed by the south line of the property of Southern University if extended; thence westerly along the south property line of Southern University to the east boundary line of Southern Heights Subdivision; thence southerly along the east boundary of said Southern Heights Subdivision a distance of 300 feet; thence westerly along the south boundary of said subdivision a distance of 2904 feet; thence northerly along the west boundary of said Southern Heights Subdivision a distance of 300 feet to the south property line of Southern University; thence southerly along the south property line of Southern University and said line extended to the west boundary of East Baton Rouge Parish; thence southerly along the west boundary of East Baton Rouge Parish to the point of beginning.

(2) Beginning at the intersection of Scenic Highway and Thomas Road; thence easterly along the south line of Thomas Road to the west line of the right-of-way of the Illinois Central Railroad; thence southerly along the west line of said right-of-way, a distance of two thousand, six hundred and sixty-six feet more or less to a point; thence south 86 degrees 16 minutes east a distance of two thousand and three feet more or less to a point; thence south 9 degrees 40 minutes west a distance of four hundred and eighty-three feet more or less to a point; thence north 82 degrees 38 minutes east a distance of one thousand, four hundred and forty-nine feet more or less to a point; thence north 88 degrees 20 minutes east a distance of two thousand, seven hundred and fifty-four feet more or less to the west line of Gibbens Road; thence southerly along the west line of Gibbens Road a distance of two thousand and eighty-seven feet more or less to the north line of Blount Road; thence westerly along the north line of Blount Road to a point which is east one thousand, six hundred and thirty feet more or less from the intersection of Blount Road and Scenic Highway; thence north 27° 04' west a distance of four hundred and sixty-seven feet more or less to a point; thence south 73° 47' west a distance of one thousand, six hundred and thirty feet more or less to the east line of said Scenic Highway; thence northerly along the east line of said Scenic Highway to the point of beginning.

(3) A certain contiguous tract or parcel of real estate (comprised of the three tracts or parcels separately owned by United States Rubber Company, Foster Grant Company, Inc. and W. R. Grace & Company, totaling 376.649 acres, more or less) lying and being in Sections 48 and 49, T-5-S, R-I-W; and Sections 56, 57 and 58, T-6-S, R-I-W, of the Greensburg Land District of Louisiana, East Baton Rouge Parish, Louisiana, and being more particularly described as follows:

Beginning at the northwest corner monument of Section 56 proceed South 53° 00' West and along south line of Section 57 for a distance of 525.36 feet and corner, said corner being the southwest corner of Section 57; thence North 37° 48' West a distance of 300.00 feet and corner; thence North 53° 00' East a distance of 350.03 feet and corner; thence North 37° 48' West a distance of 3,515.22 feet and corner; thence North 66° 14' 37" East a distance of 791.69 feet and corner; thence North 73° 30' East a distance of 3,499.53 feet and corner, said corner being on the westerly right-of-way line of U. S. Highway No. 61 (Old Bayou Sara Road): thence South 24° 12' East along said westerly right-of-way line of U. S. Highway No. 61 a distance of 2,661.60 feet and corner; thence South 27° 12' East and continuing along said westerly right-of-way line of U. S. Highway No. 61 a distance of 1,648.57 feet and corner; thence South 73° 30' West a distance of 186.60 feet and corner; said corner being on the westerly servitude line of the South Shore Railroad Company; thence South 24° 15' West a distance of 300.00 feet and corner; thence South 73° 30' West a distance of 1,465.43 feet and corner; thence North 24° 15' East a distance of 300.00 feet and corner; thence South 73° 30' East a distance of 1,051.47 feet and corner; said corner being on the westerly line of Section 56; thence North 62° 45' West and along said westerly line of Section 56 a distance of 960.70 feet to the point of beginning; more fully shown on plat by Barnard & Burk, Inc., Consulting Engineers, Baton Rouge, Louisiana, dated March 26, 1959.

(c) Rural Area. There shall be in East Baton Rouge Parish a rural area consisting of that portion of the parish not included in either the urban or the industrial areas. Fire protection, garbage and refuse collection and disposal, street lighting, and sewers and sewerage works and the maintenance and operation thereof, shall not be provided by the parish in the rural area except through the medium of districts established by the governing body of the parish, as provided by the constitution and the general laws of the state; provided that the city may supply garbage and refuse collection for a service charge based on not less than the actual cost, to any premises in the rural area from which the parish was actually collecting garbage and other refuse prior to the first day of January 1949.

SECTION 1.09. **ADDITIONS TO THE URBAN AREA.** Whenever a majority in number and amount of property tax payers, as certified by the assessor, in any compact body of land adjoining the city of Baton Rouge but not part of an industrial area, shall petition the governing body of the city to be included in the urban area the said body shall fix a time, not less than ten nor more than thirty days after the filing of such petition, at which it shall hold a public hearing on the proposal to so extend the boundaries of the urban area. Notice of such hearing and of its time, place, objects and purposes, shall be given by publication twice in the official journal of the parish, which publication shall be completed not less than five days prior to the hearing. The valuation of the property owned by each of the signers of the petition shall be certified by the parish assessor as the valuation of such property appears in the last completed assessment of property, provided that he shall take account of subsequent changes of ownership and if in any case the property of the present owner has not been specifically assessed the assessor is authorized and directed to estimate the value of such property. After the conclusion of the hearing the governing body of the city may in its discretion add by ordinance, without additional public hearing, such body of land to the urban area and as such it shall become part of the City of Baton Rouge. Such ordinance shall be published in accordance with law and shall not go into effect until the thirtieth day following its final passage. During such period any citizen of the city or the area proposed to be added thereto may file an appeal therefrom in the district court in the manner and with the effect provided by law. After the conclusion of such period the ordinance shall not be contested or attacked for any reason or cause whatever.

SECTION 1.10. **ADDITIONAL INDUSTRIAL AREAS.** Additional industrial areas may be established by the governing body of the parish on petition of the owners of not less than ninety per cent in amount of the property in such proposed area; provided that any such additional industrial area shall consist of a compact body of land of not less than three hundred and twenty acres situated in a rural area; and provided further, that there shall be filed with the petition an undertaking on the part of the petitioners, secured by such bond as the governing body of the parish may require, to devote the area predominantly to industry, to construct in such area within five years thereafter a substantial industrial plant or plants described in the petition, and to provide at their expense in such area from and after the granting of the petition all necessary streets including the maintenance and cleaning thereof, sewers, sewerage works, fire protection, police protection, and garbage and refuse collection and disposal. Any additional area so established shall be subject to all the conditions provided in subsection (b) of section 1.08. In the event such undertaking is not faithfully carried out the area shall cease to be an industrial area and shall be subject to inclusion in the urban area as provided in subsection (b) of section 1.08.

SECTION 1.11. **LIMITATION ON TAX RATES.** The provisions of section 3 (a) of Article XIV of the constitution of Louisiana relating to the limitation of taxation shall apply in the several areas established by this plan of government, provided that for this purpose the town of Zachary and the village of Baker shall be deemed to be urban areas and municipal taxes may be levied therein as provided by law.

Chapter 2

GOVERNING BODIES

SECTION 2.01. GOVERNING BODY OF EAST BATON ROUGE PARISH —COMPOSITION.

(a) The governing body of East Baton Rouge Parish, hereinafter referred to as the parish council, shall consist of seven persons elected at large from the City of Baton Rouge as extended by this plan of government; one person elected from that district outside of the City designated as Ward Three (Ward Three comprising the old seventh and tenth wards, and portions of the old sixth, eighth and ninth wards not included in the City), and two persons elected from that district outside of the City designated as Ward Two (Ward Two comprising the old fourth and fifth wards and that portion of the old third ward not included in the City), in each case by the persons qualified to vote in such city and in each such district respectively. The additional person to be elected from Ward Two shall be elected at a special election called and held for that purpose in 1965 in accordance with law, and he shall serve through December 31, 1968, and all members of the parish council shall thereafter be elected and serve terms in accordance with the provisions of Section 2.02 of this plan of government.

(b) After the federal census of 1970, and after each census thereafter, members of the parish council shall be added in the following manner: One (1) member shall be elected for each 30,000 population or fraction exceeding one-half thereof residing in each district. The total number of members of the parish council shall not exceed thirteen (13). There shall be at least one (1) member of the parish council elected from the City of Baton Rouge and one (1) member from each of Wards Two and Three.

SECTION 2.02. **METHOD OF ELECTION AND TERM.** The members of the parish council shall be nominated and elected as provided by the general laws of the state insofar as the same are applicable. The members of the parish council shall be nominated and elected in 1948 and every fourth year thereafter at the same times as representatives in the Congress of the United States and shall hold office for terms of four years from the first day of January following their election; provided that the members of the parish council elected in 1948 shall take office for the purposes specified in section 12.02 of this plan of government immediately following the promulgation of the results of such election.

SECTION 2.03. **QUALIFICATIONS.** The members of the parish council elected from the city shall be qualified voters of the parish residing in the city, and each of the remaining members shall be a qualified voter of the parish residing in the district from which he is elected. No member of the parish council or the mayor-president shall, while he holds such office, hold any other office of profit under the United States, the State of Louisiana or any political subdivision thereof, except that of notary public or an office in the National Guard or the military or naval reserve of the United States. No such member shall, during the term for which he was elected and two years there-after, be appointed to any office of profit under the Parish of East Baton Rouge or any unit of local government therein. If any of them shall cease to possess the qualification above required his office shall at once become vacant.

SECTION 2.04. **GOVERNING BODY OF CITY.** The governing body of the City of Baton Rouge shall consist of the seven members of the parish council elected from the city and shall hereinafter be referred to as the city council.

SECTION 2.05. **COMPENSATION.** The salary of each council-man shall be $300.00 per month. Except for travel allowances authorized by law, the members of the parish council shall receive no other compensation.

SECTION 2.06. **VACANCIES.** A vacancy in the membership of the councils from whatever cause arising, occurring within one year of the expiration of the term of any member shall be filled, in the case of a person who is a member of the city council, by appointment by majority vote of the remaining members of the city council of a qualified voter residing in the city, and in other cases by appointment by majority vote of the remaining members of the parish council of a qualified voter residing in the same district as his predecessor. If the vacancy occurs more than one year prior to the expiration of the term of any member it shall be filled, in the case of a person who is a member of the city council, by the vote of the qualified voters of the city, and in other cases by the vote of the quali-fied voters of the district in which the former member resided. Special elections for these purposes shall be called by the parish council and held pursuant to law, within forty days after such vacancy occurs.

SECTION 2.07. **ORGANIZATION.** On the first day of January 1949, and on the first day of January of every fourth year thereafter, or if such first day of January fall on a Sunday then on the succeeding business day, the newly elected parish council and city council shall meet at eight o'clock P.M. in the court-house of East Baton Rouge Parish or at such other place as may be designated by the parish council as its place of meeting and shall take the oath of office before a judge of the district court or other person authorized to administer oaths. There-upon the parish council shall proceed to elect one of their own number to be president pro tempore for a term of four years.

SECTION 2.08. **PARISH CLERK.** The parish council shall appoint and fix the compensation of a parish clerk who shall act as clerk of the parish council and the city council. It shall be his duty to keep separate journals of the proceedings of the parish and city councils, and such journals shall be open to public in-spection in his office during regular business hours. He shall perform such other duties as may be prescribed by this plan of government or by resolution of the parish council or city council. He shall appoint, subject to the provisions of Chapter 9 of this plan of government, all employees in his office. The cost of this office shall be included in the parish budget.

SECTION 2.09. **VOTING.** No ordinance, resolution, motion or vote, except motions of a purely procedural nature, shall be adopted, or any appointment or removal made, by the parish council or city council, unless it shall have received the affirma-tive votes of not less than a majority of all the members of such council. No such action shall be taken except in a meeting open to the public. All voting shall be by roll call and the ayes and noes shall be recorded.

SECTION 2.10. **MEMBERS OF COUNCILS INTERESTED IN PROPOSED ORDINANCE OR RESOLUTION — DUTY TO REFRAIN FROM VOTING.**

Any member of the parish council or city council who shall have any personal or private pecuniary interest in the adoption or passage of any ordinance, resolution, motion or measure, by the body of which he is a member, shall declare such fact to said body, and shall refrain from voting on the same at any time, whether on final passage or otherwise. Any person who shall violate the above provision shall be deemed guilty of a misdemeanor and upon conviction thereof shall be punished by a fine not exceeding one hundred dollars, or imprisonment for not more than sixty days, or both fine and imprisonment, at the discretion of the court, and shall forfeit his office.

SECTION 2.11. **RULES OF PROCEDURE.** The parish and city coun-cils shall have power to adopt rules of procedure not incon-sistent with this plan of government. Such rules shall provide for the time and place of holding regular meetings which may be held at the same time and place or separately. Such rules shall provide for keeping distinct the business of the parish and city councils. They shall also provide for the calling of special meetings of either council by the mayor-president or any three members of the council concerned, and shall prescribe the method of giving notice thereof; provided that the notice of each special meeting shall contain a statement of the specific item or items of business to be transacted, and no other business shall be transacted at such meeting.

SECTION 2.12. **PROCEDURE FOR PASSING ORDINANCES AND RESOLUTIONS.** All ordinances and resolutions shall be introduced in typewritten or printed form. They shall be confined to a single subject which shall be clearly expressed in the title, ex-cept in the case of a codification or revision of ordinances, annual budget ordinances, or ordinances proposing related amendments to this plan of government or proposing the sub-stitution of an entirely new form of government, in which case they shall be deemed to embrace but one subject, and their title need only refer to the general purpose and scope thereof. No ordinance or resolution which makes an appropriation, authorizes the borrowing of money, levies a tax, creates a district which may levy a tax, requires the payment of a license or permit fee, establishes any rule or regulation for the viola-tion of which a fine or other penalty is imposed, grants a franchise, creates or abolishes any office or employment, or places any burden upon or limits the use of private property, shall be adopted at the same meeting at which it was intro-duced, but shall be read a first time and a time, not less than six days after such introduction, fixed, at which the council concerned or a committee thereof shall hold a public hearing thereon. Such hearing may be held separately or in connection with the regular or special meeting of such council and may be adjourned from time to time. The parish clerk shall cause the title of the proposed ordinance or resolution and a notice of the time and place of the hearing to be published in the parish journal at least four days prior to the time fixed for such hearing. The parish clerk shall cause copies of the proposed ordinance or resolution to be mimeographed, printed or other-wise reproduced within three business days after its introduc-tion so that copies may be available to the members of the council and the public. A proposed ordinance or resolution, unless it be an emergency ordinance as hereinafter defined, shall be read a second time, and may be finally passed at any regular or special meeting of the council concerned after the conclusion of the hearing on such ordinance or resolution. An emergency ordinance for the immediate preservation of the public peace, health and safety may be passed at any regular or special meeting, after having been published in full in the official journal of the parish. An emergency ordinance shall contain a specific statement of the emergency claimed and shall be adopted by at least seven affirmative votes in the parish council or five affirmative votes in the city council. No ordinance levying a tax, authorizing the borrowing of money, or granting a franchise shall be adopted as an emergency ordinance. The provisions of this section shall apply to both the parish council and the city council.

SECTION 2.13. **REMOVALS.** Either council may remove any officer or employee appointed by it for an indefinite term, provided it shall first give such officer or employee notice in writing of its intention to remove him, containing a clear statement of the grounds for such removal and fixing the time and place, not less than ten days after the service of the notice, at which he shall be given an opportunity to be heard thereon. After the hearing, which shall be public at the option of the person sought to be removed, and at which he may be represented by counsel, the decision of the council shall be final. Members of unsalaried boards and commissions and other persons appointed by either council for fixed terms may be removed in the same manner except that the only grounds on which they may be removed shall be neglect of duty or misconduct in office.

SECTION 2.14. **POWER OF INVESTIGATION.** Either council, or any committee thereof when authorized by such council, shall have power to investigate the official conduct of any department, office or agency under its jurisdiction. For the purpose of conducting any such investigation or any hearing in connection with the contemplated removal of any officer or employee any council member shall have power to administer oaths, and either council or an authorized committee thereof may compel the attendance of witnesses and the production of books and papers. Any person refusing to obey such an order, if lawfully given, shall upon conviction be subject to a fine of not more than one hundred dollars or imprisonment for not more than sixty days or both.

SECTION 2.15. **SUBMISSION OF ORDINANCES TO THE MAYOR-PRESIDENT.**

(1) Every ordinance, except those hereinafter enumerated, adopted by the Parish or City Councils shall be signed by the Parish Clerk and presented by said officer to the Mayor-President within two (2) calendar days of its adoption.

(2) The Mayor-President, within twelve (12) calendar days of the adoption of an ordinance, shall return it to the Parish Clerk with or without his approval, or with his disapproval. If the ordinance has been approved, it shall become law upon its return to the Parish Clerk; if the ordinance is neither approved nor disapproved, it shall become law at 12:00 o'clock Noon on the twelfth (12th) calendar day after its adoption; if the ordinance is disapproved, the Mayor-President shall submit to the Parish Council or the City Council, as the case may be, through the Parish Clerk a written statement of the reasons for his veto. The Parish Clerk shall record upon the ordinance the date of its delivery to and receipt from the Mayor-President.

(3) Ordinances vetoed by the Mayor-President shall be presented by the Parish Clerk to the appropriate Council at its next regular meeting, and should the Council then, or at its next regular meeting, adopt the ordinance by an affirmative vote of two-thirds (2/3rds) of all of its members, said ordinances shall become law irrespective of the veto thereof by the Mayor-President.

(4) The right of veto, as provided in this section shall not apply to:

(a) Any action of the Councils relating to the conduct of the Councils business or the exercise of its authority pursuant to the provisions of Section 2.13 or 2.14 hereof.

(b) To the making of appointments or the establishments of boards and divisions of government by the Councils as provided by any of the provisions of the Plan of Government, or of Act 169 of 1898, as amended, or the general laws of the State of Louisiana.

(c) To the granting of licenses, permits, or franchises, and ordinances or amendments to ordinances relating thereto.

(d) To the ordering of streets or other improvements to be paved or constructed at the cost and expense of abutting property owners, pursuant to the general laws of the State of Louisiana or of Act 169 of 1898, as amended and the various procedures relating to the awarding of contracts and the levying of special assessments under such local assessment statutes.

(e) To zoning ordinances or amendments to said ordinances.

(f) To any action which the government authority is required by law to take or perform where required to take or perform such action by a petition, or by the provisions of the Plan of Government, the general laws of the State of Louisiana, or of Act 169 of 1898, as amended.

(g) To the adoption of current expense budgets, as provided for in Chapter 9 of the Plan of Government, except that any increase, decrease, deletion of any item in, or any new item added to, or subdivision of items of appropriations in the preliminary budget as submitted by the Mayor-President shall be approved by two-thirds of the entire membership of the Council concerned.

(h) To the fixing of the number or the compensation of the members of the classified and nonclassified services.

(i) To the prescribing of general regulations for the proper operation of the departments of governments when such regulations are specifically required by the Plan of Government to be approved or adopted by the Councils.

SECTION 2.16. **COUNCIL BUDGET OFFICER.** There shall be a Council Budget Officer who shall be an unclassified employee appointed by the Parish Council for an indefinite term. The Council Budget Officer shall have graduated from an accredited four-year college or university, with courses in accounting, or have at least five years of responsible work in the field of public administration, governmental accounting, or general accounting supervision. He shall perform the duties hereinafter enumerated and shall have such other authority and power and perform such other functions as may be prescribed by the Parish and City Councils, subject only to the limitation that such authority not directly conflict with the authority vested in the Director of Finance by the provisions of Chapter 8 of this Plan of Government. The Council Budget Officer shall:

(a) Study and analyze City and Parish revenues and expenditures on a continuing basis, and report thereon to the members of the Parish Council.

(b) Study and analyze budget requests of the various departments, agencies and offices to which the Parish and City make appropriations, and make specific recommendations thereon to the members of the Parish Council.

(c) Determine and have available at all times the status of the general funds of the Parish and City and of all special accounts and funds; the status of appropriations and the amount actually expended or transferred out of all such appropriations; the amount appropriated but not expended and unencumbered during each fiscal year by each budget unit; and the amount which is encumbered but not expended at the close of each fiscal year by each budget unit; and such other budgetary information as may be requested by the members of the Parish Council from time to time.

(d) Review the budget of receipts and expenditures, as recommended by the Mayor-President, and participate in the budget hearings conducted by the Councils and make specific recommendations thereon to the members of the Councils.

(e) Review all audit reports and make specific recommendations with respect thereto.

In the performance of his duties, the Council Budget Officer, or a member of his staff designated by him, shall have the power to inspect and make copies of any books, records, documents, or files of any department, agency or office to which the Parish and City make appropriations. The Budget Officer may call upon all such departments, agencies, or offices for assistance and advice, and shall coordinate his work with that of the Director of Finance in providing budget information to the members of the Councils. He shall appoint, subject to the provisions of Chapter 9 of this Plan of Government, all employees of his office. The cost of the office shall be borne by the Parish and City budgets in such proportions as the Parish and City Councils may designate.

Chapter 3

GOVERNING BODIES — POWERS AND DUTIES

SECTION 3.01. **POWERS OF THE PARISH COUNCIL.** The parish council of East Baton Rouge Parish shall, in addition to the powers and duties conferred or imposed by other provisions of this plan of government, have:

(a) All the powers and duties of East Baton Rouge Parish as provided in section 1.02 of this plan of government.

(b) Exclusive authority, saving the authority of the State of Louisiana, throughout the parish, including the City of Baton Rouge, with regard to the constructing, opening, widening, extending, closing, narrowing, improving, grading, paving, repaving, adorning with trees, shrubs and vines, curbing, guttering, cleaning, repairing, and maintaining of streets, highways, boulevards, parkways, bridges, alleys and other public ways, and the grading, improving, constructing and reconstructing of sidewalks, including the authority to assess the whole or part of the cost of any street, alley or sidewalk improvement on the owners of the abutting property. To that end there are hereby transferred to the parish and to the parish council as the governing body thereof, except as specifically provided in this plan of government, all the powers and duties hitherto conferred or imposed on the City of Baton Rouge by its charter or by the general laws of the state relating to the above enumerated matters, but such transfer of powers shall not be taken to diminish in any respect the power and obligation of the city, from whatever source derived, to: (1) supply street lighting; (2) regulate traffic and the parking of vehicles, including the provision of facilities for off-street parking; (3) grant franchises or permits for the use of the streets, highways, boulevards, parkways, bridges, alleys and other public ways within the city; for pipes, poles, wires, conduits, street railways, bus lines, taxicabs and other vehicles for hire; (4) regulate the rates and conditions of service of any public utility or other person, firm or corporation holding any such franchise or permit; and (5) make charges and collect compensation for the privileges enjoyed by any such utility, person, firm or corporation.

(c) Power to construct, own, maintain and operate airports, and to provide for their management and control by the department of public works, by a separate bureau in the office of the mayor-president, or by a board or commission.

SECTION 3.02. **POWERS AND DUTIES OF THE CITY OF BATON ROUGE AND OF THE CITY COUNCIL.** The City of Baton Rouge as extended by this plan of government shall continue to have all the powers and duties, except as provided in this plan of government, heretofore possessed by the City of Baton Rouge under its charter and the general laws of the state, and such other powers and duties not inconsistent with this plan of government as hereafter may be conferred or imposed on municipalities of the same population class. All provisions of the charter of the City of Baton Rouge not in conflict with the provisions of this plan of government are expressly continued in force and effect and henceforth, shall be subject to amendment only to the same extent and in the same manner as hereinafter provided for the amendment of this plan of government. All ordinances of the City of Baton Rouge in force prior to the first day of January 1949 shall, insofar as they are not inconsistent with this plan of government, remain in force and effect until amended or repealed by the city council.

SECTION 3.03. **POWERS OF ENFORCEMENT.** For the purpose of carrying out the powers and duties conferred or imposed on the parish and city councils, each such council respectively shall have power, whenever it deems it necessary, to require licenses and permits and fix the fees to be paid therefor, to charge compensation for any privilege granted or service rendered, and to provide penalties for the violation of any regulation, which shall not exceed a fine of two hundred dollars, imprisonment for sixty days, or both.

SECTION 3.04. **POWER TO LEVY TAXES.** The power or duty to perform any service or provide any facility, hereby granted to the parish council or city council, shall in all cases carry with it the power to levy taxes and to borrow money within the limits prescribed by this plan of government and by the constitution and general laws of the state for the purpose of performing such service or providing such facility.

Chapter 4

MAYOR-PRESIDENT

SECTION 4.01. **ELECTION OF MAYOR-PRESIDENT.** The chief executive officer of the city and parish shall be a mayor-president who shall be elected by the qualified voters of the parish at the same time and for the same terms as the members of the parish council, provided that the mayor-president first elected shall take office for the purposes specified in section 12.02 of this plan of government immediately following the promulgation of the results of such election. Thereafter the mayor-president shall hold office for a term of four years beginning on the first day of January following his election. He shall be a qualified voter of a parish and if any time during his term of office he shall cease to reside within the parish his office shall be deemed vacant.

SECTION 4.02. **COMPENSATION.** For the term beginning on the first day of January 1949 the compensation of the mayor-president shall be fixed by the parish council at not less than ten nor more than fifteen thousand dollars. Thereafter the compensation of the mayor-president shall be fixed by the council by ordinance adopted at least one year prior to the commencement of the term of the mayor-president whose compensation is to be affected thereby and if no such ordinance be adopted the compensation of the mayor-president shall remain as previously fixed by the council.

SECTION 4.03. **CHIEF EXECUTIVE OFFICER OF THE PARISH AND CITY.** The mayor-president shall be the chief executive officer of the parish and city and shall have power, subject to this plan of government, the ordinances and resolutions of the councils adopted in pursuance thereof, and the constitution and general laws of the state, to supervise and direct the administration of all departments, offices and agencies of the parish and city governments the heads of which are appointed by him. He shall have all the powers and duties, not inconsistent with the provisions of this plan of government, conferred or imposed on the mayor of the City of Baton Rouge by its charter or which may be conferred or imposed on the mayors of cities by the general laws of the state applicable to such city. He shall have power to appoint and remove, subject to the provisions of Chapter 9, of this plan of government, the director of finance, purchasing agent, personnel administrator, director of public works, the chief of the fire department and the chief of police, and such other officers and employees as the respective councils may provide by ordinances pursuant to this plan of government. In the case of any officer or employee, who is not a member of the classified service as provided by Chapter 9 of this plan of government or by any general law applicable to the City of Baton Rouge, the mayor-president shall, before he may exercise the power of removal, first serve on the officer or employee sought to be removed a notice in writing setting forth the grounds of the proposed removal and fixing a time and place, not less than ten days after the service of such notice, at which the officer or employee shall be given an opportunity to be heard thereon. After such hearing, which shall be public at the option of the officer or employee, the action of the mayor-president shall be final. The mayor-president may suspend from duty for not more than sixty days any such officer or employee pending final action.

SECTION 4.04. DUTIES OF THE MAYOR-PRESIDENT. It shall be the duty of the mayor-president:

(a) To attend and preside over meetings of the councils with the right to speak but not to vote.

(b) To keep the councils informed of the financial condition of the parish and the city and of all other matters pertaining to their proper administration, and to make recommendations concerning actions to be taken by the council.

(c) To prepare and submit the annual budgets to the councils as provided in Chapter 8 of this plan of government.

(d) To prepare and submit to the councils not later than their first meeting in March of each year a concise and comprehensive report of the financial transactions and administrative activities of the parish and the city and all districts of which the parish council or city council is the governing body, during the fiscal year ending on the preceding thirty-first day of December, in suitable form for publication, and to cause to be printed for general distribution to all citizens or request such number of copies of the same as the councils shall direct but in no case less than one thousand.

(e) To perform such other duties as may be prescribed by this plan of government or required of him by the ordinances of the respective councils.

SECTION 4.05. PRESIDENT PRO-TEMPORE. The president pro-tempore shall preside over the councils or either of them in the absence of the mayor-president. If the mayor-president is absent from the parish and city or otherwise temporarily disabled from performing his duties the president pro-tempore shall act as mayor-president and in case of a vacancy in the office of mayor-president shall serve as such until the vacancy is filled as hereinafter provided.

SECTION 4.06. VACANCY IN THE OFFICE OF MAYOR-PRESIDENT. A vacancy in the office of mayor-president, from whatever cause arising, occurring within one year of the expiration of his term shall be filled by appointment by majority vote of all the members of the parish council, but if the vacancy occurs more than one year prior to the expiration of his term it shall be filled by a vote of the qualified voters of the parish at a special election called by the parish council and held pursuant to law within forty days after such vacancy occurs.

SECTION 4.07. DIVISION OF PURCHASING. There shall be under the immediate direction of the mayor-president a division of purchasing. The head of the division of purchasing shall be the purchasing agent. He shall be a person skilled and experienced in private business purchasing or governmental purchasing and property control and accountability. It shall be the duty of the purchasing agent to purchase all supplies, materials, equipment, and contractural services, including insurance and surety bonds, for the use of the several departments of the parish and city established by this plan of government, all districts of which the parish council or city council is the governing body, all other departments, boards, commissions, offices and boards to which this provision is constitutionally applicable, or which may request the services of the purchasing agent, henceforth referred to herein as using agencies, excepting the purchase of books for the public library. It shall be the duty of the purchasing agent to consult the head of each using agency as to the kind and quality of the supplies, materials and equipment to be purchased for it.

SECTION 4.08. FURTHER POWERS AND DUTIES OF PURCHASING AGENT. The purchasing agent, for the purpose of giving effect to the provisions of the preceding section, shall have the following powers and duties:

(a) To establish, with approval of the mayor-president and after consultation with the heads of the using agencies concerned, standard specifications for supplies, materials and equipment required by the using agencies.

(b) To prescribe the time of making requisitions and the future period which such requisitions are to cover.

(c) To inspect or cause to be inspected all deliveries of supplies, materials and equipment, and to cause tests to be made when necessary in order to determine their quality, quantity and conformance with specifications.

(d) To supervise and control such central storerooms as the parish council may establish.

(e) To transfer to or between using agencies, sell or trade in, supplies, materials and equipment determined by him, with the approval of the mayor-president and after consultation with the head of the using agency concerned, to be surplus, obsolete or unused.

(f) To maintain an adequate system of accounting for all property received and all property issued by the division of purchasing, in accordance with accepted principles of accounting for property and inventory control; and to maintain such inventory of all movable property under the control of the several using agencies as the parish council or the city council, as the case may be, may require.

SECTION 4.09. COMPETITIVE BIDDING. Before making a purchase or contract the purchasing agent shall give opportunity for competitive bidding under such rules and regulations, not in conflict with general law, as may be established by the parish council and city council respectively. With the approval of the city council where the purchase is to be made with funds appropriated by it, and the parish council in all other cases, the purchasing agent may reject any or all bids and readvertise for bids; provided that competitive bidding shall not be required in the case of contracts for professional service and for services for which the rate or price is fixed by a federal or state authority authorized by law to fix rates or prices. All sales made by the purchasing agent shall be made on the basis of competitive bids after such public notice as may be prescribed by the parish council or city council, respectively, by ordinance and all sales shall be to the highest bidder.

SECTION 4.10. ACCOUNTING CONTROL OF PURCHASING. All

purchases and contracts executed by the purchasing agent shall be pursuant to a written requisition, in such form as may be prescribed by the director of finance, from the head of the using agency whose appropriation is to be charged or from the head of a division or other operating unit thereof to whom such authority has been delegated by the head of the using agency in writing, filed with the purchasing agent. No purchase order made or contract entered into by the purchasing agent shall be valid unless there be endorsed thereon the certificate of the director of finance that there is an unexpended and unencumbered balance in the appropriation and allotment applicable thereto. Nothing herein, however, shall be taken to prevent the purchasing agent from making purchases for a stores revolving fund which the parish council is hereby authorized to establish, and to make sales from the stores account to the several using agencies based on their requisitions; provided that the director of finance certifies that there is an unexpended and unencumbered balance in the appropriation and allotment to be charged.

SECTION 4.11. RECORDS RELATING TO COMPETITIVE BIDDING. A record of all bids, showing the names of the bidders and the amounts of the bids, and indicating in each case the successful bidder, together with the originals of all sealed bids and other documents pertaining to the making of purchases and the award of contracts, shall be preserved by the purchasing agent for six years in a file which shall be open to public inspection during regular business hours.

SECTION 4.12. TRANSACTIONS NOT TO BE DIVIDED. No transaction, which is essentially a unit, shall be divided for the purpose of evading or so as to evade the intent of section 4.09.

SECTION 4.13. FINANCING MAYOR-PRESIDENT'S OFFICE. The number and compensation of the employees in the office of the mayor-president, including the division of purchasing, shall be fixed by the parish council. The compensation of the mayor-president and all other expenses of his office, including those of the division of purchasing, shall be provided by appropriations made by the parish council.

SECTION 4.14. ADMINISTRATIVE OFFICER.

(a) For the purpose of assisting in the supervision and co-ordination of the duties of the mayor-president's office, the mayor-president may appoint an administrative officer who shall be an unclassified employee in the office of the mayor-president. He shall perform the duties hereinafter enumerated and may appoint one secretary or confidential assistant who shall likewise be unclassified. All other employees assigned to his office shall be appointed and removed subject to the provisions of Chapter 9 of this plan of government.

(b) The administrative officer shall have the following minimum qualifications:

1. At least five years' experience in an administrative capacity; and,

2. Must have graduated from an accredited four-year college or university.

(c) The administrative officer shall assist the mayor-president in the duties of his office and shall have and perform the following mandatory duties:

1. Make studies of the internal organization and procedures of any office, department or board, and require such reports from any of them which he deems necessary.

2. Make reports prescribing accepted standards of administrative practice for all administrative offices, departments and boards.

3. Prepare an annual statistical report of city and parish operations for submission to the mayor-president and the parish and city councils, including appropriate recom-

mendations for revisions and changes in administrative practices and other departmental procedures.

(d) Anything in this chapter to the contrary notwithstanding, the compensation of the administrative officer and all other expenses of his office shall be provided by appropriations made by the parish and city councils in such proportions as the councils may determine.

Chapter 5

DEPARTMENT OF PUBLIC WORKS

SECTION 5.01. A SINGLE DEPARTMENT OF PUBLIC WORKS. There shall be for East Baton Rouge Parish and the City of Baton Rouge a single unified department of public works the head of which shall be the director of public works.

SECTION 5.02. DEPARTMENT OF PUBLIC WORKS — ORGANIZATION AND FUNCTIONS. The department of public works shall consist, besides the director of public works, of the following:

(a) The division of engineering which shall: (1) design and prepare plans, specifications and estimates for, and supervise the construction of or construct, all buildings, structures, works or improvements to be undertaken by the parish, the city, or any district of which the parish council or city council is the governing body, provided that nothing herein shall prevent the employment by the mayor-president of consulting engineers and architects, when empowered to do so by the city council if the building, structure, work or improvement is to be undertaken under its authority, or by the parish council in other cases; (2) make all surveys, maps, plans and drawings requested by the parish planning commission, the board of adjustment, the parish attorney, the assessor, and any other department, office or agency of the parish or the city; (3) have custody of all maps and plans of the parish and the city or any part thereof not specifically required by law to be filed in some other place, and to furnish certified copies thereof on such terms as may be prescribed by the parish council; (4) make traffic safety studies in cooperation with the planning commission, and report its findings and recommendations to the mayor-president and city council; (5) supervise the execution of the street lighting contract.

(b) The division of street maintenance which shall: (1) maintain repair and clean streets, highways, boulevards, parkways, bridges, alleys and other public ways; (2) erect street name signs; (3) erect or supervise the erection of traffic signals, lights and signs, and paint traffic directions on pavements.

(c) The division of public building maintenance which shall: (1) maintain and repair all buildings and structures belonging to the parish, the city, or any district of which the parish council or city council is the governing body, except buildings used as schools; (2) provide heat, light and janitorial service for all such buildings and structures except janitorial service in jails.

(d) The division of central garage, authority to establish which is hereby granted to the parish council, which shall, when established, store, maintain and repair cars, trucks and other movable equipment belonging to the parish, the city, or any district of which the parish council or city council is the governing body.

(e) The division of sewer maintenance which shall maintain and operate sewers and sewerage works within the urban area.

(f) The division of refuse collection which shall collect and dispose of garbage and other refuse for the urban area.

(g) The division of inspections which shall: (1) provide in the urban area building, plumbing, electrical and other safety inspections; (2) enforce zoning regulations in the urban area.

(h) Such other divisions or other units of administration, with such powers and duties as may be required by the action of the council whose budget is to provide the cost thereof.

SECTION 5.03. **DEPARTMENT OF PUBLIC WORKS—FINANCING.** The compensation of the director of public works and the number and compensation of the officers and employees in the divisions of engineering, street maintenance, public building maintenance, and central garage if established, shall be fixed by the parish council, and the number and compensation of the officers and employees in the division of sewer maintenance, refuse collection, and inspections by the city council. The divisions enumerated in the first group above shall be supported by appropriations made by the parish council, and in the second group by appropriations made by the city council. The cost, however, of operating the divisions of public building maintenance and central garage if established, shall be distributed between the several departments, divisions, offices and agencies using the services of the same, including other divisions in the department of public works, by means of a system of charges for such services, based on actual cost, to be established by the parish council. The parish council is hereby specifically authorized to establish by appropriation revolving funds for each of these divisions, to be replenished by the charges above provided.

SECTION 5.04. **DIRECTOR OF PUBLIC WORKS—QUALIFICATIONS, POWERS AND DUTIES.** The director of public works shall be a qualified civil engineer licensed to practice his profession under the laws of this state, with at least five years' practical experience in public works or highway administration. He shall have the general management and control of the several divisions of the department of public works and, subject to the provisions of Chapter 9 of this plan of government, shall appoint and remove all the officers and employees of the department and shall have power to make rules and regulations for the conduct of its business consistent with this plan of government and the ordinances of the parish and city councils.

Chapter 6

POLICE DEPARTMENT

SECTION 6.01. **POLICE DEPARTMENT FOR URBAN AREA.** There shall be a police department for the City of Baton Rouge as extended by this plan of government. It shall consist of a chief of police, who shall be the head of the department, and such other officers and employees of such ranks and grades as may be provided by the city council. The police department shall be responsible within the city limits for the preservation of public peace and order, the prevention of crime, the apprehension of criminals, the protection of the rights of persons and property, and the enforcement of the laws of the state and the ordinances of the parish and city councils. All members of the department shall have the same powers and duties with respect to the enforcement of criminal laws as are now or may hereafter be conferred by the laws of the state on police officers.

SECTION 6.02. **POLICE DEPARTMENT—ORGANIZATION.** The city council shall have, except as provided in this plan of government, all the powers and duties relating to the organization and activities of a police department conferred or imposed on the City of Baton Rouge by its charter and the general laws of the state. The chief of police shall be in direct command of the department and, subject to the provisions of Chapter 9 of this plan of government, shall have power to appoint and remove all other officers and employees of the department. He shall assign all members of the department to their respective posts, shifts, details and duties. He shall make rules and regu-

lations consistent with this plan of government, the ordinances of the city council, and the laws of the state, concerning the operation of the police department, the conduct of its officers and employees, and their equipment, training and discipline, and the penalties to be imposed for infraction of such rules and regulations, which when approved by the city council shall be binding on all members of the department.

SECTION 6.03. **CONTINUANCE OF CIVIL SERVICE STATUS OF EXISTING MEMBERS OF POLICE DEPARTMENT.** All regular full-time officers and employees of the police department of the City of Baton Rouge on the first day of January 1949 are hereby continued as members of the city police department in their then ranks and grades, and shall hold such positions until promoted, demoted, transferred or removed, as provided in Chapter 9 of this plan of government.

SECTION 6.04. **FINANCING OF POLICE DEPARTMENT.** The police department shall be supported by appropriations made by the city council.

Chapter 7

FIRE DEPARTMENT

SECTION 7.01. **FIRE DEPARTMENT FOR URBAN AREA.** There shall be a fire department for the City of Baton Rouge as extended by this plan of government. It shall consist of the fire chief, who shall be the head of the department, and such other officers and employees of such ranks and grades as may be provided by the city council. It shall be responsible for providing fire protection within the urban area and not elsewhere in the parish, and any service rendered outside such area, except in accordance with a mutual assistance agreement, shall be rendered only with the approval of the chief or acting chief, who shall not approve such outside service in any case in which the assistance given will detract from the protection provided within the urban area. The city council shall, immediately after the first day of January 1949, provide by the issuance of bonds approved by the resident property taxpayers qualified to vote in the City of Baton Rouge or by the issuance of excess revenue bonds, for the construction of fire houses and a fire alarm system and the purchase of equipment sufficient to furnish adequate fire protection throughout the city. It shall also be the duty of the city council to increase the number of employees of the department to man adequately all of the city's firefighting equipment.

SECTION 7.02. **FIRE DEPARTMENT ORGANIZATION.** The city council shall have, except as provided in this plan of government, all the powers and duties relating to the organization and activities of the fire department conferred or imposed on the City of Baton Rouge by its charter and the general laws of the state. The fire chief shall be in direct command of the department and, subject to the provisions of Chapter 9 of this plan of government, shall have power to appoint and remove all other officers and employees of the department. He shall assign all members of the department to their respective posts, shifts, details and duties. He shall make rules and regulations, consistent with this plan of government, the ordinances of the city council and the laws of the state, concerning the operation of the fire department, the conduct of its officers and employees, their equipment, training and discipline, and the penalties to be imposed for the infraction of such rules and regulations, which rules and regulations, when approved by the city council, shall be binding on all members of the department.

SECTION 7.03. **CONTINUANCE OF CIVIL SERVICE STATUS OF EXISTING MEMBERS OF THE FIRE DEPARTMENT.** All regular full-time officers and employees of the fire department of the City of

Baton Rouge and all regular full-time firemen employed by East Baton Rouge Parish on the first day of January 1949, are hereby continued as members of the city fire department in their present ranks and grades, and shall hold such positions until promoted, demoted, transferred or removed, as provided in Chapter 9 of this plan of government. All regular full-time employees of fire protection District Number One of East Baton Rouge Parish shall also be transferred to the city fire department without competitive examination, provided they meet all requirements for admisison to competitive examinations.

SECTION 7.04. **FINANCING OF FIRE DEPARTMENT.** The fire department shall be supported by appropriations made by the city council.

Chapter 8

FINANCE

SECTION 8.01. **DIRECTOR OF FINANCE.** The head of the department of finance shall be the director of finance. He shall be a person skilled in local government accounting, budgeting and financial control, and shall further have graduated from an accredited four-year college, or university, with a major course in accounting or public administration, or have six years' progressively responsible accounting experience. It shall be his duty to:

(a) Compile for the mayor-president the estimates for the current expense and capital budgets.

(b) Maintain accounting systems for the parish, the city, and districts of which the parish council or city council is the governing body, hereafter in this chapter referred to as districts, and for each department, office and agency thereof, in accordance with the best recognized practices in governmental accounting; keep records for and exercise financial and budgetary control over each such department, office, or agency; keep separate accounts for the items of appropriation contained in the budget, ordinance and the allotments thereof, and encumber such items of appropriation and their respective allotments with the amount of each purchase order, pay roll or contract, approved by him for sufficiency of funds, immediately upon such approval; and keep such records as shall show at all times for each account the amount of the appropriation and the allotments thereof, the amounts paid therefrom and remaining unpaid, all encumbrance hereof, and the unencumbered balance.

(c) Prescribe the form of receipts, vouchers, bills or claims to be used, and the accounts to be kept, by all departments, offices and agencies of the parish, the city, and districts, and provide suitable instructions for the use thereof.

(d) Prescribe the times at and the manner in which moneys received by any department, office or agency for the parish, city, or any district, shall be paid to the parish and city treasurer or deposited in a bank account under his control to the credit of the parish, city, or district, as the case may be.

(e) Examine all contracts, purchase orders and other documents which involve financial obligations against the parish, the city, or any district, and approve the same only upon ascertaining that moneys have been appropriated and allotted, and that an unexpended and unencumbered balance is available in such appropriation and allotment to meet the same.

(f) Audit before payment all bills, invoices, payrolls, and other claims, demands, or charges against the parish, the city, or any district, and approve the same only if proper, legal and correct.

(g) Inspect and audit the accounts and records of financial transactions maintained in each department, office and agency of the parish, the city, and districts.

(h) Submit not later than the tenth day of each month, to the mayor-president, for presentation to the respective councils, statements showing the amount of each appropriation with transfers to and from the same, the allotments thereof to the end of the preceding month, the encumbrances and expenditures charged against such appropriation and the allotments thereof during the preceding month, the total of such charges for the fiscal year to the end of the preceding month, and the unencumbered balance remaining in such appropriation and the allotments thereof. He shall also submit at the same time statements showing the revenue estimated to be received by the parish, the city, and districts, from each source, the actual receipts from each source for the preceding month, the total receipts from each source for the year to the end of the preceding month, and the balance remaining to be collected.

(i) Prepare for the mayor-president not later than the first day of March of each year, a complete financial statement and report of the financial transactions for the preceding year, of the parish, the city, and districts.

(j) Appoint and remove subject to the provisions of Chapter 9 of this plan of government, all employees of the department of finance.

(k) Designate, with the approval of the mayor-president, an employee of the department of finance, as deputy director of the department of finance, who may have and perform all the powers and duties herein conferred or imposed on the director of finance.

SECTION 8.02. **PARISH AND CITY TREASURER.** There shall be a parish and city treasurer who shall be appointed by the parish council for an indefinite term and which office, in the discretion of the parish council, may be combined with that of parish clerk. The parish and city treasurer shall have graduated from an accredited four-year college or university, with courses in accounting, or have at least five years of responsible work in the field of public administration, governmental accounting, or general accounting supervision. He shall have custody of all funds belonging to the parish, the city, and districts, and shall deposit the same in such banks as may be designated by the parish council, on such conditions as are provided by law for the deposit of public money. He shall also be the treasurer of all special and trust funds, with power to invest the same under such conditions as may be prescribed by ordinance by the council concerned, except where otherwise provided by law or by the terms of the trust. He shall have such other powers and duties, not inconsistent with this plan of government, as are conferred or imposed on parish treasurers by law, and shall appoint and remove, subject to the provisions of Chapter 9 of this plan of government, all employees of his office.

SECTION 8.03. **DISBURSEMENTS.** No disbursements shall be made from the funds of the Parish, the City, or any district except by check signed by the treasurer, based upon a voucher or pay roll duly audited and approved by the director of finance. The parish and city councils may by ordinance authorize the treasurer to use a check signing machine or other similar mechanical device for affixing the facsimile signature of the treasurer to checks and other negotiable instruments drawn on the various accounts subject to his control and custody. The councils shall provide in such ordinance such safeguards as may be necessary for the proper protection of the public fisc.

SECTION 8.04. **SURETY BONDS.** The mayor-president, the director of finance, the parish and city treasurer, and all other officers and employees concerned in the handling of money, shall post such surety company bonds, conditioned upon the faithful performance of their duties, as are prescribed by law, or shall be required by ordinance of the city council if the salary of the officer or employee is paid from city funds exclusively, and in all other cases of the parish council.

SECTION 8.05. **COLLECTION OF TAXES.** All taxes levied by the parish council as the governing body of the parish or as the governing body of any district shall be collected by the sheriff as provided by law. The city council may by resolution enter into an agreement with the sheriff for the collection by the sheriff of taxes levied by it. Otherwise they shall be collected by the director of finance and the actual cost of such collection shall be paid from an appropriation thereof made by the city council.

SECTION 8.06. **FISCAL YEAR.** The fiscal year of the parish, the city, and districts shall commence on the first day of January in each year and end on the last day of the succeeding December.

SECTION 8.07. **DEPARTMENTAL ESTIMATES.** The head of every department, office or agency receiving financial support from the parish council or the city council shall file with the director of finance, not later than the tenth day in October in each year, estimates of revenue cash receipts to be received by that department, office or agency for or on account of the parish, city, or any district, and of the expenditures of that department, office or agency for the ensuing year. Such estimates shall be submitted upon forms furnished by the director of finance and shall contain all information which the mayor-president shall require. The mayor-president, with the assistance of the director of finance, shall review these estimates and revise them as he may deem advisable.

SECTION 8.08. **SUBMISSION OF THE BUDGETS.** Not later than the fifth day of November in each year the mayor-president shall submit to the parish council and the city council a current expense budget and a capital budget for the parish and the city respectively. He shall also submit to the parish council or city council, as the case may be, a current expense budget and capital budget for each district of which such council is the governing body, in which district current expenditures or capital outlays are to be made in the ensuing year.

SECTION 8.09. **SCOPE OF CURRENT EXPENSE BUDGETS.** Each current expense budget shall contain in respect of the unit of local government to which it is applicable; (a) an estimate of all revenue cash receipts anticipated from sources other than taxes on property; (b) an estimate of the cash surplus or deficit from the current fiscal year; (c) debt service requirements for the ensuing fiscal year; (d) all other estimated expenditures for the ensuing fiscal year to be met from current revenues; (e) an estimate of the sum required to be raised by the tax levy for the ensuing fiscal year, allowance being made for commissions to be paid to the sheriff, and assuming a rate of collection not greater than the average rate of collection of parish taxes or city taxes, as the case may be, in the year of levy for the last three completed fiscal years; provided that the estimated tax levy shall not in any case exceed the limit established by Section 3 (a) of Article XIV of the constitution of Louisiana; and provided, further, that in no event shall the total estimated expenditures exceed total anticipated cash receipts taking into account the estimated cash surplus or deficit at the end of the current fiscal year and the sheriff's commissions. Revenue cash receipts shall be shown by sources and expenditures by organization units and activities, and the budgets shall be so arranged as to show comparative figures for

receipts and expenditures for prior years, for the current year, and the mayor-president's recommendations for the ensuing year. The current expense budgets shall be accompanied by such supplementary schedules supporting the estimates of receipts and expenditures as the mayor-president may supply or the councils, respectively, may request.

SECTION 8.10. **ALLOCATIONS OF PARISH REVENUES TO MUNICIPALITIES.** The parish council as authorized by Section 3.(a) of Article XIV of the Constitution of Louisiana, shall allocate parish revenues annually to the three municipalities of the Parish by including in the current expense budget for the parish items of appropriation to these municipalities. The total of such allocations shall not be less, in any one fiscal year, than the equivalent of three mills on the taxable valuation of the industrial areas.

All allocations of parish revenues made under authority of this section shall be appropriated and distributed to the municipalities of the parish in the proportion that the population of each said municipality, based upon the last federal census, bears to the total population of the three municipalities in the parish. All amounts so appropriated to the municipalities by the parish council shall be treated as anticipated revenue in the current expense budgets of the respective municipalities. Adjustments of allocations based upon changes in population as determined by the latest federal census shall be effective on the first day of January after the promulgation of each succeeding census.

SECTION 8.11. **CAPITAL BUDGETS.** Each capital budget shall present a program of capital expenditures for the unit of local government concerned, previously considered by the parish planning commission as provided by Chapter 10 of this plan of government, proposed for the ensuing fiscal year and the next four fiscal years thereafter. The mayor-president shall recommend those projects to be undertaken during the ensuing fiscal year and the method of financing them and shall include in the appropriate current expense budget any projects to be financed from current revenues for the ensuing fiscal year. The council concerned shall have power to accept, with or without amendment, or reject, the proposed program and proposed means of financing, but such council shall not authorize any expenditure for the construction of any building, structure, work or improvement, unless the appropriation for such project is included in its capital budget, except to meet a public emergency threatening the lives, health or property of the inhabitants, when passed by seven votes in the parish council or five votes in the city council. The capital budget must be acted upon finally by the council concerned not later than the fifteenth day of December following its submission.

SECTION 8.12. **BUDGET MESSAGE.** The mayor-president shall submit, together with the current expense and capital budgets, a budget message containing his recommendations concerning the fiscal policy of the parish and the city, a description of the important features of the budgets, and an explanation of all major increases or decreases in budget recommendations as compared with expenditures for prior years.

SECTION 8.13. **BUDGETS PUBLIC RECORDS.** All the budgets and supplementary schedules submitted by the mayor-president shall be public records and shall be open to inspection in the office of the parish clerk during regular business hours. The budget message and the current expense and capital budgets shall be published in the official journal of the parish not later than the sixth day following their submission, together with notice of public hearings therein to be held not later than the fourteenth day following such publication.

SECTION 8.14. **PUBLIC HEARINGS.** The public hearing on each budget shall be conducted separately by the council concerned but all such hearings may be announced for the same time and place. The hearings, or any of them, may be adjourned from time to time.

SECTION 8.15. **ACTION BY THE COUNCILS ON CURRENT EXPENSE BUDGETS.** After the conclusion of such public hearings the councils may amend their respective current expense budgets by inserting new items of expenditure, or increasing, decreasing or striking out items of expenditure, except that no item of appropriation for dept service shall be reduced below the amount certified by the director of finance as necessary therefor. Neither council shall alter the mayor-president's estimate of receipts except to correct errors and omissions in which event a full explanation shall be spread on the minutes of the council concerned, but either council may decrease the amount of the tax levy for the ensuing fiscal year as proposed in its current expense budget by the mayor-president in proportion to such decrease as it may make in the total expenditures proposed by the mayor-president. In no event shall a council cause the total proposed expenditures to exceed total anticipated receipts. Not later than the fifteenth day of December and not earlier than the thirty-first day following its publication the councils shall adopt their respective current expense budgets. If either council shall fail to adopt its current expense budget by the fifteenth day of December it shall be presumed to have adopted the budget submitted by the mayor-president. On and after the first day of January the current expense budgets as adopted shall be in effect for the fiscal year beginning on that day. A copy of each of such budgets, certified by the parish clerk, shall be filed in the office of the director of finance. The totals in each current expense budget for each organization unit and activity shall constitute appropriations for their respective purposes, and no expenditure shall be made except in accordance therewith. Each current expense budget as finally adopted shall be published once in the official journal of the parish.

SECTION 8.16. **WORK PROGRAMS AND ALLOTMENTS.** After the current expense budgets have been adopted and before the beginning of the fiscal year to which they are applicable the head of each department, office or agency to which any appropriation is made thereby, shall submit to the mayor-president, in such form as he shall prescribe, a work program which shall show requested allotments of each such appropriation for such department, office or agency, for such fiscal year by quarterly or monthly periods as the mayor-president may direct. Before the beginning of the fiscal year the mayor-president shall approve, with such amendments as he shall determine, the allotments for each department, office and agency, and shall file the same with the director of finance who shall not authorize any expenditure to be made from any appropriation except on the basis of an approved allotment; provided such approved allotments shall conform to the salary schedules provided by the parish council and city council respectively, that the allotments requested by parish officers elected by the people shall not be altered by the mayor-president, and that allotments shall not be enforced prior to the first day of February 1949. Any approved allotment may be revised during the fiscal year in the same manner as the original allotment was made; and if the mayor-president shall at any time ascertain that there will not be for the parish, the city, or the district, sufficient funds to meet total appropriations, it shall be his duty to revise the allotments so as to forestall the incurring of a deficit.

SECTION 8.17. **TRANSFERS OF APPROPRIATIONS.** The mayor-president may at any time authorize the transfer of any unencumbered balance of an appropriation, or portion thereof, to supplement another appropriation made in the same budget to the same department, office or agency. At the request of the mayor-president, but only within the last three months of the fiscal year, either council may by resolution transfer any unencumbered balance of an appropriation made by it, or portion thereof, to supplement on appropriation made in the same budget to another department, office or agency.

SECTION 8.18. **ADDITIONAL APPROPRIATIONS.** Appropriations in addition to those contained in any current expense budget shall be made only on the recommendation of the mayor-president and only if the director of finance certifies that there is available an unappropriated cash surplus sufficient to meet such appropriation.

SECTION 8.19. **LAPSE OF APPROPRIATIONS.** Any portion of a current expense appropriation remaining unexpended and unencumbered at the close of the fiscal year shall lapse. Capital budget appropriations shall not lapse until the purpose for which the appropriation was made shall have been accomplished or abandoned; provided that any project shall be deemed to have been abandoned if three fiscal years pass without any expenditure from or encumbrance of the appropriation therefor.

SECTION 8.20. **CERTIFICATION OF FUNDS, PENALITIES FOR VIOLATION.** No payment shall be made and no obligation incurred against any allotment or appropriation unless the director of finance shall first certify that there is a sufficient unexpended and unencumbered balance in such allotment or appropriation to meet the same. Every expenditure or obligation authorized or incurred in violation of the provisions of this chapter shall be void. Every payment made in violation of the provisions of this chapter shall be deemed illegal, and every official who shall knowingly authorize or make such payment or take part therein, and every person who shall knowingly receive such payment or any part thereof, shall be jointly and severally liable to the parish, the city, or district concerned, for the full amount so paid or received. If any officer or employee of the parish, the city, or any district, shall knowingly incur any obligation or shall authorize or make any expenditure in violation of the provisions of this chapter or knowingly take part therein, such action shall be cause for his removal.

SECTION 8.21. **ANNUAL AUDIT.** The parish council shall provide for an annual audit of the accounts of the director of finance, the parish and city treasurer, and all other officers and employees of the parish, the city, and districts, having to do with the handling of money, by a firm of certified public accountants.

SECTION 8.22. **EXPENSE OF FINANCIAL ADMINISTRATION TO BE SHARED.** The compensation of the director of finance and the parish and city treasurer and the number and compensation of the employees in their respective offices shall be fixed by the parish council. The cost of financial administration, as provided in this chapter, including the annual audit, but excepting the collection of taxes, shall be shared equally by the parish and the city.

Chapter 9

PERSONNEL

SECTION 9.01. **SYSTEM FOR POLICEMEN AND FIREMEN.** Appointments, transfers, promotions, demotions, removals, and all other matters relating to the management of personnel in and for the fire department and police department shall be subject to the general laws of the state applicable to the City of Baton Rouge; provided that wherever in such laws the term mayor is used it shall be interpreted to mean mayor-president as far as the application of such laws to the City of Baton Rouge is concerned.

SECTION 9.02. **PARISH AND CITY PERSONNEL SYSTEM.** There shall be a parish and city personnel system, as provided in this chapter, for all departments, officers and agencies, except the police and fire departments, supported by appropriations made by the parish council or city council, and all other parish offices and boards to which the provisions of this chapter are constitutionally applicable. For the management and operation of the parish and city personnel system there shall be a personnel administrator appointed by the mayor-president for an indefinite term, and a personnel board of three members appointed by the parish council for terms of three years from the first day of January 1949, provided that of those first appointed one shall hold office for one year, one for two years, and one for three years. One member of the board shall always be a member of the classified service and shall be appointed from a list of three nominated by the members of such service at a meeting to be held at a time fixed by the parish council. The other two members of the board shall be known to be in sympathy with the merit principle as applied to the civil service and shall not hold or be a candidate for any other public office or position.

SECTION 9.03. **PERSONNEL ADMINISTRATOR—POWERS AND DUTIES.** The personnel administrator shall have power and be required to:

(a) Prepare and recommend to the personnel board rules to carry out the provisions of this chapter.

(b) Conduct open competitive examinations for all original appointments and, whenever it shall be determined in accordance with the rules of the personnel board to be practicable, for promotions, in the classified service; provided that in formulating examinations he shall consult with the officers having the power of appointment, as to their personnel requirements.

(c) Restrict, in accordance with such rules, eligibility to take such examinations, to persons reasonably qualified, by education, experience, age, and physical condition, to perform their respective duties.

(d) Maintain eligible lists based on such examinations for each class of position in the classified service, and whenever a vacancy is to be filled certify the names of the three persons standing highest on the eligible list applicable to the position concerned. If there are on such eligible list less than three names it shall be the duty of the personnel administrator to give notice of and hold an examination for the recruitment of such list, and if after such notice and examination there still are fewer than three names on such eligible list the personnel administrator shall certify all such names. No appointment shall be made except from an eligible list so certified by the personnel administrator, except as provided in the following subsection; provided that the personnel administrator, with the approval of the personnel board, may enter into agreements with other public personnel departments or agencies for the joint administration of examinations and the joint use of eligible lists.

(e) Authorize in writing temporary appointments to vacancies in positions for which there is no eligible list provided that no such temporary appointment shall be for a longer period than three months and shall not be subject to renewal.

(f) Prepare and recommend to the personnel board a classification plan covering all positions in the classified service.

(g) Prepare and submit to the mayor-president separate pay plans covering the members of the classified service whose compensation is provided from appropriations by the parish council and city council, respectively.

(h) Maintain a roster of all persons in the classified service in which there shall be set forth as to each such person: (1) the class title of the position held; (2) the salary or pay; (3) any changes in class title, pay or status; and (4) such other data as may be deemed desirable or useful.

(i) Certify all pay rolls for persons in the classified service and no payment for personal services to any person in the classified service shall be made unless the pay roll voucher bears the certificate of the personnel administrator that the persons mentioned therein have been appointed and employed in accordance with the provisions of this chapter.

(j) Direct and enforce the maintenance by all departments, offices and agencies in which members of the classified service are employed, of such personnel records and service ratings of members of the classified service as it shall prescribe.

(k) Organize plans for the recruitment of trained personnel for the service of the parish and city, and promote a systematic program of in-service training for members of the classified service to qualify them for advancement.

SECTION 9.04. **PERSONNEL BOARD—POWERS AND DUTIES.** The personnel board shall have power and be required to:

(a) Adopt and amend, on the recommendation of the personnel administrator, rules consistent with this plan of government and the ordinances of the city and parish councils, for the purpose of carrying out the provisions of this chapter. Among other things they shall provide for the method of holding competitive examinations; the method of certifying eligibles for appointment; the establishment, maintenance, consolidation and cancellation of eligible lists; the administration of the classification plan and the pay plan; methods of promotion and the application of service ratings thereto; probationary periods of employment; the transfer of employees within the classification plan; hours of work, vacations, sick leaves, and other leaves of absence, overtime pay; the order and manner in which layoffs shall be effected, and suspensions and dismissal and appeals therefrom; and such other rules as may be necessary to provide an adequate and systematic procedure for handling the personnel affairs of the parish and the city.

(b) Adopt, after public hearings, a classification plan as provided in section 9.06.

(c) Hear appeals from members of the classified service affected by the classification, reclassification, and allocation of positions, and also hear appeals from any disciplinary action suspending, reducing in rank or pay, or removing any member of the classified service, as hereinafter provided.

(d) Investigate any or all matters relating to conditions of employment in all departments, offices and agencies in which members of the classified service are employed, and make at least annually a report of its findings to the parish council.

SECTION 9.05. **CLASSIFIED AND UNCLASSIFIED SERVICES.** The service of all departments, offices, and agencies, except the police and fire departments, supported by appropriations made by the parish council or city council, shall be divided into the unclassified and the classified services. The unclassified service shall comprise: (a) officers elected by the people and persons appointed to fill vacancies in elective offices; (b) persons appointed by the parish council or city council; (c) the heads of departments appointed by the mayor-president, the chief executive officer of each board and commission appointed by the council, and not more than one assistant or confidential secretary to the mayor-president and each head of a department; (d) the clerk of the parish court and deputies of the parish constable; (e) assistant parish attorneys; (f) persons employed in a professional or scientific capacity to make or conduct a temporary or special inquiry, investigation or examination, including special counsel. The classified service shall comprise all positions included in the parish and city personnel system as defined in Section 9.02 not specifically included by this section in the unclassified service. All appointments and promotions in the classified service shall be made as provided in Section 9.03. No member of the classified service shall be suspended for more than thirty days, reduced in rank or pay, or removed, except after notice in writing of the grounds of the proposed disciplinary action and an opportunity to be heard thereon by the personnel board at a hearing which may be public at his option, and at which he may be represented by counsel, to be held not less than ten nor more than twenty days after the service of such notice at a time to be specified therein. The decision of the personnel board either sustaining, reversing or modifying the disciplinary action appealed from shall be final. At all such hearings, and as otherwise required for the purpose of the administration of the provisions of this chapter and of the rules and regulations of the Personnel Board, the Personnel Administrator shall have the power to make services and to administer oaths, for disobedience of which the penalities prescribed in Section 9.11 shall apply.

SECTION 9.06. **CLASSIFICATION PLAN.** The personnel administrator first appointed shall, as soon as practicable after his appointment, prepare and submit to the personnel board a classification plan for all positions in the classified service, according to similarity of authority, duties and responsibilities. The personnel board shall hold a public hearing thereon at least ten days' notice of which shall be given by publication in the official journal of the parish, and within thirty days after the submission of the plan by the personnel administrator it shall reject or adopt the same with or without modification. Changes in the classification plan may thereafter be recommended from time to time by the personnel administrator and shall take effect when approved by the personnel board. After the adoption of the classification plan the class titles set forth therein shall be used to designate such positions in all official records, documents, vouchers and communications, and no person shall be appointed to or employed in a position in the classified service under any class title which has not been recommended by the personnel administrator and approved by the personnel board as appropriate to the duties to be performed. Employees affected by the allocation or reallocation of a position to a class or by any change in the classification plan shall be afforded an opportunity to be heard thereon by the personnel board after filing with the personnel administrator a request for such hearing.

SECTION 9.07. **PAY PLANS.** The personnel administrator shall prepare and recommend to the mayor-president, within thirty days after the adoption of the classification plan by the personnel board, separate pay plans which shall be transmitted by the mayor-president with his recommendations to the parish and city councils respectively. Each such pay plan shall consist of a salary range for each class of position in the classification plan, which shall provide for regular increase within each such range, to be earned by length of service and satisfactory service ratings. Each such range shall be determined with due regard to the salary ranges for other classes and to the relative difficulty and responsibility of characteristic duties of positions in the class, the minimum qualifications required, the prevailing rate paid for similar employment outside the service of local government, and any other factors that may properly be considered to have a bearing on the fairness and adequacy of the range. The councils shall have power to adopt their respective pay plans, with or without modification. When so adopted each pay plan shall remain in effect until amended by the council concerned. When a pay plan has been adopted by either council such council shall not increase or decrease the salaries of individual members of the classified service but shall act in fixing the salaries of members of the classified service only by amendment of the pay plan.

SECTION 9.08. **PROMOTIONS.** Vacancies in higher positions in the classified service shall, as far as practicable, be filled by promotion from lower classes upon the basis of competitive examinations including a consideration of service ratings; provided that in case the personnel administrator so determines, with the approval of the mayor-president, such positions shall be filled by competitive examination open not only to persons in the classified service but also to all other qualified persons. The provisions of subsection (d) of section 9.03, relating to eligible lists, shall be applicable to filling vacancies under this section.

SECTION 9.09. **STATUS OF PRESENT EMPLOYEES.** All regular full-time employees of the City of Baton Rouge and East Baton Rouge Parish at the effective date of this plan of government, except policemen and firemen, shall be given preference over all other applicants in the determination of eligible lists for appointment to positions in the classified service as defined in section 9.05; provided that they possess the qualifications as to education, age, and physical condition, required by the personnel board for the admission of candidates to competitive examination for the class of position concerned.

SECTION 9.10. **PROHIBITED PRACTICES.** No person in the classified service or seeking admission thereto shall be appointed, promoted, reduced, removed, or in any way favored or discriminated against because of his political or religious opinions or affiliations. No person shall willfully or corruptly make any false statement, certificate, mark, rating or report in regard to any test, certification, promotion, reduction, removal or appointment held or made under the provisions of this chapter, or in any manner commit or attempt to commit any fraud preventing the impartial execution thereof or of the rules and regulations made in accordance therewith. No officer or employee in the classified service shall continue in such position after becoming a candidate for election to any public office. No person shall either directly or indirectly pay, render or give any money, service or other valuable thing to any person for or on account of or in connection with any test, appointment, promotion, reduction or removal in which he is concerned. No person shall orally, by letter, or otherwise solicit or be in any manner concerned in soliciting any assessment, subscription or contribution for any political party or political purpose whatever from any person holding a position in the classified service. No person holding a position in the classified service shall make any contribution to the campaign funds of any political party or candidate for public office or take any part in the management, affairs or campaign of any political party or candidate further than in the exercise of his rights as a citizen to express his opinion and to cast his vote. Any person who by himself or with others willfully or corruptly violates any of the provisions of this section shall upon conviction thereof be punished by a fine of not more than five hundred dollars or by imprisonment for a term not exceeding six months or by both. Any person who is convicted under this section shall for a period of five years be ineligible for appointment to or employment in a position in the service of the parish, the city, or any district of which the parish council or city council is the governing body, and shall, if he be an officer or employee of any of the above, immediately forfeit the office or position he holds.

SECTION 9.11. **POWER OF PERSONNEL BOARD TO CONDUCT INVESTIGATIONS.** For the purpose of the administration of the provisions of this chapter each member of the personnel board shall have the power to administer oaths and the board may by majority vote compel the attendance of witnesses and the production of books and papers. Any person disobeying such order of the personnel board shall be subject to a fine of not more than one hundred dollars or imprisonment for not more than sixty days or both.

SECTION 9.12. **VETERANS' PREFERENCE.** Any person who has served in time of war in the army, navy, marine corps, or coast guard of the United States and has been honorably discharged therefrom shall be entitled to have added to his rating in any examination held under the provisions of this chapter ten points on a scale of one hundred if he is eligible for or actually receiving disability compensation, pension, or other benefits from the United States, or five points on a scale of one hundred if he is not so eligible, provided that he shall be within the age limit specified for appointment to the position or class of position for which the examination is held, is physically capable of performing the duties of such position, and attains in the examination without such added points the minimum rating prescribed for passage of such examination.

SECTION 9.13. **FINANCING PERSONNEL SYSTEM.** The cost of the parish and city personnel system shall be included in the parish budget.

SECTION 9.14. **APPLICABILITY OF GENERAL STATE LAW.** If at any time a general state law providing a personnel system for city employees becomes applicable to the City of Baton Rouge and the provisions of such personnel system shall be applied to the employees of all departments, offices and agencies supported by appropriations made by the parish council as fully as if such employees were employees of the City of Baton Rouge; provided that the unclassified service of the parish shall include all elective officers of the parish, all persons appointed by the parish council, heads of departments appointed by the mayor-president, the chief executive officer of each board or commission appointed by the parish council, and one assistant or confidential secretary to the mayor-president and to each head of a department.

SECTION 9.15. **PENSIONS.** It shall be the duty of the Mayor-President, as soon as practicable after the first day of January 1949 to cause to be made at the joint expense of the Parish and City an actuarial study by a competent actuary of the requirements of the Police and Fire pension systems established by the charter of the City of Baton Rouge and of the requirements of an actuarially sound and reasonable pension system for all regular full-time employees whose compensation is derived from appropriations by the Parish Council or City Council. Upon the completion of such actuarial study the Parish and City are hereby authorized to establish by concurrent ordinances and amendments thereto a pension system for all regular full-time employees including policemen and firemen, whose compensation is derived from appropriation by the Parish Council and City Council. Such ordinances and the amendments thereto shall provide for contributions to a pension fund by all employees included in the system, and by the Parish and the City, sufficient to establish an actuarially sound reserve from which pensions shall be paid. Such ordinances shall also provide the conditions for retirement and fix the amount of retirement allowances. Such ordinances or amendments thereto shall also provide the administration of the pension system and the creation of a pension board composed of not more than seven members of whom four shall be members of the pension system, two selected by those employee members other than policemen and firemen, and one each selected from among the members of said system in the Police and Fire Departments. The remaining membership of the board shall consist of the Director of Finance, and two persons with business and accounting experience appointed by the Parish Council. The board shall administer the pension system and have custody and invest the pension reserve. As of the effective date of the pension system established by said concurrent ordinances and amendments thereto and as authorized by this section, the pension board shall be responsible for the administration of the funds held at that date by the police pension board and the board of trustees of the firemen's pension and relief fund, and shall employ such funds, respectively, in paying the pensions of those actually receiving pensions or entitled to receive pensions at such date in accordance with the provisions of the charter of the City of Baton Rouge, Policemen and firemen actually receiving or entitled to receive pensions at the effective date of the pension system authorized by this section are hereby guaranteed the payment of such pensions from the police pension fund and the firemen's pension and relief fund, respectively, and if such funds prove insufficient for the purpose the City Council shall appropriate sufficeint funds annually to pay such pensions. Policemen and firemen in the service of the city prior to the effective date of this plan of government shall be given full credit for the length of such service in determining their eligibility for retirement under the pension system authorized by this section. After the adoption of such pension system the pension systems for policemen and firemen provided by the charter of the City of Baton Rouge shall cease to exist. The pension system heretofore established by the concurrent ordinances and amendments thereto adopted by the parish and city councils pursuant to the provision of this section shall constitute the Employees' Retirement System for the City of Baton Rouge and the Parish of East Baton Rouge, and the parish and city councils shall hereafter be prohibited from making any amendment, revision, or change thereto which would have the effect of reducing the benefits, whether accrued or not, of the members of said system. The parish and city councils may, in the event social security benefits are legally authorized in the case of policemen and firemen, amend, revise or change the provisions of said system so as to provide for the integration of benefits accruing to such employees with federal social security, provided, however, that it be first determined by a competent actuary that greater benefits to the members of the police and fire departments would result from such integration will not have the effect of reducing the benefits of said employees. The parish and city councils shall annually appropriate such funds as may be required, in addition to those contributed by the employees, to maintain the system on an actuarially sound basis, and to provide the employer's contribution, if any, as required by federal social security.

Chapter 10

PLANNING AND ZONING

SECTION 10.01. **PLANNING COMMISSION—COMPOSITION.**

(a) There shall be a planning commission which shall consist of nine members. One member shall be a member of the parish council who shall be appointed by the latter for a term coincident with his term on the council; one member shall be the mayor-president or an officer or employee of the city designated by the mayor-president from time to time; one member shall be a member of the school board for a term coincident with his term on the school board; one member shall be a member of the recreation and park commission of East Baton Rouge Parish who shall be appointed by the commission for a term coincident with his term on the commission;

and five members shall be qualified voters and taxpayers of East Baton Rouge Parish, two residing in the rural area and three residing in the City of Baton Rouge, appointed by the parish council for a term of five years. The citizen members shall be appointed for terms of five years. Members may be removed by the parish council only for official misconduct or neglect of duty. Membership on the planning commission shall be forfeited by any member who has been absent without a valid excuse for more than five meetings, general or special, during one year of service. Vacancies arising among the appointive members shall be filled by the appointing body for the unexpired portion of the term.

(b) If the Parish of East Baton Rouge is authorized to zone property outside of incorporated municipalities, the planning commission, in its capacity as the parish planning commission, shall constitute the zoning commission provided for by such laws. No ordinance, nor resolution, adopting, amending, supplementing, changing or modifying any regulation or restriction or district boundary authorized by such laws to be made by the governing authority of the Parish shall be passed by that body until such ordinance or resolution has been submitted to and approved or disapproved by the planning commission acting in its capacity as zoning commission of the Parish of East Baton Rouge.

SECTION 10.02. **PLANNING COMMISSION—ORGANIZATION.** The first planning commission appointed under the provisions of this chapter shall meet as soon as practicable after its appointment and organize by election one of its members to be chairman for a term of one year from the first day of January 1949 and until his successor is elected and qualified. Thereafter the commission, at its first meeting in January of each year, shall elect one of its members to be chairman for a term of one year, who shall be eligible for re-election. The commission shall adopt rules of procedure in which it shall fix the time for its regular meetings which shall be held at least as frequently as once a month. It shall appoint a secretary who shall keep a journal of its proceedings, in which shall be recorded all actions taken by the commission and which shall be a public record. The commission shall appoint and remove, subject to the provisions of Chapter 9 of this plan of government, such other employees as it may deem necessary for its work, and shall have authority to contract with planning experts, engineers, architects, and other consultants; provided that the expenditures of the commission, exclusive of amounts received by contribution, shall be limited to the appropriations for the purpose made by the parish council and city council.

SECTION 10.03. **PLANNING COMMISSION—POWERS AND DUTIES.** The planning commission shall constitute a parish planning commission in respect of that portion of the parish outside the City of Baton Rouge and other municipalities and shall in that capacity have all the powers and duties conferred or imposed on parish planning commissions by the general laws of the state. The planning commission shall likewise constitute a city planning commission for the City of Baton Rouge and in that capacity shall have all the powers and duties conferred or imposed on city planning commissions by the general laws of the state.

SECTION 10.04. **CAPITAL BUDGET.** It shall be the duty of the planning commission to prepare and revise annually a program of capital improvements, for the parish and city respectively, for the ensuing five years, and it shall submit the same annually to the mayor-president at such time as he shall direct, together with estimates of the cost and recommendations as to the means of financing such capital improvements to be

undertaken in the ensuing fiscal year and in the next four years, as the basis of the capital budgets to be submitted by the mayor-president to the councils. In the preparation of its capital budget recommendations the planning commission shall consult with the mayor-president, the heads of departments, the school board, state officials, and interested citizens and organizations, and shall hold such hearings as it shall deem necessary.

SECTION 10.05. **ZONING.** The city council shall have all the powers and duties relating to zoning which are conferred or imposed on the legislative bodies of cities by the general laws of the state. The planning commission, in its capacity as the city planning commission, shall constitute the zoning commission provided for by such laws. No ordinance or resolution adopting, amending, supplementing, changing or modifying any regulation or restriction or district boundary authorized by such laws to be made by the city council shall be passed by the city council until such ordinance or resolution has been submitted to and approved by the planning commission; provided that failure of the planning commission to act on any ordinance or resolution submitted to it within sixty days of such submission shall be deemed to constitute approval thereof; and provided further that an ordinance or resolution disapproved by the planning commission may be adopted by the city council by not less than five affirmative votes.

Chapter 11

MISCELLANEOUS

SECTION 11.01. **PARISH ATTORNEY.** There shall be a parish attorney who shall be appointed by the parish council for an indefinite term. He shall be an attorney-at-law and shall have actively practiced his profession in the state for at least five years immediately preceding his appointment. He shall appoint such assistant parish attorneys as may be authorized, at least one of whom shall, at all times, be assigned to the prosecution of ordinance violations, as hereinafter provided. He shall be the legal advisor of the parish and city councils, the mayor-president, and all departments, offices and agencies appointed by or under the jurisdiction of any of the above and shall furnish them on request a written opinion on any question of law involving their official powers and duties. At the request of the mayor-president or any member of either council he shall prepare ordinances and resolutions for introduction. He shall draw or approve all bonds, deeds, leases, contracts, or other instruments to which the parish, the city or any district of which the parish council or city council is the governing body is a party or in which any of them has an interest. He shall represent the parish, the city and any district of which the parish council or city council is the governing body in all civil litigation. He shall, in person or through an assistant parish attorney assigned to such duty, represent the city in the prosecution of all ordinance violations in the city court, except that he shall have no authority to nolle prosequi. He shall further represent both the parish and city in any criminal case in which the constitutionality or validity of any ordinance or resolution of either council is in issue. He shall appoint and remove all employees of his office, subject, except in the case of assistant attorneys, to the provisions of Chapter 9 of this plan of government. The compensation of the parish attorney and of all employees in his office shall be fixed by the parish council and the whole cost of the office shall be provided by appropriations made by the parish council, except that the cost of any assistant parish attorney and other employees assigned to prosecute ordinance violations shall be included in the city budget. Nothing herein shall be taken to prevent the employment of special counsel when authorized by the parish council or city council in any matters relating to their respective jurisdictions.

SECTION 11.02. **RECREATION AND PARK COMMISSION.** The recreation and park commission for East Baton Rouge Parish shall consist of: the mayor-president, or an officer or employee of the city or parish designated by the mayor-president from time to time; a member of the school board of East Baton Rouge Parish appointed by the school board for a term coincident with his term on the school board; a member of the planning commission appointed by the latter for a term coincident with his term on the planning commission; and six qualified voters of the parish appointed by the parish council for terms of three years. The six members of the commission appointed by the parish council in office on January 1, 1953, shall each continue to hold office until the expiration of the term for which he was appointed, and thereafter his successor shall be appointed for a term of three years. Vacancies among the appointive members shall be filled by the appointing body for the unexpired portion of the term.

The recreation and park commission shall have exclusive responsibility for the provision of park and recreation facilities in East Baton Rouge Parish. It shall have the maintenance, management and control of all the parks, playgrounds, play fields, or other property permanently devoted to recreational purposes, and the cemeteries, belonging to the City of Baton Rouge and to East Baton Rouge Parish, and no such property shall be alienated, sold leased or otherwise disposed of by the city so long as it continues to be used by the recreation and park commission for recreational purposes. The recreation and park commission shall succeed to all the powers and duties relating to parks and recreation heretofore conferred or imposed on the City of Baton Rouge by its charter or the general laws of the state, including the power to make charges for the use of recreational facilities and incidental services and shall have all the powers and duties conferred or imposed on such commission by section 3 (b) of Article 14 of the constitution of Louisiana and Act No. 246 of 1946 and all future acts amendatory thereof and supplementary thereto. The parish and city councils are hereby authorized to make appropriations for the support of the recreation and park commission.

The recreation and park commission is hereby authorized to make use of the accounting services of the director of finance as described in section 8.01 (b-k inclusive) hereof, the services of the engineering, building maintenance and central garage divisions of the department of public works, of the purchasing division, and to become a part of and subject to the personnel systems established by chapter 9 of this plan of government or any personnel system for city employees in general provided by a general law of the state applicable to the City of Baton Rouge, on such terms and conditions as may be agreed to by the council out of whose appropriations the cost of any such service is provided.

The recreation and park commission shall prepare and submit to the planning commission, not later than October 10 of each year, a capital budget presenting a program of capital expenditures recommended to be undertaken during the ensuing fiscal year, and proposing the method of financing them. The planning commission shall approve or disapprove each item on this capital budget, and shall return the latter to the recreation and park commission not later than December 15 of each year. The recreation and park commission shall not issue any bonds or other certificates of indebtedness, nor authorize any expenditure for the purchase of land or the construction of any building, structure, work or improvement unless the appropriation for such project either has been included in the capital budget and approved by the planning commission, or shall be authorized by a vote of at least six members of the recreation and park commission.

SECTION 11.03. **PUBLIC LIBRARY.** There shall continue to be a public library for East Baton Rouge Parish, with such branches and other services as may be established by the board of control thereof. The board of control shall, after the first day of January, 1949, consist of the mayor-president exofficio and five citizens of the parish appointed by the parish council for terms of five years, provided that the five citizen members of the board of control in office on the said first day of January, 1949, shall each continue in office until the expiration of his term and that thereupon his successor shall be appointed for a term of five years. Vacancies shall be filled by the parish council for the unexpired portion of the term. The board of control shall have all the powers and duties conferred or imposed by the general laws of the state on boards of control of parish public libraries, and the cost of maintaining the parish public library and its several branches and services shall be provided by appropriations made by the parish and city councils, such appropriations to be in such amounts and proportions as the respective governing authorities may determine.

SECTION 11.04. **CITY COURT AND JUDGE.** There shall continue to be a city court of the City of Baton Rouge, which shall have jurisdiction over the territorial area of the City of Baton Rouge, as extended by this plan of government, and the provisions of Title 13, Sections 2071 through 2080 of the Louisiana Revised Statutes of 1950, shall continue in full force and effect except to the extent that they are in conflict with the provisions of this section. The city court shall be a court of record except where the amount in dispute is less than $100.00, exclusive of interests. The city court shall exercise such jurisdiction within the territorial limits of the City of Baton Rouge as may be conferred upon it by the constitution of the State of Louisiana.

The city court shall have but one judge, unless the number be increased by a vote of two-thirds (2/3rds) of the members of the city council. If there be more than one judge, the senior in point of service on the court shall be the chief or presiding judge.

Judges of the court must be electors of the City of Baton Rouge, and have been admitted to the practice of law in Louisiana at least three (3) years prior to their selection. Unless otherwise provided by the Legislature of the State of Louisiana pursuant to the provisions of Article 7, Section 51 of the Constitution of the State of Louisiana, the judges of the city court shall be elected for terms of four (4) years, such elections to take place at the same time and in the same manner as provided for election of members of the parish council and the mayor-president. The judges of the city court shall receive such salary as the city council may from time to time determine, but such salary shall not be decreased during their tenure of office and moreover, shall not be less than $10,000.00 per annum. For the term beginning January 1, 1953, the annual salary of the city judge or judges shall be fixed by the city council not later than December 1, 1952. Thereafter the annual salary of the city judge or judges shall be fixed by the city council by ordinance adopted at least one year prior to the commencement of the term of the city judge or judges whose compensation is to be affected thereby, and if no such ordinance be adopted, the compensation for the city judge or judges shall remain as previously fixed by the city council.

Judges of the court shall not practice law, nor shall they or any officer or employee of the court receive any fees.

The clerk of the city court shall be appointed by the city judge at a salary fixed by the city council. The number and compensation of deputy clerks and employees, who shall be members of the classified service as provided in Chapter 9 of this plan of government or any personnel system for city employees in general applicable to the City of Baton Rouge, shall be fixed by the city council.

All expenses of the court, including the compensation of the judge, clerk and other employees, shall be paid from appropriations made by the city council.

The court shall have full power to make and promulgate its own rules of Court within the limitations as might otherwise be imposed by the Constitution or Legislature of Louisiana.

SECTION 11.05. CITY CONSTABLE. There shall continue to be a city constable for the City of Baton Rouge as extended by this plan of government and the provisions of the charter of the City of Baton Rouge relating to such city constable shall continue in full force and effect, except to the extent that they are in conflict with the provisions of this section.

The city constable shall receive no remuneration for the performance of his official duties except the salary mentioned hereinafter. The annual salary of the city constable shall be fixed by the city council by ordinance adopted at least one year prior to the commencement of the term of the city constable whose compensation is to be affected thereby, and if no such ordinance be adopted the compensation of the city constable shall remain as previously fixed by the city council.

The chief deputy constable shall be appointed by the city constable at a salary fixed by the city council. In the event of the city constable's absence or inability to act for any cause, the chief deputy constable shall have the power and authority to act in his capacity, and to perform all the powers and duties conferred or imposed on the constable. The number and compensation of other deputy constables, who shall be members of the classified service as provided in Chapter 9 of this plan of government or any personnel system for city employees in general applicable to the City of Baton Rouge, shall be fixed by the city council.

All expenses of the city constable office, including the compensation of the constable and his deputies, shall be paid from appropriations made by the city council.

SECTION 11.06. JUSTICES OF THE PEACE AND WARD CONSTABLES. From and after the first day of January 1949 no justice of the peace or ward constable shall be elected for or exercise jurisdiction in the City of Baton Rouge as extended by this plan of government, but justices of the peace and constables shall be elected from justice of the peace wards outside the city, to be determined by the governing body of the parish, which may consist of the whole or part of any pre-existing police jury ward or of a combination of such wards or parts of such wards, provided that the justices of the peace and constables elected in 1948 for any ward shall retain and exercise their powers, duties and jurisdictions within the limits of such ward, or the portion of such ward outside the City of Baton Rouge, for the term for which they were elected.

SECTION 11.07. PARISH AND SCHOOL BOARD NOT AFFECTED. Nothing in this plan of government shall be taken to affect in any way the rights, powers and duties of the East Baton Rouge Parish school district or the East Baton Rouge Parish school board.

SECTION 11.08. CERTAIN OFFICERS TO HOLD OFFICES UNTIL THEIR SUCCESSORS ARE ELECTED OR APPOINTED AND QUALIFIED.

The mayor-president, the members of the parish and city councils, the judge of the city court, the city constable, and all officers or members of boards and commissions appointed for fixed terms, shall hold office until their successors are elected or appointed and qualified.

SECTION 11.09. AMENDMENT. Amendments of this plan of government may be proposed by majority vote of all the members elected to the parish council or by a petition containing the full text of the proposed amendment signed by qualified voters of East Baton Rouge Parish in number equal to ten per cent of the number of votes cast for sheriff at the last preceding election of parish officers and filed in the office of the parish clerk. A proposed amendment shall be submitted by the parish council to the qualified voters of the parish at a special election to be called and held by the parish council not less than sixty nor more than ninety days after the passage of the amendment by the parish council or the filing of the petition; provided, that if a state or congressional primary or election falls within the above period the special election may be held in connection with such primary or election. The parish council shall call and hold such special election in the same manner as is provided for the calling and holding of elections on bond issues under Act No. 46 of the extraordinary session of the legislature of the State of Louisiana for the year 1921, as amended, except that all qualified voters of East Baton Rouge Parish shall be eligible to vote in such election and except that the form of ballot shall be prescribed by the parish council. The parish council shall promulgate the returns of said election and shall cause a proces verbal of the election to be filed with the clerk of court of the parish. If the majority of the votes cast on such amendment are in favor thereof a certified copy thereof shall be filed with the secretary of state and it shall become effective on the thirtieth day following the promulgation of the result of the election unless another time is specified in such amendment.

SECTION 11.10. SEVERABILITY. If any provision of this plan of government or the application thereof to any person or circumstance is held invalid the remainder of this plan of government and the applicability of such provision to other persons or circumstances shall not be affected thereby.

Chapter 12

TRANSITIONAL PROVISIONS

SECTION 12.01. ELECTION OF PARISH COUNCIL, CITY COUNCIL, MAYOR-PRESIDENT, CITY JUDGE, AND CITY CONSTABLE. The provisions of this plan of government relating to the election of the parish council, city council, mayor-president, city judge, and city constable, including the division of the parish outside the city into districts for the purpose of electing members of the parish council, shall take effect upon the promulgation of the result of the special election at which this plan of government is submitted. For the purpose of electing members of the parish council the City of Baton Rouge as extended by this plan of government shall be regarded as a police jury ward electing seven members, and the remaining two districts shall each be regarded as a police jury ward electing one member. It shall be the duty of the police jury of East Baton Rouge Parish, within a time sufficiently in advance of the primary election of September 1948, in order to give full effect to the provisions of this plan of government relating to the election of the officers enumerated above, to create such additional precincts and make such changes in precinct boundaries as may be necessary, and of the registrar of voters to revise the lists of voters in accordance therewith.

SECTION 12.02. POWERS OF PARISH AND CITY COUNCILS AND MAYOR-PRESIDENT PRIOR TO JANUARY 1, 1949. The parish and city councils and the mayor-president shall take office immediately following the promulgation of the results of the election to be held on the first Tuesday after the first Monday in November 1948, for the following purposes only;

(a) To prepare and adopt, prior to the first day of January 1949, current expense budgets for the year 1949, for the parish, the city, and any district of which the parish council or the city council is the governing body. It shall be the duty of all existing city and parish offcers to supply on request such information pertinent to the preparation of such budgets as may be requested by the mayor-president. It shall be the duty of the mayor-president to submit such current expense budgets to the councils, in as nearly as practicable the form prescribed in Chapter 8 of this plan of government, at a time which will allow such budgets to be published at least thirty days prior to the thirty-first day of December 1948. The councils shall announce and hold public hearings on their respective budgets and take such action with regard thereto as is provided in said Chapter 8, and the totals of such budgets for each organization unit and activity shall constitute appropriations for the year 1949. Upon the adoption of their respective budgets for the year 1949, the councils shall fix tax rates for the parish and the city respectively. No capital budgets shall be adopted for the year 1949 but the parish council and city council shall have authority during the year 1949 to make appropriations for the construction of buildings, structures, works and improvements to be financed by the issuance of excess revenue or voted bonds as expressly authorized and required by Chapter 7 of this plan of government, and in other cases upon the recommendation of the planning commission and the mayor-president.

(b) To adopt ordinances necessary or useful in effecting an orderly transition to this plan of government. The city council and parish council are hereby authorized to adopt such ordinances within their respective jurisdictions, to be effective on the first day of January 1949.

(c) To set up the personnel system provided in Chapter 9 of this plan of government so that it may be ready to function on the first day of January 1949. The parish council is hereby authorized to appoint the members of the personnel

board, and the mayor-president to appoint the personnel administrator, to function in a preparatory capacity, and the compensation of the personnel administrator and any clerical or other assistants for services prior to the first day of January 1949 authorized by the parish council shall be paid by the parish treasurer from the parish funds.

SECTION 12.03. EXTENSION OF THE TERM OF POLICE JURORS. There shall be no election of police jurors in East Baton Rouge Parish at the general election of 1948. The terms of the police jurors in office prior to the first day of June 1948 shall be extended to the first day of January 1949, and the police jury so constituted shall continue to exercise all its powers and duties under the laws of the state, except as to the budget and tax levy for 1949, until that date.

SECTION 12.04. FINAL EFFECTIVE DATE OF REMAINING PROVISIONS OF THIS PLAN OF GOVERNMENT. The provisions of this plan of government, except where a specific time for their taking effect is provided in this plan of government and except as otherwise provided in this chapter, shall take effect on the first day of January 1949. No election of city commissioners shall be held in the fall of 1948 and no budget or tax levy for the year 1949 shall be adopted by the city commission-council.

SECTION 12.05. FORM OF QUESTION ON BALLOT. There shall be printed on the official ballot to be used in the election on the proposed plan of government, the following question:

"Shall the plan of government for East Baton Rouge Parish and the several municipal corporations and other political subdivisions and districts situated therein, prepared and submitted in accordance with Section 3(a) of Article 14 of the constitution of Louisiana, be adopted?"

NOTICE TO VOTERS

To vote in favor of the proposition submitted on this ballot place a cross (X) mark in the square after the word YES following such proposition: to vote against it, place a similar mark (X) after the word NO in the square following such propositions.

The Metropolitan Government
Of Nashville and Davidson County

The Metropolitan Government of Nashville and Davidson County was established by voter approval of a charter providing for city-county consolidation effective April 1, 1963.

The first post-war attempt to restructure the system of local government in the Nashville area was made in 1951 when the Tennessee Legislature established the Community Services Commission to study the governmental problems of Nashville and Davidson County. The Commission's report of June 1, 1952 recommended city and county home rule, functional consolidation of the health and welfare programs, and that Nashville annex a sizable amount of territory.

In 1953, Tennessee voters approved constitutional amendments which granted home rule and authorized the consolidation of city and county functions. Concurrent majorities in the central city and the remainder of the county are required to implement city-county consolidation.

The Legislature, in 1957, created a ten-member Metropolitan Government Charter Commision to draft a charter for submission to Davidson County voters. The Commission, on March 28, 1958, proposed a charter which would (1) consolidate Nashville and Davidson County, (2) create a twenty-one member metropolitan council, (3) establish an expandable urban services district and a general services district, and (4) establish a tax rate for each district based upon services rendered. The chief executive would be a metropolitan mayor elected for a four year term.

On June 17, 1958, the proposed charter was approved by Nashville by a vote of 7,802 to 4,803, but was rejected by the remainder of the county by a vote of 19,235 to 13,794. Approximately twenty-two percent of Nashville's voters and forty-four per cent of the voters in the balance of Davidson County voted in the referendum. The defeat of the proposed charter induced Nashville to turn to annexation as a solution for its problems. Seven square miles of territory were annexed on July 16, 1958 and 42.46 square miles on April 29, 1960.

A 1961 act passed by the Legislature authorized the creation of a new Davidson County charter commission subject to voter approval. On August 17, 1961, the creation of a charter commission was authorized by a vote of 11,096 to 3,730 in Nashville and 7,324 to 3,848 outside the city limits.

The charter commission filed, on April 6, 1962, a proposed charter which closely resembled the proposed 1958 charter. The new charter consolidating the City of Nashville and Davidson County was approved on June 28, 1962, by a vote of 21,064 to 15,599 in Nashville and 15,914 to 12,514 in the remainder of the county. Six small cities were permitted to exit, but were forbidden to expand their boundaries by annexation. The cities may choose to disincorporate and join the urban services district when it expands to their area.

Article 1

GENERAL PROVISIONS

SECTION 1.01. CONSOLIDATION OF COUNTY AND CITY. CREATION OF METROPOLITAN GOVERNMENT. NAME — The governmental and corporate functions now vested in the City of Nashville, a municipal corporation created by Chapter 246, Private Acts of 1947, and amendments thereto, are hereby consolidated with the governmental and corporate functions of the County of Davidson, such consolidation being pursuant to constitutional power granted by Article XI, Section 9 of the Constitution of Tennessee, as amended, and in conformity with Sections 6-3701, et seq. of Tennessee Code Annotated, as amended. Said consolidation shall result in the creation and establishment of a new Metropolitan Government to perform all, or substantially all, of the governmental and corporate functions previously performed by the County and by the City, to be known as "The Metropolitan Government of Nashville and Davidson County," herein sometimes called "the Metropolitan Government." The Metropolitan Government shall be a public corporation, with perpetual succession, capable of suing and being sued, and capable of purchasing, receiving and holding property, real and personal, and of selling, leasing or disposing of the same, to the same extent as other governmental entities.

SECTION 1.02 AREA OF METROPOLITAN GOVERNMENT. The territory embraced in the Metropolitan Government shall be the total area of Davidson County, as the same may be fixed and established upon the effective date of this Charter.

SECTION 1.03. TWO SERVICES DISTRICTS AND THEIR AREAS. The Metropolitan Government shall, within the geographical limits thereof, comprise two service districts, to-wit: A General Services District and an Urban Services District, as to both of which Districts the Metropolitan Government shall have jurisdiction and authority. The General Services District shall consist of the total area of the Metropolitan Government, the same being the total area of Davidson County as fixed and established upon the effective date of this Charter. The Urban Services District shall consist originally of the total area of the City of Nashville at the time of the filing of this Charter with the County Commissioners of Election, which area is more specifically described and set forth in Appendix One hereto.

SECTION 1.04. EXPANSION OF URBAN SERVICES DISTRICT. The area of the Urban Services District may be expanded and its territorial limits extended by annexation whenever particular areas of the General Services District come to need urban services, and the Metropolitan Government becomes able to provide such service within a reasonable period, which shall not be greater than one year after ad valorem taxes in the annexed area became due. The tax levy on property in areas hereafter annexed shall not include any item for the payment of any deficit in the pension or retirement funds of the former City of Nashville. Said tax levy shall not include any item (except pursuant to and subject to the provisions of Section 7.04 of this charter), for the payment of urban bonds of the Metropolitan Government issued prior to the effective date of such annexation, or debts of the former City of Nashville allocated to the Urban Services District under Section 7.20 of this charter, except to the extent that it shall be found and determined by the Metropolitan County Council that the property within the newly annexed area will benefit, in the form of urban services, from the expenditures for which the debt, or a specified portion of the debt, was incurred, to substantially the same extent as the property within the Urban Services District as same existed prior to such annexation.

Annexation shall be based upon a program set forth in the Capital Improvements Budget provided for by Section 6.13. Such annexation shall be accomplished and the validity of the same may be contested, by the methods and procedures specified in Tennessee Code Annotated, Sections 6-308 to 6-312, with respect to annexation by municipalities.

SECTION 1.05. FUNCTIONS WITHIN GENERAL SERVICES DISTRICT AND URBAN SERVICES DISTRICT. The Metropolitan Government may exercise within its General Services District those powers and functions which have heretofore been exercised by the County of Davidson or the City of Nashville, or both, and shall supply the residents of said General Services District with those governmental services which are now, or hereafter may be, customarily furnished by a county government in a metropolitan area.

The Metropolitan Government may exercise within its Urban Services District those powers and functions which have heretofore been exercised by the City of Nashville or the County of Davidson, and shall supply the residents of said Urban Services District with those kinds of governmental services which are now, or hereafter may be, customarily furnished by a city government in a metropolitan area.

The functions of the Metropolitan Government to be performed, and the governmental services to be rendered throughout the entire General Services District shall include: General Administration; Police; Courts; Jails; Assessment; Health; Welfare; Hospitals; Housing for the Aged; Streets and Roads; Traffic; Schools; Parks and Recreation; Library; Auditorium, Fair Grounds; Airport; Public Housing; Urban Redevelopment; Urban Renewal; Planning; Electrical Code; Building Code; Plumbing Code; Housing Code; Electricity; Transit; Refuse Disposal; Beer Supervision, and Taxicab Regulation.

The additional functions of the Metropolitan Government to be performed and the additional governmental services to be rendered within the Urban Services District shall include: Additional Police Protection; Fire Protection; Water; Sanitary Sewers; Storm Sewers; Street Lighting; Street Cleaning; Refuse Collections; and Wine and Whiskey Supervision.

Nothing in the foregoing enumeration and assignment of functions shall be construed to require the continued maintenance or furnishing of any governmental service which the Council by ordinance has determined to be obsolete and unnecessary.

Nothing in this Section shall be deemed to limit the power of the Metropolitan Government to exercise other governmental functions in either the Urban Services District or the General Services District, or to provide new and additional governmental services in either the Urban Services District or the General Services District.

SECTION 1.06. DEPARTMENTS OF METROPOLITAN GOVERNMENT. The governmental and corporate authority of the Metropolitan Government shall be vested in a Metropolitan County Mayor, who shall be the chief executive officer; a Metropolitan County Council, which shall be the chief legislative body; an Urban Council, which shall levy a property tax within the Urban Services District; the Judges of the Metropolitan Court; the Justices of the Peace; the departments, boards and commissions herein provided; and such officers, agencies, boards and commissions as may be provided by the Constitution or general laws of the State of Tennessee, or by ordinance enacted pursuant to this Charter.

Article 2

POWERS

SECTION 2.01. SPECIFIC POWERS. The Metropolitan Government of Nashville and Davidson County shall have power:

1. To levy and collect taxes upon all property excepting any property exempt from taxation by general law.
2. To levy and collect taxes upon all taxable privileges and to license and regulate such privileges and privileged occupations.
3. To make appropriations for the support of the Metropolitan Government, for any other purpose authorized by this Charter and for any purpose for which a county or city is authorized by general law to appropriate; and to provide for the payment of the debts and expenses of the Metropolitan Government and also the debts and expenses of the county and the city of which it is the successor.
4. To borrow money for the purposes and in the manner provided by Article 7, or other provisions of this Charter.
5. To purchase, lease, construct, maintain or otherwise acquire, hold and operate any building or other property, real or personal, for any public purpose, and to sell, lease or otherwise dispose of any property, real or personal, belonging to the Metropolitan Government.
6. To establish, maintain and regulate, free of sectarian influences, a system of free schools.
7. To make regulations to secure the general health of the inhabitants and to prevent, abate and remove nuisances.
8. To lay out, open, extend, widen, narrow, establish or change the grade of, close, construct, pave, curb, gutter, adorn with shade trees, otherwise improve, maintain, repair, clean and light streets, roads, alleys and walkways of the Metropolitan Government.
9. To provide for the creation, maintenance, building or purchase and operation of waterworks, electric power system, gas plants, transportation facilities, public airports, and any other public utility, including sewers and a sewage system; to fix such rates and provide for the making of such charges and assessments as are deemed necessary for the proper furnishing of such services; and to provide liens or penalties and withdrawal of service for refusal or failure to pay same.
10. To provide for the prevention and punishment of vice, obscenity, immorality, vagrancy, drunkenness, riots, disturbances, disorderly houses, bawdy houses, gambling and gambling houses, lewd exhibitions, disorderly conduct, the carrying of concealed weapons, and breaches of the peace.
11. To regulate or prohibit junk dealers; pawn shops; the manufacture, sale or transportation of intoxicating liquors, the

use and sale of firearms; the use and sale of firecrackers, fireworks and to regulate the transportation, storage and use of combustible, explosive and inflammable materials, the use of lighting and heating equipment, and any other business or situation which may be dangerous to persons or property.

12. To provide for the taking and appropriation of real property within the area of the Metropolitan Government for any public purpose, when the public convenience requires it and in accordance with the provisions of Tennessee Code Annotated, Section 23-1401, et seq.

13. To provide and maintain a system of pensions and retirement for officers and employees of the Metropolitan Government and of the county and the city to which it is successor.

14. To accept or refuse gifts, donations, bequests or grants from any source for any purpose related to the powers and duties of the Metropolitan Government.

15. To establish, maintain and operate public hospitals, sanatoria, convalescent homes, clinics and other public institutions, homes and facilities for the care of the sick, of children, the aged and the destitute.

16. To establish, maintain and operate a jail and a workhouse.

17. To make special assessments within the Urban Services District, pursuant to Tennessee Code Annotated, Sections 6-1101 through 6-1141.

18. To acquire, own, maintain and operate public parks and playgrounds, and to equip and improve them with all suitable devices, buildings and other structures.

19. To collect and dispose of garbage and other refuse within the Urban Services District, and to regulate the collection and provide for disposal of garbage and other refuse within the General Services District.

20. To provide, or aid in the support of, public libraries.

21. To regulate the erection of buildings and all other structures, to compel the owner to provide and maintain fire escapes and other safety features, and to provide fire districts or zones and building zones; to prohibit, regulate or suppress, or provide for the destruction and removal of any building or other structure which may be or become dangerous or detrimental to the public.

22. To fix the fares or rates to be charged for carriage of persons and property by any vehicle held out to the public use for hire within the area of the Metropolitan Government and not operated over a fixed route; to require indemnity bonds issued by surety companies or indemnity insurance policies to be filed by the owner or operator of such vehicle for the protection of any person against loss by injury to person or property; and to make all needful regulations with respect to the operation of such vehicles.

23. To grant rights-of-way through the streets and roads, and over the bridges and viaducts, for the use of public utilities.

24. To improve and preserve the navigation of the Cumberland River, within the Metropolitan Government; to erect, repair and regulate public wharfs, docks and landings, and to fix the rate of wharfage thereat; to regulate ferries; and to regulate the stationary anchorage and the mooring of vessels or rafts.

25. To regulate zoning.

26. To establish standard weights and measures; and to provide standards of quality for all food products used for human consumption.

27. To provide for the inspection and weighing or measuring of lumber, building material, stone, coal, wood, fuel, hay, corn and other grain.

28. To regulate, tax, license or suppress the keeping and going at large of animals, including domestic fowls; and to impound the same and in default of redemption to sell or kill the same.

29. To provide for the protection of animals and children, and to prevent cruelty to same.

30. To regulate the operation of motor vehicles and exercise control over all traffic, including parking, upon or across the streets, roads, alleys and walkways of the Metropolitan Government.

31. To regulate, by license or otherwise, plumbers and electricians and plumbing and electrical work.

32. To examine and license stationary engineers engaging in operating steam plants within the Metropolitan Government.

33. To regulate the emmission of smoke, the installation and maintenance of fuel burning equipment, and the methods of firing and stoking furnaces and boilers.

34. To regulate the operations, fees and services of private fire departments maintained outside the area of the Urban Services District; and to enter into contracts for the furnishing of fire protection outside the Urban Services District.

35. To collect service charges to defray installation and operation costs for furnishing services beyond the limits of the Urban Services District when such services are a function of the Urban Services District.

36. To create, alter or abolish departments, boards, commissions, offices and agencies other than those specifically established by this Charter, and to confer upon the same necessary and appropriate authority for carrying out of all powers, including the promulgation of building, plumbing, zoning, planning and other codes; but when any power is vested by this Charter in a specific officer, board, commission or other agency, the same shall be deemed to have exclusive jurisdiction within the particular field.

37. To enter into contracts and agreements with other governmental entities and also with private persons, firms and corporations with respect to furnishing by or to the other services and the payments to be made therefor.

38. To determine such offices for which bond shall be required and the amount thereof.

39. To provide penalties for violations of any ordinance adopted pursuant to the authority of this Charter or of general law.

40. To pass all ordinances necessary for the health, convenience, safety and general welfare of the inhabitants, and to carry out the full intent and meaning of this Charter, as fully as if specifically authorized.

SECTION 2.02. **GENERAL POWERS.** In addition to other powers herein granted, the Metropolitan Government shall be vested with (1) any and all powers which cities are, or may hereafter be, authorized or required to exercise under the Constitution and general laws of the State of Tennessee, as fully and completely as though the powers were specifically enumerated herein, except only for such limitations and restrictions as are provided in Tennessee Code Annotated, Sections 6-3701, et seq., as amended, or in this Charter; and (2) any and all powers which counties are, or may hereafter be, authorized or required to exercise under the Constitution and general laws of the State of Tennessee, as fully and completely as though the powers were specifically enumerated herein, except only for such limitations and restrictions as are provided in Tennessee Code Annotated, Sections 6-3701, et seq., as amended, or in this Charter; and (3) any and all powers possessed by the County of Davidson or the City of Nashville immediately prior to the effective date of this Charter.

Article 3

THE METROPOLITAN COUNTY COUNCIL

SECTION 3.01. **METROPLOITAN COUNTY COUNCIL CREATED. COUNCILMEN-AT-LARGE AND DISTRICT COUNCILMEN.** The legislative authority of the Metropolitan Government of Nashville and Davidson County, except as otherwise specifically provided in this Charter, shall be vested in the Metropolitan County Council, sometimes hereinafter called "Council", which shall have a total membership of forty (40), including five (5) councilmen-at-large, and thirty-five (35) district councilmen. The entire electorate of the Metropolitan Government shall elect the five (5) councilmen-at-large and each of the thirty-five (35) councilmanic districts shall elect one (1) district councilman. There shall be thirty-five (35) councilmanic districts in the Metropolitan Government, which are hereby created and established in accordance with the detailed descriptions thereof by metes and bounds as set forth in Appendix Two hereto attached as a part of this Charter.

SECTION 3.02. **TERMS. COMPENSATION. AGE AND RESIDENCE QUALIFICATION.** Members of the Council shall serve for a term of four (4) years and until their successors are elected and qualified; and shall be compensated at the rate of Three Hundred ($300) Dollars per month. No person shall be eligible to serve as councilman-at-large or district councilmen unless he shall have attained the age of twenty-five (25) at the beginning of his term and unless he shall have been a resident of the area of the Metropolitan Government for a period of one (1) year and shall continue to reside therein during his period of service. No person shall be eligible to serve as district councilman unless he shall have been a resident of the district for which elected for a period of six (6) months and shall continue to reside therein during his period of service. Members of the Council shall hold no other elective or appointive office in the Metropolitan Government or employment by said Government, except as expressly provided in this Charter.

SECTION 3.03. **QUORUM. RULES OF PROCEDURE. PRESIDING OFFICER.** Not less than two-thirds (2/3rds) of all the members to which the Council shall be entitled shall constitute a quorum for the transaction of business. The Council may determine its rules of procedure. The Vice County Mayor shall be the presiding officer of the Council, but without vote therein except in the event of a tie vote when he may cast the deciding vote.

SECTION 3.04 **REGULAR MEETINGS. ADJOURNED MEETINGS. SPECIAL MEETINGS.** The Council shall hold regular meetings only on the first and third Tuesday of each month and may hold an adjourned meeting of a regular meeting on any week day or hour it may fix. At such adjourned meeting the Council may transact any business which it might transact at a regular meeting. Special meetings of the Council may be held when called by the Mayor, and shall be called by him whenever in his judgment the public welfare requires it or whenever requested in writing by a majority of the members of the Council. At least forty-eight (48) hours written notice shall be given for any special meeting, stating the object or objects thereof, and the business of such meeting shall be restricted to the objects so stated. All meetings of the Council shall be open to the public and shall be held in a Metropolitan Building unless by reasons of casualty a different meeting place shall be select-ed, with public announcement thereof.

SECTION 3.05. **LEGISLATIVE AUTHORITY EXERCISED BY ORDINANCE. REQUIREMENTS AS TO, AND FORM OF, ORDINANCES.** The Council shall exercise its legislative authority only by ordinance, except as otherwise specifically provided by this Charter or by general law. No ordinance shall become effective until it shall have passed by a majority vote on three (3) different days, on the final passage of which it shall have received a majority vote of all the members to which the Council is entitled and until it shall have been signed by the Metropolitan County Mayor or become a law without his signature as otherwise provided in Article 5 hereof. On final passage of an ordinance or resolution, a vote shall be taken by ayes and noes, and the names of the councilmen voting for or against the same shall be entered on the minutes. Each ordinance shall begin "Be it enacted by the Council of the Metropolitan Government of Nashville and Davidson County", and no ordinance shall take effect until twenty (20) days after its passage, unless the same shall state that the welfare of the Metropolitan Government of Nashville and Davidson County requires that it should take effect sooner.

SECTION 3.06. **AUTHORITY AND POWER OF THE COUNCIL.** The Council is authorized to legislate with respect to the powers of the Metropolitan Government granted by Article 2 hereof, except as otherwise provided in this Charter; and by ordinance to provide for the organization, conduct and operations of all departments, boards, commissions, offices and agencies of the Metropolitan Government, when the same has not been provided for by this Charter.

In addition to the foregoing and in aid of its legislative function, the Council is authorized by resolution passed by a three-fourths (¾ths) majority of its entire membership and not subject to the veto power of the Mayor to conduct investigations by the whole Council or any of its committees; to employ and compensate personnel necessary for such purpose; and to make appropriations therefor.

SECTION 3.07. **NO PENSIONS FOR COUNCILMEN.** Members of the Council shall not be eligible to receive and shall not receive any pension by reason of their service as members of said Council.

Nothing in this Section shall be deemed to abrogate or diminish the obligation of the Metropolitan Government to pay pensions to those persons who upon the effective date of this Charter are entitled to receive pensions by reason of their years of service as councilmen of the City of Nashville or who upon the expiration of the terms for which they have been elected as such councilman would become entitled to receive such pensions.

Article 4

THE URBAN COUNCIL

SECTION 4.01. **SELECTION, TERM AND FUNCTION OF THE URBAN COUNCIL.** The Urban Services District shall be and constitute a municipal corporation, with a three member Urban Council, whose sole function shall be a mandatory obligation to levy a property tax adequate with other available funds to finance the budget for urban services, as determined by the Metropolitan Council. The members of the Urban Council shall be those three (3) individuals elected to the Metropolitan Council as councilmen-at-large who receive the highest votes, who reside within the area of the Urban Services District and who continue to be members of the Metropolitan Council. If only three councilmen-at-large reside in the Urban Services District, then they shall constitute the Urban Council; and if less than three councilman-at-large reside in the Urban Services District, they shall be members of the Urban Council, together with other members selected by the Metropolitan Council from its own membership so as to constitute a three member Urban Council. Members of the Urban Council so chosen by the Metropolitan Council shall be members a portion of whose district lies within the area of the Ubran Services District. The term of members of the Urban Council shall be co-extensive with the term of the members of the Metropolitan Council. Vacancies in the membership of the Urban Council shall be filled by the Metropolitan Council, which shall elect to any such vacancy one of its own members a portion of whose district lies within the area of the Urban Services District.

The Urban Council shall meet immediately following any meeting of the Metropolitan Council, at which an annual budget is adopted or amended, or at which the annual tax rate for the General Services District is adopted or amended. The Minutes for the Urban Council shall be kept by the Metropolitan Clerk.

Article 5

THE METROPOLITAN COUNTY MAYOR AND VICE MAYOR

SECTION 5.01. EXECUTIVE AND ADMINISTRATIVE POWER. CHIEF EXECUTIVE OFFICER. The executive and administrative power of the Metropolitan Government shall be vested in and exercised by a Metropolitan County Mayor and such other departments, boards, commissions, officers and agencies as are created or authorized in this Charter. The Metropolitan County Mayor, sometimes hereinafter called "Mayor", shall be responsible for the conduct of the executive and administrative work of the Metropolitan Government and for the law enforcement within its boundaries.

SECTION 5.02. TERM. QUALIFICATION. COMPENSATION. The Mayor shall be elected for a term of four (4) years and until his successor is elected and qualified. He shall have attained the age of thirty (30) at the beginning of his term and shall have been a resident of the area of the Metropolitan Government for at least three (3) years preceding his election and shall continue to reside therein during his period of service. He shall be compensated at the rate of Twenty-five Thousand ($25,000) Dollars per annum, payable semimonthly.

SECTION 5.03. POWER AND AUTHORITY OF MAYOR. The Mayor is authorized to administer, supervise and control all departments created by this Charter, except as otherwise specifically provided, and also all departments created by ordinance pursuant hereto. Such administration shall be by and through departmental directors under the supervision and control of the Mayor.

Except as otherwise provided in this Charter, the Mayor shall appoint all directors of departments, subject to limitations of civil service provided by this Charter, if any. All departmental directors not under civil service limitations appointed by the Mayor shall be confirmed by the Council and may be removed by the Mayor as provided herein or in the creating ordinance.

The Mayor shall appoint all members of boards and commissions created by this Charter or by ordinance enacted pursuant hereto, except as otherwise specifically provided, and he shall fill vacancies on said boards and commissions. Appointments to membership on boards and commissions shall not require confirmation by the Council except as the same may be specifically required by this Charter or by ordinance creating such board or commisison.

The Mayor shall have and may exercise in person or through agent, all the powers of a fiscal agent and financial officer heretofore possessed by the County Judge of Davidson County, acting either under general law or private act. The Mayor shall also be vested with and possess all executive powers and functions, exclusive of judicial functions, heretofore performed by the County Judge acting either under general law or private act, except to the extent that such powers and functions may be vested in other officers or agencies by the provisions of this Charter; and also shall be vested with and possess all executive powers and functions hereafter vested by general law in the office of the County Judge.

The Mayor shall be authorized at any reasonable time to examine and inspect the books, records, and official papers of any department, board, commission, officer or agency of the Metropolitan Government; and to attend the meeting of any board or commission and make suggestions thereto.

The Mayor is authorized to require any department, board, commission, officer or agency to submit to him written reports and information in connection with the business and affairs of the Metropolitan Government which the same handles or administers; and he shall, from time to time, submit reports and recommendations to the Council with respect to the financial condition, other business and general welfare of the Metropolitan Government.

The Mayor shall submit an annual budget as provided for in Article 6 of this Charter.

The Mayor is authorized to call special meetings of the Council as provided for in Section 3.04 of this Charter.

SECTION 5.04. MAYOR'S VETO POWER. VETO OF ITEMS IN APPROPRIATIONS AND BUDGET. The Mayor is authorized to approve or to disapprove ordinances and resolutions adopted by the Council and no ordinance or resolution shall become effective without his approval except as herein provided. Every ordinance or resolution adopted by the Council shall be presented to the Mayor for his consideration. If he approves, he shall sign the same, and it shall become effective according to the terms thereof. If he disapproves, he shall return the same to the Council without his signature, which return may be accompanied by a message indicating the reasons for his disapproval. Any resolution or ordinance so disapproved shall become effective when subsequent to its return it shall be adopted by two-thirds (⅔rds) of all the members to which the Council is entitled, with the ayes and noes and the names of the councilmen voting for and against the same entered on the minutes. Every resolution or ordinance shall become effective unless the same be approved or disapproved by the Mayor and returned to the Council at or prior to the next regular meeting of the Council occurring ten (10) days or more subsequent to the date when the same was delivered to his office for consideration.

The Mayor, while approving other portions of an ordinance, may reduce or disapprove the sum of money appropriated by any one or more items, or parts of items, in any ordinance appropriating money, except for debt service, employee benefits or independent audits, such power to be exercised with return of the ordinance to the Council within the time prescribed for disapproval of ordinances generally, accompanied by written explanation of the reasons for disapproval or reduction. The one or more items or parts of items disapproved or reduced shall be void to the extent that they have been disapproved or reduced unless any such item or parts of items so disapproved or reduced shall be restored to the ordinance in the original amount and become effective by adoption by the Council according to the rules and limitations prescribed for the passage of other ordinances over the Mayor's veto.

SECTION 5.05. **VICE MAYOR. ELECTION. PRESIDING OFFICER OF COUNCIL.** The Vice-Mayor shall be elected for a term of four (4) years and until his successor is elected and qualified. He shall possess the qualifications of the Mayor and shall be compensated at the rate of Forty-two Hundred ($4,200) Dollars per annum, payable semimonthly. In the event the office of Mayor becomes vacant, the Vice-Mayor shall serve as Mayor and be compensated as such until the vacancy is filled at a special election or at a general election, as provided in Section 15.03 of this Charter. During the time that the Vice-Mayor shall serve as Mayor, he shall cease to act as presiding officer of the Council.

SECTION 5.06. **LIMITATION ON TERMS OF SERVICE.** No Mayor elected and qualified for three (3) consecutive four (4) year terms shall be eligible for the succeeding term.

SECTION 5.07. **PENSION FOR MAYOR.** After the Mayor shall have served two (2) full terms, he shall receive an annual pension equivalent to ten (10%) percent of his salary during the last year of his second term, and after he shall have served three (3) full terms (in lieu of the lesser pension) he shall receive an annual pension equivalent to twenty-five (25%) percent of his salary during the last year of his third term. The amount of this pension shall not be increased by subsequent years of service as Mayor. The pension herein provided shall be suspended during any subsequent period that the Mayor shall be a compensated officer or employee of the Metropolitan Government and, if accepted, shall be in lieu of any pension which said Mayor may be entitled to receive from the Metropolitan Government by reason of service as an officer or employee of the City of Nashville.

Any pension which a person may be entitled to receive from the Metropolitan Government by reason of services as Mayor of the City of Nashville shall also be suspended during the period that such person shall be a compensated officer or employee of the Metropolitan Government.

Article 6

THE BUDGETS AND FINANCIAL MATTERS

SECTION 6.01. **FISCAL YEAR.** The fiscal year of the Metropolitan Government shall begin on the 1st day of July of each year and shall end on the 30th day of June next following. Said fiscal year shall constitute the budget year and the year for financial accounting and reporting of each and every office, department, institution, activity and agency of the Metropolitan Government; but the aforesaid provision shall be in addition to, and not in lieu of, any accounting and reporting required of any official or agency by state or federal laws.

SECTION 6.02. **PREPARATION OF ANNUAL OPERATING BUDGET.** The Director of Finance shall obtain from all officers, departments, boards, commissions and other agencies for which appropriations are made by the Metropolitan Government, or which collect revenues for such government, such information as shall be necessary for him to compile the Annual Operating Budget; and it shall be the duty of all such officers, departments, boards, commissions and agencies to furnish the Director such information as he may require at such time or times and in such form as the Director may prescribe.

Not later than three months prior to the end of each fiscal year said Director shall distribute to each of the agencies identified in the preceding paragraph all forms necessary for the preparation of the Operating Budget for the succeeding fiscal year. Such forms shall be returned to the Director with the information desired not later than two months prior to

the end of the current fiscal year. On the basis of the information so received and otherwise secured by him, said Director shall prepare and transmit to the Mayor a Proposed Operating Budget for the next fiscal year of the kind and scope set forth in Section 6.03 hereof. In preparing the proposed budget the Director may revise, as he may deem necessary, the estimates or requests made by the various officers, departments, boards, commissions and agencies, but any such agency shall be entitled to a hearing before the Director with reference to any contemplated changes in its budget requests or estimates.

SECTION 6.03. **SCOPE OF THE ANNUAL OPERATING BUDGET.**
Section I of the Annual Operating Budget shall apply only to the General Services District and shall deal with those services and functions appertaining to the General Services District as set out by this Charter, or by ordinance of the Council.

Section II of the Annual Operating Budget shall apply only to the Urban Services District and shall deal with those services and functions appertaining to such Urban Services District as set out in this Charter, or by ordinance of the Council.

Each of the above described Sections of the Annual Operating Budget shall contain with respect to each of the operating funds of the Metropolitan Government to which they are applicable:

(a) An estimate of the unencumbered fund balance or deficit at the beginning of the ensuing fiscal year, and the amount of any reserves for designated purposes or activities includable in the operating budget.

(b) A reasonable estimate of revenues to be received during the ensuing year, classified according to source; but the estimated revenues from current and from delinquent property taxes shall not exceed the percentage of the total receivable from each such source collected during the last completed fiscal year; or the current fiscal year.

(c) Proposed expenditures for each organizational unit and activity in accordance with the established classification of accounts, including those capital outlays which are to be financed from the revenues of the ensuing year, and including all debt service requirements in full for such fiscal year payable from such fund.

In no event shall the total proposed expenditures from any fund exceed the total anticipated revenues plus the estimated unappropriated surplus, or fund balance, and applicable reserves and less any estimated deficit at the end of the current fiscal year.

SECTION 6.04. **REVIEW AND REVISION OF OPERATING BUDGET BY MAYOR. SUBMISSION TO COUNCIL. BUDGET AS PUBLIC RECORD. DISTRIBUTION OF COPIES.**
The Mayor shall review the Operating Budget submitted to him by the Director of Finance, and may make any revisions in such budget as he may deem necessary or desirable, before it is submitted to the Council for consideration.

Not later than May 25th the Mayor shall submit to the Metropolitan Council the Operating Budget as approved by him in the form and with the contents specified in Section 6.03 hereof, together with a message explaining such budget, describing its important features, and outlining the proposed financial policies of the Metropolitan Government for the ensuing fiscal year and setting forth the reasons for any significant changes in policy or budgetary allocations.

The Mayor shall promptly cause copies of the budget and the budget message to be prepared for distribution to interested persons, and a summary of the budget shall be published in each of the daily newspapers in the area of the Metropolitan Government. The Operating Budget, as well as the Captial improvements Budget hereinafter provided for, the budget message, and all supporting schedules shall be public records in the office of the Metropolitan Clerk and shall be open to public inspection.

SECTION 6.05. **HEARINGS BY COUNCIL.** After the Council shall have passed the budget ordinance on first reading it shall hold hearings on the Proposed Operating Budget, as well as on the Capital Improvements Budgets as provided in Section 6.13 hereof, but the hearing on the Capital Improvements Budget shall be heard prior to those on the Proposed Operating Budget, and the hearings on either budget may be adjourned from time to time. Budget hearings shall be advertised in a daily newspaper of general circulation published in the area of the Metropolitan Government at least seven days prior to the date or dates set for the beginning of such public hearings.

SECTION 6.06. **ACTION BY COUNCIL ON OPERATING BUDGET.** After the conclusion of the public hearings, the Council may amend the Operating Budget proposed by the Mayor except that the budget as finally amended and adopted must provide for all expenditures required by law or by other provisions of this Charter and for all debt service requirements for the ensuing fiscal year as certified by the Director of Finance. Neither shall the Council alter the estimates of receipts or other fund availability included in the budget document except to correct errors and omissions, in which event a full explanation shall be spread on the minutes of the Council. In no event shall the total appropriations from any fund exceed the estimated fund balance, reserves and revenues, constituting the fund availability of such fund.

The Council shall finally adopt an Operating Budget for the ensuing fiscal year not later than the 30th day of June, and it shall be effective for the fiscal year beginning on the following July 1st. Such adoption shall take the form of an ordinance setting out the estimated revenues in detail by source and making appropriations according to fund and by organizational unit, purpose or activity as set out in the budget document. If the Council shall fail to adopt a budget prior to the beginning of any fiscal year, it shall be conclusively presumed to have adopted the budget as submitted by the Mayor.

A copy of the adopted budget, certified by the Metropolitan Clerk, shall be filed in the office of the Director of Finance.

The amount set out in the adopted Operating Budget for each organizational unit, purpose or activity shall constitute the annual appropriation for such item, and no expenditure shall be made or encumbrance created in excess of the otherwise unencumbered balance of the appropriation, or allotment thereof, to which it is chargeable. This shall not preclude the impoundment of funds or additional appropriations as provided herein.

SECTION 6.07. **PROPERTY TAX LEVIES.** The Council shall levy an annual tax on real and personal property and merchants' ad valorem in the General Services District, and the tax levy ordinance shall be the next order of business of the Council after the adoption of the Operating Budget. The tax rate set by such ordinance shall be such that a reasonable estimate of revenues from such levy shall at least be sufficient, together with other anticipated revenues, fund balances, and applicable reserves, to equal the total amount appropriated and to provide in addition, a reasonable amount of working capital for each of the several funds.

After the Council has approved the Annual Operating Budget of the Urban Services District, said Council shall determine and declare the amount of revenue which must be produced from a tax levy upon the real and personal property and merchants' ad valorem within the Urban Services District. The Urban Council shall thereupon convene and it shall have a

mandatory obligation by resolution to levy a property tax adequate with other available funds to finance the budget for urban services, as determined by the Council, subject, however, to the requirements of Section 1.04 of this Charter with respect to the tax on property in the newly annexed areas.

SECTION 6.08. **ALLOTMENTS OF APPROPRIATIONS.** All appropriations contained in the Current Operating Budget shall be allotted by the Director of Finance on a quarterly basis, and it shall be his duty to make such allotments promptly at the beginning of each quarter of the fiscal year. Such allotments shall be based upon estimated needs, and in the determination of such need the Director of Finance may require all spending agencies to submit allotments requests on such forms as he may prescribe. Such allotments shall constitute authorizations for expenditure or encumbrance, and no expenditure shall be made or encumbrance created, but in pursuance of an allotment, and within the otherwise unencumbered balance of such allotment.

SECTION 6.09. **IMPOUNDMENT OF FUNDS.** Upon certification of the Director of Finance that the revenues or other resources actually realized with respect to any fund are less than was anticipated and are insufficient to meet the amounts appropriated from such fund, it shall be the duty of the Mayor to impound such appropriations as may be necessary to prevent deficit operation.

SECTION 6.10. **ADDITIONAL APPROPRIATIONS.** The Metropolitan Council may make appropriations in addition to those contained in the Current Operating Budget, at any regular or special meeting called for such purpose, but any such additional appropriation may be made only from an existing unappropriated surplus in the fund to which it applies.

SECTION 6.11. **TRANSFER OF APPROPRIATIONS.** On request of any department head, and with his consent, the Mayor may transfer the unencumbered balance of any appropriation, or any portion thereof, for any purpose or activity to the appropriation for any other purpose or activity *within the same department,* but the same shall not be available for encumbrance or expenditure until it shall have been allotted by the Director of Finance.

At the request of the Mayor, but only at the end of any quarter of the fiscal year, the Council may by resolution approved by a majority of the membership of the Council transfer the unencumbered balance of any appropriation, or any portion thereof, to another appropriation within the same Section of the budget and within the same fund. However, the Council shall not make transfers of appropriations at any time between the General Services District and the Urban Services District, or transfer moneys from any operating fund to another fund. Provided, however, that this stipulation shall not apply to the discharge of obligations existing between governmental agencies financed from one fund and those financed through another fund, nor to the transfer of moneys from operating funds to agency or trust funds covering collections to be expended through such agency or trust funds, nor to the transfer of the unappropriated surplus in bond funds to the debt service funds set up to retire such bonds, nor to such other transfers between funds as may be authorized by law.

SECTION 6.12. **LAPSE OF APPROPRIATIONS.** All unencumbered balances of appropriations in the Current Operating Budget at the end of the fiscal year shall lapse into the unappropriated surplus or reserves of the fund or funds from which such appropriations were made.

SECTION 6.13. **CAPITAL IMPROVEMENTS BUDGET.** The Director of Finance shall obtain annually from all officers, departments, boards and commissions and other agencies requesting funds from the Metropolitan Government for capital improvements, such information as the Planning Commission shall require to enable it to prepare the Capital Improvements Budget. This data shall be delivered to the Planning Commission not later than four months prior to the end of the fiscal year. The Capital Improvements Budget shall include a program of proposed capital expenditures for the ensuing fiscal year and the next five fiscal years thereafter, accompanied by the report and recommendations of the Metropolitan Planning Commission with respect to the program. Section I of the Capital Improvements Budget shall present proposed General Services District projects. Section II shall present proposed Urban Services District projects. The Mayor shall submit the Capital Improvements Budget to the Council not later than May 15th and shall recommend those projects to be undertaken during the ensuing fiscal year and the method of financing them, noting the impact on the debt structure of the Metropolitan Government and shall include in the appropriate Current Operating Budget any projects to be financed from current revenues for the ensuing fiscal year.

The Council shall have power to accept, with or without amendment, or reject, the proposed program and proposed means of financing. The Council shall not authorize an expenditure for the construction of any building, structure, work or improvement, unless the appropriation for such project is included in its Capital Improvements Budget, except to meet a public emergency threatening the lives, health or property of the inhabitants, when passed by two-thirds vote of the membership of the Council. The Capital Improvements Budget must be acted upon finally by the Council not later than the 15th day of June following its submission.

The Mayor may submit amendments to the Capital Improvements Budget at any time during the year, accompanied by the recommendation thereon of the Planning Commission, which amendments shall become effective when adopted by a two-thirds vote of the membership of the Council.

SECTION 6.14. **GENERAL FUND RESERVE.** From all original moneys collected during any year, before making a budget ordinance, there shall be deducted five (5%) percent of the gross amount of the general fund revenue of the General Services District, which sum shall be placed in an account to be known as the General Fund Reserve and shall be kept separate and apart from other funds of the Metropolitan Government.

The Mayor and Council may by resolution make appropriations from said funds for the purchase of equipment for any department of the Metropolitan Government or for repairs to any building owned by any department of the Metropolitan Government; provided, however, that no appropriations shall be made from this fund to any department not deriving its operating funds from the General Fund Budget.

From all moneys collected during any year, and after making provisions for the five (5%) percent of the gross amount of the general fund revenue that shall establish the General Fund Reserve of the Metropolitan Government, there shall be next provided a sufficient amount, not to be less than Fifty Thousand ($50,000) Dollars, to be placed in and constituted the Metropolitan Government Advance Planning and Research Fund for the use of the Metropolitan Planning Commission of the Metropolitan Government in the preparation, in advance, of plans for capital projects, and for the making of such studies and the doing of such research as is by the Metropolitan Planning Commision deemed necessary in the performance of the duties and responsibilities given it by the Metropolitan Charter and general law. No expenditures shall be made from said fund except by resolution of the Metropolitan Planning Commission, and in no case shall expenditures be made therefrom for the payment of budgetary items or matters not concerned with research and advance planning. The resolution of the Metropolitan Planning Commision as to capital projects shall precisely define the projects concerned and amounts expended in the planning of such projects shall be provided for in the financing of construction of same and, upon the commencement of construction, the Metropolitan Government Advance Planning and Research Fund shall be repaid those sums and moneys expended from it in the advanced planning of such project. From all moneys collected during any year, and after the making of provision for the five (5%) percent of the gross amount of the Metropolitan Government's general fund revenue flowing into the General Fund Reserve of the Metropolitan Government, there shall next be provided a sufficient amount, as of the first day of each fiscal year, to bring the unencumbered balance on hand in the Metropolitan Government Advance Planning and Research Fund created herein to the minimum sum of Fifty Thousand ($50,000) Dollars.

By ordinance the Council may create a Contingent Reserve Fund not to exceed five (5%) percent of the general fund revenue of the Urban Services District. The Mayor and Council may by resolution make appropriations from said fund for the purchase of equipment for any department of the Metropolitan Government or for repairs to any building owned by any department of the Metropolitan Government which equipment or buildings are used primarily for the furnishing of services herein defined as Urban Services; provided, however, that no appropriations shall be made from this fund to any department not deriving its operating funds from the General Fund of the Urban Services District Current Operating Budget.

SECTION 6.15. **POST AUDIT.** The Council shall provide annually for an independent audit of the accounts and other evidences of financial transactions of the Metropolitan Government and of its every department, office and agency. The audit shall be made by an accountant or an accounting firm, the members of which have no personal interest, direct or indirect, in the fiscal affairs of the Metropolitan Government or of any of its departments, offices, or agencies. The designated accountant shall be a certified public accountant, or, if an accounting firm is employed, the members thereof shall be so certified and thoroughly qualified by training and experience in governmental accounting to perform the audit.

The independent audit shall be made by a firm chosen by a three member Audit Board. This Board shall consist of the Presiding Officer of the Council, the Chairman of the Finance Committee of the Council, and the Chairman of the Metropolitan Board of Education.

The audit may be conducted on a quarterly or continuing basis and the final report of the annual audit shall be completed as soon as practicable after the close of the fiscal year, and in no event later than four months after the close of the fiscal year. The audit report shall be available to the public and to the press.

The Council may at any time order an examination or special audit of any department, office or agency of the government.

Article 7

BOND ISSUES

SECTION 7.01. **BONDS AUTHORIZED BY METROPOLITAN COUNCIL. PURPOSES OF ISSUE.** The Council may cause the bonds and other obligations of the Metropolitan Government to be issued in the following manner and subject to the following restrictions:

The Council may in the name and for the use of the Metropolitan Government issue bonds or other obligations in the manner and to the extent hereinafter provided in this Article. Such bonds or other obligations may be issued for the purpose of financing the whole or any part of the cost of any public improvement or property the Metropolitan Government is authorized by this Charter or any other law to acquire, construct, reconstruct, extend or improve. Two or more improvements or properties may be combined as a single improvement or property for the purpose of the issuance of bonds.

SECTION 7.02. DEFINITIONS. For the purposes of this Article the word "bonds" shall mean and include bonds or other obligations payable from ad volorem taxes or other taxes, or from revenues derived from utilities or other revenue producing enterprises or facilities, or from any other sources, or any combination thereof; the words "revenue bonds" shall mean bonds or other obligations payable in whole or in part from the revenues derived from utilities or other revenue producing enterprises or facilities; and the words "tax bonds" shall mean bonds or other obligations payable in whole or in part from ad valorem taxes. All of the provisions of this Article relating to bonds shall apply to all such types of bonds, except where expressly or by necessary implication provided otherwise.

SECTION 7.03. COSTS INCLUDABLE. BONDS FOR FURNISHINGS AND EQUIPMENT. In any issue of bonds hereunder, there may be included as part of the cost to be financed from the proceeds of such bonds all engineering, technical and legal fees or expenses, interest upon such bonds during the period of acquisition or construction and for a reasonable period thereafter, fees of fiscal or financial agents or consultants, if any, the acquisition of necessary equipment and furnishings, working funds and reserve funds, and such other items or expenses as are necesasry and incidental to the completion and financing of the improvement or property and the placing of the same in operation or use. Tax bonds not to exceed the aggregate principal amount of Three Hundred Thousand ($300,000) Dollars outstanding at any one time may be issued for the purpose of acquiring furnishings and equipment for Metropolitan Government purposes, and such authority to issue such bonds shall be in addition to and not in limitation of the other provisions of this Charter, and the issuance of such bonds shall not be subject to approval of the voters at any referendum.

SECTION 7.04. GENERAL TAX BONDS AND URBAN TAX BONDS. Tax bonds may be issued pursuant to this Article for the General Services District, herein sometimes referred to as "general tax bonds", or for the Urban Services District, herein sometimes referred to as "urban tax bonds", but the full faith and credit of the Metropolitan Government shall be pledged for all bonds issued hereunder which are payable in whole or in part from ad valorem taxes. Ad valorem taxes shall be levied and collected in the General Services District for the payment of general tax bonds and in the Urban Services District for the payment of urban tax bonds; provided, however, that the Metropolitan Government shall be unconditionally and irrevocably obligated to levy and collect ad valorem taxes without limit as to rate or amount on all taxable property in the General Services District to the full extent necessary to pay all principal of and interest on all tax bonds, both general tax bonds and urban tax bonds, and the full faith and credit of the Metropolitan Government shall be pledged for the payment of all tax bonds. In the event, however, that it shall ever become necessary to levy ad valorem taxes in the General Services District outside the Urban Services District for the payment of urban tax bonds, then the amount of such taxes shall

be included in the next levy of ad valorem taxes in the Urban Services District and restored to the tax revenues of the General Services District, it being the express intention of this Article that the holders of any such tax bonds shall be entitled to the levy of ad valorem taxes to the full extent necessary on all the taxable property in the General Services District, but that as between the General Services District and the Urban Services District, such ad valorem taxes shall be levied in such respective districts for the full amount of debt service on bonds issued for such respective districts.

SECTION 7.05. WHEN BOND REFERENDUM NOT REQUIRED. NOTICE OF ISSUE. No vote or approval of the qualified electors at an election shall be required for the issuance of any tax bonds hereunder if the initial resolution authorizing such tax bonds is adopted by two-thirds of the whole membership of the Council, unless within twenty days after the date of the first publication of such initial resolution, with the notice set forth below, in a newspaper published and having general circulation in the area of the Metropolitan Government, a petition protesting the issuance of such tax bonds signed by at least six per centum of the qualified electors in the General Services District in the case of general tax bonds, or in the Urban Services District in the case of urban tax bonds, is filed in the office of the Metropolitan Clerk. If a petition protesting the issuance of such tax bonds shall be filed as aforesaid within such twenty day period, then the tax bonds proposed by such initial resolution shall not be issued without the approval of a majority of the qualified electors residing in the General Services District in the case of general tax bonds or in the Urban Services District in the case of urban tax bonds, who vote on a proposition for the issuance of such tax bonds at a regular or special election held in the manner prescribed herein. For the purposes of such election a qualified elector shall be any resident of the Metropolitan Government residing in the General Services District in the case of general tax bonds or in the Urban Services District in the case of urban tax bonds, who was qualified to vote for members of the General Assembly at the general election next preceding the filing of such petition or who is on the date of the filing of such petition then qualified to vote for the members of the General Assembly. No qualified elector shall be permitted to withdraw his signature from such petition after signing the same. The notice to be published with said initial resolution shall be in substantially the following form:

NOTICE

The foregoing resolution has been adopted. Unless within twenty (20) days from the date of the first publication of this Notice a petition signed by at least six (6%) percent of the qualified electors residing in the _____ Services District of the Metropolitan Government of Nashville and Davidson County shall have been filed with the Clerk of the Metropolitan Government protesting the issuance of the Bonds authorized in such resolution, such bonds will be issued as proposed in said resolution.

_____
Clerk of the
Metropolitan Government

Notwithstanding any of the provisions of this Article, the Council may, if it desires, call an election as provided herein for the purpose of ascertaining the will of the qualified electors in the General Services District or the Urban Services District, as the case may be, with respect to the issuance of any bonds, whether payable from ad valorem taxes or other taxes, or any other revenues, or a combination thereof.

SECTION 7.06. **REFERENDUM ELECTION AFTER PETITION OF PRO-TEST.** If the filing of a petition protesting the issuance of any tax bonds with the Metropolitan Clerk shall result in the necessity of any election on the proposition to issue such tax bonds, the Council upon the filing of such petition shall adopt a resolution, herein called the election resolution, which shall direct the holding of an election for the purpose of voting for or against the tax bonds proposed to be issued, said election to be conducted by the Davidson County Election Commissioners as hereinafter provided. Such election resolution shall state the purpose or purposes for which each bond issue is authorized, the amount or maximum amount of the bonds, the maximum number of years for which the bonds are to run, and the maximum rate of interest such bonds are to bear. More than one proposition may be submitted at the same election. Said election resolution shall request the Davidson County Election Commissioners to arrange for the holding of the election on the date specified in the resolution. The election shall thereupon be held, notice thereof given and the results thereof canvassed in the manner provided by the general laws for the holding of elections under the supervision of the Election Commissioners. After the Council has received the official report of the outcome of the election from the Election Commissioners, the Council shall adopt a resolution in which there shall be contained a formal finding of the outcome of the election, which findings shall be conclusive.

No approval of the qualified electors residing in either the General Services District or the Urban Services District at any election shall be required for the issuance of any bonds unless ad valorem taxes shall be pledged for the payment of all or part of the debt service on such bonds, and the above provisions for a permissive referendum on petition shall not apply to other bonds.

SECTION 7.07. **ISSUANCE OF BONDS UNDER GENERAL LAW.** Bonds may be issued under this Article for either the General Services District or the Urban Services District pursuant to any general law of the State of Tennessee now or hereafter in effect and applicable to counties or cities or Metropolitan Governments in the State of Tennessee and it is hereby expressly provided that the Metropolitan Government may issue bonds under the provisions of all such general laws without regard to any limitations or restrictions contained in this Charter. No proceeding for the issuance of such bonds shall be required other than those required by the general law under which such bonds are authorized and no provision of any resolution, ordinance or notice, and no election or opportunity for referendum shall be required except as may be specifically required by the provisions of such general law.

SECTION 7.08. **LIMITATIONS ON URBAN BONDS.** No urban tax bonds shall be issued pursuant to this Article which shall cause the total net bonded indebtedness payable from ad valorem taxes incurred for the Urban Services District (including all tax bonds theretofore issued for the Urban Services District and then outstanding, and the amount of any tax bonds theretofore issued by the City of Nashville and then outstanding which are allocated to the Urban Services District by this Article), after deduction of all sinking funds on hand for the payment of principal, to exceed fifteen (15%) percent of the assessed valuation of taxable property in the Urban Services District as last completed and determined prior to the issuance of such tax bonds. In computing the bonded indebtedness incurred for the Urban Services District for the purpose of this paragraph there shall be excluded:

(a) All urban bonds issued in anticipation of the collection of special assessments whether or not such urban bonds are also payable from ad valorem taxes.

(b) All revenue bonds issued for the Urban Services District or any part thereof which are payable solely from the revenues derived from the operation of any utility or other revenue producing enterprise or facility.

(c) All urban bonds payable from both ad valorem taxes and revenues derived from the operation of any utility or other revenue producing enterprise or facility, to the extent that such utility or other revenue producing enterprise or facility was selfliquidating during the immediately preceding fiscal year, in that the revenues derived therefrom, after deducting all current expenses of operation and maintenance, were sufficient to pay all principal of and interest on such bonds due in such fiscal year; or if such utility or other revenue producing enterprise or facility was not fully selfliquidating in such fiscal year, then a part of such bonds shall be excluded, which part shall be the same proportion of the total amount of such bonds which the amount of net revenues derived from such utility or revenue producing enterprise or facility in such fiscal year bears to the amount of net revenues which would have been required to make such utility or revenue producing enterprise or facility fully selfliquidating in such fiscal year.

(d) Urban bonds issued under the authority of any general law of the State of Tennessee as distinguished from urban bonds issued under sole authority of this Article.

(e) Urban bonds not exceeding Two Hundred Thousand ($200,000) Dollars in any year, issued to provide funds to repair or to replace any public building, work or structure rendered unsuitable for use by disaster when determined by the Council to be essential to the public health, safety or convenience.

(f) Urban tax bonds in the aggregate principal amount of Three Hundred Thousand ($300,000) Dollars issued for the purpose of acquiring furnishings and equipment for Metropolitan Government purposes.

No approval of qualified electors at an election shall be required for the issuance of any bonds referred to in subparagraphs (a) to (f) above, and the referendum upon petition provisions of this Article shall not apply to such bonds.

SECTION 7.09. **LENGTH OF TIME AND INTEREST RATE. CALL OF BONDS. COUPON OR REGISTERED. MODE OF EXECUTION.** No bonds issued hereunder may run for a longer period than forty (40) years nor bear interest at a greater rate than six (6%) per centum per annum, nor be sold at a price which will cause the actual interest thereof to the Metropolitan Government to exceed six (6%) per centum per annum when computed to maturity.

The Council may, in its discretion, by appropriate provisions inserted in the proceedings and in the bonds, provide that any bonds shall be redeemable prior to their stated dates of maturity, at the option of the Metropolitan Government at such time or times, at such premium or premiums not exceeding five (5%) per centum of the par value thereof, and on such other terms and conditions as may be provided in such proceedings.

Bonds issued hereunder may be issued either in coupon form or in fully registered form, may be registerable as to principal only or as to both principal and interest, and said bonds and any coupons attached thereto shall be executed, either manually or by facsimile signatures, in such manner as the Council shall determine; provided, however, that at least one manual signature shall be required on said bonds. Only one coupon shall be attached to each bond for each installment of interest thereon, and bids providing for supplemental coupons will be rejected. The seal of the Metropolitan Government shall be affixed, imprinted or reproduced on said bonds, and attested by the Metropolitan Clerk, either manually or with his facsimile signature. Any bonds or coupons executed by the proper officers of the Metropolitan Government at the time of execution thereof may be delivered notwithstanding that at the time of such delivery such officers have ceased to hold such office. The Council shall have power to provide for the issuance of substituted bonds in exchange or pay if matured any outstanding bonds which have been lost or stolen or become mutilated, defaced or destroyed, upon the giving of such indemnity and under such other terms and conditions as the Council shall prescribe.

SECTION 7.10. **METROPOLITAN BONDS NEGOTIABLE AND TAX EXEMPT.** All bonds of the Metropolitan Government shall be and constitute and have all the qualities and incidents of negotiable instruments under the law merchant and the negotiable instruments law of the State of Tennessee, regardless of the source or sources of payment of such bonds. No bonds issued hereunder shall be invalid for any irregularity or defect in the proceedings for the issuance and sale thereof, and all such bonds, upon the delivery thereof and payment therefor, or exchange in the case of refunding bonds, shall be conclusively deemed to be the valid and legally binding obligations of the Metropolitan Government in accordance with the terms thereof, and shall be incontestable in the hands of the purchasers or holders from time to time thereof.

All bonds of the Metropolitan Government, and the interest thereon, and all properties, revenues and other assets of any utility or other revenue producing enterprise or facility of the Metropolitan Government shall be exempt from all taxation by the State of Tennessee, or any County, Municipality, political subdivision or taxing agency thereof, except for inheritance, transfer and estate taxes.

SECTION 7.11. **REFUNDING BONDS.** Bonds may be issued hereunder for the purpose of refunding not more than a like principal amount of any outstanding bonds of the Metropolitan Government, including any bonds heretofore issued by the County of Davidson or the City of Nashville. Such refunding bonds may be issued without regard to the amount of bonded indebtedness of the Metropolitan Government, either for general bonds or urban bonds, and without the necessity of the approval of the qualified electors or the holding of any election, and shall not be subject to the referendum on petition provisions of this Article. Where the bonds to be refunded have become due, or become due or are called for redemption not more than six months after the delivery of the refunding bonds, the refunding bonds may be delivered and the proceeds thereof escrowed with the fiscal agent of the Metropolitan Government for the payment of the bonds to be refunded in such manner as the Council may prescribe.

SECTION 7.12. **PUBLIC SALE.** All bonds issued under this Article, except refunding bonds delivered in exchange for the bonds refunded thereby, shall be sold by the Council at public sale to the highest responsible bidder, after such advertisement as may be prescribed by the Council.

SECTION 7.13. **TEMPORARY FINANCING.** The Council may provide for temporary financing of any improvement or property by the issuance of bond anticipation notes in anticipation of the sale of bonds which have been duly authorized hereunder or under any other law, but all such bond anticipation notes, including any renewals thereof, shall finally mature not later than three years from the date of the original notes. All such bond anticipation notes shall have the same security as the bonds in anticipation of which such notes are issued. The Council may also provide for the issuance of interim certificates or tem-

porary bonds pending the delivery of bonds which have been duly awarded and sold. The Council shall prescribe the dates of issue and maturity, form and all other details of such bond anticipation notes, interim certificates or temporary bonds. The Council may also provide that short term financing be done with competitive bidding on the open market.

SECTION 7.14. **BONDS ISSUED BY RESOLUTION OF COUNCIL. NOTICE OF RIGHT TO CONTEST.** All bonds issued under this Article shall be authorized by resolution or resolutions adopted by a majority vote of all the members of the Council, at any properly convened regular, adjourned or special meeting, which may be the same meeting at which they are introduced. No publication of any resolution, proceeding or notice shall be necessary, except as specifically required by this article.

The Council in the resolution authorizing any bonds may provide that after the adoption of such resolution there shall be published in a newspaper published and having general circulation in the area of the Metropolitan Government, a notice in substantially the following form:

NOTICE

On   , 19   , the Metropolitan Council of the Metropolitan Government of Nashville and Davidson County adopted a resolution authorizing the issuance of $ bonds for the purpose of   a copy of which said resolution is on file in the office of the Metropolitan Clerk and open to inspection by any voter or citizen residing in the area of the Metropolitan Government.

For a period of twenty (20) days following the date of the first publication of this notice, any taxpayer or other interested person may file an appropriate suit or proceeding questioning the validity of the bonds proposed to be issued or the legality of the proceedings had in the authorization of such bonds. After the expiration of said twenty days, no one shall have any cause or right of action to contest in any court the legality of said bonds or proceedings or the power and obligation of the Metropolitan Government to pay said bonds from the taxes or other revenues provided in such proceedings or bonds.

_____

Metropolitan Clerk

In the case of tax bonds, however, such notice shall not be published until after the expiration of the period for the filing of a petition for a referendum, or, if such petition shall be filed, then not until after the approval of such bonds at such referendum.

If, pursuant to direction of the Council, such notice is published, no one shall have any cause or right of action after the expiration of said twenty-day period, to contest the legality, formality or regularity of such bonds or proceedings in any court for any cause whatsoever, and the authority to issue such bonds, the legality thereof and the legality of the taxes or other revenues pledged to pay the same, shall be conclusively presumed, and no court shall have any jurisdiction or authority to inquire into such matters.

SECTION 7.15. **BOND PROCEEDS CONSTITUTE TRUST FUND.** The proceeds of the sale of bonds issued under the provisions of this Article shall constitute a trust fund, and each issue shall be accounted for separate and apart, to be used exclusively for the purpose or purposes for which said bonds are authorized but the purchaser of such bonds shall be under no obligation or responsibility to see to the application thereof, and the manner of an application of such proceeds shall in no way affect the rights, remedies or security and sources for payment of the holders of such bonds.

SECTION 7.16. **UNISSUED BONDS OF COUNTY OR CITY.** Any

bonds duly authorized but unissued by the County of Davidson or the City of Nashville at the effective date of this Charter may be issued in the name of and sold by the Metropolitan Government in accordance with the provisions of the statutes and resolutions under which such bonds were authorized in the same manner and with like effect as though this Charter had not been enacted, it being the intent hereof that the enactment of this Charter shall in no way affect or impair the right of the Metropolitan Government to complete the sale and issuance of such bonds.

SECTION 7.17. REVENUE BONDS. In addition to revenue bonds authorized to be issued by any other provision of this Charter or by the provisions of any general law of the State of Tennessee, the Council shall have power to authorize the issuance of revenue bonds to finance all or part of the cost of any utility or other revenue producing enterprise or facility, where such revenue bonds are to be payable in whole or in part from the revenues of such utility or other revenue producing enterprise or facility, and to pledge all or any part of such revenues for the payment of such revenue bonds. All of the applicable provisions of this Article shall be complied with in the issuance of such revenue bonds. The Council may in the proceedings authorize the issuance of such revenue bonds make and enter into valid and binding covenants with the holders of such revenue bonds including, but not limited to, the appointment of trustees to hold and secure the proceeds of such revenue bonds and such revenues and the application thereof, the fixing and revision of the fees, rates or other charges for the services and facilities of such utility or other revenue producing enterprise or facility, including reasonable margins of safety, the creation and maintenance of reserve funds, sinking funds and depreciation funds, the appointment of a receiver in case of defaults in payment of debt service or performance of such covenants and such other covenants as are deemed necessary and advisable for the marketability of such revenue bonds and the security of the holders thereof.

SECTION 7.18. COMBINED TAX AND REVENUE BONDS. The Council may also issue combined tax and revenue bonds if deemed advisable, or pledge any other security permitted by law to the payment of such revenue bonds in addition to such revenues from such utility or other revenue producing enterprise or facility; provided, however, that if ad valorem taxes are pledged for the payment of all or any part of bonds for which such revenues are also pledged, the provision for a referendum on petition on issuance of tax bonds provided herein shall apply to such revenue bonds for which ad valorem taxes are also pledged.

SECTION 7.19. REFUNDING REVENUE BONDS. The Council shall also have power to issue refunding revenue bonds to refund any revenue bonds theretofore issued, including any revenue bonds theretofore issued by the County of Davidson or the City of Nashville, or to issue refunding and improvement revenue bonds for the combined purpose of refunding outstanding revenue bonds and to finance additions, extentions and improvements to such utility or other revenue producing enterprise or facility, and all of the applicable provisions of this Article shall be complied with in the issuance of said refunding revenue bonds or combined refunding and improvement revenue bonds.

SECTION 7.20. DEBT SERVICE FUNDS. There shall be a General Services District Debt Service Fund and an Urban Services District Debt Service Fund for the amortization of general bonds and urban bonds respectively, including bonds issued prior to the effective date of this Charter by the County of Davidson and the City of Nashville which have been allocated to such districts under the provisions of this Article. Such debt service funds shall consist of the cash and securities in the debt service funds for bonds issued by the County of Davidson and the City of Nashville prior to the effective date of this Charter and such funds hereinafter required to be paid into such funds and the interest earned on the investment thereof. The debt service funds for the bonds heretofore issued by the County of Davidson and the City of Nashville shall be transferred to the debt service fund of the district to which such bonds are allocated by this Article. Nothing contained herein, however, shall affect any debt service funds for any revenue bonds or other bonds which are required by the proceedings which authorized any bonds to be maintained as separate and segregated debt service funds for such bonds, and such sinking funds shall be transferred to the Metropolitan Government and segregated and maintained in the manner provided in the proceedings which authorized the issuance of such bonds.

All such debt service funds may be invested only in bonds which are full faith and credit general obligations of the Metropolitan Government, the State of Tennessee, the County of Davidson, the City of Nashville, the United States of America, or in such securities as may be provided in the proceedings which authorize such bonds.

There shall be included in the annual tax levy ordinances for the General Services District and the Urban Services District, over and above all other taxes assessed therein, a sum sufficient to meet the interest and redemption charges on all tax bonds due or to be paid in the ensuing year and issued for or allocated to such districts respectively, together with a sum sufficient to reimburse the general fund for any appropriation made or to be made therefrom for the payment of any such interest or redemption charges.

All moneys paid into any debt service fund shall be used exclusively for the purchase, retirement or payment of the outstanding bonds for which such debt service funds are created and maintained, and the Metropolitan Treasurer shall keep a record of all receipts and disbursements of the debt service funds and shall report the same to the Mayor and Council quarterly in each fiscal year.

Should any levy for debt service fund purposes, except in the case of bonds payable solely from revenues, fail for any reason whatsoever to provide sufficient funds to meet the redemption and interest charges for bonds in any year, sufficient amounts shall be paid from either the general fund of the General Services District or the Urban Services District for such redemption and interest charges, subject to reimbursement from subsequent levies in the General Services District or the Urban Services District, as the case may be.

If either the General Services District Debt Service Fund or the Urban Services District Debt Service Fund shall accumulate a surplus sufficient to retire bonds callable and chargeable to such funds, the Metropolitan Treasurer, with the approval by resolution of the Mayor and Council, may purchase any of such bonds at a price not exceeding the redemption price thereof on the next ensuing redemption date or may call for prior redemption any of such bonds on the next ensuing redemption date in the manner provided in the proceedings which authorized the issuance of such bonds.

The Metropolitan Treasurer shall deduct monthly, or cause to be deducted monthly, the amounts realized from the inclusion in the annual tax levy ordinances of the General Services District and the Urban Services District of the necessary sums in conformity with the subject to the above debt service fund provisions and shall deposit, or cause to be deposited, the same in the Metropolitan Government depositories to the credit of the appropriate district debt service fund accounts, which funds shall be kept separate and apart from all other funds of the Metropolitan Government.

All bonds issued prior to the effective date of this Charter by the County of Davidson, and all bonds authorized but un-issued by the County of Davidson at the effective date of this Charter and thereafter issued by the Metropolitan Government, shall be allocated to the General Services District and the principal of and interest on such bonds shall be paid from ad valorem taxes or other revenues collected in the General Services District.

All bonds issued prior to the filing date of this Charter by the City of Nashville, except for the bonds described in the next paragraph, shall be allocated to the General Services District and the principal of and interest on such bonds shall be paid from ad valorem taxes or other revenues collected in the General Services District, and it is hereby found and determined that all such bonds were issued to finance all or part of the cost of improvements or properties which render or will render services or benefits to all or substantially all the inhabitants of the General Services District. All debt service funds for such bonds shall be transferred to the General Services District Debt Service Fund.

The following described bonds issued prior to the filing date of this Charter by the City of Nashville shall be allocated to the Urban Services District and the principal of and interest on such bonds shall be paid from ad valorem taxes or other revenues collected in the Urban Services District:

CITY OF NASHVILLE BONDS - URBAN SERVICES DISTRICT

Original Date of Issue	Final Maturity	Title of Issue	Principal Outstanding June 30, 1962
		Fire Department	
12-4-33	12-1-63	Fire Hall Improvement Bonds of 1933	$ 10,000
6-15-57	6-15-77	Fire Department Improvement Bonds of 1957	85,000
6-15-60	6-15-90	Fire Department Construction, Improvement and	
		Equipment Bonds of 1960	985,000
		Total	1,080,000
		Street, Alley and Sewer	
6-1-45	6-1-74	Street, Alley and Sewer Bonds of 1945-A	795,000
6-1-45	6-1-74	Street, Alley and Sewer Bonds of 1945-B	795,000
6-1-48	6-1-78	Street, Alley and Sewer Bonds of 1948-A	607,000
6-1-48	6-1-78	Street, Alley and Sewer Bonds of 1948-B	285,000
6-1-48	6-1-78	Street, Alley and Sewer Bonds of 1948-C	465,000
6-1-48	6-1-78	Street, Alley and Sewer Bonds of 1948-D	464,000
		Total	3,411,000
		Sewers	
4-1-26	4-1-66	Sanitary Sewer Bonds of 1925 Series A	44,000
11-1-27	11-1-67	Sanitary Sewer Bonds of 1925 Series B	65,000
11-1-28	11-1-68	Sanitary Sewer Bonds of 1925 Series C	108,000
8-1-29	8-1-69	Lateral Sanitary Sewer Bonds of 1929	77,000
12-4-33	12-1-63	Sewer Extension Bonds of 1933	30,000
9-1-47	9-1-77	Sewer Bonds of 1947	260,000
5-1-53	5-1-93	Sewer Bonds of 1953	420,000
3-1-54	3-1-64	Sewer Construction and Improvement Bonds of 1954	20,000
11-1-54	11-1-85	Sewer Bonds of 1954	770,000
5-1-56	5-1-86	Sanitary Sewer Bonds of 1956	750,000
7-1-58	7-1-78	Airport Sewer Construction Bonds of 1958	220,000
7-1-58	7-1-88	Sanitary Sewer Bonds of 1958	960,000
6-15-60	6-15-90	Sewer and Utility Relocation and Land	
		Acquisition Bonds of 1960	485,000
6-15-61	6-15-00	Sewer Bonds of 1961	5,500,000
		Total	9,709,000
		Capitol Hill	
9-1-50	9-1-90	Capitol Hill Improvement Bonds of 1950	775,000
9-1-55	9-1-95	Capitol Hill Improvement Bonds of 1955	2,050,000
		Total	2,825,000

CITY OF NASHVILLE BONDS - URBAN SERVICES DISTRICT (CONTINUED)

Original Date of Issue	Final Maturity	Title of Issue	Principal Outstanding June 30, 1962
		Waterworks	
8-1-29	8-1-69	Water Extension Bonds of 1929	$ 61,000
12-4-33	12-1-63	Waterworks Extension Bonds of 1933	20,000
6-1-45	6-1-74	Waterworks Bonds of 1945-A	135,000
6-1-45	6-1-74	Waterworks Bonds of 1945-B	135,000
4-1-48	4-1-68	Waterworks Bonds of 1948	70,000
12-1-48	12-1-88	Waterworks Bonds of 1948-A	1,525,000
12-1-48	12-1-88	Waterworks Bonds of 1948-B	1,525,000
1-1-52	1-1-92	Combined Water and Sewer Bonds of 1952	920,000
		Total	4,391,000
		Miscellaneous	
5-1-24	5-1-64	T. C. Railroad Refunding Bonds of 1924	64,000
4-1-42	4-1-64	Public Improvement Repair and Replacement Bonds of 1942	20,000
6-15-57	6-15-77	Garbage Collection and Disposal System Bonds of 1957	107,000
6-15-57	6-15-77	Equipment and Improvements Bonds of 1957	130,000
1-15-60	1-15-90	Urban Renewal Bonds of 1960 Series A-1	1,375,000
1-15-60	1-15-90	Urban Renewal Bonds of 1960 Series A-2	950,000
		Total	2,646,000
		Grand Total	$24,062,000

Any bonds issued by the City of Nashville after the filing date of this Charter and before the effective date of this Charter, and any bonds authorized but unissued by the City of Nashville at the effective date of this Charter and thereafter issued by the Metropolitan Government, shall be allocated either to the General Services District or the Urban Services District in such manner and amounts as the Council shall determine, consistent with the allocation of functions between the General and the Urban Services Districts, and the principal of and interest on such bonds shall be paid from ad valorem taxes or other revenues collected in the district so determined by the Council.

Any revenue bonds issued prior to the effective date of this Charter by the County of Davidson or the City of Nashville, and any revenue bonds authorized but unissued by said County or said City at the effective date of this Charter and thereafter by the Metropolitan Government, shall be payable as to principal and interest from the revenues or other sources and in in the manner provided in the proceedings which authorized the issuance of such revenue bonds.

Neither the allocation of bonds to the General Services District or the Urban Services District nor any of the other provisions of this Charter shall impair or diminish any of the rights, remedies or security and sources for payment of any of such bonds or revenue bonds issued by the County of Davidson or the City of Nashville prior to the effective date of this Charter, or authorized but unissued by the County of Davidson or the City of Nashville at the effective date of this Charter and thereafter issued by the Metropolitan Government, and such holders of such bonds or revenue bonds shall have and be entitled to enforce any and all rights, remedies and security and sources for payment granted such holders by the proceedings which authorized the issuance of such bonds or revenue bonds as fully and to the same extent as if this Charter had not been adopted.

Article 8

METROPOLITAN DEPARTMENTS

Chapter 1

Department of Metropolitan Finance

SECTION 8.101. DEPARTMENT OF METROPOLITAN FINANCE CREATED. FUNCTIONS. There shall be a Department of Metropolitan Finance, which shall consist of the Director thereof, of other personnel hereinafter mentioned and of such other positions and employees as may be provided by ordinance or by regulations of the Director consistent with ordinance. The Department of Finance shall administer the financial affairs of the Metropolitan Government in accordance with the provisions of this Charter and applicable ordinances.

SECTION 8.102. THE DIRECTOR OF FINANCE—QUALIFICATIONS, APPOINTMENT, COMPENSATION. The Director of Finance shall have proven administrative ability and a well founded reputation in public finance, or a record of exceptional performance for at least five (5) years as a comptroller or financial head of a large business. The Mayor shall appoint the Director of Finance subject to confirmation by a majority of the whole membership of the Council. He shall serve at the pleasure of the Mayor making the appointment and until his successor is qualified. The Director's salary shall be Fifteen Thousand ($15,000) Dollars per annum, payable semimonthly.

SECTION 8.103. POWERS AND DUTIES OF THE DIRECTOR OF FINANCE. The Director of Finance shall be responsible to the Mayor for the administration of the financial affairs of the Metropolitan Government and to that end shall supervise the Division of Budgets, the Division of Accounts, the Division of Collections, the Division of Treasury, the Division of Purchases, and such other units as may be established by ordinance.

The Director of Finance or his designated Divisional Director shall:

(a) Compile for the Mayor the current budget of estimated revenues and proposed expenditures for each of the operating funds of the Metropolitan Government; and assist in the preparation of the capital improvements budget, as provided by Section 6.13 of this Charter.

(b) Maintain accounting systems for the General Services District and the Urban Services District of the Metropolitan Government, and for each department, office and agency thereof, in accordance with generally recognized governmental accounting principles and procedures, keeping accounting records for and exercising financial and budgeting control over such department, office or agency.

(c) Prescribe the accounts to be kept by all departments, offices and agencies of the Metropolitan Government, the form of receipts, vouchers, bills or claims, warrants, requisitions, purchase orders or any financial stationery to be used, and provide suitable instructions for the use thereof, and to review and approve the forms and procedures of the Trustee and the Tax Assessor.

(d) Prescribe the times and the manner in which moneys received by any department, office or agency shall either be paid to the Metropolitan Treasurer or deposited in a bank account to the credit of the Metropolitan Government.

(e) Examine all contracts, purchase orders and other documents which would result in or involve financial obligations against the Metropolitan Government, and approve the same only upon ascertaining that there is an unexpended, unencumbered and unimpounded balance in each such appropriation and allotment to which they are applicable, sufficient to cover such potential obligation.

(f) Audit before payment all bills, invoices, payrolls and other claims, demands or charges against the Metropolitan Government and approve the same only if proper, legal and correct, and duly authorized by appropriations or allotments of appropriations.

(g) Periodically inspect and audit the accounts and records of financial transactions maintained in each department, office and agency of the Metropolitan Government.

(h) Submit a monthly financial report to the Mayor, for presentation to the Council, showing the financial condition of the various funds of the Metropolitan Government, as well as the condition of all items included in the adopted annual operating budget, including estimated revenues, revenues received, appropriations and allotments for such appropriations.

(i) Prepare a complete annual report of the financial activities of all funds and all departments, boards, commissions, and agencies of the Metropolitan Government.

(j) Subject to the approval of the Mayor, instruct the Treasurer to invest the moneys of any fund in securities of the Metropolitan, State or Federal Government and/or place them on interest bearing deposit in a bank or banks where it is anticipated that the funds will not be needed for a period of ninety days or more.

(k) With the assistance of the Department of Law and the Metropolitan Planning Commission, establish standard procedures for acquiring and disposing of land for Metropolitan Departments, Boards and Commissions, exclusive of land acquisition for the Nashville Electric Service and the Nashville Housing Authority.

(l) Maintain an inventory of public property and equipment.

(m) Provide for a central records retention program.

(n) Perform such other duties as may be assigned by this Charter or by ordinance.

SECTION 8.104. DIVISION OF BUDGETS CREATED. FUNCTIONS OF BUDGET OFFICER. There shall be in the Department of Finance a Division of Budgets, which shall consist of the Budget Officer and such other officers and employees, organized into such units, as may be provided by ordinance or by the Director of Finance consistent with ordinance. The Budget Officer shall be appointed for an indefinite term by the Mayor, subject to the civil service provisions of this Charter, and he shall be the head of the Division of Budgets. The Budget Officer shall have at least five (5) years experience in which budget preparation, administration, and/or accounting systems shall have been his major responsibility. The Budget Officer's salary shall be Twelve Thousand ($12,000) Dollars per annum, payable semimonthly. The Budget Officer shall compile, under the supervision of the Director of Finance, the departmental estimates and other data necessary or useful to the Mayor and the Director of Finance, and assist in the preparation of the budgets. He shall examine from time to time the departments, boards, commissions, officers and agencies of the Metropolitan Government in relation to their organization, personnel and other requirements; ascertain the manner in which their respective budgets are carried out and their functions performed; call the attention of the department heads and the Mayor to any improvements or economies which might be made in their administrative practices and cooperate with the heads thereof in the preparation of their budget estimates for the ensuing fiscal year.

He shall carry on a continuous research program in systems and methods so as to keep current in all phases of data processing, business methods and the like; and make recommendations from time to time to the Director of Finance for utilizing to advantage the newest equipment and methods. The Budget Officer, with the advice and assistance of the Chief Accountant, shall write, revise and maintain a proper Standard Procedure Instruction Manual to be followed by all officers, departments, boards and other agencies of the Government to insure uniform accounting and budgetary procedures.

SECTION 8.105. DIVISION OF ACCOUNTS CREATED. DUTIES OF CHIEF ACCOUNTANT. There shall be in the Department of Finance a Division of Accounts, which shall consist of the Chief Accountant and such other officers and employees, organized into such units, as may be provided by ordinance or by the Director of Finance consistent with ordinance. The Chief Accountant shall be appointed for an indefinite term by the Mayor, subject to the civil service provisions of this Charter, and he shall be the head of the Division of Accounts. The Chief Accountant shall have at least five (5) years of responsible supervisory experience in general accounting and/or internal auditing. The Chief Accountant's salary shall be Twelve Thousand ($12,000) Dollars per annum, payable semimonthly. The Chief Accountant shall maintain (1) a general accounting system and such cost accounting records as shall be required by the Director of Finance, and (2) budgetary control records designed to prevent expenditures in excess of appropriations or allotments. He shall prepare disbursement warrants and conduct a thorough pre-audit to all claims on all funds, including payrolls, before payment and shall maintain a current audit control over cash receipts. The Chief Accountant shall perform such other duties as may be assigned him by ordinance or by the Director of Finance.

SECTION 8.106. DIVISION OF TREASURY CREATED. DUTIES OF METROPOLITAN TREASURER. There shall be in the Department of

Finance a Division of Treasury, which shall consist of the Metropolitan Treasurer and such other officers and employees as may be provided by ordinance or by the Director of Finance consistent with ordinance. The Metropolitan Treasurer shall be appointed for an indefinite term by the Mayor, subject to the civil service provisions of this Charter, and he shall be the head of the Division of Treasury. The Metropolitan Treasurer shall have at least five (5) years experience in which the supervision of fiscal affairs or treasury management shall have been his major responsibility. The Metropolitan Treasurer's salary shall be Twelve Thousand ($12,000) Dollars per annum, payable semimonthly. The Metropolitan Treasurer shall supervise and be responsible for the custody and disbursement of all funds belonging to the Metropolitan Government and all funds handled by Metropolitan Government officers as agents or trustees except as otherwise provided in this Charter or by ordinance or general law not inconsistent with this Charter. He shall pay moneys out of the Treasury only by checks which have been approved by the Division of Accounts.

SECTION 8.107. DIVISION OF COLLECTIONS CREATED. DUTIES OF COLLECTIONS OFFICER.

There shall be in the Department of Finance a Division of Collections, which shall consist of the Collections Officer and such other officers and employees, organized into such units, as may be provided by ordinance or by the Director of Finance consistent with ordinance. The Collections Officer shall be appointed for an indefinite term by the Mayor, subject to the civil service provision of this Charter, and he shall be the head of the Division of Collections. The Collections Officer shall have at least five (5) years experience in which the supervision of financial activities shall have been his major responsibility. The Collections Officer's salary shall be Twelve Thousand ($12,000) Dollars per annum, payable semimonthly. It shall be the duty of the Collections Officer to collect and receive delinquent real and personal property taxes or tax equivalents and all merchants' ad valorem taxes that have been delinquent for more than six (6) months as well as any interest and penalties thereon. The Collections Officer shall collect and receive all revenues, income and moneys due the Metropolitan Government accruing to the Urban Services District, the General Services District, or any other source, except as otherwise provided for by other parts of this Charter, by ordinance, or by the General Law.

SECTION 8.108. DIVISION OF PURCHASES CREATED. APPOINTMENT AND QUALIFICATION OF PURCHASING AGENT.

There shall be in the Department of Finance a Division of Purchases which shall consist of the Purchasing Agent and such other officers and employees, organized into such units, as may be provided by ordinance or by the Director consistent with ordinance. The Purchasing Agent shall be appointed for an indefinite term by the Mayor, subject to the civil service provisions of this Charter. The Purchasing Agent's salary shall be Twelve Thousand ($12,000) Dollars per annum, payable semimonthly. He shall be a person with at least five (5) years experience in private business or government purchases and property management, control and accountability. The Purchasing Agent shall have the responsibility of the general management and control of the Division and shall have the power to make rules and regulations for the administration of the Division subject to the approval of the Director of Finance.

SECTION 8.109. FUNCTION OF DIVISION OF PURCHASES.

Except as provided in this Section, the Division of Purchases shall purchase, or obtain by lease or rental, for the use of the Metropolitan Government and its departments, boards, commissions, officers and agencies all necessary and appropriate supplies, materials, equipment, other personal property, contractual services, insurance and surety bonds. The Council may establish by ordinance rules and regulations, defining emergencies, under which designated items, including perishables, may be purchased or obtained without compliance with purchasing procedures established in this Chapter. The Electric Power Board, the Nashville Housing Authority, the Board of Education and such other agencies as may be specified by ordinance shall be excluded from the purchasing procedures established in this Chapter, except to the extent otherwise herein specifically provided.

SECTION 8.110. POWERS AND DUTIES OF PURCHASING AGENT.

The Purchasing Agent for the purpose of giving effect to the provisions of the preceding Section shall have the following powers and duties:

(a) With the approval of the Director of Finance and the Mayor, and after consultation with the heads of the using agencies concerned, to establish and enforce standard specification for all supplies, materials and equipment required by the Metropolitan Government which the Purchasing Agent has authority to purchase or lease.

(b) To prescribe the time of making requisitions for such supplies, materials and equipment and the future period which such requisitions are to cover.

(c) To inspect, or cause to be inspected, all deliveries of such supplies, materials and equipment, and to cause tests to be made when necessary in order to determine their quality, quantity and conformance with specifications.

(d) To supervise and control storerooms, mailing, messenger, central duplicating and printing services and facilities provided for the various agencies of the Metropolitan Government as provided by ordinance.

(e) To transfer to or between using agencies, with the approval of Public Property Director, sell or trade in supplies, materials or equipment determined by him, after consultation with the head of the using departments or agencies concerned, to be surplus, obsolete or unused.

(f) To perform such duties with regard to the letting of contracts for public works or improvements as are provided in this Charter, and to have such other powers and to perform such other duties as may be provided by ordinance.

(g) To submit a monthly report of his activities to the Director of Finance. The Director of Finance may assign the functions set forth in subsections (c), (d) and (e) of this Section to some other Division in his department.

SECTION 8.111. COMPETITIVE BIDDING FOR PURCHASES OR SALES.

Before making a purchase or contract requiring expenditure of a sum in excess of One Thousand ($1,000) Dollars, the Purchasing Agent shall take competitive bids under such rules and regulations as may be established by ordinance. Before making a sale the Purchasing Agent shall require competitive bids. The making of all other purchases or contracts by the Purchasing Agent shall be under such conditions, rules and regulations as may be prescribed by ordinance. The Purchasing Agent may reject any and all bids received for purchases or sales.

SECTION 8.112. DIVISION OF PUBLIC PROPERTY ADMINISTRATION.

There shall be in the Department of Finance a Division of

Public Property Administration, which shall consist of the Director of Public Property and such other officers and employees, organized into such units as may be provided by ordinance or by the Director consistent with ordinance. The Director of Public Property Administration shall be appointed for an indefinite term by the Mayor, subject to the civil service provisions of this Charter. The Director of Public Property Administration shall administer the duties of the Department of Finance arising from Section 8.103 (k) and (1) of this Charter and shall perform such other duties as may be assigned by the Director of Finance or by ordinance.

Related Fiscal Provisions

SECTION 8.113. **DIVISION OF TAX ASSESSMENT CREATED. METROPOLITAN TAX ASSESSOR.** There shall be, as an independent agency of the Metropolitan Government, a Division of Tax Assessment, the head of which is designated as the Metropolitan Tax Assessor. The county tax assessor, elected for a term of four (4) years and provided for by general law in Tennessee Code Annotated, Sections 67-301 to 67-312, inclusive, shall be the Metropolitan Tax Assessor. He shall have the same powers, duties and liabilities with respect to assessment of properties in the area of the Metropolitan Government as by general law and private act are possessed by or imposed upon county and municipal tax assessors, except as herein provided in this Charter. In ascertaining the value of property, the Tax Assessor shall give particular consideration to the extent to which availability or nonavailability of sewers and other governmental services affects the actual cash value of the property. The Metropolitan Tax Assessor shall make merchants' ad valorem assessments in and for both the General Services District and the Urban Services District. The assessments made by him shall be the assessments to which the tax levy by the Council for the General Services District shall apply and to which the tax levy by the Urban Council for the Urban Services District shall apply. The Assessor may assess all property annually and he shall separately total the assessments in the Urban Services District and the General Services District.

SECTION 8.114. **COMPENSATION, SURETY BOND, OATH OF OFFICE AND ASSISTANTS OF TAX ASSESSOR.** The Metropolitan Tax Assessor's salary shall be Fifteen Thousand ($15,000) Dollars per annum, payable semimonthly. This salary may not be changed during the four years for which the tax assessor is elected.

The Metropolitan Tax Assessor shall give surety bond as provided by Tennessee Code Annotated, Section 67-304, in the case of county tax assessors, the same to be approved by the Mayor. He shall take an oath of office as provided by Tennessee Code Annotated, Section 67-307 for county tax assessors, the same to be filed in the office of the Metropolitan Clerk.

The Metropolitan Tax Assessor shall be furnished with such deputies, office personnel, material and supplies as he may need for the proper functioning of his office and as may be provided by ordinance and by his annual budget appropriations. Deputies appointed by him shall have the powers and duties and liabilities of the Tax Assessor. All employees of the Assessor other than these deputies shall be employed in accordance with civil service regulations.

SECTION 8.115. **VACANCIES IN OFFICE.** Vacancies in the office of the Metropolitan Tax Assessor shall be filled by the Metropolitan County Council. The person so appointed to fill a vacancy shall serve the remainder of the unexpired term, or until the first of September following the next regular August election, whichever is earlier. When a vacancy occurs more

than thirty (30) days prior to a regular August election, at which a Tax Assessor is not to be elected for a full term, then a Tax Assessor shall be elected at such election for the remainder of the term.

SECTION 8.116. **DIVISION OF PROPERTY TAX COLLECTIONS CREATED. DESIGNATION OF COLLECTIONS OFFICER.** There shall be as an agency of the Metropolitan Government, a Division of Property Tax Collections, the head of which shall be the County Trustee, sometimes herein called Metropolitan Trustee. He shall be elected for a four (4) year term as provided by general law. The Trustee shall be furnished with such deputies, office personnel, material and supplies as he may need for the proper functioning of his office and as may be provided by ordinance within his annual budget appropriations or as may be approved by rulings of Chancery Court. Deputies appointed by him as approved in rulings by Chancery Court shall have the powers, duties and liabilities of the Trustee. All employees of the Trustee other than these deputies shall be employed in accordance with civil service regulations.

The Trustee shall collect and receive real and personal property taxes or tax equivalents and all merchants' ad valorem taxes due the Metropolitan Government for the General Services District and the Urban Services District. He shall daily remit the same to the Metropolitan Treasurer. With respect to said real and personal property taxes and merchants' ad valorem taxes, the Trustee shall have all the powers, duties and responsibilities vested by general law in county trustees as to state, county and municipal taxes, except as otherwise provided in this Charter.

For six (6) months after the aforementioned taxes shall become delinquent the Trustee shall collect such taxes, as well as interest and penalties thereon. At the end of said six (6) months period, the Trustee shall transmit to the Collections Officer or to such other agency as may be designated by ordinance a balanced and reconciled report of all taxes remaining delinquent. Prior to such transmittal there shall be an internal audit by the Division of Accounts and after such transmittal it shall be the duty and responsibility of the Collections Officer or other designated agency to collect said delinquent taxes.

SECTION 8.117. **BOND OF THE METROPOLITAN TRUSTEE.** The official bond of the Metropolitan Trustee shall be executed by a surety company authorized to transact business in Tennessee. The minimum amount of bond shall be fixed by ordinance, however it shall be at least equal to the minimum set forth in Tennessee Code Annotated, Section 8-1103 for County Trustees.

It shall be the duty of the Mayor to examine into the solvency of the Trustee's bond and if the bond be found to be insufficient, as provided by law it shall be the duty of the Mayor to notify him of the fact and to require him to give new or additional security in such sum as may be fixed upon by the Council on the recommendation of the Mayor. If the required bond or security be not given within one month, it shall be the duty of the Council, and it shall have the power, to declare the office vacant.

SECTION 8.118. **POWERS AND DUTIES OF THE COUNTY COURT CLERK.** There shall be as an independent agency of the Metropolitan Government, the Office of County Court Clerk, the head of which shall be the County Court Clerk, elected for a term of four (4) years as provided by the constitution and the general laws of the state. The County Court Clerk shall be furnished with such deputies, office personnel, material and supplies as he may need for the proper functioning of his office and as may be provided by ordinance and within his annual budget appropriations. Deputies appointed by him as approved in rulings by Chancery Court shall have the powers and duties and liabilities of the County Court Clerk. All employees of the County Court Clerk, other than these deputies, shall be employed in accordance with civil service regulations. Nothing in this Charter is intended or shall be construed to alter or affect the powers, duties and responsibilities of the County Court Clerk as a Collector of State privilege licenses or other state revenues or as the Clerk of the Probate Court or Monthly County Court. However, all fees, revenues, incomes, commissions, emoluments and perquisites of the Office of County Court Clerk shall accrue to the Metropolitan Government and shall be deposited with the Metropolitan Treasurer daily except as otherwise provided by ordinance.

Nothing in this Section shall be construed as authorizing or empowering the County Court Clerk to assess or collect such taxes as may be provided for in the Division of Tax Assessment, Division of Property Tax Collections and Division of Collections of the Department of Finance.

SECTION 8.119. APPOINTMENT OF DEPUTIES OF METROPOLITAN TRUSTEE AND COUNTY COURT CLERK.
The Metropolitan Trustee and the County Court Clerk shall make application for the employment of deputies in accordance with the provisions of Tennessee Code Annotated, Section 8-2001. The above named officer in his petition shall name the Mayor as the party defendant thereto.

SECTION 8.120. DATE TAXES PAYABLE. INTEREST AND PENALTY FOR DELINQUENCY.
Ad valorem taxes, including merchants' ad valorem, due by reason of the tax levied in the General Services District shall become due and payable on the first Monday in October in each year. The general laws with respect to collection, delinquency, interest, penalties and the lien of taxes shall be applicable to the General Services District.

All ad valorem taxes, including merchants' ad valorem, due by reason of the tax levy in the Urban Services District shall become due and payable on the first of August of the year for which they are assessed, and that such taxes may be paid in two installments, as follows: One-half of the tax to be paid between August 1st and September 30th of the year for which they are assessed, without interest or penalty; and the remaining one-half after the first half is paid to be paid not later than January 10th without interest and penalty. The general laws with respect to collection, delinquency, interest, penalties and the lien of taxes shall be applicable to the Urban Services District except that the date of delinquency shall be January 11th.

Article 8
METROPOLITAN DEPARTMENTS

Chapter 2
Department of Metropolitan Police

SECTION 8.201. DEPARTMENT OF METROPOLITAN POLICE CREATED.
There shall be a Department of Metropolitan Police, which shall consist of the Director thereof, and such other officers and employees of such ranks and grades as may be established by ordinance and which shall include such bureaus, divisions and units as may be provided by ordinance or by regulations of the Director consistent therewith.

SECTION 8.202. RESPONSIBILITY AND POWERS OF DEPARTMENT.
The Department of the Metropolitan Police shall be responsible within the area of the Metropolitan Government for the preservation of the public peace, prevention and detection of crime, apprehension of criminals, protection of personal and property rights and enforcement of laws of the State of Tennessee and ordinances of the Metropolitan Government. The Director and other members of the Metropolitan Police Force shall be vested with all the power and authority belonging to the office of constable by the common law and also with all the power, authority and duties which by statute may now or hereafter be provided for police and law enforcement officers of counties and cities.

SECTION 8.203. CHIEF OF POLICE IS DIRECTOR. HIS POWERS AND DUTIES.
The Department of Metropolitan Police shall be under the general management and control of a Director thereof, who is designated the Chief of Police. The Chief of Police shall establish zones and precincts and assign members of the Department to their respective posts, shifts, details and duties consistent with their rank. He shall make regulations, with the approval of the Mayor and in conformity with applicable ordinances, concerning the operation of the Department, the conduct of the officers and employees thereof, their uniforms, arms and other equipment for their training. The Chief of Police shall be responsible for the efficiency, discipline and good conduct of the Department. Orders of the Mayor relating to the Department shall be transmitted in all cases through the Chief of Police or in his absence or incapacity through an officer designated as Acting Chief. Disobedience to the lawful commands of the Chief of Police or violations of the rules and regulations made by him with the approval of the Metropolitan Mayor shall be grounds for removal or other disciplinary action as provided in such rules and regulations, subject to the civil service provisions of Article 12 of this Charter.

SECTION 8.204. APPOINTMENT OF DIRECTOR. FILLING OTHER VACANCIES IN DEPARTMENT.
A permanent vacancy in the office of Director shall be filled by appointment of the Mayor subject to the civil service provisions of this Charter and subject to qualifications to be prescribed by the Civil Service Commission designed to secure a person especially qualified for the position by training and experience. A temporary vacancy in the office of Director due to sickness, absence or other disability shall be filled by appointment of the Mayor.

A vacancy in any office, position or employment in the Department shall be filled by appointment of the Chief of Police, subject to the approval of the Mayor and consistent with the civil service provisions of this Charter.

SECTION 8.205. SPECIAL POLICE.
The Chief of Police may appoint, in his discretion and upon the application of any individual, firm or corporation showing the necessity thereof, one or more special policemen, to be paid by the applicant, who shall have the powers and duties of policemen while in or on the premises of such applicant or in the actual performance of the duties for which employed. Special policemen shall be subject to the rules and regulations of the Department of Metropolitan Police and their appointments shall be revocable at any time by the Chief of Police with the approval of the Mayor. Before entering upon the performance of their duties, special policemen shall execute and file with the Metropolitan Clerk a public officer's liability bond in such amount as may be fixed by resolution of the Metropolitan Council.

SECTION 8.206. SCHOOL MOTHERS' PATROL.
The Chief of Police may establish, and shall establish if directed by ordinance, a School Mothers' Patrol Division in the Department, which shall assume the duties and functions of the School Mothers' Patrols of the former City of Nashville and the former County of Davidson.

SECTION 8.207. VOLUNTEER POLICE RESERVE AUTHORIZED.
The Director may, and if directed by ordinance, shall establish a voluntary Auxiliary Police Reserve to serve without compen-

sation in cases of emergency and in aid of civil defense. Where established by the Director, he shall promulgate rules, to be approved by the Mayor, for the organization and operation thereof.

SECTION 8.208. **QUALIFICATIONS OF PERSONNEL.** After the effective date of this Charter no person shall be eligible to appointment to any position in the Department except as a regular salaried employee in the classified service. Every appointee shall be a citizen of the United States of America; shall meet the physical requirements for admission to either the United States Army or Navy at the time of appointment and again at the close of the working probationary period; and shall comply with all applicable rules and regulations of the Civil Service Commission.

To determine whether applicants for positions in the Department possess the required physical qualifications, the Chief Medical Director may provide for conducting physical examinations and report his findings to the Civil Service Commission.

SECTION 8.209. **SALARIES.** The annual compensation of the Director, payable semimonthly, shall be Twelve Thousand ($12,000) Dollars. The salaries of the other officers and employees of the Department shall be as fixed in the pay plan adopted pursuant to Article 12 of this Charter.

SECTION 8.210. **WORK WEEK AND VACATIONS.** Every member of the Department shall be entitled to two (2) days off each week and to an annual vacation of twenty (20) days without deduction of pay. The time for vacations shall be determined and assigned by the Chief of Police. All members of the Department shall be subject to call and assignment to duty at any time during an emergency.

Article 8
METROPOLITAN DEPARTMENTS
Chapter 3
Department of Fire

SECTION 8.301. **DEPARTMENT OF FIRE CREATED.** There shall be a Department of Fire, which shall consist of the Director thereof, and such other officers and employees of such ranks and grades as may be established by ordinance and which shall include such bureaus, divisions and units as may be provided by ordinance or by regulations of the Director consistent therewith.

SECTION 8.302. **FUNCTION OF DEPARTMENT.** The Department of Fire shall be responsible for the protection against fire of life and property within the Urban Services District and within other areas covered by contracts authorized by ordinance.

SECTION 8.303. **FIRE CHIEF IS DIRECTOR. POWERS AND DUTIES.** The Department of Fire shall be under the management and control of a Director thereof, who is designated the Fire Chief. He shall assign members of the Department to stations, shifts, details and duties consistent with their rank. He shall make regulations, with the approval of the Metropolitan Mayor and in conformity with applicable ordinances, concerning the operation of the Department, the conduct of the officers and employees thereof, their uniforms, arms and other equipment and their training. The Fire Chief shall be responsible for the efficiency, discipline and good conduct of the Department. Orders of the Mayor relating to the Department shall be transmitted in all cases through the Fire Chief or in his absence or incapacity through an officer designated as Acting Chief. Disobedience to the lawful commands of the Fire Chief or viola-

tions of the rules and regulations made by him with the approval of the Mayor shall be grounds for removal or other disciplinary action as provided in such rules and regulations, subject to the civil service provisions of Article 12 of this Charter.

SECTION 8.304. **APPOINTMENT OF DIRECTOR. FILLING OTHER VACANCIES IN DEPARTMENT.** A permanent vacancy in the office of Director shall be filled by appointment of the Mayor subject to the civil service provisions of this Charter and subject to qualifications to be prescribed by the Civil Service Commission designed to secure a person especially qualified for the position by training and experience. A temporary vacancy in the office of Director due to sickness, absence or other disability shall be filled by appointment of the Mayor.

A vacancy in any office, position or employment in the Department shall be filled by appointment of the Fire Chief, subject to the approval of the Mayor and consistent with the civil service provisions of this Charter.

SECTION 8.305. **FIRE PREVENTION.** The Department of Fire shall recommend to the Council for adoption as ordinances such rules and regulations for the prevention of fire as may appear necessary and proper. In the enforcement of such rules and regulations when adopted the Department shall act through the Fire Marshal.

SECTION 8.306. **QUALIFICATION OF PERSONNEL.** After the effective date of this Charter, no person shall be eligible to appointment to any position in the Department except as a regular salaried employee in the classified service. Every appointee shall be a citizen of the United States of America; shall meet such physical requirements as shall be prescribed by the Civil Service Commission; and shall comply with all applicable rules and regulations of the Civil Service Commission.

To determine whether applicants for positions in the Department possess the required physical qualifications, the Chief Medical Director may provide for conducting physical examinations and report his findings to the Civil Service Commission.

SECTION 8.307. **SALARIES.** The annual compensation of the Director, payable semimonthly, shall be Twelve Thousand ($12,000) Dollars. The salaries of the other officers and employees of the Department shall be as fixed in the pay plan adopted pursuant to Article 12 of this Charter.

SECTION 8.308. **WORK WEEK AND VACATIONS.** Every member of the Department shall be entitled to two days off each week and to an annual vacation of twenty days without deduction of pay. The time for vacations shall be determined and assigned by the Fire Chief. All members of the Department shall be subject to call and assignment to duty at any time during an emergency.

Article 8
METROPOLITAN DEPARTMENTS
Chapter 4
Department of Public Works

SECTION 8.401. **DEPARTMENT OF PUBLIC WORKS CREATED.** There shall be a Department of Public Works, which shall consist of the Director of Public Works and such other officers and employees organized into such divisions and other units as may be provided by ordinance or by the orders of the Director consistent therewith and approved by the Mayor.

SECTION 8.402. **FUNCTIONS.** The Department of Public Works shall be responsible for:

(a) The design, construction, maintenance, repair and cleaning of roads, highways, streets, alleys, storm sewers, other public places, bridges, viaducts and other related structures.

(b) The collection and disposal of garbage and other refuse, and maintenance and operation of facilities for the disposal of same.

(c) Control of the servicing, maintenance and repair of automotive equipment, except as the same by ordinance may be assigned in whole or in part to another department or agency of the Metropolitan Government.

(d) Construction of capital improvement projects by its own employees, whenever so authorized or directed by ordinance or by the Mayor.

(e) Making and preparing such plans, specifications, estimates, surveys, maps, designs, drawings and reports as may be requested from time to time by the Council, by the Mayor or by the head of any department or any board, commission or agency of the Metropolitan Government acting with the approval of the Mayor, and supervision of the execution and performance of all contracts for capital improvement projects, the plans and specifications, for which were prepared by the Department of Public Works.

(f) The administration and enforcement of all laws, ordinances and regulations relating to permits and licenses, including those relating to weights and measures, electrical installations, building and construction, plumbing, taxicabs, miscellaneous industrial and commercial uses, elevators, water, sewer and gas installations, public gatherings and tourist camps; provided, that all licenses and permits issued shall be approved or regulated by such other offices, agencies or boards of the Metropolitan Government as may be provided from time to time by ordinance; and provided further that the Council may by ordinance transfer and assign this function to a newly created Department of Licenses and Permits.

(g) Such other powers and duties as are assigned to the Department by this Charter or may be assigned thereto by ordinance or by action of the Mayor.

SECTION 8.403. **SUPERVISION. CERTIFICATION AND APPROVAL OF PAYMENT FOR CERTAIN CAPITAL IMPROVEMENT PROJECTS.** Unless otherwise specifically provided for in this Charter, no payment upon any contract for capital improvement projects shall be made by the Metropolitan Government without the written certification of the Director of Public Works that the work or the portion thereof for which such payment is to be made has been satisfactorily performed in accordance with the terms of such contract. Unless otherwise specifically provided in this Charter, when the plans and specifications for any capital improvement project have been prepared by some person or agency other than the Department of Public Works, the performance of the contract may be supervised and certification required by the Department of Public Works before payment shall be made in accordance with the terms and provisions of the contract.

SECTION 8.404. **DIRECTOR OF PUBLIC WORKS; QUALIFICATIONS AND COMPENSATION.** The head of the Department of Public Works shall be the Director, whose annual compensation, payable semimonthly, shall be Fifteen Thousand ($15,000) Dollars. A permanent vacancy in the office of Director shall be filled by appointment made by the Mayor, subject to the civil service provisions of this Charter. He shall have had at least five (5) years experience in industry or in municipal or metropolitan public works and shall be licensed for the practice of engineering in Tennessee by the State Board of Architectural and Engineering Examiners. In the event of temporary vacancy in the office of Director due to sickness, absence or other disability, a temporary appointment may be made by the Mayor, subject to the civil service provisions of this Charter.

SECTION 8.405. **DIRECTOR OF PUBLIC WORKS; POWERS AND DUTIES.** The Director of Public Works shall have general management and control of the several divisions and units of the department. He shall appoint and remove, subject to the civil service provisions of Article 12 of this Charter, all officers and employees of the department and shall have power to make rules and regulations for the conduct of the business of the department consistent with this Charter and the ordinances of the Metropolitan Government.

SECTION 8.406. **CUSTODY OF MAPS AND PLANS.** The Department of Public Works shall have custody of all maps or plans or any part thereof which were on file immediately prior to the effective date of this Charter in the offices of the Director of Public Works of the City of Nashville or the County Highway Engineer of the County of Davidson and all such maps and plans hereafter made and not expressly required by law or ordinance to be filed in some other place; provided that all plans, records, etc., pertaining to the Sanitary Sewerage System which are in the custody of the Department of Public Works on the effective date of this Charter shall be turned over to the Department of Water and Sewerage Services.

Article 8
METROPOLITAN DEPARTMENTS
Chapter 5
Department of Water and Sewerage Services

SECTION 8.501. **DEPARTMENT OF WATER AND SEWERAGE SERVICES CREATED.** There shall be a Department of Water and Sewerage Services, which shall consist of the Director and such other officers and employees, organized into such divisions and other units as may be provided by ordinance or by the orders of the Director consistent therewith.

SECTION 8.502. **FUNCTIONS.** The Department of Water and Sewerage Services shall be responsible for: (1) The construction, operation and maintenance of all water and sanitary sewer facilities of the Metropolitan Government; (2) The collection of all charges for the services of such utilities; (3) Such other powers and duties as may be assigned to the department by ordinance.

SECTION 8.503. **DIRECTOR OF WATER AND SEWERAGE SERVICES; QUALIFICATIONS AND COMPENSATION.** The head of the Department of Water and Sewerage Services shall be the Director, whose annual compensation, payable semimonthly, shall be Fifteen Thousand ($15,000) Dollars. A permanent vacancy in the office of Director shall be filled by appointment made by the Mayor, subject to the civil service provisions of this Charter. He shall be a graduate engineer who is trained and skilled in public utility problems and shall have had at least five (5) years experience in an executive or major administrative position in a public utility operation or public utility administration.

SECTION 8.504. **DIRECTOR OF WATER AND SEWERAGE SERVICES; POWERS AND DUTIES.** The Director of Water and Sewerage Services shall have general management and control of the several divisions and units of the Department, including the approval of all departmental requisitions for purchases and services. No payment from the funds of the Department of Water and Sewerage Services shall be made until such payments shall have been certified as due and correct by the Director of the said Department; this includes the certification as to the satisfactory performance of all contracts and services in connection with the operation, maintenance and expansion of the said Department. The Director shall approve all plans and specifications relating to the expansion, operation, and maintenance of the water and sewerage system. He shall appoint and remove, subject to the civil service provisions of Article 12 of this Charter, all officers and employees of the Department and shall have power to make rules and regulations for the conduct of the business of the Department consistent with this Charter and the ordinances of the Metropolitan Government.

SECTION 8.505. **DIVISION OF BILLING AND COLLECTION.** There shall be established within the Department, a Division of Billing and Collection, which shall be responsible for the collection of all charges for the use of water, sewage disposal, and other services incident thereto.

SECTION 8.506. **ACCOUNTING SYSTEM.** The accounting system established by the Department shall be in conformity with accepted Utility Accounting practices and shall be approved by the Director of Finance and generally correlated with the central finance and accounting system of the Metropolitan Government.

SECTION 8.507. **REVOLVING FUNDS.** The Revolving Fund used in the operation of the water works system of the former City of Nashville as provided in Section 15 of Article 22 of Chapter 246 of the Private Acts of 1947 is hereby continued in full force and effect for the use and benefit of the Department of Water and Sewerage of the Metropolitan Government. This fund shall be used solely for paying the cost of improvements or extensions of the water system of the Metropolitan Government and for the purpose of making replacements in said system or purchasing and installing new capital equipment as part of said system. Whenever money in such fund shall be used for said purposes, the money so used shall be replaced in said fund from the first revenues received from the operation of the waterworks system which are not pledged for some other purpose until the fund is again restored to the amount of Two Hundred Thousand ($200,000) Dollars; provided, however, that revenues so used for the purpose of replacing money expended from such fund shall not be required to be so used in any one year in an amount exceeding ten (10%) percent of the gross revenues received from the operation of the waterworks system in such year. The Council, in its discretion, may provide for the placing of additional revenue in such fund for the purpose of establishing it in a larger amount than the minimum of Two Hundred Thousand ($200,000) Dollars herein provided. No proceeds of such fund shall be used for the payment of current costs of operating and maintaining the waterworks system of the Metropolitan Government or for the purchase of tools, operating supplies or similar equipment. No provision of this Section shall be construed to authorize the issuance of additional bonds for the foregoing purposes.

SECTION 8.508. **ESTABLISHMENT OF AND CHANGES IN RATES.** The Mayor and Council are authorized and directed to establish the rates for water and sewerage services and to provide the methods for changes therein.

Article 8
METROPOLITAN DEPARTMENTS
Chapter 6
Department of Law

SECTION 8.601. **DEPARTMENT OF LAW CREATED.** There shall be a Department of Law, which shall consist of the Director thereof, of other personnel hereinafter mentioned and of such other positions and employees as may be provided by ordi-

nance or by regulations of the Director consistent with ordinance.

SECTION 8.602. **FUNCTIONS.** The Department of Law shall have the power and its duty shall be to perform the following functions:

(a) Supervise, direct and control all the law work of the Metropolitan Government, except with respect to the Electric Power Board which, having its own General Counsel, is excepted from the provisions of this Chapter.

(b) Furnish legal advice to the Mayor, to the Council and to all officers, departments, boards and commissions concerning any matters arising in connection with the exercise of their official powers or performance of their official duties.

(c) Represent the Metropolitan Government in all litigation.

(d) Collect by suit or otherwise all debts, taxes and accounts due the Metropolitan Government which shall be placed with it for collection by any officer, department, board or commission.

(e) Prepare or approve all contracts, bonds, deeds, leases or other instruments in writing in which the Metropolitan Government is concerned.

(f) Prepare or assist in preparing for introduction any proposed ordinance upon request of the Mayor or any member of the Council.

(g) Codify and cause to be published in convenient book form once in every five (5) years all of the general ordinances which are still in effect, with compilation and publication annually of a supplement thereto. The first general codification shall be published within one (1) year after the first Director of Law assumes office under this Charter, unless the Council by resolution shall extend the time therefor.

(h) Perform such other duties as may be assigned to it by ordinance.

SECTION 8.603. **DIRECTOR OF LAW. HIS APPOINTMENT, QUALIFICATIONS, COMPENSATION, POWERS AND DUTIES.** The Department of Law shall be under the supervision and control of the Director of Law, who is designated the Metropolitan Attorney. The Metropolitan Attorney shall be appointed by the Mayor for a term which terminates with the term of the Mayor making the appointment. He shall be confirmed by a majority vote of the total membership of the Council. He shall have been a member of the Bar of Tennessee for at least five (5) years preceding his appointment and also have been a resident of the area of the Metropolitan Government for a like period. His annual compensation, payable semimonthly, shall be Fifteen Thousand ($15,000) Dollars. The Metropolitan Attorney shall appoint all officers and employees of the Department and may remove them, subject to the civil service provisions of Article 12 of this Charter. The Director of Law shall determine and assign to the members of his staff and other employees of the Department their respective duties and responsibilities, except as provided in the transitional provisions of this Charter.

SECTION 8.604. **DEPUTY DIRECTOR OF LAW.** There shall be a Deputy Director of Law, designated as the Deputy Metropolitan Attorney, who shall be appointed by the Director of Law, subject to the approval of the Mayor. The qualifications of the Deputy Director of Law shall be those hereinabove specified for the Director of Law and his compensation shall be Twelve Thousand ($12,000) Dollars per annum, payable semimonthly. The Deputy Director of Law shall be under the supervision and direction of the Metropolitan Attorney and shall assist him in the organization, administration and control of the Department of Law. In the absence of the Director of Law or in the event of a vacancy in his office, the Deputy Director of Law shall perform the duties thereof until the Director returns or the vacancy is filled.

SECTION 8.605. **ASSISTANT METROPOLITAN ATTORNEYS.** There shall be four (4) Assistant Metropolitan Attorneys who shall be appointed by the Director of Law, subject to the approval of the Mayor, and each of whose compensation shall be Seventy-five Hundred ($7500) Dollars per annum, payable semimonthly. The Council may by ordinance create additional positions of Assistant Metropolitan Attorney and fix the compensation of such positions, not to be higher than the minimum salary then being paid to an Assistant Metropolitan Attorney. All Assistant Metropolitan Attorneys shall perform such work of the Department as may be assigned to them by the Director.

SECTION 8.606. **DIRECTOR OF LAW AND OTHERS NOT TO ENGAGE IN PRIVATE PRACTICE.** The Metropolitan Attorney, the Deputy Metropolitan Attorney and all Assistant Metropolitan Attorneys shall devote their entire time and attention to the business of the Department of Law and shall not engage in the private practice of Law.

SECTION 8.607. **EMPLOYMENT OF SPECIAL COUNSEL RESTRICTED AND PROVIDED FOR.** No department, board, commission or other agency of the Metropolitan Government may employ special counsel. Whenever the interests of the Metropolitan Government require special counsel, the Council by resolution may authorize the Mayor to employ such counsel, who shall be paid such compensation for his service as the Mayor, the Director of Law and the Director of Finance shall determine to be reasonable compensation for the services rendered, and as the Council shall by resolution approve. The employment of bond counsel shall not be considered as the employment of special counsel for purposes of this Section.

SECTION 8.608. **CERTAIN PERSONNEL OF DEPARTMENT NOT UNDER CIVIL SERVICE.** The Metropolitan Attorney, the Deputy Metropolitan Attorney, their respective private secretaries and Assistant Metropolitan Attorneys shall not hold civil service status, except as expressly provided in the transitional provisions of this Charter.

Article 8
METROPOLITAN DEPARTMENTS

Chapter 7

Department of Aviation

SECTION 8.701. **DEPARTMENT OF AVIATION CREATED.** There shall be a Department of Aviation, which shall consist of the Director of Aviation and such other officers and employees as may be provided by ordinance.

SECTION 8.702. **FUNCTIONS.** The Department of Aviation shall be responsible (1) for the operation, maintenance and control of the Nashville Metropolitan Airport and other airports owned or operated in whole or in part by the Metropolitan Government, and (2) for such related activities and duties as may be prescribed by ordinance.

SECTION 8.703. **DIRECTOR OF AVIATION. QUALIFICATIONS, APPOINTMENT AND COMPENSATION.** The head of the Department of Aviation shall be the Director, whose annual compensation, payable semimonthly, shall be Twelve Thousand ($12,000) Dollars. A permanent vacancy in the office of the Director shall be filled by appointment made by the Mayor, subject to the civil service provisions of this Charter. He shall be a person with experience in an executive or major administrative po-

sition in municipal or other public airport operations and familiar with the rules and regulations of the authorized governmental agencies concerning airport operations and aeronautic requirements.

SECTION 8.704. **POWERS AND DUTIES OF DIRECTOR.** The Director of Aviation shall have the general management and supervision of the Department of Aviation. He shall appoint and remove, subject to the civil service provisions of Article 12 of this Charter, all other officers and employees. He shall have power to make rules and regulations consistent with this Charter and with applicable ordinances for the conduct of the business of the Department.

Article 9
PUBLIC SCHOOLS

SECTION 9.01. **PUBLIC SCHOOL SYSTEM ESTABLISHED.** A system of public schools for the Metropolitan Government of Nashville and Davidson County is hereby established, which shall be administered and controlled by the Metropolitan County Board of Education, sometimes in this Article called "the Board".

SECTION 9.02. **BOARD OF EDUCATION, TERM AND SELECTION OF MEMBERS.** The Metropolitan Board of Education shall be composed of nine (9) members whose terms of office shall be six (6) years each and shall be so staggered that the terms of three (3) members expire every two (2) years. One (1) member of the Board shall be appointed from each of the school districts herein defined and no member shall be appointed from a school district wherein another incumbent member resides. Any member who shall change his place of residence from one school district to another shall thereby vacate his office. The school districts from each of which one (1) member shall be appointed shall be as follows:

School District No. 1 shall include Councilmanic Districts Nos. 1, 2, 3 and 11.

School District No. 2 shall include Councilmanic Districts Nos. 7, 8, 9 and 10.

School District No. 3 shall include Councilmanic Districts Nos. 4, 5 and 6.

School District No. 4 shall include Councilmanic Districts Nos. 16, 17, 26 and 28.

School District No. 5 shall include Councilmanic Districts Nos. 18, 19, 20 and 21.

School District No. 6 shall include Councilmanic Districts Nos. 22, 23, 24 and 35.

School District No. 7 shall include Councilmanic Districts Nos. 25, 27, 33 and 34.

School District No. 8 shall include Councilmanic Districts Nos. 29, 30, 31 and 32.

School District No. 9 shall include Councilmanic Districts Nos. 12, 13, 14 and 15.

The school districts herein established may be altered in a plan for redistricting Councilmanic Districts adopted pursuant to Section 18.06 of this Charter.

Members of the Board shall be appointed by the Mayor and confirmed by a two-thirds majority of the whole membership of the Council. Of the nine (9) members originally appointed to the Board, three (3) shall be appointed for terms of six (6) years, three (3) for terms of four (4) years, and three (3) for terms of two (2) years. Thereafter as vacancies occur by expiration of the term, a successor shall be appointed for a term of six (6) years. Appointments to fill other vacancies shall be for the remainder of the term of the former member.

SECTION 9.03. **POWERS OF BOARD OF EDUCATION.** The Board is authorized to do all things necessary or proper for the establishment, operation and maintenance of an efficient and accredited consolidated school system for the Metropolitan Government, not inconsistent with this Charter or with general law, including but not limited to the following actions, all to be taken after receiving the recommendations thereon of the Director of Schools: The employment and fixing of the compensation of all persons necessary for the proper conduct of the public schools; the maintenance and preservation of school property, the management and safeguarding of school funds; the acquisition of school sites; the erection, maintenance and improvement of school buildings and additions thereto; the purchase of school equipment, furniture, apparatus, supplies and the like; the provision of group insurance of not less than Five Hundred ($500) Dollars each on its employees and teachers; and the promulgation of plans, rules and regulations for the administration, operation and maintenance of a public school system.

Purchases of the Board shall be consistent with the procedures established concerning competitive bidding as provided in Section 8.111 of this Charter. In that respect, the Board shall adopt appropriate rules and regulations concerning purchasing, including the establishment and enforcement of standard specifications for all supplies, materials and equipment required by the Board and which it has authority to purchase or lease.

The Board shall also have all powers and duties conferred by general law upon county boards of education and city boards of education, including, but not limited to, Tennessee Code Annotated, Sections 49-214 and 49-215, excepting only as otherwise provided in this Charter.

The system of furnishing free textbooks in the public schools of the City and County and receiving and accepting State Aid therefor in effect at the time of the adoption of this Charter shall be continued, unless and until changed by ordinance of the Council upon recommendation of the Board.

SECTION 9.04. **DUTIES OF METROPOLITAN BOARD OF EDUCATION. REFERENDUM AS TO SCHOOL BUDGET.** In addition to other duties imposed by this Charter or by general law, it shall be the duty of the Metropolitan Board of Education to:

1. Hold regular monthly meetings which shall be open to the public.
2. Adopt and make available for distribution rules, regulations and a statement of policies, including (a) the manner and method of operating the Metropolitan School System and its properties, (b) the manner and method of employing personnel, (c) all personnel policies and any requirements with reference to teaching personnel or nonteaching personnel, salaries, vacations, sick leave, job security and retirement policy; and (d) the manner and extent of use which may be made of the public buildings under the control of the Board.
3. Hold public hearings on the operational school budget prior to its approval by the Board, and thereafter to submit to the Mayor through the Director of Finance the budget for schools. If the operational school budget adopted by the Council is in the opinion of a two-thirds majority of the entire membership of the Board insufficient and inadequate to meet the needs of public education, then the Board is authorized to take the following action with respect thereto:

Not later than thirty (30) days prior to the first Thursday in August, the Board by a two-thirds majority of its entire membership shall adopt a resolution declaring that in addition to funds appropriated for the operational school budget as adopted by the Council, an amount of money (to be specified in the resolution) is necessary; that the specified amount will be produced by an additional tax levy of a stated number of mills (to be specified in the resolution), and that the Board by such resolution calls for and initiates a referendum election to determine whether such additional tax shall be levied and the total revenues thereby raised shall be added to the operational school budget. For the purpose of calculating the tax increase necessary, the Board shall procure from the Director of Finance, who shall furnish the same immediately upon request, the amount of revenue which an additional tax of one (1) mill is anticipated to produce, and on this basis calculate the additional tax necessary to raise the additional school funds sought. A certified copy of such resolution shall immediately be transmitted to the Council and to the Board of County Commissioners of Election, which shall order and conduct a special referendum election on the first Thursday in August, the same to be held simultaneously with, and as a part of, the general August election if the year be an even one.

The notice of election and the ballot for such referendum shall provide substantially as follows:

"Referendum Election as to increased school budget of $ _____ (here fill in the additional amount which the Board has certified as necessary) and an increase of _____ (here fill in amount which the Board has certified as necessary) mills in tax rate thereby necessitated.

For Increase _____
Against Increase _____ "

The result of said special election shall be certified by the Commissioners of Election to the Director of Finance and to the County Trustee. If the majority of voters favor said increase, then the previously adopted tax levy for the General Services District shall be deemed accordingly amended and increased and the previously adopted operational school budget shall be deemed accordingly amended and increased. If the majority of voters do not favor said increase, then both the tax levy and the operational school budget shall remain as previously adopted.

The cost of said special election shall be paid out of the general fund of the General Services District.

SECTION 9.05. **EMPLOYMENT BY BOARD OF DIRECTOR OF SCHOOLS.** The Metropolitan Board of Education is authorized to designate a person experienced in public school management and supervision and possessing a certificate of qualification issued by the State Board of Education pursuant to Tennessee Code Annotated, Section 49-220, as the chief administrative employee of the Board and to enter into an employment contract with such person for a period not exceeding five (5) years and for a compensation to be determined therein. The person so designated and employed shall be known as the "Metropolitan Director of Schools". The Metropolitan Board of Education is authorized to assign to the Metropolitan Director of Schools such duties and responsibilities as are necessarily, usually or properly assigned to a city superintendent of schools or to a county superintendent of schools.

SECTION 9.06. **PENSION RIGHTS OF EDUCATIONAL EMPLOYEES OF COUNTY AND CITY PROTECTED.** All rights and benefits which any person has acquired under a pension plan established for the benefit of teachers in the school system of Davidson County shall be preserved and continued; and all rights and benefits which any person has acquired as a non-teaching employee of the county board of education in the Davidson County Pension Fund shall be preserved and continued. All rights and benefits which any person has acquired under the Teachers Pension Department and Fund of the City of Nashville shall be preserved and continued, and all rights and benefits which any person has acquired as a non-teaching employee of the city board of education in the Civil Service Employees Pension Fund of the City of Nashville shall be preserved and continued. Every person whose rights are preserved and continued by this Section shall be entitled to participate in the applicable pension plan or fund on the terms and conditions in effect immediately prior to the effective date of this Charter, except as such terms and conditions may be changed by applicable general law.

SECTION 9.07. **PENSION AND RETIREMENT PLAN FOR METROPOLITAN TEACHERS. VOLUNTARY TRANSFER THEREUNDER OF CITY AND COUNTY TEACHERS.** The Metropolitan Board of Education shall establish an actuarially sound Pension and Retirement Plan for teachers. Such Plan shall be applicable to teachers employed by the Metropolitan Board of Education who were not employed in the county school system or the city school system immediately prior to the effective date of this Charter. Such Plan shall make provision for the transfer thereunder of teachers who were employed in either the school system of the City of Nashville or the school system of Davidson County when such teachers apply for such transfer and meet conditions of transfer specified by the Plan. The Metropolitan Board of Education is authorized in its discretion to integrate its Pension and Retirement Plan for Teachers with the Federal Insurance Contributions Act, or other applicable State or Federal Legislation.

SECTION 9.08. **TENURE RIGHTS OF COUNTY AND CITY TEACHERS PROTECTED.** Any person employed in the school systems of the City of Nashville and of Davidson County who has acquired tenure as a teacher under Sections 49-1401 to 49-1420, inclusive, of Tennessee Code Annotated, or under any Private Act, shall retain such tenure in the Metropolitan School System established by the consolidation of said school system.

SECTION 9.09. **DISABILITIES OF BOARD MEMBERS AND COUNCIL MEMBERS TO MAKE ADVERSE CONTRACTS OR OWN SCHOOL WARRANTS.** Members of the Metropolitan Board of Education and members of the Council shall be under the same disabilities as to making adverse contracts with the Metropolitan Board of Education or as to owning school warrants as are established by general law for members of county boards of education and justices of the peace.

SECTION 9.10. **CIVIL SERVICE AS TO TEACHERS AND OTHER EDUCATIONAL EMPLOYEES.** The Metropolitan Board of Education shall constitute a Civil Service Board for the purpose of investigating and hearing charges against any teacher and for the purpose of dismissing, suspending or otherwise disciplining the same and for the purpose of Section 12.09 of this Charter. In the discharge of its duty as a Civil Service Board the Metropolitan Board of Education is authorized to make rules and regulations. The provisions of Section 12.11 of this Charter with reference to offenses against civil service and disabilities of civil service employees shall be applicable to all nonteaching employees of the Board of Education.

Any teacher suspended or dismissed may obtain a judicial review as provided in Section 49.1417 of Tennessee Code Annotated, the same being a portion of the Teachers' Tenure Act. Any nonteaching employee of the Board may have his dismissal reviewed by the Court in the same manner provided by section 12.07 (h) for classified employees.

SECTION 9.11. **NO DIVERSION OF FUNDS.** No funds which have been appropriated for the use of, or transferred to, the Metropolitan School System shall be diverted from that use for any other purpose.

SECTION 9.12. **TRANSFER OF SCHOOL FUNDS WITHIN SCHOOL BUDGET.** The Board shall have power at any time to transfer funds within the major items of its budget. It shall also have power to make transfers of funds to, from or between major items in its budget, provided such transfers are not inconsistent with the general law.

SECTION 9.13. **TRANSFERS TO SCHOOL FUND FROM GENERAL FUNDS. BORROWING MONEY.** The Metropolitan Council by resolution approved by the Mayor, may transfer funds to the School Fund from the General Fund or general accounts of the Metropolitan Government, or may issue short term anticipation notes to provide such funds if in its judgement it is necessary and proper to provide temporary advances or transfers for the maintenance and operation of the schools. Such temporary advances or transfers shall be repaid or restored out of school funds during the ensuing year.

SECTION 9.14. **ACQUISITION AND SALE OF PROPERTY.** All school property heretofore belonging to the County of Davidson and all school property heretofore belonging to the City of Nashville shall belong to the Metropolitan Government of Nashville and Davidson County for the use and benefit of the Board of Education, and the title to all school property hereafter acquired shall be vested in the Metropolitan Government of Nashville and Davidson County for the use and benefit of the Board of Education. The Board of Education is hereby designated as the legal custodian of all school property and when in the judgement of said Board any property held by it is no longer suited or needed for school purposes, said Board is hereby authorized, with the approval of the Council and Mayor, to sell such property and have the proceeds credited to the unappropriated School Fund of the Metropolitan Government.

In acquiring or selling property, the Board shall cooperate closely with the Planning Commission, whose recommendation shall be sought and carefully considered by the Board.

Article 10
PUBLIC HEALTH AND HOSPITALS

Chapter 1

Public Health

SECTION 10.101. **METROPOLITAN BOARD OF HEALTH CREATED.** There shall be a Metropolitan Board of Health which sometimes in this Article may be called the "Department of Health" and sometimes called the "Board". The Board shall administer and control public health for the Metropolitan Government as herein provided.

SECTION 10.102. **BOARD OF HEALTH, QUALIFICATIONS, TERM AND SELECTION OF MEMBERS.** The Board shall be composed of five (5) members. Three members shall be doctors of medicine certified for practice as such by the State Board of Medical Examiners and licensed by the State Licensing Board for the Healing Arts, and each of whom shall have had not less than five years experience in the active practice of his profession. One of said doctors of medicine shall also have had special training, practice and experience in the field of psychiatric medicine. The two remaining members of the Board shall be chosen without reference to occupation, except that they shall not come from the medical profession. Members of the Board shall serve without compensation.

The members of the Board shall be appointed by the Mayor and confirmed by a majority of the whole membership of the Council. They shall serve terms of five (5) years each, provided that of the first five members, one shall serve for five years, one for four years, one for three years, one for two years and one for one year. Any vacancy other than by expiration of term shall be filled for the unexpired term.

SECTION 10.103. **THE METROPOLITAN BOARD OF HEALTH, FUNCTIONS.** The Board of Health, through its Chief Medical Director, shall exercise all the administrative functions of the Metropolitan Government pertaining to:

1. The physical and mental health of the people.
2. The investigation and control of communicable disease.
3. The regulation of publicly and privately owned institutions for the purpose of sanitation and public health.
4. The enforcement of reasonable rules and regulations promulgated as herein provided.
5. The collection, compilation, tabulation, analyzing and reporting of statistics and data concerning births, still births, deaths and such vital statistics.
6. The performance of the functions previously assigned by law to the Health Officers or the Health Departments of the City of Nashville and Davidson County, or such as hereafter may be assigned to City or County Health Officers or City Health Departments or County Health Departments in Tennessee.
7. The inspection of all charitable institutions, all jails and all institutions of the Metropolitan Government where sick, insane, destitute or other persons are confined. The Board may cause any person convicted of violating any law or ordinance and who is confined, or who is on parole, to be examined as to the causes contributing to the delinquency and shall make and keep a record of such examinations.

SECTION 10.104. **THE METROPOLITAN BOARD OF HEALTH, DUTIES.** In addition to the duties otherwise imposed by this Charter or by general law, it shall be the duty of the Board of Health to:

1. Determine and establish the policies to be followed in the exercise of its functions.
2. Establish within the Department of Health such divisions, branches, or subdivisions, and plan of organization as may be consistent with efficient administration, which organizational plan shall be submitted by the Board to the Council for approval by ordinance, and which organizational plan may be amended from time to time in like manner.
3. After public hearing adopt reasonable rules and regulations or amend rules and regulations previously adopted as necessary for the protection of the health of the people, which rules and regulations, among other things, shall set standards and procedures and requirements of conduct not less than as set out in regulations of the Commissioner of Public Health of Tenessee. No such rule or regulation shall be contrary to any Metropolitan ordinance.
4. Hear and act upon complaints of persons affected by decisions of the Chief Medical Director and to amend or set aside such decisions as are contrary to policies or regulations of the Board.
5. Cause to be prepared, with the aid of the Department of Law, for submission to the Council for its consideration, a comprehensive health code which shall embrace all matters with relation to public health to which the powers and duties of the Board extend, and which shall have as its purpose the preservation and promotion of the health of the people of the Metropolitan Government.
6. Submit to the Mayor, within six months after the beginning of each new term of office, a report upon the activities of the Metropolitan Board of Health and a comprehensive program of public health and indigent medical care.
7. Conduct inquiries, make investigations and hold hearings for the purpose of investigating nuisances, establishing the basis for the abatement of existing nuisances, preventing the creation of nuisances, taking other preventive steps to protect the health of the community and for other purposes herein set forth in connection with the powers, duties and authorities of the Board. In conducting any such inquiry and making of any such investigation the Board shall have and may exercise the same investigative powers as are vested by this Charter in other Metropolitan agencies which are given investigative powers.
8. Contract with other governmental agencies, or with public or private institutions, subject to confirmation by the Council by resolution for such services as will further the program and policies of the Board.
9. Cause to be prepared by the Chief Medical Director, subject to review and revision by the Board, the proposed annual budget for the Metropolitan Board of Health.
10. Cooperate with agencies of the United States and of the State of Tennessee in all matters of public health and sanitation and accept, receive and provide for the use of Federal and State grants in aid, State aid and matching funds.
11. Cooperate with privately endowed or operated institutions, funds or foundations in all matters of public health and sanitation and receive and accept and provide for the use of grants from any such institutions, funds or foundations.
12. Exercise such other authority and perform such other duties as may be required by ordinance consistent with the general law and the provisions of this Charter.

SECTION 10.105. **THE CHIEF MEDICAL DIRECTOR OF HEALTH. APPOINTMENT AND QUALIFICATION.** The Board shall appoint a Chief Medical Director of Health, herein sometimes called "Chief Medical Director", and may enter into an employment contract with such person for a period not exceeding five (5) years, and at a compensation to be fixed by the Board. Such compensation so fixed shall be subject to approval by the Council by resolution. The Chief Medical Director shall be a doctor of medicine certified for practice as such by the State Board of Medical Examiners, and licensed by the State Licensing Board for the Healing Arts. He shall have had not less than ten years previous experience in the active practice of his profession, or in the field of public health administration. He shall devote his entire time to the duties of his office.

SECTION 10.106. **THE CHIEF MEDICAL DIRECTOR. POWERS AND DUTIES.** The Chief Medical Director shall be the chief administrative officer of the Board. He shall be responsible to the Board for the administration and execution of its program and policies. Within the policies set forth by the Board, he shall have general management and control of any divisions of the department and such other administrative units as may be created by the Board or by ordinance. With the approval of the Board, pursuant to established personnel policies, and subject to the provisions of this Article, he shall appoint and remove the heads of the divisions and other officers and employees of the Board. He shall have such other powers and duties as may be authorized by general law, by this Charter or by ordinance.

SECTION 10.107. **THE METROPOLITAN BOARD OF HEALTH, PERSONNEL RULES AND REGULATIONS.** The Metropolitan Board of Health, consistent with the standards of the merit system of the United States Public Health Service, shall establish, adopt and make available for distribution, its rules, regulations and policy statement concerning its personnel policy, the manner and method of employing personnel, the requirements with reference to the qualifications of both professional and non-professional personnel, salaries, vacations, sick leave, job security, retirement policy, and other related terms and conditions of employment by the Board.

The Board shall constitute a Civil Service Board with respect to employees of the Board of Health for the purpose of Section 12.09 of this Charter and for the purpose of investigating and hearing charges against any professional or non-professional employee, and for the purpose of dismissing, suspending or otherwise disciplining any such employee, or reviewing any decision of the Chief Medical Director affecting the employment status of such employee. In the discharge of its duties as a Civil Service Board, the Board shall act pursuant to its rules and regulations governing personnel policies promulgated as hereinabove stated, and shall have the same investigative powers as vested by this Charter in other agencies of the Metropolitan Government in which investigative power is vested. Any employee of the Board dismissed or discharged pursuant to the action of the Board after hearing, may have such discharge or dismissal reviewed in the same manner as is provided in this Charter for the review of actions of the Civil Service Commission under certain conditions.

SECTION 10.108. **METROPOLITAN BOARD OF HEALTH BUDGET.** The Board shall submit to the Mayor, through the Director of Finance, the budget for the Metropolitan Board of Health. If the Mayor shall make any change therefrom in the budget submitted by him to the Council, it shall be his duty to inform the Council with respect to such change and the original proposals of the Board.

SECTION 10.109. **PENSION AND RETIREMENT RIGHTS UNDER PLANS.** All rights and benefits which any officer or employee of the County Board of Health of Davidson County or of the County Health Office has acquired under any pension plan established before the effective date of this Charter are preserved and continued, as otherwise provided in this Charter.

SECTION 10.110. **CIVIL SERVICE MEDICAL EXAMINER. CIVIL SERVICE EXAMINATIONS.** The Chief Medical Director shall designate a qualified professional member of his medical staff as Civil Service Medical Examiner to conduct physical examinations for civil service personnel, including applicants for appointments, to conduct examinations for persons in retired status and applicants for retirement benefits, and to conduct periodical examinations for drivers of vehicular equipment of the Metropolitan Government. In addition, the Civil Service Medical Examiner shall conduct physical examinations when requested by any board or agency of the Metropolitan Government but solely for Metropolitan Government purposes; or as provided by ordinance.

Article 10
PUBLIC HEALTH AND HOSPITALS
Chapter 2
Public Hospitals

SECTION 10.201. **METROPOLITAN BOARD OF HOSPITALS CREATED.** There shall be a Metropolitan Board of Hospitals, which sometimes in this Article is called the "Board". The Board shall administer and control hospitals for the Metropolitan Government of Nashville and Davidson County as herein provided.

SECTION 10.202. **BOARD OF HOSPITALS, QUALIFICATIONS, TERM AND SELECTION OF MEMBERS.** The Board shall be composed of seven (7) members. Three (3) members shall be doctors of medicine certified for practice as such by the State Board of Medical Examiners and licensed by the State Licensing Board for the Healing Arts, and each of whom shall have had not less than five years experience in the active practice of his profession. One of said doctors of medicine shall also have had special training, practice and experience in the field of psy-

chiatric medicine. One member shall be a registered nurse. The three remaining members of the Board shall be chosen without reference to occupation or profession. Members of the Board shall serve without compensation.

The members of the Board shall be appointed by the Mayor and confirmed by a majority of the whole membership of the Council. They shall serve terms of five years each, provided that of the first seven members, two shall serve for five years, one for four years, two for three years, one for two years and one for one year. Any vacancy other than by expiration of term shall be filled for the unexpired term.

SECTION 10.203. **FUNCTION OF BOARD OF HOSPITALS.** The Board of Hospitals, through the Director of Hospitals, shall exercise all the administrative functions of the Metropolitan Government pertaining to the operation of all institutions owned, maintained or operated by the Metropolitan Government for the examination, treatment, convalescence or detention of the sick, injured or physically or mentally ill. Said Board shall determine and establish the policies to be followed in the exercise of its function and it may receive, accept and provide for the use of funds from any governmental agency, by any public or private institution or by any individual.

SECTION 10.204. **THE DIRECTOR OF HOSPITALS, APPOINTMENT AND QUALIFICATIONS.** The Board of Hospitals shall appoint a Director of Hospitals, herein sometimes called "Director", and may enter into an employment contract with such person for a period not exceeding five (5) years, and at a compensation to be fixed by the Board. The Director shall be a person who has had at least five (5) years experience in hospital administration or at least ten (10) years experience in some other executive or major administrative position.

SECTION 10.205. **THE DIRECTOR. POWERS AND DUTIES.** The Director shall be the chief administrative officer of the Board of Hospitals. He shall be responsible to the Board for the administration and execution of its program and policies. Within the policies set forth by the Board, he shall have general management and control of all hospitals and institutions administered by the board. With the approval of the Board, pursuant to established personnel policies, and subject to the provisions of this Article, he shall appoint and remove the other officers and employees of the Board. He shall have such other powers and duties as may be authorized by general law, by this Charter or by ordinance.

SECTION 10.206. **THE BOARD OF HOSPITALS. PERSONNEL RULES AND REGULATIONS.** The Board of Hospitals shall establish, adopt and make available for distribution its rules, regulations and policy statement concerning its personnel policy, the manner and method of employing personnel, the requirements with reference to the qualifications of both professional and non-professional personnel, salaries, vacations, sick leave, job security, retirement policy, and other related terms and conditions of employment by the Board.

The Board shall constitute a Civil Service Board with respect to employees of said Board for the purpose of Section 12.09 of this Charter and for the purpose of investigating and hearing charges against any professional employee, and for the purpose of dismissing, suspending or otherwise disciplining any such employee, or reviewing any decision of the Director affecting the employment status of such employee. In the discharge of its duties as a Civil Service Board, the Board shall act pursuant to its rules and regulations governing personnel policies promulgated as hereinabove stated, and shall have the same investigative powers as vested by this Charter in other agencies of the Metropolitan Government in which investigative power is vested. Any employee of the Board dismissed or discharged pursuant to the action of the Board after hearing may have such discharge or dismissal reviewed in the same manner as is provided by this Charter for review of actions of the Civil Service Commission under certain conditions.

SECTION 10.207. PENSION AND RETIREMENT RIGHTS UNDER PLANS. All rights and benefits which any person has acquired as an employee of any hospital or institution owned, maintained or operated by the City of Nashville or the County of Davidson are preserved and continued as otherwise provided in this Charter.

Article 11

ADMINISTRATIVE BOARDS AND COMMISSIONS

Chapter 1

General Provisions

SECTION 11.101. GENERAL PROVISIONS CONTROL EXCEPT AS SPECIFIED. The following general provisions shall apply to all administrative boards and commissions established by this Article or other provisions of this Charter, except as specific provisions as to a particular board or commission otherwise provide.

SECTION 11.102. QUALIFICATIONS. Every member shall have been a resident of the area of the Metropolitan Government or have had his principal place of business or employment therein for not less than one (1) year prior to his appointment and shall continue to be so eligible so long as he shall serve.

SECTION 11.103. QUORUM. A majority of the membership shall constitute a quorum for the purpose of meeting and transacting business.

SECTION 11.104. REGULAR AND SPECIAL MEETINGS. Each Board or commission shall hold regular meetings at least quarterly for the conduct of its business and may hold more frequent regular meetings as its by-laws may provide; and it may hold special meetings as may be deemed necessary, the same to be called or held as provided in its by-laws.

SECTION 11.105. ELECTION OF CHAIRMAN, VICE-CHAIRMAN AND SECRETARY. Each board or commission shall elect one of its members as chairman and another as vice-chairman, who shall serve for a period of one (1) year or until his successor shall have been chosen; and it may elect as its secretary one of its own members or it may appoint as secretary one of its employees.

SECTION 11.106. MEMBERS TO HOLD NO OTHER METROPOLITAN OFFICE OR POSITION. No appointive member of any board or commission shall hold any other remunerative public office or position in the Metropolitan Government, except as otherwise specifically provided in this Charter.

SECTION 11.107. BY-LAWS, RULES AND REGULATIONS TO BE FILED WITH METROPOLITAN CLERK. Each board or commission may make such by-laws, rules and regulations, not inconsistent with law, as it deems appropriate for the conduct of its business, copies of which shall be filed with the Metropolitan Clerk and with the Secretary of the board or commission.

SECTION 11.108. EMPLOYMENT OF PERSONNEL. Except as otherwise provided in this Charter, each board or commission is authorized to employ such personnel as may be necessary to perform its functions and as may be within the limits of its budget appropriations.

Article 11

ADMINISTRATIVE BOARDS AND COMMISSIONS

Chapter 2

Board of Equalization

SECTION 11.201. BOARD OF EQUALIZATION ESTABLISHED. MEMBERS, APPOINTMENT, QUALIFIATIONS AND VACANCIES. There is hereby established a Metropolitan Board of Equalization, which shall consist of five (5) members appointed by the Mayor for a term of two (2) years, and confirmed by a majority vote of the whole membership of the Council. Said members shall be owners of taxable real property within the territorial limits of the Metropolitan Government and shall have been residents therein for a period of at least six (6) years prior to their appointment. At least two members shall reside within and own taxable real property within the Urban Services District; and at least two members shall reside without and own taxable real property without the Urban Services District. A member shall create a vacancy on the Board if during his term of office he does not meet the requirements of appointment. All vacancies shall be filled for the unexpired term in the same manner as original appointments.

SECTION 11.202. POWERS AND DUTIES. Said Board shall meet in a Metropolitan public building on the second Monday in April of each year, and sit in regular session as necessity may require until the equalization has been completed, which shall not be later than June 1st. The Board shall give notice in a principal newspaper of daily circulation published in the Metropolitan area at least five (5) days prior to the initial meeting, stating the time, place, and hours of such meeting.

It shall be the duty of the Metropolitan Board of Equalization carefully to examine, compare and equalize the assessments of property and merchants' ad valorem assessments within the territorial limits of the Metropolitan Government, and in so doing, together with the performance of all its other functions, be governed by the general laws regulating County or City Boards of Equalization, except as otherwise specified in this Charter.

Not later than fifteen (15) days after its adjournment, the Board shall cause to be published in a principal daily newspaper published in the Metropolitan area, a list of all taxpayers whose assessments were increased or decreased by said Board, giving the names of taxpayers, location of property, and the amount of increase or decrease as compared with the assessment of the Metropolitan Tax Assessor.

Not later than fifteen (15) days after its adjournment said Board shall certify the assessments. The tax rolls shall then be turned over to the Division of Collections in the Metropolitan Department of Finance at least fifteen (15) days prior to the date that taxes become due and payable.

SECTION 11.203. RIGHT OF COMPLAINT. Any owner of taxable property shall have the right to make complaint before the Metropolitan Board of Equalization. Upon such complaint, the Board may hear any evidence or witnesses offered by the complainant or take other such steps as it may deem necessary to the investigation of the complaint, and pass upon the question justly and equitably. The Board shall pass upon each complaint and either dismiss the complaint or grant all or part of the relief requested.

All decisions of the Board of Tax Equalization shall be final and conclusive unless within the time permitted by law the taxpayer appeal from said decision to the State Board of Equalization and the action of the latter Board shall be final, but always subject to such judicial review as may be permitted by law.

SECTION 11.204. **COMPENSATION OF BOARD MEMBERS.** Members of the Board shall receive compensation as provided by Tennessee Code Annotated, Section 67-211, for members of county boards of equalization.

SECTION 11.205. **GENERAL LAW APPLICABLE.** The Metropolitan Board of Equalization shall be governed by general laws regulating county or city boards of equalization except as specified in this Charter.

Article 11
ADMINISTRATIVE BOARDS AND COMMISSIONS
Chapter 3
Electric Power Board

SECTION 11.301. **ELECTRIC POWER BOARD OF NASHVILLE PROVIDED FOR AND CONTINUED AS METROPOLITAN AGENCY.** The Electric Power Board of Nashville created and established by Chapter 246, Private Acts of 1947, and amendatory Acts, the same being the Charter of the City of Nashville, shall continue to exist as the Electric Power Board of the Metropolitan Government of Nashville and Davidson County and to function as an agency of the Metropolitan Government, and shall have all the rights, duties, powers, obligations, privileges and responsibilities as are contained in the terms and provisions of said Private Acts or Municipal Charter. A copy of the terms and provisions of said Private Acts or Municipal Charter, with modifications limited to those changes necessary and proper to constitute said Electric Power Board an agency of the Metropolitan Government, is attached to this Charter and made a part hereof as Appendix Three hereto.

Article 11
ADMINISTRATIVE BOARDS AND COMMISSIONS
Chapter 4
Nashville Transit Authority

SECTION 11.401. **NASHVILLE TRANSIT AUTHORITY PROVIDED FOR AND CONTINUED AS METROPOLITAN AGENCY.** Nashville Transit Authority, created and established by Chapter 487, Private Acts of 1953 and amendatory Acts, the same being amendments to the Charter of the City of Nashville, shall continue to exist and to function as an agency of the Metropolitan Government and shall have all the rights, duties, powers, obligations, privileges and responsibilities as are contained in the terms and provisions of said Private Acts or Municipal Charter, provided that members of said Authority shall be appointed by the Mayor and confirmed by a majority vote of the whole membership of the Council. A copy of the terms and provisions of said Private Acts or Municipal Charter, with modifications limited to those changes necessary and proper to constitute said Nashville Transit Authority an agency of the Metropolitan Government is attached to this Charter and made a part hereof as Appendix Four hereto.

Article 11
ADMINISTRATIVE BOARDS AND COMMISSIONS
Chapter 5
Metropolitan Planning Commission

SECTION 11.501. **ESTABLISHMENT OF PLANNING COMMISSION.** There shall be a Metropolitan Planning Commission, sometimes in this Chapter called "the Commission", which shall be the official planning agency for the Metropolitan Government of Nashville and Davidson County.

SECTION 11.502. **MEMBERS, NUMBER, QUALIFICATIONS, APPOINTMENT, TERMS OF OFFICE, VACANIES.** The Commission shall consist of ten (10) members. The Mayor shall serve as a member of the Commission by virtue of his public office and one (1) member of the Metropolitan County Council shall be selected by that body from its membership to serve as a member of this Commission. The member of the Council selected to serve as a member of this Commission shall be the chairman of the Council committee on planning provided such a committee is established. Eight (8) members shall be appointed by the Mayor and shall be confirmed by a majority vote of the whole membership of the Council.

The eight (8) members appointed by the Mayor shall serve a term of four (4) years, respectively, or until a successor is duly appointed and qualified; except, of the members first appointed, two (2) shall serve for a term of one year, two (2) for a term of two years, two (2) for a term of three years, and two (2) for a term of four years. The terms of the Mayor and the member of the Council shall be coextensive with the term of their respective public positions.

Any vacancy occuring during the unexpired term of any member shall be filled in the manner prescribed herein for the original selection of the members of this Commission.

SECTION 11.503. **ORGANIZATION; OFFICERS, MEETINGS, QUORUM, BUSINESS, RECORDS.** Immediately upon appointment and qualification, the Metropolitan Planning Commission shall elect one of its appointive members as Chairman and one as Vice-Chairman, each of whom shall serve for a period of one (1) year, respectively, or until his successor shall have been chosen for the ensuing term. The Commission may choose such other officers as it deems necessary.

The Metropolitan Planning Commission shall meet regularly at a public building at least once a month and its meetings shall be open to the public. Special meetings may be called by the Chairman of the Commission or by any three (3) members thereof. Six (6) members shall constitute a quorum for the transaction of any business, which shall be accomplished in accordance with by-laws adopted by the Commission. A majority vote of the members present and constituting a quorum shall be necessary to decide any item of business requiring action by the Commission. The Commission shall maintain a record of its meetings and all actions taken and these records shall be open to the public.

SECTION 11.504. **POWERS, DUTIES AND RESPONSIBILITIES.** The Metropolitan Planning Commission shall have all of the powers, duties and responsibilities which are now or may be hereafter granted to municipal planning commissions, regional planning commissions or metropolitan planning commissions by general state law, including specifically but not limited to such powers, duties and responsibilities with respect to general planning, zoning and subdivision regulation as are granted by the following Chapters of Title 13—Public Planning and Housing of the Tennessee Code Annotated: Chapter 2 (Regional Planning Commissions); Chapter 3 (Regional Planning Regulations); Chapter 4 (County Zoning Regulations); Chapter 5 (Municipal Planning Commissions); Chapter 6 (Municipal Planning Regulations); and Chapter 7 (Municipal Zoning Regulations); provided such powers, duties and responsibilities are not in conflict with the provisions of this Article. To the extent that there is any conflict between the powers given a metropolitan planning commission and the powers given a municipal planning commission or a regional planning commission, the Commission hereby created shall be deemed a metropolitan planning commission; and to the extent that there is any conflict between the powers given a municipal planning commission and the powers given a regional planning commission, the Commission hereby created shall be deemed a municipal planning commission. In addition thereto, the Commission shall have such powers, duties and responsibilities as are provided by ordinance.

In the performance of these powers, duties and responsibilities the Metropolitan Planning Commission shall have the authority, and where appropriate to the context shall be required, to:

(a) Within its budget appropriation and other funds at its disposal employ personnel and enter into contracts for such services as it may require.

(b) Enter into agreements and receive such grants and/or assistance as may be available from the Federal or state governments for planning purposes; receive gifts for planning purposes.

(c) Require information which shall be furnished within a reasonable time from the other departments and agencies of the Metropolitan Government.

(d) Enter upon any land and make examinations and surveys and place and maintain necessary monuments and markers thereon.

(e) Make, amend and add to the master or general plan for the physical development of the entire Metropolitan Government area.

(f) Exercise control over platting or subdividing of land within the Metropolitan Government area.

(g) Draft for the Council an official map of the area and recommend or disapprove proposed changes in such map.

(h) Make and adopt a zoning plan and recommend or disapprove proposed changes in such plan.

(i) Make, in cooperation with the Metropolitan Government Housing Authority, and adopt plans for the clearance and rebuilding of slum areas and for the improvement of blighted areas within the Metropolitan Government area.

(j) Make and adopt plans for the replanning, conservation, improvements and renewal of neighborhoods, planning units and communities within the Metropolitan Government area.

(k) Submit annually to the Mayor, not less than sixty (60) days prior to the beginning of the budget year, a list of recommended capital improvements which in the opinion of the Commission are necessary or desirable to be constructed or otherwise provided during the forthcoming six (6) year period. Such lists shall be arranged in order of preference with recommendations as to which projects shall be constructed in which years.

(l) Promote public interest in and understanding of planning and its organization and operation, the master or general plan and its constituent parts, and the implementation of planning, including zoning, subdivision regulation, urban renewal, the official map and capital improvements programming.

SECTION 11.505. MANDATORY REFERRALS TO PLANNING COMMISSION. Whenever the Commission shall have adopted the master or general plan of the Metropolitan Government area or any part thereof, then and thenceforth no street, park or other public way, ground, place or space, no public building or structure, or no public utility whether publicly or privately owned, shall be constructed or authorized in the area under the jurisdiction of the Metropolitan Government until and unless the location and extent thereof shall have been submitted to and approved by the Planning Commission; provided that in case of disapproval, the Commission shall communicate its reasons to the Council and said Council by a vote of a majority of its membership, shall have the power to overrule such disapproval and, upon such overruling, said Council shall have the power to proceed. The widening, narrowing, relocation, vacation, change in the use, acceptance, acquisition, sale or lease of any street or public way, ground, place, property or structure shall be subject to similar submission and approval, and the failure to approve may be similarly overruled. The failure of the Commission to act within thirty (30) days from and after the date of official submission to it shall be deemed approval, unless a longer period be granted by the submitting body, board or official.

SECTION 11.506. DEPARTMENT OF PLANNING. EXECUTIVE DIRECTOR. There shall be a Department of Planning, headed by an Executive Director. The Planning Commission shall appoint an Executive Director and may enter into an employment contract with such person for a period not exceeding five (5) years, and at a compensation to be fixed by the Commission.

The Executive Director shall attend all meetings of the Metropolitan Planning Commission, act as its secretary, keep minutes of its proceedings, direct the staff of the Commission in its work, and shall have such other authority, duties and responsibilities as the Commission may require and establish or as may be provided by ordinance.

The Executive Director shall have such executive authority, duties and responsibilities as are now or may be hereafter provided by general state law concerning municipal planning commissions, regional planning commissions or metropolitan planning commissions.

The Department of Planning shall be organized in such manner deemed appropriate by the Planning Commission for the performance of its work.

Article 11
ADMINISTRATIVE BOARDS AND COMMISSIONS
Chapter 6
Metropolitan Board of Fair Commissioners

SECTION 11.601. METROPOLITAN BOARD OF FAIR COMMISSIONERS CREATED. NUMBER, QUALIFICATIONS, APPOINTMENT AND TERM OF OFFICE. There shall be a Metropolitan Board of Fair Commissioners, which shall consist of five (5) members to be appointed by the Mayor and confirmed by a majority of the whole membership of the Council. The members of the Board shall serve for terms of five (5) years each, except that of the members first appointed, one shall serve for terms of one (1) year, one for a term of two (2) years, one for a term of three (3) years, one for a term of four (4) years, and one for a term of five (5) years. Any vacancy occurring during the term of a member shall be filled in the manner prescribed for the original appointment and shall be for the unexpired portion of the term.

SECTION 11.602. FUNCTIONS AND DUTIES. It shall be the duty of the Metropolitan Board of Fair Commissioners to:

(a) Exercise all the powers and perform all the duties heretofore or hereafter imposed on the Board of Fair Commissioners of Davidson County, as established by Chapter 490 of the Acts of Tennessee for 1909 and Chapter 515 of the Private Acts of 1923 and amendments thereto.

(b) Within the limitation of its budget appropriation and

funds otherwise available, employ and fix the compensation of such personnel as may be necessary.

(c) Perform such other duties as may be imposed upon the Board by ordinance.

Article 11
ADMINISTRATIVE BOARDS AND COMMISSIONS
Chapter 7
Farmers Market Board

SECTION 11.701. **FARMERS MARKET BOARD CREATED. NUMBER, QUALIFICATION, APPOINTMENT AND TERM OF OFFICE.** There shall be a Farmers Market Board, which shall consist of five (5) members to be appointed by the Mayor and confirmed by a majority of the whole membership of the Council. The members of the Board shall hold no other public office or position, and shall serve for terms of five (5) years each, except that of the members first appointed, one shall serve for terms of one (1) year, one for a term of two (2) years, one for a term of three years, one for a term of four (4) years, and one for a term of five (5) years. Any vacancy occurring during the term of a member shall be filled in the manner prescribed for the original appointment and shall be for the unexpired portion of the term.

SECTION 11.702. **FUNCTIONS AND DUTIES.** It shall be the duty of the Farmers Market Board to:

(a) Exercise all the powers and perform all the duties heretofore or hereafter imposed on the "Davidson County Farmers Market Commission", as established by Chapter 400 of the Private Acts of 1949 and any amendments thereto.

(b) Within the limitation of its budget appropriation and funds otherwise available, employ and fix the compensation of such personnel as may be necessary.

(c) Perform such other duties as may be imposed upon the the Board by ordinance.

Article 11
ADMINISTRATIVE BOARDS AND COMMISSIONS
Chapter 8
Agricultural Extension Board

SECTION 11.801. **AGRICULTURAL EXTENSION BOARD CREATED. NUMBER, QUALIFICATIONS, APPOINTMENT AND TERM OF OFFICE.** There shall be an Agricultural Extension Board which shall consist of seven (7) members to be appointed by the Mayor and confirmed by a majority of the whole membership of the Council. The members of the Board shall have been residents of the area of the General Services District outside of the Urban Services District for not less than two (2) years prior to the appointment and shall continue such residence as a qualification for membership. At least two (2) members of the Board shall be female homemakers. The members of the Board shall serve for terms of three (3) years each, except that of the members first appointed, two shall serve for a term of one (1) year, two for a term of two (2) years, and three for a term of three (3) years.

SECTION 11.802. **FUNCTIONS AND DUTIES.** It shall be the duty of the Agricultural Extension Board to:

(a) Exercise all the powers and perform all the duties of the County Agricultural Extension Committee provided

for by Tennessee Code Annotated, Section 49-3406, and otherwise to carry out the purpose of Sections 49-3401 to 49-3408 of Tennessee Code Annotated by cooperating with the United States Department of Agriculture and the appropriate agencies of the State of Tennessee.

(b) Within the limitations of its budget appropriation and funds otherwise available, employ and fix the compensation of such personnel as may be necessary.

(c) Perform such other duties as may be imposed upon the the Board by ordinance.

Article 11
ADMINISTRATIVE BOARDS AND COMMISSIONS
Chapter 9
Metropolitan Traffic and Parking Commission

SECTION 11.901. **COMMISSION CREATED, QUALIFICATIONS, TERM AND SELECTION OF MEMBERS.** There shall be a Metropolitan Traffic and Parking Commission, sometimes in this Chapter called "the Commission". The Commission shall consist of nine (9) members, who shall serve as such without compensation. One member of the Commission shall be the Chief of Police. Another member shall be a member of the Council selected by the Council for a term of one (1) year. The remaining seven (7) members of the Commission shall be appointed by the Mayor and confirmed by a majority of the whole membership of the Council. Said seven members shall serve terms of five (5) years each, provided that the first members appointed shall serve terms of one, two, three, four, four, five and five years respectively. Any vacancy due to any cause shall be filled for the unexpired term in the same manner as the original appointment.

SECTION 11.902. **SECRETARY OF THE COMMISSION.** The Secretary shall serve at the pleasure of the Commission and shall be paid such compensation as shall be fixed by the Commission within its budgeted appropriation.

SECTION 11.903. **CHIEF TRAFFIC ENGINEER. HIS QUALIFICATIONS.** The Commission is authorized to select a Chief Traffic Engineer, subject to the civil service provisions of Article 12 of this Charter, who shall have such duties as may be prescribed by the Commission. The Chief Traffic Engineer shall be a graduate of a school of traffic engineering and shall have had at least five (5) years' experience in traffic administration.

SECTION 11.904. **FUNCTION OF COMMISSION AS TO TRAFFIC REGULATION.** For the purpose of making the roads, streets and other public ways safe for pedestrians, motorists and others, and for the purpose of facilitating the flow of traffic thereon, the Commission is hereby authorized to adopt and publish traffic regulations, including the erection of proper signs necessarily and properly connected with or incident to the following:

(a) The location and time when parking shall be limited.

(b) Places where parking shall be prohibited entirely or only during certain hours.

(c) The establishment of stop sign controls for through streets or isolated intersections.

(d) The establishment of traffic signal controls.

(e) The direction in which traffic may use any street or portion of a street.

(f) Restrictions on the size of vehicles using certain streets.

(g) The establishment of speed zones upon Metropolitan streets and roads based upon the findings of the Commission. When such zones are properly signposted, the speed indicated on the signs shall be the legal speed limit.

Such traffic regulations adopted by the Commission shall take effect five (5) days after they have been published in a daily newspaper of general circulation within the area of the Metropolitan Government and after a certified copy thereof has been filed with the Metropolitan Clerk and the Chief of Police. Such regulations when so adopted shall have the force and effect of an ordinance and shall be enforced by the Metropolitan Police. The Metropolitan Council shall provide by ordinance for the punishment of violators of such traffic regulations and shall fix proper and adequate fines and penalties.

SECTION 11.905. **COMMISSION'S REVIEW OF PROPOSED ORDI-NANCES.** Where a proposed ordinance affects traffic control or the use of streets by traffic and is not accompanied at introduction by a favorable recommendation of the Traffic and Parking Commission, a copy thereof shall be promptly delivered by the Metropolitan Clerk to the Commission and the same shall not be passed on second reading until the recommendation of said Commission with respect to the proposal has been received, or thirty (30) days have elapsed without such recommendation. No ordinance which affects traffic control or the use of streets by traffic and which has been disapproved by the Commission shall be finally passed or become effective unless it shall have been adopted by a two-thirds (⅔) majority of the whole membership of the Metropolitan Council and also then be approved by the Metropolitan Mayor with a three-fourths majority of the whole membership of the Metropolitan Council required to override a veto.

SECTION 11.906. **PUBLICATION OF TRAFFIC RULES AND REGU-LATIONS.** It shall be the duty of the Commission to publish the traffic rules and regulations of the Metropolitan Government in convenient pamphlet form, and in the compiling of such rules and regulations the Commission may call on the Metropolitan Department of Law for such assistance as may be required.

SECTION 11.907. **MANAGEMENT AND CONTROL OF PARKING, GARAGE AND OTHER TRAFFIC FACILITIES.** The Commission shall have power to control and manage parking facilities in any Metropolitan street or road, including the installation of parking meters or other necessary equipment in connection therewith. The Commission shall prescribe and may revise a schedule of service charges in connection with the use of parking meters, a copy of which schedule shall be kept on file and subject to public inspection at the office of the Commission and at the office of the Metropolitan Clerk.

The Commission shall also have control and management of any public parking garage or other traffic facilities, and with the acquisition, construction and establishment of the same. The Commission may enter into lease agreements with private operators to operate the parking facilities owned by the Metropolitan Government. The Commission is authorized to collect rents, fees or other charges for such parking garage and other traffic facilities as it may operate and manage.

All moneys collected by the Commission from parking meters, or any other service charges, shall be remitted by it to the Metropolitan Treasurer, who shall keep such moneys in a separate account earmarked for traffic and parking improvements.

SECTION 11.908. **POWERS OF COMMISSION BY PRIVATE ACT AND ORDINANCE CONTINUED.** In addition to other powers herein granted, the Commission shall have such powers as may have been granted by private act or ordinance to the Traffic Com-

mission of the City of Nashville or to the Parking Board of said City, until such powers may be modified or changed by ordinance of the Metropolitan Council.

Article 11
ADMINISTRATIVE BOARDS AND COMMISSIONS

Chapter 10
Metropolitan Board of Parks and Recreation

SECTION 11.1001. **METROPOLITAN BOARD OF PARKS AND REC-REATION. QUALIFICATIONS. TERM AND SELECTION OF MEMBERS.** There shall be a Metropolitan Board of Parks and Recreation, sometimes in this Chapter called "the Board". The Board shall consist of seven (7) members, who shall serve without compensation. One of the members of the Board shall be a member of the Board of Education, selected by said Board of Education for a term of one (1) year; and another member of the Board shall be a member of the Planning Commission, selected by said Planning Commission for a term of one (1) year. Five (5) members of the Board, who shall hold no other public office, shall be appointed by the Mayor and confirmed by a majority of the whole membership of the Council. Said five members shall serve terms of five (5) years each, provided that the first members appointed shall serve terms of one, two, three, four and five years, respectively. Any vacancy due to any cause, other than expiration of term, shall be filled for the unexpired term.

SECTION 11.1002. **POWERS AND DUTIES OF THE BOARD.** The Board shall have the following powers and duties:

1. The Board shall supervise, control and operate the park and recreation system of the Metropolitan Government.
2. It shall formulate the policies to be followed in the administration of the park and recreation system; and shall promulgate such rules and regulations as may be appropriate with respect to the administration of its policies.
3. It shall employ, subject to the civil service provisions of this Charter and within its budget appropriation and other available funds, a Director of Parks and Recreation and such superintendents and other employees as it deems necessary.
4. It shall review, approve, reject or amend the annual budget request as compiled by the Director.
5. It shall recommend to the Council (a) the sale of any lands owned by the Metropolitan Government for park or recreation purposes and no longer needed for such purposes, (b) the acquisition by condemnation of any additional lands needed for park or recreation purposes, and (c) the acceptance of any gift of lands offered for park or recreation purposes, and useful for such purposes. In the acquisition or disposition of land, the Board shall cooperate closely with the Planning Commission, whose recommendations shall be sought and carefully considered by the Board.
6. It shall have the authority to establish the fees and charges within the administration of the Park and Recreation Department. It shall have sole authority of all matters pertaining to the operations of concessions.

SECTION 11.1003. **DIRECTOR OF PARKS AND RECREATION. QUALI-FICATIONS.** The Director of Parks and Recreation shall have at least five (5) years experience in park or recreation administration in a supervisory or executive capacity.

SECTION 11.1004. **POWERS AND DUTIES OF DIRECTOR.** The Director shall be the chief administrative officer in charge of the management of public parks, playgrounds and other recreational areas and of a comprehensive recreation program for the area of the Metropolitan Government. He shall administer the policies of the Board, recommend rules and regulations to the Board for its consideration, and perform such other duties as may be assigned to him by the Board or by ordinance.

SECTION 11.1005. **POLICE PROTECTION FOR PARKS.** The Board may employ custodial personnel who shall be designated as special police by the Chief of Police, without obligation to give a public officer's liability bond as provided for by Section 8.205 of this Charter, and whose jurisdiction as special police shall be limited to the area of parks, playgrounds and other recreational areas. This Section shall not be deemed to interfere with the right of the Department of Police to exercise police jurisdiction within said areas, nor with the duty to provide such police personnel as may be reasonably requested by the Director of Parks and Recreation for the maintenance of law and order therein.

Article 11

ADMINISTRATIVE BOARDS AND COMMISSIONS

Chapter 11

Metropolitan Welfare Commission

SECTION 11.1101. **METROPOLITAN WELFARE COMMISSION. QUALIFICATIONS, TERM AND SELECTION OF MEMBERS.** There is hereby created and established a Metropolitan Welfare Commission, sometimes in this Chapter called "the Commission". The Commission shall consist of seven (7) members who shall serve without compensation. The members of the Commission shall be appointed by the Mayor and confirmed by a majority vote of the whole membership of the Council. The seven (7) members shall serve terms of five (5) years each, provided that two members shall be initially appointed for one year, two for two years, one for three years, one for four years and one for five years, respectively. Thereafter, as their respective terms expire, members shall be chosen for five years. Any vacancy, other than by expiration of term, shall be filled for the unexpired term.

SECTION 11.1102. **POWERS AND DUTIES OF THE COMMISSION.** The Commission shall have the following powers or duties:

1. To administer general assistance to residents of the Metropolitan Government area and emergency assistance to residents and nonresidents of such area under such terms and conditions as may be prescribed by the Commission in its rules and regulations.
2. To make social investigations and reports to the Council, the Selective Service and other governmental agencies.
3. To engage in study and research regarding the cause of financial dependency, and methods of better treating such dependency.
4. To administer public and private grants for welfare and relief purposes, and perform related welfare functions.
5. To perform such functions as may be assigned by law to county welfare agencies.
6. To supervise and/or operate welfare facilities.
7. To enter into cooperative agreements with the public welfare agencies of other local governments, the State of Tennessee and the United States Government and with voluntary welfare agencies for the administration of welfare programs.
8. To supervise the operation of the McKay Home, the Mu-

nicipal Children's Home and the Knowles Homes for the Aged of the former City of Nashville. The Knowles Homes shall be operated in conjunction with the Mayor in his capacity as Trustee of the Knowles Estate. The supervision of the operation of any or all of the institutions enumerated in this subsection may be transferred by ordinance to the Metropolitan Board of Hospitals.

9. To use in its work any funds appropriated by the Council and in its performance thereof to receive donations from firms, individuals and private or governmental agencies.
10. To perform such other functions as may be assigned by ordinance, or statute.

SECTION 11.1103. **DIRECTOR OF WELFARE COMMISSION, SELECTION AND DUTIES.** There shall be a Director of Welfare, who shall be appointed by the Commission. The Commission may enter into an employment contract with such person for a period not exceeding five (5) years at a compensation to be fixed by the Commission.

The Director shall administer the policies of the Commission, recommend rules and regulations to the Commission for its consideration, and perform such other duties as may be assigned to the Director by the Commision or by ordinance.

Article 11

ADMINISTRATIVE BOARDS AND COMMISSIONS

Chapter 12

Public Library

SECTION 11.1201. **PUBLIC LIBRARY PROVIDED FOR.** The Metropolitan Government shall provide for the maintenance and operation of the Nashville Public Library.

SECTION 11.1202. **PUBLIC LIBRARY BOARD, TERM AND SELECTION OF MEMBERS.** There shall be a Public Library Board which shall consist of seven (7) members, to be appointed by the Mayor and confirmed by a majority of the whole membership of the Council. Members of the Board shall serve for terms of seven (7) years each, except that the members first appointed shall be so appointed and designated that the term of one of them shall expire each year in each of the seven ensuing years. Any vacancy occurring during a term shall be filled for the unexpired term. Members of the Board shall serve without compensation.

SECTION 11.1203. **POWERS AND DUTIES OF BOARD.** The Public Library Board shall have direct charge of the Nashville Public Library system and shall have the power and duty to administer and control all libraries under its jurisdiction. The Board shall have exclusive authority to make expenditures out of the money appropriated for the Public Library as well as the money collected from fines or received from other sources. Said Board is authorized to accept gifts, bequests and contributions from public sources and private persons and corporations.

SECTION 11.1204. **CHIEF LIBRARIAN, APPOINTMENT, QUALIFICATIONS AND DUTIES.** For the proper administration of the Public Library, the Board shall employ a Chief Librarian and fix his compensation. He shall be a person with experience in an executive or major administrative position in public library operations. The Board may enter into an employment contract with such person for a period not exceeding five (5) years and for a compensation determined therein. The Board is authorized to assign to the Chief Librarian such duties and responsibilities as are customary or usual, including immediate control and management of the Public Library under the regulations prescribed by the Board.

SECTION 11.1205. **PUBLIC LIBRARY BUGDET.** The Board shall submit to the Mayor, through the Director of Finance, the budget for the Public Library and it shall be the duty of the Council to provide an amount which in its discretion is sufficient for the maintenance and operation of the Public Library System.

Article 12

CIVIL SERVICE

SECTION 12.01. **PERSONNEL ADMINISTRATION ESTABLISHED AND CIVIL SERVICE COMMISSION CREATED.** For the effective conduct of the public business, there is hereby established a personnel policy and administration under which entry into the service shall be on the basis of open competition and service shall be on the basis of merit, efficiency and fitness. The Civil Service Commission, sometimes called Commission, shall be responsible for developing and fostering the effectiveness of this personnel policy in the Metropolitan Government.

SECTION 12.02. **NUMBER, QUALIFICATIONS, SELECTION AND TERM OF MEMBERS OF COMMISSION.** The Commission shall consist of five (5) members who shall have an interest in civil service and merit principles in the public service, who shall otherwise have the qualifications prescribed in Section 11.102 of this Charter and who shall serve without compensation. No member of the Commission shall hold any public office or position nor be a member of any local, state or national political committee.

The members of the Commission shall be appointed by the Mayor and shall be confirmed by a two-thirds vote of the whole membership of the Council. One member of the Commission shall be initially appointed for a period of one (1) year; one for two (2) years; one for three (3) years; one for four (4) years; and one for five (5) years. Thereafter, appointments shall be for terms of five (5) years, except that when a vacancy occurs prior to the end of a term, the member appointed to fill the same shall hold under such appointment only for the unexpired term. One member of the Commission shall be a person actively engaged in the practice of law, one shall be a representative of business or industry, one shall be a representative of labor, and the remaining members shall be chosen without reference to profession or occupation.

SECTION 12.03. **DUTIES OF COMMISSION.** In addition to other duties herein specified, it shall be the duty of the Civil Service Commission to:

(a) Advise with and supervise the Director of Personnel in all continuing improvements of personnel standards and administration in the Metropolitan Government.

(b) Make any investigation or study it may deem desirable concerning the organization and administration of personnel in the Metropolitan Government.

(c) Review, approve, revise or modify any action taken by the Director of Personnel.

(d) Make annual reports and such special reports as it may consider desirable to the Mayor and Council.

(e) Upon request of an affected employee, review suspensions, demotions or separation from service of any employee in classified service, and to render decisions thereon, subject to its rules.

SECTION 12.04. **DIRECTOR OF PERSONNEL AND HIS DUTIES.** There shall be a Director of Personnel, who shall be appointed by the Commission, subject to the Civil Service provisions of this Charter, and who shall have had training and experience in personnel administration. The salary of the Director of Personnel shall be prescribed in the pay plan provisions of this

Article, with a salary of Twelve Thousand ($12,000) Dollars per annum, payable semimonthly. In addition to other duties herein specified, it shall be the duty of the Director of Personnel to:

(a) Administer the Civil Service Program of the Metropolitan Government under the supervision of the Civil Service Commission and subject to its rules.

(b) Attend all meetings of the Civil Service Commission, to act as its secretary, and keep minutes of its proceedings.

(c) Direct and supervise the Department of Personnel.

(d) Appoint, with the approval of the Commission and subject to the Civil Service provisions, such employees of the Department of Personnel as may be necessary.

(e) Establish and maintain a roster of all employees of all departments, commissions and agencies of the Metropolitan Government which shall reflect such data and information as may be deemed necessary regarding personnel organization and administration.

(f) Prepare and maintain an up-to-date record of the authority, duties and responsibilities of each position in the classified service.

(g) Develop, in cooperation with the appointing authorities of the Metropolitan Government, training and educational programs for employees in the Metropolitan service.

(h) Periodically review the operation and effect of personnel provisions of this Charter, the rules promulgated by the Commission, the classification plan and the pay plan, and to report his findings and recommendations to the Commission.

In making appropriations for the Civil Service Commission, the Council shall provide sufficient funds to maintain the up-to-date record required for job classification.

SECTION 12.05. **SELECTION AND DISMISSAL OF METROPOLITAN EMPLOYEES. LIMITATION ON NUMBER OF POSITIONS HELD.** The Civil Service Commission shall provide all candidates for appointment to the classified service. In accordance with rules and procedures which the Commission believes will best serve the personnel policy, candidates shall be rated by competitive examination as "Outstanding", "Well Qualified", "Qualified", and "Unqualified". The duration of each list shall be prescribed by the Commission, but none shall be less than six (6) months or more than three (3) years.

The appointing authority shall select his employees from those candidates available in the highest qualified rating. The employee appointed will be a probationary employee for the training period. After the minimum time prescribed by the Commission for the position, but before the end of the probationary period not to exceed six (6) months, the appointing authority may terminate an appointee whose training period performance indicates that he will not meet the job requirements. After the probationary period, each employee shall become a member of the classified service.

No employee in the Metropolitan service may hold more than one position or employment in the Metropolitan service, except that school personnel between school years may be employed to work in other departments.

No employee in the classified service may be terminated from the service except for cause. Any employee dismissed from the classified service or suspended, by his simple written request to the Commission, shall have the action reviewed by the Commission. If the Commission does not approve the action, it may modify or reverse it, and provide whatever recompense is indicated, which shall not exceed net loss of earnings. In a review by the Commission of any disciplinary action, the disciplinary authority shall bear the burden of proof of just cause for discipline.

SECTION 12.06. ADOPTION OF RULES BY CIVIL SERVICE COMMISSION. The Director of Personnel shall recommend to the Commission such rules as he considers necessary to carry out the provisions of this Article. Thereupon the Commission shall fix and hold a public hearing with respect to the rules or their amendments so recommended and within sixty (60) days after such recommendation the Commission shall act on such rules or amendment. The Commission may approve or reject such recommended rules or amendments in whole or in part, or it may modify and approve them as so modified. Thereafter, the Commission may amend or add to the rules on recommendation of the Director or on its own initiative, but only after a public hearing on proposed amendments.

The Commission shall review said rules periodically for the purpose of revision and in a manner appropriate to sound practices of personnel organization and administration. It shall arrange for the printing of said rules and for their distribution.

SECTION 12.07. SUBSTANTIVE CONTENT OF RULES OF THE COMMISSION. The rules of the Commission shall provide for the efficient organization and administration of employment and regulatory practices by the Metropolitan Government calculated to preserve the rights of employees and enhance public confidence in a merit system and shall include but not be limited to the following:

(a) Administration of the classification plan.

(b) Administration of the pay plan.

(c) The method of holding competitive examinations for positions in the classified service. In connection with such examinations the rules shall provide for open competitive examinations to be conducted by the Director of Personnel for the purpose of filling vacancies or making original appointments in the classified service; public announcement thereof after giving reasonable notice; the granting of preferences to former members of the Armed Forces of the United States; the appointment of examining boards; and the establishment of minimum standards for applicants for such examinations.

(d) The establishment, maintenance, consolidation and cancellation of eligibility and promotion lists, and the manner in which appointments shall be made. Such rules shall provide a method for establishing reemployment lists containing names of persons separated from positions for reasons other than cause or delinquency on their part; and the time such lists shall remain in effect; for the ranking of eligibles in accordance with ratings earned in tests; for consideration of records of performance, seniority and conduct; for the length of time that promotion and employment lists shall remain in force; and for the method of certifying vacancies and making appointments generally and certifying eligibility therefor; for working test periods; for a method of temporary appointments in the absence of eligible lists, and the limitations thereon, and for emergency appointments.

(e) The application of service ratings, hours of work, attendance regulations, holidays, and leaves of absence.

(f) The manner in which lay-offs shall be affected giving due consideration to the seniority rights of employees.

(g) A method of transferring employees within a department, and from one department to another, provided nothing in such rules shall authorize the transfer of an employee into the Police and Fire Departments of the Metropolitan Government from other departments unless such employees meet all the entrance requirements of these two departments as established by this Charter and by the rules of the Commission.

(h) The disciplinary action within the classified service. Rules with respect to such action shall provide that when an employee requests a review of disciplinary action taken against him, as provided in Section 12.05 above, such employee shall be furnished a copy of the basis of his discipline not less than fifteen days prior to such hearing, and said rules may provide for the amendment of grounds for discipline upon reasonable notice to the employee.

It shall be mandatory that the rules provide that the judgment and findings of the Commission on all questions of fact, in the hearing of charges preferred against any classified employee under the provisions of this Article, shall be final and shall be subject to review only for illegality or want of jurisdiction, excepting only cases where classified employees have been dismissed from the service by judgment of the Commission, in which case such dismissed employee may prepare and file the record of the proceedings, including a transcript certified by the Chairman of said Commission, in the Circuit and Chancery Courts of Davidson County, where the case may be heard de novo solely upon the record so certified; provided that such transcript must be presented to and signed by the Chairman of the Commission within thirty (30) days after the Commission shall have announced its findings, and provided that an extension of time may be granted for this purpose not to exceed thirty (30) days. Any person, other than a member of the Commission, may file and prefer charges against any classified employee.

Rules of the Commission when adopted as provided herein shall have the full force and effect of law.

Within one (1) year after adoption of the rules or any amendments thereto, any employee who deems himself adversely affected thereby, or any citizen, shall, upon written request therefor, be afforded a public hearing before the Commission. The Commission, after a hearing, may reaffirm its approval of the rules or make such modifications as it shall deem necessary.

SECTION 12.08. POSITIONS IN CLASSIFIED SERVICE AND IN UNCLASSIFIED SERVICE. All positions in the Metropolitan Government shall be in the classified service except the following, which are hereby declared to be in the unclassified service.

(a) All officers of the Metropolitan Government and of the County elected by popular vote, and officers appointed to fill vacancies in any such elective position.

(b) The Director of Finance, private secretaries of Directors as designated herein, the Administrative Assistants to the Mayor, the Metropolitan Attorney, the Deputy Metropolitan Attorney, the Assistant Metropolitan Attorneys, and employees in the office of the Mayor, exclusive of any such employees who may have otherwise attained a civil service status prior to the effective date of this Charter.

(c) Members of Boards or Commissions in the Metropolitan Government, except as otherwise provided in this Charter.

(d) The Executive Director or Secretary for every Board or Commission of the Metropolitan Government, and such principal professional personnel or professional positions on the staff not formerly under civil service of said Board or Commission as he may designate subject to the approval of said Board or Commission.

(e) All professional personnel employed by the Board of Health and the Board of Hospitals.

(f) All teachers employed by the Board of Education.

(g) Employees of the Nashville Electric Power Board, provided, however, that those employees of the Nashville Electric Power Board who are in active service on the effective date of this Act shall continue to hold all civil service rights and benefits heretofore provided for pursuant to the provisions of Chapter 246 of the Private Acts of the General Assembly of Tennessee for 1947 and any amendments thereto.

(h) Employees in the office of the County or Probate Judge of Davidson County.

(i) Officers heretofore elected by the Quarterly County Court of Davidson County.

(j) Deputies of the following officers: Circuit Court Clerk, Criminal Court Clerk, Chancery Clerk and Master, County Court Clerk, Trustee, Tax Assessor, Register; and court officers, stenographers and clerks appointed by judges; whether or not compensated by the Metropolitan Government.

(k) Employees of the Board of Fair Commissioners, of the Farmers' Market Board and of the Agricultural Extension Board.

(l) Those persons employed on special projects paid from any bond funds of the former City of Nashville or former County of Davidson or future bond funds of the Metropolitan Government; seasonal employees, who are herein defined as those whose service does not exceed four (4) months in any twelve (12) months period; and emergency employees as defined from time to time by rules and regulations of the Commission.

(m) Those persons whose professional services are needed from time to time on particular matters.

SECTION 12.09. CIVIL SERVICE COMMISSIONS FOR BOARD OF HEALTH, BOARD OF HOSPITALS AND BOARD OF EDUCATION. With respect to nonprofessional personnel employed by the Board of Health and the Board of Hospitals, and with respect to nonteaching employees of the Board of Education, the employing Board shall constitute a Civil Service Commission for its respective employees and in so acting said Boards shall, to the extent deemed practicable, conform to the provisions of this Article as to the adoption of rules, the discipline or dismissal of employees, the classification of positions and the adoption of a pay plan.

SECTION 12.10. ADOPTION OF CLASSIFICATION AND GENERAL PAY PLAN. The Commission shall direct the Director of Personnel to make or cause to be made:

(a) A job description of every position in the classified service.

(b) A classification plan which will assign each position by title to one class.

(c) Assignment of each classification to grades equitably related to each other on the basis of function, responsibility and nonwage benefits, with the percentage between the high and low salary range for each grade. Upon the approval of the Commission, any such determinations shall have the effect of law.

The Director of Personnel shall, after the approval of the Commission, recommend to the Director of Finance, the desirable salary ranges for each grade. The Director of Finance shall approve or modify the ranges for each grade, and forward the same with a statement of full budgetary implications, to the Mayor for his approval. The Mayor shall approve the plan or approve it subject to his modifications, but neither the Director of Finance nor the Mayor may alter or destroy the relationships between the grades. Thereupon, the Mayor shall submit the same to the Council with recommendation that it be adopted.

The Council shall (1) adopt the general pay plan, or (2) adopt the same as amended but without modifying the plan except by uniform modification of all grades, or (3) reject the same. Adoption or rejection shall be by resolution not requiring the approval of the Mayor. When a general pay plan is rejected by the Council, it shall be returned to the Commission which shall thereupon formulate another general pay plan and transmit the same to the Mayor for handling under the procedures above set forth.

Upon the approval of the plan by the Mayor and Council, this shall be the pay plan under which all covered employees must be paid.

Whenever it may be deemed desirable to create any new position in the Metropolitan Government, the Director or head of the department affected shall present a request in writing to the Mayor and the Civil Service Commission for investigation. Not later than fifteen days after the same is filed, if the Mayor thinks the creation of the position in the public interest, he shall transmit the ordinance for this purpose, together with the Civil Service Commission's written job description and assignment of the proposed position to the appropriate class in the classification plan. Where a proposed ordinance creates a new position and is not accompanied by such recommendation, copy thereof shall be promptly furnished by the Metropolitan Clerk to the Mayor and to the Civil Service Commission, and the same shall not be passed on second reading until their recommendations have been received or fifteen (15) days have elapsed without such recommendations.

Any position, job or employment hereafter created in the manner above provided, shall be in the classified service as herein defined and subject to all the rules of the Civil Service Commission, except as the ordinance creating the same or this Charter may otherwise provide.

The Director of Personnel shall maintain adequate records for all employees; he shall require, at least once a year, performance reviews on each employee on such form or forms as the Director provides. The Director of Personnel shall certify that each payroll in question complies with the personnel policy established by this Article. No payroll may be paid without this certification.

SECTION 12.11. OFFENSES AGAINST CIVIL SERVICE AND DISABILITIES OF CIVIL SERVICE EMPLOYEES. No person shall attempt to use any political endorsement in connection with any appointment in the classified service. No person shall use or promise to use, directly or indirectly, any official authority or influence, whether possessed or anticipated, to secure or attempt to secure for any person, an appointment or advantage in appointment to a position in the classified service, or an increase in pay or other advantage in employment in any such position, for the purpose of influencing the vote or political action of any person, or for a consideration.

No employee in the classified service, and no member of the Commission, shall directly or indirectly, pay or promise to pay any assessment, subscription, or contribution for any political organization or purposes, or solicit or take part in soliciting any such assessment, subscription or contribution. No person shall solicit any such assessment, subscription or contribution of any employee in the classified service.

No employee in the classified service shall be a member of any national, state or local committee of a political party, or an officer or member of a committee of a political party, or an officer or member of a committee of a partisan political club, or shall take any part in the management of the affairs of any political party, or in any political campaign, except to exercise his right as a citizen privately to express his opinions and cast his vote. Any classified employee who violates any of the foregoing provisions of this Section shall forfeit his office or position.

No person elected to public office within the Metropolitan Government shall, during the term for which he was elected, be appointed to any other position in the Metropolitan Government, except as otherwise specifically provided in this Charter.

No person shall, directly or indirectly, give, render, pay, offer, solicit, or accept any money, service, or other valuable consideration, for or on account of any appointment, proposed appointment, promotion, or proposed promotion to, or any advantages in, a position in the classified service.

No employee of the Department of Personnel and no member of the Commission, or other person, shall defeat, deceive, or obstruct any person in his right to examination, eligibility, certification, or appointment hereunder, or furnish to any person any special or secret information for the purposes of affecting the rights or prospects of any person with respect to employment in the classified service.

Any officer or employee of the Metropolitan Government who violates the provisions of this Section shall forfeit his office or position.

SECTION 12.12. **CONTINUANCE OF EXISTING CIVIL SERVICE RIGHTS OF COUNTY AND CITY EMPLOYEES.** Nothing in this Article or Charter shall impair or diminish the rights and privileges of existing employees of the County of Davidson or the City of Nashville under civil service; and such rights and privileges shall continue without impairment as obligations of the Metropolitan Government.

Article 13

SYSTEM OF EMPLOYEE BENEFIT PLANS

SECTION 13.01. **SYSTEM OF EMPLOYEE BENEFIT PLANS.** A system of employee benefit plans which include disability and retirement benefits and which may include medical insurance benefits and life insurance benefits, shall be adopted for officers and employees of the Metropolitan Government for whom such plans are not provided by other Sections of this Charter.

SECTION 13.02. **METROPOLITAN EMPLOYEE BENEFIT BOARD CREATED.** A Metropolitan Employee Benefit Board (sometimes in this Article called "Board") shall be created to administer, manage and coordinate the employee benefit plans of the Metropolitan Government as well as the retirement plans listed in Section 13.09 (a)-(c) of this Article.

SECTION 13.03. **COMPOSITION AND SELECTION OF BOARD, TERMS AND QUALIFICATIONS OF MEMBERS.** The Board shall be composed of seven (7) members, as follows: The Director of Finance and the Director of Personnel shall be members by virtue of their official positions. Two (2) members shall be appointed by the Mayor, subject to confirmation by the Council, and shall possess an interest in benefit and retirement programs in the public service. They shall serve for terms of three (3) years each, except that the members first appointed shall serve for terms of one (1) year and two (2) years respectively. Three (3) members shall be selected by employees of the Metropolitan Government from among their own number, one (1) from the Police Department and then one (1) from the Fire Department for alternate terms, and two (2) from all other

departments of Metropolitan Government. The employee members shall serve for terms of three (3) years each, except that the members first selected by the employee groups shall serve for terms of one (1) year (from the Police Department), two (2) years and three (3) years respectively.

The Director of Personnel, with the approval of the Metropolitan Civil Service Commission, shall announce a plan for the conduct of an election to be held by the employees of the Metropolitan Government to select the employee members of the Board. The election shall be conducted under the supervision of the Director of Personnel, who shall immediately report to the Commission the name of the employee receiving the required votes in such election, which report shall be spread upon the minutes of the Commission. Upon such certification by the Director of Personnel to the Commision, the successful candidate shall thereupon enter upon his duties as a member of the Board.

The members appointed by the Mayor, and confirmed by the Council, shall hold no public office and shall not be a member of any local, state or national political committee. All vacancies on the Board shall be filled for the unexpired portions of any term in the manner above prescribed for their respective positions.

In the performance of its staff functions, the Board, its Investments Committee and the Study and Formulating Committee hereinafter created may utilize the office and clerical staff of the Director of Personnel or there may be employed by the Board a Secretary who shall have had training and experience in pension and retirement administration.

SECTION 13.04. **THE INVESTMENTS COMMITTEE, ITS COMPOSITION, POWERS AND DUTIES.** The Director of Finance and the two members of the Employee Benefit Board selected by the Mayor shall be and constitute the Investments Committee of the Board. Said Committee shall regulate and determine all matters dealing with investment of funds committed to the Board and shall have full and complete control over all investments, subject to the provisions of this Charter and of other applicable law. No other member of the Board shall have authority to vote or participate in decisions dealing with investment of funds committed to the Board. The Investments Committee shall be and constitute an administrative board or commission for the purpose of regulations and duties prescribed by Chapter 1 of Article 11 of this Charter. All actions taken by the Investments Committee shall have the approval of at least two members thereof.

Full minutes shall be kept of all actions of the Investments Committee, which shall be public records as defined by state law. Said Investments Committee shall at least annually make a detailed accounting of its investments, income and expenditures, and file the same with the Board, the Mayor and the Council. This report shall be a public record, and shall show the time, place, company, firm, person or individual in each instance dealt with, the nature and type of transaction involved, the nature and type of investment, the nature and type of income derived from such investment and any other information reasonably required to determine the exact financial status of all transactions. Any affected employee, upon request and at his expense, shall be furnished copies of such report or of designated portions thereof.

Said Investments Committee shall manage, invest and distribute the fund or funds maintained in connection with the system of employee benefits plans for officers and employees of the Metropolitan Government, as well as the retirement plans listed in Section 13.09 (a)-(c) of this Article; provided, however, that no investment shall be made except in securities and properties which at the time of making the investment are permitted by statute for the investment of funds by fiduciaries in the State of Tennessee.

SECTION 13.05. DUTIES OF THE METROPOLITAN EMPLOYEE BENEFIT BOARD.

In addition to the other duties imposed by this Charter or by general law, it shall be the duty of the Board to:

(a) Hold regular monthly meetings, which shall be open to the public.

(b) Coordinate and communicate to officers and employees of the Metropolitan Government, the system of employee benefit plans for officers and employees of the Metropolitan Government, and to manage and administer such system of employee benefit plans as well as the retirement plans listed in Section 13.09 (a)-(c) of this Article.

(c) Make such expenditures as may be necessary in fulfilling its duties, within the limit of its budget appropriation.

(d) Construe any employee benefit plans adopted by the Metropolitan Government as well as any retirement plan listed in Section 13.09 (a)-(c) of this Article, and to determine all questions that may arise thereunder, including questions relating to the eligibility of any person employed by the Metropolitan Government to become a member of any such employee benefit plan and the amount of benefit to which such person, or any member of a retirement plan listed in Section 13.09 (a)-(c) of this Article may become entitled thereunder.

(e) Adopt such rules, regulations and procedures as it may deem necessary in fulfilling its duties.

(f) Advise the Mayor and the Council of the anticipated financial requirements of each employee benefit plan adopted by the Metropolitan Government, as well as the retirement plans listed in Section 13.09 (a)-(c) of this Article so that such financial requirements shall be included in the budget and tax levy ordinances for the ensuing fiscal year.

SECTION 13.06. STUDY AND FORMULATING COMMITTEE, PREPARATION OF PLAN FOR EMPLOYEE BENEFITS, CONSIDERATION AND ADOPTION THEREOF. SUBSEQUENT COMMITTEES PROVIDED FOR.

There shall be a Study and Formulating Committee consisting of five (5) persons appointed by the Mayor and approved by the Council. This Committee shall make a study and formulate a plan for employee benefits, which shall include disability and retirement benefits and which may include medical insurance benefits and life insurance benefits. Such study shall include the design, the possible coordination of any of the employee benefit plans of such system with the Social Security Act, the administration and financing of such system and all properly related matters. For the purposes of its study and formulation, the Committee is authorized to:

(a) Within the limits of its appropriation, employ the services of legal counsel, investment consultants, actuarial consultants, and the services of others which in the sole discretion of the Committee may be necessary to perform its duties.

(b) Obtain from any department, board, commission, agency, officer or employee of the Metropolitan Government information and data with respect to the compensation of any officer or employee; his length of service with the Metropolitan Government, the former City of Nashville or the former County of Davidson; his retirement or other cause of termination of employment; his contributions to any employee benefit plan of the Metropolitan Government as well as any retirement plan listed in Section 13.09 (a)-(c) of this

Article; and such other pertinent information and data as the Board may require.

The Council is hereby authorized and required to appropriate such funds as may be reasonably necessary for the work of said Committee.

Within one year after its appointment, unless the time be extended by resolution of the Council, the Study and Formulating Committee shall submit to the Employee Benefit Board a proposed system of employee benefit plans for officers and employees of the Metropolitan Government. Said Board shall either approve the plan or indicate the specific changes which it recommends in connection therewith. Thereupon the Board shall submit the approved plan or the original plan with recommended changes to the Council for its action thereon and for the enactment of a system of employee benefit plans.

The Mayor shall from time to time thereafter, and at least once every five years, appoint a subsequent Study and Formulating Committee to study benefits, contributions, extent of coverage, actuarial soundness and related matters in connection with the system of benefit plans and to submit to the Employee Benefits Board such amendments as such study may indicate as necessary.

SECTION 13.07. ELIGIBILITY OF OFFICERS AND EMPLOYEES OF METROPOLITAN GOVERNMENT.

Wherever used in this Article, the term "officers and employees of the Metropolitan Government" shall mean all officers, including Metropolitan judicial officers, and all employees, including classified and unclassified employees, who are regularly employed by the Metropolitan Government, who are not excluded in accordance with the provisions of Section 13.08 of this Article, or any other provision of this Charter, and who meet any other eligibility and participation requirements of the system of employee benefit plans adopted by the Metropolitan Government, but said term shall not include teachers whose benefits system is administered by the Metropolitan Board of Education, as provided in Section 13.09 hereof.

Such officers and employees of the Metropolitan Government shall be members of the system of employee benefit plans established by the Metropolitan Government and shall not be members of any of the retirement plans listed in Section 13.09 (a)-(c) of this Article, or in any teachers benefits system.

SECTION 13.08. EXCLUSION OF CERTAIN PERSONS.

Notwithstanding any provision of this Charter to the contrary, any officer or employee of the former City of Nashville or the former County of Davidson who on the day before the effective date of this Charter was an active or retired member of any retirement plan listed in Section 13.09 (a)-(c) of this Article shall not be eligible to become a member of the system of employee benefit plans for officers and employees of the Metropolitan Government; provided, however, that each such officer and employee of the former City of Nashville or the County of Davidson may elect voluntarily, subject to the written approval of the Board, to transfer his membership from the applicable retirement plan listed in Section 13.09 (a)-(c) of this Article to membership in such system of employee benefit plans for officers and employees of the Metropolitan Government. No employee of the Electric Power Board nor any teacher employed by the Metropolitan Government shall be eligible to become a member of the system of employee benefit plans for the officers and employees of the Metropolitan Government provided by this Article. Notwithstanding any provision of this Charter to the contrary, no person employed by the Metropolitan Government shall be eligible to become a member or shall continue to be a member of more than one of any of the following:

(a) The system of employee benefit plans for officers and employees of the Metropolitan Government.

(b) Any retirement plan listed in Section 13.09 (a)-(c) of this Article.

(c) The retirement plan for employees of the Electric Power Board.

(d) Any reitrement plan for teachers (1) of the former City of Nashville, (2) of the former County of Davidson or (3) of the Metropolitan Government hereafter adopted pursuant to Section 9.07 of this Charter.

SECTION 13.09. CONTINUING RIGHTS UNDER RETIREMENT PLANS OF THE FORMER CITY OF NASHVILLE OR THE FORMER COUNTY OF DAVIDSON. Pension rights under Section 9.07 of this Charter may include medical insurance benefits, and life insurance benefits. Said pension rights, together with those provided by Section 9.06 hereof, shall be administered by the Board of Education and both shall be an obligation and liability of the Metropolitan Government. In addition all benefits payable to members, retired members, and their survivors, in accordance with any of the following retirement plans of the former City of Nashville or the former County of Davidson as such plans existed prior to the effective date of this Charter shall continue unimpaired for the same duration provided in such plans as they existed prior to the effective date, and such benefits shall be an obligation and liability of the Metropolitan Government:

(a) The pension, retirement and benfit plan for policemen and firemen of the former City of Nashville created in accordance with the provisions of Article 48 of Chapter 246 of the Private Acts of 1947, and all amendatory acts thereof.

(b) The pension, retirement and benefit plan for the City Judge and civil service employees of the former City of Nashville created in accordance with the provisions of Article 48 of Chapter 246 of the Private Acts of 1947 and all amendatory acts thereof.

(c) The retirement plan for officers and employees of the former County of Davidson created in accordance with the provisions of Chapter 274 of the Private Acts of 1943, and all amendatory acts thereof.

It shall be the duty of the Investments Committee in addition to the duties herein above set forth to manage, invest and reinvest the funds and assets of the retirement plans listed in this Section 13.09 (a)-(c), which funds and assets shall be maintained as separate funds in one or more funds of the system of employee benefit plans for the officers and employees of the Metropolitan Government, as said Committee may determine in its sole discretion. It shall be the duty of the Employee Benefit Board to assume jurisdiction over, to administer, and to interpret the provisions of the retirement plans listed above in this Section 13.09; to codify and restate such retirement plans if the Board determines that such codification and restatement would be an administrative convenience, and to exercise the duties granted the Board in Section 13.05 of this Charter with respect to such retirement plans; provided, however, that no provision of this Charter shall be construed to affect in any way the benefits payable to members, retired members, and their survivors, of the retirement plans listed above in this Section 13.09 (a)-(c) or the teachers retirement plans of the former City of Nashville or the former County of Davidson; and provided, further, that the Board shall suspend, as a condition precedent to the employment of any person by the Metropolitan Government, the benefits payable under such retirement plan during the period such person is regularly employed by the Metropolitan Government.

SECTION 13.10. RETIREMENT PLANS SHALL BE ACTUARIALLY SOUND. Any retirement plan adopted by the Metropolitan Government pursuant to Section 13.06 hereof shall be actuarially sound; that is, annual contributions shall be made by members of such retirement plans and by the Metropolitan Government to a fund or funds established and invested for the sole purpose of financing benefits provided in accordance with the provisions of such retirement plans. The amount of such annual contributions by the employees and the Metropolitan Government shall be determined as the sum of normal cost and five (5) percent of the unfunded past service liability, where normal cost and past service liability shall be determined actuarially by a qualified independent actuary based on the entry age normal cost method of funding or the unit credit cost method of funding.

SECTION 13.11. SEPARATE FUND OR FUNDS, PAYMENTS FROM FUNDS. REPORTS. All assets of any fund maintained in connection with the system of employee benefit plans of the officers and employees of the Metropolitan Government as well as the retirement plans listed in Section 13.09 (a)-(c) of this Article shall be maintained separate and apart from all other funds of the Metropolitan Government. The Metropolitan Treasurer shall keep a separate account for each such fund and a separate record indicating each disbursement of such fund. Payments from such fund or funds shall be made only on order of the Board by a warrant to be signed by a person designated by the Board and to be countersigned by the Metropolitan Treasurer. The Metropolitan Treasurer shall submit to the Board monthly financial reports and such other reports as the Board may require.

SECTION 13.12. EXPENSE FOR TREATMENT OF ACCIDENTAL INJURY IN COURSE OF EMPLOYMENT TO BE BORNE BY METROPOLITAN GOVERNMENT. Any employee of the Metropolitan Government entitled to benefits under any benefit plan established for the Metropolitan Government, who is injured by accident arising out of and in the course of his employment, shall be entitled to emergency treatment at the nearest or most available doctor's office, hospital or clinic, at the expense of the Metropolitan Government. Any further treatment, in addition to the emergency treatment herein provided for, shall be furnished the employee free of charge by doctors, nurses, etc., in the employment of Board of Hospitals. In the event it is determined that specialized treatment not available at a Metropolitan hospital should be made available to such employee, then the same shall be made available at the nearest point or place where such specialized treatment is available, which treatment shall be paid for by the Metropolitan Government.

SECTION 13.13. DEATH BENEFITS. If no other death benefit financed in whole or in part by the Metropolitan Government is available, then benefits shall be paid on the death of an employee caused by any injury by accident arising out of and in the course of employment. The amount of the payment shall be the sum of Five Thousand ($5,000) Dollars, and payment shall begin within sixty (60) days after death to the surviving spouse, and if no spouse, to the next of kin without necessity for appointment of an Executor or Administrator. Determination by the Board as to who is entitled to payment of death benefits and the payments made pursuant to such determination shall be final and conclusive. No payment shall be made where the personal injuries resulting in death were due to the employee's willful misconduct or intentional self-inflicted injury, or due to intoxication, or willful failure or refusal to use a safety appliance or perform a duty required by law. No payment shall be made in the case of death due to sickness or disease. The words "employee of Metropolitan Government" as used in this Section shall not include any member of a board or commission created by this Charter or pursuant to it, and shall not include any contractor or employee of a contractor doing business with the Metropolitan Government.

Written notice of personal injury shall be given to the Board and to the Mayor on behalf of an employee within thirty (30) days after such personal injury was sustained. In the event of claim for death benefit, the Board shall make or cause to be made a full investigation of the facts and shall determine, on the basis of written opinion of the Metropolitan Attorney, whether the claim is legally and properly payable.

The death benefit payment of $5,000 shall be made as follows: The sum of Five Hundred ($500) Dollars shall be paid at the time of the initial settlement, and the balance shall be paid at the rate of One Hundred ($100) Dollars per month for forty-five (45) consecutive months. Payments made pursuant to this Section shall be free from the claims of creditors and not subject to attachment, garnishment or other process of law.

The provisions with respect to death benefits shall apply to all persons employed by the Metropolitan Government, including the employees of all departments, boards and commissions, except the employees of the Electric Power Board.

Article 14
METROPOLITAN COURTS

SECTION 14.01. **METROPOLITAN COURT CREATED. DIVISIONS. JURISDICTION AND POWERS.** There shall be a Metropolitan Court consisting of two divisions, to be designated Division I and Division II, with one judge for each division. Division I of the Court shall have exclusive jurisdiction to hear, try and dispose of cases involving the breach of any ordinance of the Metropolitan Government, excepting traffic violations, and to impose fines for the breach of such ordinances. Division II of the Court shall have the exclusive jurisdiction to hear, try and dispose of cases in which violations of the Metropolitan traffic laws, ordinances and resolutions may be charged, or in which offenses under the general laws of the State involving vehicular operations are charged, and to impose fines for the breach of any such laws, ordinances or resolutions. The Judges shall have power to remit fines and to release or suspend sentences imposed by them.

The Judges of the Metropolitan Court shall have jurisdiction to bind over offenders to the Grand Jury where probable cause is found to exist in cases involving violations of the criminal laws of the State and in lieu of bond to commit to jail the persons charged and also jurisdiction in misdemeanor cases to bind over to the General Sessions Court.

SECTION 14.02. **ELECTION, TERM, QUALIFICATIONS AND COMPENSATION OF JUDGES.** The Judge of Division I and the Judge of Division II of the Metropolitan Court shall be elected at the general judicial election on the first Thursday in August, 1966, and thereafter, every eight (8) years. A Judge of the Metropolitan Court shall have been licensed to practice law in the State of Tennessee for at least five (5) years prior to his election; shall have been a resident of the area of the Metropolitan Government for at least the same period; and shall be not less than thirty (30) years of age at the time of his qualification. Judges of the Metropolitan Court shall be paid the same compensation, and shall be under the same restrictions as to the practice of law, as is provided by general law for Judges of Circuit Courts.

SECTION 14.03. **PRESIDING JUDGE, RULES. SCHEDULE OF FINES. INTERCHANGE. CASH BONDS.** The Judge of Division I shall serve as the Presiding Judge of the Metropolitan Court. He shall

promulgate, with the approval of the Judge of Division II, all necessary rules for the conduct of the Court, which rules shall prescribe the days and hours when the Court will be in session and a system of interchange sittings between the Judges of the respective Divisions for the purpose of relieving congested dockets. The Judges of the Metropolitan Court shall fix a schedule of fines for persons who desire to waive court appearance and plead guilty to violation of traffic regulations, and such schedule shall be filed with the Chief Clerk of the Traffic Violations Bureau. The Judges shall also prescribe for the use of said Bureau rules for the acceptance of bail from persons to be heard in court. The Judges shall also prescribe a schedule of cash bonds which may be deposited for specified violations of ordinances in lieu of other types of bonds.

SECTION 14.04. **OTHER POWERS OF JUDGES.** The Judges of the Metropolitan Court shall have the power to issue subpoenas to compel the attendance of witnesses and, upon the failure of any witness so subpoenaed to attend, to compel his attendance by attachment. The Court shall also have the power to punish any person for contempt committed in the presence of the Court by a fine not exceeding Ten ($10) Dollars, in default of payment of which the guilty person may be imprisoned in the Metropolitan Workhouse or Jail for not exceeding three (3) days. In case of temporary absence, incompetency or inability of a Judge to serve, a majority of the attorneys of the Court who are present and are residents of the State shall elect one of their number then in attendance to hold the Court for the occasion, who shall have all the qualifications of the Judge of such Court and who shall accordingly preside and adjudicate. The election shall be held by the Clerk and in case of a tie, he shall cast the deciding vote.

SECTION 14.05. **PROCEDURE FOR ARRESTS.** Where arrests are made without a warrant by Metropolitan Police Officers for any offense which is a breach of any ordinance of the Metropolitan Government, the officer making the arrest shall take the offender before a Judge of the Metropolitan Court for the procurement of a warrant even though the offense charged be also a violation of State law, and it shall be a matter for determination by the Judge of the Metropolitan Court whether the offender shall be bound over for violating a State law. If a Judge of said Court is not available, then such offender shall be taken by said officer before a Judge of the General Sessions Court, but only for the purpose of obtaining a warrant for violation of the Metropolitan ordinance. Where a warrant is issued by either a Metropolitan Judge or a General Sessions Judge for breach of an ordinance of the Metropolitan Government, the offender shall be taken to the jail, booked for the offense so charged and incarcerated on failure to make bond.

SECTION 14.06. **JUDGMENTS REVIEWED BY CIRCUIT COURT.** An appeal may be taken from any judgment of the Metropolitan Court to the Circuit Court of Davidson County. Such appeal shall be prayed and granted within ten (10) days from the rendition of the judgment and shall not act as a stay or supersedeas of the judgment unless the defendant executes an appeal bond with solvent surety conditioned to pay the fine and costs adjudged upon appeal. Judgments of the Metropolitan Court may also be reviewed by certiorari to the Circuit Court. All cases appealed or taken by certiorari to the Circuit Court from the Metropolitan Court shall be tried by the Circuit Judge without the intervention of a jury.

SECTION 14.07. **VACANCIES FILLED BY MAYOR AND ELECTION.** Whenever a vacancy occurs in the office of Judge of a Division of the Metropolitan Court, the Mayor shall appoint a qualified person to fill the office until the next biennial election in

August occurring more than thirty (30) days after such vacancy, at which time an election shall be held to fill the vacancy for the remainder of the term or for the ensuing term as the case may be.

SECTION 14.08. **CLERK OF METROPOLITAN COURT. DEPUTY CLERKS AND ASSISTANTS.** There shall be a Clerk of the Metropolitan Court, appointed by the Judges thereof, who shall keep the minutes and records of the Court and perform such other duties as may be assigned to him by the Judges. The office of Clerk shall be a civil service position and the salary be as prescribed by the Metropolitan Pay Plan. There shall be provided by ordinance such deputy clerks and other assistants as may be necessary to the proper functioning of the Metropolitan Court. The positions thus created shall be under civil service and the salaries to be paid shall be as prescribed by the Metropolitan Pay Plan.

The Clerk and his deputies are authorized to administer oaths, to take appearance and appeal bonds when the amount thereof has been fixed by a Judge, and to issue all process ancillary to the original warrant. All process shall be issued in the name of the State of Tennessee and the same may be served by any police officer of the Metropolitan Government.

SECTION 14.09. **COURT OFFICERS.** Each Judge of the Metropolitan Court is authorized to appoint two court officers, who shall serve at the pleasure of the Judge and whose compensation shall be fixed in the Pay Plan. It shall be the duty of the court officers to keep order at sessions of the court, to serve process as ordered and to perform such other duties as may be prescribed by the Judge. The Court Officers shall have police power to the same extent as members of the Metropolitan Police Department.

SECTION 14.10. **PUBLIC DEFENDER. QUALIFICATIONS. SELECTION. TERM. DUTIES.** There shall be a Public Defender for the Metropolitan Government who shall be elected by the voters at the regular August election in 1966 and who shall hold office for a term of four (4) years, commencing September 1, 1966 and until his successor shall be duly elected and qualified. The Public Defender shall be a person licensed to practice law in Tennessee and he shall be at the time of his election or appointment, and shall continue to be during the term of office, a resident of the area of the Metropolitan Government. The Public Defender shall not engage in private practice of criminal law during his term, but he may conclude all matters pending when elected or appointed. A vacancy in the office of Public Defender shall be filled by the Metropolitan Council until the next general August election, when a successor shall be elected by the voters to fill the unexpired term or the ensuing term as may be the case.

Upon request by the defendant, or upon order of the Court, it shall be the duty of the Public Defender to defend, without expense, and to represent generally, all persons who are determined by the Court or the Public Defender to be without means to employ counsel and who have been indicted by the grand jury or charged with the commission of any crime. The Public Defender shall also, upon request, give counsel and advice to such person, in and about any charge against them upon which he is conducting the defense. The Public Defender shall prosecute all appeals to a higher Court on behalf of any person financially unable to employ counsel who has been convicted upon such charge, where in his opinion there is error in the conviction had, and such appeal will or might reasonably be expected to, result in the reversal or modification of the judgment or conviction. The Public Defender shall perform such other duties as may be assigned by ordinance.

SECTION 14.11. **COMPENSATION OF PUBLIC DEFENDER. APPOINTMENT, QUALIFICATIONS AND DUTIES OF ASSISTANTS.** The Public Defender shall receive a salary of Eight Thousand ($8,000) Dollars per annum, payable semimonthly.

For the proper conduct of the business of his office, the Public Defender is authorized to employ one Deputy or Assistant at a salary not to exceed Five Thousand ($5,000) Dollars per annum, payable semimonthly, and to employ one stenographer at a salary not to exceed Four Thousand ($4,000) Dollars per annum, payable semimonthly. Any person appointed Assistant Public Defender or Deputy Public Defender shall be licensed to practice law in Tennessee and shall be at the time of his appointment, and shall continue to be during the period of his service, a resident of the area of the Metropolitan Government. Any person appointed Assistant or Deputy Public Defender shall serve at the pleasure of the Public Defender and notice of his appointment or of the revocation of the same shall be in writing and filed with the Clerk of the Criminal Court. Such Assistant or Deputy Public Defender may attend all Criminal Courts and discharge the duties imposed by law upon the Public Defender. The Assistant or Deputy Public Defender designated by the Public Defender or by the Court in his absence, shall perform the duties of said office during any period when the Public Defender is disabled or otherwise unable to attend court. No Assistant or Deputy Public Defender shall engage in the private practice of criminal law during the period of his service, except to conclude matters pending when he was appointed.

The Council by ordinance may provide such additional Assistants, Investigators or other personnel as it may determine the Public Defender to require, and also by ordinance may enlarge or restrict the duties of the Public Defender as to the class of cases in which he shall act as attorney for indigent defendants.

SECTION 14.12. **GENERAL SESSIONS COURTS PROVIDED FOR.** Courts of General Sessions for Davidson County created by Chapter 12 of the Private Acts of 1937 are hereby recognized as Courts of the Metropolitan Government of Nashville and Davidson County. Pursuant to Tennessee Code Annotated, Section 6-3719, said Courts are hereby provided for and continued, with all rights, duties, powers, obligations, privileges and responsibilities as set forth in said Chapter 12 of the Private Acts of 1937 and all Acts amendatory thereof. In addition to the above enumerated powers, the General Sessions Judges shall have power to issue warrants for the breach of Metropolitan ordinances in furtherance of the authority granted in Section 14.05 of this Article.

SECTION 14.13. **JUVENILE COURT PROVIDED FOR.** The Juvenile Court for Davidson County created by Chapter 390 of the Private Acts of 1953 is hereby recognized as a Court of the Metropolitan Government of Nashville and Davidson County. Pursuant to Section 6-3719, Tenessee Code Annotated, said Court is hereby provided for and continued, with all rights, duties, powers, obligations, privileges and responsibilities as set forth in said Chapter 390 of the Private Acts of 1953 and any Acts amendatory thereof. The jurisdiction of the Metropolitan Court created by Section 14.01 of this Charter shall not extend to matters over which the Juvenile Court shall have been given exclusive jurisdiction by said Section 6-3719, or other applicable law.

Article 15

ELECTIONS AND REMOVAL OF OFFICERS

SECTION 15.01. **GENERAL METROPOLITAN ELECTION. WHO MAY VOTE. QUALIFICATION OF CANDIDATES.** For the purpose of electing a Mayor, Vice-Mayor, five (5) councilmen-at-large and thirty-five (35) district councilmen, there shall be held on the first Thursday in August, 1966, and each four years thereafter, a general Metropolitan election. At such general election each voter shall be entitled to vote for one (1) candidate for Mayor, one (1) candidate for Vice-Mayor, five (5) candidates for councilmen-at-large, and one (1) candidate for district councilman from the district wherein the voter resides; and the names of all qualified candidates shall be so placed on the ballot or voting machine as to accord the voter such right. All persons who have resided in the area of the Metropolitan Government for six months next preceding the day of the election who are lawfully registered and who are qualified to vote for members of the General Assembly of the State of Tennessee shall be qualified to vote in Metropolitan elections. The name of any candidate shall be included on the ballot or the voting machines when a written petition signed by at least twenty-five (25) qualified voters shall so request and when said petition shall be filed with the county commissioners of election at least thirty (30) days prior to the election.

SECTION 15.02. **METROPOLITAN ELECTIONS AND RUN-OFF ELECTIONS.** In the general Metropolitan election those qualified persons who receive a majority of the votes cast for Mayor, Vice-Mayor and district councilmen for each of the thirty-five (35) districts shall be elected to their respective offices; and those five (5) qualified persons who receive the highest number of votes, being also a majority of the total vote cast for the office of councilmen-at-large, shall be elected to such office.

In the general election if no candidate shall receive a majority of all the votes cast for the office of Mayor, Vice-Mayor or district councilman, a run-off election shall be held with respect to such unfilled office or offices. In the run-off election only the names of the two (2) candidates who received the highest number of votes cast for such office which failed to be filled at the general election shall be placed on the official ballot or voting machine.

In the general election if less than five (5) candidates receive a majority of the total vote cast for the office of councilmen-at-large, the number receiving a majority shall be elected and a run-off election shall be held with respect to the unfilled offices. For the purpose of this Section, "the total vote cast for the office of councilmen-at-large" shall be deemed to be one-fifth (1/5th) of the aggregate number of votes received by all candidates for the office of councilmen-at-large. In the run-off election, there shall be included on the ballot or voting machine a number of candidates which is twice the number of vacancies remaining to be filled. The candidates to be so included shall be those who in the general election received the highest vote less than a majority and the other candidates shall be eliminated. In the event of a tie vote among candidates, one of whom would be in the run-off except for such tie, then all such candidates so having tie votes shall be in the run-off. In a run-off election for councilmen-at-large it shall not be necessary to receive a majority and those candidates who have the highest vote and who equal in number those remaining to be elected shall be elected.

The run-off election shall be held on the fourth Thursday in August, being three weeks subsequent to the general election. In the case of a tie between candidates for the same office, it shall be broken as provided by Tennessee Code Annotated, Section 2-1408.

SECTION 15.03. **SPECIAL ELECTIONS.** There shall be held a special Metropolitan election to fill a vacancy for the unexpired term in the office of Mayor, Vice-Mayor or councilmen-at-large or district councilmen, whenever such vacancy shall exist more than nine (9) months prior to the date of the next general Metropolitan election. The special election shall be ordered by the County Commisisoners of Elections and they shall give notice thereof as provided by Tennessee Code Annotated, Section 2-1808. If in such special election to fill a vacancy for the unexpired term no candidate shall receive a majority of all the votes cast for such office, a run-off election shall be held three (3) weeks subsequent to the first special election for the purpose of filling such office in accordance with the provisions hereinbefore set forth in the case of a general Metropolitan election. The provisions of Section 15.01 hereof with respect to voting in general Metropolitan elections and with respect to qualifying as a candidate shall apply to special elections.

SECTION 15.04. **APPLICABILITY OF GENERAL ELECTION LAWS.** The general election laws of the State shall be applicable to all Metropolitan elections except as otherwise provided in this Article.

SECTION 15.05. **OUSTER OF METROPOLITAN OFFICERS.** The Mayor, Vice-Mayor, members of the Council, and every member of a Metropolitan Board or Commission appointed for a special term shall be subject to ouster under the terms and provisions of Tennessee Code Annotated, Sections 8-2701 to 8-2926, and within the meaning of such law Metropolitan officers are hereby declared to be county and municipal officers.

Article 16

FUNCTIONS OF CONSTITUTIONAL AND COUNTY OFFICERS

SECTION 16.01. **COUNTY JUDGE.** Nothing in this Charter is intended or shall be construed to alter or affect the judicial powers and functions of the County Judge and the same shall continue as provided by general law or private act. The compensation of the County Judge shall be as provided by general law with respect to Chancellors provided that this Section shall not alter or diminish the compensation of the incumbent County Judge prior to the expiration of his present term of office in 1966. The County Judge is hereby recognized as an officer of the Metropolitan Government in the exercise of his functions, having the same relationship to such Metropolitan Government in the performance of such judicial functions as he previously had to the County of Davidson.

SECTION 16.02. **COUNTY COURT CLERK.** Nothing in this Charter is intended or shall be construed to alter or affect the powers, duties and responsibilities of the County Court Clerk as a collector of State revenues or as the Clerk of the Probate Court. All fees, commissions, emoluments and perquisites of the office of County Court Clerk shall accrue to the Metropolitan Government as has been provided in Section 8-118 of this Charter.

SECTION 16.03. **DUTIES OF METROPOLITAN GOVERNMENT TO CERTAIN STATE AND COUNTY OFFICERS RECOGNIZED.** Nothing in this Charter is intended or shall be construed to affect the powers, duties or compensation of the District Attorney, Circuit Court Clerk, Criminal Court Clerk, Clerk and Master of the Chancery Court or County Register, except as set forth in this Section. The Metropolitan Government and its Council shall have the same relationship, including powers, duties and responsibilities, to said officers and their assistants and office personnel as the County of Davidson and its Quarterly County Court had prior to the effective date of this Charter. It being recognized that this Charter as to Metropolitan Courts may operate to reduce the fees of the office of Criminal Court Clerk, the Metropolitan Council is hereby authorized and directed to appropriate for the maintenance of such office such sum of money as may be necessary in addition to statutory fees for the proper operation of said office and for the maintenance of his salary at the present (maximum) level. Whenever by general law or private act the County of Davidson has been authorized or required to appropriate money, to contribute toward the compensation of expenses of said officers or their offices, or to perform other duties with respect thereto, the Metropolitan Government shall be vested with the same authority and obligation. Said officers and their official personnel shall also have the same relationship, including powers, duties and responsibilities with respect to the Metropolitan Government as they previously had to the County of Davidson or the City of Nashville. All fees, commissions, emoluments and perquisites of any of said offices shall accrue to the Metropolitan Government as the same formerly accrued to the County of Davidson.

The Metropolitan Government shall also have the same obligations and duties as the County of Davidson formerly had with the respect to compensation or expenses of court officers, bailiffs, secretaries and all other persons, and such duties may hereafter be changed by amendment or repeal of the respective private acts creating such duties when the amendatory or repealing act has been approved by the electorate or the Council, as provided by the Constitution of Tennessee.

SECTION 16.04. QUARTERLY COUNTY COURT. COMPOSITION, POWERS AND FUNCTIONS. The Quarterly County Court shall be composed of three (3) Justices from the civil district, consisting of the area of the Urban Services District, of two (2) Justices from the civil district consisting of the area outside the Urban Services District, of five (5) additional Justices from the Urban Services District as a municipal corporation, and of one (1) Justice for every other municipal corporation within the area of the Metropolitan Government.

The Quarterly County Court shall elect notaries public as provided by Tennessee Code Annotated, Section 8-1601, and shall elect officers and fill vacancies in office as provided by the Constitution of Tennessee. No other power or function shall be retained by the Quarterly County Court and said Quarterly County Court is hereby deprived of the power to levy taxes, to approve or to disapprove local acts, or otherwise to administer the governmental affairs of the Metropolitan Government.

SECTION 16.05. SHERIFF. The Sheriff, elected as provided by the Constitution of Tennessee, is hereby recognized as an officer of the Metropolitan Government. He shall have such duties as are prescribed by Tennessee Code Annotated, Section 8-810, or by other provisions of general law, except that within the area of the Metropolitan Government the Sheriff shall not be the prinicipal conservator of peace. The function as principal conservator of peace is hereby transferred and assigned to the Metropolitan Chief of Police, provided for by Article 8, Chapter 2 of this Charter. The Sheriff shall have custody and control of the Metropolitan Jail and of the Metropolitan Workhouse to which persons are sentenced for violation of State Law, but the Urban Jail and Workhouse in which persons are confined for violations of ordinances of the Metropolitan Government, or while awaiting trial for such violation, shall be under the custody and control of the Metropolitan Chief of Police. By ordinance the Urban Jail may be consolidated with the Metropolitan Jail and the Urban Workhouse may be consolidated with the Metropolitan Workhouse. After either or both such consolidations the Jail and the Workhouse shall be under the custody and control of the Sheriff.

All fees, commissions, emoluments and perquisites of the office of Sheriff shall accrue to the Metropolitan Government as the same formerly accrued to the County of Davidson.

Article 17
PUBLIC UTILITY FRANCHISES

SECTION 17.01. IRREVOCABLE FRANCHISES GRANTED ONLY BY ORDINANCE. All irrevocable public utility franchises and all renewals, extensions and amendments thereof shall be granted only by ordinance. No such ordinance shall be adopted before thirty (30) days after application therefor has been filed with the Council, nor until full public hearing has been held thereon.

SECTION 17.02. GRANTING ORDINANCES TO BE RATIFIED AT ELECTION. No such ordinance shall become effective until it has been submitted to the electors of the Metropolitan Government and has been approved by three-fifths of the electors voting thereon. No such ordinance shall be submitted to the electors at an election to be held less than sixty (60) days after the grantee named therein has filed its unconditional acceptance of such franchise, and it shall not be submitted to a special election unless the expense of holding the election, as determined by the Council, shall have been paid to the Metropolitan Treasurer by the grantee.

In any election held under the provisions of this Article, wherein is submitted any franchise ordinance for ratification by the voters, it shall not be necessary to print the entire ordinance on the ballot. It shall only be necessary to submit the question of ratification of such ordinance, together with a brief statement of the purpose or purposes of the same, and the date of its enactment by the Mayor and Council. The ordinance itself may provide for the form of its submission on the ballot.

SECTION 17.03. RESTRICTIONS ON ALL FUTURE PUBLIC UTILITY FRANCHISES AND RESERVED POWERS OF METROPOLITAN GOVERNMENT. No exclusive franchise shall ever be granted and no franchise shall be granted for a longer term than thirty (30) years. No such franchise shall be transferable, directly or indirectly, except with the approval of the Council expressed by ordinance.

All public utility franchises, whether it be so provided in the ordinance or not, shall be subject to the right of the Metropolitan Government:
1. To repeal the same for misuse or nonuse, or for failure to comply therewith.
2. To require proper and adequate extension of plant and service and the maintenance thereof, at the highest practicable standard of efficiency.
3. To establish reasonable standards of service and quality of products, and prevent unjust discrimination in service or rates.
4. To make independent audit and examination of accounts at any time, and to require reports annually.
5. To require continuous and uninterrupted service to the public in accordance with the terms of the franchise, throughout the entire period thereof.
6. To impose such other regulations as may be determined by the Council to be conducive to the safety, welfare and accommodation of the public.

SECTION 17.04. GENERAL REQUIREMENTS. All public utility franchises shall make provision for fixing rates, fares and charges, and for readjustments thereof at periodic intervals of not more than five (5) years, either by arbitration upon terms to be specifically set forth in the franchise, or by state agency, at the election of the Metropolitan Government. The value of the property of the utility used as a basis for fixing such rates, fares and charges shall in no event include a value predicated upon the franchise, good will or prospective profits.

Every public utility may be required by the Metropolitan Government to permit joint use of its property and appurtenances located in the streets, alleys, and public places of the Metropolitan Government, by other public utilities, in so far as such joint use may be reasonably practicable, and in accordance with the provisions of the National Electrical Safety Code upon payment of reasonable rental thereof; provided, that in the absence of agreement, upon application by any public utility, the Council shall provide for arbitration of the terms and conditions of such joint use and the compensation to be paid therefor, which award shall be final.

The right to use, control and regulate use of its streets, alleys, bridges and public places, and spaces above and beneath them, is hereby reserved to the Metropolitan Government and every public utility franchise shall be subject thereto. Every public utility shall indemnify the Metropolitan Government against and pay for such damage as it causes to streets, alleys, bridges and other public places by reason of excavations, cutting of pavements, construction work and the like, provided this obligation shall not obligate the public utility to pay for damages resulting from usual wear and tear or its ordinary use of such public places.

SECTION 17.05. ACQUIRING PROPERTY OF PUBLIC UTILITY BY CONDEMNATION. The Metropolitan Government shall have power to acquire by condemnation or otherwise the property of any public utility. This power shall be exercised in accordance with the general laws of the State pertaining to such acquisition by cities and may be exercised only after having been approved by three-fifths of the electors voting thereon under the procedure required by Section 17.02 hereof in the case of franchises. The cost of such election shall be borne by the Metropolitan Government.

SECTION 17.06. RECOGNITION OF FRANCHISES GRANTED BY COUNTY OR CITY. This Charter and this Article shall not affect valid franchises heretofore granted or transfers thereof heretofore approved by the County of Davidson or the City of Nashville, but the same shall continue in force and effect in accordance with their valid provisions, terms and conditions.

SECTION 17.07. REGULATION OF STREET RAILWAY COMPANIES. The entire and complete supervision, regulation, jurisdiction and control over street railway companies operating within the territory embraced in the Metropolitan Government and the environs thereof shall be vested solely in and exercised solely by Nashville Transit Authority as created and established under the terms and provisions of Chapter 487, Private Acts of 1953, as amended by Chapter 307, Private Acts of 1955, and Chapter 165, Private Acts of 1957, and as set forth in Appendix Four hereto to which reference is made. Neither the Mayor nor the Council nor any other officer or agency of the Metropolitan Government shall have or exercise any authority whatsoever over such street railway companies, or over Nashville Transit Authority except as expressly provided in said Appendix Four.

No franchise to operate a street railway company on the streets and highways of the Metropolitan Government shall be granted except upon referendum as hereinabove set forth and nothing in said Appendix Four shall be construed as depriving the citizens of the Metropolitan Government of the right to grant franchise by referendum through the procedure herein established.

SECTION 17.08. LIMITED SCOPE OF THIS ARTICLE. Nothing in this Article shall empower any agency of the Metropolitan Government to regulate rates, charges and services of any public utility whose rates, charges and services are regulated by the Tennessee Public Service Commission.

Article 18

MISCELLANEOUS PROVISIONS

SECTION 18.01. METROPOLITAN CLERK. There is hereby created and established the office of Metropolitan Clerk, which shall be charged with the recording and safekeeping of minutes, resolutions and ordinances of the Metropolitan Council and of all other documents relating to official actions of the Metropolitan Government. The Metropolitan Clerk shall also perform such other duties as may be imposed upon him by this Charter or by ordinance. The Metropolitan Clerk shall act under the supervision and control of the Mayor and Council.

Any vacancy in the office of Metropolitan Clerk shall be filled by appointment of the Mayor pursuant to the civil service provisions of this Charter. Such Clerk shall be at least thirty (30) years of age and shall have been a resident of the area of the Metropolitan Government for at least five (5) years preceding his appointment. His office shall be a civil service office and his compensation shall be fixed in the Metropolitan Pay Plan provided for by Article 12. He shall have such clerical help as may be provided by ordinance.

SECTION 18.02. ZONING REGULATIONS. ENACTMENT, REVISIONS, MODIFICATION OR CHANGE. Zoning regulations shall be enacted by the Council only on the basis of a comprehensive plan prepared by the Metropolitan Planning Commisison in accordance with the applicable state laws and as provided in Section 3.05 of this Charter.

Any revision, modification or change in the Zoning regulations of the Metropolitan Government as provided in this Section shall be made only by ordinance. Where a proposed ordinance revises, modifies, or changes the zoning regulations and is not accompanied at introduction by a favorable recommendation of the Metropolitan Planning Commission, a copy thereof shall be promptly furnished by the Metropolitan Clerk to said Planning Commission, and the same shall not be passed on second reading until the recommendation of said Planning Commission with respect to the proposal has been received or thirty (30) days have elapsed without such recommendation. No ordinance making any revision, modification or change in the zoning regulations which has been disapproved by the Metropolitan Planning Commission shall be finally passed or become effective unless it shall be adopted by a two-thirds majority of the whole membership of the Council and also then be approved by the Metropolitan Mayor, with a three-fourths majority of the whole membership of the Council required to override a veto.

SECTION 18.03. BOARD OF ZONING APPEALS. A Metropolitan Board of Zoning Appeals may be established as provided by state law and ordinance enacted by the Council in accordance with the provisions of this Charter. No member of said Board of Zoning Appeals shall hold any public office or position nor shall any member receive any financial compensation for serving on said Board.

SECTION 18.04. NASHVILLE HOUSING AUTHORITY PROVIDED FOR. The Nashville Housing Authority, created pursuant to Section 13-901 to Section 13-918, inclusive, of Tenessee Code Annotated, is hereby recognized as existing and functioning within the area of the Metropolitan Government and as having the same relationship to the Metropolitan Government as said

Nashville Housing Authority previously had to the City of Nashville. Said Housing Authority is hereby declared to be a City Housing Authority as provided for by Tennessee Code Annotated, Sections 13-901 to 13-918, inclusive, and also as a County Housing Authority as provided for by Tennessee Code Annotated, Sections 13-1001 to 13-1011, inclusive. The Metropolitan Mayor shall be deemed a mayor for the purposes of said City Housing Authorities Act as therein referred to. He shall have authority to designate and appoint, subject to confirmation by the Council, members of the Board of Commissioners of The Nashville Housing Authority of the Metropolitan Government as their terms expire or as their offices otherwise become vacant.

SECTION 18.05. **CHANGE IN SALARY.** Where the salary or compensation of a Metropolitan officer is fixed by this Charter, the same may be changed in the following manner: (1) An ordinance shall be enacted making the change and providing an effective date subsequent to the next general Metropolitan election; and (2) The Council meeting subsequent to such general Metropolitan election shall adopt a resolution approving the change proposed by the ordinance.

SECTION 18.06. **REDISTRICTING OF COUNCILMANIC DISTRICTS.** Redistricting of the Councilmanic Districts set forth in Appendix Two of this Charter may be accomplished in the following manner:

Within six (6) months after the decennial census of 1970 and each one thereafter is published by the United States Census Bureau showing the population in the area of the Metropolitan Government, it shall be the duty of the Planning Commission to recommend to the Council whether redistricting of the councilmanic districts is necessary to prevent substantial underrepresentaion of particular areas as the result of population changes. If the Planning Commission shall recommend that redistricting is necessary, it shall also submit a proposed ordinance designed to accomplish its recommendation. Such ordinance shall also revise the school districts to the extent, if any, that may be deemed necessary. The Council shall not amend, but may adopt without change such proposed ordinance. Upon approval thereof by the Mayor, or passage over his veto, redistricting shall be accomplished and district councilmen shall be elected accordingly at the next general Metropolitan election.

The Council may reject the proposed ordinance for redistricting, in which event, by resolution under Article 19 of this Charter, it shall submit to the people for approval at a special referendum election to be held within ninety (90) days an amendment to this Charter making effective the redistricting as recommended by the Planning Commission. At such referendum election the Council may submit to the people its own plans for redistricting as an alternative to the proposal of the Planning Commission also submitted.

At the expiration of ninety (90) days subsequent to the receipt by the Council of an ordinance of redistricting, as hereinabove provided, if such ordinance shall not have become effective and if the Council shall have failed to submit the same to a special referendum election, then the members of the Council shall not receive any further salaries until they take one action or the other.

SECTION 18.07. **TITLES AND SUBTITLES NOT PART OF CHAPTER.** It is hereby expressly declared and recognized that the titles and subtitles appearing before the Articles, Chapters and Sections of this Charter are not part hereof and are not intended to determine or to restrict the meaning of its provisions. No substantive provision of this Charter shall be construed to be unintended or ineffective because the same has not been suggested or indicated by a title or subtitle. Titles and subtitles have been placed in this Charter merely for the convenience of those who examine or index its provisions.

SECTION 18.08. **REGULATION AND SALE OF ALCOHOLIC BEVERAGES NOT AFFECTED BY CHARTER.** The creation and establishment of the Metropolitan Government of Nashville and Davidson County shall not alter the status of said county as to the legality of the manufacture, receipt, sale, storage, transportation, distribution and possession of alcoholic beverages. The local option election heretofore held in said county pursuant to Tennessee Code Annotated, Sections 57-111 and 57-112 shall continue to control until the status shall be subsequently altered by a local option election held pursuant to law. The Urban Services District, but not the General Services District, shall be deemed a municipality within the meaning of said Section 57-111.

The Council shall have power and authority (a) for the General Services District to regulate and tax the manufacture, distribution and sale of beer and other alcoholic beverages of less than five (5%) percent to the same extent that governing bodies of counties now possess, or may hereafter possess, such power and authority, and (b) for the Urban Services District to regulate and tax the manufacture, distribution and sale of beer and other alcoholic beverages of less than five (5%) percent and also the manufacture, receipt, sale, storage, transportation, distribution and possession of other alcoholic beverages to the same extent that governing bodies of cities now possess or may hereafter possess such power and authority.

SECTION 18.09. **FEDERAL, STATE AND OTHER AID.** The Metropolitan Government of Nashville and Davidson County shall be deemed a county and shall also be deemed an incorporated city or municipality for the purpose of determining its right to receive, and for the purpose of receiving, state aid or grant-in-aid from the State of Tennessee or from the United States or from any other agency. Said Metropolitan Government shall be entitled to receive as State aid or as grant-in-aid from the State of Tennessee or from the United States or from any other agency, public or private, all funds to which a county is, or may hereafter be, entitled and also all funds to which an incorporated city or municipality is or may be hereafter entitled and to receive the same without diminution or loss by reason of consolidation. When state aid or other grant-in-aid is distributed to any county on the basis of population or area, or both, then the entire population and the total area of the county in which such Metropolitan Government is established shall be considered in calculating and determining the basis of such distribution. When state aid or other grant-in-aid is distributed to any county on the basis of rural area, rural road mileage or rural population, or any combination thereof, then that area of the General Services District outside of the Urban Services District shall be deemed to constitute rural area, its road mileage to constitute rural road mileage and its population to constitute rural population. When state aid or grant-in-aid is distributed to any incorporated city or municipality on the basis of population or area, or both, then the population and the area of the Urban Services District shall be deemed the population and the area of the Metropolitan Government in calculating and determining the basis of such distribution.

SECTION 18.10. **METROPOLITAN AGENCIES AUTHORIZED TO COMPEL ATTENDANCE OF WITNESSES AND PRODUCTION OF DOCUMENTS.** The Council, the Civil Service Commission, the Board of Education and every other officer and agency of the Metropolitan Government authorized to conduct investigations or to hold hearings shall have power to compel the attendance of witnesses and the production of books, papers and records pertinent to the investigation or hearing, and to administer oaths to witnesses. If any person fails or refuses to obey a reasonable order for attendance or reasonable order for the production of books and papers, the Council, Board or other agency is authorized to apply to the Chancery Court for an order requiring that the order of the Council, Board or other agency be obeyed.

SECTION 18.11. **AUTHORIZATION TO COUNCIL WITH RESPECT TO CERTAIN SPECIAL APPROPRIATIONS.** The Council is hereby authorized to include in the annual operating budget for the General Services District the following:

(a) A sum not in excess of Twelve Thousand Five Hundred ($12,500) Dollars for any year for the use of Nashville Humane Association.

(b) A sum not in excess of Twenty-five Thousand ($25,000) Dollars for any year for the use of Nashville Children's Museum, of Nashville, Tennessee.

(c) The sum necessary for the purpose of paying dues or assessments of the Metropolitan Government for the cost of operating the following organizations and similar nonprofit organizations: The Tennessee Municipal League, Tennessee County Services Association, the National Institute of Municipal Law Officers and the Southern Building Code Congress.

(d) A sum not in excess of Fifteen Thousand ($15,000) Dollars for any year for the use of the Nashville Symphony Association of Nashville, Tennessee.

SECTION 18.12. **NO APPROPRIATION AUTHORIZED FROM BUDGET OF GENERAL SERVICES DISTRICT TO FINANCE CERTAIN DEFICITS.** Where any appropriation is made from time to time to finance any deficit in the pension or retirement funds of the former City of Nashville, the same shall be made solely from the budget of the Urban Services District.

SECTION 18.13. **COUNCILMEN DISQUALIFIED FOR MEMBERSHIP ON CERTAIN BOARDS AND COMMISSIONS.** Except as otherwise expressly provided in this Charter, no member of the Council shall be eligible during the term of office for which he was elected to serve on any Metropolitan Board or Commission created by this Charter.

SECTION 18.14. **FIDELITY BONDS.** Before entering upon the duties of their respective offices or positions, the Director of Finance, the Metropolitan Treasurer, the Collections Officer, the Chief Accountant, the Director of Personnel, the Purchasing Agent and such other officers and employees of the Metropolitan Government as shall be required by Council resolution upon the recommendation of the Mayor, shall execute corporate surety bonds and file said bonds with the Metropolitan Clerk. The sum of the individual bonds shall be fixed by the Council resolution, but the amount of the bond shall not in any case be less than One Thousand ($1,000) Dollars. The bond premiums shall be paid from the General Fund of the General Services District. All such bonds and sureties thereon shall be approved by the Department of Law before being accepted by the Metropolitan Clerk.

SECTION 18.15. **STATUS OF SMALLER CITIES AND VOLUNTARY SURRENDER OF THEIR CHARTERS. CREATION OF SUBURBAN UTILITY DISTRICTS.** Any city in Davidson County not abolished by this Charter shall continue to exist and to function the same as prior to adoption of this Charter, except that no such city shall extend its boundaries by annexation of any area of the Metropolitan Government. Any such smaller city may contract with the Metropolitan Government for the administration and handling of any of its governmental functions by the Metropolitan Government; and such smaller city may surrender its municipal charter at any time pursuant to Tennessee Code Annotated, Section 6-3722, with the aproval of a majority of those voting in the smaller city at an election with respect to such matter. After surrender of charter, the status of the smaller city in the Metropolitan Government shall be that prescribed in a resolution adopted by the Council prior to such surrender, or otherwise the status shall be that of other areas outside the Urban Services District at the time of dissolution.

It shall be the obligation of the Metropolitan Government to furnish smaller cities with governmental services so that such cities will be furnished with governmental services to no lesser extent than other areas outside the Urban Services District. In furnishing said services, the Metropolitan Government may take into consideration the governmental services available to the smaller city by the use of state aid and other distributable moneys not derived from local taxation by the smaller city; and in this respect the Metropolitan Government may contract with the smaller city as to the handling, use and expenditure of such moneys.

After the adoption of this Charter by vote of the people, no city shall be created in the area of the Metropolitan Government, and there shall exist in such area as municipalities only the Urban Services District and smaller cities existing prior to the adoption of this Charter.

Nothing in this Charter shall be deemed to prevent the creation of utility districts as provided for by Tennessee Code Annotated, Sections 6-2601, et seq., with the county judge to perform the function ascribed to such officer by said statute.

SECTION 18.16. **COUNTY EXECUTIVE COMMITTEES FOR POLITICAL PARTIES, REGULATION AND CONTINUATION.** For the purpose of selecting members of a county executive committee for a political party, as prescribed by any valid Private Act heretofore enacted affecting Davidson County, the thirty-five (35) councilmanic districts created and established by Section 3.01 of this Charter shall be deemed to be the city wards and also the county districts from which district representatives on a county political executive committee shall be selected. The total of seventy (70) representatives shall consist of one (1) man and one (1) woman from each of the thirty-five (35) districts. Nothing in this Section shall terminate or abridge the terms of office of members now serving on any county political executive committee, and except as expressly modified by this Section, any Private Act with respect to this subject matter is continued in force and effect.

SECTION 18.17. **AUTHORITY TO DEAL WITH STATE AND FEDERAL AGENCIES AS TO SPECIFIC GOVERNMENTAL SERVICES.** The Mayor and Council of the Metropolitan Government shall have the power and authority to participate in, cooperate in and take all necessary action with respect to any and all projects, programs and undertakings of any nature whatsoever authorized by any statute, rule or regulation of the United States or the State of Tennessee, or any federal or state agency or instrumentality, including, but not limited to, urban renewal, highways, aviation, aviation terminals, airports, airport facilities, river development or river terminals, municipal area or regional development, schools, colleges or any other area of education, sewers and sewage disposal, public housing, housing for the aged, and transportation or mass transit or any phase thereof, to exercise with respect thereto all the powers conferred by Section 6-1602 of Tennessee Code Annotated and any other state or federal statute, to borrow money and issue promissory notes, general obligation bonds, or revenue bonds, or a combination thereof, for any such purposes, and to execute mortgages or deeds of trust in favor of any federal agency, secured by property of which the Metropolitan Government is the legal, or beneficial or equitable owner, or in favor of any private agency where the loan is guaranteed by a federal agency.

AMENDING CHARTER

SECTION 19.01. **AMENDING CHARTER BY RESOLUTION OF COUNCIL OR PETITION AND POPULAR VOTE.** This Charter may be amended subsequent to its adoption in the following manner:

An amendment or amendments may be proposed (1) by the adoption of a resolution by the Council favoring the same and submitting it or them to the people for approval. The affirmative vote for adoption of such reslotion in the Council shall be not less than two-thirds of the membership to which the Council is entitled, and such resolution when adopted need not be submitted to the Mayor for his approval; or (2) upon petition by twenty percent of the qualified voters of the Metropolitan Government filed with the Metropolitan Clerk. Such resolution or petition shall also prescribe a date not less than eighty (80) nor more than one hundred (100) days subsequent to the date of its filing for the holding of a referendum election at which the electorate of the Metropolitan Government will vote to ratify or to reject the amendments proposed.

The Metropolitan Clerk shall immediately certify to the County Commissioners of Election copy of such resolution or petition and it shall thereupon be the duty of said Commissioners of Election to hold a referendum election with respect thereto. The ballot shall be prepared so as to set forth the exact language of each proposed amendment, numbered as the same is numbered in the resolution of the Council or in the petition, and to provide the voters a choice to vote "For Ratification" and "Against Ratification" of each proposed amendment. Each proposed amendment shall be ratified when a majority of the votes cast at the special referendum election shall be in favor of ratification and each proposed amendment shall be rejected when a majority of said votes shall be against ratification. Notice of said referendum election shall be given as provided by Tennessee Code Annotated, Section 2-1808, and the costs of said election shall be paid out of the general funds of the Metropolitan Government.

The Commissioners of Election shall canvass the returns and certify the results to the Secretary of State, who shall issue a proclamation showing the results of said election on the ratification or rejection of each proposed amendment to this Charter. One copy of the proclamation shall be attached to the copy of this Charter previously certified to said Secretary of State and one copy shall be delivered to the Metropolitan Clerk who shall attach the same to the copy of the Charter in his custody.

The Council shall not adopt a resolution proposing amendments to this Charter more often than twice during the term of office of members of said Council, nor shall any such amendment or amendments be submitted by petition more often than once in each two years.

The Council shall not adopt, except pursuant to Section 18.06 of this Charter, a resolution which proposes an amendment that redistricts the councilmanic districts unless the same be incidental to a proposed change in the number of such districts.

SECTION 19.02. **OTHERWISE AMENDING THIS CHARTER.** This Charter may also be amended in such other manner as may hereafter be provided by general law for amending the Charter of Metropolitan Governments.

SECTION 19.03. **CHARTER REVISION COMMISSION AUTHORIZED.** The Council is authorized by ordinance to establish a Charter Revision Commission to hold hearings and to make recommendations to the Council with respect to amendments to the Charter.

TRANSITION AND EFFECTIVE DATE

SECTION 20.01. **CERTAIN ORDINANCES AND RESOLUTIONS CONTINUED.** All city ordinances, resolutions and by-laws in force in the former City of Nashville, the Charter of which is repealed and abolished by this Charter, shall continue in force and effect, when not inconsistent with the provisions of this Charter, and shall have the legal effect of ordinances of the Metropolitan Government operative within the Urban Services District until repealed, modified or amended by subsequent action of the Metropolitan Government. All resolutions of the Quarterly County Court of Davidson County and regulations pertaining to said County established by Private Act, when not inconsistent with the provisions of this Charter, shall continue in force and effect and shall have the legal effect of ordinances of the Metropolitan Government until repealed, modified or amended by subsequent action of the Metropolitan Government.

SECTION 20.02. **ZONING REGULATIONS CONTINUED.** The creation and establishment of the Metropolitan Government of Nashville and Davidson County shall not alter or change the zoning regulations effective in Davidson County or the City of Nashville at the time this Charter becomes effective, but the same shall continue in force and effect until amended by the Council on the basis of recommendations by the Metropolitan Planning Commission or until revised, modified or changed by the Council on the basis of a comprehensive plan prepared by the Metropolitan Planning Commission in accordance with the applicable state laws and as provided by this Charter.

From the date of adoption of this Charter to the effective date as defined in Section 20.21 hereof, no change in zoning by action of the City Council of Nashville or of the Quarterly County Court of Davidson County shall affect or alter the zoning to become effective with this Charter, unless such change shall have been recommended by the Planning Commission or the same shall have received the affirmative vote of three-fourths of the entire membership of said City Council or said Quarterly County Court.

The Board of Zoning Appeals of the City of Nashville and the Board of Zoning Appeals of Davidson County shall continue as constituted and organized at the time of the effective date of this Charter, with their respective powers and duties as provided in the zoning regulations of the City of Nashville and Davidson County as identified in this Section. The functioning of said Boards of Zoning Appeals shall be terminated only at such time as zoning regulations for the Metropolitan Government area are enacted by the Council as provided in Section 18.02 of this Charter or at such time as a Metropolitan Board of Zoning Appeals may be established pursuant to Section 18.03 of this Charter.

SECTION 20.03. **PROPERTY RIGHTS, CONTRACTS, OBLIGATIONS, CAUSES OF ACTION AND LEGAL PROCEEDINGS CONTINUED.** All rights and titles to property, all rights and obligations under contracts or trusts, and all causes of action of any kind in any court or tribunal vested in the City of Nashville or the County of Davidson or in any officer or employee thereof in his official capacity, at the time this Charter becomes effective, as well as all liabilities in contract or tort and causes of action involving the same in so far as they affect the City of Nashville or the the County of Davidson or any officer or employee thereof in his official capacity which shall be outstanding at the time this Charter becomes effective, shall continue without abatement or modification by reason of any provision of this Charter.

SECTION 20.04. PROCEEDINGS BEFORE COUNTY AND CITY AGENCIES CONTINUED. All petitions, hearings and other proceedings pending before any agency of the City of Nashville or of the County of Davidson shall continue and remain in full force and effect, notwithstanding that such agency may have been abolished or consolidated by this Charter; and the petition, hearing or proceeding may be completed by the agency of the Metropolitan Government which succeeds to the rights, powers, duties and obligations of such abolished or consolidated agency. The word "agency" as used herein and in Sections 20.05, 20.06 and 20.07 of this Article is hereby defined to mean and to include officer, office, department, board and commission.

SECTION 20.05. RULES AND REGULATIONS CONTINUED. All orders, rules and regulations made by any agency of the City of Nashville or of Davidson County, which is abolished or consolidated by this Charter, shall remain in full force and effect until revoked or modified by the agency which succeeds to the rights, powers, duties and obligations of such abolished or consolidated agency.

SECTION 20.06. EMPLOYEES AND THEIR CIVIL SERVICE STATUS CONTINUED. Where an existing agency of the City of Nashville or of Davidson County is abolished or consolidated by this Charter, all employees thereof shall continue, as temporary appointees of the agency to which the rights, powers, duties and obligations of such abolished or consolidated agency are transferred, to perform their usual duties upon the same terms and conditions as theretofore until removed, appointed to positions in accordance with this Charter, or transferred to other agencies of the Metropolitan Government. Where the rights, powers, duties and obligations of any such agency are divided between two or more agencies of the Metropolitan Government, each of them shall receive such of the employees as have been regularly occupied in connection with the functions thereof which are by this Charter transferred to such agency. Every employee to whom this Section applies shall be placed temporarily in one of the agencies of the Metropolitan Government.

All questions and problems arising under this Section shall be determined by the Mayor, provided nothing in his determination nor in this Charter shall impair or diminish the rights and privileges of employees of the City or of the County under civil service on the date this Charter shall be adopted.

SECTION 20.07. TRANSFER OF RECORDS AND EQUIPMENT. When an agency of the City of Nashville or of Davidson County is abolished or consolidated by this Charter, all books, papers, maps, charts, plans, records, other equipment and personal property in the possession of the same shall be delivered to the agency to which its rights, powers, duties and obligations are transferred. In case of controversy between two or more agencies as to right, such books, papers, other documents, equipment and personal property shall be transferred to such agency as the Mayor may direct.

SECTION 20.08. CERTAIN METROPOLITAN OFFICERS APPOINTED.

(a) *Metropolitan Clerk.*—The person holding the position of City Clerk of the former City of Nashville, and having civil service status as such, is hereby appointed and designated as Metropolitan Clerk provided for by Section 18.01 of this Charter, and the certified copy of this Charter and proclamation deposited with the County Court Clerk pursuant to Tennessee Code Annotated, Section 6-3709, shall be delivered to said Metropolitan Clerk on the effective date of this Charter, to be kept by him as a part of the permanent records of his office.

(b) *Metropolitan Treasurer.*—The person holding the position of City Treasurer of the City of Nashville on the effective date of this Charter, and having civil service status as such, is hereby appointed and designated as the first Metropolitan Treasurer.

(c) *Chief Medical Director.*—The person holding the office of County Health Officer of Davidson County on the effective date of this Charter is hereby appointed and designated as the first Chief Medical Director of the Metropolitan Board of Health. Any contract of employment entered into between such County Health Officer and the County Board of Health of Davidson County prior to the effective date of this Charter for a term of employment as County Health Officer extending beyond such effective date shall be accepted by the Metropolitan Board of Health and shall have the effect of the employment of the Chief Medical Director, as such, for the unexpired portion of such contract term.

(d) *Director of Department of Water and Sewerage Services.*—The person holding the position of Director of Waterworks Department of the City of Nashville on the effective date of this Charter, and having civil service status as such, is hereby appointed and designated as the first Director of the Department of Water and Sewerage Services.

(e) *Public Defender.*—The person elected as Public Defender for Davidson County at the August election 1962 is hereby appointed and designated as the first Public Defender for the Metropolitan Government.

(f) *Director of Department of Police.*—The person holding holding the position of Chief of the Police Department of the City of Nashville on the effective date of this Charter, and having civil service status as such, is hereby appointed and designated as the first Director of the Department of Metropolitan Police.

(g) *Director of Department of Fire.*—The person holding the position of Chief of the Fire Department of the City of Nashville on the effective date of this Charter, and having civil service status as such, is hereby appointed and designated as the first Director of the Department of Fire.

(h) *Budget Officer, Division of Budgets.*—The person holding the office of Director of Accounts and Budgets of Davidson County on the effective date of this Charter is hereby appointed and designated as the first Budget Officer of the Division of Budgets.

(i) *Chief Accountant, Division of Accounts.*—The person holding the office of Chief Accountant of the City of Nashville on the effective date of this Charter, and having civil service status as such, is hereby appointed and designated as the first Chief Accountant of the Division of Accounts.

(j) *Metropolitan Judges.*—The Judge of the City Court and the Judge of the Traffic Court of the former City of Nashville are hereby designated and appointed respectively as the Judge of Division I and as the Judge of Division II of the Metropolitan Court, to serve until their successors are elected at the regular August election in 1964 for the remainder of the judicial term.

(k) *Clerk, Deputy Clerk and Court Officers of Metropolitan Court.*—The person holding the position of Clerk of the City Court in the former City of Nashville on the effective date of this Charter, and having civil service status as such, is hereby appointed and designated as the first Clerk of the Metropolitan Court. The person holding the position of Clerk of the Traffic Court of the former City of Nashville on the effective date of this Charter, and having civil service status as such is hereby appointed and designated as a Deputy Clerk to the Judge of Division II of the Metropolitan Court.

The members of the Police Department of the former City of Nashville serving as court officers to the judges of the City Court and Traffic Court of the former City of Nashville on the effective date of this Charter shall retain their positions and status as Court Officers of the Metropolitan Court and if they cease to serve as such court officers, they shall be returned to the Metropolitan Police Department as classified employees thereof.

(1) *Director of Welfare.*—The person holding the position of Director of Welfare for Davidson County on the effective date of this Charter is hereby appointed and designated as the first Director of Welfare under the jurisdiction and authority of the Metropolitan Welfare Commission created and provided for by Article 11, Chapter 11 of this Charter.

(m) *Collections Officer.*—The person holding the position of City Comptroller of the City of Nashville on the effective date of this Charter and having civil service status as such, is hereby appointed and designated as the first Collections Officer created and provided for by Section 8.107 of this Charter.

SECTION 20.09. DIRECTOR AND ASSISTANT DIRECTOR OF DEPARTMENT OF PUBLIC WORKS. The person holding the position of Director of the Department of Public Works of the City of Nashville on the effective date of this Charter is hereby appointed and designated as the first Director of said Department created and provided for by Section 8.404 of this Charter.

The person holding the position of Director of the Department of Public Works of Davidson County on the effective date of this Charter is hereby appointed and designated as Assistant Director of the Metropolitan Department of Public Works. When the office of Assistant Director becomes vacant, the same shall terminate and not be filled, except as may be provided by ordinance.

SECTION 20.10. DIVISION OF PUBLIC ROADS AND DIRECTOR THEREOF. The former County Highway Department of Davidson County shall continue to operate and to perform its former road functions as the Public Roads Division of the Department of Public Works and the Engineer of said former County Highway Department shall be the Divisional Director of said Public Roads Division. The functioning of said Division and the designation of its divisional director shall continue until changed by ordinance.

SECTION 20.11. CERTAIN MEMBERS OF COUNTY HIGHWAY PATROL AND OF THE PARK POLICE APPOINTED. Members of the County Highway Patrol appointed as such by the Sheriff of Davidson County are hereby appointed, and designated as members of the Metropolitan Police Department under the following terms and conditions:

All salaried members of the former County Highway Patrol who have had not less than three (3) years experience as members of said Patrol upon the effective date of this Charter shall be classified as Patrolmen Second Class in the Metropolitan Police Department and shall be eligible for promotional examinations for available positions in like manner as other Patrolmen Second Class in the Metropolitan Police Department.

All salaried members of the former County Highway Patrol who are not eligible for classification as Patrolmen Second Class, but who have had not less than six (6) months experience as members of such patrol prior to March 31, 1962, and who are members of such patrol upon the effective date of this Charter shall be classified as Patrolmen Third Class in the

Metropolitan Police Force. After service for one (1) year as Patrolmen Third Class and upon certification of the Director of the Department of Metropolitan Police, with the approval of the Mayor and the Civil Service Commission, such persons shall be advanced to the position of Patrolmen Second Class in the same manner as other Patrolmen Second Class. Members of the County Highway Patrol appointed hereunder to positions with the Metropolitan Police Department shall not be eligible for benefits under the Policemen's and Firemen's Pension Fund but shall derive any pension and retirement benefits from the Metropolitan Employees' Retirement Fund.

All salaried members of the Park Police of the former City of Nashville who are members of the same upon the effective date of this Charter and who have civil service status as such shall become custodial personnel of the Metropolitan Board of Parks and Recreation.

SECTION 20.12. CERTAIN CIVIL SERVICE EMPLOYEES TRANSFERRED TO METROPOLITAN DEPARTMENT OF LAW. All civil service employees in the Department of Law of the former City of Nashville or in the office of County Attorney of the former County of Davidson are hereby transferred to, and continued as employees of, the Metropolitan Department of Law.

SECTION 20.13. APPOINTMENTS TO ADMINISTRATIVE BOARDS AND COMMISSIONS. FORMER BOARDS AND COMMISSIONS CONTINUED. The Metropolitan Mayor shall appoint promptly and at least within thirty (30) days after he shall take office all members of boards and commisisons whom this Charter authorizes him to appoint. Unless otherwise provided by this Charter, all boards and commissions of the former City of Nashville and of the former County of Davidson are continued for a period of sixty (60) days after the effective date of this Charter or until the board, commission or other agency succeeding to its rights, powers, duties and obligations is organized, whichever date or event occurs earlier.

SECTION 20.14. TRANSITIONAL PROVISIONS AS TO PUBLIC SCHOOLS.

(a) *Temporary Administration by City and County School Boards.*—From the effective date of this Charter to and including July 31, 1962, the County and City School Boards shall each continue to administer, control and operate the school system previously under its jurisdiction in the same manner that such system was operated prior to the effective date of this Charter. Such operation may include assignment of teachers to schools for the school year 1962-1963, to the extent that such assignment is practicable on or before July 31, with such assignments to be made or completed thereafter by the Transitional Board of Education to the extent that may be necessary. The powers, duties and functions of said separate school boards shall cease and terminate after July 31, 1962.

(b) *Transitional Operation by Transitional Board of Education.*—From August 1, 1962 until June 30, 1964, the administration, operation and control of the Metropolitan School System shall be by and under a Transitional Board of Education, subject to the directives and limitations hereinafter specified. For the purpose of transitional operation, a Transitional Board of Education of nine (9) members is hereby created and constituted as follows:

Three (3) members shall be persons who were members of the Davidson County Board of Education immediately prior to the termination of said Board; and said three (3) members shall be chosen by the Davidson County Board of Education prior to August 1, 1962.

Three (3) members shall be persons who were members of the Board of Education of the City of Nashville immediately prior to the termination of said Board; and said three (3) members shall be chosen by the Board of Education of the City of Nashville prior to August 1, 1962.

The three (3) remaining members shall be Dr. Henry H. Hill, former President, George Peabody College for Teachers, who shall serve as Chairman of the Transitional Board, Dr. Walter S. Davis, President, A & I State University, and Mr. E. C. Carman, Vice-President, AVCO Corp.

Any vacancies on the Transitional Board of Education resulting from resignation or death of a former Davidson County Board of Education member shall be filled by the two remaining such members, or upon their failure to agree, by all remaining Board members.

Any vacancies on the Transitional Board of Education resulting from resignation or death of a former member of the Board of Education of the City of Nashville shall be filled by the two remaining such members, or upon their failure to agree, by all remaining Board members.

Any vacancies in membership resulting from the inability to serve, resignation or death of one of the three (3) members named herein shall be filled by the two remaining such members, or upon their failure to agree, by all remaining Board members; provided that if said vacancy is with respect to the membership of Dr. Walter S. Davis, his successor, as so chosen, shall be either the President or Acting President of A & I State University or of Fisk University or of Meharry Medical School.

During the transitional period, the Board shall operate the two separate school systems herein consolidated in the same manner as the two systems were operated prior to the adoption of this Charter, and with the same powers and authorities as the Board of Education of the City of Nashville and the Davidson County Board of Education previously acted.

During the transitional period the Board shall cause a comprehensive survey to be made of the two school systems to the end that, not later than July 1, 1964:

(1) A complete consolidation of the physical properties thereof may be effected.

(2) The consolidation of personnel and employees thereof may be effected.

The Transitional Board shall also (i) seek applications for the position of Director of Schools and assemble information with respect to the applicants, which applications and information shall be submitted to the Metropolitan Board of Education to the end that its permanent administration may be expedited; and (ii) prepare and submit to the Mayor a budget for the scholastic year 1964-1965.

Any fund to the credit of the Board of Education of the City of Nashville shall be transferred to the credit of the Transitional Board of Education but shall be earmarked and used for the benefit of that portion of the public school system previously operated as City schools. Any fund to the credit of the Davidson County Board of Education shall be transferred to the credit of the Transitional Board but shall be earmarked and used for the benefit of that portion of the public school system previously operated as County schools.

During the transitional period the person then holding the position of County Superintendent of Public Instruction by election of the Quarterly County Court of Davidson County, Tennessee, shall continue to hold such position and to perform and discharge the same duties of that office in connection with that portion of the public school system previously operated as County schools.

During the transitional period that person holding the position of Superintendent of the City School System of the City of Nashville shall continue to hold such position and discharge the duties of that office in connection with the school system previously operated as City schools.

The Transitional Board of Education may assign teachers to schools for the school year 1964-1965 to the extent that the same is practicable on or before June 30, 1964, with such assignments, when not made or completely made, to be finished by the permanent Metropolitan Board of Education.

(c) *Operation by Permanent Board of Education.*—At least sixty (60) days prior to July 1, 1964 the Mayor shall appoint, subject to confirmation by the Council as hereinabove provided in Section 9.02, the first members of the permanent Metropolitan County Board of Education, which shall assume administration, control and operation of the Metropolitan School System.

When the Metropolitan Board of Education fixes the compensation of positions in the school system to be paid after the expiration of the transitional period, consideration shall be given to the varying pay scales and classifications of the former City and of the former county, and whichever pay scale is higher for a particular classification shall be adopted as the original rate for such classification in the consolidated Metropolitan school system.

At the expiration of the transitional period, the Board shall offer professional employment to the person holding the position of County Superintendent of Public Instruction and to the person holding the position of Superintendent of Schools of Nashville. Such employment shall assure a compensation at least equal to that received by the person as County or City Superintendent, for a period of time not less than the unexpired term of office, and shall assign to the position duties and responsibilities commensurate with those attached to the abolished position.

SECTION 20.15. TRANSITION AS TO FISCAL AND RELATED MATTERS.

(a) *Supplemental Appropriations During Fiscal Year Ending June 30, 1963.*—Supplemental appropriations made by the Metropolitan Council to any department, board, commission, office or agency of the Metropolitan Government for the fiscal year ending June 30, 1963 shall be made within the budget structure of the former City of Nashville and former County of Davidson; provided nothing in this Section shall prevent the Metropolitan Government from borrowing money necessary to finance obligations of said Government for said period which may be specifically created by this Charter.

(b) *Budget and Tax Levy for Fiscal Year Ending June 30, 1963.*—The Budget and tax levy of the former City of Nashville shall serve as the Budget and tax levy for the Urban Services District for the fiscal year ending June 30, 1963. The Budget and tax levy for the former County of Davidson shall serve as the Budget and tax levy for the General Services District for the fiscal year ending June 30, 1963. Where functions have been transferred from the Urban Services District to the General Services District, or vice versa, the funds appropriated for such purpose shall follow the function.

(c) *Servicing Bonded Indebtedness During Fiscal Year Ending June 30, 1963.*—Debt service with respect to bonds issued by the City of Nashville shall be paid from the sinking funds of said City during the fiscal year ending June 30, 1963; and debt service with respect to bonds issued by the County of Davidson shall be paid from the sinking funds of said County during the same period, and after June 30, 1963 as set forth in Article 7, Section 7.20.

(d) *Transitional Provisions as to Tax Assessments and Assessors.*—Effective September 1, 1962, the County Tax Assessor shall become the Metropolitan Tax Assessor and shall assume the powers, authority and duties of such office as provided in this Charter.

The assessments made by said Assessor as of January 10, 1963 shall be and constitute the assessments on the basis of which taxes for said year shall be collected within both the Urban Services District and the General Services District and to which taxes levied by the Council for 1963 and thereafter shall apply. Said Assessor is hereby designated and constituted the Metropolitan Tax Assessor, and for this purpose the Charter shall take effect September 1, 1962.

On or after September 1, 1962, or as soon thereafter as practicable, all personnel of the office of Tax Assessor of the former City of Nashville under civil service, except those positions excluded or omitted from civil service under provisions of this Charter, shall be and become civil service employees in the office of the Metropolitan Tax Assessor.

(e) *Preparation of Transitional Forms and Procedures.*—Following the election of the Metropolitan Government officials, the Mayor elect shall request a meeting of the City Finance Director, the County Director of Budgets and Accounts, and the Executive Director of the City and County Planning Commissions for the purpose of proceeding with the preparation of forms, materials and procedures necessary to the official establishment, fiscal functioning and administrative organization of the Metropolitan Government. The services, facilities and staff personnel of the City Finance Department, the City Legal Department, the County Department of Accounts and Budgets, the County Attorney's office, and the Planning Commission of the City and County shall be made available to assist in these preparations.

(f) *The First Annual Operating Budget.*—In the preparation of the operating budget for the 1963-1964 fiscal year the following timetable shall prevail:

(1) By April 15, 1963, the Director of Finance shall distribute the operating budget request forms for both Section I and Section II of the Annual Operating Budget. Said forms to be returned on the date set by the Director of Finance.

(2) Not later than May 28 the Mayor shall submit to the Council the operating budget ordinances and tax levy ordinances following the form and content specified in Section 6.03 as closely as possible within the time available for their preparation.

(3) Public hearings on both the Capital Improvements Budget and Program and the Annual Operating Budget shall be held between June 7 and 15, 1963.

(4) Third reading and final action shall be taken on the Capital Improvements Budget and the 1963-

1964 Annual Operating Budget not later than June 29, 1963.

(g) *The First Capital Improvements Program.*— The City of Nashville and Davidson County Planning Commissions, following the November election of Metropolitan Government officials, shall proceed with gathering the data and information necessary for the preparation of the first Capital Improvements Budget and Program based on the allocation of functions between the General Services District and the Urban Services District.

The Mayor shall submit the Capital Improvements Budget to the Council not later than May 25, 1963.

SECTION 20.16. TRANSITIONAL PROVISIONS AS TO CIVIL SERVICE.

The person holding the position of Director of Personnel by appointment of the Civil Service Commission of the former City of Nashville on the effective date of this Charter, and having civil service status as such, is hereby appointed and designated as the first Director of Personnel provided for by Section 12.04 of this Charter.

Until the Metropolitan Civil Service Commission provided for by Section 12.02 of this Charter is organized by election of a Chairman, the existing City and County Civil Service Commissions shall continue to function. The existing rules, classification plans and pay plans of the City of Nashville and the County of Davidson shall remain in effect until new rules, a new classification plan and a new pay plan shall have been adopted by the Metropolitan Civil Service Commission.

Prior to July 1, 1964, the Civil Service Commission provided for by Section 12.02 of this Charter shall be, and shall function as, the Civil Service Commission with respect to nonprofessional personnel employed by the Board of Health and Board of Hospitals and nonteaching employees of the Board of Education.

SECTION 20.17. TRANSITIONAL PROVISIONS AS TO EMPLOYEE BENEFITS.

The person holding the position of Director of Personnel by appointment of the Civil Service Commission of the former County of Davidson on the effective date of this Charter is hereby appointed and designated as the first Secretary of the Metropolitan Employee Benefit Board.

Within thirty (30) days from the effective date of this Charter, the Director of Personnel, with the approval of either the former Civil Service Commissions of the City of Nashville and the County of Davidson or the Metropolitan Civil Service Commission, shall announce a plan for the conduct of an election as provided in Section 13.03 to select the employee members of the Employee Benefit Board. Said election shall be held within thirty (30) days from such announcement.

Until the Employee Benefit Board is organized by the election of a Chairman, the Civil Service Commission of the former City of Nashville shall continue to administer the Policemen's and Firemen's Pension Fund and the Civil Service Employees' Pension Fund; and the Pension Commission of the former County of Davidson shall continue to administer the Employees' Pension and Insurance Fund, for which purposes both Commissions shall continue to function under their respective rules and regulations and exercise all powers formerly vested in them.

The Metropolitan Government shall have no obligation (except as created by ordinance or resolution of the Metropolitan Council) for pension or retirement benefits of a person not under civil service in the County or City government on March 31, 1962 (except library employees) and brought under civil service by resolution or ordinance of the County or City governing body subsequent to said date. This provision shall not impair the pension and retirement benefits of any person employed by the County or City on said date and then under civil service or of any person who was in process of coming under civil service on said date by then serving a probationary period.

Where compensation for a Metropolitan office is fixed by this Charter, a person holding specified office in the City or County government is appointed thereto by this Charter and the compensation herein fixed is an increase over the compensation which such County or City officer was entitled to receive as of March 31, 1962, then the obligation of the Metropolitan Government for retirement benefits to such person shall be based upon the compensation paid him by the County or City as of March 31, 1962, until such person shall have served as a Metropolitan officer for five (5) years or more. After said five (5) years, such benefits shall be based upon compensation paid by the Metropolitan Government.

SECTION 20.18. **TRANSITION AS TO QUARTERLY COUNTY COURT.** The Quarterly County Court, composed of justices of the peace from civil districts and municipal corporations as prescribed by Section 16.04, shall be elected at the next regular August election for justices of the peace, to take office on September 1 following their election. The members of the Quarterly County Court as constituted prior to this Charter shall continue to serve until the expiration of their terms of office, but after the effective date of this Charter the functions, powers and duties of the Quarterly County Court shall be as provided by Section 16.04 hereof.

SECTION 20.19. **COMPENSATION AND PENSION RIGHTS OF CITY MAYOR AND CITY COUNCILMEN PRESERVED.** The Mayor and members of the City Council of the City of Nashville, whose terms of office are abridged by this Charter to the extent of approximately two (2) months, shall be entitled to receive salaries from the Metropolitan Government and to be eligible to receive pensions therefrom to the same extent as if they had served for the full term to which elected; provided that if any of said City officers shall be elected to office at the first election for Metropolitan officers, they shall not receive both the salary herein provided and the salary of the Metropolitan office to which elected.

SECTION 20.20. **SPECIAL METROPOLITAN ELECTION AND TERM OF OFFICE OF PERSONS THEN ELECTED.** There shall be a special Metropolitan election on the first Tuesday after the first Monday in November, 1962, for the purpose of electing the first Mayor, the first Vice-Mayor and forty (40) members of the first Met-

ropolitan Council, including five (5) councilmen-at-large and thirty-five (35) district councilmen. Said special election and a run-off election thereafter to be held twenty-one (21) days later, if necessary, shall be held under the provisions of Article 15 of this Charter with respect to Metropolitan elections. The Metropolitan officers elected at said special election shall take office on the first Monday of April, 1963, and shall serve until the first day of September, 1966, or until their successors are elected and qualified.

For the purpose of determining the eligibility for a pension of the first Mayor elected hereunder, and for the purposes of Section 5.06 of this Charter his term shall be deemed to be a term of four (4) years.

SECTION 20.21. **EFFECTIVE DATE OF CHARTER.** This Charter shall become effective immediately upon its adoption for purposes of Section 18.15, Section 20.02, Section 20.14 and Section 20.15 hereof. This Charter shall become effective for all other purposes on the first Monday in April, 1963, which date is hereby defined and designated as "the effective date of this Charter" within the meaning of such quoted phrase as used in this Charter.

Article 21

INTENT OF CHARTER AND SEPARABILITY OF PROVISIONS

SECTION 21.01. The people residing within the area of the Metropolitan Government declare and determine that by the adoption of this Charter it is their intent to exercise to the full extent possible the constitutional power granted by Amendment No. 8 to Article XI, Section 9 of the Constitution of Tennessee approved at an election on November 3, 1953, as implemented by Tennessee Code Annotated, Sections 6-3701, et seq., and in so doing to consolidate all or substantially all of the governmental and corporate functions of the County of Davidson and of the City of Nashville, so that, in the interest of modern, efficient and economical government, the same may be operated as one governmental entity. The people further declare that to achieve this remedial objective and to aid in the solution of the public problems of a metropolitan area, it is their purpose and intent in its adoption that this Charter shall continue in full force and effect even if any of its separable provisions or parts not essential to this remedial objective shall be held unconstitutional or void.

Metropolitan Dade County Government

A twelve-year attempt to cope with metropolitan growth in the Miami area preceded the creation of the metropolitan Dade County government in 1957. Proposals to consolidate the City of Miami and Dade County were made in 1945, 1947, and 1953, but were defeated.

In July 1953, the Miami City Commission created the Metropolitan Miami Municipal Board and authorized it to draft a plan for the improvement of the governmental system of Dade County. The Board contracted with the Public Administration Service of Chicago for the preparation of a report. The report, completed in 1954, recommended the creation of a metropolitan government. The Florida Legislature, on June 23, 1955, approved a Dade County home rule constitutional amendment, and Florida voters ratified the amendment by a vote of 244,817 to 120,343 on November 6, 1956. With less than one-fourth of Dade County voters participating in a May 21, 1957 referendum, the proposed charter providing for a commission-manager county government with metropolitan powers was approved by a vote of 44,404 to 42,620.

The conflict over the question of a metropolitan government was not ended by voter approval of the new charter. Various cities challenged the constitutionality of the new government and a total of 155 suits affecting the operation of the new government were decided during its first three years; none was successful.

The failure of the law suits did not dissuade the opponents of the new county government who next sought to emasculate it by charter amendments. By a vote of 74,420 to 48,893, Dade County voters on September 30, 1958 defeated an autonomy amendment, proposed by the Dade County League of Municipalities, which would have denied the county government jurisdiction over functions performed by cities prior to May 21, 1957. Approval of the amendment would have restricted Dade County's powers to unincorporated areas.

A more serious threat to the new government was the "McLeod" amendment which proposed thirty-seven changes in the charter including replacement of the commission-manager plan by a five-member commission, popular election of the sheriff and tax collector, and removal of the County's jurisdiction over a number of area-wide functions—sewage, water supply, and transportation. The proposed amendment was defeated, on October 17, 1961, by a slim margin: 105,097 to 97,170.

Attempts to weaken the new government were not terminated by the defeat of the "McLeod" amendment. On August 21, 1962, voters approved two charter amendments which weakened the power of the county manager; his appointments of department heads and administrative orders combining or creating departments were made subject to the approval of the county commission. The first amendment was approved by a vote of 32,845 to 30,804 and the second by 32,272 to 30,852. Three other proposed amendments were defeated.

On November 5, 1963, the voters approved four and defeated six proposed charter amendments. Approved amendments provide for an elective sheriff, election of one commissioner from each of eight districts by the voters of the county-at-large, an increase in the number of signatures required on petitions for charter amendments, and a new system for the selection of judges of the metropolitan courts.

PREAMBLE

We, the people of this County, in order to secure for ourselves the benefits and responsibilities of home rule, to create a metropolitan government to serve our present and future needs, and to endow our municipalities with the rights of self determination in their local affairs, do under God adopt this home rule Charter.

Article 1

BOARD OF COUNTY COMMISSIONERS

SECTION 1.01. **POWERS.**

A. The Board of County Commissioners shall be the legislative and the governing body of the county and shall have the power to carry on a central metropolitan government. This power shall include but shall not be restricted to the power to:

1. Provide and regulate arterial, toll, and other roads, bridges, tunnels, and related facilities; eliminate grade crossings; provide and regulate parking facilities; and develop and enforce master plans for the control of traffic and parking.
2. Provide and operate air, water, rail, and bus terminals, port facilities, and public transportation systems.
3. License and regulate taxis, jitneys, limousines for hire, rental cars, and other passenger vehicles for hire operating in the unincorporated areas of the county.
4. Provide central records, training, and communications for fire and police protection; provide traffic control and central crime investigation; provide fire stations, jails, and related facilities; and subject to Section 1.01A(18) provide a uniform system for fire and police protection.
5. Prepare and enforce comprehensive plans for the development of the county.
6. Provide hospitals and uniform health and welfare programs.
7. Provide parks, preserves, playgrounds, recreation areas, libraries, museums, and other recreational and cultural facilities and programs.
8. Establish and administer housing, slum clearance,

urban renewal, conservation, flood and beach erosion control, air pollution control, and drainage programs and cooperate with governmental agencies and private enterprises in the development and operation of these programs.

9. Provide and regulate or permit municipalities to provide and regulate waste and sewage collection and disposal and water supply and conservation programs.

10. Levy and collect taxes and special assessments, borrow and expend money and issue bonds, revenue certificates, and other obligations of indebtedness in such manner, and subject to such limitations, as may be provided by law.

11. By ordinance, establish, merge, and abolish special purpose districts within which may be provided police and fire protection, beach erosion control, recreation facilities, water, streets, sidewalks, street lighting, waste and sewage collection and disposal, drainage, and other essential facilities and services. All county funds for such districts shall be provided by service charges, special assessments, or general tax levies within such districts only. The Board of County Commissioners shall be the governing body of all such districts and when acting as such governing body shall have the same jurisdiction and powers as when acting as the Board.

12. Establish, coordinate, and enforce zoning and such business regulations as are necessary for the protection of the public.

13. Adopt and enforce uniform building and related technical codes and regulations for both the incorporated and unincorporated areas of the county; provide for examinations for contractors and all parties engaged in the building trades and for the issuance of certificates of competency and their revocation after hearing. Such certificates shall be recognized and required for the issuance of a license in all municipalities in the county. No municipality shall be entitled to require examinations or any additional certificate of competency or impose any other conditions for the issuance of a municipal license except the payment of the customary fee. The municipality may issue building permits and conduct the necessary inspections in accordance with the uniform codes and charge fees therefor.

14. Regulate, control, take over, and grant franchises to, or itself operate gas, light, power, telephone, and other utilities, sanitary and sewage collection and disposal systems, water supply, treatment, and service systems, and public transportation systems, provided, however, that:

(a) Franchises under this subsection may only be granted by a two-thirds vote of the members of the Board present and approved by a majority vote of those qualified electors voting at either a special or general election.

(b) The county shall not operate a light, power, or telephone utility to serve any territory in the county which is being supplied with similar service except by a majority vote of those qualified electors voting in an election held not less than six months after the Board has passed an ordinance to that effect by a two-thirds vote of the members of the Board present. Such ordinance shall contain information on cost, method of financing, agency to regulate rates, agency to operate, location, and other infor-

mation necessary to inform the general public of the feasibility and practicability of the proposed operation.

15. Use public funds for the purposes of promoting the development of the county, including advertising the area's advantages.

16. Establish and enforce regulations for the sale of alcoholic beverages in the unincorporated areas and approve municipal regulations on hours of sale of alcoholic beverages.

17. Enter into contracts with other governmental units within or outside the boundaries of the county for joint performance or performance by one unit in behalf of the other of any authorized function.

18. Set reasonable minimum standards for all governmental units in the county for the performance of any service or function. The standards shall not be discriminatory as between similar areas. If a governmental unit fails to comply with such standards, and does not correct such failure after reasonable notice by the Board, then the Board may take over and perform, regulate, or grant franchises to operate any such service. The Board may also take over and operate, or grant franchises to operate any municipal service if:

(a) In an election called by the Board of County Commissioners within the municipality a majority of those voting vote in favor of turning the service over to the county; or

(b) The governing body of the municipality requests the county to take over the service by a two-thirds vote of its members, or by referendum.

19. (a) By ordinance, abolish or consolidate the office of constables, or any county office created by the Legislature, or provide for the consolidation and transfer of any of the functions of such officers, provided, however, that there shall be no power to abolish the Superintendent of Public Instruction, Sheriff, or to abolish or impair the jurisdiction of the Circuit Court or to abolish any other Court, provided by the Constitution or by general law, or the judges or clerks thereof.

(b) A special election shall be held in Dade County, Florida, no later than 30 days from the passage of this amendment in order to elect the Sheriff. The Metropolitan Sheriff shall continue to hold office, until the election of the Sheriff, as provided above and his qualification and assuming office as provided by the general laws of the State of Florida. Election dates for the office of Sheriff will thereafter coincide with the primary and general elections of the State of Florida, and the election and duties and office of Sheriff shall be governed by the laws of the State of Florida.

(c) Upon the election of Sheriff, and his taking office, as herein provided, all existing ordinances inconsistent herewith shall no longer remain in force and effect.

20. Make investigations of county affairs, inquire into the conduct, accounts, records, and transactions of any department or office of the county, and for these purposes require reports from all county officers and employees, subpoena witnesses, administer oaths, and require the production of records.

21. Exercise all powers and privileges granted to municipalities, counties, and county officers by the Constitution and laws of the state, and all powers

not prohibited by the Constitution or by this Charter.

22. Adopt such ordinances and resolutions as may be required in the exercise of its powers, and prescribe fines and penalties for the violation of ordinances.

23. Perform any other acts consistent with law which are required by this Charter or which are in the common interest of the people of the county.

24. Supersede, nullify, or amend any special law applying to this county, or any general law applying only to this county, or any general law where specifically authorized by the Constitution.

B. No enumeration of powers in this Charter shall be deemed exclusive or restrictive and the foregoing powers shall be deemed to include all implied powers necessary and proper to carrying out such powers. All of these powers may be exercised in the incorporated and unincorporated areas, subject to the procedures herein provided in certain cases relating to municipalities.

C. The Board shall have the power of eminent domain and the right to condemn property for public purposes. The Board shall make fair and just compensation for any properties acquired in the exercise of its powers, duties, or functions. The Board shall also provide for the acquisition or transfer of property, the payment, assumption, or other satisfaction of the debts, and the protection of pension rights of affected employees of any governmental unit which is merged, consolidated, or abolished or whose boundaries are changed or functions or powers transferred.

D. The Board shall be entitled to levy in the unincorporated areas all taxes authorized to be levied by municipalities and to receive from the state any revenues collected in the unincorporated areas on the same basis as municipalities.

SECTION 1.02. RESOLUTIONS AND ORDINANCES.

A. The Board shall adopt its own rules of procedure and shall decide which actions of the Board shall be by ordinance or resolution, except as otherwise provided in this Charter and except that any action of the Board which provides for raising revenue, appropriating funds, or incurring indebtedness, or which provides a penalty or establishes a rule or regulation for the violation of which a penalty is imposed shall be by ordinance.

B. Every ordinance shall be introduced in writing and shall contain a brief title. The enacting clause shall be "Be it Ordained by the Board." After passage on first reading, a short summary of the ordinance shall be published in a daily newspaper of general circulation at least once together with a notice of the time when and place where it will be given a public hearing and be considered for final passage. The first such publication shall be at least one week prior to the time advertised for hearing. No ordinance shall be declared invalid by reason of any defect in publication or title if the published summary gives reasonable notice of its intent.

C. At the time and place so advertised, or at any time and place to which such public hearing may from time to time be adjourned, the ordinance shall be read by title and a public hearing shall be held. After the hearing, the Board may pass the ordinance with or without amendment.

D. The Board may adopt in whole or in part any published code by reference as an ordinance in the manner provided by law.

E. The effective date of any ordinance shall be prescribed therein, but the effective date shall not be earlier than ten days after its enactment.

F. To meet a public emergency affecting life, health, property, or public safety the Board by two-thirds vote of the members of the Board may adopt an emergency ordinance at the meeting at which it is introduced, and may make it effective immediately, except that no such ordinance may be used to levy taxes, grant or extend a franchise, or authorize the borrowing of money. After the adoption of an emergency ordinance, the Board shall have it published in full within ten days in a daily newspaper of general circulation.

G. Each ordinance and resolution after adoption shall be given a serial number and shall be entered by the clerk in a properly indexed record kept for that purpose.

H. Within two years after adoption of this Charter the Board shall have prepared a general codification of all county ordinances and resolutions having the effect of law. The general codification thus prepared shall be adopted by the Board in a single ordinance. After adoption the Board shall have the codification printed immediately in an appropriate manner together with the Charter and such rules and regulations as the Board may direct. Additions or amendments to the code shall be prepared, adopted, and printed at least every two years.

SECTION 1.03. DISTRICTS.

A. There shall be eight County Commission districts. The initial boundaries of these districts shall be as shown on the map attached as Exhibit A and made a part hereof.

B. The Board may by ordinance adopted by two-thirds vote of the members of the Board change the boundaries of the districts from time to time. The boundaries shall be fixed on the basis of the character, population, and geography of the districts.

SECTION 1.04. COMPOSITION OF THE BOARD.

The Board shall consist of nine members elected as follows:

1. From each of the eight districts there shall be elected by the qualified electors of the county at large a County Commissioner who shall be a qualified elector residing within the district at least six months and within the county at least three years before qualifying.

2. There shall be elected by the qualified electors of the county at large a Mayor who shall be a qualified elector residing within the county at least three years before qualifying. The Mayor shall also serve as a member of the Board and shall be subject to all restrictions provided in this Charter applying to all other Commissioners.

Beginning with the state primary elections in 1968, the Mayor and each Commissioner shall be elected for a term of four years.

SECTION 1.05. FORFEITURE OF OFFICE.

A. Any members of the Board of County Commissioners who ceases to be a qualified voter of the county or removes himself from the county or the district from which he was elected, or who fails to attend meetings without good cause for a period of six months, shall immediately forfeit his office. Any Commissioner except the Mayor who ceases to reside in the district which he represents shall also immediately forfeit his office.

B. Any elected or appointed county official who holds any other elective office, whether federal, state or municipal, shall forfeit his county position, provided that the provisions of this subsection shall not apply to any officials presently holding such other office during the remainder of their present terms.

C. Any appointed official or employee of Dade County who qualifies as a candidate for election to any federal, state or municipal office shall immediately forfeit his county position.

SECTION 1.06. SALARY.

Each County Commissioner shall receive a salary of $6,000

per year payable monthly and shall be entitled to be reimbursed for such reasonable and necessary expenses as may be approved by the Board.

SECTION 1.07. VACANCIES.

Any vacancy in the office of Mayor or the other members of the Board shall be filled by majority vote of the remaining members of the Board within 30 days, or the Board shall call an election to be held not more than 45 days thereafter to fill the vacancy. The person chosen to fill the office vacated must at the time of his appointment meet the residence requirements for the office to which he is appointed. If the person is appointed, he shall serve only until the next state primary election. If the person is elected, he shall serve for the remainder of the unexpired term of the office to which he is elected.

SECTION 1.08. ORGANIZATION OF THE BOARD.

The Mayor shall be Chairman of the Board. The Board shall select a vice-chairman who shall serve at the pleasure of the Board and who shall be known as Vice Mayor. The Clerk of the Circuit Court or his deputy shall serve as clerk of the Board. No action of the Board shall be taken except by a majority vote of those present at a meeting at which a majority of the Commissioners then in office is present. All meetings shall be public.

Article 2

ELECTIONS

SECTION 2.01. ELECTION AND COMMENCEMENT OF TERMS OF COUNTY COMMISSIONERS.

A. Except as otherwise provided in the Charter, beginning in 1968, the election for the offices of Mayor and County Commissioner shall be held every four years at the time of the state primary elections.

B. A candidate must receive a majority of the votes cast to be elected. If no candidate receives a majority of the votes cast there will be a runoff election at the time of the state second primary election between the two candidates receiving the highest number of votes. Should a tie result, the outcome shall be determined by lot.

C. Except as otherwise provided in this Charter, the terms of office of the Mayor and the other County Commissioners shall commence on the second Tuesday next succeeding the date provided for the state second primary election.

SECTION 2.02. ELECTION OF COUNTY COMMISSIONERS FROM MUNICIPALITIES.

Repealed at special election November 5, 1963.

SECTION 2.03. NONPARTISAN ELECTIONS.

All elections for Mayor and the other members of the Board shall be nonpartisan and no ballot shall show the party designation of any candidate. No candidate shall be required to pay any party assessment or state the party of which he is a member or the manner in which he voted or will vote in any election.

SECTION 2.04. QUALIFICATIONS AND FILING FEE.

All candidates for the office of Mayor or County Commissioner shall qualify with the Clerk of the Circuit Court no earlier than the 63rd day and no later than noon on the 49th day prior to the date of the election at which he is a candidate in the method provided by law or ordinance, and shall pay a filing fee of $300. All filing fees shall be paid into the general funds of the county.

SECTION 2.05. INVALIDITY.

Repealed at special election November 5, 1963.

SECTION 2.06. ADDITIONAL REGULATIONS AND STATE LAWS.

A. The Board may adopt by ordinance any additional regulations governing elections not inconsistent with this Charter.

B. Except as otherwise provided by this Charter or by ordinance adopted hereunder the provisions of the election laws of this state shall apply to elections held under this Charter.

SECTION 2.07. CANVASSING ELECTIONS.

All elections under this Charter shall be canvassed by the Board of County Commissioners, the Clerk of the Circuit Court, and one County Judge sitting as a canvassing board.

Article 3

THE COUNTY MANAGER

SECTION 3.01. APPOINTMENT AND REMOVAL.

The Board of County Commissioners shall appoint a County Manager who shall be the chief executive officer and head of the administrative branch of the county government. The Board shall fix the Manager's compensation, and he shall serve at the will of the Board.

SECTION 3.02. QUALIFICATIONS.

The Manager shall be chosen by the Board on the basis of his executive and administrative qualifications. At the time of his appointment he need not be a resident of the state. No County Commissioner shall be eligible for the position of Manager during or within two years after the expiration of his latest term as Commissioner.

SECTION 3.03. ABSENCE OF MANAGER.

The Board may designate a qualified administrative officer of the county to assume the duties and authority of the Manager during periods of temporary absence or disability of the Manager.

SECTION 3.04. POWERS AND DUTIES.

A. The Manager shall be responsible to the Board of County Commissioners for the administration of all units of the county government under his jurisdiction, and for carrying out policies adopted by the Board. The Manager, or such other persons as may be designated by resolution of the Board, shall execute contracts and other instruments, sign bonds and other evidences of indebtedness, and accept process.

B. Unless otherwise provided for by civil service rules and regulations, the Manager shall have the power to appoint and suspend all administrative department heads of the major departments of the county, to-wit: Tax Collector, Tax Assessor, Department of Public Works, Department of Public Safety, Building and Zoning Department, Planning Department, Finance Department, Park and Recreation Department and Internal Auditing Department, except that before any appointment shall become effective, the said appointment must be approved by the County Commission and if the same is disapproved the said appointment shall be void. In the event such appointment shall be disapproved by the County Commision the appointment shall forthwith become null and void and thereupon the County Manager shall make a new appointment or appointments, each of which shall likewise be submitted for approval by the County Commission. However, the right to suspend, remove or discharge any department head with or without cause, is reserved at all times to the County Manager.

SECTION 3.05. RESTRICTION ON BOARD MEMBERS.

Neither the Board nor any of its members shall direct or request the appointment of any person to, or his removal from, office by the Manager or any of his subordinates, or take part in the appointment or removal of officers and employees in the administrative services of the county. Except for the purpose of inquiry, as provided in Section 1.01A(20), the Board and its members shall deal with the administrative service solely through the Manager and neither the Board nor any members thereof shall give orders to any subordinates of the Manager, either publicly or privately. Any wilful violation of the provisions of this Section by a member of the Board shall be grounds for his removal from office by an action brought in the Circuit Court by the State Attorney of this County.

Article 4

ADMINISTRATIVE ORGANIZATION AND PROCEDURE

SECTION 4.01. DEPARTMENTS.

There shall be departments of finance, personnel, planning, law, and such other departments as may be established by administrative order of the Manager. All functions not otherwise specifically assigned to others by this Charter shall be performed under the supervision of the Manager.

SECTION 4.02. ADMINISTRATIVE PROCEDURE.

The Manager shall have the power to issue and place into effect administrative orders, rules, and regulations. The organization and operating procedure of departments shall be set forth in administrative regulations which the Manager shall develop, place into effect by administrative orders, and submit to the Board. The Board may, by resolution, modify such orders, rules, or regulations providing, however, no such orders, rules or regulations creating, merging, or combining departments, shall become effective until approved by resolution of the Board.

SECTION 4.03. FINANCIAL ADMINISTRATION.

A. The department of finance shall be headed by a finance director appointed by the Manager. The finance director shall have charge of the financial affairs of the county.

B. Not less than 120 days before the beginning of the fiscal year, the Manager shall recommend to the Board a proposed budget presenting a complete financial plan, including capital and operating budgets, for the ensuing fiscal year. A summary of the budget shall be published and the Board shall hold hearings on and adopt a budget.

C. No money shall be drawn from the county treasury nor shall any obligation for the expenditure of money be incurred except pursuant to appropriation and except that the Board may establish working capital, revolving, pension, or trust funds and may provide that expenditures from such funds can be made without specific appropriation. The Board, by ordinance, may transfer any unencumbered appropriation balance, or any portion thereof, from one department, fund, or agency to another, subject to the provisions of ordinance. Any portion of the earnings or balance of the several funds, other than sinking funds for obligations not yet retired, may be transferred to the general funds of the county by the Board.

D. Contracts for public improvements and purchase of supplies, materials, and services other than professional shall be made whenever practicable on the basis of specifications and competitive bids. Formal sealed bids shall be secured for all such contracts and purchases when the transaction involves the expenditure of $1,000 or more. The transaction shall be evidenced by written contract submitted and approved by the Board. The Board, upon written recommendation of the Manager, may by resolution adopted by two-thirds vote of the members present waive competitive bidding when it finds this to be in the best interest of the county.

E. Any county official or employee of the county who has a special financial interest, direct or indirect, in any action by the Board shall make known that interest and shall refrain from voting upon or otherwise participating in such transaction. Wilful violation of this Section shall constitute malfeasance in office, shall effect forfeiture of office or position, and render the transaction voidable by the Board.

F. Such officers and employees of the county as the Board may designate shall give bond in the amount and with the surety prescribed by the Board. The bond premiums shall be paid by the county.

G. At the end of each fiscal year the Board shall provide for an audit by an independent certified public accountant designated by the Board of the accounts and finances of the county for the fiscal year just completed.

H. The Budget Commission created by Chapter 21874, Laws of Florida, 1943, is hereby abolished, and Chapter 21874 shall no longer be of any effect.

SECTION 4.04. ASSESSMENT AND COLLECTION OF TAXES.

A. Beginning with the tax year 1961, the county tax rolls prepared by the county shall be the only legal tax rolls in this county for the assessment and collection of county and municipal taxes. Thereafter no municipality shall have an assessor or prepare an ad valorem tax roll. Each municipality shall continue to have the right to adopt its own budget, fix its own millage, and levy its own taxes. Each municipality shall certify its levies to the County Manager not later than 30 days after the county tax rolls have been finally approved by the Board. Any municipality may obtain a copy of this tax roll upon payment of the cost of preparing such a copy, and copies of the tax roll shall be available for public inspection at reasonable times. Maps showing the assessed valuation of each parcel of property may be prepared and made available for sale to the public at a reasonable price.

B. All county and municipal taxes for the tax year beginning January 1, 1961, and all subsequent tax years, shall be collected by the county on one bill prepared and sent out by the county. The amounts of county and municipal taxes shall be shown as separate items, and may be paid separately.

C. Delinquent municipal taxes shall be collected in the same manner as delinquent county taxes.

D. All the tax revenues collected for any municipality shall be returned monthly by the county to the municipality.

SECTION 4.05. DEPARTMENT OF PERSONNEL.

A. The Board of County Commissioners shall establish and maintain personnel and civil service, retirement, and group insurance programs. The personnel system of the county shall be based on merit principles in order to foster effective career service in county employment and to employ those persons best qualified for county services which they are to perform.

B. The County Manager shall appoint a personnel director who shall head the department of personnel and whose duty it shall be to administer the personnel and civil service programs and the rules governing them. The standards of such programs shall not be less than those prevailing at the time of the effective date of this Charter.

C. Except as provided herein, Chapter 30255, General Laws, 1955, as it exists on the effective date of this Charter, shall remain in effect until amended or changed by ordinance of the Board of County Commissioners adopted by two-thirds vote of the members present after recommendation from either the Personnel Advisory Board or the County Manager.

D. Employees of municipalities who, by merger, transfer, or assignment of governmental units or functions become county employees, shall not lose the civil service rights or privileges which have accrued to them during their period of employment with such municipality and the county shall use its best efforts to employ these employees within the limits of their capabilities. However, if because of the merger of a department or division of a municipality with the county, all of the employees of such department or division are unable to be employed by the county either because of lack of funds or lack of work, the employee possessing the greater amount of service shall be retained in accordance with civil service rules and regulations. Those employees who are not retained shall be placed on a priority list for employment by the county subject to seniority. Any non-retained employee shall have the option, if a vacancy occurs or exists in another department, and if he is qualified to render the service required, to either accept such employment or remain on the priority list until such time as employment shall be available for him in his own or similar classification.

E. The pension plan presently provided by the state for county employees shall not be impaired by the Board. Employees of municipalities, who by merger, transfer, or assignment of governmental units or functions become county employees shall not lose their pension rights, or any reserves accrued to their benefit during their period of employment with such municipality. The Board of County Commissioners shall provide a method by which these employees rights and reserves shall be protected, and these employees shall continue until retirement, dismissal, or death in a pension status no less beneficial than the status held by them at the time of merger or assignment.

F. The Board of County Commissioners shall provide and place into effect a practical group insurance plan for all county employees.

SECTION 4.06. DEPARTMENT OF LAW.

There shall be a county attorney appointed by the Board of County Commissioners who shall serve at the will of the Board and who shall head the department of law. He shall devote his full time to the service of the county and shall serve as legal counsel to the Board, Manager, and all county departments, offices, and agencies, and perform such other legal duties as may be assigned to him. With the approval of the Board, he may appoint such assistants as may be necessary in order that his duties may be performed properly. The Board may employ special counsel for specific needs.

SECTION 4.07. DEPARTMENT OF PLANNING.

The department of planning shall be headed by a planning director appointed by the County Manager. The planning director shall be qualified in the field of planning by special training and experience. Under the supervision of the Manager and with the advice of the Planning Advisory Board elsewhere provided for in this Charter, the planning director shall among other things:

1. Conduct studies of county population, land use, facilities, resources, and needs and other factors which influence the county's development, and on the basis of such studies prepare such official and other maps and reports as, taken together, constitute a master plan for the welfare, recreational, economic, and physical development of the county.

2. Prepare for review by the Planning Advisory Board, and for adoption by the Board of County Commissioners, zoning, subdivision and related regulations for the unincorporated areas of the county and minimum standards governing zoning, subdivision, and related regulations for the municipalities; and prepare recommendations to effectuate the master plan and to coordinate the county's proposed capital improvements with the master plan.

3. Review the municipal systems of planning, zoning, subdivision, and related regulations and make recommendations thereon with a view to coordinating such municipal systems with one another and with those of the county.

SECTION 4.08. BOARDS.

The Board of County Commissioners shall by ordinance create a Planning Advisory Board, a Zoning Appeals Board, and such other boards as it may deem necessary, prescribing in each case the number, manner of appointment, length of term, and advisory or quasi-judicial duties of members of such boards, who shall serve without compensation but who may be reimbursed for necessary expenses incurred in official duties, as may be determined and approved by the Board of County Commissioners.

Article 5

MUNICIPALITIES

SECTION 5.01. CONTINUANCE OF MUNICIPALITIES.

The municipalities in the county shall remain in existence so long as their electors desire. No municipality in the county shall be abolished without approval of a majority of its electors voting in an election called for that purpose. The right of self determination in local affairs is reserved and preserved to the municipalities except as otherwise provided in this Charter.

SECTION 5.02. MUNICIPAL POWERS.

Each municipality shall have the authority to exercise all powers relating to its local affairs not inconsistent with this Charter. Each municipality may provide for higher standards of zoning, service, and regulation than those provided by the Board of County Commissioners in order that its individual character and standards may be preserved for its citizens.

SECTION 5.03. MUNICIPAL CHARTERS.

A. Except as provided in Section 5.04, any municipality in the county may adopt, amend, or revoke a charter for its own government or abolish its existence in the following manner. Its governing body shall, within 120 days after adopting a resolution or after the certification of a petition of ten percent of the qualified electors of the municipality, draft or have drafted by a method determined by municipal ordinance a proposed charter, amendment, revocation, or abolition which shall be submitted to the electors of the municipalities. Unless an election occurs not less than 60 nor more than 120 days after the draft is submitted, the proposal shall be submitted at a special election within that time. The governing body shall make copies of the proposal available to the electors not less than 30 days before the election. Alternative proposals may be submitted. Each proposal approved by a majority of the electors voting on such proposal shall become effective at the time fixed in the proposal.

B. All municipal charters, amendments thereto, and repeals thereof shall be filed with the Clerk of the Circuit Court.

SECTION 5.04. CHANGES IN MUNICIPAL BOUNDARIES.

A. The planning director shall study municipal boundaries with a view to recommending their orderly adjustment, improvement, and establishment. Proposed boundary changes may be initiated by the Planning Advisory Board, the Board of County Commissioners, the governing body of a municipality, or by a petition of any person or group concerned.

B. The Board of County Commissioners, after obtaining the approval of the municipal governing bodies concerned, after hearing the recommendations of the Planning Advisory Board, and after a public hearing, may by ordinance effect boundary changes, unless the change involves the annexation or separation of an area of which more than 250 residents are electors, in which case an affirmative vote of a majority of those electors voting shall also be required. Upon any such boundary change any conflicting boundaries set forth in the charter of such municipality shall be considered amended.

C. No municipal boundary shall be altered except as provided by this Section.

SECTION 5.05. CREATION OF NEW MUNICIPALITIES.

The Board of County Commissioners and only the Board may authorize the creation of new municipalities in the unincorporated areas of the county after hearing the recommendations of the Planning Advisory Board, after a public hearing, and after an affirmative vote of a majority of the electors voting and residing within the proposed boundaries. The Board of County Commissioners shall appoint a charter commission, consisting of five electors residing within the proposed boundaries, who shall propose a charter to be submitted to the electors in the manner provided in Section 5.03. The new municipality shall have all the powers and rights granted to or not withheld from municipalities by this Charter and the Constitution and general laws of the State of Florida.

SECTION 5.06. CONTRACTS WITH OTHER UNITS OF GOVERNMENT.

Every municipality in this county shall have the power to enter into contracts with other governmental units within or outside the boundaries of the municipality or the county for the joint performance or performance by one unit in behalf of the other of any municipal function.

SECTION 5.07. FRANCHISE AND UTILITY TAXES.

Revenues realized from franchise and utility taxes imposed by municipalities shall belong to municipalities.

Article 6

METROPOLITAN COURT

SECTION 6.01. METROPOLITAN COURT ESTABLISHED.

A court is hereby established, the name of which shall be the Metropolitan Court.

SECTION 6.02. QUALIFICATIONS OF JUDGES.

Metropolitan Court judges shall be citizens of the United States and of the State of Florida for three years and of the County of Dade one year, licensed to practice law in the state for at least eight years and possess any additional qualifications prescribed by law.

SECTION 6.03. NOMINATION AND APPOINTMENT.

A. The Board of County Commissioners shall fill any vacancy in an office of Metropolitan Court judge by appointing one of three nominees for each vacancy presented to it by the Metropolitan Court Nominating Council.

B. If within 60 days from the date a vacancy occurs the Metropolitan Court Nominating Council fails to submit to the Board of County Commissioners three nominees for any such vacancy, then the Board of County Commissioners shall fill

such vacancy by appointment in any manner not otherwise inconsistent with the provisions of this Article.

C. If the Board of County Commissioners shall fail to make an appointment within 60 days from the date the list of nominees is presented to it, the appointment shall be made by the Chairman of the Metropolitan Court Nominating Council from the same list of nominees.

SECTION 6.04. APPROVAL OR REJECTION.

A. Declaration of Candidacy.

1. Any Metropolitan Court judge who desires to continue in office after the expiration of his term, and as a condition precedent thereto, shall file with the Clerk of the Board of County Commissioners a written Declaration of Candidacy for election to succeed himself not less than 60 days nor more than 90 days preceding the date of the first state primary election at which his name is to be submitted to the electors.

B. Term of Office.

1. Each Metropolitan Court judge shall, in the manner provided by law, be subject to approval or rejection on a nonpartisan ballot at the first state primary election held more than one year after his appointment.

2. Thereafter, each Metropolitan Court judge shall be subject to approval or rejection in a like manner every sixth year, provided, however, that upon the initial election held after the effective date of this Article the seven candidates receiving the highest number of affirmative votes shall each be elected for a six year term and the remaining six candidates shall each be elected for a four year term. Should a tie result, the outcome shall be determined by lot.

C. Form of Ballot.

At each election for judge, the ballot should be as follows: Shall Judge (name of Judge) of the Metropolitan Court be retained in office?

      YES_____ NO_____

SECTION 6.05. VACANCY.

The offices of all incumbent judges of the Metropolitan Court become vacant on May 1, 1964, provided, however, that the judges of the Metropolitan Court then in office may remain in office until their respective successors are appointed in the manner as herein provided. Thereafter, a vacancy occurs upon the happening of any of the following:

1. Ninety days after the election at which a judge is rejected by a majority of those voting on the question;

2. Upon the expiration date of the term of a judge who fails to file a written Declaration of Candidacy to succeed himself;

3. An increase in the number of judges by the Board of County Commissioners;

4. The death, resignation, retirement, removal from office or recall of any judge.

SECTION 6.06. METROPOLITAN COURT NOMINATING COUNCIL

A. Duty.

There shall be a Metropolitan Court Nominating Council, the primary duty of which shall be to prepare a list of three nominees for each vacancy occurring on the Metropolitan Court Bench for submission to the Board of County Commissioners.

B. Members, Number, Type and Selection.

1. The Metropolitan Court Nominating Council shall serve without compensation except for reimbursement for necessary expenses incurred in official duties, and shall consist of nine as follows:

(a) The Presiding Circuit Judge of the Eleventh Judicial Circuit in and for Dade County shall act as Chairman. In the event the Presiding Circuit Judge shall fail to accept the appointment, or having assumed office shall for any reason cease to continue to act or there be no Presiding Circuit Court Judge, the Board of County Commissioners shall appoint any judge of the Eleventh Judicial Circuit in and for Dade County, Florida, to act as Chairman;

(b) Three active members of The Florida Bar, in good standing, residing in Dade County, shall be elected by the active members of The Florida Bar, in good standing, residing in Dade County, under such procedure as established by the Board of County Commissioners.

(c) Five shall be residents of Dade County, not admitted to practice law, who shall be appointed by the Board of County Commisisoners.

C. Members' Terms.

The members of the Metropolitan Court Nominating Council shall be appointed or elected within 45 days of the effective date of this Article and the initial terms of office for members of the Metropolitan Court Nominating Council, other than the Chairman shall be as follows:

2 Lay Members	6 Year Term
2 Lay Members	5 Year Term
1 Lay Member	4 Year Term
1 Lawyer Member	6 Year Term
1 Lawyer Member	5 Year Term
1 Lawyer Member	4 Year Term

Thereafter, each member shall be appointed or elected, consistent with other provisions of this Article, for a six year term.

D. Vacancies.

Vacancies shall be filled for the unexpired term in like manner as provided for initial selection of members of the Metropolitan Court Nominating Council.

E. Regulation of Members.

No member of the Metropolitan Court Nominating Council, except the Chairman, shall hold any other public office for profit or office in a political party or organization and shall not be eligible for appointment to the Metropolitan Court Bench while a member of the Metropolitan Court Nominating Council and for a period of five years thereafter.

F. Additional Duties.

1. The Metropolitan Court Nominating Council is empowered to initiate removal proceedings against any Metropolitan Court judge for nonfeasance, malfeasance or misfeasance in office.

2. The Metropolitan Court Nominating Council shall conduct studies for improvement of the administration of justice and make reports and recommendations to the Board of County Commissioners at intervals of not more than two years.

3. The Metropolitan Court Nominating Council shall perform such other duties as may be assigned by law.

SECTION 6.07. INCAPACITY OF JUDGES.

Whenever the Metropolitan Court Nominating Council certifies to the Board of County Commissioners that a Metropolitan Court judge appears to be so incapacitated as substantially to prevent him from performing his judicial duties, the Board of County Commissioners shall inquire into the circumstances and may retire the judge.

SECTION 6.08. RECALL.

Metropolitan Court judges shall be subject to recall in the manner as provided in Section 7.02 of the home rule Charter.

SECTION 6.09. REMOVAL OF JUDGES.

Upon initiation of removal proceedings by the Metropolitan Court Nominating Council, or by the Board of County Commissioners, judges of the Metropolitan Court may be subject to removal for nonfeasance, malfeasance or misfeasance in the performance of official duties by two-thirds vote of the members of the Board of County Commissioners, after appropriate hearing.

SECTION 6.10. RETIREMENT OF JUDGES.

Every judge of the Metropolitan Court shall retire at the age of 70 years.

SECTION 6.11. NUMBER OF JUDICIAL POSITIONS.

The Board of County Commissioners shall determine the number of judges of the Metropolitan Court as in its opinion is deemed necessary to administer promptly and expeditiously the business of the Court.

In the event the Board of County Commissioners determines to decrease the number of judicial positions on the Metropolitan Court, such decision can only take effect upon the expiration of a regular term of office.

At such time as the decrease in the number of judicial positions on the Metropolitan Court becomes effective, those judges whose terms of office expire may run for election for the then existing offices, consistent with other provisions of this Article. In this event, those judges receiving the highest number of affirmative votes shall fill the said judicial vacancies.

SECTION 6.12. COMPENSATION OF JUDGES.

Judges of the Metropolitan Court shall receive compensation as prescribed by law. Compensation of judges shall not be diminished during their terms of office.

SECTION 6.13. RESTRICTIONS ON JUDGES.

No judge of the Metropolitan Court shall, during his term of office, engage in the practice of law. No judge shall, during his term of office, run for elective office other than the judicial office which he holds, or directly or indirectly make any contribution to, or hold any office in, a political party or organization, or take part in any political campaign.

SECTION 6.14. EFFECTIVE DATE.

The provisions of this Article shall become effective February 1, 1964.

SECTION 6.15. JURISDICTION AND PROCEDURE.

A. The Court shall have jurisdiction to try all cases arising under ordinances adopted by the Board.

B. The clerk of the Metropolitan Court shall be appointed by the Board. The clerk may appoint deputy clerks upon approval of the Manager. The Court may hold sessions in such places as the Board may designate.

C. Arrests, complaints, prosecutions, and convictions shall be instituted and processed in the manner provided by the rules of the Court. When the complaint is made in the name of the county, a formal complaint shall not be necessary to give the Court jurisdiction of offenses triable in such Court, but the accused may be tried for the offense for which he is docketed, provided such docket entry is sufficient to put the accused upon notice of the offense with which he is charged.

D. No person shall upon conviction for the violation of any county ordinance be punished by a fine exceeding $1,000 or imprisonment in the county jail for more than one year or by both such fine and imprisonment. If the offense is punishable by a fine exceeding $500 or imprisonment in the county jail for more than 60 days, the accused shall be entitled to a trial by jury upon demand.

E. All prosecutions for violations of any ordinance punishable by fine or imprisonment shall be conducted by the State Attorney of this county, if he be willing, and if not, by the department of law. The Board may by ordinance provide for a public defender.

F. Appeals will lie to the Circuit Court of this county from any final judgment. All such appeals shall be taken within 20 days from the entry of the judgment in the manner provided by the rules of the Circuit Court. The decision of the Circuit Court shall be subject to review in the same manner and within the same time as any other decision of the Circuit Court.

G. The judges of the Metropolitan Court are hereby empowered to adopt rules of procedure governing the Court, to punish for contempt of court including imprisonment not in excess of 48 hours, to issue search warrants, and to fix the amount of bail and appeal bonds. The judges and the clerks or their deputies may administer oaths, issue witness subpoenas, and warrants for arrest.

Article 7

INITIATIVE, REFERENDUM, AND RECALL

SECTION 7.01. INITIATIVE AND REFERENDUM.

The electors of the county shall have the power to propose to the Board of County Commissioners passage or repeal of ordinances and to vote on the question if the Board refuses action, according to the following procedure:

1. The person proposing the exercise of this power shall submit the proposal to the Board which shall without delay approve as to form a petition for circulation in one or several copies as the proposer may desire.

2. The person or persons circulating the petition shall, within one month of the approval of the form of the petition, obtain the signatures of voters in numbers at least equal to five percent of the total vote in the county for the office of Governor at the last preceeding gubernatorial general election, or 10,000, whichever is less. Each signer of a petition shall place thereon, after his name, the date, and his place of residence or precinct number. Each person circulating a copy of the petition shall attach to it a sworn affidavit stating the number of signers and the fact that each signature was made in the presence of the circulator of the petition.

3. The signed petition shall be filed with the Board which shall within 30 days order a canvass of the signatures thereon to determine the sufficiency of the signatures. If the number of signatures is insufficient or the petition is deficient as to form or compliance with this Section, the Board shall notify the person filing the petition and allow 30 days for filing of additional petition papers, at the end of which time the sufficiency or insufficiency of the petition shall be finally determined.

4. The Board shall within 30 days after the date a sufficient petition is presented either:
   (a) Adopt the ordinance as submitted in an initiatory petition or repeal the ordinance referred to by a referendary petition, or
   (b) Determine to submit the proposal to the electors.

5. The vote of the electors, if required, shall take place within 120 days after the date the petition is presented to the Board, preferably in an election already scheduled for other purposes, otherwise in a special election. The result shall be determined by a majority vote of the electors voting on the proposal.

6. An ordinance proposed by initiatory petition or the repeal of an ordinance by referendary petition shall be effective on the day after the election, except that:
   (a) Any reduction or elimination of existing revenue or any expenditures not provided for by the current budget or existing bond issues shall not take effect until the beginning of the next succeeding fiscal year; and
   (b) Rights accumulated under an ordinance between the time a certified referendary petition against the ordinance is presented to the Board and the repeal of the ordinance by the voters, shall not be enforced against the county; and

   (c) Should two or more ordinances adopted at the same election have conflicting provisions, the one receiving the highest number of votes shall prevail as to those provisions.

7. An ordinance adopted by the electorate through initiatory proceedings shall not be amended or repealed by the Board for a period of one year after the election at which it was adopted, but thereafter it may be amended or repealed like any other ordinance.

SECTION 7.02. RECALL.

Any member of the Board of County Commissioners or the Sheriff or any Constable may be removed from office by the electors of the county, district, or municipality by which he was chosen. The procedure on a recall petition shall be identical with that for an initiatory or referendary petition, except that:

1. The Clerk of the Circuit Court shall approve the form of the petition.

2. The person or persons circulating the petition must obtain signatures of electors of the county, district, or municipality concerned in numbers at least equal to ten percent or 10,000, whichever is smaller, of the qualified voters in the county, district, or municipality.

3. The signed petition shall be filed with and canvassed and certified by the Clerk of the Circuit Court.

4. The Board of County Commisioners must provide for a recall election not less than 45 nor more than 90 days after the certification of the petition.

5. The question of recall shall be placed on the ballot in a manner that will give the elector a clear choice for or against the recall. The result shall be determined by a majority vote of the electors voting on the question.

6. If the majority is against recall the officer shall continue in office under the terms of his previous election. If the majority is for recall he shall, regardless of any defect in the recall petition, be deemed removed from office immediately.

7. No recall petition against such an officer shall be certified within one year after he takes office nor within one year after a recall petition against him is defeated.

8. Any vacancy created by recall in the offices of Sheriff or Constables shall be filled for the remaining term by appointment by the Board of County Commissioners, or the Board may require the office to be filled at the next regular election or at a special election called for that purpose.

Article 8

GENERAL PROVISIONS

SECTION 8.01. ABOLITION OF CERTAIN OFFICES AND TRANSFER OF FUNCTIONS.

A. On May 1, 1958, the following offices are hereby abolished and the powers and functions of such offices are hereby transferred to the County Manager who shall provide for the continuation of all the duties and functions of these offices required under the Constitution and general laws of this state: County Assessor of Taxes, County Tax Collector, County Surveyor, County Purchasing Agent, and County Supervisor of Registration.

B. The County Manager may delegate to suitable persons the powers and functions of such officers, provided however that until the term of office for which they were elected shall terminate the County Assessor of Taxes, the County Tax Collector, the County Supervisor of Registration, and the County Purchasing Agent shall each if he so desires remain in his position and receive the same salary as presently provided for by statute.

C. In the event that other elective officers are abolished by the Board, the Board shall provide that any person duly elected to such office shall if he so desires remain in the same or similar position and receive the same salary for the remainder of the term for which he was elected, and shall provide for the continuation of all duties and functions of these offices required under the Constitution and general laws.

SECTION 8.02. WAIVER OF IMMUNITY.

Any county or municipal officeholder or employee who, upon being called before a grand jury to testify concerning the conduct of his office or the performance of his official duties or employment, refuses to sign a waiver of immunity against subsequent criminal prosecution, or to answer any relevant question concerning such matters before the grand jury, shall be removed from office or public employment by the appropriate authority, or upon suit by the State Attorney of this county.

SECTION 8.03. TORT LIABILITY.

The county shall be liable in actions of tort to the same extent that municipalities in the State of Florida are liable in actions in tort. However, no suit shall be maintained against the county for damages to persons or property or for wrongful death arising out of any tort unless written notice of claim shall first have been given to the county in the manner and within the time provided by ordinance, except that the time fixed by ordinance for notice shall be not less than 30 days nor more than 120 days.*

SECTION 8.04. SUPREMACY CLAUSE.

A. This Charter and the ordinances adopted hereunder shall in cases of conflict supersede all municipal charters and ordinances, except as herein provided, and where authorized by the Constitution, shall in cases of conflict supersede all special and general laws of the state.

B. All other special and general laws and county ordinances and rules and regulations not inconsistent with this Charter shall continue in effect until they are superseded by ordinance adopted by the Board pursuant to this Charter and the Constitution.

_____

Waiver of County's tort immunity held unconstitutional in Kaulakis v. Boyd, Fla. 1962, 138 So. 2d 505.

SECTION 8.05. EXISTING FRANCHISES, CONTRACTS, AND LICENSES.

All lawful franchises, contracts, and licenses in force on the effective date of this Charter shall continue in effect until terminated or modified in accordance with their terms or in the manner provided by law or this Charter.

SECTION 8.06. EFFECT OF THE CHARTER.

A. This Charter shall be liberally construed in aid of its declared purpose, which is to establish effective home rule government in this county responsive to the people. If any Article, Section, subsection, sentence, clause, or provision of this Charter or the application thereof shall be held invalid for any reason, the remainder of the Charter and of any ordinances or regulations made thereunder shall remain in full force and effect.

B. Nothing in this Charter shall be construed to limit or restrict the power and jurisdiction of the Florida Railroad and Public Utilities Commission.

SECTION 8.07. AMENDMENTS.

A. Amendments to this Charter may be proposed by a resolution adopted by the Board of County Commissioners or by petition of electors numbering not less than ten percent of the total number of electors registered in Dade County at the time the petition is submitted to the Board. Initiatory petitions shall be certified in the manner required for initiatory petitions for an ordinance.

B. Amendments to this Charter may be proposed by initiatory petitions of electors biennially, only during even numbered years in which state primary and general elections are held. All elections on charter amendments proposed by initiatory petitions shall be held in conjunction with state primary or general elections, unless the Board of County Commisisoners shall determine to call a special election by two-thirds vote of the entire membership.

C. Amendments to this Charter may be proposed by the Board of County Commissioners at any time. Elections on charter amendments proposed by the Board shall be held not less than 60 nor more than 120 days after the Board adopts a resolution proposing any amendment.

D. The result of all elections on charter amendments shall be determined by a majority of the electors voting on the proposed amendment.

SECTION 8.08. EFFECTIVE DATE.

This Charter shall become effective 60 days after it is ratified by a majority of the qualified electors of the county voting on the Charter.

Article 9

TRANSITORY PROVISIONS

SECTION 9.01. COMPOSITION OF BOARD OF COUNTY COMMISSIONERS PRIOR TO 1968 STATE PRIMARY ELECTIONS.

A. The term of each County Commissioner who was elected at large in 1960 state primary elections, of each County Commissioner who was elected by districts in the 1962 state primary elections, and of each County Commissioner who was elected from a municipality shall terminate at midnight on the third Tuesday next succeeding the date of the special election provided for in Section 9.01 (B).

B. There shall be elected by the qualified electors of the county at large a Mayor and from each of the eight districts a County Commissioner at a special election to be held on the twelfth Tuesday following the effective date of this amendment. Candidates for these offices shall be qualified electors residing within the county at least three years before qualifying and in addition candidates for the office of Commissioner from each of the eight districts must reside within the district for which they are a candidate on the date they qualify.

C. A candidate must receive a majority of the votes cast to be elected. If no candidate receives a majority of the votes cast, there will be a runoff election on the second Tuesday following such special election between the two candidates receiving the highest number of votes. Should a tie result, the outcome shall be determined by lot.

D. The terms of the Mayor and the other Commissioners shall begin at midnight on the third Tuesday next succeeding the date of the special election provided for in Section 9.01 (B) and shall end on the second Tuesday next succeeding the 1968 state second primary election.

E. The provisions of Sections 2.03, 2.04, 2.06 and 2.07 apply to such elections.

SECTION 9.02. APPOINTMENT OF COUNTY MANAGER.

The County Manager shall be appointed no later than October 31, 1957.

SECTION 9.03. REASSESSMENT.

A. Repealed at special election August 15, 1961.

B. Repealed at special election August 15, 1961.

C. Prior to January 1, 1961, each municipality shall conform its fiscal year to that of the county, and to accomplish this may levy taxes for less or more than one year but for not more than two years at once.

D. Upon petition from any municipality on grounds of hardship caused by use of the county tax rolls or prescribed fiscal year, the Board may from year to year grant that municipality an exemption, but no such exemption shall extend beyond January 1, 1966.

SECTION 9.04. APPROPRIATION.

There is hereby appropriated from the general fund, fine and forfeiture fund, or any other appropriate fund, from unanticipated receipts and unexpended balances in such funds, sufficient monies as determined by the Board to pay for the cost of establishing the various departments, positions, and procedures required by this Charter. Such apropriations and expenditures are hereby declared to be for county purposes and are legitimate expenditures, properly payable from the 1956-57 budget, as hereby amended.

SECTION 9.05. CHANGE OF COMMISSION DISTRICTS.

No County Commission district shall be changed until the results of the 1960 federal census are available.

SECTION 9.06. TRANSITION.

In order that there may be no interruption of the business of the county, all persons holding office at the time this Charter takes effect shall continue in the performance of their functions and duties until their successors are appointed, or until their functions and duties are transferred, altered, or abolished in accordance with this Charter. All laws in force when this Charter becomes effective and not inconsistent therewith shall continue in force until they are superseded by ordinances adopted by the Board in pursuance of this Charter. All ordinances and resolutions of the county in force when this Charter becomes effective, and all lawful rights, claims, actions, orders, obligations, proceedings, and contracts shall continue until modified, amended, repealed, or superseded in accordance with this Charter.

SECTION 9.07. TERMINATION OF THIS ARTICLE.

After December 31, 1968, this Article 9 shall cease to be a part of this Charter.

The Municipality of Metropolitan Toronto

A metropolitan federation was established in the Toronto area, effective January 1, 1954, by the unilateral action of the Ontario Legislature; citizens were not allowed a direct voice in the determination of whether a federal plan of government should be adopted for the 240-square-mile area, six times larger than the City of Toronto.

The first half of the twentieth century witnessed rapid population growth and concomitant governmental problems in the Toronto area as the population of the City of Toronto increased from 200,000 to 665,000 in the period 1900 to 1953 and the population of the twelve suburban communities increased from 25,000 to 507,000.

The City of Toronto opposed the total amalgamation of local governments until February 2, 1950 when it applied to the Ontario Municipal Board for an order amalgamating Toronto with ten of its suburbs and major sections of two other suburbs. The application led to the famous Cumming Report *of January 20, 1953. The* Report—*prepared by the Honorable Lorne R. Cumming, Chairman of the Ontario Municipal Board, with the assistance of Vice Chairman W. J. Moore—described federation as "the most promising avenue of approach" and served as the basis for the creation of the Municipality of Metropolitan Toronto. The Provincial Government accepted the principal recommendations of the* Cumming Report *and introduced* in the Legislature Bill 80 *which received Royal Assent on April 2, 1953 and became The Municipality of Metropolitan Toronto Act, 1953.*

The creation of the Municipality of Metropolitan Toronto did not deter the City of Toronto from pressing for the dissolution of the federation and the complete consolidation of local governments, and in 1963 The Royal Commission on Metropolitan Toronto was appointed to review the system of government. In its 1965 report, the Commission rejected the City of Toronto's position and recommended the continuance of the two-tier system of government with a reduction in the number of municipalities from thirteen to four. The Provincial Government, on the basis of the Commission's report, introduced legislation which became The Municipality of Metropolitan Toronto Act, 1966. The Act appears to represent an evolutionary aproach to the total consolidation of local governments as the number of municipalities was reduced, effective January 1, 1967, from thirteen to six: the City of Toronto and Boroughs of East York, Etobicoke, North York, Scarborough, and York. The Metropolitan Council was increased in size from twenty-four to thirty-three members; twelve seats are alloted to the City of Toronto and twenty seats to the five Boroughs. The Council continues to appoint its Chairman who need not be a member of the Council. The powerful eleven-member Executive Committee is composed of five members from the City of Toronto, five members from the Boroughs, and the Chairman of the Metropolitan Council.

INTERPRETATION

1. In this Act,

   (a) "area municipality" means the municipality or corporation of the Borough of East York, the Borough of Etobicoke, the Borough of North York, the Borough of Scarborough, the City of Toronto or the the Borough of York;

   (b) "bridge" means a public bridge, and includes a bridge forming part of a highway or on, over, under or across which a highway passes;

   (c) "chairman" means the chairman of the Metropolitan Council;

   (d) "debt" includes obligation for the payment of money;

   (e) "Department" means the Department of Municipal Affairs;

   (f) "highway" and "road" mean a common and public highway, and include a street, bridge, and any other structure incidental thereto;

   (g) "land" includes lands, tenements and hereditaments, and any estate or interest therein, and any right or easement affecting them, and land covered with water, and includes any buildings or improvements on land;

   (h) "local board" means any school board, public utility commission, transportation commission, public library board, board of park management, local board of health, board of commissioners of police, planning board or any other board, commission, com-mittee, body or local authority established or exercising any power or authority under any general or special Act with respect to any of the affairs or purposes, including school purposes, of the Metropolitan Corporation or of an area municipality or of two or more area municipalities or portions thereof;

   (i) "Metropolitan Area" means the area from time to time included within the Borough of East York, the Borough of Etobicoke, the Borough of North York, the Borough of Scarborough, the City of Toronto and the Borough of York;

   (j) "Metropolitan Corporation" means The Municipality of Metropolitan Toronto;

   (k) "Metropolitan Council" means the council of the Metropolitan Corporation;

   (l) "metropolitan road" means a road forming part of the metropolitan road system established under Part V;

   (m) "Minister" means the Minister of Municipal Affairs;

   (n) "money by-law" means a by-law for contracting a debt or obligation or for borrowing money, other than a by-law passed under section 233;

   (o) "Municipal Board" means the Ontario Municipal Board;

   (p) "roadway" means that part of the highway designed or intended for use by vehicular traffic. R.S.O. 1960, c. 260, s. 1; 1961-62, c. 88, s. 1; 1966, c. 96, s. 1.

Part I

INCORPORATION AND COUNCIL

2.—(1) The inhabitants of the Metropolitan Area are hereby continued a body corporate under the name of "The Municipality of Metropolitan Toronto."

(2) The Metropolitan Corporation shall be deemed to be a municipality for the purposes of *The Department of Municipal Affairs Act* and *The Ontario Municipal Board Act* and is a municipality in the County of York separated therefrom for municipal purposes.

(3) The Metropolitan Corporation shall be deemed to be a city for the purposes of section 410 of *The Municipal Act.* R.S.O. 1960, c. 260, s. 2.

(4) The Metropolitan Corporation shall be deemed to be a municipality as defined in *The Department of Municipal Affairs Act* for the purposes of *The Expropriation Procedures Act, 1962-63.* 1965, c. 81, s. 1.

3.—(1) The powers of the Metropolitan Corporation shall be exercised by the Metropolitan Council and, except where otherwise provided, the jurisdiction of the Metropolitan Council is confined to the Metropolitan Area.

(2) Except where otherwise provided, the powers of the Metropolitan Council shall be exercised by by-law.

(3) A by-law passed by the Metropolitan Council in the exercise of any of its powers and in good faith shall not be open to question, or be quashed, set aside or declared invalid either wholly or partly, on account of the unreasonableness or supposed unreasonableness of its provisions or any of them. R.S.O. 1960, c. 260, s. 3.

4.—(1) In every area municipality, meetings of electors for the nomination of candidates for council and for any local board, any members of which are to be elected by ballot by the electors, shall be held in the year 1966 and in every third year thereafter on the second Monday preceding the first Monday in December.

(2) The day for polling shall be the first Monday in December, and the polls shall be open between the hours of 10 o'clock in the morning and 8 o'clock in the evening.

(3) The council of every area municipality, before the 1st day of November in the year 1969 and in every third year thereafter, shall pass a by-law naming the place or places and time or times at which the nomination meeting or meetings shall be held, and, before the 1st day of November in the year 1966, the councils of the townships of North York and Scarborough shall each pass such a by-law, and the nomination meetings in the year 1966 in the area municipalities, other than the Boroughs of North York and Scarborough, shall be held as directed by the Municipal Board.

(4) The members of council and of such local boards shall hold office for a three-year term and until their successors are elected and the new council or board is organized.

(5) This section applies to members of the Metropolitan Separate School Board.

(6) Each area municipality shall be deemed to have passed a by-law providing for a resident voters' list under *The Municipal Franchise Extension Act,* and the assent of the electors as required therein shall be deemed to have been received. 1966. c. 96, s. 2.

5.—(1) On and after the 1st day of January, 1967, the area municipalities are entitled to the following membership on the Metropolitan Council:

the Borough of East York   — 2 members
the Borough of Etobicoke   — 4 members
the Borough of North York — 6 members
the Borough of Scarborough — 5 members
the City of Toronto   — 12 members
the Borough of York   — 3 members

(2) In accordance with the membership to which an area municipality is entitled under subsection 1, the Metropolitan Council shall include the mayor of each area municipality and, subject to subsection 3,

> (a) where an area municipality has a board of control,
> > (i) the controllers, or
> > (ii) if the number of members, exclusive of the mayor, to which the area municipality is entitled is less than the number of controllers, the controllers to the number necessary to complete the membership to which the area municipality is entitled who, at the municipal election next preceding the day the new Metropolitan Council is organized in any year, received the greatest number of votes, the next greatest, and so on as the case requires, or
> > (iii) if the area municipality is entitled to a greater number of members than the mayor and the other members of the board of control, the controllers and such number of alderman appointed by the council of the area municipality as is necessary to complete the membership to which the area municipality is entitled; or
> (b) where the area municipality does not have a board of control, such number of alderman appointed by the council of the area municipality as is necessary to complete the membership to which the area municipality is entitled.

(3) Where the number of wards in an area municipality is equal to the number of alderman to be appointed by the council of such area municipality,

> (a) the alderman for each ward; or
> (b) where there is more than one alderman for each ward, the alderman for each ward who, at the municipal election next preceding the day the new Metropolitan Council is organized in any year, received the greatest number of votes in such ward,

shall be members of the Metropolitan Council in lieu of the alderman to be appointed.

(4) If after any election in an area municipality, by reason of acclamation or an equality of votes, it cannot be determined which controller or controllers or alderman or aldermen is or are entitled to be a member or members of the Metropolitan Council, the matter shall be determined by resolution of the council of the area municipality passed before the organization meeting of the Metropolitan Council.

(5) At the first meeting of the Metropolitan Council in each year after an election at which a quorum is present, the Metropolitan Council shall organize as a council and elect as chairman one of the members of the Metropolitan Council, or any other person, to hold office for that year and the two following years and until his successor is elected or appointed in accordance with this section.

(6) The clerk of the Metropolitan Corporation shall preside at each such first meeting or, if there is no clerk, the members present shall select a member to preside, and the

person so selected may vote as a member.

(7) If at such first meeting for any reason a chairman is not elected, the clerk or presiding member may adjourn the meeting from time to time and, if a chairman is not elected within one week after such first meeting, the Lieutenant Governor in Council shall appoint the chairman to hold office for that year and the two following years and until his successor is elected or appointed in accordance with this section.

(8) The Metropolitan Council shall be composed of the chairman and the persons who are members pursuant to this Part.

(9) Notwithstanding subsections 2 and 3 and in lieu of the membership on the Metropolitan Council provided for the City of Toronto in such subsections, for the years 1967, 1968 and 1969, the membership of the City of Toronto on the Metropolitan Council shall consist of,

(a) the mayor of the City of Toronto;

(b) the two members of the board of control of the City of Toronto who at the municipal election next preceding the day the new Metropolitan Council is organized in the year 1967 received the greatest number of votes; and

(c) the alderman in each ward of the City of Toronto who at the municipal election next preceding the day the new Metropolitan Council is organized in the year 1967 received the greatest number of votes in such ward.

(10) For the years 1967, 1968 and 1969, the City of Toronto shall consist of nine wards, and shall have a board of control consisting of the mayor and four controllers elected by general vote. 1966, c. 96, s. 3.

6.—(1) The first meeting of the Metropolitan Council in each year after elections have been held in the area municipalities shall be held after the councils of all the area municipalities have held their first meetings in the year but in any event not later than the 15th day of January on such date and at such time and place as may be fixed by by-law of the Metropolitan Council. R.S.O. 1960, c. 260, s. 6 (1); 1962-63, c. 89, s. 1 (1).

(2) Notwithstanding anything in any general or special Act, the first meeting of the council of each area municipality in each year after elections have been held in the area municipalities shall be held not later than the 8th day of January. 1962-63, c. 89, s. 1 (2).

(3) A person entitled to be a member of the Metropolitan Council under subsection 2, 3 or 9 of section 5 shall not take his seat until he has filed with the person presiding at the first meeting a certificate under the hand of the clerk of the area municipality for which he was elected and under the seal of the area municipality certifying that he is entitled to be a member under such subsection. R.S.O. 1960, c. 260, s. 6 (3); 1966, c. 96, s. 4 (1).

(4) Where a person elected or appointed as chairman is not one of the persons mentioned in subsection 2, 3 or 9 of section 5, he shall, before taking his seat, take an oath of allegiance (Form 1) and a declaration of qualification (Form 2). R.S.O. 1960, c. 260, s. 6 (4); 1966, c. 96, s. 4 (2).

(5) No business shall be proceeded with at the first meeting until after the declarations of office in Form 20 of *The Municipal Act* have been made by all members who present themselves for that purpose, and each such declaration shall include a declaration that the member has not by himself or a partner, directly or indirectly, any interest in any contract with or on behalf of the Metropolitan Corporation or any local board thereof. R.S.O. 1960, c. 260, s. 6 (5).

(6) The Metropolitan Council shall be deemed to be organized when the declarations of office have been made by at least eleven members, and it may be organized and business may be proceeded with notwithstanding the failure of any of the other members to make such declarations. R.S.O. 1960, c. 260, s. 6 (6); 1966, c. 96, s. 4 (3).

7. Subject to section 6, all meetings of the Metropolitan Council shall be held at such place within the Metropolitan Area and at such times as the Metropolitan Council from time to time appoints. R.S.O. 1960, c. 260, s. 7.

8.—(1) Eleven members of the Metropolitan Council are necessary to form a quorum, and the concurring votes of a majority of members present are necessary to carry any resolution or other measure.

(2) Each member of the Metropolitan Council, except the chairman, has one vote only, and the chairman does not have a vote except in the event of an equality of votes. 1966, c. 96, s. 5, *part*.

9. The members of the Metropolitan Council, other than the chairman, hold office while they hold the offices that entitled them to such membership or to appointment to such membership and until their successors take office and a new Metropolitan Council is organized. 1966, c. 96, s. 5, *part*.

10. (1) When a vacancy occurs in the office of a chairman who has been appointed by the Lieutenant Governor in Council, a person shall be appointed by the Lieutenant Governor in Council to hold office as chairman for the remainder of the term of his predecessor.

(2) When a vacancy occurs in the office of a chairman who has been elected under subsection 5 of section 5, the Metropolitan Council shall, at a general or special meeting to be held within twenty days after the vacancy occurs, elect a chairman, who may be one of the members of the Metropolitan Council or any other person, to hold office for the remainder of the term of his predecessor.

(3) If the Metropolitan Council fails to elect a chairman within twenty days as required by subsection 2, the Lieutenant Governor in Council may appoint a person as chairman to hold office for the remainder of the term of his predecessor.

(4) When a vacancy occurs in the office of a member other than the chairman or a member who held office by reason of being a mayor, the council of the area municipality, of which he was a member, shall within fifteen days after the vacancy occurs appoint his successor to hold office for the remainder of the term of his predecessor, provided that, if he held office by reason of being a controller, another controller shall be appointed or, if he held office under subsection 2 of section 5 by reason of being an alderman, another alderman shall be appointed or, if he held office under subsection 3 or 9 of section 5 by reason of being an alderman for a ward, another alderman for such ward shall be appointed.

(5) Where a member of the council of an area municipality becomes chairman, he shall be deemed to have resigned as a member of such council, and his seat on such council thereby becomes vacant.

(6) The seat of a member of the Metropolitan Council becomes vacant if he absents himself continuously from the meetings of the Metropolitan Council during a period of one month without being authorized so to do by a resolution of the Metropolitan Council entered upon its minutes, and the Metropolitan Council shall forthwith declare the seat to be vacant, and, notwithstanding subsection 4, the council of the area municipality of which he is a member may appoint any one of its members as his successor. 1966, c. 96, s. 5, *part*.

11.—(1) The chairman may be paid for his services as

chairman a sum not exceeding $18,000 per annum. 1962-63, c. 89, s. 2 (1).

(2) The members of the Metropolitan Council, other than the chairman, may be paid such annual or other remuneration, not exceeding $3,000 per annum, as the Metropolitan Council may determine. R.S.O. 1960, c. 260, s. 11 (2); 1962-63, c. 89, s. 2 (2).

12.—(1) There shall be an Executive Committee of the Metropolitan Council composed of,

    (a) the chairman;

    (b) the mayor of each area municipality; and

    (c) where the City of Toronto has a board of control, the four controllers of such board; or

    (d) where the City of Toronto does not have a board of control, four alderman of the City of Toronto, who are members of the Metropolitan Council, appointed by the council of the City of Toronto,

and the chairman shall be chairman of the Executive Committee and entitled to vote as a member thereof.

(2) The Executive Committee has all the powers and duties of a board of control under subsection 1 of section 206 of *The Municipal Act,* and subsections 2 to 15 and 17 to 19 of that section apply *mutatis mutandis.*

(3) Each member of the Executive Committee shall, in addition to his remuneration as a member of the Metropolitan Council, receive such remuneration, not exceeding $2,000 per year, as may be authorized by the Metropolitan Council.

(4) In lieu of the membership of the City of Toronto provided for in clauses *c* and *d* of subsection 1, for the years 1967, 1968 and 1969, the following, in addition to the mayor, shall be members of the Executive Committee:

    (a) the two controllers of the City of Toronto who are members of the Metropolitan Council; and

    (b) two of the alderman of the City of Toronto who are members of the Metropolitan Council appointed by the members of the Metropolitan Council who are members of the council of the City of Toronto to hold office for such years.

(5) An alderman entitled to be a member of the Executive Committee under subsection 4 shall not take his seat until he has filed with the person presiding at the first meeting a certificate under the hand of the clerk of the Metropolitan Corporation certifying that he is entitled to be a member under such subsection. 1966, c. 96, s. 6.

13.—(1) The Metropolitan Council may from time to time establish such standing or other committees, and assign to them such duties, as it deems expedient.

(2) The Metropolitan Council may by by-law provide for paying an annual allowance not exceeding $100 to each chairman of a standing committee, except where such chairman is the chairman of the Metropolitan Council. R.S.O. 1960, c. 260, s. 13.

14. The Metropolitan Council may pass by-laws for governing the proceedings of the Metropolitan Council and any of its committees, the conduct of its members and the calling of meetings. R.S.O. 1960, c. 260, s. 14.

15. The chairman is the head of the Metropolitan Council and the chief executive officer of the Metropolitan Corporation. R.S.O. 1960, c. 260, s. 15.

16. When the chairman is absent from the Metropolitan Area or absent through illness, or refuses to act, the Metro-

politan Council may by resolution appoint one of its members to act in his place and stead, and such member has and may exercise all the rights, powers and authority of the chairman during such absence or refusal to act. R.S.O. 1960, c. 260, s. 16.

17.—(1) Sections 192, 193, 195, 197, 198, 199, 244, 253, 275 to 280, paragraph 61 of section 377 and section 406*a* of *The Municipal Act* apply *mutatis mutandis* to the Metropolitan Corporation. R.S.O. 1960, c. 260, s. 17; 1960-61, c. 61, s. 1 (1); 1961-62, c. 88, s. 4 (1).

(2) Sections 190, 198*a* and 198*b* of *The Municipal Act* apply *mutatis mutandis* to the Metropolitan Council and to every local board of the Metropolitan Corporation. 1960-61, c. 61, s. 1 (2); 1961-62, c. 88, s. 4 (2).

18.—(1) The Metropolitan Council shall appoint a clerk, whose duty it is,

    (a) to record truly in a book, without note or comment, all resolutions, decisions and other proceedings of the Metropolitan Council;

    (b) when a recorded vote is requested by a member, to record the name and vote of every member voting on any matter or question;

    (c) to preserve and file all accounts acted upon by the Metropolitan Council;

    (d) to keep in his office, or in the place appointed for that purpose, the originals of all by-laws and of all minutes of the preceedings of the Metropolitan Council and its committees;

    (e) to perform such other duties as may be assigned to him by the Metropolitan Council.

(2) The Metropolitan Council may appoint a deputy clerk who shall have all the powers and duties of the clerk.

(3) When the office of clerk is vacant or the clerk is unable to carry on his duties, through illness or otherwise, the Metropolitan Council may appoint an acting clerk *pro tempore* who shall have all the powers and duties of the clerk. R.S.O. 1960, c. 260, s. 18.

19.—(1) Any person may, at all reasonable hours, inspect any of the records, books or documents mentioned in section 18 and the minutes and proceedings of any committee of the Metropolitan Council, whether the acts of the committee have been adopted or not, and other documents in the possession or under the control of the clerk, and the clerk shall, within a reasonable time, furnish copies of them, certified under his hand and the seal of the Metropolitan Corporation, to any applicant on payment at the rate of 15 cents for every 100 words or at such lower rate as the Metropolitan Council may fix.

(2) A copy of any record, book or document in the possession or under the control of the clerk, purporting to be certified under his hand and the seal of the Metropolitan Corporation, may be filed and used in any court in lieu of the original, and shall be received in evidence without proof of the seal or of the signature or official character of the person appearing to have signed the same, and without further proof, unless the court otherwise directs. R.S.O. 1960, c. 260, s. 19.

20.—(1) The Metropolitan Council shall appoint a treasurer who shall keep the books, records and accounts of the Metropolitan Corporation and who shall perform such other duties as may be assigned to him by the Metropolitan Council.

(2) The Metropolitan Council may appoint a deputy treasurer who shall have all the powers and duties of the treasurer.

(3) When the office of treasurer is vacant or the treasurer is unable to carry on his duties, through illness or otherwise, the Metropolitan Council may appoint an acting treasurer *pro*

tempore who shall have all the powers and duties of the treasurer. R.S.O. 1960, c. 260, s. 20.

21.—(1) The treasurer shall receive and safely keep all money of the Metropolitan Corporation, and shall pay out the same to such persons and in such manner as the law of Ontario and the by-laws or resolutions of the Metropolitan Council direct, provided that every cheque issued by the treasurer shall be signed by the treasurer and by some other person or persons designated for the purpose by by-law or resolution of the Metropolitan Council, and any such other person before signing a cheque shall satisfy himself that the issue thereof is authorized.

(2) Notwithstanding subsection 1, the Metropolitan Council may by by-law provide that the signature of the treasurer on cheques may be stamped, lithographed or engraved, or may by by-law designate one or more persons to sign cheques in lieu of the treasurer.

(3) Except where otherwise expressly provided by this Act, a member of the Metropolitan Council shall not receive any money from the treasurer for any work or service performed or to be performed.

(4) The treasurer is not liable for money paid by him in accordance with a by-law or resolution of the Metropolitan Council, unless another disposition of it is expressly provided for by statute.

(5) The treasurer shall open an account or accounts in the name of the Metropolitan Corporation in such of the chartered banks of Canada or at such other place of deposit as may be approved of by the Metropolitan Council and shall deposit therein all money received by him on account of the Metropolitan Corporation, and he shall keep the money of the Metropolitan Corporation entirely separate from his own money.

(6) The treasurer shall prepare and submit to the Metropolitan Council, monthly, a statement of the money at the credit of the Metropolitan Corporation.

(7) Where the treasurer is removed from office or absconds, the Metropolitan Council shall forthwith give notice to his sureties. R.S.O. 1960, c. 260, s. 21.

22.—(1) The Metropolitan Council shall by by-law appoint one or more auditors who shall be persons licensed by the Department as municipal auditors and who shall hold office during good behaviour and be removable for cause upon the vote of two-thirds of the members of the Metropolitan Council, and the auditor or auditors so appointed shall audit the accounts and transactions of the Metropolitan Corporation and of every local board of the Metropolitan Corporation.

(2) Where an auditor audits the accounts and transactions of a local board, the cost thereof shall be paid by the Metropolitan Corporation and charged back to the local board, and in the event of a dispute as to the amount of the cost the Department may upon application finally determine the amount thereof.

(3) No person shall be appointed as an auditor of the Metropolitan Corporation who is or during the preceding year was a member of the Metropolitan Council or of the council of an area municipality or of any local board the accounts and transactions of which it would as auditor be his duty to audit, or who has or during the preceding year had any direct or indirect interest in any contract with the Metropolitan Corporation or an area municipality or any such local board, or any employment with any of them other than as an auditor.

(4) An auditor shall perform such duties as are prescribed by the Department, and also such duties as may be required by the Metropolitan Council or any local board of the Metropolitan Corporation that do not conflict with the duties prescribed by the Department.

(5) An auditor may administer an oath to any person concerning any account or other matter to be audited.

(6) The Metropolitan Council may provide that all accounts shall be audited before payment. R.S.O. 1960, c. 260, s. 22.

23.—(1) The Metropolitan Council may pass by-laws for appointing such officers and employees as it may deem necessary for the purposes of the Metropolitan Corporation, or for carrying into effect the provisions of any Act of the Legislature or by-law of the Metropolitan Council, and for fixing their remuneration and prescribing their duties, and the security to be given for the performance of them.

(2) Except as otherwise provided in this Act, all officers and employees appointed by the Metropolitan Council shall hold office during the pleasure of the Metropolitan Council, and shall, in addition to the duties assigned to them by this Act, perform all other duties required of them by any other Act or by by-law of the Metropolitan Council. R.S.O. 1960, c. 260, s. 23.

24.—(1) Sections 217, 234 and 236, subsections 4 and 5 of section 238, sections 240 and 248c and paragraphs 59, 60 and 61 of section 377 of *The Municipal Act* apply *mutatis mutandis* to the Metropolitan Corporation. R.S.O. 1960, c. 260, s. 24 (1); 1965, c. 81, s. 2.

(2) In addition to its powers in subsection 1, the Metropolitan Council may pass by-laws for providing pensions for employees, or any class thereof, and their wives and children.

    (a) In this subsection, "employee" means any salaried officer, clerk, workman, servant or other person in the employ of the Metropolitan Corporation or any local board thereof, or of any area municipality or local board thereof, or of the Toronto and York Roads Commission, and includes any person designated as an employee by the Minister.

    (b) No by-law establishing a pension plan or a by-law amending such a by-law shall be passed by the Metropolitan Council under this subsection except on an affirmative vote of at least two-thirds of the Metropolitan Council present and voting thereon, and no such by-law shall become operative until approved by the Minister.

    . . . . . .

    (d) A local board of the Metropolitan Corporation, an area municipality, a local board of an area municipality or the Toronto and York Roads Commission may enter into an agreement with the Metropolitan Corporation providing that a pension plan established under this subsection shall be applicable to employees or any class thereof of such local board, area municipality or the Toronto and York Roads Commission, and such agreement may provide for the incorporation of the plan of an area municipality, local board or the Toronto and York Roads Commission with the plan established under this subsection and for the transfer of any credits or assets from one plan to the other, but no pension plan established under this subsection applies to an employee of a local board, area municipality or the Toronto and York Roads Commission unless such an agreement has been entered into.

    (e) Where a pension plan established under this subsection is applicable to an employee of a local board of the Metropolitan Corporation or

an employee of an area municipality or a local board thereof or the Toronto and York Roads Commission, the local board, area municipality or the Toronto and York Roads Commission, as the case may be, shall deduct, by instalments from the salary, wages or other remuneration of each employee to whom the by-law is applicable, the amount that such employee is required to pay in accordance with the provisions of the plan and shall pay the amounts deducted to the treasurer of the Metropolitan Corporation.

(f) Where a pension plan established under this subsection is applicable to an employee of a local board of the Metropolitan Corporation or an employee of an area municipality or a local board thereof or the Toronto and York Roads Commission, the local board or area municipality or the Toronto and York Roads Commission shall pay to the treasurer of the Metropolitan Corporation the employer contributions in respect of such employee in accordance with provisions of the plan. R.S.O. 1960, c. 260, s. 24 (2); 1962-63, c. 89, s. 3.

(3) Where the Metropolitan Corporation or a local board thereof employs a person theretofore employed by an area municipality or a local board thereof, a local board of the Metropolitan Corporation, the County of York or the Toronto and York Roads Commission, the employee shall be deemed to remain an employee of the area municipality or local board or of the County of York or the Toronto and York Roads Commission for the purposes of any pension plan of such area municipality or local board or of the County of York or the Toronto and York Roads Commission, and shall continue to be entitled to all rights and benefits thereunder as if he had remained as an employee of the area municipality or local board or of the County of York or the Toronto and York Roads Commission, until the Metropolitan Corporation has provided a penison plan for its employees and such employee has elected, in writing, to participate therein or the local board of the Metropolitan Corporation has entered into an agreement under clause d of subsection 2. R.S.O. 1960, c. 260, s. 24 (3); 1961-62, c. 88, s. 5 (1).

(4) Until such election or an agreement has been entered into under clause d of subsection 2, the Metropolitan Corporation or local board thereof shall deduct by instalments from the remuneration of the employee the amount that such employee is required to pay in accordance with the provisions of the plan of the area municipality or local board or of the County of York or the Toronto and York Roads Commission and the Metropolitan Corporation or local board thereof shall pay to the area municipality or local board or to the County of York or the Toronto and York Roads Commission in instalments,

(a) the amounts so deducted;

(b) the future service contributions payable under the plan by the area municipality or local board or by the County of York or the Toronto and York Roads Commission. R.S.O. 1960, s. 24 (4); 1966, c. 96, s. 7 (1).

(5) Upon such election or upon such an agreement being entered into and such an employee becoming a member of the pension plan established by the Metropolitan Corporation, he or his beneficiaries are entitled on termination of his services with the Metropolitan Corporation or a local board thereof to all benefits under the pension plan of the area municipality, or of a local board, or of the County of York or of the

Toronto and York Roads Commission accrued up to the date of his becoming a member of the Metropolitan Corporation pension plan, and his employment by and service with the Metropolitan Corporation or a local board thereof shall be deemed to be employment by and service with the respective area municipality, or local board, or the County of York or the Toronto and York Roads Commission for the purpose of determining eligibility for any such accrued benefits. R.S.O. 1960, c. 260, s. 24 (5); 1961-62, c. 88, s. 5 (2).

(6) Where the Metropolitan Corporation or local board thereof employs a person theretofore employed by an area municipality or local board thereof or a local board of the Metropolitan Corporation or by the County of York or the Toronto and York Roads Commission, the employee shall be deemed to remain an employee of the area municipality or local board or of the County of York or the Toronto and York Roads Commission for the purposes of any sick leave credit plan of the area municipality, local board, the County of York or the Toronto and York Roads Commission until the Metropolitan Corporation or local board thereof has established a sick leave credit plan for its employees, whereupon the Metropolitan Corporation or local board thereof shall place to the credit of the employee the sick leave credits standing to his credit in the plan of the area municipality or local board or of the County of York or the Toronto and York Roads Commission. R.S.O. 1960, c. 260, s. 24 (6); 1961-62, c. 88, s. 5 (3); 1966, c. 96, s. 7 (2).

(7) Where the Metropolitan Corporation or local board thereof employs a person theretofore employed by an area municipality or local board thereof or a local board of the Metropolitan Corporation or by the County of York or the Toronto and York Roads Commission, the Metropolitan Corporation or local board thereof shall, during the first year of his employment by the Metropolitan Corporation or local board thereof, provide for such employee's holidays with pay equivalent to those to which he would have been entitled if he had remained in the employment of the area municipality or local board or of the County of York or the Toronto and York Roads Commission. R.S.O. 1960, c. 260, s. 24 (7); 1961-62, c. 88, s. 5 (4); 1966, c. 96, s. 7 (3).

(8) A person who was employed by an area municipality or a local board thereof before the 1st day of January, 1967, and who is employed by the Metropolitan Corporation or a local board thereof or by an area municipality or a local board thereof, without intervening employment, shall not be deemed to be a person who enters the employ of an employer within the meaning of clause a of subsection 1 of section 8 of *The Ontario Municipal Employees Retirement System Act, 1961-62*. 1966, c. 96, s. 7 (4).

Part II

ASSESSMENT

25.—(1) The Metropolitan Council shall appoint as many assessors as may be deemed necessary to carry out the duties of assessors in all the area municipalities.

(2) Every by-law appointing an assessor remains in force until repealed and it is not necessary to appoint the assessor annually. R.S.O. 1960, c. 260, s. 25.

26.—(1) The Metropolitan Council shall appoint an assessment commissioner and may appoint as many deputy assessment commissioners as may be deemed necessary.

(2) The assessment commissioner, with respect to the deputy assessment commissioners and assessors, has control and charge over the exercise by them of their powers and over

the performance by them of their duties in all the area municipalities.

(3) The assessment commissioner may assign to a deputy assessment commissioner or an assessor the area municipality or area municipalities, or part or parts thereof, within which he is to act. R.S.O. 1960, c. 260, s. 26.

27.—(1) The assessment commissioner and every deputy assessment commissioner and every assessor appointed by the Metropolitan Council shall be deemed for the purposes of this and every other Act to be respectively the assessment commissioner, a deputy assessment commissioner and an assessor of each area municipality.

(2) No area municipality shall, after the 31st day of December, 1953, appoint or continue to employ an assessment commissioner or assessors or constitute or continue a board of assessors. R.S.O. 1960, c. 260, s. 27.

28. Subject to section 29, the Metropolitan Corporation shall provide and pay for all office accommodation, supplies, stationery and equipment, and shall employ such staff, as may be necessary for the performance of the duties of assessors in the Metropolitan Area. R.S.O. 1960, c. 260, s. 28.

29. At the request of the Metropolitan Council, each area municipality,

(a) shall provide, at such rent as may be agreed upon, at least as much office accommodation for the assessment commissioner, deputy assessment commissioners, assessors and staff as was being provided by the municipality for its assessment department on the 1st day of March, 1953;

(b) shall transfer to the assessment commissioner without compensation all office supplies and stationery in the possession of the municipality on the 31st day of December, 1953, that was provided for the exclusive use of the assessment department of the municipality;

(c) shall transfer to the assessment commissioner without compensation all mechanical and other equipment used exclusively by the assessment department of the municipality on the 1st day of March, 1953;

(d) shall make available to the assessment commissioner, at such rent as may be agreed upon, all mechanical and other equipment the use of which was shared by the assessment department and any other department or departments of the municipality on the 1st day of March, 1953, on the same terms and to the same extent as the assessment department used the equipment before the 1st day of March, 1953. R.S.O. 1960, c. 260, s. 29.

30. Every assessment commissioner, every assessor and every other officer or servant of an area municipality shall, at the request of the assessment commissioner of the Metropolitan Corporation, turn over to such assessment commissioner all books, records and documents relating to the work of the assessment department of the municipality. R.S.O. 1960, c. 260, s. 30.

31. Section 130 of *The Assessment Act* does not apply in any area municipality after the 31st day of December, 1953. R.S.O. 1960, c. 260, s. 31.

32.—(1) The Metropolitan Council shall constitute by by-law one or more courts of revision for each area municipality.

(2) Each such court of revision shall consist of one or three members, as the by-law may provide, and each member of a court of revision shall be appointed by by-law and shall hold office during pleasure of the Metropolitan Council.

(3) A member of a court of revision constituted under subsection 1 for one area municipality may also be appointed a member of a court of revision constituted for one or more other area municipalities.

(4) No person who is or during the preceding year was,

(a) a member of the council of an area municipality or of the Metropolitan Council; or

(b) an officer or employee (other than a member of a court of revision) of an area municipality or of the Metropolitan Corporation,

may be appointed or hold office as a member of a court of revision constituted under this section.

(5) Where a court of revision consists of three members, two members are a quorum.

(6) Each member of a court of revision shall be paid such sum for his services as the Metropolitan Council may by by-law provide.

(7) A court or courts of revision constituted for an area municipality under this section shall be deemed for the purposes of this and every other Act to be a court or courts of revision for the area municipality constituted in accordance with *The Assessment Act* and no area municipality shall constitute or continue a court or courts of revision under *The Assessment Act* or any special Act after the 31st day of December, 1953.

(8) A court or courts of revision constituted for an area municipality under this section shall be deemed to be the court or courts of revision constituted for the area municipality for the purposes of *The Local Improvement Act*.

(9) All rights of appeal conferred by *The Assessment Act* upon a person assessed in an area municipality may be exercised by such area municipality, or by a person designated by resolution of the council of such area municipality, with respect to an assessment in any other area municipality and with respect to the decision of a court of revision, county judge or the Municipal Board on any appeal with respect to such assessment and, notwithstanding anything in *The Assessment Act,* notice of appeal to the court of revision may be given by such area municipality or by such designated person within twenty-one days after the day upon which the assessment roll with respect to such assessment is returned.

(10) Where an appeal is filed in respect of an assessment of land in an area municipality, the area municipality shall be given notice of such appeal by the assessment commissioner and is entitled to be heard by the court of revision, county judge, Municipal Board or any court. R.S.O. 1960, c. 260, s. 32.

33. Section 56 of *The Assessment Act* applies in each area municipality but for the purposes of that section the Metropolitan Council shall be deemed to be the council of each area municipality. R.S.O. 1960, c. 260, s. 33.

34. For the purposes of sections 9, 10, 11, 12, 20 and 22 and subsection 5 of section 32 of *The Assessment Act,* each area municipality shall be deemed to be a city having a population of not less than 100,000. R.S.O. 1960, c. 260, s. 34.

35.—(1) For the purposes of additions to the collector's roll of an area municipality under subsection 1 of section 53 of *The Assessment Act,* the 30th day of November of the preceding year is the date referred to in clauses a, b, and c of the said subsection 1 in lieu of the 1st day of January.

(2) Where an entry is made in the collector's roll of an area municipality under section 53 of *The Assessment Act*

and a notice has been given as provided in subsection 4 of the said section 53 prior to the 10th day of January in any year, the amount of taxes to be levied thereon shall be for the whole current year. R.S.O. 1960, c. 260, s. 35.

(3) Where the amount of a business assessment is entered in the collector's roll of an area municipality under clause *c* of subsection 1 of section 53 of *The Assessment Act,* the real property with respect to which such business assessment is computed is, for the number of months remaining in the current year after the month in which the notice provided for in subsection 4 of the said section 53 is delivered or sent, liable to taxation at the rate levied under clause *a* of subsection 4 of section 231, and the clerk of the municipality shall amend the collector's roll accordingly, and, where taxes are levied under the authority of this subsection, they shall be deemed to be taxes levied under section 53 of *The Assessment Act.* 1961-62, c. 88, s. 6.

36. The additions to be made to the assessment roll of an area municipality under section 54 of *The Assessment Act* shall be made after the return of the roll and on or before the 30th day of November in any year. R.S.O. 1960, c. 260, s. 36.

37.—(1) Except as otherwise provided in this Act, all the provisions of *The Assessment Act* apply in each area municipality. R.S.O. 1960, c. 260, s. 37.

(2) For the purposes of sections 27, 72, 75 and 83 of *The Assessment Act,* "school board" includes The Metropolitan Toronto School Board and an agent thereof. 1961-62, c. 88, s. 7; 1966, c. 96, s. 8.

37*a.*—(1) The council of the City of Toronto and the council of the Borough of Etobicoke may, without the assent of the electors, repeal any by-law in force in the City or Borough providing for the partial exemption of dwellings from taxation or provide for the abolition of such exemption over a period of five years in such manner as the council may determine.

(2) Any such by-law in force in the City of Toronto immediately before this section comes into force shall be deemed to be in force in the whole of the City of Toronto until repealed. 1966, c. 96, s. 9.

Part III

METROPOLITAN WATERWORKS SYSTEM

38. For the purpose of supplying to the area municipalities water for the use of the area municipalities and their inhabitants, the Metropolitan Corporation has all the powers conferred by any general Act upon a municipal corporation and by any special Act upon an area municipality or local board thereof, respecting the establishment, construction, maintenance, operation, improvement and extension of a waterworks system. R.S.O. 1960, c. 260, s. 38.

39.—(1) The Metropolitan Council shall before the 1st day of December, 1953, pass by-laws which shall be effective on the 1st day of January, 1954, assuming as part of the metropolitan waterworks system all works for the production, treatment and storage of water vested in each area municipality or any local board thereof and all trunk distribution mains connected therewith, and on the day any such by-law becomes effective the works and mains designated therein vest in the Metropolitan Corporation.

(2) A by-law under subsection 1 shall designate and describe the works and trunk distribution mains assumed.

(3) For the purpose of subsection 1, a distribution main shall be deemed to be a trunk distribution main if so declared in the by-law assuming it.

(4) Notwithstanding subsection 1, a by-law for assuming any specific work or trunk distribution main may, with the approval of the Municipal Board, be passed after the 1st day of December, 1953, and in that case the by-law becomes effective on the date provided therein.

(5) Where the Metropolitan Corporation assumes a work or trunk distribution main vested in an area municipality or local board,

      (*a*) no compensation or damages shall be payable to the area municipality or local board;

      (*b*) the Metropolitan Corporation shall thereafter pay to the area municipality before the due date all amounts of principal and interest becoming due upon any outstanding debentures issued by the area municipality in respect of such work or main, but nothing in this clause requires the Metropolitan Corporation to pay that portion of the amounts of principal and interest that under *The Local Improvement Act* is payable as the owners' share of a local improvement work.

(6) If the Metropolitan Corporation fails to make any payment as required by clause *b* of subsection 5, the area municipality may charge the Metropolitan Corporation interest at the rate of one-half of 1 per cent for each month or fraction thereof that the payment is overdue.

(7) In the event of any doubt as to whether any outstanding debenture or portion thereof was issued in respect of the work or trunk distribution main assumed, the Municipal Board, upon application, may determine the matter and its decision is final.

(8) In this section, "works" means buildings, structures, plant, machinery, equipment and appurtenances, devices, conduits, intakes and outlets and underground construction and installations and other works designed for the production, treatment and storage of water and includes lands appropriated for such purposes and uses. R.S.O. 1960, c. 260, s. 39.

40.—(1) Where an area municipality or a local board thereof has agreed with any other municipality to supply water to that other municipality, and the works and trunk distribution mains used or required in carrying out such agreement are assumed by the Metropolitan Corporation, the Metropolitan Corporation becomes liable for the supply of water in accordance with the agreement and is bound by all the terms thereof and the area municipality or local board is relieved of all liability thereunder.

(2) Notwithstanding subsection 1 and notwithstanding anything in the agreement, the Municipal Board, upon the application of the Metropolitan Council or the council of the municipality to which the water is supplied, has jurisdiction and power from time to time to confirm, vary or fix the rates charged or to be charged in connection with water supplied under the agreement. R.S.O. 1960, c. 260, s. 40.

41.—(1) Where all the works of an area municipality or any local board thereof for the production, treatment and storage of water are assumed by the Metropolitan Corporation, the area municipality or local board shall not thereafter establish, maintain or operate any such works.

(2) An area municipality that did not operate any such works on the 31st day of December, 1953, shall not, after that date, establish, maintain or operate any such works.

(3) Nothing in this section limits the powers of an area municipality or local board thereof respecting the use and

distribution of water supplied to such area municipality by the Metropolitan Corporation. R.S.O. 1960, c. 260, s. 41.

42.—(1) No municipality or local board that is supplied with water by the Metropolitan Corporation shall supply or agree to supply any of such water beyond the limits of the municipality without the approval of the Metropolitan Council.

(2) Nothing in subsection 1 prohibits an area municipality or local board from supplying water to another municipality where the area municipality or local board has agreed to supply such water before the 1st day of April, 1953, and the works and trunk distribution mains used or required in carrying out such agreement have not been assumed by the Metropolitan Corporation. R.S.O. 1960, c. 260, s. 42.

43. The Metropolitan Council may pass by-laws for regulating the time, manner, extent and nature of the supply of water from its waterworks system, and every other matter or thing related to or connected therewith that it may be necessary and proper to regulate in order to secure to the inhabitants of the Metropolitan Area a continued and abundant supply of pure and wholesome water, and to prevent the practising of frauds on the Metropolitan Corporation with regard to the water so supplied. R.S.O. 1960, c. 260, s. 43.

44. The Metropolitan Council may pass by-laws for the maintenance and management of its waterworks system and may also by by-law or resolution fix the charges to meet the cost of any work or services done or furnished for the purposes of the supply of water and the rent of or charges for fittings, apparatus, meters or other things leased or furnished to any municipality or local board. R.S.O. 1960, c 260, s. 44.

45.—(1) The Metropolitan Council may pass by-laws fixing the rates at which water will be supplied to the area municipalities, and the times and places when and where the rates shall be payable.

(2) In fixing the rates, the Metropolitan Council may use its discretion as to the rate or rates to be charged to any area municipality, and may charge different rates to the various area municipalities.

(3) The Metropolitan Council shall so fix the rates at which water is supplied to the area municipalities that the revenues of the waterworks system will be sufficient to make the system self-sustaining after providing for such maintenance, renewals, depreciation, debt charges and reserves as the Metropolitan Council may think proper.

(4) Clause k of subsection 1 of section 53 of *The Ontario Municipal Board Act* does not apply with respect to water supplied by the Metropolitan Corporation to an area municipality. R.S.O. 1960, c. 260, s. 45.

46.—(1) The Metropolitan Corporation has power to and shall supply water to the area municipalities, but, subject to subsection 2, shall not supply water to any other person.

(2) The Metropolitan Corporation may enter into a contract for the supply of water to any local municipality outside the Metropolitan Area for its use or for resale to the inhabitants thereof for any period not exceeding twenty years, and may renew such contract from time to time for further periods not exceeding twenty years at any one time. R.S.O. 1960, c. 260, s. 46.

47. The Metropolitan Council shall keep separate books and accounts of the revenues, expenditures, assets and liabilities of its waterworks system in such manner as may be prescribed by the Department. R.S.O. 1960, c. 260, s. 47.

48.—(1) Notwithstanding anything in *The Public Utilities*

Act or any other general or special Act, the revenues of the waterworks system shall be applied only for,

    (*a*) the reduction of any indebtedness assumed or incurred with respect to the system;

    (*b*) the operation, maintenance, renewal, improvement or extension of the system;

    (*c*) the establishment of such reserve funds as the Metropolitan Council may deem proper, to be used at any future time for any purpose mentioned in clause *a* or *b* or for the stabilization of rates,

and any surplus revenues not required for such purposes shall remain credited to the waterworks system accounts and shall not form part of the general funds of the Metropolitan Corporation.

(2) It is not necessary to levy any rate to provide for principal, interest or other payments on account of any debentures issued or assumed by the Metropolitan Corporation for the purposes of the waterworks system except to the extent that the revenues of the system are insufficient to meet the annual payments falling due on account of principal and interest on the debentures.

(3) The moneys forming part of a reserve fund established under subsection 1 shall be paid into a special account and may be invested in such securities as a trustee may invest in under *The Trustee Act* and the earnings derived from the investment of such moneys shall form part of the reserve fund.

(4) The moneys forming part of a reserve fund established under subsection 1 shall be applied or expended only for the purposes of the waterworks system. R.S.O. 1960, c. 260, s. 48.

49.—(1) Subject to section 56, the Metropolitan Corporaion may sell, lease or otherwise dispose of any real or personal property acquired, held or used for or in conection with the waterworks system that, in the opinion of the Metropolitan Council, is no longer required for the purposes of the waterworks system, but where the property is actually used for the purposes of the waterworks system no such sale, lease or other disposition shall be made without the approval of the Municipal Board.

(2) The proceeds of any such sale, lease or other disposition shall be applied first in redemption and payment of any indebtedness assumed or incurred in respect of the property disposed of, and the balance shall form part of the revenues of the waterworks system. R.S.O. 1960, c. 260, s. 49.

50.—(1) The Metropolitan Corporation is not liable for damages caused by the shut-off or reduction of the amount of water supplied to an area municipality in cases of emergency or breakdown or when it is necessary in maintaining or extending the system, but the Metropolitan Council shall wherever possible give to any area municipality reasonable notice of intention to shut off or reduce the supply of water.

(2) Where the supply of water by the Metropolitan Corporation to an area municipality is interrupted or reduced, the area municipality or its local board may, notwithstanding anything in any contract, allocate and distribute its available water among its customers and may interrupt or decrease the delivery of water under any contract, and nothing done under this subsection shall be deemed to be a breach of contract, or entitle any person to rescind any contract or release any guarantor from the performance of his obligation. R.S.O. 1960, c. 260, s. 50.

51.—(1) The Metropolitan Council may pass by-laws establishing standards for and regulating and governing the design, construction and maintenance of local water distribution works by the area municipalities and may provide in any such by-law for the inspection of such local works, and every area municipality and local board shall conform to such by-laws.

(2) No area municipality or local board thereof shall construct or extend any local water distribution works or connect or continue the connection of the same or any part thereof to any work or main of the Metropolitan Corporation without the approval of the Metropolitan Council. R.S.O. 1960, c. 260, s. 51.

52. If the council of an area municipality considers itself aggrieved by the refusal of the Metropolitan Corporation or the Metropolitan Council,

> (a) to assume as a metropolitan work any local work;
>
> (b) to construct any extension of the metropolitan distribution system;
>
> (c) to maintain or increase the supply of water to the area municipality;
>
> (d) to approve the construction or extension of any local water distribution works by the area municipality; or
>
> (e) to permit the connection or the continuance of a connection to the metropolitan system,

the council may appeal to the Municipal Board which may make such order as it deems advisable in the matter, and the decision of the Municipal Board is final. R.S.O. 1960, c. 260, s. 52.

53.—(1) All rates and charges against an area municipality or local board thereof imposed under the authority of this Part are a debt of the area municipality to the Metropolitan Corporation, and the treasurer of every area municipality shall pay the same to the treasurer of the Metropolitan Corporation at the times and in the amounts specified by by-law of the Metropolitan Council.

(2) The Metropolitan Council may by by-law provide for uniform rates of discount for prompt payment of charges for water supplied to the area municipalities and may by by-law provide for the payment of interest in the event of default at a rate not exceeding one-half of 1 per cent for each month or fraction thereof while such default continues. R.S.O. 1960, c. 260, s. 53.

54. The Metropolitan Corporation has, in respect of all works and trunk distribution mains assumed as part of the metropolitan waterworks system, all the rights, powers, benefits and advantages conferred either by by-law or contract or otherwise upon the area municipality or area municipalities or their local boards with respect to such works or mains before they were assumed by the Metropolitan Corporation and the Metropolitan Corporation may sue upon such rights or under such by-laws or agreements in the same manner and to the same extent as the area municipality or municipalities or local board or boards might have done if such works or mains had not been assumed. R.S.O. 1960, c. 260, s. 54.

55. Any person authorized by the Metropolitan Council has free access from time to time, upon reasonable notice given and request made, to all works for the production and distribution of water within an area municipality and to all lands, buildings and premises used in connection therewith and the right upon the like notice and request to inspect and copy all plans, records and specifications and other information relating to the construction, extension or maintenance of such local works. R.S.O. 1960, c. 260, s. 55.

56. Where a distribution main has been assumed by the Metropolitan Corporation under section 39 and, in the opinion of the Metropolitan Council, is no longer required for the purposes of the metropolitan waterworks system but is, in the opinion of the council of the area municipality in which it is situate, required as a local distribution main by the area municipality, the Metropolitan Council shall by by-law remove the main from the metropolitan waterworks system and transfer it to the area municipality. R.S.O. 1960, c. 260, s. 56.

57. The works and mains assumed by the Metropolitan Corporation under section 39, together with any extensions or additions thereto constructed by the Metropolitan Corporation, may be used by the Metropolitan Corporation for the purpose of supplying and distributing water to any or all of the area municipalities and, subject to subsection 2 of section 46, to any local municipality outside the Metropolitan Area. R.S.O. 1960, c. 260, s. 57.

58. Sections 2, 3, 4, 5, 13, 28, 31, 32, 33, 52, 53, 54 and 56 of *The Public Utilities Act* apply *mutatis mutandis* to the Metropolitan Corporation. R.S.O. 1960, c. 260, s. 58.

Part IV
METROPOLITAN SEWAGE WORKS

59.—(1) In this Part,

> (a) "capital improvement" means an addition to or an extension, enlargement, alteration, replacement or other improvement of a work of such nature or character that it is usually and properly accounted for as a capital asset;
>
> (b) "land drainage" means storm, surface, overflow, subsurface or seepage waters or other drainage from land, but does not include sewage;
>
> (c) "sewage" means domestic sewage or industrial wastes, or both;
>
> (d) "sewage works" means an integral system consisting of a sewer or sewer system and treatment works;
>
> (e) "sewer" means a public sewer for common usage for the purpose of carrying away sewage or land drainage, or both;
>
> (f) "sewer system" means a system of two or more interconnected sewers having one or more common discharge outlets and includes pumping plant, force mains, siphons and other like work;
>
> (g) "treatment works" means buildings, structures, plant, machinery, equipment, devices, intakes and outfalls or outlets and other works designed for the interception, collection, settling, treating, dispersing, disposing or discharging of sewage or land drainage, or both, and includes land appropriated for such purposes and uses;
>
> (h) "work" means a sewer, sewer system, sewage works or treatment works, or a capital improvement of any of them.

(2) For the purpose of this Part, a sewer, sewer system or sewage works, whether existing or proposed, shall be deemed to be a trunk sewer, trunk sewer system or trunk sewage works, if so declared by by-law of the Metropolitan Council. R.S.O. 1960, c. 260, s. 59.

60. For the purpose of collecting or receiving from the area municipalities, or any of them, sewage and land drainage and the treatment or disposal thereof, the Metropolitan Corporation has all the powers conferred by any general Act upon a municipal corporation and by any special Act upon an area municipality or local board thereof. R.S.O. 1960, c. 260, s. 60.

61. The Metropolitan Council may pass by-laws for constructing, maintaining, improving, repairing, widening, altering, diverting and stopping up trunk sewers, trunk sewer systems, trunk sewage works, treatment works and watercourses. R.S.O. 1960, c. 260, s. 61.

62.—(1) The Metropolitan Council shall, before the 1st day of December, 1953, pass by-laws which shall be effective on the 1st day of January, 1954, assuming as metropolitan sewage works all treatment works vested in each area municipality or any local board thereof, and on the day any such by-law becomes effective the works designated therein vest in the Metropolitan Corporation.

(2) The Metropolitan Council may at any time pass by-laws for assuming any trunk sewer, trunk sewer system, or watercourse vested in any area municipality or local board thereof, but no such by-law becomes effective before the 1st day of January, 1954.

(3) A by-law under subsection 1 or 2 shall designate and describe the works assumed.

(4) Notwithstanding subsection 1, a by-law for assuming any specific treatment works may, with the approval of the Municipal Board, be passed after the 1st day of December, 1953, and in that case the by-law becomes effective on the date provided therein.

(5) Where the Metropolitan Corporation assumes a work or watercourse vested in an area municipality or local board,

(a) no compensation or damages shall be payable to the area municipality or local board;

(b) the Metropolitan Corporation shall thereafter pay to the area municipality before the due date all amounts of principal and interest becoming due upon any outstanding debentures issued by the area municipality in respect of such work or watercourse, but nothing in this clause requires the Metropolitan Corporation to pay that portion of the amounts of principal and interest that under *The Local Improvement Act* is payable as the owners' share of a local improvement work.

(6) If the Metropolitan Corporation fails to make any payment as required by clause *b* of subsection 5, the area municipality may charge the Metropolitan Corporation interest at the rate of one-half of 1 per cent for each month or fraction thereof that the payment is overdue.

(7) In the event of any doubt as to whether any outstanding debenture or portion thereof was issued in respect of the work or watercourse assumed, the Municipal Board, upon application, may determine the matter and its decision is final. R.S.O. 1960, c. 260, s. 62.

63.—(1) Where an area municipality or a local board thereof has agreed with any other municipality to receive sewage or land drainage from that other municipality, and the works or watercourses used or required in carrying out such agreement are assumed by the Metropolitan Corporation, the Metropolitan Corporation becomes liable to receive such sewage or land drainage in accordance with the agreement and the receiving municipality or local board is relieved of all liability thereunder.

(2) Where an area municipality or a local board thereof has agreed with any person other than a municipality to receive sewage or land drainage and the works or watercourses used or required in carrying out such agreement are assumed by the Metropolitan Corporation, the Metropolitan Corpora-

tion becomes liable to receive such sewage or land drainage in accordance with the agreement and the area municipality or local board is relieved of all liability thereunder.

(3) Notwithstanding subsections 1 and 2 and notwithstanding anything in any such agreement, the Municipal Board, upon the application of the Metropolitan Council or of the council of any area municipality or of any person concerned, may by order terminate any such agreement and adjust all rights and liabilities thereunder. R.S.O. 1960, c. 260, s. 63.

64.—(1) Where all the treatment works of an area municipality or any local board thereof are assumed by the Metropolitan Corporation, the area municipality shall not thereafter establish, maintain or operate treatment works without the approval of the Metropolitan Council.

(2) No area municipality shall establish or enlarge any treatment works after the 1st day of December, 1953, without the approval of the Metropolitan Council. R.S.O. 1960, c. 260, s. 64.

65. The Metropolitan Council may pass by-laws for the maintenance and management of its sewers, sewer system, sewage works, treatment works and watercourses and regulating the manner, extent and nature of the reception and disposal of sewage and land drainage from the area municipalities and every other matter or thing related to or connected therewith that it may be necessary and proper to regulate in order to secure to the inhabitants of the Metropolitan Area an adequate system of sewage and land drainage disposal. R.S.O. 1960, c. 260, s. 65.

66.—(1) Where in the opinion of the Metropolitan Council an area municipality or a portion thereof will or may derive a special benefit from the construction and operation of a work or watercourse, the Metropolitan Council may, with the approval of the Municipal Board, in authorizing the construction, extension or improvement of the work, by by-law provide that the area municipality shall be chargeable with and shall pay to the Metropolitan Corporation such portion of the capital cost thereof as the by-law specifies, and such by-law is binding on the area municipality.

(2) Where debentures are issued for the cost of the work, the area municipality chargeable under the by-law shall make payments to the Metropolitan Corporation with respect to such debentures proportionate to its share of the capital cost as set out in the by-law in the same manner as if debentures for such share had been issued by the Metropolitan Corporation for the purposes of the area municipality.

(3) The area municipality may pay the amounts chargeable to it under this section out of its general funds or, subject to the approval of the Municipal Board, may pass by-laws under section 380 of *The Municipal Act* for imposing sewer rates to recover the whole or part of the amount chargeable to the area municipality in the same manner as if the work were being or had been constructed, extended or improved by the area municipality. R.S.O. 1960, c. 260, s. 66.

67.—(1) No municipality or person shall connect any local work, local watercourse, private drain or private sewer to a local metropolitan work or watercourse without the approval of the Metropolitan Council.

(2) The Metropolitan Corporation may enter into a contract with any local municipality outside the Metropolitan Area to receive and dispose of sewage and land drainage from the local municipality on such terms and conditions as may be agreed upon for any period not exceeding twenty years, and may renew such contract from time to time for further periods not exceeding twenty years at any one time.

(3) Any engineer or other officer of the Metropolitan Corporation has power to inspect the plans and specifications of any work referred to in subsection 1 and to inspect the work during its construction and before it is connected with the metropolitan work or watercourse. R.S.O. 1960, c. 260, s. 67.

68.—(1) The Metropolitan Council may pass by-laws establishing standards for and regulating and governing the design, construction and maintenance of local works connected or to be connected to a metropolitan work or watercourse, and every area municipality and local board shall conform to such by-laws.

(2) No area municipality or local board thereof shall enlarge, extend or alter any local work or watercourse that discharges into a metropolitan work or watercourse without the approval of the Metropolitan Council. R.S.O. 1960, c. 260, s. 68.

69. If the council of an area municipality considers itself aggrieved by the refusal of the Metropolitan Corporation or the Metropolitan Council,

> (a) to assume as a metropolitan work any local work;
> (b) to construct, extend or improve any metropolitan work;
> (c) to receive any required volume of sewage or land drainage from the area municipality;
> (d) to approve the construction, alteration, improvement or extension of a local work;
> (e) to permit a connection or the continuance of a connection to any metropolitan work,

the council may appeal to the Municipal Board which may make such order as it deems advisable in the matter, and the decision of the Municipal Board is final. R.S.O. 1960, c. 260, s. 69.

70.—(1) The Metropolitan Council may pass by-laws subject to the approval of the Municipal Board, providing for imposing on and collecting from any area municipality, in respect of the whole or any designated part or parts thereof from which sewage and land drainage is received, a sewage service rate or rates sufficient to pay such portion as the by-law may specify of the annual cost of maintenance and operation of any metropolitan work or works

(2) All such charges constitute a debt of the area municipality to the Metropolitan Corporation and shall be payable at such times and in such amounts as may be specified by by-law of the Metropolitan Council.

(3) The area municipality may pay the amounts chargeable to it under any such by-law out of its general funds or, subject to the approval of the Municipal Board, may pass by-laws under section 380 of *The Municipal Act* for imposing sewage service rates to recover the whole or part of the amount chargeable to the area municipality. R.S.O. 1960, c. 260, s. 70.

71. The Metropolitan Corporation has, in respect of all works assumed, all the rights, powers, benefits and advantages conferred either by by-law or contract or otherwise upon the area municipality or area municipalities or their local boards with respect to such works before they were assumed by the Metropolitan Corporation and the Metropolitan Corporation may sue upon such rights or under such by-laws or agreements in the same manner and to the same extent as the area municipality or municipalities or local board or boards might have done if such works had not been assumed. R.S.O. 1960, c. 260, s. 71.

72. Any person authorized by the Metropolitan Council has free access from time to time, upon reasonable notice given and request made, to all works within an area munici-

pality and to all lands, buildings and premises used in connection therewith and the right, upon the like notice and request, to inspect and copy all plans, records and specifications and other information relating to the construction, extension or maintenance of such local works. R.S.O. 1960, c. 260, s. 72.

73. Any works assumed by the Metropolitan Corporation under the authority of section 62, together with any extensions or additions thereto constructed by the Metropolitan Corporation, may be used by the Metropolitan Corporation for the purpose of receiving and disposing of sewage and land drainage from any or all of the area municipalities and, subject to subsection 2 of section 67, from any local municipality outside the Metropolitan Area. R.S.O. 1960, c. 260, s. 73.

Part IV-A
WASTE DISPOSAL

73a.—(1) In this Part,

> (a) "area municipality" includes a local board;
> (b) "waste" includes ashes, garbage, refuse and domestic or industrial waste of any kind.

(2) The Metropolitan Corporation may acquire and use land within the Metropolitan Toronto Planning Area and may erect, maintain and operate buildings, structures, machinery or equipment for the purposes of receiving, dumping and disposing of waste, and may contract with any person for such purposes, and may prohibit or regulate the dumping and disposing of waste or any class or classes thereof upon any such land, and may charge fees for the use of such property, which fees may vary in respect of different classes of waste, but no such fees shall be charged to any area municipality or its agent.

(3) The power to acquire land under subsection 2 shall not be exercised without,

> (a) the approval of the municipality in which the land is situate, which approval may be granted upon such terms and conditions as may be agreed upon; or
> (b) failing such approval or agreement, the approval of the Municipal Board.

(4) The Municipal Board, before giving its approval under clause *b* of subsection 3, shall hold a public hearing and shall give or cause to be given at least ten days notice of the hearing to the clerk of the municipality concerned and to such other persons in such manner as the Municipal Board may direct, and the Municipal Board, as a condition of giving any such approval, may by its order impose such restrictions, limitations and conditions respecting the acquisition or use of such land as to the Municipal Board may appear necessary or expedient.

(5) On and after the 1st day of January, 1967, no area municipality shall exercise any of its powers with respect to the matters provided for in subsection 2 without the consent of the Metropolitan Council.

(6) The Metropolitan Council shall, before the 1st day of January, 1697, pass by-laws, which shall be effective on the 1st day of January, 1967, assuming for the use of the Metropolitan Corporation any land, building, structure, machinery or equipment, including vehicles used primarily for the disposal of waste, that the Metropolitan Corporation may require for the purposes of subsection 2 that is vested on the 31st day of March, 1966, in any area municipality and is used on such date for the purposes set out in subsection 2 or that is acquired by any area municipality after the 31st day of March, 1966, and before the 1st day of January, 1967, for such use, and on

the day any such by-law becomes effective the property designated therein vests in the Metropolitan Corporation.

(7) No area municipality, after the 31st day of March, 1966, and before the 1st day of January, 1967, shall without the consent of the Metropolitan Council sell, lease or otherwise dispose of or encumber any property mentioned in subsection 6.

(8) Notwithstanding subsection 6, a by-law for assuming any property mentioned in subsection 6, with the approval of the Municipal Board, may be passed after the 1st day of January, 1967, and in that case the by-law shall become effective on the date provided therein.

(9) Where the Metropolitan Corporation assumes any property under subsection 6 or 8,

(a) no compensation or damage shall be payable to the area municipality except as provided in this subsection;

(b) the Metropolitan Corporation shall thereafter pay to the area municipality before the due date all amounts of principal and interest becoming due upon any outstanding debentures issued by the area municipality in respect of any property vested in the Metropolitan Corporation under subsection 6 or 8; and

(c) notwithstanding any order of the Municipal Board or any debenture by-law passed pursuant thereto, all amounts of principal and interest becoming due thereafter with respect to any debentures theretofore issued by the Metropolitan Corporation in respect of any property vested in the Metropolitan Corporation under subsection 6 or 8 shall be repaid by levies against all the area municipalities.

(10) If the Metropolitan Corporation fails to make any payment as required by clause b of subsection 9, the area municipality may charge the Metropolitan Corporation interest at the rate of one-half of 1 per cent for each month or fraction thereof that the payment is overdue.

(11) In the event of any doubt as to whether,

(a) any outstanding debenture or portion thereof was issued in respect of any property assumed under subsection 6 or 8; or

(b) any vehicle was used primarily for the disposal of waste,

the Municipal Board, upon application, may determine the matter, and its decision is final.

(12) No by-law of any municipality heretofore or hereafter passed pursuant to paragraph 112 of subsection 1 of section 379 of *The Municipal Act* or a predecessor thereof shall apply to the operations of the Metropolitan Corporation pursuant to subsection 2.

(13) Nothing in this Part shall affect any contract for the disposal of waste that is now existing between any person and any area municipality, but the Metropolitan Corporation and any such municipality may enter into an agreement providing that the Metropolitan Corporation shall assume all or part of the liability created by such contract in respect of the disposal of waste. 1966, c. 96, s. 10.

Part V

METROPOLITAN ROAD SYSTEM

74. In this Part,

(a) "approved" means approved by the Minister or of a type approved by the Minister;

(b) "Department" means the Department of Highways;

(c) "Minister" means the Minister of Highways. R.S.O. 1960, c. 260, s. 74.

75. Unless assumed as a metropolitan road by the by-law mentioned in section 76, all roads within the Metropolitan Area or on the boundary between the Metropolitan Area and an adjoining county that, on the 31st day of December, 1953, form part of the county road system of the County of York established under *The Highway Improvement Act* shall, on the 1st day of January, 1954, revert or be transferred to the corporations of the local municipalities in which they are situate. R.S.O. 1960, c. 260, s. 75.

76.—(1) Subject to the approval of the Lieutenant Governor in Council, the Metropolitan Council shall by by-law establish a metropolitan road system in the Metropolitan Area by assuming roads in any area municipality and may include in the system such boundary line roads or portions thereof between the Metropolitan Area and an adjoining county as may be agreed upon between the Metropolitan Council and the council of such county, and the by-laws shall designate the roads to be assumed as metropolitan roads and intended to form the metropolitan road system.

(2) The by-law shall be passed not later than the 31st day of October, 1953, and shall come into force on the 1st day of January, 1954.

(3) The Metropolitan Corporation shall submit the by-law to the Minister for approval by the Lieutenant Governor in Council on or before the 31st day of October, 1953, and upon receipt of the application for such approval the Minister may obtain such report thereon as he may deem necessary and may hear the council of any area municipality that may be dissatisfied therewith before presenting the application for consideration to the Lieutenant Governor in Council.

(4) The Lieutenant Governor in Council may approve the by-law in whole or in part and where the by-law is approved in part only it shall be enforced and take effect so far as approved, but it is not necessary for the Metropolitan Council to pass any further by-law amending the original by-law or repealing any portion thereof which has not been so approved.

(5) Subject to the approval of the Lieutenant Governor in Council, the Metropolitan Council may amend the by-law from time to time by adding roads to or removing roads from the metropolitan road system or in any other manner.

(6) Where a road or a part thereof is added to the metropolitan road system, the soil and freehold of such road or part is thereupon vested in the Metropolitan Corporation.

(7) Where a road or a part thereof is removed from the metropolitan road system, except by reason of it being stopped-up pursuant to section 87, such road or part is thereupon transferred to and the soil and freehold thereof is thereupon vested in the corporation of the local municipality in which it is situate.

(8) Subject to the approval of the Lieutenant Governor in Council, the Metropolitan Corporation may from time to time pass a by-law consolidating its by-laws establishing the metropolitan road system and all by-laws amending such by-law. R.S.O. 1960, c. 260, s. 76.

77.—(1) The Metropolitan Corporation shall submit a by-law covering the estimated expenditure on metropolitan roads for the calendar year to the Department for the Minister's approval, not later than the 31st day of March of the year in which the expenditure is to be made. R.S.O. 1960, c. 260, s. 77 (1).

(1a) The Metropolitan Corporation may, at any time within the calendar year in which the expenditure is to be made, submit to the Minister for his approval a by-law covering the estimated expenditure on metropolitan roads supplementing the by-law submitted under subsection 1. 1962-63, c. 89, s. 4.

(2) No subsidy shall be granted by the Department for work undertaken by the Metropolitan Corporation that has not been provided for by a by-law duly approved by the Minister. R.S.O. 1960, c. 260, s. 77 (2).

78.—(1) The Metropolitan Council shall annually and may with the consent of the Minister at any time during the progress of its work in connection with the metropolitan road system submit to the Minister,

    (a) a detailed statement of receipts and expenditures in the form prescribed by the Minister;

    (b) a declaration of the engineer or other officer of the Metropolitan Corporation who is charged with the responsibility of directing and supervising the work that the statement of receipts and expenditures is correct and that the work has been done in accordance with the requirements of the Minister and with the approval of the proper officer of the Department;

    (c) a declaration of the treasurer of the Metropolitan Corporation that the statement of receipts and expenditures is correct; and

    (d) a petition for the payment of the grant, authorized by resolution of the Metropolitan Council.

(2) Upon receipt of the statement, declarations and petition and the approval thereof by the proper officer of the Department, the Minister may direct payment to the treasurer of the Metropolitan Corporation out of moneys appropriated therefor by the Legislature of an amount equal to 50 per cent of the amount of the expenditure that is properly chargeable to road improvement and in all cases of doubt or dispute the decision of the Minister is final. R.S.O. 1960, c. 260, s. 78.

(3) Subject to section 77, the Minister may, in his discretion, direct payment to the Metropolitan Corporation under this section, on or after the 1st day of May in any year, of a sum not exceeding 25 per cent,

    (a) of the amount paid by the Minister under this section in respect of the preceding calendar year; or

    (b) of the average annual payments made by the Minister under this section in respect of the five preceding calendar years. 1962-63, c. 89, s. 5.

79. No expenditure towards which a special contribution has been or may be made from any source shall be included in a statement submitted under section 78 except with the consent of the Minister. R.S.O. 1960, c. 260, s. 79.

80. Expenditures that shall be deemed to be properly chargeable to road improvement include those made for the purpose of,

    (a) opening a new metropolitan road and acquiring the necessary land therefor;

    (b) clearing a metropolitan road of obstructions;

    (c) widening, altering or diverting a metropolitan road;

    (d) subject to section 3 of *The Public Service Works on Highways Act,* defraying 50 per cent of the cost of labour only in taking up, removing or changing the location of appliances or works placed on or under a metropolitan road by an operating corporation;

    (e) constructing and maintaining bridges, culverts or other structures, other than sanitary sewers, incidental to the construction of a metropolitan road;

    (f) grading a metropolitan road;

    (g) constructing and maintaining an approved base for the road surface on a metropolitan road, including the installing and maintaining of approved drainage;

    (h) constructing and maintaining any approved type of road surface on a metropolitan road;

    (i) constructing and maintaining necessary curbs, gutters and catch basins on a metropolitan road;

    (j) clearing snow from and applying chemicals or abrasives to icy surfaces on a metropolitan road;

    (k) establishing and laying out a new road under section 86 and constructing such new road as part of the metropolitan road system before actually assuming it is a metropolitan road by amending the by-law passed under section 76; and

    (l) such other work of road improvement as the Minister may approve. R.S.O. 1960, c. 260, s. 80; 1962-63, c. 89, s. 6.

81. Every road constructed or repaired as part of the metropolitan road system shall be so constructed and repaired in accordance with the requirements of the Minister. R.S.O. 1960, c. 260, s. 81.

82. The Metropolitan Corporation has, in respect of the roads or streets included in the metropolitan road system, all the rights, powers, benefits and advantages conferred, and is subject to all liabilities imposed, either by statute, by-law, contract or otherwise upon The Corporation of the County of York or the corporation of the area municipality or the corporations of two or more area municipalities which had jurisdiction over the roads before they were assumed by the Metropolitan Corporation, and the Metropolitan Corporation may sue upon such rights or under such agreements or by-laws in the same manner and to the same extent as the County of York or the area municipality or municipalities, as the case may be, might have done if the roads had not been assumed as metropolitan roads. R.S.O. 1960, c. 260, s. 82.

83.—(1) The Metropolitan Corporation is not by reason of assuming a road under this Act liable for the building, maintenance or repair of sidewalks on any metropolitan road or portion thereof, but the area municipality in which such sidewalks are located continues to be liable for the maintenance and repair of such sidewalks and is responsible for any injury or damage arising from the construction or presence of the sidewalks on such road or portion thereof to the same extent and subject to the same limitations to which an area municipality is liable under section 443 of *The Municipal Act,* in respect of a sidewalk on a road over which a council has jurisdiction.

(2) The council of an area municipality may construct or put down a sidewalk or other improvement or service on a metropolitan road but no such work shall be undertaken by a municipal corporation or any individual or company without first obtaining the written consent of the Metropolitan Council expressed by resolution.

(3) The cost of any sidewalk constructed on a metropolitan road may be met out of the general funds of the area municipality or the work may be undertaken as a local improvement under *The Local Improvement Act.*

(4) An area municipality when constructing a sidewalk or other improvements or service on a metropolitan road under this section shall conform to any requirements or conditions imposed by the Metropolitan Council and is responsible for any injury or damage arising from the construction or presence of the sidewalk, improvements or service on the road.

(5) Subsection 4 of section 100 of *The Highway Improvement Act* does not apply to a sidewalk constructed on a metropolitan road by the council of a township. R.S.O. 1960, c. 260, s. 83.

84. Where a metropolitan road intersects a road that is not a metropolitan road, the continuation of the metropolitan road to its full width across the road intersected, including the bridges and culverts thereon or touching thereon, is a part of the metropolitan road system except in the case of an intersection by a metropolitan road of the King's Highway, and in that case the full width of the intersection shall be deemed to be part of the King's Highway. R.S.O. 1960, c. 260, s. 84.

85. When land abutting on a metropolitan road is dedicated for highway purposes for, or apparently for, the widening of the metropolitan road, the land so dedicated is part of the metropolitan road and the soil and freehold thereof is vested in the Metropolitan Corporation subject to any rights in the soil reserved by the person who dedicated the land. R.S.O. 1960, c. 260, s. 85.

86. Subject to the approval of the Lieutenant Governor in Council, the Metropolitan Council may pass by-laws for establishing and laying out new roads and for amending the by-law passed under section 76 by assuming such new roads as part of the metropolitan road system and the provisions of *The Municipal Act* with respect to the establishment and laying out of highways by municipalities apply *mutatis mutandis*. R.S.O. 1960, c. 260, s. 86.

87. With respect to the metropolitan roads, the Metropolitan Corporation has all the powers conferred, and is subject to all the liabilities imposed, upon the council or corporation of a city under *The Municipal Act, The Highway Traffic Act* and any other Act with respect to highways. R.S.O. 1960, c. 260, s. 87.

87a.—(1) Subject to The Highway Traffic Act, the Metropolitan Corporation may,

(*a*) install signal-light traffic control systems on any highway in the Metropolitan Area;

(*b*) operate all signal-light traffic control systems heretofore or hereafter installed in the Metropolitan Area;

(*c*) control its signal-light traffic control system by electronic computers; and

(*d*) regulate traffic on highways in the Metropolitan Area within 100 feet of any signal-light traffic control system and for such purpose the Metropolitan Corporation is deemed to be a municipality under section 108 of *The Highway Traffic Act.*

(2) When a by-law passed under subsection 1 regulating traffic on any part of a highway in the Metropolitan Area is in force, any by-law passed by an area municipality that conflicts therewith has no effect to the extent of such conflict.

(3) No area municipality may, after the day this section comes into force, install or operate signal-light traffic control systems in the Metropolitan Area.

(4) All signal-light traffic control systems installed on highways in the Metropolitan Area are vested in the Metropolitan Corporation, and no compensation therefor shall be paid by the Metropolitan Corporation to any area municipality. 1961-62, c. 88, s. 8.

88.—(1) Where the name of a highway is a duplication or is similar to the name of another highway in the Metropolitan Area, the Metropolitan Council may pass by-laws for changing the name of any such highway, and no area municipality thereafter has power to change the name of such highway.

(2) A by-law passed under subsection 1 shall recite the fact of such duplication or similarity, and the change shall take effect when a certified copy of the by-law is registered in the proper registry or land titles office. R.S.O. 1960, c. 260, s. 88.

89.—(1) The Metropolitan Council may by by-law prescribe a lower or higher rate of speed for motor vehicles driven upon any metropolitan road or any portion of a metropolitan road than is prescribed in subsection 1 of section 59 of *The Highway Traffic Act,* but such rate of speed shall not be less than 25 miles per hour or more than 60 miles per hour.

(2) No by-law passed under subsection 1 shall become effective until approved by the Department of Transport and the metropolitan roads or portions thereof affected by the by-law shall be marked to comply with the regulations made under *The Highway Traffic Act.* R.S.O. 1960, c. 260, s. 89.

90. The Metropolitan Council may by by-law prescribe the rate of speed for motor vehicles driven on lands vested in the Metropolitan Corporation under Part XV in accordance with subsection 4 of section 59 of *The Highway Traffic Act,* R.S.O. 1960, c. 260, s. 90.

91. The Metropolitan Council may by by-law empower the council of any area municipality to lease or license the use of untravelled surface portions of metropolitan roads within those portions of the area municipality zoned for commercial or industrial purposes to the owners or occupants of property abutting on such roads to be used solely for the parking of vehicles. R.S.O. 1960, c. 260, s. 91.

92. The Metropolitan Council may plant trees on a metropolitan road and the cost of the work shall be deemed to be part of the cost of repairing and maintaining the road. R.S.O. 1960, c. 260, s. 92.

93.—(1) Where, in the exercise of its powers or in the performance of its obligations under this Act, the Metropolitan Corporation finds that it is necessary to expropriate land for the purpose of establishing, laying out, opening up, widening, improving, protecting from erosion, altering or diverting a metropolitan road, the Metropolitan Corporation may, instead of the procedure provided by *The Municipal Act,* proceed in the manner provided by *The Public Works Act* in the case of lands taken by the Minister of Public Works for the purposes of Ontario without the consent of the owner of such lands, and the provisions of *The Public Works Act mutatis mutandis* apply, and the powers and duties of the Minister of Public Works as set out in *The Public Works Act* may be exercised and performed in the name of the Metropolitan Corporation.

(2) The plan and description of the lands taken, required by section 17 of *The Public Works Act* to be deposited in the registry office, shall be signed by the chairman and clerk of the Metropolitan Corporation and by an Ontario land surveyor, and upon the deposit of the plan and description the land becomes and is vested in the Metropolitan Corporation. R.S.O. 1960, c. 260, s. 92.

94.—(1) Sections 452 and 454 of *The Municipal Act* do not apply to a bridge or highway crossing or forming a boundary between the Metropolitan Area and an adjoining county where such bridge or highway is included in the metropolitan road system and in the county road system of the county.

(2) When there is a difference between the Metropolitan Council and the council of a county in respect of any such bridge or highway as to the corporation upon which the obligation rests for the building, maintaining or keeping in repair of the bridge or highway, or as to the proportions in which the corporations should respectively contribute thereto, or where the Metropolitan Council and the council of the county are unable to agree as to any action, matter or thing to be taken or done in respect of such bridge or highway, every

such difference shall be determined by the Municipal Board upon an application by the Metropolitan Corporation or the corporation of the county.

(3) The Municipal Board shall appoint a day for the hearing of the application, of which ten days notice in writing shall be given to the clerk of each municipality, and shall, at the time and place appointed, hear and determine all matters in difference between the municipalities in regard to such bridge or highway, and the Municipal Board may make such order in regard to the same as it may deem just and proper, and may by the order fix and determine the amount or proportion which each municipality shall pay or contribute toward the building, maintaining and keeping in repair of such bridge or highway.

(4) An order made by the Municipal Board under this section is binding upon the municipalities for such period as the Municipal Board may determine, and is final and conclusive. R.S.O. 1960, c. 260, s. 94.

95. Clause *b* of subsection 1 of section 419 of *The Municipal Act* does not apply to a bridge over a river, stream, pond or lake forming or crossing a boundary line between area municipalities, and the councils of the area municipalities on either side of such boundary line have joint jurisdiction over every such bridge that is not included in the metropolitan road system. R.S.O. 1960, c. 260, s. 95.

96. Section 434 of *The Municipal Act* does not apply to a bridge over a river, stream, pond or lake forming or crossing a boundary line between the Metropolitan Area and an adjoining county, and the councils of the area municipality and the local municipality in the adjoining county on either side of such boundary line have joint jurisdiction over every such bridge that is not included in the metropolitan road system R.S.O. 1960, c. 260, s. 96.

97.—(1) The Metropolitan Council has, with respect to all land lying within a distance of 150 feet from any limit of a metropolitan road, all the powers conferred on the council of a local municipality by section 30 of *The Planning Act*.

(2) In the event of conflict between a by-law passed under subsection 1 by the Metropolitan Council and a by-law passed under section 30 of *The Planning Act* or a predecessor of such section by the council of the area municipality in which the land is situate, the by-law passed by the Metropolitan Council prevails to the extent of such conflict, but in all other respects the by-law passed by the council of the area municipality remains in full force and effect. R.S.O. 1960, c. 260, s. 97.

98.—(1) Subject to the approval of the Municipal Board, the Metropolitan Corporation may by by-law designate any metropolitan road, or any portion thereof, as a metropolitan controlled-access road.

(2) Subject to the approval of the Municipal Board, the Metropolitan Corporation may by by-law close any municipal road that intersects or runs into a metropolitan controlled-access road.

(3) The Municipal Board may direct that notice of any application for approval of the closing of a road under this section shall be given at such times, in such manner and to such persons as the Municipal Board may determine, and may further direct that particulars of claims in respect of land injuriously affected by the closing of the road shall be filed with the Municipal Board and the Metropolitan Corporation within such time as the Municipal Board shall direct.

(4) No claim by or on behalf of any person who has not filed the particulars of claim within the time directed by the Municipal Board shall be allowed except by leave of the Municipal Board.

(5) Upon the hearing of the application for approval of the closing of a road, the Municipal Board may make such order as it deems proper refusing its approval or granting its approval upon such terms and conditions as it deems proper, and any order of the Municipal Board approving of the closing of a road may contain provisions,

   (*a*) determining the portion or portions of the road that shall be closed;
   (*b*) providing that the approval shall be subject to the making of compensation to persons whose land is injuriously affected by the closing of the road,
       (i) by the payment by the Metropolitan Corporation to any of such persons of such damages as may be fixed by the Municipal Board,
       (ii) by the providing of another road for the use of any such persons,
       (iii) by the vesting of any portion of the road allowance so closed in any of such persons notwithstanding any other Act, and
       (iv) in such other manner as the Municipal Board may deem proper;
   (*c*) providing for the payment of the costs of any person appearing on such application and fixing the amount of such costs; and
   (*d*) providing for the doing of such other acts as in the circumstances it deems proper.

(6) Upon the approval of the Municipal Board being so obtained but subject to the provisions of the order of the Municipal Board made on the application for such approval, the Metropolitan Corporation may do all such acts as may be necessary to close the road in respect of which the application is made.

(7) Where, at any time after making application for the approval of the Municipal Board of the closing of a road, the Metropolitan Corporation discontinues its application or, having obtained such approval, does not proceed with the closing of the road and does not pay the compensation provided for in the order of the Municipal Board, the Municipal Board may, upon the application of any person whose land would be injuriously affected by the closing of the road and who has appeared upon such application for approval, make such order as to costs against the Metropolitan Corporation as it deems proper and may fix the amount of such costs.

(8) Any person who claims to be injuriously affected by the closing of a road may, by leave of the Court of Appeal, appeal to that court from any order of the Municipal Board approving the closing of such road, and the Metropolitan Corporation may, upon like leave, appeal from any order of the Municipal Board made on an application under this section.

(9) The leave may be granted on such terms as to the giving of security for costs and otherwise as the court may deem just.

(10) The practice and procedure as to the appeal and matters incidental thereto shall be the same, *mutatis mutandis,* as upon an appeal from a county court, and the decision of the Court of Appeal is final.

(11) Section 95 of *The Ontario Municipal Board Act* does not apply to an appeal under this section. R.S.O. 1960, c. 260, s. 98.

99.—(1) The Metropolitan Corporation may pass by-laws prohibiting or regulating the construction or use of any private road, entranceway, gate or other structure or facility as a means of access to a metropolitan controlled-access road and may impose penalties for contravention of any such by-law.

(2) The Metropolitan Corporation may give notice to the owner of any land requiring him to close up any private road, entranceway, gate or other structure or facility constructed or used as a means of access to a metropolitan controlled-access road in contravention of a by-law passed under subsection 1.

(3) Every notice given under subsection 2 shall be in writing and shall be served personally or by registered mail and in the case of service by registered mail shall be deemed to have been received on the second day following the mailing thereof.

(4) Where the person to whom notice is given under subsection 2 fails to comply with the notice within thirty days after its receipt, the Metropolitan Corporation may by resolution direct any officer, employee or agent of the municipality to enter upon the land of such person and do or cause to be done whatever may be necessary to close up the private road, entranceway, gate or other structure or facility as required by the notice.

(5) Every person who fails to comply with a notice given under subsection 2 is guilty of an offence and on summary conviction is liable to a fine of not less than $10 and not more than $100 for a first offence and to a fine of not less than $50 and not more than $500 for a second or subsequent offence.

(6) Where a notice given under subsection 2 has been complied with, the Metropolitan Corporation shall make due compensation to the owner of the land if the private road, entranceway, gate or other structure or facility constructed or used as a means of access to a metropolitan controlled-access road was constructed or used, as the case may be,

(a) before the day on which the by-law designating the road as a metropolitan controlled-access road became effective; or

(b) in compliance with a by-law passed under subsection 1, in which case the making of compensation is subject to any provisions of such by-law.

(7) Every claim for such compensation shall be determined in accordance with subsections 2 to 6 of section 11 of *The Highway Improvement Act,* which subsections apply *mutatis mutandis.* R.S.O. 1960, c. 260, s. 99.

100. Sections 95, 97, 98, 99, 102 and 105 of *The Highway Improvement Act* apply *mutatis mutandis* to any metropolitan road. R.S.O. 1960, c. 260, s. 100.

101. For the purposes of subsection 1 of section 45 and Part VIII of *The Highway Improvement Act,* the Metropolitan Corporation shall be deemed to be the corporation of a city having a population of more than 50,000 situate within the County of York but separated therefrom for municipal purposes, and the said Part VIII applies to the Metropolitan Corporation, but no area municipality has any liability or authority under that Part. R.S.O. 1960, c. 260, s. 101.

102. In addition to the liability of the Metropolitan Corporation for the expenditures on suburban roads under section 101, the Metropolitan Council may contribute such amount as the Metropolitan Council deems proper as its appropriate share of the administrative expenses of the Toronto and York Roads Commission. R.S.O. 1960, c. 260, s. 102.

103. The Metropolitan Council may contribute such amount as the Metropolitan Council deems proper as its share of the cost of maintenance of the part of the Malton Road in the County of Peel extending from the County of York to the Malton Airport thereby assuming the liability of The Corporation of the City of Toronto under an agreement dated July 2, 1943, but not to exceed 25 per cent of the annual maintenance costs of such part of the road. R.S.O. 1960, c. 260, s. 103.

104. The Toronto and York Roads Commission, established under Part III of *The Highway Improvement Act,* being chapter 166 of the Revised Statutes of Ontario, 1950, is continued. R.S.O. 1960, c. 260, s. 104.

105. All roads forming part of the county road system of the County of York on the 31st day of December, 1953, except those vested in a local municipality under section 75 or assumed by by-law of the Metropolitan Council under section 76, continue to form part of the county road system of the County of York, and are suburban roads for all the purposes of Part VIII of *The Highway Improvement Act,* until changed in accordance with the *The Highway Improvement Act.* R.S.O. 1960, c. 260, s. 105.

106.—(1) Where the Metropolitan Corporation assumes as a metropolitan road any road in an area municipality, other than a road mentioned in section 75,

(a) no compensation or damages shall be payable to the area municipality in which it was vested;

(b) the Metropolitan Corporation shall thereafter pay to the area municipality before the due date all amounts of principal and interest becoming due upon any outstanding debentures issued by the area municipality in respect of such road, but nothing in this clause requires the Metropolitan Corporation to pay that portion of the amounts of principal and interest that under *The Local Improvement Act* is payable as the owners' share of a local improvement work.

(2) Notwithstanding subsection 1, the Metropolitan Corporation shall, after the 1st day of January, 1956, pay to The Corporation of the Township of North York before the due date all amounts of principal and interest becoming due upon any outstanding debentures of the Bayview Avenue bridge that are payable as the owners' share of such local improvement work.

(3) If the Metropolitan Corporation fails to make any payment as required by clause *b* of subsection 1, the area municipality may charge the Metropolitan Corporation interest at the rate of one-half of 1 per cent for each month or fraction thereof that the payment is overdue.

(4) In the event of any doubt as to whether any outstanding debenture or portion thereof was issued in respect of the road assumed, the Municipal Board, upon application, may determine the matter and its decision is final. R.S.O. 1960, c. 260, s. 106.

107.—(1) Where an area municipality intends to stop up a highway or part of a highway, it shall so notify the secretary of the board of the Metropolitan Toronto Planning Area by registered mail.

(2) If the Metropolitan Toronto Planning Board objects to such stopping up, it shall so notify the council of the area municipality by registered mail within twenty-one days of the receipt of the notice under subsection 1 and the highway or part thereof concerned shall not be stopped up except by agreement between the area municipality and the board and failing agreement the Municipal Board, upon application, may determine the matter and its decision is final

(3) In the case of a township in the Metropolitan Area, it is not necessary to obtain the approval of the judge of the county court to such stopping up under section 459 of *The Municipal Act.* R.S.O. 1960, c. 260, s. 107.

Part VI

METROPOLITAN TRANSPORTATION

108. In this Part,

(a) "Commission" means the Toronto Transit Commission established under this Part;

(b) "Former Commisison" means The Toronto Transportation Commission. R.S.O. 1960, c. 260, s. 108.

109. The Toronto Transit Commission is continued with the powers, rights, authorities and privileges vested in it by this Act. R.S.O. 1960, c. 260, s. 109.

110.—(1) The Commission is a body corporate and shall consist of five members appointed, except as provided in subsection 2, by by-law of the Metropolitan Council.

(2) The first members of the Commission shall be,

(a) the three members of the former Commission in office on the 31st day of December, 1953;

(b) two members appointed by by-law of the Metropolitan Council before the 1st day of January, 1954, each of whom shall be a ratepayer and a resident of one of the area municipalities other than the City of Toronto.

(3) Of the three members of the Commission who take office under clause a of subsection 2, the Metropolitan Council shall by by-law passed before 1st day of January, 1954, designate one who shall hold office until the 31st day of December, 1956, one who shall hold office until the 31st day of December, 1957, and one who shall hold office until the 31st day of December, 1958; of the two members appointed under clause b of subsection 2, the Metropolitan Council shall by by-law passed before the 1st day of January, 1954, designate one who shall hold office until the 31st day of December, 1954, and one who shall hold office until the 31st day of December, 1955. R.S.O. 1960, c. 260, s. 110 (1-3).

(4) A member shall hold office until his successor is appointed, and, except in the case of the filling of a vacancy occuring during the term of office, a member shall be appointed for a term of three years.

(4a) For the purpose of instituting a three-year term on a staggered basis, the Metropolitan Council may designate the terms of office of the members in office on the 30th day of April, 1963.

(4b) The Metropolitan Council may provide that the Commission shall consist of not fewer than three members. 1962-63, c. 89, s. 7.

(5) No person is eligible to be appointed as a member of the Commission unless he is a resident and a ratepayer of an area municipality.

(6) No member of the Metropolitan Council or of the council of an area municipality is eligible to be appointed as a member of the Commission.

(7) No appointment of a member of the Commission shall be made except on the affirmative vote of at least two-thirds of the members of the Metropolitan Council present and voting.

(8) A member of the Commission is eligible for reappointment on the expiration of his term of office.

(9) Where the office of a member of the Commission becomes vacant during his term of office, the Metropolitan Council shall immediately appoint a member who shall hold office for the remainder of the term for which his predecessor was appointed.

(10) Three members of the Commission constitute a quorum.

(11) The members of the Commission shall be paid such salary or other remuneration as may be fixed by by-law of the Metropolitan Council. R.S.O. 1960, c. 260, s. 110 (5-11).

111.—(1) On the 1st day of January, 1954, there is hereby vested in the Commission,

(a) all the undertaking, assets and real and personal property, wherever situate, owned by, vested in or held by the former Commission, including the capital stock of Gray Coach Lines Limited held by it;

(b) all real and personal property acquired or held by The Corporation of the City of Toronto for the purposes of or on behalf of the former Commission;

(c) all real and personal property acquired or held by any area municipality in respect of any service furnished by the former Commission to such municipality or any portion thereof.

(2) The Commission, on the 1st day of January, 1954, shall assume all liabilities of the former Commission, and shall assume all liabilities of any area municipality incurred in respect of any property vested in the former Commission under subsection 1.

(3) Subject to section 121, no compensation or damages shall be payable to the former Commission or any area municipality in respect of any undertaking, assets and property vested in the Commission under this section.

(4) In the event of any doubt as to whether any particular asset or liability is vested in the Commission by this section, the Municipal Board, upon application, shall determine the matter and its decision is final and not subject to appeal.

(5) For the purposes of *The Registry Act, The Land Titles Act, The Bills of Sale and Chattle Mortgages Act* or any other Act affecting title to property, it is sufficient to cite this Act to show the transmission of title to the Commission and the vesting therein of any real or personal property or any interest therein, but, if an order has been made by the Municipal Board under subsection 4, the order shall be cited as well.

(6) The former Commission is dissolved as of the 1st day of January, 1954.

(7) On or after the 1st day of January, 1954, the Commission in relation to the Toronto Transportation Commission Pension Fund Society, a corporation subject to Part VI of *The Corporations Act* and incorporated by letters patent dated the 3rd day of January, 1940, shall stand in the place and stead of the former Commission.

(8) The name of the said Toronto Transportation Commission Pension Fund Society is changed to "Toronto Transit Commission Pension Fund Society". R.S.O. 1960, c. 260, s. 111.

112.—(1) The Commission may provide by contract with an insurer licensed under *The Insurance Act* or with an association registered under *The Prepaid Hospital and Medical Services Act* or with a corporation to be known as the Toronto Transit Commission Sick Benefit Association, to be established subject to Part VI of *The Corporations Act,* for weekly sick-pay, special service, medical and surgical benefits for employees or any class thereof of the Commission and their wives or husbands and dependent children and retired employees in accordance with this section and for contributing toward the cost thereof.

(2) No contract under subsection 1 shall authorize contributions by the Commission in excess of the total of those made by the employees.

(3) The Commission shall only make contributions in respect of,

(a) regular employees who have been employed for at least sixty days with the Commission and their wives or husbands and dependent children;

(b) retired employees who reside in Ontario and who elect to continue the benefits,

and shall not make contributions in respect of temporary or seasonal employees or dependents of regular employees other than wives or husbands and dependent children.

(4) Special service and medical and surgical benefits may be provided for dependents other than wives or husbands and dependent children of regular employees, and for dependents of retired employees, who so elect, provided the cost thereof shall be borne by such employees.

(5) Sick-pay benefits shall not be provided for other than active regular employees of the Commission.

(6) Weekly sick-pay in an amount greater than may be provided under the other provisions of this section may be provided for such employees who elect to bear the excess cost of such greater sick-pay.

(7) The Commission may assume the cost of the administration of the benefits provided under this section.

(8) The sick-pay, special service and medical and surgical benefits provided or to be provided before the 1st day of January, 1961, and contributions made in relation thereto by The Toronto Transportation Commission, the Toronto Transit Commission, the Toronto Transportation Commission Sick Benefit Association and the Toronto Transit Commission Sick Benefit Association are hereby confirmed and declared to be legal and valid. R.S.O. 1960, c. 260, s. 112.

113.—(1) Where the former Commission has agreed with any area municipality or other municipality or person, or any two or more of them, for services to be provided by the former Commission, the Commission shall, on the 1st day of January, 1954, assume all liabilities and is entitled to all benefits of the former Commission under such agreement and the former Commission is relieved of any liability thereunder.

(2) Notwithstanding subsection 1 and notwithstanding anything in any such agreement, the Municipal Board, upon the application of the Commission or of any municipality or person who is a party to such agreement, may by order terminate or vary such agreement and adjust all rights and liabilities thereunder. R.S.O. 1960, c. 260, s. 113.

114. No further investment in the capital stock of Gray Coach Lines, Limited shall be made by the Toronto Transit Commission, nor shall the capitalization of Gray Coach Lines, Limited hereafter be increased until the consent of the Metropolitan Council is first obtained thereto. R.S.O. 1960, c. 260, s. 114.

115. On and after the 1st day of January, 1954, the Commission,

(a) shall consolidate and co-ordinate all forms of local passenger transportation within the Metropolitan Area, with the exception of steam railways and taxis, and shall plan for the future development of such transportation so as to serve best the inhabitants of the Metropolitan Area;

(b) has and may exercise, with respect to the entire Metropolitan Area, all the powers, rights, authorities and privileges with respect to the construction, maintenance, operation, extension, alteration, repair, control and management of local passenger transportation which the former Commission had with respect to any part of the Metropolitan Area on the 31st day of December, 1953;

(c) has and may exercise all the powers, rights, authorities and privileges with respect to the construc-

tion, maintenance, operation, extension, alteration, repair, control and management of local passenger transportation systems heretofore or hereafter conferred upon or exercisable by the council or corporation of any area municipality, and such powers, rights, authorities and privileges shall not be exercised by any area municipality or its council or by the Metropolitan Corporation or the Metropolitan Council. R.S.O. 1960, c. 260, s. 115.

116.—(1) The Commission has, in particular, but not so as to restrict its general powers and duties, the following powers and duties:

(a) To construct, maintain, operate, extend, alter, repair, control and manage a local transportation system within the Metropolitan Area by means of surface, underground or over head railways, tramways or buses, or any other means of local transportation except steam railways and taxis.

(b) To establish new local passenger transportation services in the Metropolitan Area as and when required and to alter, curtail or abolish any services if the Commission deems it desirable so to do.

(ba) If the Commission deems it desirable, to establish, construct, manage and operate parking lots for the parking of vehicles in connection with its local passenger transportation system, and to charge fees for parking therein.

(c) Subject to section 116a, to fix such tolls and fares and establish such fare zones so that the revenue of the Commission shall be sufficient to make all transportation facilities under its control and management self-sustaining, after providing for such maintenance, renewals, depreciation, debt charges and reserves as it may think proper.

(d) To purchase, lease, acquire and use any real or personal property for its purposes, but the Commission shall not acquire any property that is to be paid for by moneys raised on the issue of debentures of the Metropolitan Corporation unless the approval of the Metropolitan Council has first been obtained.

(e) To make requisitions upon the Metropolitan Corporation for all sums of money necessary to carry out its powers and duties but nothing in this Act divests the Metropolitan Council of its authority with reference to providing the money required for such works, and when such money is provided by the Metropolitan Corporation the treasurer of the Metropolitan Corporation shall upon the certificate of the Commission pay out any money so provided. R.S.O. 1960, c. 260, s. 116 (1); 1961-62, c. 88, s. 9; 1966, c. 96, s. 11.

(2) The power of the Metropolitan Council to acquire land for the purposes of the Metropolitan Corporation includes the power to acquire land for the purposes of the Commission. R.S.O. 1960, c. 260, s. 116 (2).

116a.—(1) Subject to the approval of the Municipal Board, the Metropolitan Corporation may contribute to the capital costs of the Commission. 1961-62, c. 88, s. 10.

(2) The Metropolitan Corporation may contribute to the cost of operating the transportation system operated by the Commission. 1962-63, c. 89, s. 8.

117.—(1) The Commission may enter into an agreement with any person, or with one or more area municipalities, or with one or more other municipalities situated within twenty-five miles of the Metropolitan Area, under which the Commission will operate a local passenger transportation service upon such terms as may be agreed upon, but every such agreement shall provide that any deficit in operations shall be paid by the person or municipality or municipalities, and if the agreement is with one or more municipalities the agreement shall provide that any surplus in operations shall be credited to the municipality or municipalities.

(2) Where an agreement is entered into under subsection 1 with one or more municipalities, the council of any such municipality may pass by-laws,

    (a) providing that any deficit charged to the municipality shall be payable out of, and any surplus shall be credited to, the general funds of the municipality; or

    (b) with the approval of the Municipal Board, providing that any deficit shall be assessed against, and any surplus shall be credited to, the rateable property in any area or areas of the municipality defined in the by-law. R.S.O. 1960, c. 260, s. 117.

117a. In clauses a and b of subsection 1 of section 116 and in subsection 1 of section 118, "Metropolitan Area" shall be deemed to include the whole of Steeles Avenue where it is a boundary of an area municipality. 1965, c. 81, s. 3.

118.—(1) For the purposes of *The Public Vehicles Act* and the regulations with respect to registration fees under *The Highway Traffic Act,* the Metropolitan Area shall be deemed to be one urban municipality and, for the purpose of *The Public Commercial Vehicles Act,* the Metropolitan Area shall be deemed to be one urban zone.

(2) Except in accordance with an agreement made under subsection 3, no person other than the Commission shall, after the 1st day of July, 1954, operate a local passenger transportation service within the Metropolitan Area, with the exception of steam railways, taxis, buses owned and operated by a board of education, school board or private school and buses owned and operated by any corporation or organization solely for the purposes of the corporation or organization provided no fare or fee is charged for transportation.

(3) An agreement may be entered into between the Commission and any person legally operating a local public passenger transportation service wholly within or partly within and partly without the Metropolitan Area on the 1st day of January, 1954, under which such person may continue to operate such service or any part thereof for such time and upon such terms and conditions as such agreement provides.

(4) Where a local public passenger transportation service is legally operating wholly within the Metropolitan Area on the 1st day of April, 1953, and continues in operation, and will be required by subsection 2 to cease to operate within the Metropolitan Area on the 1st day of July, 1954, or upon the termination of an agreement made under subsection 3,

    (a) the Commission may agree with the owner of the service, not later than one month before the date upon which the service will be required to cease to operate, to purchase the assets and undertaking used in providing the service; and

    (b) if no agreement is entered into under clause a, the assets and undertaking used in providing the service, not disposed of by the owner thereof before the date upon which the service is required to cease to operate, shall vest in the Commission on that date.

(5) Where a local public passenger transportation service is legally operating partly within and partly without the Metro-

politan Area on the 1st day of April, 1953, and continues in operation, and will be required by subsection 2 to cease to operate within the Metropolitan Area on the 1st day of July, 1954, or upon the termination of an agreement made under subsection 3,

    (a) the Commission may agree with the owner of the service, not later than one month before the date upon which the service will be required to cease to operate within the Metropolitan Area, to purchase the assets and undertaking used in providing the entire service or to purchase the portion thereof that is allocated to the provision of the service within the Metropolitan Area; and

    (b) if no agreement is entered into under clause a, the portion of the assets and undertaking that is allocated to the provision of the service within the Metropolitan Area, not disposed of by the owner thereof before the date upon which the service is required to cease to operate, shall vest in the Commission on that date.

(6) Where the whole or a portion of the assets and undertaking used in or allocated to the provision of a local public passenger transportation service vests in the Commission, the Commission shall pay due compensation therefor to the owner thereof, based upon the value to the owner of the assets and undertaking used in providing the service where the service was operated wholly within the Metropolitan Area, and based upon the proportion of such value that is allocated to the provision of the service within the Metropolitan Area where the service was operated partly within and partly without the Metropolitan Area.

(7) The amount of any compensation payable under this section or any question of allocation, if not mutually agreed upon, shall be determined by the Municipal Board, and the decision of the Municipal Board on any question of allocation is final.

(8) The Commission shall be deemed to be a street railway company for the purposes of *The Railways Act.*

(9) Where a local public passenger transportation service operating partly within and partly without the Metropolitan Area is required by subsection 2 to cease to operate within the Metropolitan Area and thereupon discontinues the portion of its service beyond the Metropolitan Area, the Municipal Board may, on the application of any municipality, order the Commission to furnish a similar service upon such terms and conditions and to such extent as may be fixed by the Municipal Board.

(10) Where the Municipal Board orders the Commission to furnish a service under subsection 9, the Commission shall be deemed to have applied for an operating license under *The Public Vehicles Act,* and the Ontario Highway Transport Board shall issue a certificate of public necessity and convenience, with respect thereto.

(11) Every person who contravenes any of the provisions of subsection 2 is guilty of an offence and on summary conviction is liable to a fine of $50 for the first offence and $300 for each subsequent offence. R.S.O. 1960, c. 260, s. 118.

119. Immediately after the close of each calendar year, the Commission shall prepare, deliver to the Metropolitan Council, and publish,

    (a) a complete audited and certified financial statement of its affairs, including revenue and expense account, balance sheet and profit and loss statement;

    (b) a general report of its operations during that calendar year. R.S.O. 1960, c. 260, s. 119.

120.—(1) All claims, actions and demands arising from or relating to the construction, maintenance, operation, extension, alteration, repair, control and management of the Commission's transportation system and property, or arising from the exercise of any of the powers of the Commission, shall be made upon and brought against the Commission and not upon or against the Metropolitan Corporation or any area municipality.

(2) The Commission may sue and be sued in its own name. R.S.O. 1960, c. 260, s. 120.

121.—(1) On and after the 1st day of January, 1954, the Metropolitan Corporation shall pay to each area municipality before the due date all amounts of principal and interest becoming due upon any outstanding debentures issued by that area municipality in respect of any property vested in the Commission under subsection 1 of section 111 or issued by that area municipality for or on behalf of the former Commission.

(2) The Commission shall pay to the Metropolitan Corporation, before the date mentioned in subsection 1, the amount which the Metropolitan Corporation is liable to pay on that date under subsection 1.

(3) If the Metropolitan Corporation fails to make any payment as required by subsection 1, or if the Commission fails to make any payment as required by subsection 2, the area municipality may charge the Metropolitan Corporation, or the Metropolitan Corporation may charge the Commission, as the case may be, interest at the rate of one-half of 1 per cent for each month or fraction thereof that the payment is overdue.

(4) In the event of any doubt as to whether any outstanding debenture or portion thereof was issued in respect of any property vested in the Commission under subsection 1 of section 111 or for or on behalf of the former Commission, the Municipal Board, upon application, may determine the matter and its decision is final. R.S.O. 1960, c. 260, s. 121.

122. The Metropolitan Council may make an annual grant of not more than $80,000 to the Toronto Transit Commission toward the cost of providing free transportation for blind persons and war amputees. R.S.O. 1960, c. 260, s. 122; 1960-61, c. 61, s. 2.

123.—(1) So long as the lands and easements heretofore or hereafter acquired by the Metropolitan Corporation for the right of way of the extension to the rapid transit system of the Commission known as the Bloor-Danforth-University Avenue Subway or for the right of way of any other rapid transit project undertaken subsequent to the undertaking of the Bloor-Danforth-University Avenue Subway are owned by the Metropolitan Corporation and used by the Commission for the purpose of rapid transit, such lands and easements and any buildings and structures thereon so owned and used are exempt from business and real property taxation, and the Commission is not liable for payments in lieu thereof under section 43 of *The Assessment Act*.

(2) Subsection 1 does not apply to lands and buildings and structures thereon used as car yards or shops for or in connection with such Subway or rapid transit project nor to concessions operated, rented or leased in subway or rapid transit stations. 1965, c. 81, s. 4.

(3) The exemption provided by subsection 1 shall be deemed to be an exemption from taxation provided by section 4 of *The Assessment Act*. R.S.O. 1960, c. 260, s. 123 (3).

Part VII

EDUCATION

124. In this Part,

(*a*) "Department" means the Department of Education;

(*b*) "Minister" means the Minister of Education;

(*c*) "regulations" means regulations made under *The Department of Education Act;*

(*d*) "resident pupils" means pupils,

　　(i) who reside with their parents or guardians, or

　　(ii) who or whose parents or guardians are assessed for an amount equal to the average assessment of the ratepayers,

within the limits of a high school district for secondary school purposes, or a school section for public school purposes, within the Metropolitan Area, but does not include pupils residing with their parents or guardians on land that is exempt from taxation for school purposes, who and whose parents or guardians are not assessed for, and do not pay, taxes for secondary school purposes or public school purposes, respectively, in the high school district or school section;

(*e*) "School Board" means The Metropolitan Toronto School Board. 1966, c. 96, s. 12, *part.*

125. Each area municipality is a high school district and is deemed to be an urban school section. 1966, c. 96, s. 12, *part.*

126.—(1) On and after the 1st day of January, 1967, there shall be a board of education for each area municipality, to be known respectively as,

(*a*) The Board of Education for the Borough of East York;

(*b*) The Board of Education for the Borough of Etobicoke;

(*c*) The Board of Education for the Borough of North York;

(*d*) The Board of Education for the Borough of Scarborough;

(*e*) The Board of Education for the City of Toronto; and

(*f*) The Board of Education for the Borough of York.

(2) The members of such boards of education shall hold office for a three-year term and until their successors are elected or appointed and a new board organized.

(3) On the day on which each such new board of education holds its first meeting,

(*a*) the board or boards of education having jurisdiction in the area municipality for which such new board of education is established are dissolved; and

(*b*) all the assets and liabilities of the former board or boards of education are assets and liabilities of such new board of education. 1966, c. 96, s. 12, *part.*

127.—(1) All the provisions of *The Secondary Schools and Boards of Education Act* that are not inconsistent with this Act apply to such boards of education in the same manner and to the same extent as if such boards of education had been created by by-laws pursuant to *The Secondary Schools and Boards of Education Act*.

(2) Each such board of education has all the powers, duties and responsibilities conferred and imposed upon it by any general or special Act and regulations made thereunder that are not inconsistent with the provisions of this Act, and shall com-

ply with all the requirements of this Act that apply to them.

(3) Each such board of education may borrow money under section 100 of *The Schools Administration Act* only with the approval of the Metropolitan Council on the recommendation of the School Board.

(4) Each such board of education shall have a director of education appointed under Part VII of *The Schools Administration Act,* and he shall also be the secretary and treasurer of such board.

(5) An employee of a board of education in the Metropolitan Area or of the School Board is not eligible to be a member of any board of education in the Metropolitan Area. 1966, c. 96, s. 12, *part.*

128. The first meeting of each such board of education in the year 1967 shall be held on the first Wednesday in January in that year and thereafter shall be held not later than the second Wednesday in January in each year at such place and time as the board may determine. 1966, c. 96, s. 12, *part.*

129.—(1) The Metropolitan School Board is continued a corporation under the name of The Metropolitan Toronto School Board with the powers and duties and for the purposes set out in this Act.

(2) On and after the 1st day of January, 1967, the School Board, subject to subsection 5, shall be composed of the chairman of each board of education in the Metropolitan Area and,

(a) one member of and appointed by The Board of Education for the Borough of Etobicoke;

(b) two members of and appointed by The Board of Education for the Borough of North York;

(c) one member of and appointed by The Board of Education for the Borough of Scarborough;

(d) five members of and appointed by The Board of Education for the City of Toronto; and

(e) three members appointed by the Metropolitan Separate School Board.

(3) The appointment of members of a board of education as members of the School Board shall be made at the first meeting of the board of education in each year after elections have been held in the area municipalities.

(4) At the first meeting of the School Board in each year, at which a quorum is present, the School Board shall elect as chairman one of its members to hold office for that year and until his successor is elected in accordance with this section.

(5) No person employed by the School Board or appointed under section 54 of *The Secondary Schools and Boards of Education Act* to a board of education in the Metropolitan Area is eligible to be a member of the School Board, and, where the chairman of any such board of education is so appointed, the board of education shall appoint another member thereof as a member of the School Board. 1966, c. 96, s. 12, *part.*

130.—(1) The first meeting of the School Board in each year shall be held not later than the third Wednesday in January on such date and at such time and place as may be fixed by resolution of the School Board.

(2) At the first meeting of the School Board in each year after elections have been held in the area municipalities, at which a quorum is present, the members present shall select a member to preside, and the person so selected may vote as a member, and the School Board shall organize as a board.

(3) A person entitled to be a member of the School Board under subsection 2 or 5 of section 129 shall not take his seat until he has filed with the person presiding at the first meeting a certificate under the hand of the secretary of the board of education of which he is the chairman or by which he was ap-

pointed, or of the Metropolitan Separate School Board, as the case may be, and under the seal of such board certifying that he is entitled to be a member.

(4) No business shall be proceeded with at the first meeting until after the certificates mentioned in subsection 3 have been filed by all the members who present themselves for that purpose.

(5) The School Board shall be deemed to be organized when the certificates have been filed by at least nine members, and it may be organized and business may be proceeded with notwithstanding the failure of any of the other members to file such certificate. 1966, c. 96, s. 12, *part.*

131. Subject to section 130, all meetings of the School Board shall be held at such places within the Metropolitan Area and at such times as the School Board from time to time appoints. 1966, c. 96, s. 12, *part.*

132.—(1) Eight members of the School Board are necessary to form a quorum when the School Board is dealing with matters that affect public schools exclusively and ten members of the School Board are necessary to form a quorum in all other cases, and the concurring votes of a majority of the members of the School Board present who are entitled to vote on any matter are necessary to carry such matter.

(2) Each member of the School Board has one vote only.

(3) A member of the School Board appointed under clause *e* of subsection 2 of section 129 shall not vote or otherwise take part in any of the proceedings of the School Board exclusively affecting the public schools. 1966, c. 96, s. 12, *part.*

133.—(1) The members of the School Board appointed by boards of education shall hold office while they are members of their respective boards of education and until their successors take office and a new School Board is organized, provided that, if, as the result of a change in the chairmanship of a board of education, a member of the board of education who is also a member of the School Board becomes chairman of such board of education, his seat on the School Board, otherwise than as chairman of the board of education, becomes vacant, and another member of the board of education shall be appointed to fill the vacancy.

(2) Subsection 13 of section 56 of *The Secondary Schools and Boards of Education Act* applies to the appointment of the members of the School Board by the Metropolitan Separate School Board, and such members shall hold office for three years and until their successors are appointed. 1966, c. 96, s. 12, *part.*

134.—(1) When a vacancy occurs in the office of chairman, the School Board shall, at a general or special meeting to be held within twenty days after the vacancy occurs, elect as chairman one of its members to hold office for the remainder of the term of his predecessor.

(2) When a vacancy occurs in the office of an appointed member, other than a member appointed by the Metropolitan Separate School Board, the board of education of which he was a member shall, within fifteen days after the vacancy occurs, appoint his successor from among its members to hold office for the remainder of the term of his predecessor.

(3) When a vacancy occurs in the office of a member appointed by the Metropolitan Separate School Board, that board shall, within fifteen days after the vacancy occurs, appoint his successor to hold office for the remainder of the term of his predecessor.

(4) Where the chairman of the School Board is a member of a board of education, he may resign his office as chairman without resigning from such board of education.

(5) The seat of a member of the School Board shall be-

come vacant if he absents himself from the meetings of the School Board for three consecutive months without being authorized so to do by a resolution of the School Board entered upon its minutes, and the School Board shall forthwith declare the seat to be vacant. 1966, c. 96, s. 12, *part*.

135. It is the duty of the School Board and it has power,

(a) to require each board of education within the Metropolitan Area to prepare and submit to the School Board, from time to time as the School Board may prescribe, its proposals and recommendations with respect to the provision of adequate public elementary and secondary school accommodation within its jurisdiction, and the estimated cost thereof;

(b) to review and consolidate all such proposals, in consultation with the boards of education, the Department and the Metropolitan Council and their respective officials, and to prepare and revise from time to time a composite proposal and the recommendations of the School Board for the provision of adequate public elementary, academic secondary and vocational secondary school accommodation for the Metropolitan Area as a whole;

(c) to submit to the Metropolitan Council from time to time the composite proposal referred to in clause b, together with all relevant information with respect thereto;

(d) notwithstanding the provisions of this or any other Act, to review and to determine, in consultation with the respective boards of education, the boundaries of the attendance areas for those public elementary and secondary schools in the Metropolitan Area that are to be attended by resident pupils from more than one school section or high school district;

(e) to appoint a director who holds a certificate of qualification as a school inspector, who shall be secretary-treasurer of the School Board, and such other officers and staff as may be deemed expedient for the purposes of the School Board, to pay their salaries, and subject to the regulations, to prescribe their duties, and to provide and pay for office accommodation, furnishings, fuel, light, stationery, equipment, insurance and miscellaneous expenses, including travelling expenses of officers and members of the School Board, if authorized by the School Board;

(f) if deemed expedient, to pay to each member a mileage allowance not exceeding 10 cents for each mile necessarily travelled by him in going to the meetings of the School Board from his home and in returning to his home, and to pay to each member who is a member of a board of education an allowance not exceeding $2,400 per annum and to each member appointed by the Metropolitan Separate School Board an allowance not exceeding $1,200 per annum;

(g) to prepare, adopt and submit each year to the Metropolitan Council, on or before such date and in such form as the Metropolitan Council may prescribe, the estimates of the School Board for the current year, separately for public elementary and for secondary school purposes, of all sums required to meet its expenditures and obligations under this Act, and such estimates,

(i) shall set forth the estimated revenues and expenditures of the School Board,

(ii) shall make due allowance for a surplus of any previous year that will be available during the current year,

(iii) shall provide for a deficit of a previous year,

(iv) shall provide for the amounts of principal and interest payable during the current year in respect of all outstanding debentures issued for school purposes,

(v) may provide for expenditures to be made out of current funds for permanent improvements, such expenditures not to exceed a sum calculated at two mills in the dollar upon the total assessment in the Metropolitan Area for secondary school purposes and two mills in the dollar upon the total Assessment in the Metropolitan Area for public school purposes according to the last revised assessment rolls. 1966, c. 96, s. 12, *part*.

136.—(1) Sections 38, 39 and 41 of *The Schools Administration Act* apply *mutatis mutandis* to the School Board.

(2) Where the School Board employs or has employed a person theretofore employed by a board of education in the Metropolitan Area, the employee shall be deemed to remain an employee of the board of education for the purpose of any pension plan of such board of education, and shall continue to be entitled to all rights and benefits thereunder as if he had remained as an employee of the board of education, until the School Board has provided a pension plan for its employees and such employee has elected, in writing, to participate therein.

(3) Until such election, the School Board shall deduct by instalments from the remuneration of the employee the amount that such employee is required to pay in accordance with the provisions of the plan of the board of education, and the School Board shall pay to the board of education in instalments,

(a) the amounts so deducted; and

(b) the future service contributions payable under the plan by the board of education.

(4) Where the School Board employs or has employed a person theretofore employed by a board of education in the Metropolitan Area, the employee shall be deemed to remain an employee of the board of education for the purposes of any sick leave credit plan of such board of education until the School Board has established a sick leave credit plan for its employees, whereupon the School Board shall place to the credit of the employee the sick leave credits standing to his credit in the plan of the board of education. 1966, c. 96, s. 12, *part*.

137.—(1) The Metropolitan Corporation shall pay to the School Board, in monthly instalments, the moneys required by the School Board as shown in its estimates submitted under clause g of subsection 1 of section 135, except the moneys required for the purposes of subclauses iv and v of such clause, and the moneys required for the purposes of such subclause v shall be paid to the School Board from time to time as required.

(2) The School Board shall pay to each board of education in the Metropolitan Area, in monthly instalments, the moneys required by such board of education as shown in its estimates approved by the School Board, except moneys approved for permanent improvements, which shall be paid to such board of education from time to time as required, but the total of such monthly payments shall be reduced by the amounts, if any, that are deducted from the legislative grants for pay-

ment to the Teachers' Superannuation Fund and the Canada Pension Plan on behalf of the teachers employed by that board of education. 1966, c. 96, s. 12, *part*.

138.—(1) The special and general legislative grants, which but for this Act would be payable to boards of education in the Metropolitan Area, shall be calculated as provided in the regulations.

(2) The special and general legislative grants, except those paid to boards of education under subsection 3, shall be paid to the School Board.

(3) The legislative grants in respect of expenditures made by a board of education for the construction of classrooms and for items eligible for stimulation grants, to the extent that such expenditures were approved by the Minister and raised entirely by levies under subsection 5 of section 139 in the area municipality in which such board of education has jurisdiction, shall be paid to the board of education. 1966, c. 96, s. 12, *part*.

139.—(1) Each board of education in the Metropolitan Area, instead of submitting to a municipal council its annual estimates as provided by law, shall prepare, adopt and submit each year to the School Board, on or before such date and in such form as the School Board may prescribe, its estimates for the current year, separately for public elementary and for secondary school purposes, of all sums required during the year for the purposes of the board of education, and such estimates,

   (a) shall set forth the estimated revenues and expenditures of the board of education;

   (b) shall make due allowance for a surplus of any previous year that will be available during the current year;

   (c) shall provide for a deficit of any previous year;

   (d) may provide for expenditures to be made out of current funds for permanent improvements.

(2) Upon receipt by the School Board of the estimates of all the boards of education in the Metropolitan Area, the School Board shall consider the estimates, having regard to the limit upon the amount that it may include in its estimates for expenditures for permanent improvements out of current funds, and approve such estimates in whole or in part, and shall notify each such board of education of the extent to which its estimates have been approved by the School Board.

(3) In considering such estimates, the School Board shall endeavour to provide for all boards of education in the Metropolitan Area, having regard to their varying needs, the funds necessary for an educational programme throughout the Metropolitan Area.

(4) If the estimates of a board of education are not approved in whole by the School Board, the board of education may submit to the council of the area municipality in which it has jurisdiction, within twenty days after notice is given pursuant to subsection 2, its estimates made up as provided for in subsection 1, except that such estimates shall include and make due allowance for the revenues to be derived from the School Board pursuant to the estimates approved by the School Board, provided that, before submitting such estimates to the council, the board of education shall revise the estimates, if necessary, so that the difference between,

   (a) the aggregate estimates of all sums required for public elementary school purposes and the aggregate of the revenues for such purposes to be derived from the School Board pursuant to the estimates approved by the School Board shall not exceed a sum calculated at one and one-half mills in the dollar upon the total assessment in the area munici-

pality for public school purposes according to the last revised assessment roll; and

   (b) the aggregate estimates of all sums required for secondary school purposes and the aggregate of the revenues for such purposes to be derived from the School Board pursuant to the estimates approved by the School Board shall not exceed a sum calculated at one mill in the dollar upon the total assessment in the area municipality for secondary school purposes according to the last revised assessment roll.

(5) The council of each area municipality shall levy and collect each year and transfer to the board of education for that area municipality from time to time as required, but not later than the 15th day of December, such sums as may be required by the board of education for its purposes during the year in accordance with its estimates submitted to the council pursuant to subsection 4.

(6) The amount required to be raised by the council of each area municipality under subsection 5,

   (a) for public school purposes, shall be raised by levy upon the whole rateable property rateable for public school purposes; and

   (b) for secondary school purposes, shall be raised by levy upon the whole rateable property rateable for secondary school purposes,

within the area municipality according to the last revised assessment roll thereof.

(7) If the estimates of a board of education are not approved in whole by the School Board, the board of education may, within fifteen days after notice is given pursuant to subsection 2, appeal to the Municipal Board, provided that any amount in issue in such an appeal shall not be included in its estimates under subsection 4.

(8) The Municipal Board shall conduct a public hearing of every such appeal upon such notice as it may deem proper and may dismiss the appeal or may by order require the School Board to provide additional funds to the board of education to an extent not exceeding the amounts in issue in such appeal, and, in considering any such appeal, the Municipal Board shall have regard amongst other things to the matters referred to in subsections 2 and 3.

(9) If an order of the Municipal Board requiring the School Board to provide additional funds to a board of education,

   (a) is issued in any year before the estimates of the School Board for such year are submitted to the Metropolitan Council, the School Board shall include in its estimates for that year the amount required to be paid pursuant to the order; or

   (b) is issued in any year after the estimates of the School Board for such year are submitted to the Metropolitan Council, the Metropolitan Council shall advance to the School Board the amount required to be paid pursuant to the order and may borrow money from time to time by way of promissory note for such purpose, and the School Board shall include in its estimates for the next succeeding year the amount required to repay such advance and the interest charges on any amounts borrowed by the Metropolitan Council for the purpose of making such advance.

(10) The Municipal Board may issue an order under subsection 8 upon such terms and conditions, including terms and conditions with respect to the use of the funds to be paid to the board of education thereunder, as the Municipal Board deems appropriate. 1966, c. 96, s. 12, *part*.

140.—(1) On and after the 1st day of January, 1954, the Metropolitan Corporation shall pay to each area municipality before the due date all amounts of principal and interest becoming due upon any outstanding debentures issued by the area municipality for public or secondary school purposes.

(2) If the Metropolitan Corporation fails to make any payment as required by subsection 1, the area municipality may charge the Metropolitan Corporation interest at the rate of one-half of 1 per cent for each month or fraction thereof that the payment is overdue.

(3) In the event of any doubt as to whether any outstanding debenture or portion thereof was issued for public or secondary school purposes, the Municipal Board, upon application, may determine the matter, and its decision is final. 1966, c. 96, s. 12, *part*.

141. Notwithstanding any order of the Municipal Board or any debenture by-law passed pursuant thereto, all amounts of principal and interest becoming due on and after the 1st day of January, 1967, with respect to any debentures issued for public or secondary school purposes by the Metropolitan Corporation since the 1st day of January, 1954, or issued hereafter, shall be repaid by levies against all the area municipalities. 1966, c. 96, s. 12, *part*.

142.—(1) Notwithstanding the provisions of this or any other Act, no board of education in the Metropolitan Area,

    (*a*) shall discontinue the operation and maintenance of any school under its jurisdiction; or

    (*b*) shall sell, lease or otherwise dispose of any school site or school building, or any item of school property the cost of which was financed in whole or in part by the issue of debentures,

without the approval of the School Board.

(2) Where a board of education sells, leases or otherwise disposes of any school site or school building in accordance with clause *b* of subsection 1, it shall pay the proceeds of such sale to the School Board.

(3) The School Board shall use the proceeds of the disposal of property paid to it under subsection 2 only for permanent improvements,

    (*a*) if such property was used for public school purposes, for public school purposes; or

    (*b*) if such property used for secondary school purposes, for secondary school purposes. 1966, c. 96, s. 12, *part*.

143. A board of education with the approval of the School Board may transfer property that was acquired for public school purposes to secondary school purposes or vice versa, and, where property is so transferred, the transfer shall be made effective on the 1st day of January in any year and the principal and interest on any debentures issued with respect to such property to be raised in that year and subsequent years by levy shall be raised by levy on the whole rateable property rateable for the purposes to which such property is transferred. 1966, c. 96, s. 12, *part*.

144.—(1) Where a board of education in the Metropolitan Area desires that the sums required for permanent improvements as defined in paragraph 25 of subsection 2 of section 1 of *The Schools Administration Act* shall be raised by the issue and sale of debentures, it may apply to the School Board and it shall at the same time deliver a copy of such application to the clerk of the Metropolitan Corporation.

(2) The application shall state the purpose of the proposed borrowing, the nature and the estimated cost of the proposed work or project.

(3) The School Board, at its first meeting after receiving the application or as soon thereafter as possible, shall consider and approve or disapprove the application, and the secretary of the School Board shall forward a certified copy of its resolution in respect of the application to the secretary of the applicant board of education and to the clerk of the Metropolitan Corporation.

(4) A board of education in the Metropolitan Area may renovate any school buildings under its jurisdiction and the same shall be deemed permanent improvements for the purposes of this Act. 1966, c. 96, s. 12, *part*.

145.—(1) The Metropolitan Council, after the application referred to in section 144 has been dealt with by the School Board, shall consider and approve or disapprove the application, and the clerk of the Metropolitan Corporation shall thereupon give notice of the decision of the Metropolitan Council to the secretary of the applicant board of education and to the secretary of the School Board.

(2) If the Metropolitan Council approves the application, it shall apply to the Municipal Board for its approval under section 64 of *The Ontario Municipal Board Act* and, if the Municipal Board approves, the Metropolitan Council shall pass a by-law authorizing the borrowing of money by the issue and sale of debentures of the Metropolitan Corporation for the purposes stated in the application.

(3) Where the Metropolitan Council disapproves the application, the applicant board of education or the School Board may appeal to the Municipal Board for an order requiring the Metropolitan Council to pass a by-law for borrowing money by the issue and sale of debentures for the purpose or purposes stated in the application.

(4) The Municipal Board shall conduct a public hearing of every such appeal upon such notice as it may deem proper, and may dismiss the appeal or may by order require the Metropolitan Council to pass the by-law mentioned in subsection 3, and the decision of the Municipal Board on such appeal is final. 1966, c. 96, s. 12, *part*.

145a.—(1) At the request of the School Board, an application may be made by the Metropolitan Council to the Municipal Board for approval by the Municipal Board of expenditures and the borrowing of money and the issuing of debentures for the undertaking of any permanent improvements as defined in paragraph 25 of subsection 2 of section 1 of *The Schools Administration Act* or in subsection 4 of section 144 of this Act without specifying particular sites and projects, and the Municipal Board may dismiss the application or may approve part or all thereof, provided that no board of education in the Metropolitan Area shall make any commitment for the acquisition of a site or the undertaking of a project to be financed under an order of the Municipal Board made on such an application until the School Board has approved the cost of such acquisition or undertaking and the treasurer of the Metropolitan Corporation has certified that funds can be provided under such order in payment thereof.

(2) In any order made under this section, the Municipal Board may impose such terms and conditions as it may see fit and may permit preliminary expenditures by a board of education in the Metropolitan Area, including expenditures for the preparation of surveys, architects' plans, appraisals and other expenditures that may be necessary for the calling of tenders, prior to the approval of the School Board and the certificate of the treasurer referred to in subsection 1.

(3) The approval of the Municipal Board provided for in this section shall be deemed to be the approval of the Municipal Board required by section 64 of *The Ontario Municipal*

Board Act and sections 144 and 145 of this Act for any site acquired or project carried out under and in accordance with such order. 1966, c. 96, s. 12, *part.*

146.—(1) If it appears to the School Board that the erection of a school for pupils from more than one school section or high school district in the Metropolitan Area is or will be desirable, the School Board may acquire land for the school site by purchase or otherwise by expropriation.

(2) The Metropolitan Council may borrow money at the request of the School Board for the purpose of acquiring land under subsection 1, and the School Board shall pay the interest charges on the amount borrowed as they fall due and shall repay the principal sum within five years from the date it was made available to it.

(3) Upon being reimbursed for all expenses, including interest charges on money borrowed under subsection 2, actually incurred in acquiring and holding the land less any revenue received therefrom, the School Board may convey the land to a board of education having jurisdiction in one of the school sections or high school districts from which pupils will attend the school when erected.

(4) The School Board may sell land acquired under subsection 1 if it appears to the School Board that such land will not be required for the erection of a school and may lease or rent such land at any time if it appears to the School Board that it is not immediately so required.

(5) *The Expropriation Procedures Act, 1962-63* applies to the expropriation of land under this section and to the compensation to be paid for land so expropriated. 1966, c. 96, s. 12, *part.*

147.—(1) Nothing in this Act affects any public school board or public school section within the Metropolitan Area heretofore or hereafter established by the Minister under section 12 of *The Public Schools Act* or any high school board or high school district within the Metropolitan Area hereafter established by the Minister under subsection 5 of section 12 of *The Secondary Schools and Boards of Education Act.*

(2) The School Board shall be deemed to be a board within the meaning of *The Teachers' Superannuation Act.* 1966, c. 96, s. 12, *part.*

148.—(1) A board of education in the Metropolitan Area shall not admit to a secondary school operated by it any pupil who is not a resident pupil without prior approval of the School Board.

(2) Where a child,

    (a) who is a ward in the care of The Metropolitan Toronto Children's Aid Society or whose mother is his sole support; and

    (b) who has the right to attend a public or secondary school in an area municipality without payment of a fee,

resides in the Metropolitan Area, he has the same right to attend a school without payment of a fee as he would have if his residence was that of his parents or guardians, and, if he does so attend, he shall be deemed for all purposes to be a resident pupil of the school section or high school district in which he resides. 1966, c. 96, s. 12, *part.*

149.—(1) The council of any area municipality may grant aid to the board of education for the area municipality to pay in whole or in part for the construction by the board of education of indoor or outdoor swimming pools on the property of the board of education.

(2) An area municipality and the board of education thereof may enter into agreements with respect to the construction,

control, operation, maintenance and repair of such swimming pools and with respect to the operation and use of such swimming pools, except during school hours, by the area municipality.

(3) The council of an area municipality may charge fees for the use of or admission to such swimming pools while the operation and use of the pools is under the control of the area municipality.

(4) The Metropolitan Corporation may issue debentures for the purposes of any undertaking under this section. 1966, c. 96, s. 12, *part.*

149*a.* Insurance placed by a board of education on its property shall be deemed to have been placed on its own behalf and on behalf of the School Board, and any proceeds of such insurance shall,

    (a) if requested by the School Board, be paid to the School Board; and

    (b) be used in the manner provided in subsection 3 of section 142. 1966, c. 96, s. 12, *part.*

Part VII-A
REGIONAL LIBRARY BOARD

149*b.* In this Part,

    (a) "area board" means a public library board established for an area municipality;

    (b) "Library Board" means the Metropolitan Toronto Library Board. 1966, c. 96, s. 13, *part.*

149*c.*—(1) There is hereby established a regional library board, which is a corporation, under the name of "Metropolitan Toronto Library Board", composed of,

    (a) one person appointed by the council of each area municipality who shall be a resident in the area municipality and who may be a member of a public library board;

    (b) the chairman of the Metropolitan Council;

    (c) one person appointed by The Metropolitan Toronto School Board who shall be a resident in the Metropolitan Area; and

    (d) one person appointed by the Metropolitan Separate School Board who shall be a resident in the Metropolitan Area.

(2) Appointments of members of the Library Board shall be made in the month of January, 1967, and in the month of January in every third year thereafter.

(3) The appointed members of the Library Board shall hold office for a three-year term and until their successors are appointed.

(4) Vacancies arising from any cause shall be filled forthwith by the appointing body, and the person appointed to fill the vacancy shall hold office for the unexpired term of the person whose place has become vacant.

(5) The chairman of the Metropolitan Council may designate any member of the Metropolitan Council to be his delegate at any or all of the meetings of the Library Board.

(6) The Library Board, from among its members, shall elect a chairman and may elect a vice-chairman, and a majority of the members of the Library Board constitutes a quorum.

(7) Except as otherwise provided in this Act, the Library Board with respect to the Metropolitan Area shall be deemed to be a board of a regional library system under *The Public Libraries Act, 1966,* and may make grants in aid of capital or

current expenditures to any area board for the provision of central or regional reference library services.

(8) The Library Board shall submit annually to the Metropolitan Council an estimate of its financial requirements for the year, and the Metropolitan Council may amend such estimate and shall pay to the Library Board out of the moneys appropriated for the Library Board such amounts as may be requisitioned from time to time.

(9) The Library Board may,

    (a) with the approval of the Metropolitan Council, acquire by purchase, lease or otherwise any land required for its purposes and sell, lease or otherwise dispose of any land or buildings when no longer required for its purposes; and

    (b) erect, maintain and repair buildings on its lands and make additions to or alterations of such buildings.

(10) The power of the Metropolitan Corporation to acquire land for the purposes of the Metropolitan Corporation includes the power to acquire land for the purposes of the Library Board.

(11) All claims, actions and demands arising from or relating to the operations of the Library Board or the exercise of any of its powers shall be made upon and brought against the Library Board and not upon or against the Metropolitan Corporation.

(12) The Library Board may sue and be sued in its own name. 1966, c. 96, s. 13, *part.*

149d.—(1) At the request of the Library Board, the Metropolitan Council may, after the 1st day of January, 1967, pass by-laws assuming on behalf of the Library Board any land or building that the Library Board requires for its purposes that is vested on the 31st day of March, 1966, in any area municipality or area board and that is used on such day for public library purposes, and on the day any such by-law becomes effective the property designated therein vests in the Library Board.

(2) No area municipality or area board, after the 31st day of March, 1966, shall, without the consent of the Metropolitan Council until the Library Board is organized and thereafter without the consent of the Library Board, sell, lease or otherwise dispose of or encumber any land or building that is used for public library purposes.

(3) Where any part of a building mentioned in subsection 1 is used by the area municipality or area board for purposes other than those for which the Library Board was established, the Metropolitan Council may, at the request of the Library Board,

    (a) where practicable, assume on behalf of the Library Board only the part of the building and land appurtenant thereto used for purposes similar to those for which the Library Board was established; or

    (b) assume on behalf of the Library Board the whole building and land appurtenant thereto, and the Library Board may enter into an agreement with the area municipality or area board for the use of a part of the land or building by such area municipality or area board on such terms and conditions as may be agreed upon.

(4) Where the Metropolitan Corporation assumes any property under subsection 1 or 3,

    (a) no compensation or damage shall be payable to the area municipality or area board except as provided in this subsection;

    (b) the Metropolitan Corporation shall thereafter pay to the area municipality before the due date all amounts of principal and interest becoming due thereafter upon any outstanding debentures issued by the area municipality in respect of any property vested in the Library Board under subsection 1 or 3;

    (c) notwithstanding any order of the Municipal Board or any debenture by-law passed pursuant thereto, all amounts of principal and interest becoming due thereafter with respect to any debentures theretofore issued by the Metropolitan Corporation on behalf of such area municipality in respect of any property vested in the Library Board under subsection 1 or 3 shall be repaid by levies against all the area municipalities;

    (d) the Metropolitan Corporation shall thereafter pay to the area municipality or area board, for the portion of any land or building vested in the Library Board under this section that is not used, on the 31st day of March, 1966, for purposes similar to those for which the Library Board was established, such amount as may be agreed upon, and, failing agreement, the Municipal Board, upon application, may determine the amount, and its decision is final, provided that such amount shall not be greater than the capital expenditure for such portion of the land or building less the amount of any outstanding debentures in respect of such portion.

(5) If the Metropolitan Corporation fails to make any payment as required by clause *b* of subsection 4, the area municipality may charge the Metropolitan Corporation interest at the rate of one-half of 1 percent for each month or fraction thereof that the payment is overdue.

(6) At the request of the Library Board, each area municipality or area board shall transfer to the Library Board for its use without compensation all personal property, including books, periodicals, newspapers, manuscripts, pictures, films, recordings and catalogues in the possession of the area municipality or area board at any time during the period between the 31st day of March, 1966, and the 1st day of January, 1968, that was provided for purposes similar to those for which the Library Board was established.

(7) No area municipality or area board during the period referred to in subsection 6 shall, without the consent of the Metropolitan Council until the Library Board is organized and thereafter without the consent of the Library Board, dispose of any personal property referred to in subsection 6.

(8) In the event of any doubt as to whether,

    (a) any outstanding debenture or portion thereof was issued in respect of any property assumed; or

    (b) any personal property referred to in subsection 6 was used for purposes similar to those for which the Library Board was established,

the Municipal Board, upon application, may determine the matter and its decision is final. 1966, c. 96, s. 13, *part.*

Part VIII

AREA MUNICIPALITIES

150.—(1) On the 1st day of January, 1967,

    (a) the Township of East York and the Town of Leaside are amalgamated as a township municipality the inhabitants of which are a body corporate under the name of The Corporation of the Borough of East York;

    (b) the Township of Etobicoke, the Village of Long Branch, the Town of Mimico and the Town of New

Toronto are amalgamated as a township municipality the inhabitants of which are a body corporate under the name of The Corporation of the Borough of Etobicoke;

(c) the Township of North York is continued as a township municipality the inhabitants of which are a body corporate under the name of The Corporation of the Borough of North York;

(d) the Township of Scarborough is continued as a township municipality the inhabitants of which are a body corporate under the name of The Corporation of the Borough of Scarborough;

(e) the City of Toronto, the Village of Forest Hill and the Village of Swansea are amalgamated as a city municipality the inhabitants of which are a body corporate under the name of The Corporation of The City of Toronto;

(f) the Township of York and the Town of Weston are amalgamated as a township municipality the inhabitants of which are a body corporate under the name of The Corporation of the Borough of York.

(2) For the purposes of every Act, the municipalities amalgamated by this section shall be deemed to have been amalgamated by orders of the Municipal Board, not subject to section 42 of *The Ontario Municipal Board Act* or to petition or appeal under section 94 or 95 of such Act, made on the day this section comes into force pursuant to applications made under section 14 of *The Municipal Act,* and, subject to the provisions of this Act, the Municipal Board, upon the application of any area municipality or local board thereof or of its own motion, may exercise its powers consequent upon such amalgamations, and sections 94 and 95 of *The Ontario Municipal Board Act* do not apply to decisions or orders made in the exercise of such powers.

(3) The area municipalities are municipalities in the County of York separated therefrom for municipal purposes.

(4) The provisions of any special Act, in so far as they are not inconsistent with any of the provisions of this Act, relating to the City of Toronto, the Township of East York, the Township of Etobicoke or the Township of York shall apply to the whole of the new city or borough formed under subsection 1 of which it forms a part.

(5) The provisions of any special Act, in so far as they are not inconsistent with any of the provisions of this Act, relating to,

(a) the Village of Forest Hill or the Village of Swansea, shall continue to apply to the part of the City of Toronto formerly in the Village of Forest Hill or the Village of Swansea except where they are in conflict with any special Act relating to the City of Toronto;

(b) the Town of Leaside, shall continue to apply in the part of the Borough of East York formerly in the Town of Leaside except where they are in conflict with any special Act relating to the Township of East York;

(c) the Town of Mimico, the Town of New Toronto or the Village of Long Branch, shall continue to apply in the part of the Borough of Etobicoke formerly in the Town of Mimico, the Town of New Toronto or the Village of Long Branch except where they are in conflict with any special Act relating to the Township of Etobicoke;

(d) the Town of Weston, shall continue to apply in the part of the Borough of York formerly in the Town of Weston except where they are in conflict with any special Act relating to the Township of York.

(6) Notwithstanding subsections 1 and 2, on the 1st day of January, 1967, the provisions of any special Act respecting the composition of council relating to any area municipality are repealed. 1966, c. 96, s. 14, *part.*

151.—(1) On and after the 1st day of January, 1967, the council of each area municipality shall be composed of,

(a) a mayor elected by general vote who shall be the head of council; and

(b) a board of control, if at any time the area municipality has such a board; and

(c) alderman as follows:

(i) if elected by general vote, not fewer than four aldermen, or

(ii) if elected by wards and the area municipality has four or more wards, one, two or three aldermen for each ward, or, if the area municipality has fewer than four wards, two or three aldermen for each ward.

(2) The Borough of East York shall be deemed to have a population of not less than 100,000 for the purposes of section 202 of *The Municipal Act.*

(3) After this section comes into force, the council of the Township of North York and the council of the Township of Scarborough, and, after the 1st day of January, 1967, the council of any area municipality, may pass by-laws providing for the composition of its council in accordance with subsection 1.

(4) A by-law under this section, and a by-law amending or repealing any such by-law, shall be passed not later than the 1st day of November in the year in which an election is to be held and shall not be passed unless it has received the approval of the Municipal Board.

(5) Every such by-law, including an amending or repealing by-law, shall take effect at and for the purposes of the triennial election next after its passing. 1966, c. 96, s. 14, *part.**

Part IX

HEALTH AND WELFARE SERVICES

152.—(1) In this section, "public welfare purposes" includes any purpose in respect of which any obligation is imposed or power is conferred on the Metropolitan Corporation in relation to matters referred to in this Part.

(2) The Metropolitan Council may pass by-laws, which shall not become effective before the 1st day of January, 1967, assuming any land or building that it requires for public welfare purposes that is vested on the 31st day of March, 1966, in any area municipality and that is used on such day primarily for public welfare purposes, and on the day any such by-law becomes effective the property designated therein vests in the Metropolitan Corporation.

(3) No area municipality, after the 31st day of March, 1966, and before the 1st day of January, 1967, shall without the consent of the Metropolitan Council sell, lease or otherwise dispose of or encumber any land or building that is used primarily for public welfare purposes.

(4) Where any part of a building mentioned in subsection

Part VIII above does not affect the composition of the councils of the area municipalities of the status of the towns of Leaside, Mimico, New Toronto and Weston during the year 1966. See 1966, c. 96, s. 45.

buildings and of repairs and insurance, so far as they have been borne by one or other of the two municipalities, and the cost of maintaining and supporting the prisoners, as well as the salaries of all officers and servants connected therewith. R.S.O. 1960, c 260, s. 182.

183. After five years from the time when the amount of the compensation is agreed upon or determined by the Municipal Board under sections 180 and 182 or after a direction by the Lieutenant Governor in Council under the authority of this section, the Lieutenant Governor in Council upon the application of the county or the Metropolitan Corporation may direct that the existing arrangement shall cease after a day to be named and that the compensation to be paid from that day shall be settled by agreement or determined by the Municipal Board. R.S.O. 1960, c. 260, s. 183.

184. The jail may be used for the purposes of a lock-up house for any area municipality or any local municipality in the county, and if so used the area municipality or local municipality shall pay yearly to the treasurer of the Metropolitan Corporation a reasonable sum for such use and for the expenses incurred by such use, and in case of disagreement the amount to be paid to the Metropolitan Corporation shall be determined by the Municipal Board. R.S.O. 1960, c. 260, s. 184.

185. Sections 358 and 359 of *The Municipal Act* apply to the jail, the Metropolitan Corporation and the jailers and jail employees, and the Metropolitan Corporation shall be deemed to be a city for the purposes of those sections. R.S.O. 1960, c. 260, s. 185.

186. Sections 355 to 371 of *The Municipal Act* do not apply to the County of York or any area municipality. R.S.O. 1960, c. 260, s. 186.

187.—(1) The jail maintained by The Corporation of the City of Toronto, and all real and personal property used for the purposes of such jail, are vested in the Metropolitan Corporation and, subject to subsection 2, no compensation or damages shall be payable to the City.

(2) On and after the 1st day of January, 1954, the Metropolitan Corporation shall pay to The Corporation of the City of Toronto before the due date all amounts of principal and interest becoming due on any outstanding debentures issued by the City in respect of such jail.

(3) If the Metropolitan Corporation fails to make any payment as required by subsection 2, the City may charge the Metropolitan Corporation interest at the rate of one-half of 1 per cent for each month or fraction thereof that the payment is overdue.

(4) In the event of any doubt as to whether any debenture or portion thereof was issued in respect of the jail, the Municipal Board, upon application, may determine the matter and its decision is final. R.S.O. 1960, c. 260, s. 187.

188.—(1) Until the Metropolitan Corporation has provided, established or erected a court house and is ready to provide and pay for all matters mentioned in section 177, The Corporation of the City of Toronto shall in the first instance provide and pay for all such matters.

(2) The Metropolitan Corporation shall repay to The Corporation of the City of Toronto, in such manner as may be agreed upon, the costs incurred by the City under subsection 1. R.S.O. 1960, c. 260, s. 188.

189. The Metropolitan Corporation shall be deemed to be a city for the purposes of *The Juvenile and Family Courts Act*. R.S.O. 1960, c. 260, s. 189.

190. The Metropolitan Corporation shall be deemed to be a city for the purposes of *The Coroners Act* and no area municipality is liable for the payment of any salaries, fees or expenses under such Act. R.S.O. 1960, c. 260, s. 190.

191. The Corporation of the County of York is not liable, and the Metropolitan Corporation is liable, for the fees and allowances required to be paid by the county under section 38 of *The Coroners Act* with respect to deceased persons who were resident in the home for the aged established by the Metropolitan Corporation and known as Greenacres. R.S.O. 1960, c. 260, s. 191.

192.—(1) Nothing in this Act alters or affects the boundaries of any registry division.

(2) The building in which the Registry Office for the Registry Division of the City of Toronto is located and the lands on which such building is situated and all personal property used for the purposes of such registry office and the land titles office therein are vested in the Metropolitan Corporation and the Metropolitan Corporation shall pay to the City of Toronto such compensation therefor as may be agreed upon and failing agreement as may be determined by the Municipal Board.

(3) The surplus fees in respect of the Registry Office for the Registry Division of the City of Toronto and of the Land Titles Office in the City of Toronto to which the Metropolitan Corporation is entitled, after payment of the cost of any alterations or additions thereto, shall be paid by the Metropolitan Corporation to the City of Toronto in payment of the compensation agreed upon or determined under subsection 2 until such compensation is fully paid.

(4) The building in which the Registry Office for the Registry Division of the East and West Riding of the County of York and the lands on which such building is situated and all personal property used for the purposes of such registry office are vested in the Metropolitan Corporation and the Metropolitan Corporation shall pay such compensation therefor to the County of York and the area municipalities except the City of Toronto as may be agreed upon and failing agreement as may be determined by the Municipal Board.

(5) The total compensation under subsection 4 shall be determined on the basis of values as of the 1st day of January, 1955, and the County of York shall be entitled to 15 per cent of such total compensation and the area municipalities shall be entitled to the remainder in such proportions as may be agreed upon and failing agreement as may be determined by the Municipal Board.

(6) When the boundaries of the Registry Division of the East and West Riding of the County of York are changed so that no land within a municipality forming part of the County of York for municipal purposes is within such Registry Division, the Metropolitan Corporation shall pay to the County of York the amount of compensation to which the County is entitled under subsection 5.

(7) The surplus fees of the Registry Office for the Registry Division of the East and West Riding of the County of York to which the Metropolitan Corporation is entitled, after payment of the cost of any alterations or additions thereto, shall be paid by the Metropolitan Corporation to and distributed among the area municipalities except the City of Toronto in payment of the compensation agreed upon or determined under subsection 5 in the same proportions as are determined with respect to the compensation until such compensation is fully paid.

(8) No interest shall be payable in respect of any compensation payable by the Metropolitan Corporation under this section.

(9) For the purposes of *The Registry Act,* the Metropolitan Corporation shall be deemed to be a city and shall provide registry office accommodation and all other matters under *The Registry Act* with respect to the said registry divisions and the registry offices thereof.

(10) So long as any land within a municipality forming part of the County of York for municipal purposes is within the boundaries of the Registry Division of the East and West Riding of the County of York, the County of York shall bear and pay to the treasurer of the Metropolitan Corporation such equitable proportion of the expenses incurred under section 20 of *The Registry Act* and any other expenses with respect to the registry office for such registry division, as the Inspector of Legal Offices directs.

(11) Subject to section 5 of *The Land Titles Act,*

    (a) the Metropolitan Corporation is entitled to the surplus fees in respect of the Registry Office for the Registry Division of the City of Toronto; and

    (b) so long as any land within a municipality forming part of the County of York for municipal purposes is within the boundaries of the Registry Division of the East and West Riding of the County of York, the Metropolitan Corporation and the County of York are entitled to the surplus fees in respect of the Registry Office for the Registry Division of the East and West Riding of the County of York in the manner provided in *The Registry Act* and thereafter the Metropolitan Corporation is entitled to such surplus fees.

(12) For the purposes of *The Land Titles Act,* the Metropolitan Corporation shall be deemed to be a city and the responsibility of the City of Toronto under that Act shall hereafter be the responsibility of the Metropolitan Corporation which shall share with the County of York the expenses under that Act in the manner provided by subsection 3 of section 3 of that Act.

(13) The Metropolitan Corporation and the County of York are entitled to the surplus fees in respect of the Land Titles Office in the City of Toronto in the manner provided in *The Land Titles Act.*

(14) Where any portion of any building that is vested by this section in the Metropolitan Corporation is being used by the City of Toronto for purposes other than a registry or land titles office on the 1st day of January, 1954, the City of Toronto may continue to use any such portion on such terms and at such rental as may be agreed upon and failing agreement as may be determined by the Municipal Board and when any such portion is required by the Metropolitan Corporation it shall give to the City of Toronto at least six months notice to vacate.

(15) When the building and lands vested by subsection 2 in the Metropolitan Corporation are required by the City of Toronto for the development of a civic square, the Metropolitan Corporation shall sell and convey such building and lands to the City of Toronto within two years of being notified by the City that the building and lands are so required at a price equal to the amount of compensation therefor determined under subsection 2. R.S.O. 1960, c. 260, s. 192.

Part XI

METROPOLITAN POLICE

193. In this Part, "Metropolitan Board" means Metropolitan Board of Commissioners of Police for the Metropolitan Corporation. R.S.O. 1960, c. 260, s. 193.

194.—(1) The Metropolitan Corporation shall be deemed to be a city for the purposes of *The Police Act.*

(2) *The Police Act* does not apply to any area municipality.

(3) Notwithstanding subsection 2, any area municipality making payments under subsection 14 of section 202 may be paid a grant under Part III of *The Police Act.* R.S.O. 1960, c. 260, s. 194.

195. All boards of commissioners of police of area municipalities are dissolved. R.S.O. 1960, c. 260, s. 195.

196.—(1) The Board of Commissioners of Police for the Metropolitan Corporation shall be known as Metropolitan Board of Commissioners of Police and shall be composed of,

    (a) the chairman of the Metropolitan Council;

    (b) one member of the Metropolitan Council appointed by the Metropolitan Council;

    (c) a judge of the county court of the County of York designated by the Lieutenant Governor in Council; and

    (d) two magistrates designated by the Lieutenant Governor in Council.

(2) The Metropolitan Board may pass by-laws under paragraph 3 of section 403 of *The Municipal Act.* R.S.O. 1960, c. 260, s. 196.

197. The Metropolitan Corporation shall provide for the payment of a reasonable remuneration, not being less than the minimum prescribed by the regulations under *The Police Act,* to the members of the Metropolitan Board. R.S.O. 1960, c. 260, s. 197.

198. The Metropolitan Corporation shall provide all real and personal property necessary for the purposes of the Metropolitan Board. R.S.O. 1960, c. 260, s. 198.

199. All regulations under *The Police Act* made by the boards of commissioners of police dissolved under section 195 that are in force immediately before the 1st day of January, 1957, shall continue in force and effect and apply to the members of the Metropolitan Police Force until repealed by the Metropolitan Board. R.S.O. 1960, c. 260, s. 199.

200.—(1) Every person who is a member of a police force in an area municipality, including any chief constable, constable, police officer and assistant, on the 15th day of March, 1956, and is continuously so employed until immediately before the 1st day of January, 1957, becomes a member of the Metropolitan Police Force on the 1st day of January, 1957, and is subject to the government of the Metropolitan Board to the same extent as if appointed by the Metropolitan Board.

(2) Subsections 3 to 7 of section 24 apply to every person who becomes a member of the Metropolitan Police Force, except a chief constable, constable or other police officer, to the same extent as if such person had been an employee of an area municipality or the board of commissioners of police thereof and thereafter became employed by the Metropolitan Corporation.

(3) The Metropolitan Board and the members of the Metropolitan Police Force shall be charged with the same duties with respect to by-laws of the area municipalities as with respect to by-laws of the Metropolitan Corporation. R.S.O. 1960, c. 260, s. 200.

201.—(1) The Metropolitan Council shall, before the 1st day of January, 1957, pass by-laws which shall be effective on the 1st day of January, 1957, assuming for the use of the Metropolitan Board any such land or building that the Metropolitan Board may require that is vested on the 15th day of February, 1956, in any area municipality or local board thereof, and at least 40 per cent of which is used on such date for the purposes of the police force of that area municipality, and on the day any such by-law becomes effective the property designated therein vests in the Metropolitan Corporation.

(2) No area municipality, before the 1st day of January, 1957, shall without the consent of the Metropolitan Board sell, lease or otherwise dispose of or encumber any land or building mentioned in subsection 1.

(3) Notwithstanding subsection 1, a by-law for assuming any land or building mentioned in subsection 1, with the approval of the Municipal Board, may be passed after the 1st day of January, 1957, and in that case the by-law shall become effective on the date provided therein.

(4) Where any part of a building mentioned in subsection 1 is used by the area municipality or a local board thereof for other than police purposes, the Metropolitan Council may,

(a) where practicable assume only the part of the building and land appurtenant thereto used for the purposes of the police force of the area municipality; or

(b) vest the building and land appurtenant thereto in the Metropolitan Corporation and enter into an agreement with the area municipality or local board thereof for the use of a part of the building by the area municipality or local board on such terms and conditions as may be agreed upon.

(5) Where the Metropolitan Corporation assumes any property under subsection 1 or 3,

(a) no compensation or damage shall be payable to the area municipality or local board except as provided in this subsection;

(b) the Metropolitan Corporation shall thereafter pay to the area municipality before the due date all amounts of principal and interest becoming due upon any outstanding debentures issued by the area municipality in respect of any property vested in the Metropolitan Corporation;

(c) the Metropolitan Corporation shall thereafter pay to the area municipality for the portion of any land or building vested in the Metropolitan Corporation under this section that is not used for police purposes on the 15th day of February, 1956, such amount as may be agreed upon and failing agreement the Municipal Board, upon application, may determine the amount, and its decision is final, provided such amount shall not be greater than the capital expenditure for such portion of such land or building less the amount of any outstanding debentures in respect of such portion.

(6) If the Metropolitan Corporation fails to make any payment as required by clause b of subsection 5, the area municipality may charge the Metropolitan Corporation interest at the rate of one-half of 1 per cent for each month or fraction thereof that the payment is overdue.

(7) Where a building vested in an area municipality or local board is used partly by the police force of the area municipality and is not vested in the Metropolitan Corporation under this section, the area municipality at the request of the Metropolitan Board shall provide, at such rental as may be agreed upon, at least as much accommodation in such building for the use of the Metropolitan Board as was being provided by the area municipality for its police force on the 15th day of February, 1956.

(8) At the request of the Metropolitan Board, each area municipality, for the use of the Metropolitan Board,

(a) shall transfer to the Metropolitan Corporation without compensation all office supplies and stationery in the possession of the area municipality on the 31st day of December, 1956, that was provided for the exclusive use of the police force of the area municipality;

(b) shall transfer to the Metropolitan Corporation without compensation all personal property with the exception of office supplies and stationery in the possession of the area municipality on the 15th day of February, 1956, or thereafter that was provided for the exclusive use of the police force of the area municipality;

(c) shall make available to the Metropolitan Corporation all personal property the use of which was shared by the police and any department or departments of the area municipality on the 15th day of February, 1956, on the same terms and to the same extent as the police department used the property before the 15th day of February, 1956.

(9) No area municipality or board of commissioners of police, without the consent of the Metropolitan Board, shall dispose of any personal property referred to in subsection 8 owned by the area municipality on the 15th day of February, 1956, or thereafter.

(10) All signal and communication systems owned by any area municipality and used for the purposes of the police force of the area municipality on the 15th day of February, 1956, or thereafter are vested in the Metropolitan Corporation for the use of the Metropolitan Board on the 1st day of January, 1957, and no compensation shall be payable to the area municipality therefor and the Metropolitan Corporation shall thereafter pay to the area municipality before the due date all amounts of principal and interest becoming due upon any outstanding debentures issued by the area municipality in respect of any such signal or communication system.

(11) In the event of any doubt as to whether,

(a) any outstanding debenture or portion thereof was issued in respect of any property assumed; or

(b) any land or building is used at least 40 per cent for the purposes of a police force,

the Municipal Board, upon application, may determine the matter and its decision is final. R.S.O. 1960, c. 260, s. 201.

202.—(1) The Metropolitan Council, on the recommendation of the Metropolitan Board, shall provide such pension plan for the chief constable, constables and other police officers who are members of the Metropolitan Police Force, as the Minister may approve, and may provide for the incorporation of the plan of any area municipality and the Toronto Police Benefit Fund with the plan established under this section, and may provide for the transfer of the interests of such members who were in the service of the police force of an area municipality from the Toronto Police Benefit Fund and from the pension plan of any area municipality to the pension plan established under this section.

(2) The benefits provided in the pension plan established under this section for the services of any member of the Metropolitan Police Force performed on and after the 1st day of January, 1957, shall be on a basis not less favourable with respect to such services than the benefits provided in By-law No. 13273 of The Corporation of the City of Toronto, as amended, respecting the Toronto Police Benefit Fund.

(3) The benefits provided in the pension plan established under this section,

(a) with respect to the services performed before the 1st day of January, 1957, of members of the Toronto Police Benefit Fund shall not be less favourable than the benefits provided in the said By-law No. 13273, provided such benefits shall be limited to those purchasable with the assets transferred from the Toronto Police Benefit Fund and the payments to be made by the City of Toronto as provided in subsection 14 and any additional payments agreed to be made by the City of Toronto to the pension plan established under this section; and

(b) with respect to the services performed before the 1st day of January, 1957, by the chief constable, constables and other police officers of any area municipality shall be not less favourable than the benefits provided for the chief constable, constables and other police officers under the pension plan of such other area municipality, provided such benefits shall be limited to those purchasable with the assets transferred from the pension plan of the area municipality, the payments to be made by the area municipality as provided in subsection 14 and any additional payments agreed to be made by the area municipality to the pension plan established under this section.

(4) Every chief constable, constable and other police officer of the police force of an area municipality who has become a member of the Metropolitan Police Force pursuant to subsection 1 of section 200, or his beneficiaries, is entitled on termination of his services with the Metropolitan Police Force to all benefits accrued up to the 31st day of December, 1956, under the pension plan of the area municipality, and his employment by and service with the Metropolitan Police Force shall be deemed to be employment by and service with the police force of the area municipality for the purpose of determining eligibility for any such accrued benefits.

(5) An area municipality is liable to pay benefits accrued up to the 31st day of December, 1956, under subsection 4 only to the extent that such benefits exceed the benefits provided for services before the 1st day of January, 1957, in the pension plan established under this section.

(6) Subject to the approval of the Minister, the Metropolitan Council, on the recommendation of the Metropolitan Board, may by by-law provide benefits under the pension plan established under this section with respect to services performed prior to the 1st day of January, 1957, by the chief constables, constables and other police officers of the police forces of the area municipalities who have become members of the Metropolitan Police Force under subsection 1 of section 200 on a basis not less favourable than the basis required by subsection 2 for services after that date, and in such event the Metropolitan Council, with the like approval, may, for such purpose, determine,

(a) the extent to which the provisions of subsections 3 and 14 shall continue to apply;

(b) the payments to be made to such pension plan by each area municipality; and

(c) the assets to be assigned or transferred under subsection 12.

(7) The benefits authorized by subsection 6 may be provided for such chief constables, constables and other police officers whose services with the Metropolitan Police Force were terminated by retirement with immediate pension benefits or by death after the 1st day of January, 1957, and before the date a by-law passed under subsection 6 becomes effective.

(8) Any payments required to be made by an area municipality under subsection 6 other than assets transferred or assigned may, with the consent of the Metropolitan Council, be on a deferred basis and raised in a subsequent year or years and any such payments shall be deemed to be current expenditures.

(9) Any additional payments required to be made by the Metropolitan Corporation to provide the benefits authorized by subsection 6 may be on a deferred basis and raised in a subsequent year or years and shall be deemed to be current expenditures.

(10) Every chief constable, constable and other police officer of an area municipality who becomes a member of the Metropolitan Police Force under section 200 thereupon becomes a member of the pension plan established or to be established under this section.

(11) Until a pension plan is established under this section, the Metropolitan Board shall deduct by instalments 7 per cent of the gross salary of each member of the Metropolitan Police Force referred to in subsection 10, and the Metropolitan Corporation shall contribute an equivalent amount and shall pay over to the treasurer of the Metropolitan Corporation all deductions and contributions which shall be held by him in trust in a provisional fund.

(12) At the request of the Metropolitan Board,

(a) the ownership of the assets of the Toronto Police Benefit Fund;

(b) a sum equal to the amount standing to the credit of the chief constable, constables and other police officers of each area municipality, except the City of Toronto, in the pension plan of the area municipality; and

(c) the interest of every such police officer in the pension plan of an area municipality provided by contract with Her Majesty in accordance with the *Government Annuities Act* (Canada) or with an insurer,

shall be transferred to the provisional fund under subsection 11 until the pension plan is established under this section and thereafter to such pension plan.

(13) The ownership of all securities registered in the name of the Toronto Police Benefit Fund shall be deemed to be transferred upon the various registry books of the issuers of such securities to the name of the Metropolitan Toronto Police Benefit Fund.

(14) Where any area municipality is committed to make payments in any year into the pension plan of any area municipality or the Toronto Police Benefit Fund with respect to past services of any chief constable, constable or other police officer, the area municipality shall pay over in such year the amounts for which it is so committed to the provisonal fund under subsection 11 until the pension plan is established under this section and thereafter to such pension plan.

(15) When a pension plan is established under this section, the assets of the provisional fund shall be transferred thereto.

(16) The Metropolitan Board shall establish, effective on and after the 1st day of January, 1957, a sick leave credit plan for the chief constable, constables and other police officers who are members of the Metropolitan Police Force, and shall provide therein for sick leave credits at least equivalent to those to which each such person would have been entitled if he had remained a member of a police force in an area municipality and shall place to the credit of each such person the sick leave credits standing to his credit in the plan of the area municipality.

(17) Where a chief constable, constable or other police officer of an area municipality becomes a member of the Metropolitan Police Force under section 200, the Metropolitan Board shall provide, during the first year he is such a member, for holidays with pay at least equivalent to those to which such police officer would have been entitled if he had remained a

member of the police force of the area municipality. R.S.O. 1960, c. 260, s. 202.

MAGISTRATES

203.—(1) The Metropolitan Corporation shall be deemed to be a city for the purposes of *The Magistrates Act.*

(2) *The Magistrates Act* does not apply to the City of Toronto and any reference to the City of Toronto in that Act shall be deemed to be a reference to the Metropolitan Corporation. R.S.O. 1960, c. 260, s. 203.

204. The Metropolitan Corporation may for the purposes of the magistrates assigned to the Metropolitan Corporation continue to use any court room and office accommodation provided by The Corporation of the City of Toronto for the purposes of the magistrates assigned to the City of Toronto on the 31st day of December, 1956, on such terms and at such rental as may be agreed upon and failing agreement as may be determined by the Municipal Board. R.S.O. 1960, c. 260, s. 204.

205. At the request of the Metropolitan Corporation,

(*a*) there shall be transferred to the Metropolitan Corporation without compensation all office supplies and stationery used exclusively for the purposes of the magistrates' courts in the Metropolitan Area on the 31st day of December, 1956;

(*b*) there shall be transferred to the Metropolitan Corporation without compensation all public personal property, with the exception of office supplies and stationery, used exclusively for the purposes of the magistrates' courts in the Metropolitan Area on the 15th day of February, 1956;

(*c*) there shall be made available to the Metropolitan Corporation all personal property, the use of which was shared by the magistrates' courts and any department or departments of any area municipality on the 15th day of February, 1956, to the same extent as the magistrates used the property on the 15th day of February, 1956, on such terms as may be agreed upon and failing agreement as may be determined by the Municipal Board. R.S.O. 1960, c. 260, s. 205.

206. The Metropolitan Corporation shall be deemed to be a city for the purpose of section 151 of *The Highway Traffic Act.* R.S.O. 1960, c. 260, s. 206.

207. The Metropolitan Corporation shall be deemed to be a municipality for the purpose of section 87 of *The Liquor Licence Act.* R.S.O. 1960, c. 260, s. 207.

208. The fines and penalties that but for this Act would otherwise belong to an area municipality belong to the Metropolitan Corporation. R.S.O. 1960, c. 260, s. 208.

Part XII

LICENSING COMMISSION

209. In this Part, "Licensing Commission" means the licensing commission established for The Municipality of Metropolitan Toronto under this Part. R.S.O. 1960, c. 260, s. 209.

210.—(1) There shall be a licensing commission for The Municipality of Metropolitan Toronto to be known as Metropolitan Licensing Commission composed of,

(*a*) the chairman of the Metropolitan Council or his delegate; and

(*b*) two persons appointed by the Metropolitan Council who are not members of the council of an area municipality. R.S.O. 1960, c. 260, s. 210 (1); 1962-63, c. 89, s. 11 (1).

(2) The chairman of the Metropolitan Council may designate any member of the Metropolitan Council to be his delegate at any or all of the meetings of the Licensing Commission.

(3) The Licensing Commission shall elect a chairman and may elect a vice-chairman, and a majority of the members of the Licensing Commission constitutes a quorum. R.S.O. 1960, c. 260, s. 210 (2, 3).

211.—(1) The Licensing Commission has all the powers that may be exercised,

(*a*) by boards of commissioners of police under,

　　(i) paragraphs 1, 4 and 6 of section 395 of *The Municipal Act,*

　　(ii) paragraphs 7 and 8 of subsection 1 of section 399 of *The Municipal Act,*

　　(iii) paragraphs 4, 5, 12 and 14 of section 401 of *The Municipal Act;*

(*b*) by councils of cities under paragraph 1 of section 390 of *The Municipal Act.* R.S.O. 1960, c. 260, s. 211 (1).

(1*a*) A by-law passed by the Licensing Commission pursuant to subclause i of clause *a* of subsection 1 of this section and paragraph 1 of section 395 of *The Municipal Act* with respect to licensing, regulating and governing owners and drivers of ambulances may include provisions,

(*a*) for licensing, regulating and governing ambulance attendants and providing for examinations to be passed by ambulance drivers and attendants;

(*b*) for requiring owners of ambulances to install and maintain such means of communication with any central ambulance dispatching system maintained by or for the Metropolitan Corporation as the by-law may prescribe;

(*c*) for requiring owners and drivers of ambulances to accept and make calls as directed through such central ambulance dispatching system. 1966, c. 96, s. 27.

(2) The Metropolitan Council, by reference to the provisions of any Act, may by by-law authorize the Licensing Commission to exercise the powers of any area municipality or board of commissioners of police with respect to the licensing, revoking of a licence, regulating, governing, prohibiting or limiting of any trade, calling, business or occupation or the person carrying on or engaged in it and upon being so authorized the Licensing Commission may exercise such powers. R.S.O. 1960, c. 260, s. 211 (2).

212. The Licensing Commission has the same power to summon and examine witnesses on oath as to any matter connected with the execution of its powers and duties or as to any matter respecting any licence issued before the 1st day of January, 1957, by any body that formerly exercised the powers now vested in the Licensing Commission, to enforce their attendance and to compel them to give evidence and produce documents and things, as is vested in any court of law in civil cases. R.S.O. 1960, c. 260, s. 212.

213. Where a by-law of the Licensing Commission passed under a provision of *The Municipal Act* or any other Act is applicable to an area municipality, any by-law of the area municipality passed under the same provision of *The Municipal Act* or any other Act has no effect and the area municipality does not have power to pass such a by-law while the by-law passed by the Licensing Commission is in effect in such area municipality. R.S.O. 1960, c. 260, s. 213.

214. All the powers and duties of a board of commissioners of police under *The Municipal Act* or any other Act and all the powers and duties of the Board of Commissioners of Police for the City of Toronto under any special Act, except those which by this Act are exercised by the Licensing Commission or the Metropolitan Board of Commissioners of Police, shall after the 1st day of January, 1957, be exercised by the council of the City of Toronto. R.S.O. 1960, c. 260, s. 214.

215. Sections 247 and 248 and Part XXI of *The Municipal Act* apply *mutatis mutandis* to the Licensing Commission and to the by-laws passed by the Licensing Commission, and the Licensing Commission shall fix the fees to be paid for any licence. R.S.O. 1960, c. 260, s. 215.

216. The Metropolitan Corporation shall pay to the members of the Licensing Commission for their services such remuneration as may be determined by the Metropolitan Corporation. R.S.O. 1960, c. 260, s. 216.

Part XIII

HOUSING AND REDEVELOPMENT

217.—(1) The Metropolitan Corporation and the Metropolitan Council have all the powers conferred on the corporation or council of a municipality under *The Housing Development Act* or any other Act with respect to housing or building development, housing projects, temporary housing accommodation and redevelopment areas and with respect to any other matter concerned with the provision or improvement of housing accommodation.

(2) Nothing in subsection 1 shall be deemed to limit or interfere with the powers of the area municipalities with respect to the matters mentioned in subsection 1. R.S.O. 1960, c. 260, s. 217.

218. Without limiting its powers under subsection 1 of section 217, the Metropolitan Corporation,

  (a) shall be deemed to be a governmental authority within the meaning of section 17 of *The Housing Development Act;* and

  (b) may enter into agreements with any area municipality for sharing or contributing to the costs incurred by the area municipality in exercising any of its powers with respect to the matters mentioned in subsection 1 of section 217. R.S.O. 1960, c. 260, s. 218.

Part XIV

PLANNING

219.—(1) The Metropolitan Toronto Planning Area is hereby continued.

(2) The Metropolitan Corporation shall be the designated municipality within the meaning of *The Planning Act* for the purposes of the said planning area. R.S.O. 1960, c. 260, s. 219 (1, 2).

(3) The planning board for the planning area shall be constituted as provided in *The Planning Act,* except that the membership of the planning board shall at all times include two persons recommended by The Metropolitan Toronto School Board and approved by the Minister.

(4) On and after the 1st day of January, 1967, subject to

The Planning Act, each area municipality is a subsidiary planning area within The Metropolitan Toronto Planning Area, and the subsidiary planning areas within The Metropolitan Toronto Planning Area but outside the Metropolitan Area are continued. 1966, c. 96, s. 28.

(5) REPEALED: 1966, c. 96, s. 28.

(6) Nothing in subsection 4 affects any official plan in effect in any subsidiary planning area.

(7) When the Minister has approved an official plan adopted by the Metropolitan Council,

  (a) any official plan then in effect in a subsidiary planning area affected thereby shall be amended to conform therewith;

  (b) no official plan of a subsidiary planning area shall be adopted that does not conform therewith;

  (c) no public work, as defined in *The Planning Act,* shall be undertaken, and no by-law shall be passed, by any municipality or local board within The Metropolitan Toronto Planning Area, that does not conform therewith. R.S.O. 1960, c. 260, s. 219 (6, 7).

220.—(1) The Metropolitan Corporation shall be deemed to be a municipality for the purposes of sections 1 to 20, 22 to 25, 28, 33 and 34 of *The Planning Act,* and no area municipality shall be deemed to be a municipality for the purposes of section 7 of *The Planning Act* with respect to the financial requirements of the board of The Metropolitan Toronto Planning Area. 1966, c. 96, s. 29.

(2) The Metropolitan Corporation may enter into agreements with area municipalities or persons relating to conditions of approval of plans of subdivision and shall be deemed to have always had authority to enter into such agreements. R.S.O. 1960, c. 260, s. 220 (2).

(3) The Metropolitan Corporation, with the approval of the Minister, may enter into an agreement with any governmental authority, or any agency thereof created by statute, for the carrying out of studies relating to the physical condition of The Metropolitan Toronto Planning Area or any part thereof. 1964, c. 71, s. 2 (2).

220*a.* Before an official plan for The Metropolitan Toronto Planning Area is adopted, amended or repealed by the Metropolitan Council or by the council of any municipality within The Metropolitan Toronto Planning Area, such council shall give notice thereof to each other municipality within The Metropolitan Toronto Planning Area, including the Metropolitan Corporation, and shall give to each such municipality an opportunity to make representation thereon to the council or a committee thereof appointed for such purpose. 1966, c. 96, s. 30.

221. The scope and general purpose of the official plan for The Metropolitan Toronto Planning Area includes,

  (a) land uses and consideration generally of industrial, agricultural, residential and commercial areas;

  (b) ways of communication;

  (c) sanitation;

  (d) green belts and park areas;

  (e) public transportation,

and such other matters as the Minister of Municipal Affairs may from time to time define under *The Planning Act.* R.S.O. 1960, c. 260, s. 221.

222. Except as provided in this Part, the provisions of *The Planning Act* continue to apply. R.S.O. 1960, c. 260, s. 222.

Part XV

PARKS, RECREATION AREAS, ETC.

223.—(1) The Metropolitan Council may pass by-laws for acquiring land for and establishing, laying out and improving and maintaining public parks, zoological gardens, recreation areas, squares, avenues, boulevards and drives in the Metropolitan Area or in any adjoining local municipality in the County of Ontario or the County of Peel or in any local municipality in the County of York, and for exercising all or any of the powers that are conferred on boards of park management by *The Public Parks Act.*

(2) Paragraphs 65 and 66 of section 377 of *The Municipal Act* apply *mutatis mutandis* to the Metropolitan Corporation. R.S.O. 1960, c. 260, s. 223.

(3) The Metropolitan Corporation shall be deemed to be a municipality for the purposes of *The Parks Assistance Act.*

(4) Where, under an agreement with The Metropolitan Toronto and Region Conservation Authority, lands vested in the Authority are managed and controlled by the Metropolitan Corporation, the Metropolitan Corporation may,

(a) exercise all or any of the powers conferred on it under subsection 1 in respect of such lands;

(b) lay out, construct and maintain roads on such lands and, with the consent of the area municipality in which such lands, or any part thereof, are situate, assume the maintenance of existing roads on such lands, or any part thereof;

(c) subject to *The Highway Traffic Act,* regulate traffic on such roads and prescribe the rate of speed for motor vehicles driven on such roads in accordance with subsection 4 of section 59 of *The Highway Traffic Act;*

(d) notwithstanding the provisions of any other Act, exempt from municipal taxation any such lands for so long as they are managed and controlled by the Metropolitan Corporation and used for park purposes.

(5) An exemption from taxes under subsection 4 shall be deemed to have the same effect as an exemption from taxes under section 4 of *The Assessment Act.* 1960-61, c. 61, s. 9.

224.—(1) Where the Metropolitan Corporation has acquired land under section 223, the Metropolitan Council may agree to pay annually to the area municipality or other local municipality in which the land is situate a sum not exceeding the amount that would have been payable to the municipality as taxes in the year of acquisition if the land were not exempt from taxation.

(2) Subsection 1 does not apply where the land acquired by the Metropolitan Corporation was acquired from the municipality in which the land was situate or from a local board thereof and at the time of acquisition was used as a public park, recreation area, square, avenue, boulevard or drive. R.S.O. 1960, c. 260, s. 224.

225.—(1) For the purposes of section 223, the Metropolitan Council may with the approval of the Municipal Board by by-law assume any existing public park, zoological gardens, recreation area, square, avenue, boulevard or drive vested in any area municipality or in any local board thereof, and upon the passing of the by-law the public park, zoological gardens, recreation area, square, avenue, boulevard or drive vests in the Metropolitan Corporation.

(2) Where the Metropolitan Corporation assumes any existing public park, zoological gardens, recreation area, square, avenue, boulevard or drive vested in any area municipality or local board thereof,

(a) no compensation or damages shall be payable to the area municipality or local board;

(b) the Metropolitan Corporation shall thereafter pay to the area municipality before the due date all amounts of principal and interest becoming due upon any outstanding debentures issued by the area municipality in respect of the property assumed.

(3) If the Metropolitan Corporation fails to make any payment as required by clause b of subsection 2, the area municipality may charge the Metropolitan Corporation interest at the rate of one-half of 1 per cent for each month or fraction thereof that the payment is overdue.

(4) In the event of any doubt as to whether any outstanding debenture or portion thereof was issued in respect of the property assumed, the Municipal Board, upon application, may determine the matter and its decision is final. R.S.O. 1960, c. 260, s. 225 (1-4).

(5) REPEALED: 1966, c. 96, s. 31.

225a.—(1) The Metropolitan Council may by by-law assume any of the lands in the City of Toronto designated or known as Exhibition Park or created by fill to the south thereof, saving and excepting any lands or any interest therein of Her Majesty in right of Ontario, and the enactment of such by-law shall vest in the Metropolitan Corporation a full, clear and absolute title to the lands as described in such by-law free and clear of all conditions as to use contained in *An Act respecting the City of Toronto,* being chapter 86 of the Statutes of Ontario, 1903.

(2) No compensation or damages shall be payable by the Metropolitan Corporation to the City of Toronto for such assumed lands, but the Metropolitan Corporation shall thereafter pay before the due date all amounts of principal and interest becoming due upon any outstanding debentures issued in respect of the property assumed, and the provisions of subsections 3 and 4 of section 225 apply *mutatis mutandis.*

(3) Such assumed lands shall be used,

(a) for parks and exhibition purposes;

(b) for the purposes of trade and agricultural fairs;

(c) for the holding of displays, sporting events, public entertainments and meetings;

(d) for highway, electrical transmission or public utility purposes; or

(e) for any other purpose that the City of Toronto may approve.

(4) An exhibition shall be held annually on such assumed lands.

(5) With respect to the lands so assumed, the Metropolitan Council may exercise all or any of the powers that are conferred on boards of park management by *The Public Parks Act* and shall have all other powers required for the full and effective use of such assumed lands in accordance with subsection 3.

(6) If any of the lands vested by this section in the Metropolitan Corporation cease to be used for the purposes of subsection 3, the Metropolitan Corporation shall thereupon transfer such lands to the City of Toronto, and no compensation or damages shall be payable to the Metropolitan Corporation in respect thereof.

(7) Such assumed lands shall be exempt from taxation for municipal purposes so long as such lands continue to be owned by the Metropolitan Corporation and used for the purposes of the Canadian National Exhibition Association, provided that the full value of such lands, except the lands that are exempt

from taxation under section 4 of *The Assessment Act,* shall be included in the assessment of the City of Toronto for the purposes of the apportionment of the levies of the Metropolitan Corporation among the area municipalities.

(8) Subject to subsection 9, upon the passing of the by-law referred to in subsection 1, the Metropolitan Corporation shall be responsible for all liabilities of the City of Toronto and is entitled to all benefits under agreements made by or on behalf of the City of Toronto with respect to the use of such assumed lands, and the City of Toronto shall be relieved of any liability thereunder.

(9) Subsection 8 does not apply to agreements between the City of Toronto and the Metropolitan Corporation or to agreements for payments in lieu of taxes.

(10) The City of Toronto may continue to use, maintain, repair, reconstruct and replace watermains, sewers and sewage works in such assumed lands until and unless the area in which such watermains, sewers and sewage works are located are required by the Metropolitan Corporation, in which case the Metropolitan Corporation shall pay to the City of Toronto such amount as may be agreed upon or, failing agreement, such amount as may be determined by arbitration, and the provisions of *The Expropriation Procedures Act, 1962-63* apply to any such arbitration.

(11) The Metropolitan Corporation shall pay to the City of Toronto such amount for personal property on such assumed lands or in the buildings thereon as may be mutually agreed upon between the Metropolitan Corporation and the City of Toronto.

(12) The Metropolitan Corporation may enter into agreements with the Canadian National Exhibition Association, the Royal Agricultural Winter Fair and other bodies respecting the use of such assumed lands, the charging of entrance or admission fees and any other matter or thing that the Metropolitan Council deems desirable for the full and effective use of such assumed lands for the purposes set out in subsection 3.

(13) The Metropolitan Corporation may make grants to and erect and maintain buildings and structures for the use of the Canadian National Exhibition Association and other bodies and may enter into agreements with the Association and other bodies with respect to the operation and maintenance throughout the year of all or any part of such assumed lands and any buildings or structures now or hereafter erected thereon.

(14) The Metropolitan Corporation may enter into an agreement with the Canadian National Exhibition Association appointing the Association as its agent to carry out any of the powers of the Metropolitan Corporation under this section, and, upon the execution of such an agreement, the Association is authorized to exercise such powers subject to such restrictions as may be set out in the agreement. 1966, c. 96, s. 32.

226.—(1) For the purposes of section 223, all land comprising Toronto Islands owned by the City of Toronto and all rights of the City of Toronto to use and occupy land comprising Toronto Islands owned by The Toronto Harbour Commissioners, except such portions of all such lands as are set aside and used or required for the purposes of the Toronto Island Airport, are vested in the Metropolitan Corporation as of the 1st day of January, 1956, subject to the provisions of then existing leases, and, subject to subsection 2, no compensation or damages shall be payable to the City of Toronto in respect thereof.

(2) The Metropolitan Corporation shall pay to the City of Toronto,

   (a) before the due date all amounts of principal and interest becoming due upon any outstanding debentures issued by the City of Toronto for the pur-

poses of the land and rights vested by this section in the Metropolitan Corporation;

   (b) the amount approved by the Municipal Board and expended by the City of Toronto, but not debentured, for shore protection of Algonquin Island;

   (c) the amount approved by the Municipal Board and expended by the City of Toronto, but not debentured, for acquisition of leasehold interests and clearing of sites;

   (d) such amount for personal property, exclusive of leaseholds, transferred to the Metropolitan Corporation as may be mutually agreed upon between the Metropolitan Corporation and the City of Toronto;

   (e) the amount of the expenses incurred by the City of Toronto after the 1st day of January, 1956, with respect to the operation and maintenance of the land and rights vested by this section in the Metropolitan Corporation.

(3) Where any portion of the land and rights vested by this section in the Metropolitan Corporation is being used by the City of Toronto for the purpose of providing municipal services other than park and recreation services, the City of Toronto may continue to use such portion rent free so long as it is required to provide such municipal services.

(4) The Metropolitan Corporation shall pay to the City of Toronto annually such amount for the lighting, refuse collection and disposal services provided by the City of Toronto in respect of the land and rights vested by this section in the Metropolitan Corporation as may be mutually agreed upon between the Metropolitan Corporation and the City of Toronto.

(5) If any of the land vested by this section in the Metropolitan Corporation and any land comprising Toronto Islands, which is hereafter conveyed by The Toronto Harbour Commissioners to the Metropolitan Corporation, ceases to be used for any of the purposes of section 223, the Metropolitan Corporation shall thereupon transfer such land to the City of Toronto and no compensation or damages shall be payable to the Metropolitan Corporation in respect thereof; provided this subsection does not apply to any land so long as it continues to be used as at the 1st day of January, 1956, under any then existing lease or renewal or extension thereof.

(6) In the event of any doubt as to whether any outstanding debenture or portion thereof was issued for the purposes of the land and rights vested by this section in the Metropolitan Corporation or of failure to agree as to the amount to be paid for the personal property transferred to the Metropolitan Corporation or as to the amount to be paid for lighting, refuse collection and disposal services provided by the City of Toronto, the Municipal Board, upon application, may determine the matter, and its decision is final. R.S.O. 1960, c. 260, s. 226.

(7) Notwithstanding any other provision in this Act, the Metropolitan Corporation may establish, maintain and operate a ferry service for providing access to the lands vested in the Metropolitan Corporation under this section for so long as such lands or any part thereof remain so vested and are used for park purposes, and, for such purposes, the Metropolitan Corporation may assume the rights, equipment and other assets of the Toronto Transit Commission used in providing such service subject only to the payment of any outstanding liability in respect thereto and such adjustment as the Metropolitan Corporation may determine and may enter into agreements with any person with respect to the provision of such service. 1960-61, c. 61, s. 10.

(8) Notwithstanding any other provision in this Act, the Metropolitan Corporation may establish, maintain and operate a public bus transportation system on the Toronto Islands and for such purposes the Metropolitan Corporation may,

(a) maintain and operate buses for the conveyance of passengers;

(b) acquire by purchase or otherwise any real or personal property required for the establishment, operation, maintenance or extension of the system; and

(c) fix transportation fares and tolls and make regulations with respect to the operation and control of the system. 1961-62, c. 88, s. 13.

Part XVI

FINANCES

227. In this Part, "rateable property" includes business and other assessment made under *The Assessment Act*. R.S.O. 1960, c. 260, s. 227.

228. Section 302 of *The Municipal Act* applies *mutatis mutandis* to the Metropolitan Corporation. R.S.O. 1960, c. 260, s. 228.

Yearly Levies and Estimates

229.—(1) The Metropolitan Council shall in each year prepare and adopt estimates of all sums required during the year for the purposes of the Metropolitan Corporation, including the sums required by law to be provided by the Metropolitan Council for school purposes and for any local board of the Metropolitan Corporation, and such estimates shall set forth the estimated revenues and expenditures in such detail and according to such form as the Department may from time to time prescribe.

(2) In preparing the estimates, the Metropolitan Council shall make due allowance for a surplus of any previous year which will be available during the current year and shall provide for any operating deficit of any previous year and for such reserves within such limits as to type and amount as the Department may approve but shall not make any allowance for payments to be received during the current year under *The Municipal Unconditional Grants Act*. R.S.O. 1960, c. 260, s. 229.

230.—(1) The Metropolitan Council shall in each year levy against the area municipalities a sum sufficient,

(a) for payment of the estimated current annual expenditures as adopted;

(b) for payment of all debts of the Metropolitan Corporation falling due within the year as well as amounts required to be raised for sinking funds and principal and interest payments or sinking fund requirements in respect of debenture debt of area municipalities for the payment of which the Metropolitan Corporation is liable under this Act.

(2) The Metropolitan Council shall ascertain and by by-law direct what portion of the sum mentioned in subsection 1 shall be levied against and in each area municipality.

(3) The amount levied under subsection 1 for public school purposes shall be apportioned among the area municipalities in the proportion that the whole rateable property rateable for public school purposes in each of the area municipalities bears to the whole rateable property rateable for public school purposes in the Metropolitan Area, according to the last revised assessment rolls.

(4) The amount levied under subsection 1 for secondary school purposes shall be apportioned among the area municipalities in the proportion that the whole rateable property rateable for secondary school purposes in each of the area municipalities bears to the whole rateable property rateable for secondary school purposes in the Metropolitan Area, according to the last revised assessment rolls.

(5) All other amounts levied under subsection 1 shall be apportioned among the area municipalities in the proportion that the whole rateable property in each area municipality bears to the whole rateable property in the Metropolitan Area, according to the last revised assessment rolls.

(6) Notwithstanding subsections 3, 4 and 5, the Metropolitan Council may pass its by-law under subsection 2 before the assessment rolls of all the area municipalities are revised by the courts of revision, and in that case the levies shall be apportioned among the area municipalities according to the last revised assessment rolls of those area municipalities whose assessment rolls have been so revised and the assessment rolls as returned of those area municipalities whose assessment rolls have not been so revised.

(7) Where the by-law under subsection 2 is passed as provided in subsection 6, the Metropolitan Council shall, forthwith after the assessment rolls of all the area municipalities have been revised by the courts of revision, amend the by-law so as to make the apportionments among the area municipalities according to the assessment rolls as so revised, and,

(a) where the moneys levied against an area municipality are thereby increased, the treasurer of the area municipality shall pay the amount of the increase to the treasurer of the Metropolitan Corporation; and

(b) where the moneys levied against an area municipality are thereby decreased, the treasurer of the area municipality shall be liable to pay to the treasurer of the Metropolitan Corporation only the reduced levy or, if the original levy has been paid by the area municipality, the treasurer of the Metropolitan Corporation shall pay the amount of the decrease to the treasurer of the area municipality.

(8) The apportionment of the levy among the area municipalities as provided for in subsections 2 to 5 shall be based on the full value of all rateable property, and no fixed assessment other than a fixed assessment under section 39 of *The Assessment Act* or partial or total exemption from assessment or taxation applies thereto, except as provided in section 4 of *The Assessment Act*.

(9) Notwithstanding anything in this section, the assessment upon which the levy among the area municipalities shall be apportioned shall include the valuations of all properties for which payments in lieu of taxes are paid by the Crown in right of Canada or any province or any board, commission, corporation or other agency thereof or The Hydro-Electric Power Commission of Ontario to any area municipality. R.S.O. 1960, c. 260, s. 230 (1-9).

(9a) The clerk of an area municipality shall transmit to the clerk of the Metropolitan Corporation, within sixty days of the receipt of a grant paid in lieu of taxes, a statement of the valuations of real property in the area municipality upon which such grant was made. 1964, c. 71, s. 3.

(10) One by-law or several by-laws for making the levies may be passed as the Metropolitan Council may deem expedient.

(11) The clerk of the Metropolitan Corporation shall forthwith after the metropolitan levies have been apportioned certify to the clerk of each area municipality the amount that has been so directed to be levied therein for the then current year for metropolitan purposes showing separately the amounts required for public school purposes, secondary school purposes and general purposes.

(12) Subject to subsection 5, 6 and 7 of section 57 of *The Assessment Act,* in each area municipality, the metropolitan levy,

    (a) for public school purposes, shall be calculated and levied upon the whole rateable property rateable for public school purposes;

    (b) for secondary school purposes, shall be calculated and levied upon the whole rateable property rateable for secondary school purposes; and

    (c) for all other purposes, shall be calculated and levied upon the whole rateable property rateable for such purposes,

within such area municipality according to the last revised assessment roll thereof.

(13) All moneys levied against an area municipality under the authority of this section shall be deemed to be taxes and are a debt of the area municipality to the Metropolitan Corporation and the treasurer of every area municipality shall pay the moneys so levied to the treasurer of the Metropolitan Corporation at the times and in the amounts specified by the by-law of the Metropolitan Council mentioned in subsection 2.

(14) If an area municipality fails to make any payment as provided in the by-law, interest shall be added at the rate of one-half of 1 per cent for each month or fraction thereof that the payment is overdue. R.S.O. 1960, c. 260, s. 230 (10-14).

230*a.*—(1) Notwithstanding section 230, the Metropolitan Council may, in any year before the adoption of the estimates for that year, levy against each of the area municipalities a sum not exceeding 50 per cent of the levy made by the Metropolitan Council in the preceding year against that area municipality or against the former area municipalities included within that area municipality, and subsections 13 and 14 of section 230 apply to such a levy.

(2) The amount of any levy made under subsection 1 shall be deducted from the amount of the levy made under section 230. 1966, c. 96, s. 33, *part.*

230*b.*—(1) The council of each of the area municipalities specified in the schedule to this section shall, within the bound-

area municipality as required in subsection 1 and shall make corresponding reductions in the amounts to be levied against such area municipality under sections 230 and 231.

(3) The treasurer of each of the area municipalities specified in the schedule to this section, in each of the years set out in the schedule and prior to the adoption of estimates by the Metropolitan Council, shall certify to the treasurer of the Metropolitan Corporation the amounts of tax allowances in the former area municipalities that would result in that year from reductions in the rates of taxation for such year in accordance with subsection 1.

231.—(1) The Metropolitan Council in each year shall determine, in accordance with subsections 2 and 3, what proportion of the total of the sums to be levied against the area municipalities under section 230 shall be raised by levy,

    (a) on the total of,

        (i) the assessment for real property that is used as a basis for computing business assessment including the assessment for real property that is rented and is occupied or used by the Crown in right of Canada or any province or any board, commission, corporation or other agency thereof, or by any municipal or metropolitan corporation or local board thereof, and

        (ii) the business assessment, and

        (iii) the assessment for mineral lands, railway lands and pipe lines and the assessment of telephone and telegraph companies,

    in the Metropolitan Area, according to the last revised assessment rolls; and

    (b) on the total assessment for real property in the Metropolitan Area according to the last revised assessment rolls except the assessments for real property mentioned in subclauses i and iii of clause *a.*

(2) The amount to be raised in each year by levy on the total of the assessments under clause *a* of subsection 1 shall

SCHEDULE

Area Municipality	Former Area Municipality	1967	1968	1969	1970
			Mills in the Dollar		
City of Toronto	Village of Forest Hill				
general purposes		8	6	4	2
City of Toronto	Village of Swansea				
general purposes		10	8.5	6	3
public school purposes		1.5	----	----	----
Borough of East York	Town of Leaside				
general purposes		5.5	4.5	3	1.5
public school purposes		1	----	----	----
Borough of York	Town of Weston				
general purposes		0.5	0.5	0.5	----
public school purposes		0.5	0.5	----	----

1966, c. 96, s. 33, *part.*

aries of the former area municipalities specified in such schedule, impose lower rates of taxation on the assessment described in subsection 3 of section 294 of *The Municipal Act* than those imposed on such assessment in the remainder of such area municipality, in the years, for the purposes and by the number of mills set out in such schedule.

(2) The Metropolitan Council shall include, in the estimates to be adopted for the years specified in the schedule to this section, the amount of the reductions granted by each

be a sum equal to the proportion of the total of the sums to be levied against the area municipalities under section 230 that the total of the assessments under clause *a* of subsection 1 bears to the total assessment for real property and business assessment in the Metropolitan Area according to the last revised assessment rolls.

(3) The amount to be raised in each year by levy on the total assessment under clause *b* of subsection 1 shall be a sum equal to the proportion of the total of the sums to be levied

against the area municipalities under section 230 that the total assessment under clause *b* of subsection 1 bears to the total assessment for real property and business assessment in the Metropolitan Area according to the last revised assessment rolls less the amount of the estimated revenue from payments to be received in that year by the Metropolitan Corporation under section 7 of *The Municipal Unconditional Grants Act.*

(4) The Metropolitan Council in each year shall require each area municipality to levy,

    (a) on the whole of,

        (i) the assessment for real property that is used as the basis for computing business assessment including the assessment for real property that is rented and is occupied or used by the Crown in right of Canada or any province or any board, commission, corporation or other agency thereof, or by any municipal or metropolitan corporation or local board thereof, and

        (ii) the business assessment, and

        (iii) the assessment for mineral lands, railway lands, other than railway lands actually in use for residential and farming purposes, and pipe lines and the assessment of telephone and telegraph companies,

according to the last revised assessment roll, a sum equal to the proportion of the amount required to be raised under subsection 2 that the whole of such assessments bears to the total of such assessments in the Metropolitan Area according to the last revised assessment rolls; and

    (b) on the whole of the assessment for real property, except the assessment for real property mentioned in subclauses i and iii of clause *a,* according to the last revised assessment roll, a sum equal to the proportion of the amount required to be raised under subsection 3 that the whole of such assessment bears to the total of such assessments in the Metropolitan Area according to the last revised assessment rolls. R.S.O. 1960, c. 260, s. 231.

Reserve Funds

232.—(1) The Metropolitan Council, or The Metropolitan School Board with the approval of the Metropolitan Council, may in each year, if authorized by a two-thirds vote of the members present at a meeting of the Metropolitan Council or the School Board, as the case may be, provide in the estimates for the establishment or maintenance of a reserve fund for any purpose for which it has authority to spend funds. 1960-61, c. 61, s. 11.

(2) The moneys raised for a reserve fund established under subsection 1 shall be paid into a special account and may be invested in such securities as a trustee may invest in under *The Trustee Act,* and the earnings derived from the investment of such moneys form part of the reserve fund.

(3) The moneys raised for a reserve fund established under subsection 1 shall not be expended, pledged or applied to any purpose other than that for which the fund was established without the approval of the Department.

(4) The auditor in his annual report shall report on the activities and position of each reserve fund established under subsection 1. R.S.O. 1960, c. 260, s. 232 (2-4).

Temporary Loans

233.—(1) The Metropolitan Council may by by-law, either before or after the passing of by-laws for imposing levies on the area municipalities for the current year, authorize the chairman and treasurer to borrow from time to time by way of promissory note such sums as the Metropolitan Council may deem necessary to meet, until the levies are received, the current expenditures of the Metropolitan Corporation for the year, including the amounts required for principal and interest falling due within the year upon any debt of the Metropolitan Corporation, and the sums required by law to be provided by the Metropolitan Council for school purposes and for any local board of the Metropolitan Corporation.

(2) The amount that may be borrowed in any year for the purposes mentioned in subsection 1 shall not, except with the approval of the Municipal Board, exceed 70 per cent of the total amount of the estimated revenues of the Metropolitan Corporation as set forth in the estimates adopted for the year.

(3) Until such estimates are adopted, the limitation upon borrowing prescribed by subsection 2 shall temporarily be calculated upon the estimated revenues of the Metropolitan Corporation as set forth in the estimates adopted for the next preceding year.

(4) For the purposes of subsections 2 and 3, estimated revenues shall not include revenues derivable or derived from the sale of assets, borrowings or issues of debentures or from a surplus including arrears of levies and proceeds from the sale of assets.

(5) The lender is not bound to establish the necessity of borrowing the sum lent or to see to its application.

(6) Any promissory note made under the authority of this section shall be sealed with the seal of the Metropolitan Corporation and signed by the chairman or by some other person authorized by by-law to sign it, and by the treasurer, and may be expressed so as to bear interest only upon such money as may be borrowed thereon from the time when such money is actually lent.

(7) The Metropolitan Council may by by-law provide or authorize the chairman and treasurer to provide by agreement that all or any sums borrowed for any or all of the purposes mentioned in this section shall, with interest thereon, be a charge upon the whole or any part or parts of the revenues of the Metropolitan Corporation for the current year and for any preceding years as and when such revenues are received; provided that such charge does not defeat or affect and is subject to any prior charge than subsisting in favour of any other lender.

(8) Any agreement entered into under subsection 7 shall be sealed with the corporate seal and signed by the chairman and treasurer.

(9) If the Metropolitan Council authorizes the borrowing of or borrows any larger amount than is permitted under this section, every member who knowingly votes therefor is disqualified from holding any municipal office for two years.

(10) If the Metropolitan Council authorizes the application of any revenues of the Metropolitan Corporation charged under the authority of this section otherwise than in repayment of the loan secured by such charge, the members who vote for such application are personally liable for the amount so applied, which may be recovered in any court of competent jurisdiction.

(11) If any member of the Metropolitan Council or officer of the Metropolitan Corporation applies any revenues so charged otherwise than in repayment of the loan secured by such charge, he is personally liable for the amount so applied, which may be recovered in any court of competent jurisdiction.

(12) Subsections 9, 10 and 11 do not apply to the Metropolitan Council or any member of the Metropolitan Council or officer of the Metropolitan Corporation acting under an order

or direction issued or made under the authority of Part III of *The Department of Municipal Affairs Act,* nor do they apply in any case where application of the revenues of the Metropolitan Corporation is made with the consent of the lender in whose favour a charge exists. R.S.O. 1960, c. 260, s. 233.

Debt

234.—(1) Subject to the limitations and restrictions in this Act and *The Ontario Municipal Board Act,* the Metropolitan Council may borrow money for the purposes of,

    (a) the Metropolitan Corporation, including the purposes of the Toronto Transit Commission and of the Metropolitan Toronto Library Board;

    (b) any area municipality;

    (c) the joint purposes of any two or more area municipalities;

    (d) any board of education in the Metropolitan Area, whether under this or any general or special Act, and may issue debentures therefor on the credit of the Metropolitan Corporation. R.S.O. 1960, c. 260, s. 234 (1); 1966, c. 96, s. 34.

(2) Notwithstanding any other provision of this Part, the Metropolitan Corporation may expend moneys for the purposes of an extension to the rapid transit system of the Toronto Transit Commission and may issue debentures therefor for any term or terms not exceeding forty years and may, with the approval of the Municipal Board, provide for the refinancing of not more than one-half of the amount of any such issue at the end of the term thereof, provided that the total period for repayment of the debt created shall not exceed forty years.

(3) All debentures issued pursuant to a by-law passed by the Metropolitan Council under the authority of this Act are direct, joint and several obligations of the Metropolitan Corporation and the area municipalities notwithstanding the fact that the whole or any portion of the rates imposed for the payment thereof may have been levied only against one or more of the area municipalities but nothing in this subsection affects the rights of the Metropolitan Corporation and of the area municipalities respectively as among themselves.

(4) Notwithstanding any general or special Act, no area municipality has, after the 31st day of December, 1953, power to issue debentures.

(5) When an area municipality, prior to the 31st day of December, 1953,

    (a) has applied for and obtained the final approval of the Municipal Board in respect of any work, project or other matter mentioned in subsection 1 of section 64 of *The Ontario Municipal Board Act;* and

    (b) has entered into a contract for or authorized the commencement of such work, project or matter but

has not prior to that date issued the debentures authorized, the Metropolitan Council, upon the request of the council of the area municipality, shall pass a by-law authorizing the issue and sale of debentures of the Metropolitan Corporation for the purposes and in the amount approved by the Municipal Board and shall, if required by the area municipality, issue such debentures and provide temporary financing for the area municipality in the manner provided in section 237, and no further approval of the Municipal Board is required.

(6) Bonds, debentures and other evidences of indebtedness of the Metropolitan Corporation shall be deemed to be bonds, debentures and other evidences of indebtedness of a municipal corporation for the purposes of *The Trustee Act.* R.S.O. 1960, c. 260, s. 234 (2-6).

234a. The references in subsection 2 of section 286 of *The Municipal Act* to a two-year term and to a biennial election shall, with respect to the Metropolitan Council and the councils of each area municipality, be deemed to be references to a three-year term and to a triennial election. 1966, c. 96, s. 35.

235.—(1) Subject to the limitations and restrictions in this Act and *The Ontario Municipal Board Act,* the Metropolitan Corporation may by by-law incur a debt or issue debentures for the purposes set forth in subsection 1 of section 234 of this Act and, notwithstanding any general or special Act, such by-law may be passed without the assent of the electors of the Metropolitan Area.

(2) Where, under any general or special Act, an area municipality cannot incur a debt or issue debentures for a particular purpose without the assent of its electors or without the concurrence of a specified number of the members of its council, the Metropolitan Council shall not pass a by-law authorizing the issue of debentures on behalf of such area municipality for such purpose unless such assent or concurrence to the passing of the by-law by the Metropolitan Council has been obtained.

(3) Nothing in subsection 2 requires the assent of any electors where such assent has been dispensed with under section 63 of *The Ontario Municipal Board Act.* R.S.O. 1960, c. 260, s. 235.

236.—(1) Notwithstanding any general or special Act, the Municipal Board, before making any order under section 64 of *The Ontario Municipal Board Act* on the application of the Metropolitan Corporation or of any area municipality, shall hold a public hearing for the purpose of inquiring into the merits of the matter.

(2) Notice of the hearing shall be given to the clerk of the Metropolitan Corporation and to the clerk of each area municipality in such manner as the Municipal Board may direct.

(3) The Municipal Board may dispense with the public hearing if the applicant files with the secretary of the Municipal Board a certified copy of a resolution of the council of each corporation entitled to notice under subsection 2 consenting to such dispensation. R.S.O. 1960, c. 260, s. 236.

(4) The Municipal Board may direct that an applicant give, by registered mail, to the persons mentioned in subsection 2 notice of any application including a requirement that the Metropolitan Corporation or any area municipality file with the applicant, within such time as may be specified by the Municipal Board, any objection to the application, and, if no objection is filed within the time specified, the Municipal Board may dispense with the public hearing. 1961-62, c. 88, s. 14.

237.—(1) When the Municipal Board has authorized the borrowing of money and the issue of debentures by the Metropolitan Corporation for its purposes, the Metropolitan Council pending the issue and sale of the debentures may agree with a bank or person for temporary advances from time to time to meet expenditures incurred for the purpose authorized, and may by by-law pending the sale of such debentures or in lieu of selling them authorize the chairman and treasurer to raise money by way of loan on the debentures and to hypothecate them for the loan.

(2) When the Municipal Board has authorized the borrowing of money and the issue of debentures by the Metropolitan Corporation for the purposes of an area municipality or a board of education, the Metropolitan Council pending the issue and sale of the debentures may, and on the request of the area municipality or board of education shall, agree with a bank or person for temporary advances from time to time

to meet expenditures incurred for the purposes authorized, and may, or on the request of the area municipality or board of education shall, pending the sale of such debentures or in lieu of selling them, authorize the chairman and treasurer to raise money by way of loan on the debentures and to hypothecate them for the loan, and shall transfer the proceeds of such advance or loan to the area municipality or board of education. R.S.O. 1960, c. 260, s. 237 (1, 2).

(2a) The Metropolitan Corporation may charge interest on any proceeds of an advance or loan transferred under subsection 2 at a rate sufficient to reimburse it for the cost of such advance or loan. 1965, c. 81, s. 7.

(3) The proceeds of every advance or loan under this section shall be applied for the purposes for which the debentures were authorized, but the lender shall not be bound to see to the application of the proceeds and, if the debentures are subsequently sold, the proceeds of the sale shall be applied first in repayment of the loan and, where the debentures were issued for the purposes of an area municipality or board of education, the balance, subject to section 249, shall be transferred to the area municipality or board of education.

(4) Subject to subsection 3, the redemption of a debenture hypothecated does not prevent the subsequent sale thereof. R.S.O. 1960, c. 260, s. 237 (3, 4).

238.—(1) Subject to subsection 2, a money by-law for the issuing of debentures shall provide that the principal shall be repaid in annual instalments with interest annually or semi-annually upon the balances from time to time remaining unpaid, but the by-law may provide for annual instalments of combined principal and interest.

(2) A money by-law for the issuing of debentures may provide that the principal shall be repaid at a fixed date with interest payable annually or semi-annually, in which case debentures issued under the by-law shall be known as sinking fund debentures.

(3) Notwithstanding any general or special Act, the whole debt and the debentures to be issued therefor shall be made payable within such term of years as the Municipal Board may approve.

(4) The by-law may provide for raising in each year, by special levy or levies against one or more area municipalities, the whole or specified portions of the sums of principal and interest payable under the by-law in such year, and each such area municipality shall pay to the Metropolitan Corporation such sums at the times and in the amounts specified in the by-law.

(5) The by-law shall provide for raising in each year, by a special levy on all the area municipalities, the sums of principal and interest payable under the by-law in such year to the extent that such sums have not been provided for by any special levy or levies against any area municipality or municipalities made especially liable therefor by the by-law.

(6) Any special levy against an area municipality imposed by the by-law under the authority of subsection 4 may be levied by the area municipality against persons or property in the same maner and subject to the same limitations as if it were passing a by-law authorizing the issue of debentures of the area municipality, for the same purpose, for the portion of the debt levied against it under subsection 4.

(7) All levies imposed by the by-law against an area municipality are a debt of the area municipality to the Metropolitan Corporation.

(8) The Metropolitan Council may by by-law authorize a change in the mode of issue of the debentures, and may provide that the debentures be issued with coupons instead of in amounts of combined principal and interest or *vice versa,*

and where any debentures issued under the by-law have been sold, pledged or hypothecated by the Metropolitan Council, upon again acquiring them, or at the request of any holder of them, may cancel them and issue one or more debentures in substitution for them, and make such new debenture or debentures payable by the same or a different mode on the instalment plan, but no change shall be made in the amount payable in each year.

(9) All the debentures shall be issued at one time and within two years after the passing of the by-law unless, on account of the proposed expenditure for which the by-law provides being estimated or intended to extend over a number of years and of its being undesirable to have large portions of the money in hand unused and uninvested, in the opinion of the Metropolitan Council it would be of advantage to so issue them, and in that case the by-law may provide that the debentures may be issued in sets of such amounts and at such times as the circumstances require, but so that the first of the sets shall be issued within two years, and all of them within five years after the passing of the by-law.

(10) All the debentures shall bear the same date, except where they are issued in sets, in which case every debenture of the same set shall bear the same date.

(11) Notwithstanding the provisions of the by-law, the debentures may bear date at any time within the period of two years or five years, as the case may be, mentioned in subsection 9 and the debentures may bear date before the date the by-law is passed if the by-law provides for the first levy being made in the year in which the debentures are dated or in the next succeeding year.

(12) The Municipal Board, on the application of the Metropolitan Council, the council of any area municipality, a board of education or any person entitled to any of the debentures or of the proceeds of the sale thereof, may at any time extend the time for issuing the debentures beyond the two years, or the time for the issue of any set beyond the time authorized by the by-law.

(13) The extension may be made although the application is not made until after the expiration of the two years or of the time provided for the issue of the set.

(14) Unless the by-law names a later day when it is to take effect, it takes effect on the day of its passing.

(15) Notwithstanding any general or special Act, the Metropolitan Council may borrow sums for two or more purposes in one debenture by-law and provide for the issue of one series of debentures therefor.

(16) Section 283 of *The Municipal Act* applies *mutatis mutandis* to the Metropolitan Corporation.

(17) The by-law may provide that all the debentures or a portion thereof shall be redeemable at the option of the Metropolitan Corporation on any date prior to maturity subject to the following provisions:

    1. The by-law and every debenture that is so redeemable shall specify the place or places of payment and the amount at which such debenture may be so redeemed.

    2. The principal of every debenture that is so redeemable becomes due and payable on the date set for the redemption thereof, and from and after such date interest ceases to accrue thereon where provision is duly made for the payment of the principal thereof, the interest to the date set for redemption, and any premium payable on redemption.

    3. Notice of intention so to redeem shall be sent by post at least thirty days prior to the date set for

such redemption to the person in whose name the debenture is registered at the address shown in the Debenture Registry Book.

4. At least thirty days prior to the date set for such redemption, notice of intention so to redeem shall be published in *The Ontario Gazette* and in a daily newspaper of general circulation in the City of Toronto and in such other manner as the by-law may provide.

5. Where only a portion of the debentures issued under the by-law is so to be redeemed, such portion shall comprise only the debentures that have the latest maturity dates, and no debentures issued under the by-law shall be called for such redemption in priority to any such debenture that has a later maturity date.

6. Where a debenture is redeemed on a date prior to maturity, such redemption does not affect the validity of any by-law by which special assessments are imposed or instalments thereof levied, the validity of such special assessments or levies, or the powers of the Metropolitan Council to continue to levy and collect from any area municipality the subsequent payments of principal and interest payable by it to the Metropolitan Council in respect of the debenture so redeemed.

(18) The by-law may provide that the debentures to be issued thereunder shall be expressed and be payable,

(a) in lawful money of Canada and payable in Canada; or

(b) in lawful money of the United States of America and payable in the United States of America; or

(c) in lawful money of Great Britain and payable in Great Britain.

(19) Where under the provisions of the by-law debentures issued thereunder are expressed and made payable in lawful money of the United States of America or of Great Britain, the Metropolitan Council may in such by-law or in any amending by-law, in lieu of providing for the raising in each year during the currency of the debentures specific sums sufficient to pay interest thereon or instalments of principal falling due in such year, provide that there shall be raised such yearly amount as may be necessary for such purposes and as the requirements for such purposes may from year to year vary.

(20) When sinking fund debentures are issued, the amount of principal to be raised in each year shall be a specific sum which, with the estimated interest at a rate not exceeding 3½ per cent per annum, capitalized yearly, will be sufficient to pay the principal of the debentures or any set of them, when and as it becomes due.

(21) When sinking fund debentures are issued, the sinking fund committee shall keep one or more consolidated bank accounts in which,

(a) the treasurer of the Metropolitan Corporation shall deposit each year during the term of the debentures the moneys raised for the sinking fund of all debts that are to be paid by means of sinking funds; and

(b) there shall be deposited all earnings derived from, and all proceeds of the sale, redemption or payment of, sinking fund investments.

(22) When sinking fund debentures are issued, there shall be a sinking fund committee which shall be composed of the treasurer of the Metropolitan Corporation and two members appointed by the Lieutenant Governor in Council, and the two appointed members shall be paid, out of the current fund of the Metropolitan Corporation, such annual remuneration as the Lieutenant Governor in Council may determine.

(23) The Lieutenant Governor in Council may appoint an alternate member for each of the appointed members and any such alternate member has all the powers and duties of the member in the absence or inability to act of such member.

(24) The treasurer of the Metropolitan Corporation shall be the chairman and treasurer of the sinking fund committee and in his absence the appointed members may appoint one of themselves as acting chairman and treasurer.

(25) Each member of the sinking fund committee shall, before entering into the duties of his office, give security for the faithful performance of his duties and for duly accounting for and paying over all moneys that come into his hands, in such amount as the auditor of the Metropolitan Corporation shall determine, and in other respects the provisions of section 234 of *The Municipal Act* apply with respect to such security.

(26) Two members of the sinking fund committee are a quorum, and all investments and disposals of investments must be approved by a majority of all the members of the committee.

(27) All assets of the sinking funds, including all consolidated bank accounts, shall be under the sole control and management of the sinking fund committee.

(28) All withdrawals from the consolidated bank accounts shall be authorized by the sinking fund committee, and all cheques on the consolidated bank accounts shall be signed by the chairman or acting chairman and one other member of the sinking fund committee.

(29) The sinking fund committee shall invest any moneys on deposit from time to time in the consolidated bank accounts and may at any time or times vary any investments.

(30) The moneys in the consolidated bank accounts shall be invested in one or more of the following forms:

(a) in securities in which a trustee may invest under *The Trustee Act;*

(b) in debentures of the Metropolitan Corporation;

(c) in temporary advances to the Metropolitan Corporation pending the issue and sale of any debentures of the Metropolitan Corporation;

(d) in temporary loans to the Metropolitan Corporation for current expenditures, but no loan for such purpose shall be made for a period ending after the end of the calendar year in which the loan is made.

(31) Any securities acquired by the sinking fund committee as investments for sinking fund purposes may be deposited with the Treasurer of Ontario.

(32) The Treasurer of Ontario shall release, deliver or otherwise dispose of any security deposited with him under subsection 31 only upon the direction in writing of the sinking fund committee.

(33) All sinking fund debentures issued on the same date, payable in the same currency, and maturing on the same date, notwithstanding they are issued under one or more by-laws, shall be deemed one debt and be represented by one sinking fund account.

(34) That proportion of the amount of all earnings in any year, on an accrual basis, from sinking fund investments, obtained by,

(a) multiplying the amount of all such earnings by the amount of the capitalized interest for that year under subsection 20 with respect to the principal raised up to and including such year for all sinking fund debentures represented by any sinking fund account; and

(b) dividing the product obtained under clause a by the amount of all capitalized interest for that year under subsection 20 with respect to all principal raised up to and including such year for all outstanding sinking fund debentures,

shall be credited to the sinking fund account mentioned in clause a.

(35) The treasurer of the Metropolitan Corporation shall prepare and lay before the Metropolitan Council in each year, before the annual metropolitan levies are made, a statement showing the sums that the Metropolitan Council will be required, by by-law, to raise for sinking funds in that year.

(36) If the treasurer contravenes subsection 21 or 35, he is guilty of an offence and on summary conviction is liable to a fine of not more than $250.

(37) If the Metropolitan Council neglects in any year to levy the amount required to be raised for a sinking fund, each member of the Metropolitan Council is disqualified from holding any municipal office for two years, unless he shows that he made reasonable efforts to procure the levying of such amount. R.S.O. 1960, c. 260, s. 238 (1-37).

(38) Notwithstanding this or any other Act or by-law, if it appears at any time that the amount at the credit of any sinking fund account will be more than sufficient, with the estimated earnings to be credited thereto under subsection 34 together with the levy required to be made by the by-law or by-laws that authorized the issue of the debentures represented by such sinking fund account, to pay the principal of the debt represented by such sinking fund account when it matures, the Municipal Board on the application of the sinking fund committee, the Metropolitan Council, the council of an area municipality, The Metropolitan School Board or a board of education in the Metropolitan Area may authorize the Metropolitan Council or the council of an area municipality to reduce the amount of money to be raised with respect to such debt in accordance with the order of the Municipal Board. 1961-62, c. 88, s. 15 (1).

(39) No money collected for the purpose of a sinking fund shall be applied towards paying any part of the current or other expenditure of the Metropolitan Corporation or otherwise than is provided in this section. R.S.O. 1960, c. 260, s. 238 (39).

(40) When there is a surplus in a sinking fund account, the sinking fund committee shall,

(a) use the surplus to increase the amount at the credit of another sinking fund account; or

(b) authorize the withdrawal of the surplus from the consolidated bank accounts, and the surplus shall be used for one or more of the following purposes:

(i) to retire unmatured debentures of the Metropolitan Corporation or of an area municipality,

(ii) subject to the approval of the Municipal Board, to reduce the next annual levy on account of principal and interest payable with respect to debentures of the Metropolitan Corporation or of an area municipality,

(iii) to reduce the amount of debentures to be issued for other capital expenditures for which the issue of debentures has been approved by the Municipal Board,

and the surplus shall be used under either clause a or b for the purposes of the Metropolitan Council, the council of an area municipality, The Metropolitan School Board for public schools, The Metropolitan School Board for secondary schools, a board of education for public schools, a board of education for secondary schools, the Toronto Transit Commission, a hydro-electric system and the metropolitan waterworks in the proportion that the amount of the contribution for the pur-

poses of each bears to the total contributions to the sinking fund account in connection with which the surplus arose. 1961-62, c. 88, s. 15 (2).

(41) Notwithstanding that any sinking fund debentures have been issued for the purposes of one or more area municipalities or of a board of education, any deficit in the sinking fund account shall be provided by the Metropolitan Corporation out of its current funds and any surplus in the sinking fund account shall be used as provided in subsection 40. R.S. O. 1960, c. 260, s. 238 (41).

239.—(1) If the Municipal Board is of opinion that the current rate of interest so differs from the rate of interest payable on any debentures that remain unsold or undisposed of that the sale or disposal thereof may substantially decrease or increase the amount required to be provided under the by-law under which such debentures were issued, the Municipal Board may authorize the Metropolitan Council to pass a by-law to amend such by-law so as to provide for,

(a) a different rate of interest;

(b) a change in the amount to be raised annually and, if necessary, in the special levies;

(c) such other changes in such by-law or any other by-law as to the Municipal Board may seem necessary to give effect thereto;

(d) the issue of new debentures to bear interest at the amended rate in substitution and exchange for such first-mentioned debentures; and

(e) the cancellation of such first-mentioned debentures upon the issue of such new debentures in substitution and exchange therefor.

(2) For the purposes of this section, the hypothecation of debentures under section 237 shall not constitute a sale or other disposal thereof.

(3) The Metropolitan Council may by one by-law authorized under subsection 1 amend two or more by-laws and provide for the issue of one series of new debentures in substitution and exchange for the debentures issued thereunder.

(4) A by-law passd under this section does not affect the validity of any by-law by which special assessments are imposed or instalments thereof levied, the validity of such special assessments or levies, or the powers of the Metropolitan Council to continue to levy and collect from any area municipality the subsequent payments of principal and interest payable by it to the Metropolitan Council. R.S.O. 1960, c. 260, s. 239.

240.—(1) Where part only of a sum of money provided for by a by-law has been raised, the Metropolitan Council may repeal the by-law as to any part of the residue, and as to a proportionate part of the amounts to be raised annually.

(2) The repealing by-law shall recite the facts on which it is founded, shall be appointed to take effect on the 31st day of December in the year of its passing, shall not affect any rates or levies due or penalties incurred before that day and shall not take effect until approved by the Municipal Board. R.S.O. 1960, c. 260, s. 240.

241.—(1) Subject to section 240, after a debt has been contracted under a by-law, the Metropolitan Council shall not, until the debt and interest have been paid, repeal the by-law or any by-law appropriating, for the payment of the debt or the interest, the surplus income from any work or any interest therein, or money from any other source, and shall not alter any such by-law so as to diminish the amount to be raised annually, and shall not apply to any other purpose any money of the Metropolitan Corporation that has been directed to be applied to such payment.

(2) When the Metropolitan Corporation, by or under the

authority of this Act, pays to an area municipality any amount of principal and interest becoming due upon any outstanding debentures issued by the area municipality, neither the council of the area municipality, nor any officer thereof shall apply any of the money so paid for any purpose other than the payment of the amounts of principal and interest so becoming due. R.S.O. 1960, c. 260, s. 241.

242. Any officer of the Metropolitan Corporation whose duty it is to carry into effect any of the provisions of a money by-law of the Metropolitan Corporation, who neglects or refuses to do so, under colour of a by-law illegally attempting to repeal or amend it, so as to diminish the amount to be raised annually under it, is guilty of an offence and on summary conviciton is liable to a fine of not more than $100. R.S.O. 1960, c. 260, s. 242.

243.—(1) Within four weeks after the passing of a money by-law, the clerk of the Metropolitan Corporation may register a duplicate original or a copy of it, certified under his hand and the seal of the Metropolitan Corporation, in the Registry Office for the Registry Division of the City of Toronto.

(2) Subject to section 61 of *The Ontario Municipal Board Act,* every by-law registered in accordance with subsection 1, or before the sale or other disposition of the debentures issued under it, and the debentures are valid and binding, according to the terms thereof, and the by-law shall not be quashed, unless within one month after the registration in the case of by-laws passed under *The Municipal Drainage Act* or *The Local Improvement Act,* and in the case of other by-laws, within three months after the registration, an application or action to quash the by-law is made to or brought in a court of competent jurisdiction, and a certificate under the hand of the proper office of the court and its seal, stating that such application has been made or action brought is registered in such registry office within such period of three months, or one month, as the case may be.

(3) After the expiration of the period prescribed by subsection 2, if no application or action to quash the by-law is made or brought, the by-law is valid and binding according to its terms.

(4) If an application or action to quash the by-law is made or brought within the period prescribed by subsection 2, but part only of the by-law is sought to be quashed, the remainder of it, if no application or action to quash it is made or brought within that period, is, after the expiration of that period, valid and binding according to its terms.

(5) If the application or action is dismissed in whole or in part, a certificate of the dismissal may be registered, and after such dismissal and the expiration of the period prescribed by subsection 2, if it has not already expired, the by-law, or so much of it as is not quashed is valid and binding according to its terms.

(6) Nothing in this section makes valid a by-law passed without the assent of the electors of an area municipality as required by subsection 2 of section 235, or a by-law where it appears on the face of it that any of the provisions of subsection 5 of section 238 have not been substantially complied with.

(7) Failure to register a by-law as prescribed by this section does not invalidate it. R.S.O. 1960, c. 260, s. 243.

244.—(1) A debenture or other like instrument shall be sealed with the seal of the Metropolitan Corporation, which seal may be engraved, lithographed, printed or otherwise mechanically reproduced thereon, and, subject to subsection 3, shall be signed by the chairman, or by some other person authorized by by-law of the Metropolitan Corporation to sign it, and by the treasurer.

(2) A debenture may have attached to it interest coupons which shall be signed by the treasurer and his signature to them may be engraved, lithographed, printed or otherwise mechanically reproduced thereon and such interest coupons are sufficiently signed if they bear the signature of the treasurer on the date the Metropolitan Council authorized the execution of the debenture or on the date the debenture bears or at the time the debenture was issued and delivered.

(3) The signature of the chairman, or such other person authorized by by-law to sign the debentures or other like instruments, may be engraved, lithographed, printed or otherwise mechanically reproduced thereon and, if the debentures or other like instruments are countersigned in writing by a person authorized by by-law of the Metropolitan Corporation to countersign, the signature of the treasurer may be engraved, lithographed, printed or otherwise mechanically reproduced thereon.

(4) The seal of the Metropolitan Corporation when so engraved, lithographed, printed or otherwise mechanically reproduced has the same force and effect as if manually affixed and the signature of the chairman or such other person authorized by by-law to sign the debentures or other like instruments and, if the debentures or other like instruments are countersigned, the signature of the treasurer when so engraved, lithographed, printed or otherwise mechanically reproduced shall be deemed the signature of the chairman or other person so authorized to sign or of the treasurer, as the case may be, and is binding upon the Metropolitan Corporation.

(5) Any debenture or other like instrument is sufficiently signed and countersigned if it bears the signatures of the persons provided in this section if such persons had authority to sign and countersign as provided in this section either on the date the Metropolitan Council authorized the execution of such instrument or on the date such instrument bears or at the time it was issued and delivered. R.S.O. 1960, c. 260, s. 244.

245. Where the interest for one year or more on the debentures issued under a by-law and the principal of any debenture that has matured has been paid by the Metropolitan Corporation, the by-law and the debentures issued under it are valid and binding upon the Metropolitan Corporation. R.S.O. 1960, c. 260, s. 245.

246.—(1) Where a debenture contains or has endorsed upon it a provision to the following effect:

> This debenture, or any interest therein, is not, after a certificate of ownership has been endorsed thereon by the treasurer of this Corporation (or by such other person authorized by by-law of this Corporation to endorse such certificate of ownership), transferable except by entry by the treasurer (or by such other person so authorized) in the Debenture Registry Book of the Corporation at the _____
> _____
> of _____

the treasurer (or such other persons so authorized), on the application of the owner of the debenture or of any interest in it, shall endorse upon the debenture a certificate of ownership and shall enter in a book, to be called the Debenture Registry Book, a copy of the certificate and of every certificate that is subsequently given, and shall also enter in such book a memorandum of every transfer of such debenture.

(2) A certificate of ownership shall not be endorsed on a debenture except by the written authority of the person last entered as the owner of it, or of his executors or administrators, or of his or their attorney, and, if the person last en-

tered as owner of it is a corporation, the written authority of such corporation, or its successors, which authority shall be retained and filed by the treasurer.

(3) After a certificate of ownership has been endorsed, the debenture, if it contains or has endorsed upon it a provision to the like effect of the provision contained in subsection 1, is transferable only by entry by the treasurer (or by such other person so authorized) in the Debenture Registry Book as and when a transfer of the debenture is authorized by the then owner of it or his executors or administrators or his or their attorney and, if the then owner of it is a corporation, the written authority of such corporation, or its successors. R.S.O. 1960, c. 260, s. 246.

247. Where a debenture is defaced, lost or destroyed, the Metropolitan Council may by by-law provide for the replacing of the debenture on the payment of such fee and on such terms as to evidence and indemnity as the by-law may provide. R. S.O. 1960, c. 260, s. 247.

248.—(1) On request of the holder of any debenture issued after the 3rd day of April, 1957, by the Metropolitan Corporation, the treasurer of the Metropolitan Corporation may issue and deliver to such holder a new debenture or new debentures in exchange therefor for the same aggregate principal amount.

(2) On the request of the sinking fund committee, the treasurer of the Metropolitan Corporation may, as provided in this section, exchange debentures heretofore or hereafter issued by the Metropolitan Corporation.

(3) Any new debenture mentioned in subsection 1 may be registered as to principal and interest but in all other respects shall be of the same force and effect as the debenture or debentures surrendered for exchange.

(4) The treasurer and auditor of the Metropolitan Corporation shall cancel and destroy all debentures surrendered for exchange and shall certify in the Debenture Registry Book that they have been cancelled and destroyed and shall also enter in the Debenture Registry Book particulars of any new debenture issued in exchange. R.S.O. 1960, c. 260, s. 248.

249.—(1) The moneys received by the Metropolitan Corporation from the sale or hypothecation of any debentures to the extent that such moneys are required for the purpose or purposes for which the debentures were issued, and for the repayment of any outstanding temporary loans with respect thereto, shall be used only for such purpose or purposes.

(2) None of the moneys received by the Metropolitan Corporation from the sale or hypothecation of any debentures shall be applied towards payment of the current or other expenditures of the Metropolitan Corporation, an area municipality or a board of education in the Metropolitan Area.

(3) Where on the sale of any debentures an amount is realized in excess of that required for the purpose or purposes for which the debentures were issued, the excess amount shall be applied,

(a) if any such debentures are redeemable prior to maturity at the option of the Metropolitan Corporation, to redeem one or more of the debentures having the latest maturity date; or

(b) to reduce the next annual levy on account of principal and interest payable with respect to such debentures; or

(c) to reduce the amount of debentures to be issued for other capital expenditures of a similar nature for which the issue of debentures has been approved by the Municipal Board, provided that the principal and interest charges of such debentures are levied upon the assessment of the same class of

ratepayers as was levied upon for the principal and interest charges of the debentures with respect to which the excess arose.

(4) Where on the sale of any debentures a deficiency in the amount required for the purpose or purposes for which the debentures were issued is sustained, the amount of such deficiency shall be added to the sum to be raised for the first annual payment of principal and interest with respect to the debentures and the levy made in the first year for such purpose or purposes shall be increased accordingly or shall be raised by the issue of other debentures approved by the Municipal Board for the same or any similar purpose or purposes. R.S.O. 1960, c. 260, s. 249.

249a. Where real or personal property acquired out of moneys received by the Metropolitan Corporation from the sale or hypothecation of any debentures is disposed of by sale or otherwise, the net proceeds of such disposal shall be applied as an excess in accordance with subsection 3 of section 249 or, with the approval of the Municipal Board, may be applied to meet the whole or a portion of any other capital expenditure the debt charges for which, if raised by taxation, would be raised by taxation levied upon the assessment of the same class of ratepayers as was levied upon for the principal and interest charges of the debentures issued in respect of the property disposed of or sold. 1961-62, c. 88, s. 16.

250. When the Metropolitan Corporation intends to borrow money on debentures under this or any other Act, the Metropolitan Council may prior to the issue thereof call for tenders for the amount of money required and the person tendering shall specify the rate of interest the debentures shall bear when issued at par. R.S.O. 1960, c. 260, s. 250.

251.—(1) The Metropolitan Council shall,
(a) keep a separate account of every debt;
(b) where the whole of the debt is not payable in the current year, keep in respect thereof,
(i) an additional account for the interest, if any, and
(ii) an additional account for the sinking fund or the instalments of principal,
distinguished from all other accounts by a prefix designating the purpose for which the debt was contracted; and
(c) keep the accounts so as to exhibit at all times the state of every debt, and the amount of money raised, obtained and appropriated for the payment of it.

(2) The Metropolitan Council may by by-law provide and direct that instead of a separate account of the interest upon every debt being kept, a consolidated account of the interest upon all debts may be kept, but which consolidated account shall be so kept that it will be possible to determine therefrom the true state of the interest account upon every debt and that provision has been made to meet the interest upon every debt. R.S.O. 1960, c. 260, s. 251.

252. If in any year after paying the interest and appropriating the necessary sum in payment of the instalments there is a surplus properly applicable to such debt, it shall so remain until required in due course for the payment of interest or in payment of the principal. R.S.O. 1960, c. 260, s. 252.

253.—(1) If the Metropolitan Council applies any money raised for a special purpose or collected for a sinking fund in paying current or other expenditure, the members who vote for such application are personally liable for the amount so applied, which may be recovered in any court of competent jurisdiction.

(2) If the Metropolitan Council, upon the request in writing of a ratepayer of any area municipality, refuses or neglects for one month to bring an action therefor, the action may be brought by any such ratepayer on behalf of himself and all other ratepayers in the Metropolitan Area.

(3) The members who vote for such application are disqualified from holding any municipal office for two years. R.S.O. 1960, c. 260, s. 253.

254. When, by or under the authority of this Act, the Metropolitan Corporation is or becomes liable for the payment to an area municipality of all amounts of principal and interest becoming due upon any outstanding debentures issued by the area municipality, the Metropolitan Corporation may, with the approval of the Municipal Board,

(a) cancel all such debentures that have not been sold and issue new debentures of the Metropolitan Corporation in substitution and exchange therefor and apply the proceeds thereof, as may be directed by the Municipal Board, for the purposes for which such debentures were issued;

(b) arrange with the area municipality for the redemption of all such debentures as are redeemable and issue new debentures of the Metropolitan Corporation to raise the moneys required for such redemption;

(c) purchase, by agreement with the owner or owners thereof, all such debentures of a single issue of the area municipality, and issue new debentures of the Metropolitan Corporation to raise the money required to complete such purchase. R.S.O. 1960, c. 260, s. 254.

Part XVII

GENERAL

255.—(1) Section 5, Parts XV, XVI, XVII and XXI, section 248*b* and paragraphs 3, 22 and 27 of section 377 of *The Municipal Act* apply *mutatis mutandis* to the Metropolitan Corporation. R.S.O. 1960, c. 260, s. 255 (1); 1961-62, c. 88, s. 17 (1); 1966, c. 96, s. 36 (1).

(2) For the purposes of subsection 2 of section 482 of *The Municipal Act,* the by-laws of the Metropolitan Corporation or of any local board thereof shall be deemed to be by-laws passed by the council of a city. R.S.O. 1960, c. 260, s. 255 (2).

(3) Sections 10 and 11 and, subject to subsection 2 of section 150, section 14 of *The Municipal Act* do not apply to any area municipality except in relation to alterations of boundaries, within the Metropolitan Area, of area municipalities, which alterations, in the opinion of the Municipal Board, are of a minor nature. 1966, c. 96, s. 36 (2).

(3*a*) 1962-63, c. 89, s. 13 (1) REPEALED: 1966, c. 96, s. 36 (3).

(4) The Metropolitan Corporation and each local board thereof shall be deemed to be a municipality for the purpose of section 89 of *The Labour Relations Act.*

(5) Nothing in this Act alters or affects the powers of The Toronto Harbour Commissioners.

(6) Where a by-law passed by the Metropolitan Council under section 399 of *The Municipal Act,* being chapter 243 of the Revised Statutes of Ontario, 1950, is applicable to an area municipality, any by-law passed by the council of such area municipality under paragraph 70 of subsection 1 of section 388 or under section 399 of *The Municipal Act,* being

chapter 243 of the Revised Statutes of Ontario, 1950, or any predecessor of such paragraph or section, has no effect while the by-law passed by the Metropolitan Council is in effect in such area municipality.

(7) The Metropolitan Corporation shall be deemed to be a local municipality for the purpose of paragraph 116 of subsection 1 of section 379 of *The Municipal Act.* R.S.O. 1960, c. 260, s. 255 (4-7).

(8) By-laws may be passed by the Metropolitan Council,

(a) for the establishment and maintenance of emergency measures civil defence organizations in the Metropolitan Area; and

(b) for providing moneys for emergency measures and civil defence, for the purposes of emergency measures civil defense organizations and for the cost of the operation of such organizations, and for other similar work in the Metropolitan Area,

and, when a by-law passed under this subsection is in force in the Metropolitan Area, any by-law passed by the council of an area municipality under subclauses ii and iii of clause *b* of section 378 of *The Municipal Act* has no effect. 1960-61, c. 61, s. 13.

(8*a*) When a by-law passed under clause *a* of subsection 8 is in force, the Metropolitan Council may pass by-laws,

(a) with the consent of the area municipality or local board concerned, for appointing heads of departments and alternates to be members of the Metropolitan Toronto Emergency Measures Organization or any committee thereof;

(b) with the consent of the area municipality or local board concerned, for training employees of the area municipality or local board in their functions under the Metropolitan Toronto Emergency Measures Organization;

(c) for appointing members of the Metropolitan Toronto Emergency Measures Organization, or of any committee thereof, to be in charge of such departments or utilities throughout the Metropolitan Area, as the by-law may provide, when an emergency has been proclaimed under the *War Measures Act* (Canada) or under *The Emergency Measures Act, 1962-63;*

(d) for acquiring alternative headquarters for the metropolitan government outside the Metropolitan Area;

(e) for designating evacuation routes and empowering members of the Metropolitan Police Force to require persons to use such routes;

(f) for obtaining and distributing emergency materials, equipment and supplies; and

(g) for complying with any request of the Government of Canada or Ontario in the event of a nuclear attack. 1961-62, c. 88, s. 17 (3); 1962-63, c. 89, s. 13 (2).

(9) Notwithstanding any other provision in this Act, the Metropolitan Council may pass by-laws authorizing the head of the department concerned to grant such of the approvals and consents required by subsection 2 of section 51, subsection 1 of section 67, subsection 2 of section 68 and subsection 2 of section 83 as are designated in the by-law, and any such by-law may prescribe terms and conditions under which any such approval or consent may be granted. R.S.O. 1960, c. 260, s. 255 (9).

256. The Metropolitan Corporation may make expenditures not exceeding $125,000 in any one year for the purpose of diffusing information respecting the advantages of the municipality as an industrial, business, educational, residential or vacation centre and may make annual grants for a period not exceeding five years, and upon the expiration of any such period may make similar grants for a further period not exceeding five years. R.S.O. 1960, c. 260, s. 256.

257. REPEALED: 1966, c. 96, s. 37.

258. The Metropolitan Council may make annual grants, not to exceed in any year a sum calculated at one-tenth of one mill in the dollar upon the total assessment upon which the metropolitan levy is apportioned among the area municipalities under subsection 5 of section 230, to institutions, associations and persons carrying on or engaged in works that in the opinion of the Metropolitan Council are for the general advantage of the inhabitants of the Metropolitan Area and for which grant or grants there is no express authority provided by any other Act. 1966, c. 96, s. 38.

258a. The Metropolitan Corporation may assume the whole or any part of the capital and operating costs of the fire boat and the marine fire boat station of the City of Toronto. 1965, c. 81, s. 8.

259. The Metropolitan Corporation may pass by-laws prohibiting the driving or operating of motor vehicles in the Metropolitan Area that create undue noise and for the purposes of any such by-law may define the expressions motor vehicles and undue noise. R.S.O. 1960, c. 260, s. 259.

260. Where in an action or by the settlement of a claim arising out of an injury to an employee or to any person deemed an employee for the purposes of *The Workmen's Compensation Act* the Metropolitan Corporation recovers damages from a third person, such damages or any portion thereof may be paid to such employee or person or, in the event of his death, to one or more of his dependents upon such terms and conditions as the Metropolitan Corporation may impose. 1962-63, c. 89, s. 14.

261.—(1) Where the Metropolitan Council passes a resolution requesting a judge of the county court of the County of York, or a judge of the county court of a county adjoining the County of York, to investigate any matter relating to a supposed malfeasance, breach of trust or other misconduct on the part of a member of the Metropolitan Council, or an officer or employee of the Metropolitan Corporation, or of any person having a contract with it, in regard to the duties or obligations of the member, officer, employee or other person to the Metropolitan Corporation, or to inquire into or concerning any matter connected with the good government of the Metropolitan Corporation or the conduct of any part of its public business, including any business conducted by a local board of the Metropolitan Corporation, the judge shall make the inquiry and for that purpose has all the powers that may be conferred on a commissioner under *The Public Inquiries Act,* and he shall, with all convenient speed, report to the Metropolitan Council the result of the inquiry and the evidence taken.

(2) The judge shall be paid by the Metropolitan Corporation the same fees as he would be entitled to if the inquiry had been made by him as a referee under *The Judicature Act.*

(3) The Metropolitan Council may engage and pay counsel to represent the Metropolitan Corporation, and may pay all proper witness fees to persons summoned to give evidence at the instance of the Metropolitan Corporation, and any person charged with malfeasance, breach of trust or other misconduct, or whose conduct is called in question on such investigation or inquiry, may be represented by counsel. R.S.O. 1960, c. 260, s. 261.

262.—(1) The Lieutenant Governor in Council, upon the recommendation of the Minister, may issue a commission to inquire into the affairs of the Metropolitan Corporation or a local board thereof, and any matter connected therewith, and the commissioner has all the powers that may be conferred on a commissioner under *The Public Inquiries Act.*

(2) A commission may be recommended at the instance of the Department, or upon the request in writing of not less than one-third of the members of the Metropolitan Council, or of not less than fifty ratepayers of an area municipality assessed as owners and resident therein.

(3) The expenses of and incidental to the execution of the commission, including the fees and disbursements of the commissioner, shall be fixed and certified by the Minister and are subject to such division between the Metropolitan Corporation and the Province as the Lieutenant Governor in Council may direct. R.S.O. 1960, c. 260, s. 262.

263. The Metropolitan Corporation for its purposes may enter, break up, dig and trench in, upon and under the highways, lanes and other public communications of any area municipality and may construct and maintain therein pipes, sewers, drains, conduits and other works necessary for its purposes, without making compensation therefor, but all such highways, lanes and other public communications shall be restored to their original condition without unnecessary delay. R.S.O. 1960, c. 260, s. 263.

264. The Metropolitan Corporation and any area municipality may enter into agreements for the use within any part of the Metropolitan Area of the services of their respective officers, employees and equipment. R.S.O. 1960, c. 260, s. 264.

265.—(1) For the purposes of paragraph 9 of section 4 and section 43 of *The Assessment Act,* the Metropolitan Corporation shall be deemed to be a municipality.

(2) For the purposes of paragraph 9 of section 4 of *The Assessment Act,* where property belonging to the Metropolitan Corporation is occupied by an area municipality or where property belonging to an area municipality is occupied by the Metropolitan Corporation or another area municipality, the occupant shall not be deemed to be a tenant or lessee, whether rent is paid for such occupation or not. R.S.O. 1960, c. 260, s. 265.

(3) In subsection 2, "Metropolitan Corporation" and "area municipality" include a local board thereof. 1966, c. 96, s. 39.

266.—(1) An execution against the Metropolitan Corporation may be endorsed with a direction to the sheriff to levy the amount thereof by rate, and the proceedings therein shall then be the following:

1. The sheriff shall deliver a copy of the writ and endorsement to the treasurer of the Metropolitan Corporation, or leave such copy at the office or dwelling place of that officer, with a statement in writing of the sheriff's fees and of the amount required to satisfy the execution, including the interest calculated to some day as near as is convenient to the day of the service.

2. If the amount with interest thereon from the day mentioned in the statement is not paid to the sheriff within one month after the service, the sheriff shall examine the assessment rolls of all the area municipalities and shall, in like manner as the levies of the Metropolitan Council for general purposes are apportioned among the area municipalities, determine the portion of the amount men-

tioned in the statement that shall be levied against and in each area municipality.

3. The sheriff shall then in like manner as rates are struck for general municipal purposes within each area municipality strike a rate sufficient in the dollar to cover its share of the amount due from the execution and in determining such amount he may make such addition to the same as the sheriff deems sufficient to cover its share of the interest up to the time when the rate will probably be available and his own fees and poundage.

4. The sheriff shall thereupon issue a precept under his hand and seal of office directed to the collector of the area municipality, and shall annex to the precept the roll of such rate, and shall by the precept, after reciting the writ and that the Metropolitan Corporation has neglected to satisfy the same, and referring to the roll annexed to the precept, command the collector to levy such rate at the time and in the manner by law required in respect to the general annual rates.

5. If, at the time for levying the annual rates next after the receipt of such report, the collector has a general rate roll delivered to him for the year, he shall add a column thereto, headed "Execution rate in A.B. *vs.* The Municipality of Metropolitan Toronto" (adding a similar column for each execution if more than one), and shall insert therein the amount by such precept required to be levied upon each person respectively, and shall levy the amount of such execution rate as aforesaid, and shall, within the time within which he is required to make the return of the general annual rate, return to the sheriff the precept with the amount levied thereon.

6. The sheriff shall, after satisfying the execution and all the fees and poundage thereon, pay any surplus, within ten days after receiving the same, to the treasurer of the area municipality.

(2) The clerk, assessor and collector of each area municipality shall, for all purposes connected with carrying into effect, or permitting or assisting the sheriff to carry into effect, the provisions of this Act with respect to such execution, be deemed to be officers of the court out of which the writ issued, and as such are amendable to the court and may be proceeded against by attachment, mandamus or otherwise in order to compel them to perform the duties imposed upon them. R.S.O. 1960, c. 260, s. 266.

267.—(1) Except as provided in this Act, the Municipal Board, upon the application of any area municipality, The Corporation of the County of York or the Metropolitan Corporation, may exercise any of the powers conferred on it by clauses *a* and *d* of subsection 10 of section 14 of *The Municipal Act.*

(2) In addition to its powers under subsection 1, the Municipal Board has power to direct the Metropolitan Corporation to pay to The Corporation of the County of York, in a lump sum or in its discretion over a period of years from the 1st day of January, 1954, on a progressively reduced basis, such amount as it deems just and equitable to relieve the County from any undue burden caused by the separation from the County of the municipalities mentioned in section 149. R.S.O. 1960, c. 260, s. 267.

268. The Lieutenant Governor in Council, upon the recommendation of the Municipal Board, may authorize the Metropolitan Corporation to do all such acts or things not specifically provided for in this Act that are deemed necessary or advisable to carry out effectively the intent and purposes of this Act. R.S.O. 1960, c. 260, s. 268.

269. The provisions of this Act apply notwithstanding the provisions of any general or special Act and, in the event of any conflict between this Act and any general or special Act, this Act prevails. R.S.O. 1960, c. 260, s. 269.

270.—(1) Notwithstanding anything in *The Power Commission Act* or in *The Public Utilities Act* or in any other special or general Act, the whole of the Township of Scarborough, the whole of the Township of North York and the whole of the Township of Etobicoke shall each be deemed to be an area established under subsection 1 of section 70 of *The Power Commission Act,* and The Public Utilities Commission of the Township of Scarborough, The Hyrdo-Electric Commission of the Township of North York and The Hydro-Electric Commission of the Township of Etobicoke shall each be deemed to have been established for the whole of the said respective areas.

(2) If any of such corporations desire to enter into a contract with The Hydro-Electric Power Commission of Ontario for the supply of electrical power or energy for the use of the municipality and inhabitants thereof, the assent of the municipal electors is not necessary.

(3) Subject to this section and where not inconsistent therewith, Part II of *The Power Commission Act* shall be deemed to apply to each of such commissions and areas. R.S.O. 1960, c. 260, s. 270.

271.—(1) The Metropolitan Corporation or an area municipality or the Metropolitan Corporation and one or more area muncipalities,

    (a) may acquire land for the purposes of constructing municipal buildings; and

    (b) may construct municipal buildings for the use of the Metropolitan Corporation or the Metropolitan Corporation and one or more area municipalities. R.S.O. 1960, c. 260, s. 271 (1); 1961-62, c. 88, s. 18.

(2) Section 252 of *The Municipal Act* applies *mutatis mutandis* to any joint undertaking under this section. R.S.O. 1960, c. 260, s. 271 (2).

272.—(1) The Metropolitan Corporation shall be deemed to be a municipality for the purposes of paragraphs 67 and 68 of section 377 of *The Municipal Act.*

(2) The Metropolitan Corporation and the Corporation of the City of Toronto may enter into an agreement to provide for the operation by The Parking Authority of Toronto of any or all of the parking lots of the Metropolitan Corporation or the parking authority established by the Metropolitan Corporation. R.S.O. 1960, c. 260, s. 272.

273. For the purposes of section 59 of *The Highway Traffic Act,* the Boroughs of East York, Etobicoke, North York, Scarborough and York shall be deemed to be cities. 1966, c. 96, s. 40.

Metropolitan London Government

The government of rapidly growing metropolitan London was a subject of considerable concern in the nineteenth century. The first inquiry into the government of the London area was that of the Royal Commisison on Municipal Corporations which issued reports in 1835 and 1837. Its 1837 report recommended expansion of the Corporation of the City of London, but Parliament failed to act upon the recommendation. The government of the London area was studied by other Royal Commissions which issued reports in 1854, 1894, and 1923.

The lack of an area-wide authority and the overlapping functions of various units of local government led to the appointment, on December 10, 1957, of the Royal Commission on Local Government in Greater London to study the structure of the governmental system and the distribution of functions in an area with a population of over eight million or approximately one-fifth of the population of England. In its October 1960 report, the Commission rejected the transference of functions to the central government and recommended the reorganization of the single-tier system of local government into a two-tier system.

The Government accepted the basic recommendations of the Royal Commisison and introduced legislation which became the London Government Act 1963. With the exception of the ancient City of London, all units of local government were dissolved in an area extending thirty-eight miles east to west and twenty-eight miles north to south; the Greater London Council was established to perform a number of area-wide functions and thirty-two London Boroughs ranging in population from 146,000 to 341,000 were created to perform local functions.

The London Government Act 1963 assigns sole responsibility for a number of functions such as the ambulance service, land drainage, and refuse disposal to the Greater London Council, and sole responsibility for many other functions to the London Boroughs. The Greater London Council and the London Boroughs share responsibility for other functions—housing, planning, roads, and traffic.

Be it enacted by the Queen's most Excellent Majesty, by and with the advice and consent of the Lords Spiritual and Temporal, and Commons, in this present Parliament assembled, and by the authority of the same, as follows:—

Part I

LOCAL GOVERNMENT IN AND AROUND GREATER LONDON

1.—(1) There shall be established new administrative areas, to be known as London boroughs, which shall comprise the areas respectively described (by reference to existing administrative areas) in column 2 of Part I of Schedule 1 to this Act; and in this and any other Act—

    (*a*) any reference to an inner London borough shall be construed as a reference to one of the London boroughs numbered from 1 to 12 in the said Part I;

    (*b*) any reference to an outer London borough shall be construed as a reference to one of the London boroughs numbered from 13 to 32 in the said Part I.

(2) If in the case of any London borough, on representations in that behalf made to the Privy Council by the Minister, Her Majesty by the advice of Her Privy Council thinks fit to grant a charter of incorporation of the inhabitants of that borough, Her Majesty may by that charter—

    (*a*) make provision with respect to the name of the borough; and

    (*b*) subject to the provisions of this Act, make any provision such as may be made by virtue of section 131 of the Local Government Act 1933 by a charter granted under Part VI of that Act;

and any charter which purports to be granted in pursuance of the Royal prerogative and this subsection shall be deemed to be valid and within the powers of this Act and Her Majesty's prerogative and the validity thereof shall not be questioned in any legal proceeding whatever.

(3) In the case of any London borough whose inhabitants are not incorporated by such a charter as is referred to in the last foregoing subsection, provision for their incorporation shall be made by the Minister by order (hereafter in this Act referred to as an "incorporation order") which may include any such provision as is mentioned in paragraph (*a*) or (*b*) of that subsection.

(4) The provisions of Part III of Schedule 1 to this Act shall have effect for the purpose of the revocation or alteration of the provisions with respect to the matters mentioned in paragraph 1 of the said Part III of any charter or incorporation order under subsection (2) or (3) of this section; but nothing in any such charter or order or in any order under the said Part III shall authorise the number of councillors of any London borough to exceed sixty.

(5) Before the Minister makes as respects a London borough either representations under subsection (2) of this section for the grant of a charter or an incorporation order under subsection (3) thereof, the Minister or, as may be appropriate, the Secretary of State shall cause such notices to be given and such, if any, inquiries to be held with respect to the matters to be dealt with by the charter or order as may appear to the Minister or, as the case may be, the Secretary of State to be expedient.

(6) The Municipal Corporations Act 1882 shall apply to every London borough and section 15 of the Interpretation Act 1889 shall have effect accordingly, that is to say, the expression "borough" when used in relation to local government in any enactment whether passed before or after this Act (and in particular, subject to section 8 (2) of this Act, in the Local Government Act 1933) shall except where the context otherwise requires (and except in particular in the expressions "county borough" and "non-county borough") include a London borough; and the council of a London borough shall be a local authority within the meaning of the said Act of 1933.

(7) The first election of councillors of each London borough shall be held, under arrangements to be made by its charter or incorporation order, on the day in May 1964 fixed by the Secretary of State as the day of election of borough councillors

in England and Wales; and the persons declared to be elected councillors at that election shall come into office on the fourth day after the day of election.

2.—(1) The area comprising the areas of the London boroughs, the City and the Temples shall constitute an administrative area to be known as Greater London.

(2) There shall be established for Greater London a council consisting of a chairman, alderman and councillors which shall be a body corporate under the name of the Greater London Council with perpetual succession and a common seal and shall have all such functions as are vested in that Council by this Act or otherwise.

(3) Notwithstanding anything in subsection (1) or (2) of this section, the Greater London Council may with the consent of the Minister change the name of the Council or the name by which the area referred to in the said subsection (1) is to be known or both those names, or make provision as to the titles by which the chairman, vice-chairman and any deputy chairman of the Council are to be known, and any change of name made in pursuance of this subsection shall take effect as from such date as the Minister may by order appoint; and any such order—

    (a) shall not affect any rights or obligations of any council, authority or person, and

    (b) shall not be taken as invalidating any instrument (whether made before or after the date appointed by the order) which refers to the Council or the said area by the previous name.

but the new name shall be substituted for the previous name in all enactments relating to the Council or, as the case may be, that area and in all instruments and legal proceedings made or commenced before the said date which refer to that previous name, so, however, that nothing in this subsection shall be construed as affecting the title of any Act or instrument.

(4) The provisions of Schedule 2 to this Act shall have effect with respect to the constitution and general functions of the Greater London Council; and the first election of councillors of that Council shall be held on 9th April 1964, and the persons declared elected at that election shall come into office on the fourth day after the day of election.

3.—(1) As from 1st April 1965—

    (a) no part of Greater London shall form part of any administrative county, county district or parish;

    (b) the following administrative areas and their councils (and, in the case of a borough, the municipal corporation thereof) shall cease to exist, that is to say, the counties of London and Middlesex, the metropolitan boroughs, and any existing county borough, county district or parish the area of which falls wholly within Greater London;

    (c) the urban district of Potters Bar shall become part of the county of Hertfordshire;

    (d) the urban districts of Staines and Sunbury-on-Thames shall become part of the county of Surrey.

(2) As from the passing of this Act, in the Local Government Act 1958—

    (a) in sections 17 (1) and 53 (1), for any reference to the metropolitan area there shall be substituted a reference to Greater London;

    (b) section 53 (2) shall cease to have effect;

    (c) in section 28, subsection (6) shall cease to have effect, but—

        (i) subsection (1) shall not apply to the county of London or of Middlesex;

        (ii) no county review under that section shall

extend to any part of Greater London;

        (iii) subject to any order under section 23 or 24, any such review by the Hertfordshire county council shall extend to the urban district of Potters Bar and any such review by the Surrey county council shall extend to the urban districts of Staines and Sunbury-on-Thames;

    (d) in relation to a county district to which Part III applies as from the date of the passing of this Act only by virtue of this subsection, that date shall be deemed to be specified in sections 47 (3) and 52 (2) as a further day on which the periods mentioned in those provisions may begin.

4.—(1) Subject to any provision to the contrary effect made by, or by any instrument made under, this Act or any other Act passed during the same session as this Act (and in particular any provision conferring functions on the Greater London Council), and without prejudice to any express provision so made, the provisions of this section (being provisions designed to confer on the councils of London boroughs as respects their boroughs and on the Common Council as respects the City the functions exercisable by the councils of county boroughs as respects their boroughs or by the existing London county council as respects the metropolitan boroughs or, as the case may be, the City) shall have effect as from 1st April 1965 as respects any enactment (hereafter in this section referred to as an "existing enactment") contained in any public general Act passed before this Act or in any other such Act passed during the same session as this Act.

(2) Subject to subsection (7) of this section, where any existing enactment refers to, or to the councils of, county boroughs, then—

    (a) if it also refers in the same context to, or to the councils of, metropolitan boroughs, any reference in that enactment in that context to, or to the council of, a metropolitan borough shall be construed as a reference to, or to the council of, a London borough;

    (b) if it also refers (or, but for section 3 (1) (b) of this Act, would have referred) in the same context to the London county council (whether expressly or by virtue of a reference to councils of counties) but not to councils of metropolitan boroughs, any reference in that enactment in that context to a county borough or the council thereof shall be construed as including a reference to a London borough or the council thereof and, where that enactment extends to the City but does not refer to the Common Council, as including also a reference to the City or the Common Council.

(3) Any reference in any existing enactment which, by virtue of any other existing enactment passed subsequently thereto, falls to be construed as a reference to authorities of a particular class shall be deemed for the purposes of subsection (2) of this section to be a reference to authorities of that class.

(4) Any existing enactment to the effect that any provision does not apply or refer, or applies or refers only, to the administrative county of London or to that county other than the City or other than the City and the Temples shall have effect as if it provided that the provision in question does not apply or refer, or, as the case may be, applies or refers only, to Greater London other than the outer London boroughs, or other than those boroughs and the City, or other than those boroughs, the City and the Temples, as the case may be.

(5) Where, under any existing enactment which by virtue of

subsection (4) of this section applies to Greater London other than the outer London boroughs or other than those boroughs and the City with or without the Temples, any functions were exercisable immediately before 1st April 1965 as respects a metropolitan borough by the London county council or by the council of that borough or as respects the City by the London county council, those functions shall be exercisable as respects an inner London borough by the council of that borough or, as the case may be, as respects the City by the Common Council.

(6) In any existing enactment which by virtue of subsection (4) of this section applies to the outer London boroughs but not to the rest of Greater London, any reference to, or to the council of, a county borough shall be construed as including a reference to, or to the council of, an outer London borough.

(7) Without prejudice to any exclusion by virtue of subsection (1) of this section and to any amendment of the enactment in question by or under any subsequent provision of this Act, subsection (2) of this section shall not apply to any existing enactment contained in—

    (a) the Local Goverment Act of 1888, 1929, 1933 or 1958; or

    (b) the enactments to which section 40 of this Act applies or would apply but for the provisio to subsection (4) of that section; or

    (c) the Representation of the People Acts; or

    (d) any enactment relating to rating and valuation in England and Wales; or

    (e) the Town and Country Planning Act 1962; or

    (f) any of the Acts amended by Schedule 5, 6, 8 or 13 to this Act;

and this section shall not apply to any enactment contained in an Act passed with respect only to the whole or part of the existing county of London.

5.—(1) Subject to any provision to the contrary effect made by, or by any instrument made under, this Act or any other Act passed during the same session as this Act, and without prejudice to any express provision so made, the Greater London Council may, with the concurrence of the council in question, delegate to any London borough council or to the Common Council, with or without restrictions or conditions as the Greater London Council think fit, any of the functions of the Greater London Council except—

    (a) functions for which the Greater London Council are required by any enactment for the time being in force to appoint a committee;

    (b) functions in respect of which specific powers of delegation to that council are conferred by any enactment; and

    (c) the power of borrowing money or issuing a precept for the levy of a rate;

and where any functions are delegated to a London borough council or the Common Council under this section, that council shall, in the discharge of those functions, act as agents for the Greater London Council.

(2) The Common Council and the council of any London borough which is adjacent to the City may agree together for the discharge by that borough council, as agent for the Common Council, of such of the functions of the Common Council as may be specified in the agreement.

(3) Without prejudice to any other provision of this or any other Act, any of the following councils, that is to say, the Greater London Council, the London borough councils and the Common Council, may, for the better performance of their respective functions, agree with any one or more of the others of those councils and any other local authority within the meaning of the Local Government Act 1933 whose area is contiguous with any part of Greater London for—

    (a) the undertaking by one party for another of any administrative, clerical, professional, scientific or technical services;

    (b) the use or maintenance by one party of any vehicle, plant, equipment or apparatus of another party and, if it appears convenient, the services of any staff employed in connection therewith;

    (c) the carrying out of works of maintenance by one party in connection with land or buildings for the maintenance of which another party is responsible,

on such terms as may be agreed between them; and in this subsection the expression "maintenance" includes minor renewals, improvements and extensions.

6.—(1) Section 140 of the Local Government Act 1933 shall not apply to the alteration of the boundary between a county or county borough and Greater London, and nothing in section 253 of that Act shall authorise any local authority within the meaning of that Act to include in any Bill promoted by them any provision making an alteration of the boundaries of any London borough or of Greater London; but the following provision of this section shall have effect for the purposes of such an alteration.

(2) If proposals are made to the Minister—

    (a) by the council of the London borough affected and the Greater London Council acting jointly, or by the council of the county or county borough affected, for the making of an alteration of the boundary of Greater London; or

    (b) by the council of a London borough for the making of an alteration of the boundary between that and some other London borough; or

    (c) by the council of the London borough affected or by the Common Council, for the making of an alteration of the boundary between a London borough and the City; or

    (d) under subsection (4) of this section,

the Minister shall, unless he is satisfied that the proposals ought not to be entertained, cause a local inquiry to be held, and may make an order giving effect to the proposals or making such other alteration of the boundary in question as he may deem expedient, or may refuse to make any such order; but no order shall be made under this subsection unless a draft thereof has been laid before, and approved by a resolution of, each House of Parliament.

(3) If joint representations are made to the Minister—

    (a) by all or, as the case may be, both of the councils referred to in paragraph (a), (b) or (c) of subsection (2) of this section for the making of such an alteration as is mentioned in that paragraph; or

    (b) by the Common Council or the council of a London borough and the Honourable Society of the Inner Temple or of the Middle Temple for the making of an alteration of the boundary between the City or that borough and the Inner Temple or the Middle Temple, as the case may be,

the Minister shall, unless he is satisfied that it is unnecessary so to do, cause a local inquiry to be held and, after considering the report of any such inquiry, may by order give effect to the representations.

(4) In the case of a London borough contiguous with a county, at any time after 31st March 1965 and before 1st April 1970 proposals for the transfer from that borough to

that county of a part of that borough which is so contiguous may be made to the Minister by any three hundred or more local government electors residing in that part of the borough and together constituting not less than ten per cent, of the total number of local government electors so residing.

(5) Any order by the Minister under subsection (2) or (3) of this section shall be deemed for the purposes of sections 148 and 149 of the said Act of 1933 to be an order made in pursuance of powers conferred by Part VI of the said Act of 1933.

7.—(1) The powers of the Greater London Council under section 253 of the Local Government Act 1933 shall include power subject to subsection (2) of this section to promote a Bill in Parliament for any purpose which is for the public benefit of the inhabitants of Greater London or of any part thereof; and without prejudice to the generality of those powers any provision included in a Bill promoted by that Council—

(a) for such a purpose as aforesaid; or

(b) subject to subsection (3) of this section, at the request of a London borough council or the Common Council,

may alter the functions of any London borough council or the Common Council or, as the case may be, of the council making the request notwithstanding that no alteration is made thereby in the functions of the Greater London Council.

(2) Before the Greater London Council include in any Bill to be promoted by them any provision altering the functions of the Common Council or a London borough council, they shall consult with the Common Council or, as the case may be, with that borough council or, if the provision relates to all the London borough councils, with any association or committee which appears to the Greater London Council to be representative of those borough councils.

(3) Where, in the case of any provision which, by virtue of subsection (1) (b) of this section, is or is proposed to be included at the request of a borough council or the Common Council in a Bill promoted or to be promoted by the Greater London Council, it is or will be a condition of the inclusion of that provision in the Bill that the borough council or, as the case may be, Common Council shall make a contribution towards the expenses incurred or to be incurred by the Greater London Council in connection with the promotion of the Bill, sections 254 and 255 of, and Schedule 9 to, the said Act of 1933 shall apply in relation to the making of the request aforesaid—

(a) as if any reference in the said sections or Schedule to the promotion of, or of any provision of, a Bill were a reference to the making of the request aforesaid for the inclusion of, or, as the case may be, of any part of, that provision in the Bill in question and, in relation to the Common Council, as if the City were a borough and the Common Council the council of that borough;

(b) as if the deposit of the Bill in question in Parliament by the Greater London Council were such a deposit of that Bill by the borough council or, as the case may be, Common Council;

and where the borough council or Common Council are required by either of the said sections as modified by this subsection to take all necessary steps to withdraw the Bill or some provision thereof, that council shall forthwith notify the Greater London Council to that effect and the Greater London Council shall thereupon take all necessary steps to withdraw the provision or part of a provision in question.

(4) A London borough council or the Common Council may in compliance with any such condition as is referred to in subsection (3) of this section make such contribution towards the expenses incurred by the Greater London Council in connection with the promotion of the Bill in question as may be agreed between the councils concerned.

8.—(1) The provisions of Part I of Schedule 3 to this Act, being provisions necessary or expedient in consequence of the foregoing provisions of this Part of this Act, shall have effect with respect to parliamentary and local government elections in and around Greater London; and the Representation of the People Acts shall have effect subject to the modifications specified in Parts II and III of that Schedule, being modifications consequential on the provisions of the said Part I or modifications of those Acts in their application to Greater London; and the said Schedule 3 shall be included among the enactments which may be cited together as the Representation of the People Acts.

(2) The Local Government Act 1933 shall have effect subject to the modifications specified in Schedule 4 to this Act, being—

(a) modifications consequential on other provisions of this Act; or

(b) modifications designed to assimilate the provisions of the said Act of 1933 to provisions for corresponding purposes contained in the London Government Act 1939; or

(c) modifications designed to make the said Act of 1933 apply in appropriate cases in relation to the Greater London Council as it applies in relation to a county council or in relation to a London borough as it applies in relation to a county borough or as it applies in relation to a metropolitan borough; or

(d) modifications of the said Act of 1933 in its application either to all London boroughs or to the inner London boroughs.

Part II

ROAD TRAFFIC, HIGHWAYS AND MOTOR VEHICLES

9.—(1) The provisions of this Part of this Act shall have effect for the purpose of redistributing functions with respect to road traffic in Greater London and assimilating the law with respect to highways in Greater London to that in force in the rest of England and Wales.

(2) It shall be the duty of the Greater London Council so to exercise the functions conferred on them by or by virtue of sections 10 to 19 of this Act as, so far as practicable having due regard to—

(a) the desirability of securing and maintaining reasonable access to premises;

(b) the effect on the amenities of any locality affected; and

(c) any other matters appearing to the Council to be relevant,

to secure the expeditious, convenient and safe movement of vehicular and other traffic (including foot passengers) and the provision of suitable and adequate parking facilities on and off the highway; and the Minister of Transport shall not—

(i) give any direction to the Council under section 10 (7) (a) or (b), 11 (7) or 13 (2) (a) of this Act; or

(ii) exercise his power under section 10 (2) (b), 11 (2) (a) or 13 (2) (c) of this Act to revoke or vary any order made by the Council,

unless he is satisfied, having regard to any matters appearing to him to be relevant, that the Council's duty aforesaid is not being satisfactorily discharged by the Council and that it is necessary for him so to do in order to secure compliance with that duty.

(3) The Greater London Council shall before 1st April 1965 consult with the Minister of Transport with regard to the administrative arrangements to be made by the Council for the discharge of the Council's functions by virtue of sections 10 to 15 of this Act.

(4) Any person appointed by the Greater London Council to hold a local inquiry for the purposes of any of the Council's functions by virtue of sections 10 to 15 of this Act shall have the like powers as a person appointed to hold an inquiry to which section 290 of the Local Government Act 1933 applies.

(5) Without prejudice to any power of delegation conferred by or by virtue of the provisions of sections 10 to 20 of this Act, section 5 (1) of this Act shall not apply to any function conferred on the Greater London Council by or by virtue of those provisions.

(6) The London Traffic Area and the London and Home Counties Traffic Advisory Committee shall cease to exist; and any reference in the Road Traffic Act 1960, the Road Traffic and Roads Improvement Act 1960 or the Road Traffic Act 1962—

    (a) to the London Traffic Area; or

    (b) except in sections 85 (1) and (8), 135 and 141 of the Road Traffic Act 1960, to an area comprising the metropolitan police district and the City of London,

shall be construed as a reference to Greater London.

10.—(1) Subject to subsections (4) to (7) of this section, the Greater London Council (hereafter in this section referred to as "the Council") may by order make provision for controlling vehicular and other traffic (including foot passengers) on roads in Greater London, being—

    (a) roads other than trunk roads; or

    (b) trunk roads with respect to which the Minister of Transport has consented to the making of the order in question,

and in particular, but without prejudice to the generality of the foregoing words, for any of the purposes, or with respect to any of the matters, mentioned in Schedule 4 to the Road Traffic Act 1960; but no such order shall contain any provision for regulating the speed of vehicles on roads, and paragraph 16 of the said Schedule 4 and section 62 of the London Passenger Transport Act 1933 shall cease to have effect.

(2) The powers of the Minister of Transport under section 34 of the said Act of 1960 shall be exercisable only—

    (a) with respect to trunk roads in Greater London; or

    (b) for the revocation or variation, after giving notice to the Council and, if he thinks fit, after holding a public inquiry, of any order by the Council under subsection (1) of this section; or

    (c) for securing the object of any direction with respect to any road other than a trunk road or a special road given by that Minister to the Council under subsection (7) of this section with which the Council have failed to comply,

and shall be exercisable by order made by statutory instrument instead of by regulations; and the powers of the said Minister by virtue of this subsection to make orders under the said section 34 shall include power to make such an order varying or revoking any such order previously made by him; and so much of section 26 of the Road Traffic Act 1962 as limits the duration of the powers conferred thereby shall cease to have effect.

(3) The provisions of subsections (2) to (4) and (7) to (9) of the said section 34 shall apply to an order made by the Council under subsection (1) of this section as they apply to an order made by the Minister of Transport under the said section 34 and, in relation to such an order by the Council, shall have effect as if in those provisions—

    (a) for any reference to that Minister there were substituted a reference to the Council;

    (b) any reference to the said section 34 included a reference to subsection (1) of this section.

(4) Before making any order under subsection (1) of this section otherwise than in pursuance of a direction given by the Minister of Transport under subsection (7) thereof, the Council shall consult with the appropriate commissioner of police and with any other council, being a London borough council or the Common Council, within whose area any road affected by the proposed order lies or whose area appears to the Greater London Council likely to be affected by that order.

(5) Subject to the next following subsection, any order made by the Council under subsection (1) of this section may be revoked or varied by a subsequent order of the Council under that subsection.

(6) If the provisions as respects any length of road of any order made by the Council under subsection (1) of this section are revoked or varied by an order of the Minister of Transport under the said section 34, then, except with the consent of that Minister, the Council shall not make any further order under the said subsection (1) as respects the same length of road within twelve months after the making of the Minister's order.

(7) The Minister of Transport may after consultation with the Council give to the Council—

    (a) a direction to make an order under subsection (1) of this section for a specified purpose and coming into force before the expiration of a specified period; or

    (b) a direction prohibiting, either generally or except with the consent of that Minister or for a specified period, the making or bringing into force of such an order with respect to specified matters or a specified area,

and may also give directions, either generally or with respect to any particular case or class of cases, as to the procedure to be followed in connection with any order under the said subsection (1).

(8) The Greater London Council as well as the Minister of Transport shall have power to make an order under section 11 (1) of the Road Traffic Act 1962 (which relates to speed limits on roads other than restricted roads) as respects any road in Greater London other than a trunk road.

11.—(1) The Greater London Council as well as the Minister of Transport shall have power to make an experimental traffic order under section 28 of the Road Traffic Act 1962 with respect to any road in Greater London, being—

    (a) a road other than a trunk road; or

    (b) a trunk road with respect to which that Minister has consented to the making of the order in question.

(2) The Minister of Transport shall not make an order under the said section 28 with respect to any road in Greater London which is not a trunk road except for the purpose of—

    (a) the revocation or variation, after giving notice to the Greater London Council, of any order by that Council under that section; or

    (b) securing the object of any direction given to that Council by that Minister by virtue of subsection (3) of this section with which that Council have failed to comply.

(3) The provisions of section 10 (6) and (7) of this Act

shall have effect for the purposes of subsection (1) of this section as if—

(a) any reference in those provisions to, or to an order made by the Greater London Council under, subsection (1) of that section were a reference to, or to an order made by that Council by virtue of, subsection (1) of this section;

(b) any reference to an order of the Minister of Transport under section 34 of the Road Traffic Act 1960 were a reference to an order of that Minister under the said section 28.

(4) An order made by the Greater London Council under the said section 28 may include provision whereby a specified officer, or some person authorised in that behalf by a specified officer, of the Council may, if it appears to that officer or person essential in the interests of the expeditious, convenient and safe movement of traffic and after consulting with the appropriate commissioner of police and giving such public notice as the Minister of Transport may direct, modify or suspend the order or any provision thereof.

(5) Before the Greater London Council make any order under the said section 28 they shall—

(a) except where the order is made in pursuance of a direction by the Minister of Transport by virtue of subsection (3) of this section, consult with the appropriate commissioner of police; and

(b) give such public notice as that Minister may direct.

(6) The Minister of Transport may repay to the Greater London Council any expenses incurred by that Council in connection with any order made by them under the said section 28.

(7) The powers with respect to the carrying out of experimental traffic schemes conferred by section 35 of the Road Traffic Act 1960 on the commissioner of police of the metropolis shall be exercisable only within Greater London; and the authority for the giving of any consent or direction under subsection (1) or (5) of that section shall be the Greater London Council instead of the Minister of Transport; but the Greater London Council shall not give their consent to any such scheme affecting a trunk road except with the agreement of that Minister; and in the case of any particular scheme that Minister may after consultation with the Greater London Council direct that Council to consent thereto within a specified period or to withhold their consent therefrom.

12.—(1) The Minister of Transport or the Greater London Council may, to such extent as that Minister or Council may consider necessary in connection with any order under section 34 of the Road Traffic Act 1960, section 10 (1) of this Act or section 28 of the Road Traffic Act 1962 made or proposed to be made by that Minister or, as the case may be, that Council—

(a) exercise as respects any road in Greater London which is not a trunk road any powers exercisable by the highway authority for that road in connection with the placing of traffic signs on or near that road in pursuance of section 52 of the said Act of 1960 and affix any such sign to any lamp-post or other structure in the highway, whether or not belonging to that Minister or Council;

(b) authorise or require the highway authority for any such road to place in the carriageway such bollards or other obstructions as that Minister or Council may consider appropriate for preventing the passage of vehicles, or vehicles of any class or description, at any point at which their passage (whether in any direction or in one direction only) is prohibited by any such order as aforesaid and to

maintain and light those obstructions;

(c) authorise or require any highway authority to remove any obstruction placed by that authority in pursuance of an authorisation or requirement under the last foregoing paragraph.

(2) To such extent as the Minister of Transport or, as the case may be, the Greater London Council may consider necessary in connection with any order such as is mentioned in subsection (1) of this section, whether made or proposed to be made by that Minister or by that Council, that Minister may do with respect to any trunk road, or as the case may be that Council may do with respect to any metropolitan road, anything which the authority making or proposing to make the order might under subsection (1) (b) of this section require to be done with respect to any other road by the highway authority therefor.

(3) The Greater London Council or, to such extent as the Minister of Transport may consider necessary in connection with any order made or proposed to be made by him under the said section 34 or 28, that Minister may give to the highway authority for any road in Greater London which is not a trunk road such directions with respect to the adjustment, modification or replacement of, or of any part of, the mechanism of traffic signs, being light signals controlled by that authority, as that Council or Minister may consider expedient in the interests of the movement of traffic.

(4) If a highway authority fail to comply with any requirement or direction under subsection (1) or (3) of this section the Minister of Transport or, as the case may be, the Greater London Council may carry out the work required by the requirement or direction, and the expense incurred by that Minister or Council in so doing shall be recoverable summarily as a civil debt from the authority.

(5) As respects any traffic sign placed by the Minister of Transport or the Greater London Council in the exercise of the powers conferred by subsection (1) (a) of this section, it shall be the duty of that Council—

(a) to take such steps to maintain, and to make such alteration of, that sign as may be necessary or expedient in connection with the order in connection with which it was placed;

(b) to remove that sign upon that order ceasing to have effect;

and that Minister may recover from that Council summarily as a civil debt any expenses incurred by him by virtue of the said subsection (1) (a).

(6) As respects any road in Greater London other than a trunk road the Greater London Council shall be the competent authority for the purposes of section 22 of the said Act of 1960 with respect to signs for indicating speed restrictions.

(7) References in this section to a highway authority include references to any person who, not being a highway authority, is responsible for the maintenance of a road.

(8) The power of the Minister of Transport under section 63 of the Road Traffic Act 1960 to make advances towards expenses incurred in relation to traffic signs shall be exercisable with respect to any expenses incurred by the Greater London Council in relation to the erection, maintenance, alteration or removal of traffic signs or by virtue of subsection (2) of this section; and the said section 63 shall apply in relation to any such obstruction as is mentioned in subsection (1) of this section as it applies in relation to traffic signs.

13.—(1) Section 81 of the Road Traffic Act 1960 (which relates to the power of local authorities to provide parking places) shall extend to the whole of Greater London and to the use as a parking place of any place other than a road in

Greater London; and the Greater London Council as respects the whole of Greater London, the council of a London borough as respects the borough, and the Common Council as respects the City, shall be the local authority for the purposes of that section; but the Greater London Council shall not exercise their powers under that section—

    (*a*) as respects any London borough, without the consent of the council of that borough, or

    (*b*) as respects the City, without the consent of the Common Council,

except with the consent of the Minister of Transport.

(2) The functions as respects Greater London conferred on the Minister of Transport by section 85 (1) and (2) of the said Act of 1960 (which relate to the designation on the application of local authorities of parking places on highways where charges are made), the functions of that Minister under section 85 (5) of that Act (which relates to the designation of parking places without an application by the local authority) and, in respect of any site in Greater London, the supplementary functions of that Minister under sections 86 and 87 of that Act and section 3 of the Road Traffic and Roads Improvement Act 1960 shall be exercisable by the Greater London Council (hereafter in this section referred to as "the Council") as well as by that Minister; and that Minister—

    (*a*) subject to subsection (3) of this section, may after consultation with the Council direct the Council—

        (i) to make under any provision of the said sections 85, 86, 87 and 3 (hereafter in this section referred to as "the relevant provisions") such order as may be specified in the direction in respect of any site in Greater London so specified to come into force before the expiration of a period so specified, being in the case of an order under the said section 85 (1) an order either in the form applied for by the local authority or in that form with specified modifications; or

        (ii) not to make under any of the relevant provisions a particular order which has been applied for or proposed;

    (*b*) shall not himself make an order under any of the relevant provisions except for the purpose of securing the object of any direction given to the Council under paragraph (*a*) (i) of this subsection with which the Council have failed to comply;

    (*c*) may, after giving notice of his intention to the Council and any other person appearing to that Minister to be likely to be concerned, by order revoke or vary any order made by the Council under any of the relevant provisions.

(3) Before giving any direction under subsection (2) (*a*) (*j*) of this section—

    (*a*) in the case of a direction to make with or without modifications—

        (i) an order applied for under the said section 85 (1); or

        (ii) an order under the said section 85 (5) or 3 (4) which has already been proposed by the Council,

    the Minister of Transport shall consider any objections made to the order applied for or proposed;

    (*b*) in the case of a direction to make an order under the said section 85 (5) or 3 (4) which has not already been proposed by the Council, that Minister instead of the Council shall comply with the requirements of Part II of Schedule 10 to the Road Traffic

Act 1960 in like manner as if the order were to be made to him instead of by the Council;

    (*c*) in the case of a direction to make any order in the form of an order applied for by a local authority or proposed by the Council but with modifications which appear to that Minister to affect substantially the character of the order, that Minister shall take such steps as appear to him to be sufficient and reasonably practicable for informing any local authority concerned and any other person likely to be concerned.

(4) Any application by a local authority in Greater London for an order under the said section 85 (1) shall be made to the Council and not to the Minister of Transport, but a London borough council shall not make such an application in respect of a site on a trunk road except with the consent of that Minister and, for the purposes of subsection (2) (*b*) of this section, and such application made to the Council shall be deemed to have been made to that Minister.

(5) In relation to an order of the Council—

    (*a*) any reference in the relevant provisions or in the said Schedule 10 to the Minister of Transport (other than the reference in the said section 86 (2) (*a*)) shall be construed as a reference to the Council;

    (*b*) the said section 85 (5) shall have effect as if paragraph (*a*) and, in paragraph (*b*), the words "with the consent of the Treasury", the words from "or the" to "Council" where first occurring and the words "or Council" were omitted; and

    (*c*) the said section 3 (4) shall have effect as if the reference to section 90 (3) and (5) of the Road Traffic Act 1960 were omitted;

and in relation to parking places designated by virtue of the said section 85 (5) by an order of the Council, references in sections 85 (3), 86 to 89 and 232 (2) (*a*) (ii) of the Road Traffic Act 1960 and sections 6 and 15 of the Road Traffic and Roads Improvement Act 1960 to the local authority shall be construed as references to the Council.

(6) Where—

    (*a*) the Council make an order under any of the relevant provisions in pursuance of a direction under subsection (2) (*a*) (i) of this section; or

    (*b*) the Minister of Transport makes an order under any of the relevant provisions for the purpose specified in subsection (2) (*b*) of this section; or

    (*c*) that Minister makes an order under subsection (2) (*c*) of this section; or

    (*d*) that Minister enters into an agreement under the said section 85 (5) (*b*) for the transfer of a parking place designated by an order of that Minister,

the powers of the Council to vary or revoke orders made by them under the relevant provisions shall extend to the variation or revocation of any such order as aforesaid notwithstanding that it is made by, or by direction of, that Minister but, except with the consent of that Minister—

        (i) any order such as is mentioned in paragraph (*a*), (*b*), (*c*) or (*d*) of this subsection shall not be revoked or varied by the Council, and

        (ii) where an order of the Council under the said section 85 with respect to parking places on any length of highway has been varied or revoked by that Minister by virtue of the said subsection (2) (*c*), the Council shall not make a further order under the said section 85 as respects that length of highway,

within twelve months of the making of the order referred to

in paragraph (*a*), (*b*) or (*c*) or the transfer referred to in paragraph (*d*), as the case may be, of this subsection.

(7) The Minister of Transport may give directions to the Council, either generally or with respect to any particular case or class of cases, as to the procedure to be followed in connection with—

> (*a*) any application to the Council for an order under the said section 85 (1);
>
> (*b*) the making of any order by the Council under any of the relevant provisions,

including directions modifying the provisions of the said Schedule 10 in their application to, or applying those provisions with modifications to, any such order of the Council; but, except in the case of an order revoking and re-enacting the provisions of a previous order, whether or not made by the same authority, no direction given by virtue of this subsection shall reduce the opportunities afforded by the said Schedule 10 to object to any application or proposal.

(8) In the Road Traffic and Roads Improvement Act 1960, the following provisions shall cease to have effect, that is to say—

> (*a*) so much of section 4 (1) as limits the duration of the powers conferred by the said section 85 (5);
>
> (*b*) so much of section 4 (2) as limits the duration of the power conferred thereby on the Minister of Transport to make grants towards the provision and maintenance of off-street parking places;
>
> (*c*) section 10 (which relates to the provision by that Minister of temporary parking accommodation in Greater London).

14.—(1) The functions of the Minister of Transport under the following enactments shall, as respects Greater London, become functions of the Greater London Council, that is to say—

> (*a*) sections 137 and 138 of the Highways Act 1959 (which relate to half-yearly schemes of repair and improvement works);
>
> (*b*) except as respects trunk roads, section 21 of the Road Traffic Act 1960 (which relates to directions with respect to speed limits on restricted roads);
>
> (*c*) sections 49 and 50 of the Road Traffic Act 1960 (which relate to the use of roads as playgrounds);
>
> (*d*) section 18 of the Road Traffic and Roads Improvement Act 1960 (which relates to road improvements),

and so much of the said section 18 as restricts the duration thereof shall cease to have effect.

(2) The Greater London Council shall have as respects Greater London the like powers as are conferred on the Minister of Transport by section 19 of the Road Traffic and Roads Improvement Act 1960 (which relates to road improvements) and so much of that section as restricts the duration thereof shall cease to have effect; and, without prejudice to the extent of the powers of the Greater London Council by virtue of the foregoing provisions of this subsection, that Minister shall exercise his powers under the said section 19 only if he considers it necessary in connection with any order made or proposed to be made by him under section 34 of the Road Traffic Act 1960 or section 28 of the Road Traffic Act 1962 for a purpose specified in section 10 (2) (*b*) or (*c*) or, as the case may be, 11 (2) of this Act.

(3) In exercising their functions by virtue of subsection (1) (*a*) of this section, the Greater London Council, before drawing up a scheme under section 137 (3) of the said Act of 1959, shall instead of referring the statements mentioned in the said section 137 (3) to the body so mentioned consult with the appropriate commissioner of police and the London Transport Board; and no such scheme confirmed by that Council shall be binding on the Minister of Transport.

(4) The consent of the Greater London Council for the purposes of section 138(2) of the said Act of 1959 shall not be unreasonably withheld, and any question whether the withholding of such consent is unreasonable shall be determined in like manner as any question arising under section 136(4) of that Act; and section 136(6) and (7) of the said Act of 1959 shall apply to a contravention of section 138(2) thereof as they apply to a contravention of section 136(1) thereof.

(5) In the application to Greater London of section 44 of the Road Traffic Act 1960 (which relates to schemes for the establishment of pedestrian crossings on roads other than trunk roads) the expression "local authority" in that section shall mean—

> (*a*) as respects a metropolitan road, the Greater London Council;
>
> (*b*) as respects any other road in a London borough, the council of the borough;
>
> (*c*) as respects any other road in the City, the Common Council;

but before the Greater London Council submit any scheme under that section with respect to a metropolitan road they shall consult with any other of the councils aforesaid within whose area that road is situated.

(6) In the Road Traffic Act 1960—

> (*a*) section 17 (which relates to the control of the use of footpaths and bridleways for motor-vehicle trials) shall apply to the council of a London borough as it applies to the council of a county borough;
>
> (*b*) section 49 (which empowers local authorities to prohibit traffic on roads to be used as playgrounds) shall apply to the Common Council as it applies to the council of a borough;
>
> (*c*) section 65 (3) (which relates to the appointment of authorized examiners of vehicles) shall apply to the Greater London Council as it applies to the council of a county and to the Common Council as it applies to the council of a borough;
>
> (*d*) sections 135 (8) and 141 (2) to (6) (which relate respectively to road service licences and to the approval of routes in the London special area) shall apply to the Greater London Council as they apply to the commissioners of police therein mentioned;
>
> (*e*) section 202 (2) (*a*) (which relates to the bodies excepted from the requirement of third-party insurance or security) and section 221 (3) (which relates to the institution of proceedings for an offence under that section in respect of protective helmets for motor cyclists) shall apply to the Greater London Council as they apply to the council of a county.

15.—(1) The Road Traffic Act 1960, the Road Traffic and Roads Improvement Act 1960 and the Road Traffic Act 1962 shall have effect subject to the modifications specified in relation thereto in Parts I, II and III respectively of Schedule 5 to this Act, being modifications consequential on other provisions of this Act.

(2) Any expression used in sections 10 to 14 of this Act which is also used in the Road Traffic Act 1960 shall have the same meaning as in that Act.

16.—(1) The Greater London Council shall be the highway authority for all metropolitan roads; and the council of a London borough or the Common Council shall be the highway authority for all highways in the borough or, as the case may be, in the City, whether or not maintainable at the public expense, which are not for the time being metropolitan roads or highways for which under section 1 (1) of the Highways Act 1959 the Minister of Transport is the highway authority.

(2) The Highways Acts 1959 and 1961 shall extend to the whole of Greater London, and—

(a) the Highways Act 1959 shall have effect subject to the amendments specified in Schedule 6 to this Act, being amendments—

(i) consequential on other provisions of this Act; or

(ii) designed to apply in relation to highway authorities in Greater London, in appropriate cases and with appropriate modifications, provisions of that Act applicable to comparable authorities elsewhere;

(b) in section 2 (2) of the Private Street Works Act 1961, the reference to a county borough shall include a reference to a London borough;

and in the application of section 153 of the Highways Act 1959 to Greater London the words "the carriageway of" in subsection (1) thereof shall be omitted.

(3) The power conferred on a local highway authority by section 26 (2) of the Highways Act 1959 to construct new highways shall be exercisable by the Greater London Council for the purpose of constructing a new highway communicating with a metropolitan road notwithstanding that the new highway will not itself be such a road; but before so exercising that power that Council shall give notice of their proposals for the construction of the new highway to, and consider any representations by, the council which will be the highway authority for that new highway.

(4) Where a new highway to be constructed by virtue of the said section 26(2) by a London borough council or the Common Council will communicate with a metropolitan road, the communication shall not be made unless the manner in which it is to be made has been approved by the Greater London Council.

(5) It shall be the duty of every London borough council and of the Common Council to furnish, and to instruct their officers to furnish, any information in their power which may reasonably be required by the Greater London Council for the purpose of enabling that Council to discharge their functions under or by virtue of this and the two next following sections.

(6) Any expression used in this or the two next following sections which is also used in the Highways Act 1959 shall have the same meaning as in that Act.

17.—(1) The following shall be metropolitan roads, that is to say—

(a) subject to subsection (2) of this section, the highways specified in Schedule 7 to this Act;

(b) subject as aforesaid, any highway constructed or proposed to be constructed by the Greater London Council the construction of which as a metropolitan road has been approved by the Minister of Transport;

(c) any other highway or proposed highway which is for the time being designated as a metropolitan road by an order under subsection (2) of this section or by an order under section 7 of the Highways Act 1959 directing that the highway shall cease to be a trunk road.

(2) Subject to subsection (3) of this section, the Minister of Transport may, on the application of the Greater London Council, a London borough council or the Common Council, by order designate as a metropolitan road any highway or proposed highway specified in the order or direct that any highway or proposed highway so specified which is for the time being a metropolitan road shall cease to be such a road.

(3) The council by whom an application for an order under subsection (2) of this section is made shall send a copy of the application to any other council who, if the order were to be made, would become or cease to be the highway authority for the highway in question and, before determining whether or not to make the order, the Minister of Transport shall consider any representation which any such other council may make to him with reference to the making of the order and, if so requested by any such other council, shall hold a local inquiry.

(4) Where a highway in a London borough or the City becomes (otherwise than by virtue of subsection (1) (a) of this section) or ceases to be a metropolitan road, the council of the borough or the Common Council, as the case may be, and the Greater London Council may agree for the transfer to the new highway authority for the highway of such property and liabilities relating thereto of the former highway authority therefor on such terms and conditions as may be specified in the agreement.

(5) The drains belonging to a highway which is for the time being a metropolitan road shall vest in the Greater London Council and, where any other drain or sewer was, at the date when the highway became a metropolitan road, used for any purpose in connection with the drainage of that highway, that Council shall continue to have the right of using that drain or sewer for that purpose; and any difference arising under this subsection between the Greater London Council and a London borough council or the Common Council as to the council in whom a drain is vested, or as to the use of a drain or sewer, shall, if either council so elect, be referred to and determined by the Minister.

(6) An order—

(a) under subsection (2) of this section; or

(b) under section 7 of the Highways Act 1959 directing that a highway shall cease to be a trunk road and designating that highway as a metropolitan road,

may be made before 1st April 1965 so as to come into force at any time not earlier than that date.

18.—(1) The Greater London Council may agree with the council of any London borough or the Common Council for the delegation to the borough council or Common Council of any of the functions of the Greater London Council with respect to the maintenance and improvement of, and other dealing with—

(a) the whole or any part of so much of any metropolitan road as lies within the borough or, as the case may be, the City;

(b) any land which does not form part of a metropolitan road but has been acquired by the Greater London Council in connection with such a road under section 214 (5) or (6) or 215 (2) of the Highways Act 1959.

(2) A London borough council or the Common Council shall, in the discharge of any functions delegated by virtue of subsection (1) of this section, act as agents for the Greater London Council; and it shall be a condition of the delegation—

(a) that the works to be executed and the expenditure to be incurred by the borough council or the Common Council in the discharge of the delegated functions shall be subject to the approval of the Greater London Council; and

(b) that the borough council or Common Council shall comply with any requirement of the Greater London Council as to the manner in which, and the persons by whom, any works are to be carried out, and with any general directions of the Greater London Council as to the terms of contracts to be entered into for the purposes of the discharge of the delegated functions; and

(c) that any such works shall be completed to the satisfaction of the Greater London Council;

and, if at any time the Greater London Council are satisfied on the report of some officer of the Council or other person appointed by them for the purpose that the road or land with respect to which the functions are delegated is not in proper repair or condition, they may give notice to the borough council or Common Council requiring them to place it in proper repair or condition and, if the notice is not complied with within a reasonable time, may themselves do anything which seems to them necessary to place it in proper repair or condition.

(3) A delegation to a London borough council or the Common Council under subsection (1) of this section may be determined by notice given to that council by the Greater London Council, or the functions so delegated may be relinquished by notice given by the borough council or Common Council to the Greater London Council; but—

(a) the determination or relinquishment shall not take effect until 1st April in the calendar year next following that in which the notice is given; and

(b) such a notice shall not be given during the last three months of a calendar year.

(4) The Greater London Council may enter into an agreement with the council of a London borough or the Common Council for the construction of a metropolitan road in the borough or, as the case may be, in the City, or for the carrying out by the borough council or Common Council of any particular work of improvement of, or other dealing with, such a road or part thereof or such land as is mentioned in subsection (1) of this section; and subsection (2) of this section shall apply to the discharge of the functions of the borough council or Common Council under any such agreement and to the conditions to be included in the agreement as it applies to the discharge of functions delegated by virtue of the said subsection (1) and to the conditions to be attached to any such delegation.

(5) The council of a London borough or the Common Council shall, if so required by the Greater London Council, undertake the maintenance of any metropolitan road within the borough or, as the case may be, within the City in consideration of such payments by the Greater London Council as may from time to time be agreed between them or, in default of such agreement, as may be determined by the Minister of Transport; and while that requirement remains in force the borough council or Common Council shall have the like powers and be subject to the like duties and liabilities with respect to the maintenance of that road as if they were the highway authority therefor.

(6) Plant or materials belonging to a council by whom functions fall to be exercised by virtue of a delegation, agreement or requirement under this section may be used by them for the purposes of the exercise of those functions, subject to the terms of any delegation or of any agreement between that council and the Greater London Council.

(7) Nothing in this section shall be construed as limiting the power of the Greater London Council to enter into and carry into effect agreements with any person for any purpose connected with the construction, improvement or maintenance of, or other dealing with, a metropolitan road or otherwise connected with any functions of that Council relating to metropolitan roads; but no such agreement shall provide for the delegation of any powers or duties of the Greater London Council except in accordance with the provisions of this section.

19.—(1) The Public Utilities Street Works Act 1950 shall have effect subject to the modifications hereafter specified in this section.

(2) For the purposes of the operation of Part II in relation to a street in Greater London, the reference in section 21 (1) to a county council shall be construed as including a reference to the Greater London Council.

(3) In section 35 (2), for the words "the administrative county of London" there shall be substituted the words "Greater London".

(4) In paragraph 1 (b) of Schedule 7, for the words "conferred on the London County Council" there shall be substituted the words "in default of their execution by the undertakers conferred".

(5) In paragraph 5 of schedule 7, for the words "in London" there shall be substituted the words "in Greater London".

(6) In paragraph 6 of Schedule 7, for the word "London" there shall be substituted the words "any part of London other than an outer London borough".

20.—(1) The functions of a county council under the Vehicles (Excise) Act 1962 (being functions as to the collection of excise duties on, and the licensing and registration of, mechanically propelled vehicles) shall be exercised as respects Greater London by the Greater London Council; and accordingly, in section 24 (1) of that Act, for the definition of "county" there shall be substituted—

" 'county' includes a county borough and Greater London, and references to the council of a county shall be construed, in relation to a county borough, as references to the council of the borough and, in relation to Greater London, as references to the Greater London Council."

(2) The Greater London Council shall be the licensing authority for Greater London for the purposes of Part II of the Road Traffic Act 1960 (which relates to driving licenses).

Part III

HOUSING AND PLANNING

Housing

21.—(1) Subject to subsection (3) of this section, the council of a London borough shall be the local authority as respects that borough for all purposes of the Small Dwellings Acquisition Act 1899, the Housing Act 1957, the Housing (Financial Provisions) Act 1958, the House Purchase and Housing Act 1959 and the Housing Act 1961 for which the council of a county borough are the local authority as respects that county borough.

(2) The Common Council shall be the local authority as respects the City for the purposes of the said Act of 1899 and, subject to subsection (3) of this section, shall continue to be the local authority as respects the City for all purposes of the other enactments referred to in subsection (1) of this section.

(3) The council of a London borough or the Common Council shall not exercise any powers under Part V of the Housing Act 1957 outside Greater London for the purposes of a scheme prepared by that council unless, on an application

made to the Minister for the purpose by that council, it appears to the Minister expedient that the needs of that borough or, as the case may be, the City with respect to the provision of housing accommodation should be satisfied by the provision of such accommodation by that council outside Greater London and he consents to the scheme.

(4) Without prejudice to the powers of a London borough council or the Comomn Council, the Greater London Council shall be a local authority as respects the whole of Greater London for the purposes of the Small Dwellings Acquisition Act 1899, Part V of the Housing Act 1957 (as regards housing accommodation both inside and outside Greater London), section 9 of the Housing (Financial Provisions) Act 1958 and section 13 of the House Purchase and Housing Act 1959; but the Greater London Council—

(a) except—

(i) for the purpose of the carrying out by them of the provisions of a development plan within the meaning of the Town and Country Planning Act 1962 relating to an area of comprehensive development; or

(ii) for the purpose of rehousing persons displaced by, or in consequence of, action taken by them in the exercise of any of their powers,

shall not exercise their powers to provide housing accommodation under the said Part V by the development or redevelopment of land in a London borough except with the consent of the council of that borough or, if that consent is withheld, with the consent of the Minister, who, in deciding whether or not to give his consent, shall have regard to the needs of that borough as well as the needs of Greater London as a whole; and

(b) subject to subsections (7) and (11) of this section, shall not exercise any powers by virtue of this section in the City;

and in Schedule 2 to the Land Compensation Act 1961 (which relates to the payments to be made on the compulsory acquisition of houses as being unfit for human habitation) after paragraph 2 (1) (e) there shall be inserted—

"(f) an acquisition by the Greater London Council under Part V of the Act of 1957".

(5) Until such date as the Minister may by order appoint, the Greater London Council may exercise any of the powers of a local authority under any of the enactments referred to in subsection (1) of this section in any circumstances in which that power might have been exercised by the London county council if this Act had not been passed; and different days may be appointed under this subsection for different purposes or for different areas.

(6) Any review by the Greater London Council in pursuance of their duty under section 91 of the Housing Act 1957 shall be made in consultation with the London borough councils and the Common Council, who shall keep the Greater London Council supplied with information as to their assessment of the needs of their respective districts and as to any action proposed to be taken by them, or any arrangements made between any of them, to meet those needs, and with such other information relevant to that duty in such form as the Greater London Council may require; and the Greater London Council shall inform the Minister of any proposed exercise of their powers under Part V of the Housing Act 1957 in a London borough to which the council of that borough have given their consent.

(7) Section 5 (1) of this Act shall not apply to any func-
tions of the Greater London Council by virtue of this or the next following section, but the Greater London Council and the council of any London borough may agree together for the carrying out of any action under Part V of the Housing Act 1957 in that borough—

(a) by the Greater London Council as agent of the borough council; or

(b) by the borough council as agent of the Greater London Council;

and, without prejudice to subsection (11) of this section, the Greater London Council and the Common Council may agree together for the carrying out of any such action in the City by the Greater London Council as agents of the Common Council.

(8) It shall be the duty of the council of any London borough in carrying out their functions under Parts II and III of the Housing Act 1957 to have regard to any proposals in that behalf as respects the area of that borough submitted before 1st April 1965 under the Housing Repairs and Rents Act 1954 or section 2 of the Housing Act 1957 by any existing council to whom section 3(1)(b) of this Act applies or jointly by the London county council and a metropolitan borough council, but subject to any modifications made by subsequent proposals approved by the Minister under the said section 2.

(9) In section 93 (3) of the Housing Act 1957, references to the London county council, a metropolitan borough council and the administrative county of London shall be construed as references respectively to the Greater London Council, a London borough council and Greater London.

(10) Arrangements may be made by any of the London borough councils or the Common Council for the rehousing of any person by another of those councils; and any such arrangements may include provision for the payment of contributions by that council to that other council.

(11) The Greater London Council and any of the following other councils, that is to say, the Common Council and any borough or urban or rural district council whose area lies outside but adjacent to or in the vicinity of Greater London, may enter into agreements for the provision by the Greater London Council of houses outside the London boroughs to meet the special needs of that other council, or for the provision by that other council of houses within their area to meet the needs of the Greater London Council, and for the payment in either case of such contributions as may be agreed by the council needing the houses to the council providing them.

(12) The enactments referred to in subsection (1) of this section shall have effect subject to the modifications respectively specified in Schedule 8 to this Act, being modifications necessary or expedient in consequence of the foregoing provisions of this section or other provisions of this Act.

22.—(1) The Greater London Council shall establish and maintain in such form and manner as they think appropriate records showing the needs for the time being of Greater London with respect to housing accommodation.

(2) Any application for housing accommodation maintained by a housing authority in Greater London—

(a) if the applicant is resident in a London borough, whether or not the accommodation is sought in that borough, shall be made to the council of that borough; or

(b) in any other case, shall be made to the Greater London Council who may, if they think fit, transmit the application to such of the London borough councils as they think apropriate,

and shall include information on such matters as the Greater

London Council may require for the purposes of their functions under subsection (1) of this section.

(3) Each London borough council shall establish and maintain a register of all applications duly made to them under subsection (2) (*a*) or transmitted to them under subsection (2) (*b*) of this section which are for the time being outstanding, and shall furnish to the Greater London Council such particulars in such form as the Greater London Council may require for the purposes of their functions under subsection (1) of this section—

(*a*) of any such application as aforesaid; and

(*b*) of the steps taken by the borough council to satisfy the needs of persons requiring housing accommodation maintained by that borough council.

(4) Subsections (2) and (3) of this section shall apply to the City as if it were a London borough and the Common Council were the council of that London borough.

(5) The Greater London Council shall establish and maintain facilities for the exchange of housing accommodation in Greater London for other housing accommodation, whether in or outside Greater London, between persons requiring such an exchange and, notwithstanding anything in the Accommodation Agencies Act 1953, may require the payment of a charge by any person making use of those facilities.

23.—(1) On 1st April 1965 there shall vest in the Greater London Council all land which immediately before that date was held by the London county council for the purposes of their functions as a local authority under the Housing Act 1957.

(2) On 1st April 1965 there shall vest in the council of each London borough all land which immediately before that date was held for the purposes of functions as such a local authority as aforesaid—

(*a*) by any council to whom section 3 (1) (*b*) of this Act applies whose area falls wholly within that London borough;

(*b*) in the case of land within the London borough, by the Chigwell urban district council.

(3) The Minister shall if so requested by both the parties concerned, or if so requested by one of those parties may after consultation with the other of those parties, or if he thinks fit after consultation with both parties may without any such request, by order provide for the transfer—

(*a*) from or to the Greater London Council to or from any London borough council or the Common Council of any land for the time being held by the council in question for the purpose of development or redevelopment as housing accommodation; or

(*b*) from the Greater London Council or the council of a London borough to the local authority (not being the Greater London Council) for the purposes of the Housing Act 1957 or to a housing association of any housing accommodation for the time being vested in that council, being, in the case of the council of a London borough, housing accommodation outside that borough;

and any such order shall include such terms as may have been agreed between the two parties concerned or, in default of such agreement, determined by the Minister and provision for arbitration as to the value of the property transferred; and in the case of an order made by virtue of paragraph (*b*) of this subsection—

(i) the said terms may include the retention by the transferor of a right to nominate tenants to the transferred accommodation and, where such a right is retained, provision for the

payment of contributions by the transferor to the transferee; and

(ii) the order shall be subject to annulment in pursuance of a resolution of either House of Parliament.

(4) The Greater London Council shall submit to the Minister by such date, if any, as the Minister may at any time after 1st April 1965 require and in any event by not later than 1st April 1970 a programme for any transfers of housing accommodation vested in that Council such as are mentioned in subsection (3) (*b*) of this section which they propose to make and have not yet made; and the Minister may at any time after 1st April 1965 require any London borough council to submit a similar programme for such transfers of accommodation vested in them.

(5) References in this section to land or housing accommodation shall be construed as including references to any other property held in connection therewith and any rights or liabilities attaching thereto.

(6) Any contributions which the Greater London Council carry to the credit of their Housing Revenue Account under paragraph 1 (5) or (6) of Schedule 5 to the Housing (Financial Provisions) Act 1958 for the year 1965-66 shall be treated as expenditure for special London purposes and be chargeable only on the inner London boroughs, the City and the Temples; and so much of any such contributions for the years hereinafter mentioned shall be treated and chargeable as aforesaid as is necessary to ensure that the amounts in the pound required to be levied for special London purposes and for general London purposes respectively by way of rates in respect of those contributions are as near as may be in the following proportions, that is to say—

(*a*) for the year 1966-67, six to one;

(*b*) for the year 1967-68, five to two;

(*c*) for the year 1968-69, four to three;

(*d*) for the year 1969-70, three to four;

(*e*) for the year 1970-71, two to five;

(*f*) for the year 1971-72, one to six;

and so much of paragraph 5 of the said Schedule 5 as authorises the Greater London Council to apply any surplus shown in their Housing Revenue Account at the end of a financial year towards making good to their general fund any such contributions as aforesaid for earlier years shall not apply to contributions for any year earlier than 1972-73.

Application of Town and Country Planning Act 1962 to Greater London

24.—(1) The provisions of this section shall have effect with respect to the local planning authority for the purposes of the Town and Country Planning Act 1962 (hereafter in this Part of this Act referred to as "the Planning Act") in its application to Greater London.

(2) Subject to subsections (3) and (5) of this section, the Greater London Council shall be the local planning authority for Greater London as a whole.

(3) Subject to subsection (4) of this section and to sections 25 to 29 of this Act, for all purposes of the Planning Act except sections 7 (2), (5) and (6) the local planning authority as respects any London borough shall be the council of the borough and as respects the City shall be the Common Council; and any application under Part III of the Planning Act for planning permission for any development shall be made to, and, subject to the said subsection (4) and section 22 of the Planning Act, shall be determined by, such as may be appropriate of those councils; but, except in any case or class of cases with respect to which the Greater London Council other-

wise direct, each London borough council and the Common Council shall cause a copy of every decision made by them on such an application to be sent to the Greater London Council, together with a copy of the application and such other information relating thereto and to the decision as the Greater London Council may reasonably require.

(4) In relation to development of such a class in such area of Greater London as the Minister may by regulations prescribe the Greater London Council shall be the local planning authority for all relevant purposes of the Planning Act other than the reception of applications for, or with respect to the need for, planning permission for such development, and accordingly, subject to subsection (5) of this section, the council by whom there is received—

(a) any application for planning permission for such development; or

(b) any application under section 43 of the Planning Act in the case of which it appears to that council that the proposed action to which the application relates would constitute or involve such development if it constituted or involved development at all,

shall forward the application to the Greater London Council, who shall deal with it in like manner as if it had been made to them; and such development of land in such an area by the Greater London Council shall be deemed for the purposes of sections 42 (1) and 66 of that Act to be development by that Council of land in respect of which they are the local planning authority; but, without prejudice to the said subsection (5), the Greater London Council may in any particular case by instrument in writing authorise a London borough council or the Common Council to discharge on their behalf any functions under sections 45 to 51 of that Act with respect to such development of land in such an area.

(5) Section 5 (1) of this Act shall not apply to any functions of the Greater London Council under the Planning Act or under or by virtue of sections 24 to 29 of this Act, but the Greater London Council may with the consent of the Minister, and shall if so required by the Minister, delegate to the council of a London borough or the Common Council any of those functions so far as exercisable in that borough or, as the case may be, in the City, and any council to whom functions are so delegated shall perform those functions on behalf of the Greater London Council.

(6) Without prejudice to his powers by virtue of section 19 (2) or 22 of the Planning Act, the Minister may by regulations make with respect to applications for planning permission for development in Greater London provision for particular applications or applications of a particular class to be referred before they are dealt with by the local planning authority—

(a) in the case of an application falling to be dealt with by the Greater London Council, to the Minister;

(b) in the case of an application falling to be dealt with by a London borough council or the Common Council—

(i) to the Greater London Council; or

(ii) in such cases as the regulations may prescribe, to the Minister;

(c) in the case of an application referred to the Greater London Council by virtue of paragraph (b)(i) of this subsection, to the Minister,

and for the giving to the referring council by the Greater London Council or, as the case may be, the Minister of directions as to the manner in which the application is to be dealt with; and in particular the Minister shall make regulations under this subsection with respect to any application which the local planning authority consider should be granted for permission for development inconsistent with the Greater London development plan referred to in section 25 (3) (or, as respects any period before that plan becomes operative, with the initial development plan referred to in section 25 (2)) of this Act.

(7) The Greater London Council may agree with a London borough council or the Common Council for the transfer to the borough council or Common Council of any liability of the Greater London Council to pay compensation under the Planning Act in respect of anything done by the borough council or Common Council in the exercise of functions delegated to them under subsection (5) of this section and for the transfer of any officers of any of those councils; and any such agreement shall include provisions in accordance with section 85(3) of this Act for the protection of the interests of such officers.

(8) In relation to land in a London borough or the City—

(a) references to local planning authorities in any of the following enactments, that is to say—

(i) sections 33 and 34 of, and Schedule 2 to, the Electricity Act 1957;

(ii) section 108 of, and Schedule 12 to, the Highways Act 1959;

(iii) Schedule 1 to the Pipe-lines Act 1962,

shall be construed as including references to the Greater London Council but not to the borough council or the Common Council;

(b) the reference in section 86(4) of the Transport Act 1962 to the local planning authority to whom application is made for permission for the development in question shall be construed as a reference to the local planning authority by whom that application falls to be dealt with;

(c) references in section 3(2) of the Acquisition of Land (Authorisation Procedure) Act 1946 to the local planning authority shall be construed as including references both to the Greater London Council and to the borough council or, as the case may be, the Common Council;

(d) any reference in section 17 or 20 of the Caravan Sites and Control of Development Act 1960 to the local planning authority shall be construed as a reference to the borough council or, as the case may be, the Common Council;

(e) any reference in Part III of the Land Compensation Act 1961 to the local planning authority shall be construed as a reference to the borough council or, as the case may be, the Common Council; but that council shall consult with the Greater London Council before issuing a certificate under section 17 of that Act in any case where an application for planning permission for any development to which the certificate would relate would fall to be dealt with by the Greater London Council.

(9) The Greater London Council may direct that any expenses incurred by them under any of the provisions specified in paragraph 1 of Schedule 8 to the Planning Act or by virtue of sections 24 to 29 of this Act shall be treated as expenses for special London purposes chargeable upon such part of Greater London as may be specified in the direction.

25.—(1) In the application of the Planning Act to Greater London, sections 4 (1) and (5) and 6 (1) and (2) (which relate to the submission or amendment of development plans) shall not apply but the provisions of this and the next following section shall have effect in place thereof.

(2) Subject to the provisions of any order under section 84

of this Act, any development plans under the Planning Act operative on 31st March 1965 which relate, or so far as they relate, to any part of Greater London shall together constitute as from 1st April 1965 the initial development plan for Greater London.

(3) The Greater London Council shall cause to be carried out a survey of Greater London and shall, within such period as the Minister may allow, submit to the Minister a report of that survey and a general development plan for Greater London, to be known as the Greater London development plan, which, subject to any regulations made (by virtue of section 27 (5) (e) of this Act) under section 10 of the Planning Act, shall lay down considerations of general policy with respect to the use of land in the various parts of Greater London, including in particular guidance as to the future road system, and may make any necessary consequential modifications in the initial development plan aforesaid; and as from the date when the Greater London development plan becomes operative, that plan and the initial development plan aforesaid with any modifications therein made by the Greater London development plan shall together constitute the interim development plan for Greater London.

(4) Within such period as the Minister may allow after the Greater London development plan becomes operative, each London borough council shall as respects their borough, and the Common Council shall as respects the City, carry out on behalf of the Greater London Council such further survey, if any, as the borough council or Common Council may consider necessary or as the Greater London Council may direct, and submit to the Greater London Council a report on any such further survey and a local development plan which, subject to any such regulations as aforesaid, shall restate as respects the borough or, as the case may be, the City the relevant provisions of the initial development plan aforesaid as modified by the Greater London development plan with any alterations and additions appearing to them necessary or expedient which are consistent with the Greater London development plan; and, without prejudice to section 27 (1) of this Act, the Greater London Council shall within such further period as the Minister may allow forward any such reports and those local development plans to the Minister with any observations thereon by that Council.

(5) The development plan for the purposes of the Planning Act for any London borough or, as the case may be, the City shall be the following, as amended from time to time by virtue of any provision of the two next following sections, that is to say—

(a) as from 1st April 1965 until the Greater London development plan becomes operative, the relevant provisions of the initial development plan aforesaid;

(b) as from the date when the Greater London development plan becomes operative until the date when the local development plan submitted by the borough council or Common Council becomes operative, the relevant provisions of the interim development plan aforesaid;

(c) as from the date when the said local development plan becomes operative, that plan together with the Greater London development plan;

and accordingly section 101 (5) of the Planning Act shall not apply to Greater London.

26.—(1) The Greater London Council shall from time to time cause fresh surveys of Greater London to be carried out and, not less than once in every five years after the approval of the Greater London development plan by the Minister, submit to the Minister a report of any such surveys together with proposals for any alterations or additions to that plan which appear to that Council to be required having regard to those surveys.

(2) Without prejudice to the provisions of the foregoing subsection, the Greater London Council may at any time, and shall at any time when so directed by the Minister, submit to the Minister proposals for such alterations or additions as appear to the Council to be expedient or as may be required by that direction—

(a) in the case of proposals made before the date of the Minister's approval of the Greater London development plan, to the initial development plan referred to in section 25 (2) of this Act; or

(b) in the case of proposals made after that date, to the Greater London development plan.

(3) After the Greater London development plan has become operative, the council of any London borough or the Common Council may at any time, and shall at any time when so directed by the Minister or, with the approval of the Minister, by the Greater London Council, after carrying on behalf of the Greater London Council such, if any, fresh survey of the borough or, as the case may be, the City as may appear to the borough council or Common Council to be expedient or as may be required by that direction, submit to the Greater London Council proposals for such alterations or additions as may appear expedient or as may be so required—

(a) in the case of proposals made before the date of the Minister's approval of their local development plan under section 25 (4) of this Act, to the initial development plan aforesaid as modified by the Greater London development plan; or

(b) in the case of proposals made after that date, to that local development plan;

and, without prejudice to section 27 (1) of this Act, the Greater London Council shall, within such time as the Minister may allow, forward any such proposals to the Minister together with any observations thereon by that Council.

27.—(1) If any local development plan submitted to the Greater London Council under section 25 (4) of this Act, or any proposal so submitted under section 26 (3) of this Act, contains any provision which in the opinion of the Greater London Council involves a departure from the Greater London development plan, that Council may, if they think fit, require the council submitting the plan or proposal to reconsider that provision within such period as may be specified in the requirement, and thereupon—

(a) unless within the period so specified the submitting council agree that the provision involves such a departure, the question shall be referred to the Minister for decision;

(b) if the submitting council agree as aforesaid, or if on such a reference to the Minister the Minister decides that the provision involves such a departure, the Greater London Council may if they think fit cause that provision to be struck out from the local development plan or proposal for the purpose of its consideration by the Minister;

(c) if on such a reference to the Minister the Minister decides that the provision does not involve such a departure, the provision shall be included in the local development plan or proposal for the purpose of its consideration by the Minister, but the Minister, if so required by the Greater London Council, shall afford that Council an opportunity to make further observations thereon.

(2) Any survey under section 25 (3) or 26 (1) of this Act shall, unless for special reasons the Greater London Council decide to carry it out themselves, be carried out on behalf of that Council by the London borough councils and the Common Council as respects their respective areas; and subject to subsection (6) of this section any such survey and any survey under section 25 (4) or 26 (3) of this Act shall be carried out on such lines as the Greater London Council may direct.

(3) The Greater London Council, before preparing the Greater London development plan or any proposals under section 26 (1) or (2) of this Act, shall consult with the London borough councils and the Common Council or, in the case of any such proposals, with such of those councils as are affected by the proposals, and before submitting the plan or proposals to the Minister shall give to each of those councils an opportunity to make representations with respect to the plan or proposals and shall consider any representations so made.

(4) A London borough council or the Common Council—

(a) when preparing their local development plan under section 25(4) or any proposal under section 26(3) of this Act shall give to the Greater London Council any information which that Council may require with respect to the matters to be included in that plan or proposal; and

(b) before submitting that plan or proposal to the Greater London Council shall give that Council an opportunity to make representations in the light of that information and shall consider any representations so made.

(5) The following provisions of Part II of the Planning Act, that is to say—

(a) section 4 (2), (3) and (4) (which relate to the contents of development plans);

(b) section 5 (which relates to the approval of development plans by the Minister);

(c) section 6 (3) and (4) (which relate to proposals for amendments to development plans);

(d) section 7 (which confers additional powers on the Minister with respect to development plans);

(e) section 10 (2), (3) and (5) (which contain supplementary provisions as to development plans);

(f) section 11 (which relates to the publication and date of operation of development plans),

shall apply for the purposes of sections 25 and 26 of this Act with the modifications specified in subsection (7) of this section as if any report or plan submitted or forwarded under section 25 (3) or (4) of this Act were a report or plan submitted under section 4 (1) of that Act and any report or proposal submitted or forwarded under section 26 of this Act were a report or proposal submitted under section 6 of that Act.

(6) Section 10(4) of the Planning Act shall not apply to Greater London but, subject to any express provision contained in or having effect by virtue of this or either of the two last foregoing sections, the Minister may give directions—

(a) to the Greater London Council with respect to the form and content of any directions by the Greater London Council under subsection (2) of this section;

(b) to that Council, to any London borough council and to the Common Council—

(i) with respect to the procedure for the carrying out of the functions exercisable under or by virtue of those sections by any of those councils; and

(ii) with respect to the furnishing to the Minister

by those councils of information required for the purpose of the functions exercisable under or by virtue of those sections by the Minister.

(7) In the application by virtue of subsection (5) of this section of the provisions of the Planning Act hereinafter mentioned—

(a) any reference in section 4 (3) or (4) to the opinion of the local planning authority shall be construed as a reference to the opinion of either the Greater London Council or the council of the London borough in which the land in question is situated (or, if it is situated in the City, the Common Council);

(b) the reference in section 7 (1) (b) to the local planning authority shall be construed as a reference to any of the following councils, that is to say, the Greater London Council, the London borough councils and the Common Council, by whom there fall to be taken the steps necessary to enable the plan, report or proposal in question to be submitted within the period in question;

(c) the reference in section 7 (4) to the preceding provisions of Part II of the Planning Act shall be construed as including a reference to the provisions of sections 25 and 26 of this Act and subsections (1) to (4) of this section;

(d) any reference in section 10 (2), (3) or (5) to objections or representations shall be construed as a reference only to objections or representations arising from—

(i) any addition, modification or alteration to the initial development plan referred to in section 25 (2) of this Act which is proposed to be effected by the Greater London development plan or which is proposed under section 26 (2) (a) of this Act;

(ii) any addition or alteration to the initial development plan aforesaid as modified by the Greater London development plan which is proposed to be effected by any local development plan forwarded to the Minister under section 25 (4) of this Act or which is proposed under section 26 (3) (a) thereof;

(iii) any alteration or addition to the Greater London development plan proposed under section 26 (1) or (2) (b) of this Act;

(iv) any alteration or addition to such a local development plan as aforesaid proposed under section 26 (3) (b) of this Act;

(e) the reference in section 11 (1) to the local planning authority shall be construed—

(i) in relation to any amendment of the initial development plan aforesaid made before the Greater London development plan becomes operative or made by the Greater London development plan, as a reference to the Greater London Council;

(ii) in relation to any amendment of the provisions with respect to any London borough or the City of the initial development plan aforesaid as modified by the Greater London development plan, as a reference to the council of that borough or, as the case may be, the Common Council;

(iii) in relation to the Greater London development plan, as a reference to the Greater

London Council;

(iv) in relation to a local development plan under section 25 (4) of this Act, as a reference to the council of the London borough in question or, as the case may be, the Common Council.

28.—(1) The Minister shall cause a copy, certified by or on his behalf to be a true copy, of so much of, and of any amendment to, any list of buildings of special architectural or historic interest compiled or approved by him under section 32 of the Planning Act as relates to any London borough or the City to be deposited—

(a) with the clerk of the borough council or, as the case may be, the town clerk of the City; and

(b) with the clerk to the Greater London Council,

and any such copy shall be so deposited, in the case of a list compiled or approved or amendment made before 1st April 1965, as soon as may be after that date or, in any other case, as soon as may be after the list has been compiled or approved or the amendment has been made; and any such copy deposited with the clerk of a London borough council or the town clerk of the City shall be registered in the register of local land charges in such manner as may be prescribed by rules made for the purposes of the said section 32 under section 15 (6) of the Land Charges Act 1925 by the proper officer so prescribed:

Provided that nothing in this subsection shall require the deposit with the town clerk of the City of a further copy of any document so deposited before 1st April 1965.

(2) As respects buildings in Greater London—

(a) any reference to a local planning authority in section 30 of the Planning Act (which relates to building preservation orders) or in section 62 or 125 of that Act so far as it relates to such orders shall be construed as including a reference to the Greater London Council;

(b) except in any case or class of cases with respect to which the Greater London Council otherwise direct, each London borough council and the Common Council shall supply the Greater London Council with copies of any notices received by the borough council or Common Council under section 33 of that Act;

(c) any reference in sections 52 to 55 of that Act to the local planning authority shall be construed as including a reference to the Greater London Council;

(d) section 69 of that Act shall have effect as if Greater London were a county and the Greater London Council were the council of that county and as if the London boroughs and the City were county boroughs and, in the case of the City, the Common Council were the council of that county borough.

(3) In section 33 (3) of the Planning Act, for the words from "to the Minister" onwards there shall be substituted the words—

"(a) to the Minister; and

(b) if the building to which the notice relates is situated in a county district, to the council of that district; and

(c) to such other persons or bodies of persons as may be specified by directions of the Minister either generally or with respect to the building in question."

29.—(1) In the application to Greater London of the following provisions of the Planning Act, that is to say, sections

68 (1), 71, 74, 75 (7), 112 (4) and (5), 129 (1), 135 (1), 136 (1) and 207 (5), any reference therein to a county borough or the council thereof shall be construed as including a reference to a London borough or the council thereof and to the City or the Common Council, as the case may be.

(2) Where under section 68 (1) of the Planning Act the Minister has power to authorise a London borough council or the Common Council to acquire any land compulsorily, he may, if after consultation with that council and with the Greater London Council he thinks it expedient so to do, authorise the land to be so acquired by the Greater London Council instead of the borough council or Common Council, and in that case shall have the like powers under section 207 (5) of that Act in relation to the Greater London Council as in relation to the borough council or Common Council.

(3) The powers conferred on London borough councils and the Common Council by section 71 of the Planning Act shall be exercisable also by the Greater London Council—

(a) in a London borough, with the consent of the council of the borough; or

(b) in the City, with the consent of the Common Council; or

(c) in the Inner Temple or the Middle Temple, with the consent of the Sub-Treasurer or, as the case may be, Under-Treasurer thereof; or

(d) in any of the areas aforesaid, if the appropriate consent aforesaid is withheld, with the consent of the Minister; or

(e) in relation to land in any of the areas aforesaid, without any such consent as aforesaid, if the land is used for the purposes of an industrial or commercial undertaking and is to be acquired incidentally to the removal of that undertaking from Greater London.

(4) In section 154 (7) of the Planning Act (which defines the expression "local authority" for the purposes of certain orders relating to highways) after the words "rural district" there shall be inserted the words "the Greater London Council, the council of a London borough, the Common Council of the City of London".

(5) In section 221 (1) of the Planning Act, in the definition of "local authority" for the words "and any other authority being" there shall be substituted the words "the Greater London Council, the council of a London borough and any other authority (except the Receiver for the Metropolitan Police District) who are".

(6) For the purposes of sections 8, 86 (5), 178 (1) and (2), 179, 189 (2), 199, 211 (1) (a) and 217 (2) of the Planning Act, the provisions of sections 24 to 29 of this Act shall be deemed to be included in that Act and, in the case of sections 25 to 27 of this Act, to be included in Part II of that Act.

(7) In paragraph 6 (1) of Schedule 11 to the Planning Act, after the words "that council" there shall be inserted the words "or by the Greater London Council in relation to any road for the time being designated by or under section 17 of the London Government Act 1963 as a metropolitan road".

Part IV

EDUCATION AND YOUTH EMPLOYMENT SERVICE

30.—(1) As from 1st April 1965, any reference in the Education Acts 1944 to 1962 or in any other Act to the local education authority shall be construed—

(a) in relation to any outer London borough, as a reference to the council of that borough;

(b) subject to subsections (6) and (7) of this section, in

154

relation to the remainder of Greater London (which remainder shall be known as the Inner London Education Area) as a reference to the Greater London Council acting by means of a special committee thereof constituted as mentioned in subsection (2) of this section;

and the Greater London Council, when acting as aforesaid as the local education authority for the said Area, shall, except for the purposes of any document of title, be known as the Inner London Education Authority, and any reference in this or any other Act to a member or officer of that Authority or, in relation to that Authority, to a member or officer of a local education authority shall be construed as a reference to a member of the special committee aforesaid or, as the case may be, an officer appointed for the purposes of the functions of the Greater London Council as a local education authority.

(2) The special committee aforesaid shall consist of—

(a) such of the councillors of the Greater London Council as have been elected by local government electors for an inner London borough or the City;

(b) one representative of each inner London borough council appointed by that borough council from among the members thereof;

(c) one representative of the Common Council appointed by the Common Council from among the members thereof;

and any person appointed in pursuance of paragraph (b) or (c) of this subsection shall, unless re-appointed, retire on the fourteenth day after the ordinary day of retirement of London borough councillors falling next after his appointment, but may resign his membership of the Inner London Education Authority at any time by notice in writing to the clerk of the council by whom he was appointed thereto.

(3) The Greater London Council shall not act by means of the special committee aforesaid for the purpose of issuing any precept or borrowing any money, but shall so act for the purpose of determining—

(a) the amount for which the Council are to precept upon rating authorities in the Inner London Education Area in respect of expenditure of the Inner London Education Authority; and

(b) what amount, if any, is to be borrowed by the Council in respect of such expenditure,

and for the purpose of the making of the arrangements for the handling of receipts and payments required by section 58 of the Local Government Act 1958 so far as those arrangements relate to moneys paid or payable in connection with the functions of the Greater London Council as a local education authority, and shall also so act for the purpose of the appointment of any officer employed solely for the purposes of those functions, and in particular the appointment of the officer referred to in subsection (4) of this section.

(4) The officers to be appointed by the Greater London Council under paragraph 12 of Schedule 2 to this Act shall include a chief education officer of the Inner London Education Authority; and section 88 of the Education Act 1944 shall apply to the appointment of that officer as it applies to the appointment of any similar officer under the Local Government Act 1933.

(5) Part II of Schedule 1 to the Education Act 1944 shall have effect in its application to the Inner London Education Area as if—

(a) paragraph 7 from "or has been" onwards and paragraph 11 were omitted;

(b) in paragraph 8, the reference to the power to borrow money or to raise a rate included a reference to the power to make such a determination as is referred to in subsection (3) of this section;

and Part III of the said Schedule 1 (which relates to the delegation of functions of local education authorities to divisional executives) shall not apply to Greater London.

(6) The Minister of Education shall carry out, and not later than 31st March 1970 lay before Parliament a report on, a review of the administration of education in the Inner London Education Area for the purpose of determining whether, and if so to what extent, in what part or parts of that Area, and subject to what, if any, conditions, all or any of the functions of the local education authority relating to education should be transferred to, or to a body including a member or members appointed by, the appropriate council, that is to say, as respects the City the Common Council or as respects an inner London borough the council of that borough; and in the light of that review the Minister of Education may by regulations make provision for such a transfer as aforesaid of such of those functions, in such part of the Area aforesaid, and subject to such conditions, if any, as may be specified in the regulations; but no such regulations shall be made unless a draft thereof has been laid before, and approved by a resolution of, each House of Parliament.

(7) Any regulations under subsection (6) of this section may include such incidental, consequential, transitional or supplementary provisions, including in particular provisions with respect to finance, the transfer and management or custody of property (whether real or personal) and the transfer of liabilities (but, without prejudice to sections 84(1) and 85 of this Act, excluding provisions with respect to the transfer of officers), as may appear to the Minister of Education to be necessary or proper for the purpose or in consequence of the regulations; and where any such regulations provide as respects any part of the Inner London Education Area for the transfer of all the functions of the local education authority relating to education to some authority other than the Inner London Education Authority, the regulations may also provide for that other authority to become, and for the Inner London Education Authority to cease to be, the local education authority for that part of that Area for the purposes of all enactments except (without prejudice to section 34 (4) of this Act) section 10 of the Employment and Training Act 1948.

(8) In section 97 of the Children and Young Persons Act 1933, in proviso (b), for the words "London County Council as local authority" there shall be substituted the words "local education authority".

31.—(1) For the purposes of the Education Acts 1944 to 1962—

(a) the development plan under section 11 of the Education Act 1944 in force for the county of London immediately before 1st April 1965, so far as it relates to the Inner London Education Area, shall continue on and after that date to be the development plan approved by the Minister of Education for that Area;

(b) until replaced by a revised development plan submitted to and approved by the said Minister under subsection (2) of this section, any development plan under the said section 11 in force immediately before 1st April 1965 which relates, or so far as it relates, to the area of any outer London borough shall, or, if more than one, shall together, constitute as from that date the development plan approved by the said Minister for that borough;

(c) subject to subsection (4) of this section, any scheme of further education under section 42 of the said Act of 1944 in force immediately before 1st April 1965 which relates, or so far as it relates, to the Inner London Education Area or to the area of any outer London borough, shall, or, if more than one, shall together, continue to be, or, as the case may be, constitute, on and after that date the scheme of further education approved by the Minister of Education under the said section 42 for that Education Area or, as the case may be, that borough.

(2) The council of each outer London borough shall, by 1st April 1966 or within such period thereafter as the Minister of Education may in any particular case allow, prepare and submit to that Minister a revised development plan for the borough for the purposes of the said Acts of 1944 to 1962 which shall be in such form and contain such particulars with respect to existing primary and secondary schools in their area and as to the action the authority propose to take to secure that there shall be sufficient schools available for their area as that Minister may require; and subsections (3) to (5) of section 11 of the said Act of 1944 shall apply to any revised development plan submitted under this subsection as they apply to a development plan submitted under subsection (1) of that section.

(3) Before preparing a revised development plan for their borough under subsection (2) of this section, the council of each outer London borough shall consult with any other local education authority whose area is contiguous with that borough with a view to ensuring that the revised plan has regard both to the use made of schools outside that borough by children resident therein and to the use of schools within that borough by children resident outside it.

(4) Within such period as the Minister of Education may allow, the council of each outer London borough shall for the purposes of section 42 of the said Act of 1944 submit to that Minister a restatement of the scheme or schemes of further education referred to in subsection (1) (c) of this section so far as relating to that borough; and that restatement when submitted to that Minister shall be deemed for the purposes of the said section 42 to be a scheme of further education which has been submitted to that Minister under subsection (1) of that section.

(5) As from 1st April 1965 it shall be the duty of the local education authority for any area in Greater London to maintain, and that authority shall not except in accordance with section 13 or 14 of the said Act of 1944 or subsection (6) of this section cease to maintain, any county or voluntary school maintained immediately before that date by the former local education authority for that area, being a school which is situated in that area or of which that former local education authority were, or in case of dispute are determined by the Minister of Education to have been, the main user immediately before that date.

(6) Any authority who by virtue of section 30(1) of this Act are, or are to become, the local education authority for any area in Greater London may agree with any other local education authority for the maintenance by that other authority of any school which under subsection (5) of this section would otherwise fall to be maintained by the first-mentioned authority.

(7) In the case of any school maintained immediately before 1st April 1965 by a local education authority who in consequence of this Act will not continue to maintain it on and after that date—

    (a) any instrument or rules of management or instru-

ment or articles of government made by an order under section 17 of the said Act of 1944 and any arrangement made under section 20 of that Act, being an order or arrangement in force immediately before that date, shall continue in force on and after that date, subject to any further such order or arrangement and to any agreement under subsection (6) of this section, as if—

    (i) any reference therein to that local education authority were a reference to the authority by whom by virtue of subsection (5) or (6) of this section the school falls to be maintained on and after that date or, if there is no such authority or if there is any doubt as to the identy of that authority, such local education authority as the Minister of Education may direct;

    (ii) any reference therein to any other existing local authority, being the council of a metropolitan borough, non-county borough or urban district to whom section 3 (1) (b) of this Act applies, were a reference, if the school falls to be maintained by the council of a borough, to that council or, in any other case, to the council of the London borough which includes the area of that existing authority or, if different parts of that area are included in different London boroughs, the council of such of those boroughs (or, if more than one, the councils thereof acting jointly) as appears to the local education authority to be served by the school;

    (b) any direction of the local education authority under section 22 of the said Act of 1944 and any agreed syllabus of religious instruction under section 29 of that Act, being a direction or syllabus in force immediately before that date, shall continue in force on and after that date until replaced by a further direction under the said section 22 or, as the case may be, by the adoption of a new syllabus under the said section 29.

(8) For the purposes of any duty imposed by or under the Education Acts 1944 to 1962 or section 3 (4) of the Local Government Act 1958 with respect to the admission of pupils to—

    (a) county or voluntary schools; or

    (b) institutions maintained or assisted by local education authorities for the purpose of providing further education,

it shall not be a ground for refusing a pupil admission to, or excluding a pupil from, any such school or institution maintained or assisted by a local education authority in Greater London that the pupil resides in the area of some other local education authority if that area is within, or is contiguous with any part of, Greater London; and where any provision for further education is made by a local education authority in Greater London in respect of a pupil who resides in Greater London, or in some other local education authority's area which is contiguous with any part of Greater London, but belongs to the area of a local education authority other than the providing authority, and the Minister of Education is satisfied that, having regard to all the circumstances of the case, it is right so to do, that Minister may on the application of the providing authority direct that section 7(1) of the Education (Miscellaneous Provisions) Act 1953 (which relates to the recoupment of the providing authority by the authority to whose area the pupil belongs) shall apply notwithstanding that the last-mentioned authority have not consented to the making of the provision.

(9) Section 7(4) and (5) of the Education (Miscellaneous

Provisions) Act 1953 (which relate to the determination of the local education authority to whose area any pupil belongs for the purposes of further education) shall apply for the purposes of subsection (8) of this section as they apply for the purposes of the said section 7.

(10) In relation to any school maintained by the Inner London Education Authority, the expression "minor authority" in the said Act of 1944 shall be construed as a reference to any of the following councils whose area appears to that Authority to be served by the school, that is to say, the councils of the inner London boroughs and the Common Council; and before approving any proposals submitted to him under section 13 of the said Act of 1944 with respect to any school which is, or is to be, situated within the City or an inner London borough, the Minister of Education shall afford to the Common Council or, as the case may be, the borough council, an opportunity of making representations to him with respect to the proposal.

32.—(1) The Inner London Education Authority and each respectively of the following councils, that is to say, the councils of the inner London boroughs and the Common Council, shall as soon as may be jointly prepare and submit to the Minister of Education and the Minister of Health for their approval a scheme with respect to—

(a) the joint use of professional staff, premises and equipment for the purposes of the health services falling to be provided by the local education authority and the local health authority respectively; and

(b) consultation as to the qualifications, experience, conditions of service and appointment of professional staff concerned with both those health services.

(2) If in the case of any of the councils aforesaid no such scheme as aforesaid has been submitted to the Ministers aforesaid under the foregoing subsection within such period as those Ministers think reasonable, those Ministers may themselves prepare such a scheme with respect to that council.

(3) In the case of any of the councils aforesaid—

(a) the Inner London Education Authority and the council concerned may from time to time jointly prepare and submit to the Ministers aforesaid for their approval, or

(b) the Ministers aforesaid may from time to time, after consultation with the said Authority and council, themselves prepare,

a further scheme with respect to the matters mentioned in subsection (1) of this section, and any such further scheme may vary or revoke any scheme under subsection (1) or (2) of this section and any previous scheme under this subsection.

(4) The Ministers aforesaid shall act jointly for the purpose of approving any scheme submitted to them under subsection (1) or (3) (a) of this section and may approve the scheme either without modification or with such modifications as, after consultation with the Inner London Education Authority and the council concerned, they consider necessary or expedient; and after the scheme has been so approved, then, while that scheme remains in force, no professional staff to whom the scheme applies shall be appointed or employed except in accordance therewith.

(5) The Ministers aforesaid shall act jointly for the purpose of themselves preparing any scheme under subsection (2) or (3) (b) of this section, and the Inner London Education Authority and the council concerned shall comply with any such scheme while it remains in force.

(6) In this section the expression "professional staff" in relation to any scheme thereunder means medical officers, dental officers, nurses, health visitors and such other specialist staff as may be specified in that scheme.

(7) In its application to the Inner London Education Authority, section 54 (4) of the Education Act 1944 shall have effect as if for the words "the council of any county district in the area of the authority" there were substituted the words "the council of any inner London borough or the Common Council of the City of London".

33.—(1) Where, in the case of any grant made before 1st April 1965 under section 50, 61 (2) or 81 of the Education Act 1944, section 6 of the Education (Miscellaneous Provisions) Act 1953 or section 1 or 2 of the Education Act 1962 in respect of a pupil who has not completed his course by that date, the local education authority by whom that grant was made—

(a) cease on that date in consequence of this Act to be a local education authority; or

(b) if the authority's area at the date of the making of the grant had been the same as on 1st April 1965, would not have been the appropriate authority to make it,

it shall on and after 1st April 1965 be the duty of the authority specified in subsection (2) of this section to make the remaining payments in pursuance of that grant, subject to the same conditions, if any, as to satisfactory work, financial need or other matters as were attached to the grant or as would be attached to such a grant by the authority specified as aforesaid, whichever are the most favourable.

(2) The authority referred to in the foregoing subsection shall be—

(a) the local education authority to whose area the pupil would have belonged (or, in the case of an award under section 1 of the Education Act 1962, in whose area he would have been ordinarily resident) at the date immediately before the grant was made if at that date the changes taking place under Parts I and IV of this Act on 1st April 1965 had already taken place; or

(b) if there is no local education authority to whose area the pupil would have belonged (or, as the case may be, in whose area he would have been ordinarily resident) as aforesaid, then, without prejudice to any right to recoupment, such local education authority as the Minister of Education may determine;

and section 6 (2) to (4) of the Education (Miscellaneous Provisions) Act 1948 or section 7 (4) and (5) of the Education (Miscellaneous Provisions) Act 1953 (which relate to the determination of the local education authority to whose area any pupil belongs for the purposes of primary or secondary education or, as the case may be, further education) or Schedule 1 to the said Act of 1962 (which relates to the determination of ordinary residence for the purposes of the said section 1), as the case may be, shall apply for the purposes of this subsection as they apply for the purposes of the said Act of 1948, the said section 7 or the said section 1, as the case may be.

34.—(1) Subject to the provisions of this section, as from 1st April 1965 the local education authority for any area in Greater London shall undertake in that area, in accordance (subject to any necessary modification thereof in consequence of this Act) with any scheme in force immediately before that date under section 10 of the Employment and Training Act 1948 which relates, or so far as it relates, to that area, the functions with respect to the youth employment service to which the scheme relates; and for the purposes of any such modification as aforesaid the powers of the Minister of Labour upon the failure of the local education authority to comply with any direction with respect to the amendment of that scheme given by that Minister under section 12 (2) of the said Act of 1948 shall include power by a further direction to amend the scheme himself.

(2) If before 1st January 1966 any authority who by virtue of section 30 (1) of this Act are, or are to become, the local education authority for any area in Greater London give notice in writing to the Minister of Labour that they wish this subsection to have effect, any such scheme as aforesaid, so far as it relates to that area, shall cease to be in force as from such date as that Minister may determine.

(3) Any such authority as are mentioned in the last foregoing subsection who have not given such notice as is so mentioned shall, within such period as the Minister of Labour may allow, submit to that Minister for his approval under the said section 10 a revised scheme for the purposes of that section, and any such revised scheme shall be deemed for the purposes of the said Act of 1948 to be such an amending scheme as is mentioned in section 12 (1) of that Act.

(4) Unless notice in respect of the Inner London Education Area has been given under subsection (2) of this section, the Minister of Labour shall, in conjunction with the review to be carried out by the Minister of Education under section 30 (6) of this Act, carry out, and not later than 31st March 1970 lay before Parliament a report on, a review of the administration of the youth employment service in that Area for the like purpose as the Minister of Education's review aforesaid and shall have as respects the functions of the local education authority under the said section 10 the like power to make regulations in the light of that review as are conferred by section 30 (6) and (7) of this Act on the Minister of Education as respects that authority's functions relating to education.

(5) In paragraph 1 (b) of Schedule 1 to the said Act of 1948 (which provides for the nomination by certain bodies of members of the National Youth Employment Council), for the words "The London County Council" there shall be substituted the words "The Inner London Education Authority".

Part V

SEWERAGE AND TRADE EFFLUENTS

35.—(1) On 1st April 1965 there shall vest in the Greater London Council all sewers and all sewage disposal works which immediately before that date were vested in the London or Middlesex county council, the Wandle Valley Main Drainage Authority, the North Surrey Joint Sewage Board or the Richmond Main Sewerage Board, and the said Authority and Boards shall cease to exist.

(2) On 1st April 1965 there shall vest—

    (a) in the council of each London borough all sewers and sewage disposal works primarily serving an area in the borough which immediately before that date were vested in the council of a county borough, metropolitan borough or county district the area of which falls wholly or partly within the borough;

    (b) in the council of a London borough all drains in the borough which immediately before that date fell within paragraph (a) or (b) of the definition of "drain" in section 81 (1) of the Public Health (London) Act 1936.

(3) As respects the sewerage area of the Greater London Council—

    (a) the provision of main sewers and of sewage dis-

posal works shall be the function of the Greater London Council; and

    (b) the provision of public sewers other than main sewers shall, as respects a London borough, be the function of the council of the borough and, as respects a county district, be the function of the council of that district;

and any power of the Common Council, the Sub-Treasurer of the Inner Temple or the Under-Treasurer of the Middle Temple to provide sewers (whether conferred by any enactment or otherwise) shall be exercisable subject to paragraph (a) of this subsection.

(4) As respects a London borough which, or a part thereof which, falls outside the sewerage area of the Greater London Council the provision of all public sewers and sewage disposal works shall be the function of the council of the borough; but this subsection shall have effect subject to any enactment or agreement with respect to such sewers and works and subject to the provisions of subsection (9) of this section.

(5) It shall be the duty of the Greater London Council as soon as practicable after 1st April 1965 to take into consideration the public sewers and sewage disposal works primarily serving their sewerage area or (subject to subsection (9) of this section) any part of Greater London not forming part of that area, being sewers or works vested in some other local authority, with a view to determining whether a declaration should be made under this subsection, and if they are satisfied that any such sewer is or should become a main sewer or that any such works should be transferred to them, they shall, subject to the provisions of section 17 (1) and (3) of the Public Health Act 1936 as applied by subsection (7) of this section, declare that that sewer or works shall as from such date as may be specified in the declaration vest in them, giving the requisite notice of their proposal to do so not later that 1st April 1970.

(6) It shall be the duty of the Greater London Council to keep under consideration after 1st April 1970 the sewers and works mentioned in the last foregoing subsection, and if at any time they are satisfied that any such sewer constructed or acquired by any other local authority since that date should become a main sewer or that there has been a change of circumstances since that date affecting any other sewer so mentioned or any works so mentioned which makes it expedient that the sewer or works should be transferred to them, they shall, subject to the provisions of the said section 17(1) and (3), declare that the sewer or works shall as from such date as may be specified in the declaration vest in them.

(7) The following provisions of section 17 of the Public Health Act 1936 (as amended by Schedule 9 to this Act) shall apply to a declaration under this section as they apply to a declaration under subsection (1) of that section, that is to say, subsections (1), (3), (5) and (6); and in deciding on an appeal under that section whether a declaration shall be made under this section, the Minister shall have regard to all the circumstances of the case and in particular to the considerations—

    (a) whether or not the sewer or works in question primarily serves the sewerage area of the Greater London Council or a part of Greater London not forming part of that area; and

    (b) whether or not the sewer in question is or should become a main sewer, or as the case may be, whether or not any machinery, equipment, pumping station, pipe or other thing is or should be used in connection with the works in question.

(8) If any land used for the purposes of a sewage disposal works is vested by virtue of a declaration under this section in

the Greater London Council and subsequently the land ceases to be used for that purpose the Greater London Council shall if so requested by the council in whom it was previously vested reconvey the land to that council on such terms as may be agreed between the two councils or in default of agreement as may be determined by the Minister.

(9) Nothing in this section shall affect any sewer, sewage disposal works or other property, or any powers or duties, of the West Kent Main Sewerage Board.

36.—(1) The expenses incurred by the Greater London Council in the discharge of their functions relating to sewerage and sewage disposal shall be chargeable on the London boroughs and county districts falling wholly or partly within the sewerage area of the Greater London Council and on the City and the Temples, and where part only of such a borough or district falls within the said sewerage area those expenses shall be chargeable only on that part of the borough or district.

(2) The expenses so incurred shall be expenses for special London purposes notwithstanding that those expenses are chargeable on areas outside Greater London; and in relation to those expenses paragraph 19 (2) (*b*) of Schedule 2 to this Act shall have effect as if the reference to part only of Greater London included a reference to the sewerage area of the Greater London Council.

(3) Where any expenses so incurred are by virtue of subsection (1) of this section chargeable on part of a London borough or county district, any expenses incurred by the council of that borough or district in connection with main sewers or sewage disposal works primarily serving another part of the borough or district shall be chargeable only on that other part of the borough or district and, in the case of a rural district, notwithstanding anything in section 6 of the Rural Water Supplies and Sewerage Act 1944, shall not be general expenses.

(4) The foregoing provisions of this section shall have effect subject to section 67 of this Act.

(5) The Greater London Council shall reimburse to the council of a London borough or county district any expenses (including an appropriate proportion of administrative expenses) agreed by the two councils, or in default of agreement determined by the Minister, to have been reasonably incurred by the borough or district council in the discharge of their functions in connection with a main sewer which is vested in the borough or district council and primarily serves the sewerage area of the Greater London Council, and any sums reimbursed by the Greater London Council under this subsection shall be treated as expenses incurred by the Council in the discharge of their functions relating to sewerage and sewage disposal.

37.—(1) The following enactments relating to sewerage, drainage and sewage disposal, that is to say—
  (*a*) the provisions of sections 14 to 42 and 330 of the Public Health Act 1936 and sections 1 (2) and 90 and Part XII of that Act so far as they relate to those provisions;
  (*b*) section 13 of the Local Government (Miscellaneous Provisions) Act 1953; and
  (*c*) sections 12 to 15 of, and Schedule 2 to, the Public Health Act 1961,
shall, subject to the exceptions and modifications specified in Parts I and II of Schedule 9 to this Act, apply to all parts of the sewerage area of the Greater London Council and shall so apply instead of any other enactments in that behalf and, in particular in the case of the inner London boroughs, the City and the Temples, instead of any corresponding provisions contained in Parts II and XIV of the Public Health (London) Act 1936.

(2) The provisions of Part III of the said Schedule 9 shall, except so far as the contrary intention appears, have effect in all parts of the sewerage area of the Greater London Council (being provisions reproducing, with modifications designed amongst other things to enable them to operate in that area or to bring them into conformity with this Act or the enactments mentioned in the foregoing subsection, provisions of Part II of the Public Health (London) Act 1936 and other enactments relating to sewerage, sewage disposal and drainage in the administrative county of London which do not correspond to any enactments mentioned in that subsection but which it is expedient to apply to that area).

(3) The enactments mentioned in subsection (1) of this section shall apply to any part of Greater London outside the sewerage area of the Greater London Council as they apply elsewhere in England and Wales, subject, however, in the case of section 21 of the Public Health Act 1936 to the modifications specified in paragraph 5 of Part II of Schedule 9 to this Act, and accordingly the local authority for the purposes of those enactments in their application to any such part of Greater London shall as respects a London borough be the council of the borough; but the foregoing provision shall not affect the application of any local statutory provision having effect in the district of the West Kent Main Sewerage Board.

(4) Paragraphs 1 and 2 of Part 1 of the said Schedule 9 shall extend outside the sewerage area of the Greater London Council.

38.—(1) On and after 1st April 1965 the following enactments relating to trade effluents, that is to say, the Public Health (Drainage of Trade Premises) Act 1937, Part V of the Public Health Act 1961 and sections 1 (2) and 90 and Part XII of the Public Health Act 1936 so far as they relate to the said Act of 1937 and the said Part V shall, without prejudice to section 37 of this Act but subject to the exceptions and modifications specified in Schedule 10 to this Act, apply to all parts of the sewerage area of the Greater London Council (including the City and the Temples) and to any part of Greater London which does not form part of that area, and shall so apply instead of Part II of the London County Council (General Powers) Act 1953 and Part II of the London County Council (General Powers) Act 1962 in the areas in which the two last mentioned Acts applied immediately before 1st April 1965.

(2) The provision made by an order under section 84 of this Act may include—
  (*a*) provision continuing in force any agreement, condition or liability to pay charges subsisting immediately before 1st April 1965 under Part II of the said Act of 1953 or Part II of the said Act of 1962 notwithstanding that the agreement could not have been made, the condition imposed or the liability incurred under the enactments relating to trade effluents specified in subsection (1) of this section;
  (*b*) provision for varying or revoking any such agreement or condition or varying or abrogating any such liability, in either case to such extent as appears to the Minister to be necessary or proper to effect the transition from the provisions of the said Parts II to the said enactments relating to trade effluents;
  (*c*) provision exempting the owner or occupier of any premises with respect to which any such agreement or condition is in force from compliance with any requirement imposed by or by virtue of the said enactments to obtain the consent of the local authority with respect to all or any of the matters to which

the agreement or condition relates or any other such requirement with respect to all or any of those matters.

39.—(1) In this Part of this Act, except where the context otherwise requires—

    (a) "main sewer" means a public sewer used for the general reception of sewage from other public sewers and not substantially used for the reception of sewage from private sewers and drains;

    (b) "sewerage area of the Greater London Council" means an area defined by an order made by the Minister as being the area drained by the sewers for the time being vested in the Council by virtue of section 35 of this Act and by any other sewers the sewage from which is directly or indirectly discharged into the sewers or sewage disposal works so vested in the Council, exclusive of any area in the district of the West Kent Main Sewerage Board and any area outside Greater London the sewage from which is so discharged in pursuance only of an agreement under section 28 of the Public Health Act 1936;

    (c) any expression which is also used in Part II of the Public Health Act 1936 shall have the same meaning as in the said Part II.

(2) An order under subsection (1) (b) of this section defining the sewerage area of the Greater London Council as constituted on 1st April 1965 shall be made so as to come into force on that date and subsequent orders redefining that area shall be made thereunder as occasion may require.

(3) The Greater London Council shall keep, together with the documents relating to the business of the Council, a map or other document showing the extent for the time being of their sewerage area, and that map or other document shall be open to inspection by members of the public.

(4) Any installation or equipment installed or used for the purpose of treating any overflow of sewage from a sewer caused by an excess of storm water shall be deemed for the purposes of this Part of this Act to form part of that sewer and not to be or form part of a sewage disposal works.

(5) Any dispute between two authorities having functions with respect to sewers as to whether a sewer primarily serving the sewerage area of the Greater London Council is or is not a main sewer or whether or not a sewer or sewage disposal works primarily serves a part of that area or a part of Greater London not forming part of that area (other than a dispute which falls to be determined under section 17 of the Public Health Act 1936) shall in default of agreement be determined by the Minister.

Part VI

APPLICATION OF PUBLIC HEALTH ACTS AND RELATED ACTS

40.—(1) The enactments to which this section applies shall apply or, as the case may be, continue to apply throughout Greater London as they apply elsewhere in England and Wales, but those enactments shall have effect subject to the provisions of subsection (2) of this section and to the modifications specified in Part I of Schedule 11 of this Act.

(2) Subject to any provision to the contrary in the said Part I, and in particular the provisions of the said Part I conferring on the Greater London Council functions with respect to refuse disposal and other matters, the local authority and

the urban sanitary authority for the purposes of the said enactments shall—

    (a) for a London borough, be the council of the borough;

    (b) for the City, be the Common Council; and

    (c) for the Inner Temple and the Middle Temple, be the Sub-Treasurer and the Under-Treasurer thereof respectively.

(3) The provisions of Part II of Schedule 11 to this Act shall have effect in Greater London (being provisions reproducing, with modifications designed to bring them into conformity with this Act or the enactments to which this section applies, certain provisions of the Public Health (London) Act 1936 and certain other enactments having effect only in the administrative county of London).

(4) This section applies to the following enactments:—

    (a) the Public Health Acts 1875 to 1925;

    (b) the Public Health Act 1936;

    (c) the Water Acts 1945 and 1948 and the Water Act 1958;

    (d) sections 8 and 12 of the Local Government (Miscellaneous Provisions) Act 1953;

    (e) the Clean Air Act 1956;

    (f) sections 14 to 18 and 23 of the Mental Health Act 1959;

    (g) the Noise Abatement Act 1960; and

    (h) the Public Health Act 1961:

Provided that this section shall not apply to any enactment applied by or mentioned in section 37, 38, 44 or 58 of, or Schedule 9 or 10 to, this Act, except that it applies to sections 1 (2) and 90 and Part XII of the Public Health Act 1936 so far as relating to other enactments to which this section applies.

41.—(1) For the purposes of the Public Health Act 1936 the Port of London shall be a port health district and the Common Council shall be the port health authority for that district; and the Minister of Health may by order—

    (a) confer on the said authority jurisdiction over all waters within the Port of London and also over the the whole or part of the district of any riparian authority within the meaning of Part I of that Act as amended by subsection (3) of this section;

    (b) assign to the said port health authority any of the functions, rights and liabilities of a local authority under any of the enactments to which section 40 of this Act applies or would apply but for the proviso to subsection (4) of that section and under any provision of Part II of Schedule 11 to this Act or any local statutory provision continued in force by section 87 of this Act and any of the functions, rights and liabilities of a local authority or a food and drugs authority under any provision of the Food and Drugs Act 1955; and

    (c) extend to all waters mentioned in paragraph (a) of this subsection and the whole or part of any district so mentioned any such provision as aforesaid or any instrument made under any such provision, being a provision or instrument which would not otherwise so extend.

(2) In the foregoing subsection the references to a local authority and the district of an authority shall include references respectively to the Greater London Council and, in relation to that Council, Greater London.

(3) Part I of the Public Health Act 1936, so far as it relates to port health districts and authorities, shall have effect subject to the following modifications:—

    (a) references in sections 2 and 4 to a local authority

and the district of an authority shall be construed in accordance with the last foregoing subsection;

(b) no order under the said Part I constituting a port health district shall include any part of the Port of London in that district or confer jurisdiction over any area for the time being subject to the jurisdiction of the port health authority for that port;

(c) section 9 shall apply to any order under subsection (1) of this section as it applies to an order under the said Part I constituting a port health district; and

(d) in Schedule 1, in its application to the Port of London, paragraphs 2 (1) and 3 and, in paragraph 4 (2), the words from "in respect of" to "foregoing paragraph" shall be omitted.

42.—(1) The provisions of sections 106, 108, 110, 115 and 116 of the Local Government Act 1933 relating to medical officers of health and public health inspectors shall apply to the City, the Inner Temple and the Middle Temple, and accordingly in those sections, so far as they apply to such officers and inspectors, references to a borough and to a borough council or a local authority shall be construed as including references to the City, the Inner Temple and the Middle Temple and to the Common Council, the Sub-Treasurer of the Inner Temple and the Under-Treasurer of the Middle Temple respectively.

(2) The provisions of the said sections 106, 115 and 116 relating to medical officers of health and public health inspectors shall also apply to the port health district of the Port of London, and accordingly in those sections, so far as they apply to such officers and inspectors, references to a borough and to a borough council or a local authority shall also be construed as including references to that district and to the port health authority therefor respectively.

43.—(1) Without prejudice to the application to any part of Greater London by section 40 of this Act of any enactments relating to building control and to buildings and structures, but subject to any order under section 84 of this Act, the relevant provisions of the London Building Acts shall continue to have effect in Greater London other than the outer London boroughs, and Part II of the Act of 1939 and any regulations thereunder and any other relevant provisions of the London Building Acts which relate to the said Part II shall, notwithstanding anything in section 4 of the Act of 1930, extend to the outer London boroughs; and—

(a) the Greater London Council shall have the functions of the London county council under all the aforementioned provisions; and

(b) the councils of the inner London boroughs and, in the case of provisions which extend to the outer London boroughs, the councils of the outer London boroughs shall have the functions of metropolitan boroughs under the said provisions.

(2) In accordance with the foregoing subsection, in the relevant provisions of the London Building Acts and any byelaws and regulations made thereunder—

(a) for references to London or the administrative county of London there shall be substituted references to Greater London other than the outer London boroughs;

(b) for references to the London county council there shall be substituted references to the Greater London Council, except that for references to instruments of any description made by, or resolutions of, the London county council there shall be substituted references to instruments of that descrip-

tion made by, or resolutions of, that county council or the Greater London Council;

(c) for references to the council of a metropolitan borough there shall be substituted references to the council of an inner London borough or, in the case of a provision which extends to the outer London boroughs, references to the council of any London borough, and references to a local authority shall be construed accordingly;

(d) for references to the London Building Acts or the provisions of those Acts there shall be substituted references to the relevant provisions of those Acts, and for references to the Act of 1930, 1935 or 1939 (other than references to a specified provision thereof) there shall be substituted references to so much of the said relevant provisions as are contained in that Act.

(3) If the Minister, after consultation with the Greater London Council and any other council concerned, so directs, the Greater London Council shall in the exercise of the power conferred on them by section 5 (1) of this Act delegate such of their functions under the relevant provisions of the London Building Acts as the Minister may specify in the direction.

(4) The expenses incurred by the Greater London Council in the discharge of their functions under the relevant provisions of the London Building Acts which do not extend to the outer London boroughs (including any expenses incurred by the council of an inner London borough or the Common Council as agent for the Greater London Council by virtue of section 5 (1) of this Act) shall be chargeable only on the inner London boroughs and the City.

(5) In this section "the relevant provisions of the London Building Acts" means—

(a) the London Building Acts 1930 to 1939, except the provisions repealed by the next following subsection;

(b) sections 6 and 7 of the London County Council (General Powers) Act 1954, and section 3 of that Act so far as it relates to those sections;

(c) sections 5 to 13 of, and Schedules 1 and 2 to, the London County Council (General Powers) Act 1955, and section 3 of that Act so far as it relates to those sections and Schedules;

(d) section 62 of the London County Council (General Powers) Act 1956; and

(e) sections 15 to 17 of the London County Council (General Powers) Act 1958, and sections 3 and 13 of that Act so far as they relate to the said sections 15 to 17;

and references to the Acts of 1930, 1935 and 1939 shall be construed as references respectively to the London Building Act 1930, the London Building Act (Amendment) Act 1935 and the London Building Acts (Amendment) Act 1939.

(6) The following provisions of the London Building Acts 1930 to 1939 shall cease to have effect, that is to say—

(a) Parts II and III and sections 51 to 53 of the Act of 1930;

(b) section 4 (1) (a) of the Act of 1935;

(c) sections 128 to 131 and 156 of the Act of 1939, and section 148 of that Act so far as it relates to other provisions of the London Building Acts 1930 to 1939 repealed by this subsection.

44.—(1) The council of a London borough shall as respects the borough and the Common Council shall as respects the City be the local authority for the purposes of the Public Health (Interments) Act 1879 and the Cremation Acts 1902 and 1952, and—

(a) the powers conferred by the Burial Acts 1852 to 1906 to provide burial grounds shall not be exercisable by the council of any London borough or the Common Council; and

(b) any burial board constituted for an area wholly within Greater London shall cease to exist on 1st April 1965.

(2) No new cemetery shall be provided in Greater London without the previous approval of the Minister.

(3) Subsection (1) of this section shall not affect the power to make an Order in Council under section 1 of the Burial Act 1853 or section 1 of the Burial Act 1855 with respect to the discontinuance of burials; and—

(a) the power to make any such Order shall, notwithstanding anything in section 5 of the said Act of 1853 (which precludes the exercise of that power in the case of cemeteries provided under any Act of Parliament or with the approval of the Minister), be exercisable in relation to all cemeteries provided in or for an area in Greater London, whether provided by virtue of the Public Health (Interments) Act 1879 or otherwise; and

(b) section 51 of the Burial Act 1852 shall apply to cemeteries in which burials are discontinued by virtue of this subsection as it applies to burial grounds in which interments are discontinued under that Act:

Provided that nothing in any such Order shall prevent the interment of the body of any person in the cathedral church of St. Paul's, London, or in the collegiate church of St. Peter's, Westminster, if Her Majesty signifies Her pleasure that the body be so interred.

(4) In the Burial Acts 1852 to 1906 any reference to the Metropolis shall be construed as a reference to Greater London; and in those Acts in their application to Greater London—

(a) any reference to a parish (not being a reference which is to be taken as a reference to an ecclesiastical parish) shall, without prejudice to section 68 (5) of the Rating and Valuation Act 1925, as amended by paragraph 13 of Schedule 15 to this Act, be construed as a reference to a London borough or the City, as the case may be; and

(b) any reference to a burial board shall be construed as a reference to the council of a London borough or the Common Council, as the case may be.

(5) Notwithstanding anything in section 7 of the Burial Act 1900 and without prejudice to section 3 of the Public Health (Interments) Act 1879, the provisions of sections 27 to 31 of the Cemeteries Clauses Act 1847 shall, so far as applicable, continue to apply to the City of London Cemetery, but the foregoing provisions of this subsection shall not affect the right of the incumbent of any ecclesiastical parish in the City to perform funeral services in respect of his own parishioners.

(6) The provision made by an order under section 84 of this Act may include provision that a burial ground provided under the Burial Acts 1852 to 1906 for any area the whole or part of which is included in a London borough, or a cemetery provided by virtue of the said Act of 1879 for any such area, shall be treated as if it were provided for the whole of that borough or, if the area is included partly in one and partly in another borough, as if it were provided for the whole of one or both of those boroughs.

(7) In this section "cemetery" includes a burial ground or any other place for the interment of the dead.

Part VII

FUNCTIONS AS TO HEALTH AND WELFARE SERVICES AND OTHER MATTERS

45.—(1) Subject to section 19 (2) and (3) of the National Health Service Act 1946 (which relate to joint boards and health committees of local health authorities) and subject to subsection (3) of this section, the local health authority for each London borough shall be the council of that borough and for the City shall be the Common Council.

(2) It shall be the duty of every local health authority in Greater London (so far as concerns the functions conferred or imposed on them by virtue of subsection (1) of this section) to continue to provide for their area on and after 1st April 1965 the services corresponding (with any necessary modifications) with the services which were required or authorised to be provided for that area immediately before that date by the local health authority or authorities for the whole or any part of that area in pursuance of Part III of the said Act of 1946 and of any proposals or arrangements thereunder; and—

(a) any such proposals and arrangements in force immediately before that date shall continue in force accordingly until revoked or modified by further proposals or arrangements under the said Part III;

(b) such further proposals or, as the case may be, particulars of such further arrangements shall be submitted to the Minister of Health by each local health authority in Greater London within such period after 1st April 1965 as that Minister may direct.

(3) In its application to Greater London, section 27 of the said Act of 1946 (which imposes a duty on local health authorities to provide ambulance services) shall have effect as if for any reference to the local health authority there were substituted a reference to the Greater London Council; and so far as concerns the duty imposed on that Council by virtue of this subsection—

(a) subsection (2) of this section shall apply to that Council as it applies, so far as concerns functions conferred or imposed by virtue of subsection (1) of this section, to a local health authority;

(b) the following provisions shall apply to that Council as if they were the local health authority for the whole of Greater London, that is to say—
   (i) in the said Act of 1946, sections 2, 20, 57, 58, 63, 65, 66, 71, 72 and 74;
   (ii) section 24 of the National Health Service (Amendment) Act 1949;
   (iii) the National Health Service (Amendment) Act 1957.

(4) The Greater London Council shall have the like powers of contributing to voluntary organisations as are conferred on local health authorities by sections 22 (5) and 28 (3) of the said Act of 1946.

(5) Section 55 (1) of the said Act of 1946 (which relates to the accounts of local health authorities who are county borough councils) shall apply to the Common Council as it applies to a county borough council.

(6) In section 79 (1) of the said Act of 1946, in the definition of "local authority", for the words "metropolitan borough" there shall be substituted the words "London borough, the Greater London Council"; and in section 20 (2) (*c*) of that Act and in paragraph 6 of Part II of Schedule 4 to that Act, for the words "forming part of" there shall be substituted the words "the whole or part of which is included in".

(7) In paragraph 2 of Part II of Schedule 4 to the said Act of 1946, any reference to the council of a county borough shall be construed as including a reference to the council of a London borough and to the Common Council.

46.—(1) The council of each London borough shall as respects the borough and the Common Council shall as respects the City—

(a) be the local authority for the purposes of the National Assistance Act 1948 (including Part III thereof);

(b) have the functions conferred by or by virtue of that Act on councils of county boroughs;

(c) be the local authority for the purposes of section 3 of the Disabled Persons (Employment) Act 1958.

(2) In accordance with the foregoing subsection, but subject to the subsequent provisions of this section, the following references, that is to say—

(a) references in any enactment to the local authority or registration authority within the meaning or for the purposes of either of the said Acts or any provision thereof;

(b) references to a local authority, so far as concerns the functions of such an authority under either of those Acts or any provision thereof;

(c) references in the said Act of 1948 to the council of a county borough,

shall be construed in relation to Greater London as references to the council of a London borough or the Common Council, as the case may be; and references in any enactment to the area of any such authority, and references in the said Act of 1948 to a county borough, shall be construed accordingly.

(3) The Greater London Council shall have the like powers of contributing to the funds of voluntary organizations as are conferred on the councils of London boroughs by sections 26 (6), 30 (2) and 31 (3) of the said Act of 1948.

(4) The functions of the council of a county borough under section 47 of the said Act of 1948 (which relates to the removal to suitable premises of persons in need of care and attention) and section 50 of that Act (which relates to the burial and cremation of the dead) shall, as respects the Inner Temple and the Middle Temple, be exerciseable by the Sub-Treasurer and the Under-Treasurer thereof respectively, and those persons shall be included among the appropriate authorities specified in sections 47 (12) and 50 (2) of that Act.

(5) Without prejudice to paragraph 27 (a) of Schedule 4 to this Act, section 59 of the said Act of 1948 (which relates to the accounts of county borough councils) shall not apply to the London borough councils.

(6) It shall be the duty of each London borough council and of the Common Council to continue to provide for the area of the council on and after 1st April 1965 the accommodation and the services and facilities for disabled persons corresponding (with any necessary modifications) with those which were required or authorised to be provided for that area immediately before that date by the local authority or authorities for the whole or any part of that area in pursuance of the provisions of Part III of the said Act of 1948 or of section 3 of the said Act of 1958 and of any schemes made under those provisions; and any such schemes in force immediately before that date shall continue in force until revoked or modified by further schemes under the relevant provisions of the next following subsection.

(7) It shall be the duty of each London borough council and of the Common Council, within such period after 1st April 1965 as the Minister of Health may by directions specify, to submit schemes for the exercise of the council's functions with respect to the provision for the area of the council of accommodation and of services and facilities for disabled persons and section 34 of the said Act of 1948 shall apply to schemes under this section as it applies to schemes under sections 21 and 29 of that Act:

Provided that in relation to the provision of facilities for disabled persons this subsection shall have effect as if for the references therein and in the said section 34 to the Minister of Health there were substituted references to the Minister of Labour.

(8) In this section—

(a) references to accommodation provided under Part III of the said Act of 1948 and to a local authority providing accommodation shall be construed as if they were contained in the said Part III;

(b) references to services for disabled persons shall be construed as references to the services required or authorised to be provided under section 29 of that Act for persons who are substantially and permanently handicapped, including persons suffering from any form of mental disorder; and

(c) references to facilities for disabled persons are references to facilities for employment for them or work on their own account, or for their training for such employment or work, required or authorised to be provided under section 3 of the Disabled Persons (Employment) Act 1958.

47.—(1) Subject to subsection (2) of this section, the council of each London borough shall as respects the borough, and the Common Council shall as respects the City, have the functions of the council of a county borough under the enactments to which this section applies and be the local authority for the purposes of such of those enactments as refer to a local authority; and accordingly references to the council of a county borough or a local authority in those enactments, in the amendment of section 96 of the Children and Young Persons Act 1933 made by Schedule 4 to the Acquisition of Land (Authorisation Procedure) Act 1946 and in the definition of "remand home" in any enactment shall, subject as aforesaid, be construed as including references to the council of a London borough and the Common Council.

(2) Section 96 (4) of the Children and Young Persons Act 1933 shall not apply to expenses incurred by the Common Council, and, without prejudice to paragraph 27 (a) of Schedule 4 to this Act, subsections (2) and (3) of section 49 of the Children Act 1948 shall not apply to the accounts kept by a London borough council under that section.

(3) The enactments to which this section applies are—

(a) Parts III, IV and V of the Children and Young Persons Act 1933 and Part VI of that Act so far as it relates to the said Parts III, IV and V;

(b) the Children Act 1948;

(c) sections 48 and 49 of the Criminal Justice Act 1948;

(d) Part I of the Children Act 1958;

(e) the Adoption Act 1958;

(f) any other enactment conferring functions for the purposes of which a local authority are required to establish a children's committee under section 39 of the Children Act 1948.

(4) The Greater London Council may make contributions to any voluntary organisation—

(a) whose object or primary object is to promote the welfare of children; or

(b) who are providing advice, guidance and assistance such as to promote the welfare of children by diminishing the need to receive children into or keep them in care under the Children Act 1948 or the Children and Young Persons Act 1933 or to bring children before a juvenile court.

48.—(1) The Greater London Council shall be the fire authority for Greater London for the purposes of the Fire Services Acts 1947 to 1959, and accordingly—

(a) references in those Acts to a county and to a county council shall be construed as including references to Greater London and the Greater London Council respectively;

(b) references in any other enactment to a fire authority or to a fire authority constituted by, or for the purposes of, the Fire Services Act 1947 shall, in the application of that enactment to Greater London, be construed as references to the Greater London Council.

(2) Not later than the end of 1964, the Greater London Council shall prepare and submit to the Secretary of State for his approval an establishment scheme for a fire brigade for Greater London under section 19 of the Fire Services Act 1947 to come into force on 1st April 1965, and the Secretary of State shall not later than 15th March 1965 approve that scheme either as submitted or subject to such modifications as he may direct.

(3) The Metropolitan Fire Brigade Act 1865 shall have effect as if references to the Metropolitan Board of Works were references to the Greater London Council and references to the metropolis were references to Greater London other than the outer London boroughs.

49.—(1) Subject to subsection (2) of this section, the functions conferred or imposed by or by virtue of any provision of the Civil Defence Acts 1937 and 1939 or of regulations under the Civil Defence Act 1948 on a local authority within the meaning of that provision or on a council of a specified description shall—

(a) if expressed to be conferred or imposed on a fire authority or if relating to ambulance services or a service for the collection and removal of casualties or to the section of the Civil Defence Corps formed for stretcher bearing and giving first aid, be exercisable throughout Greater London by the Greater London Council;

(b) if relating to the making and carrying out of plans for the dispersal of members of the civil population or for their maintenance and temporary accommodation when dispersed, be exercisable as respects a London borough or the City by the Greater London Council as well as by the council of the borough or the Common Council, as the case may be;

(c) in any other case be exercisable as respects a London borough by the council of that borough and as respects the City by the Common Council;

and accordingly any reference in the said Acts of 1937 and 1939 and in those regulations to a local authority or a council of a specified description shall, so far as relates to the exercise of any such function in Greater London, be construed as a reference to the council or councils to whom the function is transferred by this subsection.

(2) The foregoing subsection shall not apply to functions conferred or imposed on police authorities, statutory water undertakers or sewerage authorities.

(3) For the purpose of determining whether any, and if so what, deduction should be made from grants payable in accordance with regulations under section 3 of the Civil Defence Act 1948 to a local authority to whom functions are transferred by

subsection (1) of this section from another authority, any land or article acquired by, or article provided for, that other authority for the purposes of those functions shall be treated as having been acquired or, as the case may be, provided for the first mentioned authority for those purposes.

(4) Any power to vary or revoke regulations made under the Civil Defence Act 1948 shall include power to amend or repeal subsections (1) and (3) of this section so far as those subsections amend those regulations.

(5) For section 58 (4) of the Civil Defence Act 1939 there shall be substituted the following subsection:—

"(4) The Greater London Council may be authorised by a scheme submitted by them under this section to exercise, for the purpose of securing supplies of water for extinguishing fires in Greater London caused by hostile attack, any powers exercisable under paragraph 1 (1) of Part III of Schedule 9 to the London Government Act 1963 in connection with the functions there mentioned, and to exercise those powers in any part of Greater London, notwithstanding that it is outside the sewerage area of the Greater London Council as defined by section 39 of that Act, and without compliance with any requirement mentioned in paragraph 1 (4) of the said Part III; and where they are authorised to exercise such powers paragraph 9 of the said Part III shall apply accordingly";

and in section 58 (5) of the said Act of 1939 for the reference to the London county council there shall be substituted a reference to the Greater London Council.

(6) In section 33 (4) (a) of the Civil Defence Act 1939 (as amended by Part III of Schedule 1 to the Public Health Act 1961) for the words "outside the administrative county of London" there shall be substituted the words "outside Greater London and in the outer London boroughs".

50.—(1) Subject to subsection (3) of this section, the council of a London borough shall be the local authority for the borough for the purposes of the Explosives Acts 1875 and 1923 and the Fireworks Act 1951.

(2) Subject to subsection (3) of this section, the Greater London Council shall be the local authority empowered to grant petroleum-spirit licences as respects Greater London under the Petroleum (Consolidation) Act 1928; and accordingly for section 2 (1) (a) and (b) of that Act there shall be substituted—

"(a) in Greater London, the Greater London Council".

(3) Subsections (1) and (2) of this section shall not affect the jurisdiction exercisable in any harbour wholly or partly in Greater London by a harbour authority within the meaning of the Explosives Act 1875 or, as the case may be, the Petroleum (Consolidation) Act 1928.

51.—(1) The council of a London borough shall as respects the borough, and the Common Council shall as respects the City, be the local authority for the purposes of the Offices, Shops and Railway Premises Act 1963, and the Greater London Council shall have the functions of the London county council under that Act; and accordingly—

(a) in the definition of "local authority" in section 90 (1) of that Act, for the words "or a county district, the council of a metropolitan borough" there shall be substituted the words "a London borough or a county district"; and

(b) for the words "London County Council" wherever they occur in that Act there shall be substituted the words "Greater London Council".

(2) The said Act of 1963 shall be further amended as follows:—

(a) in section 41(1) for the words "administrative county of London" there shall be substituted the words "inner London boroughs, the City of London, the Inner Temple and the Middle Temple";

(b) in section 41(3) for the words "administrative county of London" there shall be substituted the words "inner London boroughs, the City of London, the Inner Temple or the Middle Temple";

(c) in section 52(3)(a) after the word "county" there shall be inserted the words "or the Greater London Council";

(d) in section 52(5) for the words "administrative county of London" there shall be substituted the words "Greater London".

(3) No order shall be made under section 54 of the Shops Act 1950 other than an order revoking, either generally or as respects a specified area, a previous order under that section; and, in relation to any area outside the City and the Temples, the power of making such an order under that section shall be exercisable by the council of the London borough in which that area falls, and references in subsections (2) to (4) of that section and in any order made thereunder to the London county council shall be construed as references to that borough council.

(4) Until finally repealed as respects all classes of premises and for all purposes by the said Act of 1963—

(a) section 72(2) of the Shops Act 1950 shall have effect throughout Greater London as originally enacted and not as amended by section 18 of the London County Council (General Powers) Act 1958;

(b) the definition of "sanitary authority" in section 74 (1) of the Shops Act 1950 shall have effect as if for the words from "means" onwards there were substituted the words "means the council of a borough or an urban or rural district or, as respects the City of London, the Common Council".

52.—(1) The authority under the Theatres Act 1843 for the licensing of houses or places for the public performance of stage plays in any part of Greater London in which the lord chamberlain of Her Majesty's household is not that authority shall be the Greater London Council.

(2) The provisions of the Cinematograph Act 1909, except section 5 thereof, shall apply to Greater London as if it were a county and the Greater London Council were the council of that county; and section 1 of the Sunday Entertainments Act 1932 shall extend to the whole of Greater London and, in its application to Greater London, have effect as if subsection (5) were omitted.

(3) Schedule 12 to this Act shall have effect with respect to the licensing of the public entertainments referred to in that Schedule in Greater London and with respect to the functions of the Greater London Council by virtue of subsections (1) and (2) of this section.

53.—(1) The authority empowered to grant licences under Schedule 3 to the Betting, Gaming and Lotteries Act 1963 authorising the provision of betting facilities on tracks shall, in relation to Greater London, be the Greater London Council; but that council may delegate their functions under that Schedule to a committee consisting of members thereof, and in that case—

(a) if the committee are specially appointed for the purpose, the number and term of office of the members thereof shall be fixed by the Greater London Council; and

(b) subject to the provisions of that Schedule and to any directions given by the Greater London Council, the procedure of the committee shall be such as they may themselves determine;

and section 5 (1) of this Act shall not apply to any functions of the Greater London Council by virtue of this section.

(2) Where, apart from this subsection, the betting days within the meaning of paragraph 14 of the said Schedule 3 for Greater London would fall to be fixed for the period of twelve months beginning with 1st July in any year in accordance with paragraph 15 (4) of that Schedule, then, if within the period of one month from the date of the publication of the notice referred to in paragraph 15 (2) of that Schedule the authority referred to in subsection (1) of this section receive written notice signed by all the holders of licences under that Schedule for the time being in force in respect of tracks in Greater London, being tracks—

(a) which, immediately before 1st April 1965, were in the same licensing area for the purposes of that Schedule; and

(b) in respect of which such licences were in force immediately before that date,

stating that the signatories unanimously desire that the betting days for that period of twelve months for those tracks should be the days specified in the notice given under this subsection, and those days are days which might lawfully be fixed under that Schedule as the betting days for that period, that authority shall fix as the betting days for those tracks for that period the days so specified and the said paragraph 15 (4) shall not apply thereto.

(3) Where in the case of any particular track or group of tracks the betting days for any such period of twelve months as aforesaid are fixed by virtue of subsection (2) of this section, so much of paragraph 14 (3) of the said Schedule 3 as requires the betting days or, as the case may be, the four of those days fixed as special betting days for the purposes of section 7 (2) of the said Act of 1963 to be the same for the whole of Greater London shall be construed in relation to that period as a requirement that—

(a) those of any betting days fixed by virtue of subsection (2) of this section which are fixed as special betting days shall be the same for all the tracks for which those betting days are fixed;

(b) any betting days fixed otherwise than by virtue of subsection (2) of this section and those of them fixed as special betting days shall be the same for the whole of Greater London;

and unless the betting days fixed for that period are the same for the whole of Greater London, any reference in section 6 (3) or 15 (1) (a) of the said Act of 1963 to one of the betting days fixed as mentioned in that provision shall be construed in relation to any track in Greater London as a reference to one of the days fixed in accordance with that Schedule or subsection (2) of this section as the days on which betting facilities may be provided on that particular track.

54.—(1) The council of a London borough shall, as respects that borough, be—

(a) both the food and drugs authority and the local authority for the purposes of the Food and Drugs Act 1955;

(b) the authority responsible for enforcing section 31 of that Act (which prohibits the sale of milk from diseased cows); and

(c) the local authority for the purposes of the Slaughterhouses Act 1958 and the Slaughter of Animals Act 1958;

and the Common Council shall, as respects the City, be the authority responsible for enforcing the said section 31 and the local authority for the purposes of each of the said Acts of 1958; and in the said Act of 1955 Part III (which relates to the provision and regulation of markets) shall extend to all the London boroughs, Part IV (which relates to slaughterhouses, knackers' yards, and cold-air stores) shall extend to the whole of Greater London, and so much of section 15 (2) as restricts the power of local authorities in London to make bylaws under that section shall cease to have effect.

(2) Notwithstanding anything in subsection (1) of this section, neither the council of any London borough nor the Common Council shall be required to carry out a review of, or submit a report on, slaughterhouse facilities under section 3 of the Slaughterhouses Act 1958, and section 4 (3) of that Act shall not apply to any such council; but—

> (a) in relation to the council of an inner London borough or the Common Council, section 4 (1) and (2) of that Act shall have effect as if the following provisions thereof were omitted, that is to say—
>> (i) in the said section 4 (1), the words from the beginning to "last foregoing section" and paragraphs (a) and (b);
>> (ii) in the said section 4 (2), the words from "after" to "apply and";
> (b) in relation to the council of an outer London borough, sections 4 (1) and (2) and 6 (1) of that Act shall have effect as if any report submitted under section 3 of that Act which relates, or so far as it relates, to the area of that borough had been submitted by that council and any application refused under the said section 6 (1) by the authority by whom that report was submitted had been so refused by that council.

(3) For the purposes of the Diseases of Animals Act 1950—

> (a) subject to paragraph (b) of this subsection, the council of a London borough shall be the local authority for the borough;
> (b) for the purpose of the provisions of that Act relating to imported animals, the Common Council shall be the local authority in and for the whole of Greater London.

(4) The Diseases of Animals Act 1950, the Food and Drugs Act 1955 and the Slaughter of Animals Act 1958 shall have effect subject to the modifications specified in relation thereto in Parts I, II and III respectively of Schedule 13 to this Act, being modifications consequential on the foregoing provisions of this section.

55.—(1) Part IV of the Agriculture Act 1947 (which relates to smallholdings) shall apply to the Greater London Council as it applies to a county council, and accordingly in section 47 (1) of that Act (which makes it the duty of every county council other than the London county council to provide smallholdings) for the words "other than the London County Council" there shall be substituted the words "and of the Greater London Council".

(2) The Greater London Council shall have the like powers as a county council under section 12 of the Agricultural Land (Utilisation) Act 1931 with respect to the provision of cottage holdings; and any remaining functions under the provisions of the Small Holdings and Allotments Acts 1908 to 1931 repealed by the Small Holdings and Allotments Act 1926 or saved by proviso (a) to section 67 (2) of the Agriculture Act 1947 which, by virtue of section 19 (1) of the said Act of 1926 or the said section 67 (2), were exercisable immediately before 1st

April 1965 by the Middlesex county council shall as from that date become functions of the Greater London Council.

(3) Section 61 (3) of the Agriculture Act 1947 (which relates to the matters which may be referred by a smallholdings authority to the smallholdings committee constituted by that authority under section 61 (1) of that Act) shall apply to the Greater London Council as it applies to the council of a county; and in section 71 (8) (c) of that Act (which relates to the discharge of the functions of County Agricultural Executive Committees in the existing county of London) for the words "the county of London" there shall be substituted the words "Greater London".

(4) In its application to an inner London borough, section 23 of the Small Holdings and Allotments Act 1908 shall have effect as if—

> (a) in subsection (1) for the word "shall" wherever it occurs there were substituted the word "may"; and
> (b) subsection (2) were omitted;

and in section 20 of the Allotments Act 1922 for the words "Metropolitan borough" there shall be substituted the words "outer London borough".

56.—(1) The Public Libraries Act 1892 shall be deemed to have been adopted in every London borough and each London borough shall be a library district within the meaning of that Act; and—

> (a) in section 13 (2) (e) of that Act, for the words "the administrative county of London" there shall be substituted the words "Greater London";
> (b) section 20 of that Act, section 8 of the Public Libraries Act 1901 and section 3 of the Public Libraries Act 1919 shall not apply to any London borough;
> (c) section 6 of the Public Libraries Act 1919 shall apply to a London borough council whether or not they are the local education authority.

(2) In section 13 of the Public Libraries Act 1901, for the words "administrative county" there shall be substituted the word "City".

57.—(1) The Greater London Council shall be a local authority for the purposes of section 132 of the Local Government Act 1948 (which relates to the powers of local authorities with respect to the provision of entertainments).

(2) Any property (including the Royal Festival Hall) which immediately before 1st April 1965 was held by the London county council by virtue of any of the following enactments, that is to say—

> (a) section 46 of the London County Council (General Powers) Act 1901 (which relates to the Horniman museum);
> (b) the Iveagh Bequest (Kenwood) Act 1929;
> (c) section 3 of the London County Council (General Powers) Act 1940 (which relates to certain ponds at Ken Wood, Hampstead Heath and Parliament Hill);
> (d) section 4 of the London County Council (General Powers) Act 1947 (which relates to the provision of concert halls, etc.);
> (e) the London County Council (Crystal Palace) Act 1951;
> (f) section 29 of the London County Council (General Powers) Act 1959 (which relates to the Geffrye museum),

shall on that date vest in the Greater London Council; and the functions of the London county council by virtue of the enactments referred to in paragraph (a), (b), (e) or (f) of this subsection or by virtue of section 20 of the London County Council (General Powers) Act 1952 (which relates to the exhibition at Ken Wood of drawings from Sir John Soane's museum) shall on that date become functions of the Greater London Council.

58.—(1) The following provisions (being provisions relating to the powers of local authorities with respect to parks and open spaces), that is to say, section 164 of the Public Health Act 1875, the Open Spaces Act 1906 (other than section 14 thereof) and sections 52 to 54 of the Public Health Act 1961 and, for the purposes of the said section 54, the provisions therein mentioned of the Public Health Act 1936, shall have effect as if—

    (a) the London borough councils, and

    (b) for the purposes of any park or open space for the time being vested in the Greater London Council or of the provision of further parks or open spaces where that provision is—

        (i) by way of the appropriation of land held for other purposes, being, notwithstanding anything in section 23 of the Town and Country Planning Act 1959, an appropriation made with the consent of the Minister; or

        (ii) approved by the Minister as being for the benefit of an area of Greater London substantially larger than the London boroughs in or near which the park or open space is proposed to be provided,

    the Greater London Council,

were included among the local authorities to whom the provision in question applies.

(2) Any land which immediately before 1st April 1965 was vested in the London or Middlesex county council and used as a park or open space, not being land to which section 57(2) or 59(1) of this Act applies, shall on that date vest in the Greater London Council; but, not later than 31st March 1970 or such later date before 1st April 1975 as the Minister may direct, the Greater London Council shall, after consultation with the London borough councils, prepare and submit to the Minister a scheme with respect to that land—

    (a) containing proposals as to what part, if any, of that land should, in the opinion of the Greater London Council, be retained by that Council and giving their grounds for that opinion;

    (b) providing with respect to the remainder of that land for the transfer of any park or open space comprised therein to one, or to two or more jointly, of the London borough councils, and, in the case of a transfer to two or more councils jointly, providing for the management and control of the park or open space by a body representative of both or all of those councils;

    (c) in the case of any of that land proposed to be transferred, indicating any necessary modifications of any local Act or other instrument with respect to the land in question;

and the Minister may by order, after consultation with the Greater London Council and any London borough council to whom the order relates or in whose area any of the land is situated, give effect to the scheme without modification or with such modifications as the Minister thinks fit or make such other provision for the retention by the Greater London Council, or the transfer to one, or to two or more jointly, of the London borough councils, of any of that land as appears to the Minister appropriate; and any reference in this subsection to a London borough council shall be construed as including a

reference to the Common Council and, in relation to any land outside Greater London, as including a reference to the council of any county or county district in whose area any of the land is situated.

(3) Until the coming into operation of the Minister's order under subsection (2) of this section, one half of the expenditure of the Greater London Council in the exercise of functions with respect to parks and open spaces, being functions which immediately before 1st April 1965 were functions of the London county council, shall be treated as expenditure for special London purposes and be chargeable only on the inner London boroughs, the City and the Temples.

59.—(1) Where, in the case of any Green Belt land within the meaning of the Green Belt (London and Home Counties) Act 1938, immediately before 1st April 1965—

    (a) that land, not being land to which section 81 (1) of this Act applies, was vested in the London or Middlesex county council; or

    (b) any functions, rights or liabilities were exercisable with respect to that land by either of those councils,

then on that date that land shall vest in, or, as the case may be, those functions, rights and liabilities shall become functions, rights and liabilities of, the Greater London Council.

(2) In the said Act of 1938—

    (a) in section 2 (1), in the definition of "the area", for the words from "London" onwards there shall be substituted the words "and Surrey, and Greater London";

    (b) the expression "local authority" shall include the Greater London Council;

    (c) the expression "contributing local authority" in relation to any land in relation to which, if this Act had not been passed, any existing council to whom section 3 (1) (b) of this Act applies would have been such an authority, shall, if that existing council is the London or Middlesex county council, include the Greater London Council or, in any other case, include the London borough council whose area includes the whole or any part of the area of that existing council;

    (d) in sections 5, 6, 12, 15 and 32, the expression "the county council" in relation to any land in Greater London shall mean the Greater London Council;

    (e) in section 17 (7) for the words "county or borough or district or parish" there shall be substituted the word "area".

60.—(1) Subject to the provisions of this section, as respects any part of the existing county of Hertfordshire, Essex, Kent or Surrey which on 1st April 1965 ceases to be part of that county and as respects any part of the existing county of Middlesex, any functions under sections 27 to 34 of the National Parks and Access to the Countryside Act 1949 (which relate to the ascertainment of footpaths, bridleways and certain other highways) which on 31st March 1965 still remained to be discharged by the county council shall on 1st April 1965 become functions—

    (a) in the case of any area falling within a London borough, of the council of that borough;

    (b) in the case of any part of the urban district of Potters Bar, of the Hertfordshire county council;

    (c) in the case of any part of the urban district of Staines or Sunbury-on-Thames, of the Surrey county council;

and, in the case of an area mentioned in paragraph (b) or (c) of this subsection, the county council so mentioned shall not be required to discharge as respects that area any functions under the said sections 27 to 34 already discharged by the Middlesex county council.

(2) As respects any part of a London borough to which the said sections 27 to 34 do not apply by virtue of subsection (1) of this section and as respects any part of the City, sub-sections (2), (3) and (5) of section 35 of the said Act of 1949 (which relate to the extension of the said sections 27 to 34 to county boroughs) and, as respects any part of any London borough or the City, subsection (4) of that section (which relates to the exclusion of parts of a county from the operation of those sections) shall apply in relation to that London borough and the council thereof or to the City and the Common Council, as the case may be, as they apply in relation to a county borough (or, in the case of the said subsection (4), a county) and the council thereof.

(3) The London borough council to whom any functions of any county council other than the Middlesex county council are transferred by virtue of subsection (1) of this section may agree with the county council for the performance of any of those functions by that county council on behalf of the borough council; and where by virtue of subsection (1) or (2) of this section the said sections 27 to 34 for the time being apply to any part of any London borough or the City, the borough council or Common Council, as the case may be, may agree with the Greater London Council for the functions of the borough council or Common Council under the said sections 27 to 34 to be discharged by the Greater London Council, and while such an agreement with the Greater London Council is in force—

(a) references in Part IV of the said Act of 1949 to the surveying authority shall be construed accordingly;

(b) section 28 (1) of the said Act of 1949 shall have effect in relation to a survey carried out by the Greater London Council as if the reference therein to the councils of county districts and parishes were a reference to the borough council or Common Council, as the case may be.

(4) In section 23 of the said Act of 1949, the reference to the local planning authority shall be construed in relation to land in a London borough or the City as a reference to the borough council or, as the case may be, the Common Council.

(5) The provisions of Part V of the said Act of 1949 with respect to access agreements and access orders and section 90 of that Act shall not apply to the inner London boroughs or the City; and in relation to land in an outer London borough references in sections 64 to 82 and 90 of that Act to the local planning authority shall be construed as references to the borough council.

(6) In section 89 of the said Act of 1949 the expression "local planning authority", and in section 99 of that Act the expression "local authority", shall include the Greater London Council, a London borough council and the Common Council; and in section 102 of that Act—

(a) the expression "local planning authority" shall include the council of an outer London borough; and

(b) the expression "local authority" shall include the Greater London Council.

61.—(1) As respects participation in town development within the meaning of the Town Development Act 1952, and as respects the power to contribute towards expenses of such development conferred by sections 4 and 10(3) of that Act on the council of a county borough, the Greater London Council shall be in the same position under that Act as the council of

a county borough, and accordingly references in that Act to the council of a county borough as an authority participating or eligible to participate and the references to the council of a county borough in sections 4, 10(3) and 12(1) of that Act shall include references to the Greater London Council; and, for the purposes of any such development in respect of which the Greater London Council have power under the said section 4 to make a contribution to the council of any receiving district within the meaning of that Act, they shall also have power to make available to that council the services of any of their officers or servants.

(2) In section 2(1)(b) of the said Act of 1952, for sub-paragraphs (ii) and (iii) there shall be substituted the following—

"(ii) Greater London; or

(iii) a county district in an area of continuous urban development adjacent to any big centre of population other than Greater London; or".

(3) It shall be the duty of the Greater London Council—

(a) to implement, or complete the implementation of, any undertaking given before 1st April 1965 with the approval of the Minister—

(i) under section 4, 10(3) or 19(3) of the said Act of 1952 (including the said section 4 as extended by section 34(2) of the Housing Act 1961) by any council to whom section 3(1)(b) of this Act applies; or

(ii) under the said section 4 (as extended as aforesaid) by the Hertfordshire, Essex, Kent or Surrey county council in a case where the undertaking was in respect of development relieving congestion in any area falling within Greater London;

(b) to take or complete any action which was agreed to be taken by any council to whom section 3(1)(b) of this Act applies in pursuance of an agreement made before 1st April 1965, being an agreement made with the authority of the Minister under section 8(1) of the said Act of 1952 or an agreement such as is referred to in section 8(2) of that Act;

and the Greater London Council shall have the like rights under any agreement to which paragraph (b) of this subsection applies as the council whose liabilities thereunder they assume by virtue of that paragraph.

(4) References in subsection (3) of this section to an undertaking given or action agreed to be taken by any council shall be construed as including references to any undertaking or action which, having regard to the established practice of that council, should properly be deemed to have been so given or to have been so agreed to be taken; and any dispute as to the existence or extent of any duty, right or liability of the Greater London Council by virtue of the said subsection (3) or as to whether or not any particular undertaking or action should properly be deemed as aforesaid shall be referred to and determined by the Minister.

(5) Any action authorised by an order under section 9 of the said Act of 1952 to be taken by any council to whom section 3(1)(b) of this Act applies may be taken by the Greater London Council; and that Council shall have the like liabilities and rights in connection with any obligation with respect to that action imposed by the order as the council originally authorised by the order to take that action.

62.—(1) The London borough councils and (where not

already so) the Common Council shall be local authorities for the purposes of the following enactments—

(a) the Canals Protection (London) Act 1898, which shall extend to the whole of Greater London;

(b) the Celluloid and Cinematograph Film Act 1922, which shall extend to the whole of Greater London;

(c) the Pharmacy and Poisons Act 1933;

(d) section 17 of the Restriction of Ribbon Development Act 1935;

(e) the Riding Establishments Act 1939;

(f) the Schedule to the Consumer Protection Act 1961, including that Schedule as applied by section 6 (3) (b) of that Act.

(2) Schedule 14 to this Act shall have effect with respect to the discharge in Greater London and the adjoining areas of functions with respect to land drainage and flood prevention and other functions under the enactments therein mentioned.

(3) Without prejudice to the operation in Greater London of the Places of Worship Registration Act 1855, nothing in this Act shall transfer to any local authority in Greater London any functions under the Places of Religious Worship Act 1812.

(4) Unless provision for the purpose is made by some other Act passed during the same session as this Act, the Board of Trade may, as respects Greater London or any part thereof, by order make provision as to the authority by whom there shall be exercised on and after 1st April 1965 any function conferred on local authorities by the enactments relating to weights and measures.

(5) The confirmation and record of the rules of loan societies under the Loan Societies Act 1840 shall as respects any such society formed in Greater London be functions of the Greater London Council; and accordingly in relation to that Act sections 3 and 78 of the Local Government Act 1888 shall have effect as if Greater London were a county and the Greater London Council were the council of that county.

Part VIII

RATING AND VALUATION AND ASSOCIATED MATTERS

63.—(1) Each London borough shall be a rating area and the rating authority therefor shall be the council of the borough; and, subject to subsection (2) of this section, the Rating and Valuation Act 1925 shall apply in Greater London as it applies elsewhere in England and Wales.

(2) The enactments relating to rating and valuation in England and Wales shall have effect subject to the modifications thereof specified in Schedule 15 to this Act, being—

(a) modifications consequential on the foregoing subsection and other provisions of this Act; or

(b) modifications of the said Act of 1925 in its application to Greater London; or

(c) modifications extending to the whole of Greater London provisions applicable to the existing county of London.

64.—(1) The authorities to whom general grants are payable under Part I of the Local Government Act 1958 shall include the London borough councils and the Common Council, and accordingly references in the said Part I to recipient authorities shall include references to those councils.

(2) The expenditure which qualifies as relevant expenditure for the purposes of the said Part I shall include expenditure incurred by or on behalf of the Greater London Council in respect of the carrying out of that Council's functions by

virtue of section 45(3) of this Act and any expenditure by way of contributions by that Council—

(a) by virtue of section 45(4) or 47(4) of this Act; or

(b) by virtue of section 46(3) of this Act so far as it relates to section 26(6) of the National Assistance Act 1948.

(3) Where the provision of any service giving rise to relevant expenditure within the meaning of the said Part I as amended by the last foregoing subsection is a function of the the Greater London Council or of a joint board whose district is wholly or partly comprised in a London borough or in the City, section 3 (1) of the said Act of 1958 (which enables the Minister to reduce a general grant in the case of default by a recipient authority) shall in relation to that borough or the City, as the case may be, apply to a failure on the part of the Greater London Council or the joint board to achieve or maintain reasonable standards as it would apply if the failure were that of the council of that borough or the Common Council, as the case may be.

(4) In its application to the council of an inner London borough or the Common Council, paragraph 4 of Part III of Schedule 1 to the said Act of 1958 shall have effect as if in sub-paragraph (1) thereof—

(a) for any reference to the local education authority there were substituted a reference to the Inner London Education Authority;

(b) the reference to the centres provided as mentioned in that sub-paragraph were a reference to such centres provided by the council of any of the inner London boroughs or the Common Council;

(c) for the first reference to the area of the authority there were substituted a reference to the Inner London Education Area and the second such reference were a reference to the inner London borough in question or, as the case may be, the City;

and, for the purposes of sub-paragraph (2) (b) of that paragraph, as if the Inner London Education Area were the area of a single local health authority.

(5) In paragraph 8 (3) of the said Part III, for the words "the administrative county of London" there shall be substituted the words "Greater London".

65.—(1) The authorities to whom rate-deficiency grants under Part I of the Local Government Act 1948 may become payable shall include the London borough councils, and accordingly references to those councils shall be substituted for references to metropolitan borough councils in sections 5 and 6 of the Local Government Act 1958 (which regulate the cases in which and conditions subject to which such grants are payable).

(2) For the purposes of the said section 5, sums payable by an authority by virtue of a precept issued by the Greater London Council, in so far as payable in respect of expenditure of that Council for general London purposes, shall not be treated as expenditure of the authority paying those sums.

(3) Section 6 of the said Act of 1958 (which provides for disregarding the amount of abnormal expenditure in determining the amount of any rate-deficiency grant) shall not affect the payment of rate-deficiency grants to a London borough council or the Common Council for the years 1965-66, 1966-67 and 1967-68.

66.—(1) The Minister may, subject to and in accordance with the subsequent provisions of this section, make as respects the whole or any part or parts of Greater London a scheme or schemes for the purpose of reducing disparities in the rates levied in different rating areas of Greater London other than the Temples.

(2) Any such scheme shall take the form of provision for the making of contributions by rating authorities in Greater London elsewhere than the Temples to other such authorities, either directly, or through the Greater London Council, or by means of adjustments by the Greater London Council in the amounts for which they precept on those rating authorities respectively, or, in the case of rating authorities in the Inner London Education Area, by a re-allocation between those authorities of the aggregate amount payable to them by virtue of section 64 of this Act, or by a combination of any two or more of those methods.

(3) Rules made under section 9 of the Rating and Valuation Act 1925 and regulations made under section 15 of the Local Government Act 1948 may make the like provision for the purpose of schemes under this section as may be made by such rules or regulations for the purposes of the said section 9 or Part I of the said Act of 1948, as the case may be; and for the purposes of section 14 of the said Act of 1948 (which relates to investigations into the working of Part I of that Act) this section shall be deemed to be included in the said Part I and the expression "local authority" in the said section 14 shall include the Greater London Council.

(4) Any scheme under this section may, subject to the next following subsection, be revoked or varied by any subsequent scheme under this section.

(5) Before making a scheme under this section, the Minister shall consult with any association or committee which appears to him to be representative of the London borough councils and with the Common Council and the Greater London Council.

(6) In section 5 (6) of the Local Government Act 1958 (which, among other things, provides for disregarding payments under section 10 of the Local Government Act 1948 in determining the expenditure of an authority for the purpose of computing rate-deficiency grants) for the words "and, in the case of a local authority within the administrative county of London, no payments under section ten of the Act of 1948 were payable" there shall be substituted the words "were payable and, in the case of a local authority in Greater London, section 66 of the London Government Act 1963 had not been passed".

67.—(1) Where, in the case of any rating area to which this section applies, different parts of that area would, apart from this section, be chargeable with expenses incurred by different authorities or bodies in the discharge of the like functions, then, if the rating authority so resolve, the aggregate of those expenses shall be chargeable on the whole of that area or, if those parts do not together comprise the whole of that area, on so much of that area as consists of those parts.

(2) This section applies to any rating area in Greater London and to any other rating area which falls partly in—

(a) the metropolitan police district; or

(b) the sewerage area of the Greater London Council; or

(c) some other area comprising the whole or part of Greater London prescribed for the purposes of this section by an order of the Minister.

68.—(1) The Common Council may levy a general rate for the purpose of defraying any expenses incurred by them under any enactment, being expenses which do not fall to be defrayed out of the poor rate.

(2) The Common Council may for the purposes of any enactment borrow money under the City of London Sewers Acts 1848 to 1897 in accordance with the provisions of those Acts or any other Acts regulating the mode of borrowing money by the Council.

(3) In any enactment passed after 1st August 1958 and applying or subsequently applied to the Common Council any reference to the general rate fund of a local authority or any description of local authority shall, except where the context otherwise requires, be construed in relation to the Council as a reference to the general rate of the City.

(4) The foregoing provisions of this section apply to the Common Council as local authority, as police authority and as port health authority.

(5) In this section any reference to any enactment includes a reference to any instrument made under an enactment and any reference to any enactment or instrument includes a reference to any enactment or instrument contained in or made under this Act, or passed or made after this Act.

69.—(1) As soon as may be after the first election of councillors of the Greater London Council or, as the case may be, of any London borough, each existing rating authority whose area, or part of whose area, falls within Greater London or, as the case may be, that London borough shall, in accordance with arrangements made by the Minister by regulations, cause the appropriate contribution to be paid into the general fund of the Greater London Council or, as the case may be, the general rate fund of that London borough.

(2) In the foregoing subsection, the expression "the appropriate contribution" in relation to any existing rating area or any part of such an area means an amount equal to the product of a rate of a penny in the pound levied in that rating area or, as the case may be, that part thereof for the year 1964-65, being—

(a) in the case of the area of a county borough, that product ascertained in accordance with the rules for the time being in force under section 16 of the Local Government Act 1958;

(b) in a case where that product has been estimated by the rating authority for the purposes of section 9 (2) (d) of the Rating and Valuation Act 1925, that product as so estimated;

(c) in any other case, that product estimated by the rating authority in like manner as it would fall to be estimated for the purposes of the said section 9 (2) (d).

(3) Any expenses incurred by any returning officer in relation to the holding of the first election of councillors of the Greater London Council or, as the case may be, of any London borough which, apart from this subsection, would under paragraph 19 of Schedule 3 to this Act fall to be paid by the Greater London Council or, as the case may be, the council of that London borough shall be paid by the existing rating authorities whose areas fall wholly or partly within Greater London or, as the case may be, that London borough, the amount payable by each of those authorities being an amount bearing the same proportion to the aggregate amount of those expenses as the appropriate contribution of that authority to the general fund of the Greater London Council or, as the case may be, the general rate fund of that London borough under the foregoing provisions of this section bears to the aggregate amount of the appropriate contributions so payable to the fund in question.

(4) The Greater London Council and the London borough councils may borrow for the purpose of meeting any expenditure incurred by them before 1st April 1965.

70.—(1) If the county of Essex, Hertfordshire, Kent or

Surrey incurs an additional rate burden consequential on this Act which exceeds the estimated product of a rate of fivepence in the pound for the county for the year 1965-66, the Greater London Council shall pay as part of their expenditure for general London purposes to the council of that county as part of their receipts for general county purposes—

(a) in the year 1965-66, an amount equal to that excess;

(b) in the year 1966-67, an amount equal to seven-eighths of that excess;

(c) in the year 1967-68, an amount equal to three-quarters of that excess;

(d) in the year 1968-69, an amount equal to five-eighths of that excess;

(e) in the year 1969-70, an amount equal to half that excess;

(f) in the year 1970-71, an amount equal to three-eighths of that excess;

(g) in the year 1971-72, an amount equal to a quarter of that excess;

(h) in the year 1972-73, an amount equal to one-eighth of that excess.

(2) The provisions of Schedule 16 to this Act shall have effect for the purpose of determining whether any, and if so what, additional rate burden consequential on this Act has been incurred by any of the counties aforesaid.

(3) Any payments made by the Greater London Council under this section shall be disregarded in ascertaining the expenditure of any county council for the purposes of section 5 of the Local Government Act 1958.

Part IX

MISCELLANEOUS AND GENERAL

Common services

71.—(1) The Greater London Council shall establish an organisation for the purpose of conducting, or assisting in the conducting of, investigations into, and the collection of information relating to, any matters concerning Greater London or any part thereof and making, or assisting in the making of, arrangements whereby any such information and the results of any such investigation are made available to any authority concerned with local government in Greater London, any government department or the public; and without prejudice to the foregoing provisions of this subsection the Greater London Council shall be a local authority for the purposes of sections 134 and 135 of the Local Government Act 1948 (which relate respectively to information centres and to instruction and information on questions relating to local government).

(2) The appropriate Minister with respect to any matter may require the Greater London Council to provide him with any information with respect to that matter which is in the possession of, or available to, that Council, any London borough council or the Common Council in consequence of the exercise of any power conferred by or under any enactment; and where such a requirement is made in respect of any information which is so in the possession of, or available to, any London borough council or the Common Council but not the Greater London Council, the Greater London Council may require that borough council or, as the case may be, the Common Council to furnish the Greater London Council with that information.

72.—(1) The Greater London Council may purchase and store and supply to any authority such as is mentioned in subsection (2) of this section any goods or materials required for the discharge of the functions of that authority, and that Coun-

cil and any such authority may enter into and carry into effect agreements and do all such other acts as may be necessary or convenient for the purpose of any such purchase, storage or supply.

(2) The authorities referred to in the foregoing subsection are—

(a) any of the following, and any joint committee appointed by any two or more of the following, that is to say, the London borough councils, the Common Council and, in relation to any functions exercisable by them which are exercisable elsewhere in Greater London by the said councils, the Sub-Treasurer of the Inner Temple and the Under-Treasurer of the Middle Temple;

(b) any body of persons discharging functions relating to education or public health in Greater London and receiving financial aid in relation to those functions from any of the councils aforesaid or from the Greater London Council or the Inner London Education Authority;

(c) any person or body of persons responsible for the management or government of any school or other educational institution in Greater London in the case of which the fees or expenses of any person receiving education, instruction or training thereat are wholly or partly defrayed by a local education authority in Greater London;

(d) any voluntary organisation with which a local authority in Greater London have made such arrangements as are referred to in section 26 of the National Assistance Act 1948;

(e) any body of persons concerned with the promotion of the welfare of persons ordinarily resident in Greater London who are aged or to whom section 29 of the said Act of 1948 applies;

(f) any of the following bodies constituted under the National Health Service Act 1946, that is to say, any Regional Hospital Board or Executive Council constituted for an area which falls wholly or partly within Greater London, and any Hospital Management Committee appointed by, and the Board of Governors of any teaching hospital situated in the area of, any such Regional Hospital Board;

(g) the British Postgraduate Medical School.

73.—(1) Subject to subsection (2) of this section the Greater London Council may, for the purpose of giving publicity to the amenities and advantages of Greater London—

(a) enter into and carry into effect agreements for the purpose with any person approved by the Minister;

(b) make reasonable contributions towards the expenses incurred by any such person in giving effect to any such agreement;

(c) incur reasonable expenditure on the use of suitable media of advertising;

(d) incur reasonable expenditure on the establishment and maintenance of office accommodation for the dissemination of information relating to Greater London.

(2) Nothing in the foregoing subsection shall authorise the Greater London Council to give publicity in the United Kingdom, whether by advertising or otherwise, to the commercial and industrial advantages of Greater London; and nothing in paragraph (c) or (d) of that subsection shall authorise the publication of any advertisement, or the establishment or maintenance of office accommodation, by the Greater London Council themselves in any place outside the United Kingdom.

74.—(1) Without prejudice to section 106 of the Local Government Act 1933, the officers of each London borough council and the Common Council shall as soon as reasonably practicable, and in any event not later than 1st April 1968, include an architect for the borough or, as the case may be, the City.

(2) The architect aforesaid shall be appointed from among fit persons by, and hold office during the pleasure of, the borough council or Common Council and shall perform such duties as that council may direct, and shall be paid such reasonable remuneration as that council may determine.

75.—(1) Any of the following councils, that is to say, the Greater London Council, the London borough councils and the Common Council, may pay compensation—

    (a) to any of their officers who sustains an injury in the course of his employment; or

    (b) to the widow or widower or child of any of their officers who, in the course of his employment, dies or sustains an injury resulting in death.

(2) Any compensation payable under this section may be paid either—

    (a) by way of a lump sum; or

    (b) by way of periodical payments of such amounts and payable at such times and for such periods as the council in question may from time to time determine having regard to all the circumstances of the case.

(3) The payment of compensation under this section shall not affect any right or claim to damages or compensation which an officer of any of the councils aforesaid or his widow or widower or child may have against any person other than that council or, except so far as may be agreed when the compensation is granted, against that council.

76.—(1) As from 1st April 1965, the metropolitan police district shall consist of the following areas, that is to say—

    (a) Greater London, excluding the City of London, the Inner Temple and the Middle Temple;

    (b) in the county of Essex, the urban districts of Chigwell and Waltham Holy Cross;

    (c) in the county of Hertfordshire, the urban districts of Bushey, Cheshunt and Potters Bar, the rural district of Elstree, and the parishes of Northaw in the rural district of Hatfield and Aldenham in the rural district of Watford;

    (d) in the county of Surrey the borough of Epsom and Ewell, and the urban districts of Banstead, Esher, Staines and Sunbury-on-Thames,

and section 16 of, and Schedule 4 to, the Police Act 1946 shall cease to have effect.

(2) This section and the Metropolitan Police Acts 1829 to 1959 may be cited together as the Metropolitan Police Acts 1829 to 1963 and this section shall be construed as one with those Acts.

77.—(1) In the Local Government Superannuation Act 1937—

    (a) in section 1 (which relates to the local authorities who are required to maintain superannuation funds under Part I of that Act), in subsection (1) *(a)*, for the words "metropolitan borough" there shall as from 1st April 1965 be substituted the words "London borough and the Greater London Council";

    (b) in section 40(1), in the definition of "local authority", after the word "district" there shall be inserted the words "the council of a London borough, the Greater London Council";

    (c) in Part I of Schedule 1 (which relates to the local authorities whose whole-time officers are to be compulsorily superannuable), after the paragraph beginning "The council" there shall be inserted the following paragraphs—

        "The council of a London borough.

        The Greater London Council.".

(2) For the purpose of the making before 1st April 1965 under section 2 of the said Act of 1937 of a combination scheme to come into force on or after that date, the Greater London Council or a London borough council shall be deemed to be an administering authority notwithstanding that they are not for the time being required to maintain a superannuation fund under Part I of that Act.

(3) Notwithstanding anything in section 4 of the said Act of 1937 (which relates to the funds to which contributions are payable), if in the case of any contributory employee or class of contributory employees of the Greater London Council or a London borough council it appears to the Minister expedient so to do, the Minister may by order, which shall be subject to annulment in pursuance of a resolution of either House of Parliament, provide that for the purposes of that Act the appropriate superannuation fund in relation to that employee or class shall be such fund as may be specified in or determined under the order; and any such order may make such incidental, consequential, transitional or supplementary provision as may appear to the Minister to be necessary or proper for the purposes or in consequence of the order and for giving full effect thereto.

78.—(1) Subject to the following provisions of this section, the enactment relating to coroners, and in particular the Coroners Act 1844 and the Coroners Acts 1887 to 1954, shall apply in relation to Greater London (exclusive of the City and the Temples) as if that area were a county and the Greater London Council were the council of that county, and references in those enactments to a county alderman or a county councillor shall be construed accordingly.

(2) In their application to the said area of Greater London, the said enactments shall have effect subject to the following modifications:—

    (a) the requirements as to residence contained in section 5 of the Coroners Act 1844 shall not apply;

    (b) any sum required by section 27 (2) of the Coroners Act 1887 to be paid out of the local rate and any salary or pension required by section 8 of the Coroners (Amendment) Act 1926 to be defrayed as expenses for special county purposes, shall in the first instance be defrayed by the Greater London Council and shall be charged on the London boroughs;

    (c) any provision of the said enactments defining a county shall not apply.

(3) The Greater London Council may provide and maintain proper accommodation for the holding of inquests.

(4) It shall be the duty of the Greater London Council as respects the area of Greater London mentioned in subsection (1) of this section, and of the council of each county adjoining Greater London as respects their county review area, to take into consideration the division of that area into coroners' districts and, unless they consider it inexpedient to do so, to exercise before the end of 1964 the power conferred on them by section 12 of the Coroners (Amendment) Act 1926 of submitting a draft order providing for the division, or alteration of any division, of that area into coroners' districts; and the

Greater London Council shall not later than 1st April 1965 appoint a sufficient number of coroners for the said area of Greater London and section 2 of the said Act of 1926 shall apply to any such appointment as if a vacancy had occurred in the office of coroner for that area.

(5) This section, except so far as it relates to the appointment of corners and to corners' districts, shall not come into force until 1st April 1965; and until that date the fact that any powers relating to the appointment of coroners and coroners' districts are exercisable by the Greater London Council shall not prevent the exercise of the like powers by the authorities by whom they were exercisable immediately before the passing of this Act.

79. Subject to any order under section 84 of this Act, as respects any local land charge within the meaning of section 15 of the Land Charges Act 1925 which affects land situated in any London borough or in the City, the proper officer to act as local registrar under that section shall, as from 1st October 1964, be the clerk, or the person for the time being authorised to act as clerk, of the council of that London borough or, as the case may be, the town clerk, or the person for the time being authorised to act as town clerk, of the City.

80.—(1) Notwithstanding anything in section 120 of the Land Registration Act 1925, the registration of title to land shall continue at all times on and after 1st April 1965 to be compulsory on sale—

> (a) in any part of Greater London in which immediately before that date such registration was so compulsory; and
>
> (b) in the areas comprised in the existing urban districts of Potters Bar, Staines and Sunbury-on-Thames.

(2) Her Majesty may by Order in Council declare as respects any other part of Greater London specified in the Order that registration of title to land is to be compulsory on sale on and after such date as may be so specified; and nothing in section 122 of the said Act of 1925 shall apply to the making of an Order under this subsection.

(3) Nothing in any Order under subsection (2) of this section shall render compulsory the registration of the title to an incorporeal hereditament or to mines and minerals apart from the surface, or to corporeal hereditaments parcel of a manor and included in the sale of a manor as such.

(4) As soon as the registration of title to land has become compulsory on sale in the whole of Greater London as for the time being constituted at any time on or after 1st April 1965, any area which subsequently becomes part of Greater London shall be deemed to be included in an Order under subsection (2) of this section.

(5) The registration of title to land shall continue to be compulsory on sale in any area by virtue of subsection (1) (a), (2) or (4) of this section notwithstanding that the area in question ceases to be part of Greater London.

(6) Section 123 of the said Act of 1925 (which relates to the effect of that Act in areas where registration is compulsory) shall have effect as if the provisions of subsection (1) of this section were contained in an Order in Council; and section 124 of that Act (which provides that Part XI of that Act shall bind the Crown) shall have effect as if this section were included in the said Part XI.

81.—(1) Where immediately before 1st April 1965 any property (not being property to which section 57 (2) of this Act applies) was held exclusively for charitable purposes by the London or Middlesex county council as sole trustee, that property shall on that date vest in the Greater London Council for the like purposes, so, however, that where that property

was so held by the London county council for the purposes of a charity registered in the register established under section 4 of the Charities Act 1960 in any part of that register which is maintained by virtue of section 2 of that Act by the Minister of Education, the charity trustees on and after that date shall be the Inner London Education Authority.

(2) Where immediately before 1st April 1965 any property was held exclusively for charitable purposes as sole trustee by any existing council to whom section 3 (1) (b) of this Act applies other than the London or Middlesex county council, that property shall on that date vest for the like purposes in the council of the appropriate London borough, that is to say, the London borough whose area includes the whole or the greater part of the area of the existing council in question.

(3) Where immediately before 1st April 1965 any power with respect to any charity, not being a charity incorporated under the Companies Acts or by charter, was under the trusts of the charity or by virtue of section 37 (5) (c) of the said Act of 1960 vested in, or in the holder of any office connected with, any such existing council as aforesaid, that power shall at that date vest in, or in the holder of the corresponding office connected with, the council of the appropriate London borough aforesaid.

(4) Where under the trusts of any charity established for purposes which are by their nature or by the trusts of the charity directed wholly or mainly to the benefit of an area which falls wholly or mainly within Greater London, not being a charity incorporated as aforesaid, any power with respect to that charity was immediately before 1st April 1965 vested in, or in the holder of any office connected with, the London, Middlesex, Essex, Hertfordshire, Kent or Surrey county council, then, if the conditions specified in paragraph (a) or (b) of this subsection are satisfied, that power shall on that day vest in, or in the holder of the corresponding office connected with, the authority specified in that paragraph, that is to say—

> (a) if that area falls wholly or mainly within a single London borough and, where that borough is an inner London borough, the charity was immediately before that date registered in the register aforesaid in any part thereof which is maintained by the Charity Commissioners but not in any part thereof which is maintained as aforesaid by the Minister of Education, the council of that borough;
>
> (b) if the conditions specified in the foregoing paragraph are not satisfied but that area falls wholly or mainly within the Inner London Education Area, and subject to the next following subsection, the Inner London Education Authority.

(5) Where under subsection (4) (b) of this section any power vests or is to vest in, or in the holder of any office connected with, the Inner London Education Authority, that Authority or, as the case may be, the holder of that office may, with the consent of the Charity Commissioners and of the council or office-holder nominated, nominate for the purposes of this subsection the council of any inner London borough or, as the case may be, the holder of the corresponding office connected with any such council, and thereupon, or, if the nomination is made before 1st April 1965, on that date, that power shall vest in that council or, as the case may be, in the holder of that corresponding office.

(6) Where under the trusts of any charity, not being a charity incorporated as aforesaid, any power with respect to that charity was immediately before 1st April 1965 vested in, or in the holder of any office connected with, the London or Midddlesex county council and neither paragraph (a) nor paragraph (b) of subsection (4) of this section applies, that

power shall vest in, or in the holder of the corresponding office connected with, such of the following authorities, that is to say, the councils of the London boroughs, the Greater London Council and the Inner London Education Authority, as the charity trustees may not later than 1st April 1967 with the consent of that council or, as the case may be, of the holder of that corresponding office appoint or, in default of such appointment, as may be appointed by the Charity Commissioners or, in the case of an exempt charity, by the Minister.

(7) References in the foregoing provisions of this section to a power with respect to a charity shall not include references to any power of any person by virtue of being a charity trustee thereof; but where under the trusts of any charity, not being a charity incorporated as aforesaid, the charity trustees immediately before 1st April 1965 included the holder of an office connected with any council to whom section 3 (1) (b) of this Act applies, then, as from that date, those trustees shall instead include the holder of such office connected with such of the following authorities, that is to say, the councils of the London boroughs, the Greater London Council and the Inner London Education Authority, as the Charity Commissioners may appoint.

(8) Nothing in the foregoing provisions of this section shall affect any power of Her Majesty, the court or any other person to alter the trusts of any charity.

(9) As from 1st April 1965—

> (a) sections 6, 10, 11 and 12 of the said Act of 1960 shall apply to the Greater London Council and to the Inner London Education Authority as if Greater London or, as the case may be, the Inner London Education Area were a county and that Council or, as the case may be, Authority were the council of that county and, for the purposes of subsection (4) of the said section 10, as if for the reference to any county district there were substituted a reference to any London borough;
>
> (b) the said sections 10 and 11 shall apply to the City as if it were a London borough and the Common Council were the council of that borough;
>
> (c) in Schedule 3 to that Act any reference to the county of London shall be construed as a reference to Greater London.

(10) In this section, the expressions "charitable purposes", "charity", "charity trustees", "exempt charity", "court" and "trusts" have the same meanings respectively as in the said Act of 1960.

General

82.—(1) Her Majesty may at any time, whether before or after 1st April 1965, by Order in Council coming into force not earlier than that date provide that any functions exercisable as respects a London borough by the council of that borough, not being functions for the exercise of which as respects the Temples specific provision is made elsewhere in this Act and, without prejudice to the foregoing provision, not being functions for which provision is made by Part V or VI of this Act, shall be exercisable—

> (a) as respects the Inner Temple by the Sub-Treasurer thereof and as respects the Middle Temple by the Under-Treasurer thereof; or
>
> (b) as respects both the Temples by the Common Council.

(2) Any Order in Council under this section may make such incidental, consequential, transitional or supplementary provision as appears to Her Majesty to be necessary or proper for the purposes or in consequence of any of the provisions of the Order, including provision—

> (a) applying any enactment relating to the functions in question (including any enactment in this Act or in any other Act passed during the same session as this Act) to the Inner Temple or the Middle Temple;
>
> (b) modifying any such enactment in its application thereto;
>
> (c) excluding the application of any such enactment thereto;
>
> (d) repealing any such enactment applying thereto.

(3) Any Order in Council under this section shall be subject to annulment in pursuance of a resolution of either House of Parliament.

(4) Any expenses incurred by the Sub-Treasurer of the Inner Temple or the Under-Treasurer of the Middle Temple under this Act or any enactment applied to the Temples by or under this Act may be defrayed out of a rate in the nature of a general rate levied in the Inner Temple or the Middle Temple, as the case may be.

83.—(1) As from 1st April 1965, the enactments specified in Schedule 17 to this Act shall have effect subject to the provisions of that Schedule, being provisions necessary or expedient in consequence of other provisions of this Act.

(2) Her Majesty may at any time, whether before or after 1st April 1965, in any case where it appears to Her appropriate in consequence of the provisions of this Act, by Order in Council coming into force not earlier than 1st April 1965 make such further modifications of any enactment contained in any other public general Act passed before 1st April 1965 (not being an Act passed with respect only to the whole or part of the existing county of London) as may appear to Her to be necessary to make that enactment apply—

> (a) in relation to Greater London or the Greater London Council as it applies in relation to, or to the council of, a county (or a particular county to which section 3 (1) (b) of this Act applies); or
>
> (b) in relation to a London borough or the council thereof or, as the case may be, in relation to the City or the Common Council, as it applies in relation to, or to the council of, a county borough (or a particular county borough to which the said section 3 (1) (b) applies); or
>
> (c) in relation to a London borough or the council thereof as it applies in relation to, or to the council of, a metropolitan borough (or a particular metropolitan borough),

or, in the case of an enactment conferring on the London county council power to appoint members of any body, to make that power exercisable by some body appearing to Her to be representative of all or any of the councils of the London boroughs and the Common Council or by the Inner London Education Authority; but no such Order shall be made unless a draft thereof has been laid before, and approved by a resolution of, each House of Parliament.

84.—(1) The Minister or any appropriate Minister may at any time, whether before or after 1st April 1965, by order, which shall be subject to annulment in pursuance of a resolution of either House of Parliament, make such incidental, consequential, transitional or supplementary provision as may appear to him—

> (a) to be necessary or proper for the general or any particular purposes of this Act or in consequence of any of the provisions thereof or for giving full effect thereto; or
>
> (b) to be necessary or proper in consequence of such

of the provisions of any other Act passed in the same session as this Act as apply to Greater London or any authority therein or any other area or authority affected by Part I of this Act;

and nothing in any other provision of this Act shall be construed as prejudicing the generality of this subsection.

(2) Any such order may in particular include provision—

(a) with respect to the transfer and management or custody of property (whether real or personal) and the transfer of rights and liabilities;

(b) with respect to the membership of any body so far as that membership consists of persons elected by, or appointed by or on the nomination of—

(i) any council affected by Part I of this Act; or

(ii) any two or more bodies who include such a council;

(c) for applying, amending or repealing or revoking, with or without savings, any Act passed or any instrument under an Act made before 1st April 1965;

(d) for requiring the council of any London borough, with a view to securing that the introduction of a general rate of uniform amount per pound of rateable value throughout the borough is gradual, to make and levy during a limited period beginning on 1st April 1965 differential rates determined by reference to the circumstances of the existing rating areas and parts of such areas included in the borough;

(e) for any of the matters specified in section 148(1) (a) to (h) and (2) of the Local Government Act 1933;

(f) for anything duly done before 1st April 1965 by any authority in the exercise of functions which on and after that date become functions of some other authority to be deemed as from that date to have been duly done by that other authority, and for any instrument made before that date, if or so far as it was made in the exercise of those functions, to continue in force on and after that date until varied or revoked in the exercise of those functions by that other authority.

(3) The provision which may be made by virtue of paragraph (e) of the last foregoing subsection shall include the making, in relation to any association mentioned in section 2 of the Auxiliary Forces Act 1953, of the like provision as may be made in relation to a public body under section 148(1)(a) to (h) of the Local Government Act 1933, including provision for continuing in existence any such association and the area for which it is established or authorising the establishment of any such association under the said Act of 1953 for the whole or any part of Greater London and in either case for the appointment of a president and vice-president of any such association.

(4) Notwithstanding anything in the foregoing provisions of this section, the Minister shall not make an order under this section (or this section as extended by section 87 of this Act) affecting any Act or instrument applying only to the City (with or without the Temples) or to things or persons connected therewith except after consultation with the Common Council.

(5) Section 151 of the said Act of 1933 (which relates to financial adjustments by agreement between public bodies affected by any alteration of areas or authorities made by an order under Part VI of that Act) shall apply for the purposes of this Act as if the reference to such an order included a reference to any provision of, or of any instrument made under, this Act.

(6) The provisions of Part I of this Act shall not affect the liability of any person whose name was immediately before 1st April 1965 included in a jurors book for any county or other area to serve on a jury for that area, and any such person (unless duly exempted or excused) shall, so long as the jurors book in which his name was then included remains in force for any area affected by the said Part I, continue to be liable to serve on a jury for that area.

85.—(1) Any order under section 6 or 84 of this Act may contain provisions as to the transfer of any person who is, on such date as may be specified in relation to him in the order, the holder of any place, situation or employment and who is affected by any provision of, or of any instrument made under, this Act, and shall contain provisions for the protection of the interests of such persons.

(2) In the case of any person who on the 31st March 1965 is in the employment of one or more local authorities who are or include a council to whom section 3 (1) (b) of this Act applies, being employment which, or which in the aggregate, is wholetime employment, the Minister shall by order make such provision as is necessary to ensure that, to the extent, if any, to which, by reason only of the said section 3 (1) (b), that person would apart from the order cease on 1st April 1965 to be in employment which, or which in the aggregate, would be wholetime employment by one or more local authorities, that person is transferred on 1st April 1965 to the employment of such local authority as may be specified in or determined under the order.

(3) The provision required by subsection (1) or (2) of this section or by section 24(7) of this Act shall include such provision with respect to any person who is transferred under this Act (or, as the case may be, in pursuance of any agreement under the said section 24(7)) from the employment of one authority to that of another as to secure that—

(a) so long as he continues in the employment of that other authority by virtue of the transfer and until he is served with a statement in writing of new terms and conditions of employment, he enjoys terms and conditions of employment not less favourable than those he enjoyed immediately before the date of transfer; and

(b) the said new terms and conditions are such that—

(i) so long as he is engaged in duties reasonably comparable to those in which he was engaged immediately before the date of transfer, the scale of his salary or remuneration, and

(ii) the other terms and conditions of his employment,

are not less favourable than those he enjoyed immediately before the date of transfer.

(4) The appropriate Minister shall by regulations make provision for the payment by such authority as may be prescribed by or determined under the regulations, but subject to such exceptions or conditions as may be so prescribed, of compensation to or in respect of persons who are, or who but for any such service by them as may be so prescribed would be, the holders of any such place, situation or employment as may be so prescribed and who suffer loss of employment or loss of diminution of emoluments which is attributable to any provision of this Act or of any instrument (including any agreement under section 24(7)) made under this Act; and any such regulations—

(a) may include provision as to the manner in which and the person to whom any claim for compensation is to be made, and for the determination of all questions arising under the regulations; and

(b) shall be subject to annulment in pursuance of a resolution of either House of Parliament.

(5) The Minister, after consulting with such bodies representative of local authorities or of staff employed by local authorities as appear to him to be concerned and with any local authority with whom consultation appears to him to be desirable, shall not later than one month after the passing of this Act establish a staff commission for the purpose of—

(a) considering and keeping under review the arrangements for the recruitment of staff by the Greater London Council and the London borough councils and for the transfer in consequence of the provisions of this Act or any instrument made thereunder of staff employed by other local authorities affected by Part I of this Act;

(b) considering such staffing problems arising in consequence of, and such other matters relating to staff employed by any body affected by, any provision of, or of any instrument made under, this Act as may be referred to the commission by the Minister; and

(c) advising the Minister on the steps necessary to safeguard the interests of such staff;

and the Minister may give directions to the commission as to their procedure and to any local authority (including any existing local authority) in Greater London with respect to the furnishing of any information requested and the implementation of any advice given by the commission and with respect to the payment by such authorities of any expenses incurred in connection with the commission.

86.—(1) In the case of any London borough other than the borough numbered 29 in Part I of Schedule 1 to this Act, for the purpose of the consideration of the matters to be included in the borough's charter or incorporation order or to be dealt with under section 84, 85(5) or 87(2) of this Act, the councils of the existing boroughs, metropolitan boroughs or urban districts which, or parts of which, are to be included in that London borough, and the council of any existing county in which the whole or any part of the area of that London borough is situated, may, and within four weeks of being so required by the Minister shall, appoint such number of representatives respectively to a joint committee for the purpose as may be agreed between those councils, or, in default of such agreement, determined by the Minister.

(2) For the purpose of the consideration of the matters in connection with the establishment of the Greater London Council to be dealt with under section 84, 85(5) or 87(2) of this Act the councils of the existing counties and county boroughs whose areas lie wholly or partly within Greater London may, and within four weeks of being so required by the Minister shall, appoint such number of representatives respectively to a joint committee for the purpose as may be agreed between those councils or, in default of such agreement, determined by the Minister.

(3) Any expenses incurred by any joint committee established under this section shall be defrayed by the councils represented thereon in such proportions respectively as may be agreed between them, or in default of such agreement, determined by the Minister.

87.—(1) Subject to the provisions of this Act and any Act passed after this Act and before 1st April 1965 and of any order under section 84 of this Act or this section, any local statutory provision to which this section applies and which is not continued in force by any other provision of this Act shall—

(a) notwithstanding the changes of administrative areas and abolition of local authorities effected by Part

I of this Act and, in the case of an instrument made under any enactment, notwithstanding the repeal of that enactment, continue to apply on and after that date to, but only to, the area, things or persons to which or to whom it applies before that date;

(b) have effect subject to any necessary modifications, including in particular—

(i) in the case of a Greater London statutory provision, the substitution for any reference to an existing county borough, metropolitan borough or county district situated wholly or partly within Greater London or the council thereof of a reference to so much of the London borough or boroughs as comprise that existing borough or district or any part thereof or, as the case may be, the council of that London borough or the councils of those London boroughs;

(ii) in the case of an urban district statutory provision, the substitution for any reference to the county of Middlesex or the council thereof of a reference to the county in which the district in question is included by virtue of this Act or, as the case may be, the council of that county;

but the continuation by this subsection of an instrument made under any enactment shall not be construed as prejudicing any power to vary or revoke the instrument which is exercisable apart from this subsection.

(2) An order made under section 84 of this Act by any Minister may—

(a) repeal or revoke any Greater London statutory provision which appears to that Minister to have become spent, obsolete or unnecessary or to have been substantially superseded by any enactment or instrument which applies or may be applied to the area, persons or things to which or to whom that provision applies;

(b) transfer to any authority appearing to that Minister to be appropriate any functions of an existing local authority under a Greater London statutory provision which are not to become functions of some other authority under any provision of this Act except section 84 and this section, or under any other instrument made under this Act, being functions exercisable by any existing local authority abolished by this Act or exercisable in, or with respect to things or persons connected with, the relevant area by any other existing local authority;

(c) without prejudice to the last foregoing paragraph, make such modifications of any Greater London statutory provision in its application to any part of the relevant area as appears to that Minister to be expedient;

(d) extend any such provision, with or without further modifications, to a part of the relevant area to which it did not previously extend.

(3) For the purpose of securing uniformity in the law applicable with respect to any matter in different parts of the relevant area, or in the relevant area or any part thereof and other parts of England and Wales, any appropriate Minister may, after consultation with such of the appropriate councils as appear to the Minister to be interested, by provisional order made after 1st April 1965 amend, repeal or revoke any Greater London statutory provision and extend it, with or without modifications, to a part of the relevant area to which it did not previously extend; and any such order may include such

incidental, consequential, transitional or supplementary provision as may appear to the Minister to be necessary or proper for the purposes of the order or in consequence of any provisions thereof.

The appropriate councils for the purposes of this subsection are—

(a) in relation to sewerage and sewage disposal so far as they concern the sewerage area of the Greater London Council, the Common Council and the councils of the London boroughs and county districts wholly or partly within that area;

(b) in relation to land drainage, flood prevention and the like matters so far as they concern the London excluded area within the meaning of Schedule 14 to this Act, the Common Council and the councils of the London boroughs and county districts wholly or partly within that area;

(c) in relation to any matters not falling within paragraphs (a) and (b) of this subsection, the Common Council and the councils of the London boroughs;

and also, in relation to any matter with respect to which the Greater London Council have functions, that Council.

(4) Where any Greater London statutory provision is continued in force in any area by subsection (1) of this section or is amended or modified in its application, or extended, to any area by an order under section 84 of this Act or subsection (3) of this section, any appropriate Minister may by that order or, in the case of a provision continued as aforesaid, by an order under this subsection provide that that provision as so continued, amended, modified or extended shall have effect in that area to the exclusion of any enactment for corresponding purposes (including any enactment contained in or applied by this Act), or may make such modifications of any such enactment in its application to that area as will secure that the enactment will operate harmoniously with the said provision in that area.

(5) Any appropriate Minister may by order provide that any Greater London statutory provision continued in force by subsection (1) of this section, being a provision of an instrument made under an enactment, shall cease to have effect, either generally or as respects any area, persons or things specified in the order, at the end of a period so specified.

(6) Any order under subsection (4) or (5) of this section shall be subject to annulment in pursuance of a resolution of either House of Parliament.

(7) No order shall be made as respects any part of Greater London after the passing of this Act under section 303 of the Public Health Act 1875 or any other enactment which authorises the making in relation to any local statutory provision of provision corresponding to that which may be made in relation thereto by an order under section 84 of this Act or this section:

Provided that the foregoing provisions of this subsection shall not affect—

(a) any order made under any such enactment before the passing of this Act; or

(b) the power of the Minister to make an order under section 82 of the Public Health Act 1961 with respect to any provision which appears to him to be inconsistent with, or unnecessary in consequence of, any provision of Part II of that Act as regards building regulations.

(8) This section applies to any local statutory provision in force immediately before 1st April 1965 and not expressly repealed or revoked by this Act, being a provision—

(a) applying to any part of the relevant area or to

things or persons connected with a part of the relevant area; or

(b) conferring on an existing local authority abolished by this Act functions the exercise of which is not restricted to a part of Greater London or to things or persons connected therewith; or

(c) applying to the urban district of Potters Bar, Staines or Sunbury-on-Thames or to things or persons connected with one of those districts.

(9) In this section—

"the relevant area" means Greater London except that—

(a) in relation to sewerage and sewage disposal, it includes so much of any county district as is in the sewerage area of the Greater London Council;

(b) in relation to land drainage, flood prevention and the like matters, it includes so much of any county district as is in the London excluded area within the meaning of Schedule 14 to this Act;

"Greater London statutory provision" means any statutory provision to which this section applies, being a provision mentioned in subsection (8)(a) or (b) of this section;

"local authority" means the council of a county, county borough, metropolitan borough or county district or the Common Council or any joint committee, joint board, joint authority or other combined body all the members of which are representatives of any such council;

"urban district statutory provision" means any statutory provision to which this section applies, being a provision mentioned in subsection (8)(c) of this section.

88.—(1) Any Minister may cause a local inquiry to be held for the purpose of any of his functions under this Act in any case where there is no duty and no power apart from this section to hold an inquiry.

(2) Section 290 (2) to (5) of the Local Government Act 1933 (which subsections relate to the giving of evidence at inquiries and the payment of costs) shall apply to any local inquiry caused to be held for the purpose of this Act by any Minister as if that Minister were a department for the purposes of that section, but shall not apply to any such inquiry so far as some other provision with respect to the subject-matter of those subsections is applicable to that inquiry by virtue of any other enactment.

89.—(1) In this Act, except where the context otherwise requires the following expressions have the following meanings respectively, that is to say—

"appropriate Minister", in relation to the making of an order or regulation with respect to any matter, means the Minister in charge of any government department concerned with that matter; but the validity of any order or regulation purporting to be made by any Minister by virtue of a power conferred on the appropriate Minister by this Act shall not be affected by any question as to whether or not that Minister was the appropriate Minister for the purpose;

"the City" means the City of London;

"the Common Council" means the Common Council of the City of London;

"county" means an administrative county;

"county review area" in relation to the county of Essex, Hertfordshire, Kent or Surrey, means the area with respect to which, by virtue of section 3 (2) of this

177

Act, a county review by the council of that county under section 28 of the Local Government Act 1958 may for the time being be made;

"existing" in relation to a local government area or authority, means that area or authority as it existed immediately before the passing of this Act;

"functions" includes powers and duties;

"Inner London Education Area" and "Inner London Education Authority" have the meanings respectively assigned to them by section 30 (1) of this Act;

"land" includes land covered by water and any interest or right in, to or over land;

"local statutory provision" means a provision of a local Act (including an Act confirming a provisional order) or a provision of a public general Act passed with respect only to the whole or part of the existing county of London or a provision of an instrument made under any such local or public general Act or of an instrument in the nature of a local enactment made under any other Act;

"metropolitan road" means a road for the time being designated by or under section 17 of this Act as a metropolitan road;

"Minister" includes the Board of Trade;

"the Minister" means the Minister of Housing and Local Government;

"Port of London" means the port of that name established for the purposes of the enactments relating to customs or excise;

"relevant year of election" means the first year of election occurring after the first Order in Council is made after the passing of this Act under the House of Commons (Redistribution of Seats) Act 1949 giving effect to a report of the Boundary Commission for England under that Act with respect to the parliamentary constituencies situated wholly or partly in Greater London; and for the purposes of this definition "year of election" means the year 1967 or any third year thereafter;

"sewerage area of the Greater London Council" has the meaning assigned to it by section 39 of this Act;

"the Temples" means the Inner Temple and the Middle Temple.

(2) In this Act, except where the context otherwise requires, references to any enactment shall be construed as references to that enactment as amended, extended or applied by or under any other enactment, including any enactment contained in this Act.

(3) References in any other Act to any enactment modified by this Act shall, except when the context otherwise requires, be construed as a reference to that enactment as so modified.

90. Any power to make orders, rules or regulations conferred by this Act on any Minister shall be exercisable by statutory instrument, and any power to make an order under any provision of this Act shall include power to make an order varying or revoking any order previously made under that provision.

91.—(1) There shall be defrayed out of moneys provided by Parliament—

(a) any expenses incurred by any Minister under this Act; and

(b) any increase attributable to the provisions of this Act in the sums payable out of moneys so provided under any other enactment.

(2) Any sums received by any Minister under this Act shall be paid into the Exchequer.

92.—(1) The House of Commons Disqualification Act 1957 shall be amended in accordance with the following provisions of this section.

(2) In Part II of Schedule 1, in its application to the House of Commons of the Parliament of the United Kingdom, after the entry relating to the South of Scotland Electricity Board there shall be inserted the words "The Staff Commission established under section 85(5) of the London Government Act 1963".

(3) In Part III of Schedule 1, both in its application to the House of Commons of the Parliament of the United Kingdom and in its application to the Senate and House of Commons of Northern Ireland, in the entry relating to local government officers—

(a) after the words "England and Wales" where they first occur there shall be inserted the words "of the Greater London Council";

(b) the words "of a metropolitan borough" shall cease to have effect; and

(c) the words "outside London" shall cease to have effect:

Provided that the repeal made by paragraph (b) of this subsection shall not take effect until 1st April 1965.

93.—(1) In addition to the repeals by virtue of paragraph 70 of Schedule 6 to this Act, the enactments specified in Schedule 18 to this Act are hereby repealed to the extent mentioned in the third column of that Schedule—

(a) in the case of the enactments specified in Part I of that Schedule, as from the passing of this Act;

(b) in the case of the enactments specified in Part II of that Schedule, as from 1st April 1965:

Provided that the repeal of any enactment specified in the said Part I shall not affect the operation of that enactment in relation to an election held on or after the date of the passing of this Act to fill a casual vacancy occurring before that date.

(2) Without prejudice to section 38(1) of the Interpretation Act 1889, where this Act repeals any enactment making provision with respect to a particular matter or particular matters and either makes, or applies some other enactment making, corresponding or different provision with respect to that matter or those matters, then, unless the contrary intention appears and, in particular, subject to any order under section 82, 83, 84, 85 or 87 of this Act, references in any enactment other than this Act, or in any instrument made under any enactment other than this Act, to the repealed enactment shall be construed as references to the enactment contained in or applied by this Act which makes the corresponding or different provision.

(3) Nothing in this Act shall effect the boundary of the area for the supply of electricity or gas of any Area Board within the meaning of the Electricity Act 1947 or the Gas Act 1948.

(4) Nothing contained in, or done by virtue of, any provision of this Act other than section 84(2)(b) or paragraph 35 of Schedule 4 shall affect the functions of the conservators of any common.

(5) Any enabling provision contained in this Act shall be deemed to be in addition to, and not in derogation of, any powers exercisable by Her Majesty by virtue of Her Royal prerogative.

94.—(1) This Act may be cited as the London Government Act 1963.

(2) The following provisions of this Act shall not come into force until 1st April 1965, that is to say, Parts II, III, and V to VIII other than sections 17(6), 48(2), 62(4), 66, 69, and 70.

(3) Except for section 4(4) and section 92 of this Act and the repeals made by this Act in the House of Commons Dis-

qualification Act 1957, the provisions of this Act other than this subsection shall not extend to Scotland; and as from 1st April 1965 in paragraph 8 of Schedule 6 to the Valuation and Rating (Scotland) Act 1956 for the words "the Administrative County of London" there shall be substituted the words "Greater London other than the outer London boroughs".

(4) Except for the said section 92 and the said repeals, the provisions of this Act other than this subsection shall not extend to Northern Ireland.

The Port of New York Authority

In 1834, the States of New Jersey and New York signed an agreement specifying the obligations and rights of the two states in the Hudson River and Bay of New York. The rapid growth of commerce and trade in the Bay of New York induced the Governors of the two states to create, in 1917, the New York-New Jersey Port Development Commission to review the 1834 agreement.

Accepting the Commission's recommendations, the New Jersey and New York Legislature on April 20, 1921 approved an interstate compact* which created the Port of New York Authority to develop and operate transportation and terminal facilities in an area radiating twenty-five miles out from the Statute of Liberty in New York City harbor. The Compact, which subsequently was ratified by Congress and signed by the President, provides for the Authority to be governed by a Board of Commissioners: Six Commissioners are appointed by the Governor of each state for overlapping six-year terms.

WHEREAS, In the year eighteen hundred and thirty-four the states of New York and New Jersey did enter into an agreement fixing and determining the rights and obligations of the two states in and about the waters between the two states, especially in and about the bay of New York and the Hudson river; and

WHEREAS, Since that time the commerce of the port of New York has greatly developed and increased and the territory in and around the port has become commercially one center or district; and

WHEREAS, It is confidently believed that a better co-ordination of the terminal, transportation and other facilities of commerce in, about and through the port of New York, will result in great economies, benefiting the nation, as well as the states of New York and New Jersey; and

WHEREAS, The future development of such terminal, transportation and other facilities of commerce will require the expenditure of large sums of money and the cordial co-operation of the states of New York and New Jersey in the encouragement of the investment of capital, and in the formulation and execution of the necessary physical plans; and

WHEREAS, Such result can best be accomplished through the co-operation of the two states by and through a joint or common agency.

Now, therefore, The said states of New Jersey and New York do supplement and amend the existing agreement of eighteen hundred and thirty-four in the following respects:

ARTICLE I.

They agree to and pledge, each to the other, faithful co-operation in the future planning and development of the port of New York, holding in high trust for the benefit of the nation the special blessings and natural advantages thereof.

ARTICLE II.

To that end the two states do agree that there shall be created and they do hereby create a district to be known as the "Port of New York District" (for brevity hereinafter referred to as "The District") which shall embrace the territory bounded and described as follows:

The district is included within the boundary lines located by connecting points of known latitude and logitude. The approximate courses and distances of the lines enclosing the district are recited in the description, but the district is determined by drawing lines through the points of known latitude and longitude. Beginning at a point A of latitude forty-one degrees and four minutes north and longitude seventy-three degrees and fifty-six minutes west, said point being about sixty-five hundredths of a mile west of the westerly bank of the Hudson river and about two and one-tenth miles northwest of the pier at Piermont, in the county of Rockland, state of New York; thence due south one and fifteen-hundredths miles more or less to a point B of latitude forty-one degrees and three minutes north and longitude seventy-three degrees and fifty-six minutes west; said point being about one and three-tenths miles northwest of the pier at Piermont, in the county of Rockland, state of New York; thence south fifty-six degrees and thirty-four minutes west six and twenty-six hundredths miles more or less to a point C of latitude forty-one degrees and no minutes north and longitude seventy-four degrees and two minutes west, said point being about seven-tenths of a mile north of the railroad station at Westwood, in the county of Bergen, state of New Jersey; thence south sixty-eight degrees and twenty-four minutes west nine and thirty-seven-hundredths miles more or less to a point D of latitude forty degrees and fifty-seven minutes north and longitude seventy-four degrees and twelve minutes west, said point being about three miles northwest of the business center of the city of Paterson, in the county of Passaic, state of New Jersey; thence south forty-seven degrees and seventeen minutes west eleven and eighty-seven-hundredths miles more or less to a point E of latitude forty degrees and fifty minutes north and longitude seventy-four degrees and twenty-two minutes west, said point being about four and five-tenths miles west of the borough of Caldwell, in the county of Morris, state of New Jersey; thence due south nine and twenty-hundredths miles more or less to a point F of latitude forty degrees and forty-two minutes north and longitude seventy-four degrees and twenty-two minutes west, said point being about one and two-tenths miles southwest of the passenger station of the Delaware, Lackawana and Western railroad in the city of Summit, in the county of Union, state of New Jersey; thence south forty-two degrees and twenty-four minutes west, seven and seventy-eigth-hundredths miles more or less to a point G of latitude forty degrees and thirty-seven minutes north and longitude seventy-four degrees and twenty-eight minutes west, said point being about two and two-tenths miles west of the business center of the city of Plainfield, in the county of Somerset, state of New Jersey; thence due south twelve and sixty-five-hundredths miles more or less on a line passing about one mile west of the business center of the city of New Brunswick to a point H of latitude forty degrees and twenty-six minutes north and longitude seventy-

**Laws of New York, 1921,* chapter 154 and *Laws of New Jersey, 1921,* chapter 151.

four degrees and twenty-eight minutes west, said point being about four and five-tenths miles southwest of the city of New Brunswick, in the county of Middlesex, state of New Jersey; thence south seventy-seven degrees and forty-two minutes east ten and seventy-nine-hundredths miles more or less to a point I of latitude forty degrees and twenty-four minutes north and longitude seventy-four degrees and sixteen minutes west, said point being about two miles southwest of the borough of Matawan, in the county of Middlesex, state of New Jersey; thence due east twenty-five and forty-eight-hundredths miles more or less, crossing the county of Monmouth, state of New Jersey, and passing about one and four-tenths miles south of the pier of the Central Railroad of New Jersey at Atlantic Highlands to a point J of latitude forty degrees and twenty-four minutes north and longitude seventy-three degrees and forty-seven minutes west, said point being in the Atlantic ocean; thence north eleven degrees fifty-eight minutes east twenty-one and sixteen-hundredths miles more or less to a point K, said point being about five miles east of the passenger station of the Long Island railroad at Jamaica and about one and three-tenths miles east of the boundary line of the city of New York, in the county of Nassau, state of New York; thence in a north-easterly direction passing about one-half mile west of New Hyde Park and about one and one-tenth miles east of the shore of Manhasset bay at Port Washington, crossing Long Island Sound to a point L, said point being the point of intersection of the boundary line between the states of New York and Connecticut and the meridian of seventy-three degrees, thirty-nine minutes and thirty seconds west longitude, said point being also about a mile northeast of the village of Port Chester; thence northwesterly along the boundary line between the states of New York and Connecticut to a point M, said point being the point of intersection between said boundary line between the states of New York and Connecticut and the parallel of forty-one degrees and four minutes north latitude, said point also being about four and five-tenths miles northeast of the business center of the city of White Plains; thence due west along said parallel, of forty-one degrees and four minutes north latitude, the line passing about two and one-half miles north of the business center of the city of White Plains and crossing the Hudson river to the point A, the place of beginning.

The boundaries of said district may be changed from time to time by the action of the legislature of either state concurred in by the legislature of the other.

ARTICLE III.

There is hereby created "The Port of New York Authority" (for brevity hereinafter referred to as the "Port Authority"), which shall be a body corporate and politic, having the powers and jurisdiction hereinafter enumerated, and such other and additional powers as shall be conferred upon it by the legislature of either state concurred in by the legislature of the other, or by act or acts of congress, as hereinafter provided.

ARTICLE IV.

The port authority shall consist of six commissioners— three resident voters from the state of New York, two of whom shall be resident voters of the city of New York, and three resident voters from the state of New Jersey, two of whom shall be resident voters within the New Jersey portion of the district, the New York members to be chosen by the state of New York and the New Jersey members by the state of New Jersey in the manner and for the terms fixed and determined

from time to time by the legislature of each state respectively, except as herein provided.

Each commissioner may be removed or suspended from office as provided by the law of the state for which he shall be appointed.

ARTICLE V.

The commissioners shall, for the purpose of doing business, constitute a board and may adopt suitable by-laws for its management.

ARTICLE VI.

The port authority shall constitute a body, both corporate and politic, with full power and authority to purchase, construct, lease and/or operate any terminal or transportation facility within said district; and to make charges for the use thereof; and for any of such purposes to own, hold, lease and/or operate real or personal property, to borrow money and secure the same by bonds or by mortgages upon any property held or to be held by it. No property now or hereafter vested in or held by either state, or by any county, city, borough, village, township or other municipality, shall be taken by the port authority, without the authority or consent of such state, county, city, borough, village, township or other municipality, nor shall anything herein impair or invalidate in any way any bonded indebtedness of such state, county, city, borough, village, township or other municipality, nor impair the provisions of law regulating the payment into sinking funds of revenues derived from municipal property, or dedicating the revenues derived from any municipal property to a specific purpose.

The powers granted in this article shall not be exercised by the port authority until the legislatures of both states shall have approved of a comprehensive plan for the development of the port as hereinafter provided.

ARTICLE VII.

The port authority shall have such additional powers and duties as may hereafter be delegated to or imposed upon it from time to time by the action of the legislature of either state concurred in by the legislature of the other. Unless and until otherwise provided, it shall make an annual report to the legislature of both states, setting forth in detail the operations and transactions conducted by it pursuant to this agreement and any legislation thereunder. The port authority shall not pledge the credit of either state except by and with the authority of the legislature thereof.

ARTICLE VIII.

Unless and until otherwise provided, all laws now or here-after vesting jurisdiction or control in the public service commission, or the public utilities commission, or like body, within each state respectively, shall apply to railroads and to any transportation terminal or other facility owned, operated, leased or constructed by the port authority, with the same force and effect as if such railroad, or transportation, terminal or other facility were owned, leased, operated or constructed by a private corporation.

ARTICLE IX.

Nothing contained in this agreement shall impair the powers of any municipality to develop or improve port and terminal facilities.

ARTICLE X.

The legislatures of the two states, prior to the signing of this agreement, or thereafter as soon as may be practicable, will adopt a plan or plans for the comprehensive development of the port of New York.

ARTICLE XI.

The port authority shall from time to time make plans for the development of said district, supplementary to or amendatory of any plan theretofore adopted, and when such plans are duly approved by the legislatures of the two states, they shall be binding upon both states with the same force and effect as if incorporated in this agreement.

ARTICLE XII.

The port authority may from time to time make recommendations to the legislatures of the two states or to the congress of the United States, based upon study and analysis, for the better conduct of the commerce passing in and through the port of New York, the increase and improvement of transportation and terminal facilities therein, and the more economical and expeditious handling of such commerce.

ARTICLE XIII.

The port authority may petition any interstate commerce commission (or like body), public service commission, public utilities commission (or like body), or any other federal, municipal, state or local authority, administrative, judicial or legislative, having jurisdiction in the premises, after the adoption of the comprehensive plan as provided for in article X for the adoption and execution of any physical improvement, change in method, rate of transportation, system of handling freight, warehousing, docking, lightering or transfer of freight, which, in the opinion of the port authority, may be designed to improve or better the handling of commerce in and through said district, or improve terminal and transportation facilities therein. It may intervene in any proceeding affecting the commerce of the port.

ARTICLE XIV.

The port authority shall elect from its number a chairman, vice-chairman, and may appoint such officers and employees as it may require for the performance of its duties, and shall fix and determine their qualifications and duties.

ARTICLE XV.

Unless and until the revenues from operations conducted by the port authority are adequate to meet all expenditures, the legislatures of the two states shall appropriate, in equal amounts, annually, for the salaries, office and other administrative expenses, such sum or sums as shall be recommended by the port authority and approved by the governors of the two states, but each state obligates itself hereunder only to the extent of one hundred thousand dollars in any one year.

ARTICLE XVI.

Unless and until otherwise determined by the action of the legislatures of the two states, no action of the port authority shall be binding unless taken at a meeting at which at least two members from each state are present and unless four votes are cast therefor, two from each state. Each state reserves the right hereafter to provide by law for the exercise of a veto power by the governor thereof over any action of any commissioner appointed therefrom.

ARTICLE XVII.

Unless and until otherwise determined by the action of the legislatures of the two states, the port authority shall not incur any obligations for salaries, office or other administrative expenses, within the provisions of article XV, prior to the making of appropriations adequate to meet the same.

ARTICLE XVIII.

The port authority is hereby authorized to make suitable rules and regulations not inconsistent with the constitution of the United States or of either state, and subject to the exercise of the power of congress, for the improvement of the conduct of navigation and commerce, which, when concurred in or authorized by the legislatures of both states, shall be binding and effective upon all persons and corporations affected thereby.

ARTICLE XIX.

The two states shall provide penalties for violations of any order, rule or regulation of the port authority, and for the manner of enforcing the same.

ARTICLE XX.

The territorial or boundary lines established by the agreement of eighteen hundred and thirty-four, or the jurisdiction of the two states established thereby, shall not be changed except as herein specifically modified.

ARTICLE XXI.

Either state may by its legislature withdraw from this agreement in the event that a plan for the comprehensive development of the port shall not have been adopted by both states on or prior to July first, nineteen hundred and twenty-three; and when such withdrawal shall have been communicated to the governor of the other state by the state so withdrawing, this agreement shall be thereby abrogated.

ARTICLE XXII.

Definitions. The following words as herein used shall have the following meaning: "Transportation facility" shall include railroads, steam or electric, motor truck or other street or highway vehicles, tunnels, bridges, boats, ferries, car-floats, lighters, tugs, floating elevators, barges, scows or harbor craft of any kind, air craft suitable for harbor service, and every kind of transportation facility now in use or hereafter designed for use for the transportation or carriage of persons or property. "Terminal facility" shall include wharves, piers, slips, ferries, docks, dry docks, bulkheads, dock-walls, basins, car-floats, float-bridges, grain or other storage elevators, warehouses, cold storage, tracks, yards, sheds, switches, connections, overhead appliances, and every kind of terminal or storage facility now in use or hereafter designed for use for the handling, storage, loading or unloading of freight at steamship, railroad or freight terminals. "Railroads" shall include railways, extensions thereof, tunnels, subways, bridges, elevated structures, tracks, poles, wires, conduits, power houses, substations, lines for the transmission of power, car-barns, shops, yards, sidings, turn-outs, switches, stations and approaches thereto, cars and motive equipment. "Facility" shall include all works, buildings, structures, appliances and appurtenances necessary and convenient for the proper construction, equipment, maintenance and operation of such facility or facilities or any one or more of them. "Real property" shall include land under water, as well as uplands, and all property either now commonly or legally defined as real property or which may hereafter be so defined. "Personal property" shall include choses in action and all other property now commonly or legally defined as personal property or which may hereafter be so defined. "To lease" shall include to rent or to hire. "Rule or regulation," until and unless otherwise determined by the legislatures of both states, shall mean any rule or regulation not inconsistent with the constitution of the United States or of either state, and, subject to the exercise of the power of congress, for the improvement of the conduct of navigation and commerce within the district, and shall include charges, rates, rentals or tolls fixed or established by the port authority; and until otherwise determined as aforesaid, shall not include matters relating to harbor or river pollution. Wherever action by the legislature of either state is herein referred to, it shall mean an act of the legislature duly adopted in accordance with the provisions of the constitution of the state.

Plural or singular. The singular wherever used herein shall include the plural.

Consent, approval or recommendation of municipality; how given. Wherever herein the consent, approval or recommendation of a "municipality" is required, the word "municipality" shall be taken to include any city or incorporated village within the port district, and in addition in the state of New Jersey any borough, town, township or any municipality governed by an improvement commission within the district. Such consent, approval or recommendation whenever required in the case of the city of New York shall be deemed to have been given or made whenever the board of estimate and apportionment of said city or any body hereafter succeeding to its duties shall by majority vote pass a resolution expressing such consent, approval or recommendation; and in the case of any municipality now or hereafter governed by a commission, whenever the commission thereof shall by a majority vote pass such a resolution; and in all other cases whenever the body authorized to grant consent to the use of the streets or highways of such municipality shall by a majority vote pass such a resolution.

IN WITNESS WHEREOF we have hereunto set our hands and seals under Chapter 154 of the Laws of 1921 of the State of New York and Chapter 151 of the Laws of 1921 of the State of New Jersey, this thirtieth day of April, 1921.

WILLIAM R. WILLCOX	(L. S.)
EUGENIUS H. OUTERBRIDGE	(L. S.)
CHARLES D. NEWTON	(L. S.)
J. SPENCER SMITH	(L. S.)
DEWITT VAN BUSKIRK	(L. S.)
FRANK R. FORD	(L. S.)
THOMAS F. MCCRAN	(L. S.)

IN THE PRESENCE OF:

NATHAN L. MILLER	CLARENCE E. CASE
WALTER E. EDGE	D. P. KINGSLEY
ALFRED E. SMITH	IRVING T. BUSH
CHARLES S. WHITMAN	ARTHUR N. PIERSON
WILLIAM M. CALDER	JULIUS HENRY COHEN
LEWIS H. POUNDS	

in whose presence Messrs. Willcox, Outerbridge, Smith, Van Buskirk, Ford and McCran signed in the Great Hall of the Chamber of Commerce in the City of New York on the thirtieth day of April, 1921. Attorney General Newton being at that time absent from the City, he signed on the sixth day of May, 1921, at the Chamber, in the presence of:—

WILLIAM LEARY	CHAS. T. GWYNNE

The Municipality of Metropolitan Seattle

The origin of the Municipality of Metropolitan Seattle primarily may be traced to the need for governmental action to end the pollution of Lake Washington caused by communities discharging thirty million gallons of sewage into the Lake daily.

The League of Women Voters and the Municipal League of Seattle and King County proposed a revision of the County charter to enable the County to solve the problem of water pollution and other problems, but the proposed charter was rejected by the voters in 1952.

In September 1956, a seventy-five member Metropolitan Problems Advisory Committee was appointed by the Mayor of Seattle and the Board of King County Commissioners after consultation with city, county, and special district officials. In December 1956, the Committee concluded the existing system of local government was unable to solve area-wide problems. Consequently, the Committee prepared a metropolitan municipal corporation bill for introduction in the 1957 Washington Legislature. The bill was passed unanimously by the Senate and by a two-vote margin in the House of Representatives. On March 22, 1957, Governor Albert D. Rossellini signed the Act* which provides a metropolitan municipal corporation may be created by a referendum to perform any one or more of the following functions: Sewage disposal, water supply, public transportation, garbage disposal, parks and parkways, and comprehensive planning. A concurrent majority vote in the central city and the remainder of the area is required to create a corporation.

A referendum on the question of creating a metropolitan municipal corporation responsible for planning, rapid transit, and sewage disposal in a 471-square-mile area was held on March 11, 1958—101,947 votes were cast for and 85,590 votes against the creation of the corporation. Seattle voted overwhelmingly in favor of the creation of a metropolitan municipal corporation, but the remainder of the area rejected the proposal.

On September 9, 1958, a referendum was held on the question of establishing a metropolitan municipal corporation responsible only for sewage disposal. The proposal was approved by the voters.

Other functions may be assigned the Municipality of Metropolitan Seattle without a referendum by a concurrent resolution of the King County Board of Commissioners, Seattle City Council, and City Council of two-thirds of the other component cities.

AN ACT Relating to municipal corporations, providing for the creation and operation of metropolitan municipal corporations to provide and coordinate certain specified public services and functions for prescribed geographic areas including two or more cities and towns and all or part of one or more counties.

BE IT ENACTED BY THE LEGISLATURE OF THE STATE OF WASHINGTON:

Section 1. It is hereby declared to be the public policy of the state of Washington to provide for the people of the populous metropolitan areas in the state the means of obtaining essential services not adequately provided by existing agencies of local government. The growth of urban population and the movement of people into suburban areas has created problems of sewage and garbage disposal, water supply, transportation, planning, parks and parkways which extend beyond the boundaries of cities, counties and special districts. For reasons of topography, location and movement of population, and land conditions and development, one or more of these problems cannot be adequately met by the individual cities, counties and districts of many metropolitan areas.

It is the purpose of this act to enable cities and counties to act jointly to meet these common problems in order that the proper growth and development of the metropolitan areas of the state may be assured and the health and welfare of the people residing therein may be secured.

Sec. 2. As used herein:

(1) "Metropolitan municipal corporation" means a municipal corporation of the state of Washington created pursuant to this act.

(2) "Metropolitan area" means the area contained within the boundaries of a metropolitan municipal corporation, or within the boundaries of an area proposed to be organized as such a corporation.

(3) "City" means an incorporated city or town.

(4) "Component city" means an incorporated city or town within a metropolitan area.

(5) "Component county" means a county, all or part of which is included within a metropolitan area.

(6) "Central city" means the city with the largest population in a metropolitan area.

(7) "Central county" means the county containing the city with the largest population in a metropolitan area.

(8) "Special district" means any municipal corporation of the state of Washington other than a city, county, or metropolitan municipal corporation.

(9) "Metropolitan council" means the legislative body of a metropolitan municipal corporation.

(10) "City council" means the legislative body of any city or town.

(11) "Population" means the number of residents as shown by the figures released for the most recent official state, federal, or county census, or population determination made under the direction of the state census board.

(12) "Metropolitan function" means any of the functions of government named in section 5 of this act.

(13) "Authorized metropolitan function" means a metropolitan function which a metropolitan municipal corporation shall have been authorized to perform in the manner provided in this act.

*Laws of Washington, 1957, chapter 213.

Sec. 3. Any area of the state containing two or more cities, at least one of which is a city of the first class, may organize as a metropolitan municipal corporation for the performance of certain functions, as provided in this act.

Sec. 4. No metropolitan municipal corporation shall include only a part of any city, and every city shall be either wholly included or wholly excluded from the boundaries of such corporation. No territory shall be included within the boundaries of more than one metropolitan municipal corporation.

Sec. 5. A metropolitan municipal corporation shall have the power to perform any one or more of the following functions, when authorized in the manner provided in this act:

(1) Metropolitan sewage disposal.

(2) Metropolitan water supply.

(3) Metropolitan public transportation.

(4) Metropolitan garbage disposal.

(5) Metropolitan parks and parkways.

(6) Metropolitan comprehensive planning.

Sec. 6. All functions of local government which are not authorized as provided in this act to be performed by a metropolitan municipal corporation, shall continue to be performed by the counties, cities and special districts within the metropolitan area as provided by law.

Sec. 7. A metropolitan municipal corporation may be created by vote of the qualified electors residing in a metropolitan area in the manner provided in this act. An election to authorize the creation of a metropolitan municipal corporation may be called pursuant to resolution or petition in the following

(1) A resolution or concurring resolutions calling for such an election may be adopted by either:

(a) The city council of a central city; or

(b) The city councils of two or more component cities other than a central city; or

(c) The board of commissioners of a central county.
A certified copy of such resolution or certified copies of such concurring resolutions shall be transmitted to the board of commissioners of the central county.

(2) A petition calling for such an election shall be signed by at least four percent of the qualified voters residing within the metropolitan area and shall be filed with the auditor of the central county.

Any resolution or petition calling for such an election shall describe the boundaries of the proposed metropolitan area, name the metropolitan function or functions which the metropolitan municipal corporation shall be authorized to perform initially and state that the formation of the metropolitan municipal corporation will be conducive to the welfare and benefit of the persons and property within the metropolitan area. After the filing of a first sufficient petition or resolution with such county auditor or board of county commissioners respectively, action by such auditor or board shall be deferred on any subsequent petition or resolution until after the election has been held pursuant to such first petition or resolution.

Upon receipt of such a petition, the auditor shall examine the same and certify to the sufficiency of the signatures thereon. For the purpose of examining the signatures on such petition, the auditor shall be permitted access to the voter registration books of each component county and each com-

ponent city. No person may withdraw his name from a petition after it has been filed with the auditor. Within thirty days following the receipt of such petition, the auditor shall transmit the same to the board of commissioners of the central county, together with his certificate as to the sufficiency thereof.

Sec. 8. Upon receipt of a duly certified petition or a valid resolution calling for an election on the formation of a metropolitan municipal corporation, the board of commissioners of the central county shall fix a date for a public hearing thereon which shall be not more than sixty nor less than forty days following the receipt of such resolution or petition. Notice of such hearing shall be published once a week for at least four consecutive weeks in one or more newspapers of general circulation within the metropolitan area. The notice shall contain a description of the boundaries of the proposed metropolitan area, shall name the initial metropolitan function or functions and shall state the time and place of the hearing and the fact that any changes in the boundaries of the metropolitan area will be considered at such time and place. At such hearing or any continuation thereof, any interested person may appear and be heard on all matters relating to the effect of the formation of the proposed municipal metropolitan corporation. The commissioners may make such changes in the boundaries of the metropolitan area as they shall deem reasonable and proper, but may not delete any portion of the proposed area which will create an island of included or excluded lands, may not delete a portion of any city, and may not delete any portion of the proposed area which is contributing or may reasonably be expected to contribute to the pollution of any water course or body of water in the proposed area when the petition or resolution names metropolitan sewage disposal as a function to be performed by the proposed metropolitan municipal corporation. If the commissioners shall determine that any additional territory should be included in the metropolitan area, a second hearing shall be held and notice given in the same manner as for the original hearing. The commissioners may adjourn the hearing on the formation of a metropolitan municipal corporation from time to time not exceeding thirty days in all. At the next regular meeting following the conclusion of such hearing the commissioners shall adopt a resolution fixing the boundaries of the proposed metropolitan municipal corporation, declaring that the formation of the proposed metropolitan municipal corporation will be conducive to the welfare and benefit of the persons and property therein and calling a special election on the formation of the metropolitan municipal corporation to be held not more than one hundred twenty days nor less than sixty days following the adoption of such resolution.

Sec. 9. The election on the formation of the metropolitan municipal corporation shall be conducted by the auditor of the central county in accordance with the general election laws of the state and the results thereof shall be canvassed by the county canvassing board of the central county, which shall certify the result of the election to the board of county commissioners of the central county, and shall cause a certified copy of such canvass to be filed in the office of the secretary of state. Notice of the election shall be published in one or more newspapers of general circulation in each component county in the manner provided in the general election laws. No person shall be entitled to vote at such election unless he is a qualified voter under the laws of the state in effect at the time of such election and has resided within the metropolitan area for at least thirty days preceding the date of the election. The ballot proposition shall be in substantially the following form:

"FORMATION OF METROPOLITAN MUNICIPAL CORPORATION

"Shall a metropolitan municipal corporation be established for the area described in a resolution of the board of commissioners of _____ county adopted on the _____ day of _____, 19 _____, to perform the metropolitan function of _____ (here insert the title of each of the functions to be authorized as set forth in the petition or initial resolution)

| YES | _____ | ☐ |
| NO | _____ | ☐" |

If a majority of the persons voting on the proposition residing within the central city shall vote in favor thereof and a majority of the persons voting on the proposition residing in the metropolitan area outside of the central city shall vote in favor thereof, the metropolitan municipal corporation shall thereupon be established and the board of commissioners of the central county shall adopt a resolution setting a time and place for the first meeting of the metropolitan council which shall be held not later than thirty days after the date of such election. A copy of such resolution shall be transmitted to the legislative body of each component city and county and of each special district which shall be affected by the particular metropolitan functions authorized.

At the same election there shall be submitted to the voters residing within the metropolitan area, for their approval or rejection, a proposition authorizing the metropolitan municipal corporation, if formed, to levy at the earliest possible time permitted by law on all taxable property located within the metropolitan municipal corporation a general tax, for one year, of one mill in excess of any constitutional or statutory limitation for authorized purposes of the metropolitan municipal corporation. The proposition shall be expressed on the ballots in substantially the following form:

"ONE YEAR ONE MILL LEVY

"Shall the metropolitan municipal corporation, if formed, levy a general tax of one mill for one year upon all the taxable property within said corporation in excess of the forty mill tax limit for authorized purposes of the corporation?

| YES | _____ | ☐ |
| NO | _____ | ☐" |

Such proposition to be effective must be approved by a majority of at least three-fifths of the persons voting on the proposition to levy such tax and the number of persons voting on the proposition shall constitute not less than forty percent of the total number of votes cast in the area of the proposed metropolitan municipal corporation at the last preceding county or state general election.

Sec. 10. A metropolitan municipal corporation may be authorized to perform one or more metropolitan functions in addition to those which it has previously been authorized to perform, with the approval of the voters at an election, in the manner provided in this section.

An election to authorize a metropolitan municipal corporation to perform one or more additional metropolitan functions may be called pursuant to a resolution or a petition in the following manner:

(1) A resolution calling for such an election may be adopted by:

(a) The city council of the central city; or

(b) The city councils of two or more component cities other than a central city; or

(c) The board of commissioners of the central county.

Such resolution shall be transmitted to the metropolitan council.

(2) A petition calling for such an election shall be signed by at least four percent of the registered voters residing within the metropolitan area and shall be filed with the auditor of the central county.

Any resolution or petition calling for such an election shall name the additional metropolitan functions which the metropolitan municipal corporation shall be authorized to perform.

Upon receipt of such a petition, the auditor shall examine the signatures thereon and certify to the sufficiency thereof. For the purpose of examining the signatures on such petition, the auditor shall be permitted access to all voter registration books of any component county and of all component cities. No person may withdraw his name from a petition after it has been filed with the auditor. Within thirty days following the receipt of such petition, the auditor shall transmit the same to the metropolitan council, together with his certificate as to the sufficiency of signatures thereon.

Upon receipt of a valid resolution or duly certified petition calling for an election on the authorization of the performance of one or more additional metropolitan functions, the metropolitan council shall call a special election to be held not more than one hundred and twenty days nor less than sixty days following such receipt. Such special election shall be conducted and canvassed as provided in this act for an election on the question of forming a metropolitan municipal corporation. The ballot proposition shall be in substantially the following form:

"Shall the _____ metropolitan municipal corporation be authorized to perform the additional metropolitan functions of _____ (here insert the title of each of the additional functions to be authorized as set forth in the petition or resolution)?

| YES | _____ | ☐ |
| NO | _____ | ☐" |

If a majority of the persons voting on the proposition shall vote in favor thereof, the metropolitan municipal corporation shall be authorized to perform such additional metropolitan function or functions.

Sec. 11. A metropolitan municipal corporation may be authorized to perform one or more metropolitan functions in addition to those which it previously has been authorized to perform, without an election, in the manner provided in this section. A resolution providing for the performance of such additional metropolitan function or functions shall be adopted by the metropolitan council. A copy of such resolution shall be transmitted by registered mail to the legislative body of each component city and county. If, within ninety days after the date of such mailing, a concurring resolution is adopted by the legislative body of each component county, of each component city of the first class, and of at least two-thirds of all other component cities, and such concurring resolutions are transmitted to the metropolitan council, such council shall by resolution declare that the metropolitan municipal corporation has been authorized to perform such additional metropolitan function or functions. A copy of such resolution shall be transmitted by registered mail to the legislative body of each component city and county and of each special district which will be affected by the particular additional metropolitan function authorized.

Sec. 12. A metropolitan municipal corporation shall be governed by a metropolitan council composed of the following:

(1) One member selected by, and from, the board of commissioners of each component county;

(2) One additional member selected by the board of commissioners of each component county for each county commissioner district containing twenty thousand or more persons residing in the unincorporated portion of such commissioner district lying within the metropolitan municipal corporation who shall be a resident of such unincorporated portion: PROVIDED, That one additional member shall be selected by and from, the board of county commissioners for each county commissioner district containing less than twenty thousand persons in its unincorporated area.

(3) One member who shall be the mayor of the central city.

(4) One member from each of the three largest component cities containing a population of ten thousand or more other than the central city, selected by, and from, the mayor and city council of each of such cities.

(5) One member representing all component cities other than the four largest cities with a population of ten thousand or more, to be selected from the mayors and city councils of such smaller cities by the mayors of such cities in the following manner: The mayors of all such cities shall meet on the second Tuesday following the establishment of a metropolitan municipal corporation and thereafter on the third Tuesday in June of each even-numbered year at two o'clock p.m. at the office of the board of county commissioners of the central county. The chairman of such board shall preside. After nominations are made, successive ballots shall be taken until one candidate receives a majority of all votes cast.

(6) One member selected by, and from, the city council of the central city.

(7) One member selected by, and from, the city council of each component city containing a population of fifty thousand or more.

(8) One additional member selected by and from the city council of each component city containing a population of one hundred thousand or more.

(9) One additional member selected by, and from, the city council of each component city containing a population of one hundred thousand or more for each one hundred thousand population over and above the first one hundred thousand.

(10) One member, who shall be chairman of the metropolitan council, selected by the other members of the council. He shall not hold any public office other than that of notary public or member of the military forces of the United States or of the state of Washington not on active duty.

Sec. 13. At the first meeting of the metropolitan council following the formation of a metropolitan municipal corporation, the mayor of the central city shall serve as temporary chairman. As its first official act the council shall elect a chairman. The chairman shall be a voting member of the council and shall preside at all meetings. In the event of his absence or inability to act the council shall select one of its members to act as chairman pro tempore. A majority of all members of the council shall constitute a quorum for the transaction of business. A smaller number of council members than a quorum may adjourn from time to time and may compel the attendance of absent members in such manner and under such penalties as the council may provide. The council shall determine its own rules and order of business, shall provide by resolution for the manner and time of holding all regular and special meetings and shall keep a journal of its proceedings which shall be a public

record. Every legislative act of the council of a general or permanent nature shall be by resolution.

Sec. 14. Each member of a metropolitan council except those selected under the provisions of section 12 (3), (5) and (10), shall hold office at the pleasure of the body which selected him. Each member, who shall hold office ex officio, may not hold office after he ceases to hold the position of mayor, commissioner, or councilman. The chairman shall hold office until the second Tuesday in July of each even-numbered year and may, if reelected, serve more than one term. Each member shall hold office until his successor has been selected as provided in this act.

Sec. 15. A vacancy in the office of a member of the metropolitan council shall be filled in the same manner as provided for the original selection. The meeting of mayors to fill a vacancy of the member selected under the provisions of section 12 (5) shall be held at such time and place as shall be designated by the chairman of the metropolitan council after ten days' written notice mailed to the mayors of each of the cities specified in section 12 (5).

Sec. 16. The chairman of the metropolitan council shall receive such compensation as the other members of the metropolitan council shall provide. Members of the council other than the chairman shall receive compensation for attendance at metropolitan council or committee meetings of twenty-five dollars per diem but not exceeding a total of two hundred dollars in any one month, in addition to any compensation which they may receive as officers of component cities or counties: PROVIDED, That elected public officers serving in such capacities on a full time basis shall not receive compensation for attendance at metropolitan, council or committee meetings. All members of the council shall be reimbursed for expenses actually incurred by them in the conduct of official business for the metropolitan municipal corporation.

Sec. 17. The name of a metropolitan municipal corporation shall be established by its metropolitan council. Each metropolitan municipal corporation shall adopt a corporate seal containing the name of the corporation and the date of its formation.

Sec. 18. In addition to the powers specifically granted by this act a metropolitan municipal corporation shall have all powers which are necessary to carry out the purposes of the metropolitan municipal corporation and to perform authorized metropolitan functions. A metropolitan municipal corporation may contract with the United States or any agency thereof, any state or agency thereof, any other metropolitan municipal corporation, any county, city, special district, or governmental agency for the operation by such entity of any facility or the performance of any service which the metropolitan municipal corporation may be authorized to operate or perform, on such terms as may be agreed upon by the contracting parties.

A metropolitan municipal corporation may sue and be sued in its corporate capacity in all courts and in all proceedings.

Sec. 19. The metropolitan council shall provide by resolution the effective date on which the metropolitan municipal corporation will commence to perform any one or more of the metropolitan functions which it shall have been authorized to perform.

Sec. 20. If a metropolitan municipal corporation shall be authorized to perform the function of metropolitan sewage disposal, it shall have the following powers in addition to the general powers granted by this act:

(1) To prepare a comprehensive sewage disposal and storm water drainage plan for the metropolitan area.

(2) To acquire by purchase, condemnation, gift, or grant and to lease, construct, add to, improve, replace, repair, maintain, operate and regulate the use of metropolitan facilities for sewage disposal and storm water drainage within or without the metropolitan area, including trunk, interceptor and outfall sewers, whether used to carry sanitary waste, storm water, or combined storm and sanitary sewage, lift and pumping stations, sewage treatment plants, together with all lands, properties, equipment and accessories necessary for such facilities. Sewer facilities which are owned by a city or special district may be acquired or used by the metropolitan municipal corporation only with the consent of the legislative body of the city or special districts owning such facilities. Cities and special districts are hereby authorized to convey or lease such facilities to metropolitan municipal corporations or to contract for their joint use on such terms as may be fixed by agreement between the legislative body of such city or special district and the metropolitan council, without submitting the matter to the voters of such city or district.

(3) To require counties, cities, special districts and other political subdivisions to discharge sewage collected by such entities from any portion of the metropolitan area into such metropolitan facilities as may be provided to serve such areas when the metropolitan council shall declare by resolution that the health, safety, or welfare of the people within the metropolitan area requires such action.

(4) To fix rates and charges for the use of metropolitan sewage disposal and storm water drainage facilities.

(5) To establish minimum standards for the construction of local sewer facilities and to approve plans for construction of such facilities by component counties or cities or by special districts wholly or partly within the metropolitan area. No such county, city, or special district shall construct such facilities without first securing such approval.

(6) To acquire by purchase, condemnation, gift, or grant, to lease, construct, add to, improve, replace, repair, maintain, operate and regulate the use of facilities for the local collection of sewage or storm water in portions of the metropolitan area not contained within any city or sewer district and, with the consent of the legislative body of any city or sewer district, to exercise such powers within such city or sewer district and for such purpose to have all the powers conferred by law upon such city or sewer district with respect to such local collection facilities. All costs of such local collection facilities shall be paid for by the area served thereby.

Sec. 21. If a metropolitan municipal corporation shall be authorized to perform the function of metropolitan sewage disposal, the metropolitan council shall, prior to the effective date of the assumption of such function, cause a metropolitan sewer advisory committee to be formed by notifying the legislative body of each component city which operates a sewer system to appoint one person to serve on such advisory committee and the board of commissioners of each sewer district, any portion of which lies within the metropolitan area, to appoint one person to serve on such committee who shall be a sewer district commissioner. The metropolitan sewer advisory committee shall meet at the time and place provided in the notice and elect a chairman. The members of such committee shall receive no compensation other than reimbursement for expenses actually incurred in the performance of their duties. The function of such advisory committee shall be to advise the metropolitan council in matters relating to the performance of the sewage disposal function.

Sec. 22. If a metropolitan municipal corporation shall be authorized to perform the function of metropolitan water supply, it shall have the following powers in addition to the general powers granted by this act:

(1) To prepare a comprehensive plan for the development of sources of water supply, trunk supply mains and water treatment and storage facilities for the metropolitan area.

(2) To acquire by purchase, condemnation, gift or grant and to lease, construct, add to, improve, replace, repair, maintain, operate and regulate the use of metropolitan facilities for water supply within or without the metropolitan area, including buildings, structures, water sheds, wells, springs, dams, settling basins, intakes, treatment plants, trunk supply mains and pumping stations, together with all lands, property, equipment and accessories necessary to enable the metropolitan municipal corporation to obtain and develop sources of water supply, treat and store water and deliver water through trunk supply mains. Water supply facilities which are owned by a city or special district may be acquired or used by the metropolitan municipal corporation only with the consent of the legislative body of the city or special district owning such facilities. Cities and special districts are hereby authorized to convey or lease such facilities to metropolitan municipal corporations or to contract for their joint use on such terms as may be fixed by agreement between the legislative body of such city or special district and the metropolitan council, without submitting the matter to the voters of such city or district.

(3) To fix rates and charges for water supplied by the metropolitan municipal corporation.

(4) To acquire by purchase, condemnation, gift or grant and to lease, construct, add to, improve, replace, repair, maintain, operate and regulate the use of facilities for the local distribution of water in portions of the metropolitan area not contained within any city or water district and, with the consent of the legislative body of any city or water district, to exercise such powers within such city or water district and for such purpose to have all the powers conferred by law upon such city or water district with respect to such local distribution facilities. All costs of such local distribution facilities shall be paid for by the area served thereby.

Sec. 23. If a metropolitan municipal corporation shall be authorized to perform the function of metropolitan water supply, the metropolitan council shall, prior to the effective date of the assumption of such function, cause a metropolitan water advisory committee to be formed by notifying the legislative body of each component city which operates a water system to appoint one person to serve on such advisory committee and the board of commissioners of each water district, any portion of which lies within the metropolitan area, to appoint one person to serve on such committee who shall be a water district commissioner. The metropolitan water advisory committee shall meet at the time and place provided in the notice and elect a chairman. The members of such committee shall serve at the pleasure of the appointing bodies and shall receive no compensation other than reimbursement for expenses actually incurred in the performance of their duties. The function of such advisory committee shall be to advise the metropolitan council with respect to matters relating to the performance of the water supply function.

Sec. 24. If a metropolitan municipal corporation shall be authorized to perform the function of metropolitan transportation, it shall have the following powers in addition to the general powers granted by this act:

(1) To prepare and develop a comprehensive plan for public transportation service which will best serve the residents of the metropolitan area.

(2) To acquire by purchase, condemnation, gift or grant and to lease, construct, add to, improve, replace, repair, maintain, operate and regulate the use of metropolitan transportation facilities within or without the metropolitan area, including systems of surface, underground or overhead railways, tramways, busses, or any other means of local transportation except taxis, and including passenger terminal and parking facilities, together with all lands, rights of way, property, equipment and accessories necessary for such systems and facilities. Public transportation facilities which are owned by any city may be acquired or used by the metropolitan municipal corporation only with the consent of the city council of the city owning such facilities. Cities are hereby authorized to convey or lease such facilities to metropolitan municipal corporations or to contract for their joint use on such terms as may be fixed by agreement between the city council of such city and the metropolitan council, without submitting the matter to the voters of such city.

(3) To fix rates and charges for the use of such facilities.

Sec. 25. Except in accordance with an agreement made as provided herein, upon the effective date on which the metropolitan municipal corporation commences to perform the metropolitan transportation function, no person or private corporation shall operate a local public passenger transportation service within the metropolitan area with the exception of taxis, busses owned or operated by a school district or private school, and busses owned or operated by any corporation or organization solely for the purposes of the corporation or organization and for the use of which no fee or fare is charged.

An agreement may be entered into between the metropolitan municipal corporation and any person or corporation legally operating a local public passenger transportation service wholly within or partly within and partly without the metropolitan area and on said effective date under which such person or corporation may continue to operate such service or any part thereof for such time and upon such terms and conditions as provided in such agreement. Where any such local public passenger transportation service will be required to cease to operate within the metropolitan area, the commission may agree with the owner of such service to purchase the assets used in providing such service, or if no agreement can be reached, the commission shall condemn such assets in the manner provided herein for the condemnation of other properties.

Wherever a privately owned public carrier operates wholly or partly within a metropolitan municipal corporation, the Washington Public Service Commission shall continue to exercise jurisdiction over such operation as provided by law.

Sec. 26. If a metropolitan municipal corporation shall be authorized to perform the metropolitan transportation function, it shall, upon the effective date of the assumption of such power, have and exercise all rights with respect to the construction, acquisition, maintenance, operation, extension, alteration, repair, control and management of passenger transportation which any component city shall have been previously empowered to exercise and such powers shall not thereafter be exercised by such component cities without the consent of the metropolitan municipal corporation. PROVIDED, That any city owning and operating a public transportation system on such effective date may continue to operate such system within such city until such system shall have been acquired by the metropolitan municipal corporation and a metropolitan municipal corporation may not acquire such system without the consent of the city council of such city.

Sec. 27. If a metropolitan municipal corporation shall be authorized to perform the function of metropolitan trans-

portation, a metropolitan transit commission shall be formed prior to the effective date of the assumption of such function. Except as provided in this section, the metropolitan transit commission shall exercise all powers of the metropolitan municipal corporation with respect to metropolitan transportation facilities, including but not limited to the power to construct, acquire, maintain, operate, extend, alter, repair, control and manage a local public transportation system within and without the metropolitan area, to establish new passenger transportation services and to alter, curtail, or abolish any services which the commission may deem desirable, to fix tolls and fares, so that the revenue of the system shall be sufficient to meet all operating transportation costs but not necessarily sufficient to meet the cost of construction or acquisition of new facilities and depreciation of facilities, unless the commission shall elect to do so.

The metropolitan transit commission shall authorize expenditures for transportation purposes within the budget adopted by the metropolitan council. Bonds of the metropolitan municipal corporation for public transportation purposes shall be issued by the metropolitan council as provided in this act.

The metropolitan transit commission shall consist of five members appointed by the metropolitan council. Three members of the first metropolitan transit commission shall be selected from the existing transit commission of the central city, if there be a transit commission in such city. The terms of first appointees shall be for one, two, three, four and five years, respectively. Thereafter, commissioners shall serve for a term of four years. Compensation of transit commissioners shall be determined by the metropolitan council.

Sec. 28. If a metropolitan municipal corporation shall be authorized to perform the function of metropolitan garbage disposal, it shall have the following powers in additional to the general powers granted by this act:

(1) To prepare a comprehensive garbage disposal plan for the metropolitan area.

(2) To acquire by purchase, condemnation, gift, or grant and to lease, construct, add to, improve, replace, repair, maintain, operate and regulate the use of metropolitan facilities for garbage disposal within or without the metropolitan area, including garbage disposal sites, central collection station sites, structures, machinery and equipment for the operation of central collection stations and for the hauling and disposal of garbage by any means, together with all lands, property, equipment and accessories necessary for such facilities. Garbage disposal facilities which are owned by a city or county may be acquired or used by the metropolitan municipal corporation only with the consent of the legislative body of the city or county owning such facilities. Cities and counties are hereby authorized to convey or lease such facilities to metropolitan municipal corporations or to contract for their joint use on such terms as may be fixed by agreement between the legislative body of such city or county and the metropolitan council, without submitting the matter to the voters of such city or county.

(3) To fix rates and charges for the use of metropolitan garbage disposal facilities.

(4) With the consent of any component city, to acquire by purchase, condemnation, gift or grant and to lease, construct, add to, improve, replace, repair, maintain, operate and regulate the use of facilities for the local collection of garbage within such city, and for such purpose to have all the powers conferred by law upon such city with respect to such local collection facilities. Nothing herein contained shall be deemed to authorize the local collection of garbage except in component cities.

All costs of such local collection facilities shall be paid for by the area served thereby.

Sec. 29. If a metropolitan municipal corporation shall be authorized to perform the function of metropolitan parks and parkways, it shall have the following powers in addition to the general powers granted by this act:

(1) To prepare a comprehensive plan of metropolitan parks and parkways.

(2) To acquire by purchase, condemnation, gift or grant, to lease, construct, add to, improve, delevop, replace, repair, maintain, operate and regulate the use of metropolitan parks and parkways, together with all lands, rights of way, property, equipment and accessories necessary therefor. A park or parkway shall be considered to be a metropolitan facility if the metropolitan council shall by resolution find it to be of use and benefit to all or a major portion of the residents of the metropolitan area. Parks or parkways which are owned by a component city or county may be acquired or used by the metropolitan municipal corporation only with the consent of the legislative body of such city or county. Cities and counties are hereby authorized to convey or lease such facilities to the metropolitan municipal corporations or to contract for their joint use on such terms as may be fixed by agreement between the legislative bodies of such city or county and the metropolitan council, without submitting the matter to the voters of such city or county. If parks or parkways which have been acquired or used as metropolitan facilities shall no longer be used for park purposes by the metropolitan municipal corporation, such facilities shall revert to the component city or county which formerly owned them.

(3) To fix fees and charges for the use of metropolitan park and parkway facilities.

Sec. 30. If a metropolitan municipal corporation shall be authorized to perform the function of metropolitan parks and parkways, a metropolitan park board shall be formed prior to the effective date of the assumption of such function. Except as provided in this section, the metropolitan park board shall exercise all powers of the metropolitan municipal corporation with respect to metropolitan park and parkway facilities.

The metropolitan park board shall authorize expenditures for park and parkway purposes within the budget adopted by the metropolitan council. Bonds of the metropolitan municipal corporation for park and parkway purposes shall be issued by the metropolitan council as provided in this act.

The metropolitan park board shall consist of five members appointed by the metropolitan council at least two of whom shall be residents of the central city. The terms of first appointees shall be for one, two, three, four and five years, respectively. Thereafter members shall serve for a term of four years. Compensation of park board members shall be determined by the metropolitan council.

Sec. 31. If a metropolitan municipal corporation shall be authorized to perform the function of metropolitan comprehensive planning, it shall have the following powers in addition to the general powers granted by this act:

(1) To prepare a recommended comprehensive land use and capital facilities plan for the metropolitan area.

(2) To review proposed zoning ordinances and resolutions or comprehensive plans of component cities and counties and make recommendations thereon. Such proposed zoning ordinances and resolutions or comprehensive plans must be submitted to the metropolitan council prior to adoption and may not be adopted until reviewed and returned by the metropolitan council. The metropolitan council shall cause such ordinances, resolutions and plans to be reviewed by the planning staff of

the metropolitan municipal corporation and return such ordinances, resolutions and plans, together with their findings and recommendations thereon within sixty days following their submission.

(3) To provide planning services for component cities and counties upon request and upon payment therefor by the cities or counties receiving such service.

Sec. 32. A metropolitan municipal corporation shall have power to acquire by purchase and condemnation all lands and property rights, both within and without the metropolitan area, which are necessary for its purposes. Such right of eminent domain shall be exercised by the metropolitan council in the same manner and by the same procedure as is or may be provided by law for cities of the first class, except insofar as such laws may be inconsistent with the provisions of this act.

Sec. 33. A metropolitan municipal corporation shall have power to construct or maintain metropolitan facilities in, along, on, under, over, or through public streets, bridges, viaducts and other public rights of way without first obtaining a franchise from the county or city having jurisdiction over the same: PROVIDED, That such facilities shall be constructed and maintained in accordance with the ordinances and resolutions of such city or county relating to construction, installation and maintenance of similar facilities in such public properties.

Sec. 34. Except as otherwise provided herein, a metropolitan municipal corporation may sell, or otherwise dispose of any real or personal property acquired in connection with any authorized metropolitan function and which is no longer required for the purposes of the metropolitan municipal corporation in the same manner as provided for cities of the first class. When the metropolitan council determines that a metropolitan facility or any part thereof which has been acquired from a component city or county without compensation is no longer required for metropolitan purposes, but is required as a local facility by the city or county from which it was acquired, the metropolitan council shall by resolution transfer it to such city or county.

Sec. 35. All the powers and functions of a metropolitan municipal corporation shall be vested in the metropolitan council unless expressly vested in specific officers, boards, or commissions by this act. Without limitation of the foregoing authority, or of other powers given it by this act, the metropolitan council shall have the following powers:

(1) To establish offices, departments, boards and commissions in addition to those provided by this act which are necessary to carry out the purposes of the metropolitan municipal corporation, and to prescribe the functions, powers and duties thereof.

(2) To appoint or provide for the appointment of, and to remove or to provide for the removal of, all officers and employees of the metropolitan municipal corporation except those whose appointment or removal is otherwise provided for by this act.

(3) To fix the salaries, wages and other compensation of all officers and employees of the metropolitan municipal corporation unless the same shall be otherwise fixed in this act.

(4) To employ such engineering, legal, financial, or other specialized personnel as may be necessary to accomplish the purposes of the metropolitan municipal corporation.

Sec. 36. A metropolitan municipal corporation shall have power to adopt by resolution such rules and regulations as shall be necessary or proper to enable it to carry out authorized metropolitan functions and may provide penalties for the violation thereof. Actions to impose or enforce such penalties may be brought in the superior court of the state of Washington in and for the central county.

Sec. 37. The metropolitan council shall establish and provide for the operation and maintenance of a personnel merit system for the employment, classification, promotion, demotion, suspension, transfer, layoff and discharge of its appointive officers and employees solely on the basis of merit and fitness without regard to political influence or affiliation. The person appointed or body created for the purpose of administering such personnel system shall have power to make, amend and repeal rules and regulations as are deemed necessary for such merit system. Such rules and regulations shall provide:

(1) That the person to be discharged or demoted must be presented with the reasons for such discharge or demotion specifically stated; and

(2) That he shall be allowed a reasonable time in which to reply thereto in writing and that he be given a hearing thereon within a reasonable time.

Sec. 38. A metropolitan municipal corporation shall offer to employ every person who on the date such corporation acquires a metropolitan facility is employed in the operation of such facility by a component city or county or by a special district.

Sec. 39. Where a metropolitan municipal corporation employs a person employed immediately prior thereto by a component city or county, or by a special district, such employee shall be deemed to remain an employee of such city, county, or special district for the purposes of any pension plan of such city, county, or special district, and shall continue to be entitled to all rights and benefits thereunder as if he had remained as an employee of the city, county, or special district, until the metropolitan municipal corporation has provided a pension plan and such employee has elected, in writing, to participate therein.

Until such election, the metropolitan municipal corporation shall deduct from the remuneration of such employee the amount which such employee is or may be required to pay in accordance with the provisions of the plan of such city, county, or special district and the metropolitan municipal corporation shall pay to the city, county, or special district any amounts required to be paid under the provisions of such plan by employer or employee.

Sec. 40. Where a metropolitan municipal corporation employs a person employed immediately prior thereto by a component city or county or by a special district, the employee shall be deemed to remain an employee of such city, county, or special district for the purposes of any sick leave credit plan of the component city, county, or special district until the metropolitan municipal corporation has established a sick leave credit plan for its employees, whereupon the metropolitan municipal corporation shall place to the credit of the employee the sick leave credits standing to his credit in the plan of such city, county, or special district.

Where a metropolitan municipal corporation employs a person theretofore employed by a component city, county, or by a special district, the metropolitan municipal corporation shall, during the first year of his employment by the metropolitan municipal corporation, provide for such employee a vacation with pay equivalent to that which he would have been entitled if he had remained in the employment of the city, county, or special district.

Sec. 41. On or before the third Monday in June of each year, each metropolitan municipal corporation shall adopt a budget for the following calendar year. Such budget shall include a separate section for each authorized metropolitan function. Expenditures shall be segregated as to operation and maintenance expenses and capital and betterment outlays. Administrative and other expense general to the corporation shall be allocated between the authorized metropolitan functions. The budget shall contain an estimate of all revenues to be collected during the following budget year, including any surplus funds remaining unexpended from the preceding year. The remaining funds required to meet budget expenditures, if any, shall be designated as "supplemental income" and shall be obtained from the component cities and counties in the manner provided in this act. The metropolitan council shall not be required to confine capital or betterment expenditures made from bond proceeds or emergency expenditures to items provided in the budget. The affirmative vote of three-fourths of all members of the metropolitan council shall be required to authorize emergency expenditures.

Sec. 42. Each component city shall pay such proportion of the supplemental income of the metropolitan municipal corporation as the assessed valuation of property within it limits bears to the total assessed valuation of taxable property within the metropolitan area. Each component county shall pay such proportion of such supplemental income as the assessed valuation of the property within the unincorporated area of such county lying within the metropolitan area bears to the total assessed valuation of taxable property within the metropolitan area. In making such determination, the metropolitan council shall use the last available assessed valuations. The metropolitan council shall certify to each component city and county, prior to the fourth Monday in June of each year, the share of the supplemental income to be paid by such component city or county for the next calendar year. The latter shall then include such amount in its budget for the ensuing calendar year, and during such year shall pay to the metropolitan municipal corporation, in equal quarterly installments, the amount of its supplemental income share from whatever sources may be available to it.

Sec. 43. The treasurer of each component county shall create a separate fund into which shall be paid all money collected from taxes levied by the metropolitan municipal corporation on property in such county and such money shall be forwarded quarterly by the treasurer of each such county to the treasurer of the central county as directed by the metropolitan council. The treasurer of the central county shall act as the treasurer of the metropolitan municipal corporation and shall establish and maintain such funds as may be authorized by the metropolitan council. Money shall be disbursed from such funds upon warrants drawn by the auditor of the central county as authorized by the metropolitan council. The central county shall be reimbursed by the metropolitan municipal corporation for services rendered by the treasurer and auditor of the central county in connection with the receipt and disbursement of such funds. The expense of all special elections held pursuant to this act shall be paid by the metropolitan municipal corporation.

Sec. 44. It shall be the duty of the assessor of each component county to certify annually to the metropolitan council the aggregate assessed valuation of all taxable property in his county situated in any metropolitan municipal corporation as the same appears from the last assessment roll of his county.

Sec. 45. A metropolitan municipal corporation shall have the power to issue general obligation bonds and to pledge the full faith and credit of the corporation to the payment thereof, for any authorized capital purpose of the metropolitan municipal corporation: PROVIDED, That a proposition authorizing the issuance of such bonds shall have been submitted to the electors of the metropolitan municipal corporation at a special election and assented to by three-fifths of the persons voting on said proposition at said election at which such election the total number of persons voting on such bond proposition shall constitute not less than forty percent of the total number of votes cast within the area of said metropolitan municipal corporation at the last preceding state general election. Both principal of and interest on such general obligation bonds shall be payable from annual tax levies to be made upon all the taxable property within the metropolitan municipal corporation in excess of the forty mill tax limit.

General obligation bonds shall bear interest at a rate of not to exceed six percent per annum. The various annual maturities shall commence not more than five years from the date of issue of the bonds and shall as nearly as practicable be in such amounts as will, together with the interest on all outstanding bonds of such issue, be met by equal annual tax levies.

Such bonds shall be signed by the chairman and attested by the secretary of the metropolitan council, one of which signatures may be a facsimile signature and the seal of the metropolitan corporation shall be impressed thereon. Each of the interest coupons shall be signed by the facsimile signatures of said officials. General obligation bonds shall be sold at public sale as provided by law for sale of general obligation bonds of cities of the first class and at a price not less than par and accrued interest.

Sec. 46. A metropolitan municipal corporation may issue revenue bonds to provide funds to carry out its authorized metropolitan sewage disposal, water supply, garbage disposal or transportation purposes, without submitting the matter to the voters of the metropolitan municipal corporation. The metropolitan council shall create a special fund or funds for the sole purpose of paying the principal of and interest on the bonds of each such issue, into which fund or funds the metropolitan council may obligate the metropolitan municipal corporation to pay such amounts of the gross revenue of the particular utility constructed, acquired, improved, added to, or repaired out of the proceeds of sale of such bonds, as the metropolitan council shall determine. The principal of, and interest on, such bonds shall be payable only out of such special fund or funds, and the owners and holders of such bonds shall have a lien and charge against the gross revenue of such utility.

Such revenue bonds and the interest thereon issued against such fund or funds shall be a valid claim of the holders thereof only as against such fund or funds and the revenue pledged therefor, and shall not constitute a general indebtedness of the metropolitan municipal corporation.

Each such revenue bond shall state upon its face that it is payable from such special fund or funds, and all revenue bonds issued under this act shall be negotiable instruments within the provisions of the negotiable instruments law of this state. Such revenue bonds may be registered either as to principal only or as to principal and interest, or may be bearer bonds, shall be in such denominations as the metropolitan council shall deem proper; shall be payable at such time or times and at such places as shall be determined by the metropolitan council; shall bear interest at such rate or rates as shall be determined by the metropolitan council, shall be signed by the chairman and attested by the secretary of the metropolitan council, one of which signatures may be a facsimile signature, and the seal of the metropolitan municipal corporation shall be impressed thereon; each of the interest coupons shall be signed by the facsimile signatures of said officials.

Such revenue bonds shall be sold in such manner as the metropolitan council shall deem to be for the best interests

of the metropolitan municipal corporation, either at public or private sale. The aggregate interest cost to maturity of the money received for such revenue bonds shall not exceed seven percent per annum.

The metropolitan council may at the time of the issuance of such revenue bonds make such covenants with the purchasers and holders of said bonds as it may deem necessary to secure and guarantee the payment of the principal thereof and the interest thereon, including but not being limited to covenants to set aside adequate reserves to secure or guarantee the payment of such principal and interest, to maintain rates sufficient to pay such principal and interest and to maintain adequate coverage over debt service, to appoint a trustee or trustees for the bondholders to safeguard the expenditure of the proceeds of sale of such bonds and to fix the powers and duties of such trustee or trustees and to make such other covenants as the metropolitan council may deem necessary to accomplish the most advantageous sale of such bonds. The metropolitan council may also provide that revenue bonds payable out of the same source may later be issued on a parity with revenue bonds being issued and sold.

The metropolitan council may include in the principal amount of any such revenue bond issue an amount for working capital and an amount necessary for interest during the period of construction of any such metropolitan facilities plus six months. The metropolitan council may, if it deems it to the best interest of the metropolitan municipal corporation, provide in any contract for the construction or acquisition of any metropolitan facilities or additions or improvements thereto or replacements or extensions thereof that payment therefor shall be made only in such revenue bonds at the par value thereof.

If the metropolitan municipal corporation shall fail to carry out or perform any of its obligations or covenants made in the authorization, issuance and sale of such bonds, the holder of any such bond may bring action against the metropolitan municipal corporation and compel the performance of any or all of such covenants.

Sec. 47. The metropolitan council may, by resolution, without submitting the matter to the voters of the metropolitan municipal corporation, provide for the issuance of funding or refunding general obligation bonds to refund any outstanding general obligations bonds or any part thereof at maturity, or before maturity if they are by their terms or by other agreement subject to prior redemption, with the right in the metropolitan council to combine various series and issues of the outstanding bonds by a single issue of funding or refunding bonds, and to issue refunding bonds to pay any redemption premium payable on the outstanding bonds being refunded. The funding or refunding general obligation bonds shall, except as specifically provided in this section, be issued in accordance with the provisions of this act with respect to general obligation bonds.

The metropoolitan council may, by resolution, without submitting the matter to the voters of the metropolitan municipal corporation, provide for the issuance of funding or refunding revenue bonds to refund any outstanding revenue bonds or any part thereof at maturity, or before maturity if they are by their terms or by agreement subject to prior redemption, with the right in the metropolitan council to combine various series and issues of the outstanding bonds by a single issue of refunding bonds, and to issue refunding bonds to pay any redemption premium payable on the outstanding bonds being refunded. The funding or refunding revenue bonds shall be payable only out of a special fund created out of the gross revenue of the particular utility, and shall be a valid claim only as against such special fund and the amount of the revenue of the utility pledged to the fund. The funding or refunding revenue bonds shall, except as specifically provided in this section, be issued in accordance with the provisions of this act with respect to revenue bonds.

The net interest cost to maturity on funding or refunding bonds issued under this act shall not exceed seven percent per annum. The amount of premium, if any, to be paid on the redemption of such funding or refunding bonds prior to maturity thereof shall not be considered in determining such net interest cost. The metropolitan council may exchange the funding or refunding bonds at par for the bonds which are being funded or refunded, or it may sell them in such manner as it deems for the best interest of the metropolitan municipal corporation.

Sec. 48. A metropolitan municipal corporation shall have the power when authorized by a majority of all members of the metropolitan council to borrow money from any component city or county and such cities or counties are hereby authorized to make such loans or advances on such terms as may be mutually agreed upon by the legislative bodies of the metropolitan municipal corporation and any such component city or county to provide funds to carry out the purposes of the metropolitan municipal corporation.

Sec. 49. If a metropolitan municipal corporation shall have been authorized to levy a general tax on all taxable property located within the metropolitan municipal corporation in the manner provided in this act, either at the time of the formation of the metropolitan municipal corporation or subsequently, the metropolitan council shall have the power to authorize the issuance of interest bearing warrants on such terms and conditions as the metropolitan council shall provide, same to be repaid from the proceeds of such tax when collected.

Sec. 50. The metropolitan municipal corporation shall have the power to levy special assessments payable over a period of not exceeding twenty years on all property within the metropolitan area specially benefited by any improvement, on the basis of special benefits conferred, to pay, in whole, or in part, the damages or costs of any such improvement, and for such purpose may establish local improvement districts and enlarged local improvement districts, issue local improvement warrants and bonds to be repaid by the collection of local improvement assessments and generally to exercise with respect to any improvement which it may be authorized to construct or acquire the same powers as may now or hereafter be conferred by law upon cities of the first class. Such local improvement districts shall be created and such special assessments levied and collected and local improvement warrants and bonds issued and sold in the same manner as shall now or hereafter be provided by law for cities of the first class. The duties imposed upon the city treasurer under such acts shall be imposed upon the treasurer of the county in which such local improvement district shall be located.

A metropolitan municipal corporation may provide that special benefit assessments levied in any local improvement district may be paid into such revenue bond redemption fund or funds as may be designated by the metropolitan council to secure the payment of revenue bonds issued to provide funds to pay the cost of improvements for which such assessments were levied. If local improvement district assessments shall be levied for payment into a revenue bond fund, the local improvement district created therefor shall be designated a utility local improvement district.

Sec. 51. All banks, trust companies, bankers, savings banks, and institutions, building and loan associations, savings and loan associations, investment companies and other persons carrying on a banking or investment business, all insurance companies, insurance associations, and other persons carrying on an insurance business, and all executors, administrators, curators, trustees and other fiduciaries, may legally invest any sinking funds, moneys, or other funds belonging to them or within their control in any bonds or other obligations issued by a metropolitan municipal corporation pursuant to this act. Such bonds and other obligations shall be authorized security for all public deposits. It is the purpose of this section to authorize any persons, political subdivisions and officers, public or private, to use any funds owned or controlled by them for the purchase of any such bonds or other obligations. Nothing contained in this section with regard to legal investments shall be construed as relieving any person of any duty of exercising reasonable care in selecting securities.

Sec. 52. A metropolitan municipal corporation shall have the power to invest its funds held in reserves or sinking funds or any such funds which are not required for immediate disbursement, in property or securities in which mutual savings banks may legally invest funds subject to their control.

Sec. 53. Territory annexed to a component city after the establishment of a metropolitan municipal corporation shall by such act be annexed to such corporation. Any other territory adjacent to a metropolitan municipal corporation may be annexed thereto by vote of the qualified electors residing in the territory to be annexed, in the manner provided in this act. An election to annex such territory may be called pursuant to a petition or resolution in the following manner:

(1) A petition calling for such an election shall be signed by at least four percent of the qualified voters residing within the territory to be annexed and shall be filed with the auditor of the central county.

(2) A resolution calling for such an election may be adopted by the metropolitan council.

Any resolution or petition calling for such an election shall describe the boundaries of the territory to be annexed, and state that the annexation of such territory to the metropolitan municipal corporation will be conducive to the welfare and benefit of the persons or property within the metropolitan municipal corporation and within the territory proposed to be annexed.

Upon receipt of such a petition, the auditor shall examine the same and certify to the sufficiency of the signatures thereon. For the purpose of examining the signatures of such petition, the auditor shall be permitted access to the voter registration books of each city within the territory proposed to be annexed and of each county a portion of which shall be located within the territory proposed to be annexed. No person may withdraw his name from a petition after it has been filed with the auditor. Within thirty days following the receipt of such petition, the auditor shall transmit the same to the metropolitan council, together with his certificate as to the sufficiency thereof.

Sec. 54. Upon receipt of a duly certified petition calling for an election on the annexation of territory to a metropolitan municipal corporation, or if the metropolitan council shall determine without a petition being filed, that an election on the annexation of any adjacent territory shall be held, the metropolitan council shall fix a date for a public hearing thereon which shall be not more than sixty nor less than forty days following the receipt of such petition or adoption of such resolution. Notice of such hearing shall be published once a week for at least four consecutive weeks in one or more newspapers of general circulation within the territory proposed to be annexed. The notice shall contain a description of the boundaries of the territory proposed to be annexed and shall state the time and place of the hearing thereon and the fact that any changes in the boundaries of such territory will be considered at such time and place. At such hearing or any continuation thereof, any interested person may appear and be heard on all matters relating to the proposed annexation. The metropolitan council may make such changes in the boundaries of the territory proposed to be annexed as it shall deem reasonable and proper, but may not delete any portion of the proposed area which will create an island of included or excluded lands and may not delete a portion of any city. If the metropolitan council shall determine that any additional territory should be included in the territory to be annexed, a second hearing shall be held and notice given in the same manner as for the original hearing. The metropolitan council may adjourn the hearing on the proposed annexation from time to time not exceeding thirty days in all. At the next regular meeting following the conclusion of such hearing, the metropolitan council, shall if it finds that the annexation of such territory will be conducive to the welfare and benefit of the persons and property therein and the welfare and benefit of the persons and property within the metropolitan municipal corporation, adopt a resolution fixing the boundaries of the territory to be annexed and calling a special election on such annexation to be held not more than one hundred twenty days nor less than sixty days following the adoption of such resolution.

Sec. 55. An election on the annexaton of territory to a metropolitan municipal corporation shall be conducted and canvassed in the same manner as provided for the conduct of an election on the formation of a metropolitan municipal corporation except that notice of such election shall be published in one or more newspapers of general circulation in the territory proposed to be annexed and the ballot proposition shall be in substantially the following form:

"ANNEXATION TO _____
(here insert name of metropolitan municipal corporation)

"Shall the territory described in a resolution of the metropolitan council of _____
(here insert name of metropolitan municipal corporation)
adopted on the _____ day of _____, 19_____, to be annexed to such incorporation?"

YES _____ ☐
NO _____ ☐"

If a majority of those voting on such propositions vote in favor thereof, the territory shall thereupon be annexed to the metropolitan municipal corporation.

Sec. 56. The rule of strict construction shall have no application to this act, but the same shall be liberally constructed in all respects in order to carry out the purposes and objects for which this act is intended.

Sec. 57. If any provision of this act, or its application to any person or circumstance is held invalid, the remainder of the act, or the application of the provision to other persons or circumstances is not affected.